ANCIENT SANSKRIT LITERATURE

ANCIENT SANSKRIT LITERATURE

By

F. MAX MÜLLER

BKP

BHARATIYA KALA PRAKASHAN
DELHI (INDIA)

First Published : 1859
Revised Edition : 2007
New Edition : 2023

Published by C.P. Gautam *for*
BHARATIYA KALA PRAKASHAN
3480/1, Ground Floor, Narang Colony,
Tri Nagar, Delhi - 110035,
Phone No. : 011 71522860, 9811642997, 8595139625
E-mail : info@bkpbooks.com; sales.bkpbooks@gmail.com
Website: www.bkpbooks.com

ISBN : 978-81-8090-162-1

Laser Type Setting by
A-ONE GRAPHICS
Pitampura, Delhi-110088

Printed by :
G.S. Offset Printers
Delhi

TO

HORACE HAYMAN WILSON, ESQ,

SODEN PROFESSOR OF SANSKRIT, ASSOCIATE OF THE INSTITUTE OF FRANCE, ETC.

This Work is Inscribed

AS A TOKEN OF ADMIRATION AND GRATITUDE BY HIS PUPIL AND FRIEND

MAX MÜLLER

PREFACE

A few words of personal explanation are due to those who may have seen, in the Preface to the First Volume of my edition of the Rig-Veda,[1] a note announcing as ready for publication an Introductory Memoir on the Literature of the Veda. Ten sheets of this Memoir were printed when, in the beginning of the year 1851, 1 was appointed Deputy Professor, and, after the death of my lamented friend, Francis Trithen, in the year 1854, Professor of Modern European Languages and Literature -in the University of Oxford. In compliance with the statutes of the Foundation of Sir Robert Taylor, I had to write "Three Courses of Lectures in every year, on the Philology or Literature of some of the principal Languages of Europe." These new and unexpected duties rendered it necessary for me to discontinue for a time my favourite studies. And when, after the first years of my new office, 1 was able to employ again a greater amount of leisure on their prosecution, I felt that I should better serve the interests of Sanskrit Philology by devoting all my spare time to editing the text and commentary of the Veda, than by publishing the results, more or less fragmentary, of my own researches into the language, literature, and religion of the ancient Brahmans.

In resuming now, after the lapse of nearly ten years, the pub-

1. Rig-Veda-Sanhita, the sacred songs of the Brahmans, together with the Commentary of Sayanacharya, edited by Max Müller, Vol. I., 1849; Vol. H., 1864; Vol. III., 1856. There will be three more volumes, the first of which is to be published next year. The first volume of Professor Wilson's Translation was published 1850; the second, 1854, the third, 1857.

lication of these Essays, I may regret that on many points 1 have been anticipated by others, who during the interval have made the Veda the special subject of their studies. But this regret is fully balanced by the satisfaction I feel in finding that in the main, my original views on the literature and religion of the Vedic age have not been shaken, either by my own continued researches or by the researches of others; and that the greater part of this work could be printed, as it now stands, from the original manuscript. It will be seen, however, that in the notes, as well as in the body of the work, I have availed myself, to the best of my ability, of all the really important and solid information that could be gathered from the latest works of Sanskrit philologists. The frequent references to the works of Wilson, Burnouf, Lassen, Benfey, Roth, Boehtlingk, Kuhn, Regnier, Weber, Aufrecht, Whitney, and others, will show where I have either derived new light from the labours of these eminent scholars, or found my own conclusions confirmed by their independent testimony. Believing, as I do, that literary controversy is more apt to impede than to advance the cause of truth, I have throughout carefully abstained from it. Where it seemed necessary to controvert unfounded statements or hasty conclusions, I have endeavoured to do so by stating the true facts of the case, and the legitimate conclusions that may be drawn from these facts.

My readers have to thank Dr. Buhler, a pupil of Professor Benfey of Gottingen, for the alphabetical index at the end of this Volume.

MAX MÜLLER

CONTENTS

INTRODUCTION

Full seventy years have passed since Sir William Jones published his translation of Śakuntalā,[1] a work which may fairly be considered as starting point of Sanskrit philology. The first appearance of this beautiful specimen of dramatic art created at the time a sensation throughout Europe, and the most rapturous praise was bestowed upon it by men of high authority in matters of taste.[2] At the same time the attention of the historian, the philologist, and the philosopher was roused to the fact that a complete literature had been preserved in India, which promised to open a new leaf in the ancient history of mankind, and deserved to become the object of serious study. And although the enthusiasm with which works like Śakuntalā were at first received by all who took an interest in literary curiosities could scarcely be expected to last, the real and scientific interest excited by the language, the literature, the philosophy, and antiquities of India has lasted, and has been increasing ever since. England, France, Germany, Italy, Denmark, Sweden, Russia and Greece have each contributed their share towards the advancement of Sanskrit Philology, and names like those of Sir W. Jones, Colebrooke, Wilson, in England, Burnouf in France, the two Schlegels, W. von Humboldt, Bopp, and Lassen, in Germany, have secured to this branch of modern scholarship a firm standing and a universal reputation. The number of books that have been published by Sanskrit scholars in the course of the last seventy years is but small.[3] Those works, however, represent large and definite results, important not only in)' their bearing on Indian antiquities, but, as giving birth to a new system of Comparative Philology, of the highest possible importance to philology in general.[4] In little more than half a century, Sanskrit has gained its proper place in the republic of learning, side by side with Greek and Latin. The privileges which these two languages enjoy in the educational system of modern Europe will scarcely ever be shared by Sanskrit. But no one who wishes to acquire a thorough knowledge of these or any other of the Indo-European languages,—no one who takes an interest in the philosophy and the historical growth of human speech, no one who desires to study the history of that branch of mankind to which we ourselves belong, and to discover in the first germs of the language, religion, and mythology of our forefathers, the wisdom of him who is not the God of the Jews only, can, for the future, dispense with some knowledge of the language and ancient literature of India.

HISTORY OF SANSKRIT PHILOLOGY

And yet Indian philology is still in its infancy, and the difficulties with which it has had to contend have been great, much greater, indeed, than those which lay in the way of Greek philology after its revival in the fifteenth century. Seventy years after the fall of Constantinople, the classical works of Greek literature were not only studied from manuscripts: they had been edited and printed. There were men like Reuchlin, Erasmus, and Melanchthon, who had investigated the most important documents in the different periods of Greek literature, and possessed a general knowledge of the historical growth of the Greek mind. Learned Greeks who were taking refuge in the west of Europe, particularly in Italy, had brought with them a sufficient knowledge to teach their language and literature; and they were able and ready to guide the studies of those who were afterwards to contribute to the revival of classical learning in Europe. Men began where they ought to begin, namely, with Homer, Herodotus, and Thucydides and not with Anacreontic poetry or Neo-Platonist philosophy. But when our earliest Sanskrit scholars directed their attention to Indian literature, the difficulties they had to struggle with were far greater. Not to mention the burning and enervating sky of India, and the burden of their official occupations, men like

Halhed, Wilkins, and Sir W. Jones could hardly find a single Brāhmaṇa who would undertake to teach them his sacred idiom. When, after some time, learned Paṇḍits became more willing to impart their knowledge to Europeans, their own views of Indian history and literature were more apt to mislead their pupils than to guide them, in a truly historical direction. Thus it happened that, at the beginning of Sanskrit philology, preference was given either to works which still enjoyed amongst the Hindus themselves a great, but frequently undeserved, popularity, or to those which by their poetical beauty attracted the attention of men of taste. Everything Indian, whether Manu's Code of Laws, the Bhagavadgītā, Śakuntalā, or the Hitopadeśa, was at that time considered to be of great and extravagant antiquity, and it was extremely difficult for European scholars to form a right opinion on the real merits of Indian literature. The literary specimens received from India were generally fragments only of larger works: or, if not, they had been chosen so indiscriminately from different and widely distant periods, that it was impossible to derive from them an adequate knowledge of the rise and fall of the national literature of India.

Herder, in other respects an excellent judge of ancient national poetry, committeed himself to some extraordinary remarks on Indian literature. In his criticism on Śakuntalā, written in the form of letters to a friend, he says : "Do you not wish with me, that instead of these endless religious books of the Vedas, Upavedas and Upāṅgas, they would give us the more useful and more agreeable works of the Indians, and especially their best poetry of every kind ? It is here the mind and character of a nation is best brought to life before us, and I gladly admit, that I have received a truer and more real notion of the manner of thinking among the ancient Indians from this one Śakuntala, than from all their Upnekats (Upanisads) and Bagavedams."[5] The fact is that at that time Herder's view on the endless religious books of the Vedas, could only have been formed from a wretched translation of the Bagavedam, as he calls it—that is, the Bhāgavatapurāṇa,—a Sanskrit work composed as many centuries after as the Vedas were before Christ; or from the Ezour-vedam, a very coarse forgery, if, indeed, it was intended as such, written, as it appears, by a native servant, for the use of the famous Jesuit missionary in India, Roberto de Nobilibus.[6]

Even at a much later time, men who possessed the true tact of an historian like Niebuhr, have abstained from passing sentence on the history of a nation whose literature had only just been recovered, and had not yet passed through the ordeal of philological criticism. In his Lectures on Ancient History, Niebuhr leaves a place open for India, to be filled up when the pure metal of history should have been extracted from the ore of Brāhmaṇic exaggeration and superstition.

Other historians, however, thought they could do what Niebuhr had left undone; and after perusing some poems of Kālidāsa, some fables of the Hitopadeśa, some verses of the Ānanda-laharī, or (the mystic poetry of the Bhagavadgītā, they gave, with the aid of Megasthenes and Apollonius of Tyana, a so-called historical account of the Indian nation, without being aware that they were using as contemporary witnesses, authors as distant from each other as Dante and Virgil. No nation has, in this respect, been more unjustly treated than the Indian. Not only have general conclusions been drawn from the most scanty materials, but the most questionable and spurious authorities have been employed without the least historical investigation or the exercise of that critical ingenuity, which, from its peculiar character, Indian literature requires more than any other.[7]

There is another circumstance which has retarded the progress of Sanskrit philology : an affectation of that learned pedantry which has done so much mischief to Greek and Latin scholarship. We have much to learn, no doubt, from classical scholars, and nothing can be a better preparation for a Sanskrit student than to have passed through the school of a Bentley or a Hermann. But in Greek and Latin scholarship the distinction between useful and useless knowledge has almost disappeared, and the real objects of the study of these ancient languages have been well nigh forgotten. More than half of the publications of classical scholars have tended only to impede our access to the master-works of the ancients; and a sanction has been given to a kind of learning, which, however creditable to the individual, is of no benefit to the public at large. A similar spirit has infected Sanskrit philology. Sanskrit texts have been edited, on which no rational man ought to waste his time. Essays have been written on subjects on which it is folly to be wise. These remarks are not intended to disparage critical scholarship or to depreciate the results which have been obtained by minute and abstruse erudition. But scholars who devote all their time to critical niceties and recondite subtleties are apt to forget that these are but accessories. Knowledge which has no object beyond itself is, in most cases, but a pretext for vanity. It is so easy, even for the most superficial scholar, to bring together a vast mass of information, bearing more or less remotely on questions of no importance whatsoever. The test of a true scholar is to be able to find out what is really important, to state with precision and clearness the results of long and tedious researches, and to suppress altogether lucubrations, which, though they might display the laboriousness of the writer, would but encumber his subject with needless difficulty.

AIM OF SANSKRIT PHILOLOGY

The object and aim of philology, in its highest sense, is but one,—to learn what man is, by learning what man has been. With this principle for our pole-star, we shall never lose ourselves, though engaged in the most minute and abstruse inquiries. Our own studies may seemingly refer to matters that are but secondary and preparatory, to the clearance, so to say, of the rubbish which passing ages have left on the monuments of the human mind. But we shall never mistake that rubbish for the monuments which it covers. And if, after years of tiresome labour, we do not arrive at the results which we expected,—if we find but suprious and unimportant fabrications of individuals, where we thought to place ourselves face to face with the heroes of an ancient world, and among ruins that should teach us the lessons of former ages, —we need not be discouraged nor ashamed, for in true science even a disappointment is a result.

If, then, it is the aim of Sanskrit philology to supply one of the earliest and most important links in the history of mankind, we must go to work historically; that is, we must begin, as far as we can, with the beginning, and then trace gradually the growth of the Indian mind, in its various manifestations, as far as the remaining literary monuments allow us to follow this course. What has been said with regard to philosophy, that we must acquire a knowledge of the beginning and first principles, because then we say that we understand any thing when we believe we know its real beginnings," applies with equal force to history. Now every one acquainted with Indian literature, must have observed how impossible it is to open any book on Indian subjects without being thrown back upon an earlier authority, which is generally acknowledged by the Indians as the basis of all their knowledge, whether sacred or profane. This ealier authority, which we find alluded to in theological and philosophical works, as well as in poetry, in codes of law, in astronomical, grammatical, metrical, and lexicographic compositions, is called by one comprehensive name, the Veda.

It is with the Veda, therefore, that Indian philology ought to begin if it is to follow a natural and historical course. So great an influence has the Vedic age (the historical period to which we are justified in referring the formation of the Sacred texts) exercised upon all succeeding periods of Indian history, so closely is every branch of literature connected with Vedic traditions, so deeply have the religious and moral ideas of that primitive era taken root in the mind of the Indian nation, so minutely has almost every private and public act of Indian life been regulated by old traditionary precepts, that it is impossible to find the right point of view for judging of Indian religion, morals, and literature without a knowledge of the literary remains of the Vedic age. No one could fairly say that those men who first began to study Sanskrit, now seventy years ago, ought to have begun with reading the Veda. The difficulties connected with the study of the Veda would have made such a course utterly impossible and useless. But since the combined labours of Sanskrit scholars have now rendered the study of that language of more easy access, since the terminology of Indian grammarians and commentators, which not long ago was considered unintelligible, has become more familiar to us, and manuscripts can be more readily procured at the principal public libraries of Europe, Sanskrit philology has no longer an excuse for ignoring the Vedic age.

THE VEDIC AGE

It might be inferred from the very variety of subjects upon which, as has been just observed, the Veda is quoted as the last and highest authority, that by Veda must be understood something more than a single work. It would be, indeed, much nearer the truth to take *Veda* as a collective name for the sacred literature of the Vedic age which forms, so to speak, the background of the whole Indian world. Many of the works which belonged to that period of literature have been irrecoverably lost. With regard to many of them, though their existence cannot be doubted, it is even uncertain whether they were ever committed to writing. A large number, however, of Vedic works does still exist; and it will require many years before they can be edited together with their commentaries. Till then it will be impossible to arrive at definite results on many questions connected with Vedic literature, and it would not be safe to take a comprehensive view of the whole Vedic age before all the sources have been exhausted from which its history and character can be studied. Nothing could be farther from the purpose of this historical essay than to attempt anything of this kind at present. What I have to offer are but Prolegomena to the Veda, or treatises on some preliminary questions connected with the history of the Vedic age. There are points which can be settled with complete certainty, though it may be impossible to bring, as yet, the whole weight of evidence to bear upon them; and the general question as to the authenticity, the antiquity, and the different periods of Vedic literature, ought to be answered even before beginning an edition of Vedic works. Again, there are many questions of special interest for Sanskrit literature, in which even now, with the materials that have been published and with the help of manuscripts that are accessible in the public libraries of Europe, it is possible to arrive at certain results; while other points are such that even after the complete publication of all Vedic texts and commentaries, they will remain open to different views, and will necessarily become the subject of literary discussions. The principal object of the following essays will be to put the antiquity of the Veda in its proper light. By antiquity, however, is meant, not only the chronological distance of the Vedic age from our own, measured by the revolutions and the progress of the heavenly bodies, but also and still more, the distance between the intellectual, moral, and religious state of men as represented to us during the Vedic age, compared with that of other periods of history, —a distance which can only be measured by the revolutions and the progress of the human mind.

No one who is at all acquainted with the position which India occupies in the history of the world, would expect to grid many synchronisms between the history of the *Brāhmaṇas* and that of other nations before the date of the origin of Buddhism in India. Although the *Brāhmaṇas* of India belong to the same family, the Āryan or Indo-European family, which civilized the whole of Europe, the two great branches of that primitive race were kept asunder for centuries after their first separation. The main stream of the Āryan nations has always flowed towards the north-west. No historian can tell us by what impulse those adventurous Nomads were driven on through Asia towards the isles and shores of Europe. The first start of this world-wide migration belongs to a period far beyond the reach of documentary history; to times when the soil of Europe had not been trodden by either Celts, Germans, Slavonians, Romans, or Greeks. But whatever it was, the impulse was as irresistible as the spell which, in our own times, sends the Celtic tribes towards the prairies or the regions of gold across the Atlantic. It requires a strong will, or a great amount of inertness, to be able to withstand the impetus of such national, or rather ethnical movements. Few will stay behind when all are going. But to let one's friends depart and then to set out ourselves—to take a road which, lead where it may, can never lead us to join those again who speak our language and worship our gods - is a course which only men of strong individuality and great self–dependence are capable of pursuing. It was the course adopted by the southern branch of the Āryan family, the Brāhmanic Āryas of India and the Zoroastrians of Iran.

THE ĀRYAN FAMILY

At the first dawn of traditional history we see these Āryan tribes migrating across the snow of the Himālaya southward toward the "Seven Rivers" (the Indus, the five rivers of the Panjāb and the Sarasvatī), and ever since India has been called their home. That before that time they had been living in more northern regions, within the same precincts with the ancestors of the Greeks, the Italians, Slavonians, Germans, and Celts, is a fact as firmly established as that the Normans of William the Conqueror were the Northmen of Scandinavia. The evidence of language is irrefragable, and it is the only evidence worth listening to with regard to ante-historical periods. It would have been next to impossible to discover any traces of relationship between the swarthy natives of India and their conquerors, whether Alexander or Clive, but for the testimony borne by language. What other evidence could have reached back to times when Greece was not peopled by Greeks, nor India by Hindus ? Yet these are the times of which we are speaking. What authority would have been strong enough to persuade the Grecian army, that their gods and their hero ancestors were the same, as those of King Porus, or to convince the English soldier that the same blood was running in his veins and in the veins of the dark Bengalese ? And yet there is not an English jury nowadays, which, after examining the hoary documents of languagc, would reject the claim of a common descent and a legitimate relationship between Hindu, Greek, and Teuton. Many words still live in India and in England, that have witnessed the first separation of the northern and southern Āryans, and these are witnesses not to be shaken by cross-examination. The terms for God, for house, for father, mother, son, daughter, for dog and cow, for heart and tears, for axe and tree, identical in all the Indo-European idioms, are like the watchwords of soldiers. We challenge the seeming stranger;

and whether he answer with the lips of a Greek, a German, or an Indian, we recognise him as one of ourselves. Though the historian may shake his head, though the physiologist may doubt, and the poet scorn the idea, all must yield before the facts furnished by language. There was a time when the ancestors of the Celts, the Germans, the Slavonians, the Greeks, and Italians, the Persians and Hindus, were living together within the same fences, separate from the ancestors of the Semitic and Turanian races.

It is more difficult to prove that the Hindu was the last to leave this common home, that he saw his brothers all depart towards the setting sun, and that then, turning towards the south and the east, he started alone in search of a new world. But as in his language and in his grammar he has preserved something of what seems peculiar to each of the northern dialects singly, as he agrees with the Greek and the German seem to differ from all the rest, and as no other language has carried off so large a share of the common Āryan heirloom – whether roots, grammar, words, myths, or legends – it is natural to suppose that, though perhaps the eldest brother, the Hindu was the last to leave the central home of the Āryan family.

The Āryan nation who pursued a north-westerly direction, stand before us in history as the principal nations of north-western Asia and Europe. They have been the prominent actors in the great drama of history, and have carried to their fullest growth all the elements of active life with which our nature is endowed. They have perfected society and morals, and we learn from their literature and works of art, the elements of science, the laws of art, and the principles of philosophy. In continual struggle with each other and with Semitic and Turanian races, these Āryan nations have become the rulers of history, and it seems to be their mission to link all parts of the world together by the chains of civilization, commerce, and religion. In a word, they represent the Āryan man in his historical character.

But while most of the members of the Āryan family followed this glorious path, the southern tribes were slowly migrating towards the mountains which gird the north of India. After crossing the narrow passes of the Hindukuś or the Himālaya, they conquered or drove before them, as it seems without much effort, the aboriginal inhabitants of the Trans-Himālayan countries. They took for their guides the principal rivers of Northern India, and were led by them to new homes in their beautiful and fertile valleys. It seems as if the great mountains in the north had afterwards closed for centuries their Cyclopean gates against new immigrations, while, at the same time, the waves of the Indian Ocean kept watch over the southern borders of the peninsula. None of the great conquerors of antiquity – Sesostris, Semiramis, Nebuchadnezzar, or Cyrus, who waged a kind of half-nomadic warfare over Asia, Africa, and Europe, and whose names, traced in characters of blood, are still legible on the threshold of history8, disturbed the peaceful seats of these Āryan settlers. Left to themselves in a world of their own, without a past, and without a future before them, they had nothing A but themselves to ponder on. Struggles there must have been in India also. Old dynasties were destroyed, whole families annihilated, and new empires founded. Yet the inward life of the Hindu was not changed by these convulsions. His mind was like the lotus leaf after a shower of rain has passed over it; his character remained the same, passive, meditative, quiet, and full of faith.

The chief elements of discord amongst the peaceful inhabitants of this rich country were, the struggle for supremacy between the different classes of society, the subjugation of the uncivilized inhabitants, particularly in the south of India, and the pressure of the latest comers in the north upon the possessors of the more fertile countries in the south.

GREECE AND INDIA

These three struggles took place in India at an early period, and were sufficiently important to have called forth the active faculties of any but the Indian nation. In these struggles we may recognise almost the same elements by which the Greek character was perfected and matured. But how different have been the results upon the Indian mind. The struggle for supremacy between the different classes, which in Greece ended with the downfall of the tyrannies and the rising of well-organised republics, has its counterpart in India in the extirpation of the Kṣatriya race and the triumph of the Brāhmaṇas through Paraśu-Rāma.[8]

The second struggle, or the war against the uncivilized inhabitants of the south, is represented by the Indian poet of the Rāmāyaṇa as the battle of a divine hero against evil spirits and uncouth giants. What this is to India, the war of Persia was to Greece; the victory of patriotic valour over brute force. The Muses of Herodotus are the Rāmāyaṇa of Hellas.

In the third of these parallel struggles the contrast is no less striking. We follow, with a mournful interest, the narrative of international jealousies between the different states of Greece; we see how one tries to crush the power of the other, while all are preparing the common ruin of the country. But what characters are here presented to our analysis, what statesmanship, what eloquence, what bravery. In India the war of the Mahābhārata was, perhaps, more , bloody than the Peloponnesian war : but in the hands of the Brāhmaṇas the ancient epic has been changed into a didactic legend.

Greece and India are, indeed, the two opposite poles in the historical development of the Āryan man. To the Greek, existence is full of life and reality; to the Hindu it is a dream, an illusion. The Greek is at home where he is born; all his energies belong to his country : he stands and falls with his party, and is ready to sacrifice even his life to the glory and I independence of Hellas. The Hindu enters this world as a stranger; all his thoughts are directed to another world; he takes no part even where he is driven to act; and when he sacrifices his life, it is but to be delivered from it.

THE INDIAN MIND

No wonder that a nation like the Indian cared so little for history; no wonder that social and political virtues were little cultivated, and the ideas of the Useful and the Beautiful scarcely known to them. With all this, however, they had what the Greek was as little capable of imagining as they were of realising the elements of Grecian life. They shut their eyes to this world of outward seeming and activity, to open them full on the world of thought and rest. Their life was a yearning after eternity; their activity a struggle to return into that divine essence from which this life seemed to have severed them. Believing as they did in a divine and really existing eternal Being (τσ οντως ον), they could not believe in the existence of this passing world. If the one existed, the other could only seem to exist; if they lived in the one, they could not live in the other. Their existence on earth was to them a problem, their eternal life a certainty. The highest object of their religion was to restore that bond[10] by which their own self.(Ātman) was linked to the eternal Self (paramātman); to recover that unity which had been clouded and obscured by the magical illusions of reality, by the so called *Māyā* of creation. It scarcely entered their mind either to doubt or to affirm the immortality of the soul,[11] except in later times, and then only for philosophical and controversial purposes.[12] Not only their religion and literature, but their very language, reminded them daily of that relation between the real and the seeming word. The word ātman, for instance, which in the Veda occurs often as tman, means life, particularly animal life. Thus we read, (Ṛv. i, 63, 8). "Increase, O bright Indra ! this our manifold food, like water all over the earth; by which, O Hero! you give us life, like sap, to move everywhere." Here *tman* means the vital principle and is compared with the juice that circulates in plants. In another hymn, addressed to the horse which is to be sacrificed (Ṛv. i. 162. 20.), the poet says, "Mā tvā tapat priya ātmapiyantam," literally, "Let not your dear self burn or afflict you as you approach the sacrifice." Here *priya ātma* corresponds to the Greek φιλον ητορ. But we find ātman used also in a higher sense in the Veda. For instance, (Ṛv. i, 115. 1.), "*Surya ātma jagatas tasthuṣhaśeha*:" "the sun is the soul of all that moves and rests."13 Most frequently, however, tman and ātman are employed for self, just as we say, My soul praises, rejoices, for I praise, I myself rejoice. This is the most usual signification of ātman in the later Sanskrit, where it is used like a pronoun. Yet ātman means there also the soul of the universe, the highest soul or Self (paramātman) of which all other souls partake, from which all reality in this created world emanates, and into which every thing will return. Thus a Hindu speaking of himself (ātman) spoke also, though unconsciously, of the soul of the universe (Paramātman); and to know himself was to him to know both his own self and the universal Self, or to know himself in the divine Self. The Sanskrit, "ātmānam ātmanā paśya," "see (your) self by (your) self," had a deeper signification than the Greek γυθτ σεαυτσυ,[12] because it has not only a moral, but also a metaphysical meaning. How largely this idea of the Ātman, as the Divine spirit, entered into the early religious and philosophical speculations of the Indians, may be seen from the following dialogue between Yājñavalkya and Maitreyī, which forms part of the Bṛhadāraṇyaka.

"Maitreyī,"[13] said Yājñavalkya, "I am going away from this my house (into the forest). Forsooth, I must make a settlement between you and my other wife Kātyāyani."

Maitreyī said, "My Lord, if this whole earth full of wealth belonged to me, should I be immortal by it ?"

"No," replied Yājñavalkya; "like the happy life of rich people will be thy life. But there is no hope of immortality by wealth."

And Maitreyī said, "What should I do with that by which I do not become immortal ? What my Lord knoweth (of immortality) may he tell that to me."

Yājñavalkya replied, "You, who art truly dear to me,[14] your speakest dear words. Sit down, I will explain it to your, and listen well to what I say."And he said," A husband is loved, not because you love the husband, but because you love (in him) the Divine Spirit (ātmā, the absolute Self). A wife is loved, not because we love the wife, but because we love (in her) the Divine Spirit. Children are loved, not because we love the children, but because we love the Divine Spirit in them. This spirit it is which we love when we (seem to) love wealth, Brāhmaṇas,

Kṣatriyas, this world, the gods, all beings, this universe. *The Divine Spirit, O beloved wife, is to be seen, to be heard, to be perceived, and to be meditated upon.* If we see, hear, perceive, and know him, O Maitreyī, then this whole universe is known to us."

"Whosoever looks for Brahmahood elsewhere than in the Divine Spirit, should be abandoned by the Brāhmaṇas. Who-soever looks for the Kṣātra-power elsewhere than in the Divine Spirit, should be abandoned by the Kṣātras. Whosoever looks for this world, for the gods, for all beings, for this universe, elsewhere in the Divine Spirit, should be abandoned by them all. This Brahmahood, this Kṣātra-power, this world, these gods, these beings, this universe, all is the Divine Spirit."

"Now, as we cannot seize the sounds of a drum externally by themselves, but seize the sound by seizing the drum, or the beating of it, as we cannot seize the sounds of a conch-shell by themselves, but seize the sound by seizing the conch-shell, or the shell-blower, as we cannot seize the sounds of a lute by themselves, but seize the sound by seizing the lute, or the lutanist,—so is it with the Divine Spirit."

"As clouds of smoke rise out of a fire kindled with dry fuel, thus, O Maitreyi, have all the holy words been breathed out of that Great Being."

"As all the waters find their centre in the sea, so all sensations find their centre in the skin, all tastes in the tongue, all smells in the nose, all colours in the eye, all sounds in the ear, all thoughts in the mind, all knowledge in the heart, all actions in the hands, and all the Holy Scriptures in speech."

"It is with us, when we enter into the Divine Spirit, as if a lump of salt was thrown into the sea; it becomes dissolved into the water (from which it was produced), and is not to be taken out again. But wherever you take the water and taste it, it is salt. Thus is this great, endless, and boundless Being but one mass of knowledge. As the water becomes salt, and the salt becomes water again, thus has the Divine Spirit appeared from out the elements and disappears again into them. When we have passed away, there is no longer any name. This I tell your, my wife," said Yājñavalkya.

Maitreyī said, "My Lord, here thou hast bewildered me, saying that there is no longer any name when we have passed away."

And Yājñavalkya replied, "My wife, what I say is not bewildering, it is sufficient for the highest knowledge. For if there be as it were two beings, then the one sees the other, the one hears, perceives, and knows the other. But if the one Divine Self be the whole of all this, whom or through whom should he see, hear, perceive, or know? How should he know (himself), by whom he knows every thing (himself) ? How, my wife, should he know (himself) the knower?[16] Thus you have been taught, Maitreyī; this is immortality." Having said this Yājñavalkya left his wife for ever, and went into the solitude of the forests.

It must be observed that the work from which this dialogue is taken belongs to a later period of Vedic literature. In the earlier times which are represented to us in the hymns of the Veda, these mystic tendencies are not yet so strongly developed. In the songs of the Ṛg-veda we find but little of philosophy, but we do occasionally meet with wars of kings, with rivalries of ministers, with triumphs and defeats, with war-songs and imprecations. The active side of life is still prominent in the genuine poetry of the Ṛṣis, and there still exists a certain equilibrium between the two scales of human nature. It is only after the Āryan tribes had advanced southward, and taken quiet possession of the rich plains and beautiful groves of Central,[18] India, that they seem to have turned all their energies and thoughts from the world without them to that ,more wonderful nature which they perceived within,

ALEXANDER IN INDIA

Such was their state when the Greeks first became acquainted with them after the discovery of India by Alexander. What did these men, according to Megasthenes, most think and speak about ? Their most frequent conversations, he says,[16] were about life and death. This life they considered as the life of an embryo in the womb; but death as the birth to a real and happy life for those who had thought, and had prepared themselves to be ready to die.[18] Good and bad was nothing to them; not that they denied the distinction between good and bad in a moral sense. They recognised law and virtue, as we see in their sacred poetry as well as in their codes of law. But they denied that anything that happened to men in this life could be called either good or bad, and they maintained that philosophy consisted in removing the affections of pleasure as well as of pain. Liking pain and hating pleasure was what they considered the highest state of indifference that man could arrive at *

We are told by the same author that the Indians did not communicate their metaphysical doctrines to women; thinking that, if their wives understood these doctrines, and learned to be indifferent to pleasure and pain, and to consider life and death as the same, they would no longer continue to be the slaves of others: or, if they failed to understand them, they would be talkative, and communicate their knowledge to those who had no right to it. This statement of the Greek author is fully borne out by the later Sanskrit authorities. We find, for instance, in the ceremonial Sëtras (*Śrauta and gṛhya-Sūtras*), that women were not allowed to learn the sacred songs of the Vedas, the knowledge of which constituted one of the principal requirements for a Brāhmaṇa before he was admitted to the performance of the sacrifices. Indeed, the whole education of a Brāhmaṇa consisted in learning the old sacred literature by heart, and many years were spent for this purpose by every Brahmācārin in the house and under the severe discipline of his Guru, or of an Aeliarya. As it was necessary[19] however, for a husband to perform sacrifices together with his lawful wife, and passages of thc hymns[20] as well as of the Brāhmaṇas, speak clearly of man and wife as performing sacrifices in common, it was laid down in the Sūtras that the husbanr or the priest should, at the sacrifice itself, make his wife recite those hymns which were necessary for the ceremony. But although women were thus allowed to participate in the sacrifices of their husbands, they were not initiated, still less were they admitted to the highest knowledge of the Ātman or the Braḥmān[21]. Cases like that of Maitreyī were exceptions not the rule.

Thus the account which Megasthenes gives of the Indians shows us the same abstract and passive character which we find throughout the whole classical or post-Vedic literature of the Brāhmaṇas, and which, to a great extent, explains the absence of anything like historical literature among this nation of philosophers.

INDIAN CHARACTER

A people of this peculiar stamp of mind was never destined to act a prominent part in what is called, the history of the world. This exhausting atmosphere of transcendental ideas could not but exercise a detrimental influence on the active and the moral character of the Indians. But if we admire in classical history even those heroes in whom the love of country was driven to the highest pitch of fanaticism, we have scarcely a right to despise a nation, in whom the love of a purer and higher life degenerated sometimes into reckless self-sacrifice. No people certainly made a more favourable impression upon the Greeks than the Indians. And when we read the account of their moral and intellectual condition at the time of Alexander, we are obliged to admit that if some of their good qualities are no longer to be met with among the Indians of later times, this is owing, not entirely to an original defect of character, but to that continual system of oppression exercised upon them by foreign conquerors, to whose physical power they submitted, while they could not help despising their masters as barbarians. Of the demoralising influence of a foreign occupation we have an instance in the time of Alexander, in the story of Kalānas (Kalyāṇa), who yielded to the flattering offers of the European conqueror, and left his sacred home to follow his royal master as a piece of curiosity. But Megasthenes was afterwards informed that the behaviour of Kalānas was strongly disapproved of by his friends, as ambitious and servile; while Maṇḍanis was praise. for his manly answer to Alexander's messengers, not only by his countrymen, but by Alexander himself. It was not long before Kalānas repented his unworthy ambition, for he burnt himself soon after at Pasargada, in the same manner as the only other Brāhmaṇa who reached Europe in ancient times burned himself at Athens to the astonishment of the Greeks, who erected a tomb to him, with the inscription, "Here lies the Indian Sarman Cheya (Śarman Ācārya ?), from Barygaza, who sought immortality after the old custom of the Indians."

The genius of the Greek nation owes its happy and healthy growth to liberty and national independence. The Homeric songs were addressed to a people, proud of his heroes, whether real or legendary. If Persia had crushed the chivarly of Greece, we should never have heard the names of Herodotus, Æschylus, Sophocles, Phidias, and Pericles. Where the feeling of nationality has been roused, the poet is proud to be listened to by his nation, and a nation is proud to listen to her poet. But in times of national degradation the genius of great men turns away from the realities of life, and finds its only consolation in the search after truth, in science and philosophy. Socrates, Plato, and Aristotle arose when the Greek nation began to decline; and, under the heavy grasp first of Macedonian sway, then of Roman tyranny, the life of the Greek genius ebbed away, while its immortal productions lived on in the memory of other and freer nations. The Indian never knew the feeling of nationality and his heart-never trembled in the expectation of national applause. There were no heroes to inspire a poet, no history to call forth a historian. The only sphere where the Indian mind found itself at liberty to act, to create, and to worship, was the sphere of religion and philosophy; and nowhere have religious and metaphysical ideas struck roots so deep in the mind of a nation as in India. The Hindus were a nation of philosophers. Their struggles were the struggles of thought; their past, the problem of creation; their future, the problem of existence. The present alone, which is the real and living solution of the problems of the past and the future, seems never to have attracted their thoughts or to have called out their energies. The shape which metaphysical ideas take amongst the different classes of society, and at different periods of civilization, naturally varies from coarse superstition to sublime spiritualism. But, taken as a whole, history supplies no second instance where the inward life of the soul has so completely absorbed all the practical faculties of a whole people, and, in fact, almost destroyed those qualities by which a nation gains its place in history.

INDIA'S PLACE IN HISTORY

It might, therefore, be justly sa.id that India has no place in the political history of the world. While other nations, as the Egyptians, the Jews, the Babylonians, Assyrians, Persians, the Greeks, the Romans, and the Teutonic races, have during certain periods, culminated on the political horizon of the world, India has moved in such a small and degraded circle of political existence that it remained almost invisible to the eyes of other nations. An expedition like that of Alexander could never have been conceived by an Indian king, and the ambition of native conquerors, in those few cases where it existed, never went beyond the limits of India itself.

But if India has no place in the political history of the world, it certainly has a right to claim its place in the intellectual history of mankind. The less the Indian nation has taken part in the political struggles of the world, and expended its energies in the exploits of war and the formation of empires, the more it has fitted itself and concentrated all its powers for the fulfilment of the important mission reserved to it in the history of the East. History seems to teach that the whole human race required a gradual education before, in the fulness of time, it could be admitted to the truths of Christianity. All the fallacies of human reason had to be exhausted, before the light of a higher truth could meet with ready acceptance. The ancient religions of the world were but the milk of nature, which was in due time to be succeeded by the bread of life. After the primeval physiolatry, which was common to all the members of the Āryan family, had, in the hands of a wily priesthood, been changed into an empty idolatry, the Indian alone, of all the Āryan nations, produced a new form of religion, which has well been called subjective, as opposed to the more objective worship of nature. That religion, the religion of Buddha, has spread, far beyond the limits of the Āryan world and to our limited vision, it may seem to have retarded the advent of Christianity among a large portion of the human race. But in the sight of Him with whom a thousand years are but as one day, that religion, like all the ancient religions of the world, may have but served to prepare the way of Christ, by helping, through its very errors, to strengthen and to deepen the ineradicable yearning of the human heart after the truth of God.

Though the religion of Buddha be of all religions the most hostile to the old belief of the Brāhmaṇas, – the Buddhists standing to the Brāhmaṇas in about the same relation as the early Protestants to the Church of Rome, yet the very bitterness of this opposition proves that Buddhism is peculiarly Indian. Similar ideas to those proclaimed by Buddha were current long before his time, and traces of them may be found even in other countries. But for the impressive manner in which these ideas were first proclaimed and preached throughout India, for the hold which they took on the Indian mind, for the readiness with which they were received, particularly by the lower classes, till at last they were adopted by the sovereign as the religion of state, in a word, for the historical and universal character which this doctrine there assumed, the cause must be sought in the previous history of the Indian nation. There is something in the doctrines of Buddhism that is common to all systems of philosophy or religion, which break with the traditions of an effete idol-worship and a tyrannical hierarchy. There is some truth in Buddhism as there is in every one of the false religions of the world. But it was only in India, where people had been prepared by centuries of thought and meditation, as well as by the very corruption of the old Brāhmanical system, to embrace and nurture the religious ideas of Buddha Śākya Muni; it was only in India, that those new doctrines took an historical shape, and grew into a religion which, if truth depended on majorities, would be the truest of all forms of faith.

Up to the present day there is no religion of the world more extensively prevalent than the religion of Buddha;[22] and though it has been banished from the soil of India, and no living follower of this creed is now to be met with in that country,[23] yet it has found a refuge and second home in Ceylon, Siam, Ava, Pegu, the

Burman Empire, China, Tibet, Tatary, Mongolia and Siberia, and is, even in its present corruption, looked upon and practised as the only true system of faith and worship by many millions of human beings. Truly, then, the moment when this religious doctrine took its origin in India is an era in be intellectual history of the world; and, from a historical point of view, India may be considered, at that time, passing through the meridian of history. The most accurate observers of the progress of the Indian mind have, therefore, chosen this moment as the most favourable for fixing, historically and chronologically, the position of India: Professor Wilson in his "Viṣṇu-Purāṇa," Professor Burnouf in his "Introduction to the History of Buddhism," and Professor Lassen in his – 'Indian Antiquities."

HISTORICAL ORIGIN OF BUDDHISM

It would be out of place to discuss at present all the arguments by which the historical origin of the Buddhistic religion has been fixed chronologically in the works here mentioned. The date of Buddha's death, in the middle of the sixth century B.C., and the beginning of the Ceylonese era, 543 B.C., will have to be considered hereafter. For the present, it will be sufficient to keep in mind that the Buddhistic era divides the whole history of India into two parts, in the same manner as the Christian era divides the history of the world. It is therefore of the greatest importance, with regard to the history of Vedic literature. The rise of a new religion so hostile to the hierarchical system of the Brāhmaṇas is most likely to have produced a visible effect on their sacred and theological writings. If traces of this kind can be discovered in the ancient literature of India, an important point will be gained, and it will be possible perhaps to restore to this vast mass of Brāhmanic lore a certain historical connection. After the rise of a new religious doctrine in the first centuries after Buddha, it could not be expected that trie Brāhmanic literature should cease at once. On the contrary, we should expect at first a powerful reaction and a last effort to counteract the influence of the rising doctrine. And, as in India the religion of Buddha addressed itself more especially to the lower classes of the people, and found its strongest support amongst those who had to suffer from the exclusiveness of the Brāhmanic system, a period of transition would most likely be marked by a more popular style of literature, by an attempt to simplify the old complicated system of the Brāhmanic ceremonial, till at last the political ascendency, secured to the new doctrine through its adoption by the reigning princes, like Asoka, would cause this effort also to slacken.

NON-VEDIC WORKS

Before it can be shown, however, that this really took place in India, and that traces of this religious crisis exist in the Vedic literature of the Brāhmaṇas it seems necessary to point out what Sanskrit works can be included within that literature, and what other books are to be excluded altogether when, we look for evidence with regard to the true history of the Vedic age.

Let us begin by the negative process, and endeavour to separate and reject those works which do not belong to the genuine Vedic cycle. If we examine the two epic poems of India, the Rāmāyaṇa and Mahābhārata, we shall find it impossible to use them as authorities for the Vedic age because we are not yet able to decide critically which parts of these poems are ancient, and which are modern and post-Buddhistic, or at least retouched by the hands of late compilers and editors. There are certainly Very ancient traditions and really Vedic legends in both of these poems. Some of their heroes are taken from the same epic cycle in which the Vedic poetry moves. Those, however, only form subjects for episodes in the two poems, while their principal heroes—are essentially different in their character and manners. In fact, though there are remains of the Vedic age to be found in the epic poems, like the stories of Urvaśī and Purūravas Śakuntalā and Dushyanta, Uddālaka, Śunaḥśepa. Janaka' Vaideha, and particularly of the Vedic Ṛṣis, like Vaśiṣtha, Viśvāmitra, Yājñavalkya, Dīrghatamas, Kakṣīvat, Kavaṣa' and many others, yet this would only prove that the traditions of the Vedic age were still in the mouth of the people at the time when the epic poetry of the Hindus was first composed or that they were not yet forgotten in after times, when the Brāhmaṇas began to collect all the remains of epic songs into one large body, called the Mahābhārata. If we compare the same legends as exhibited in the hymns and Brāhmaṇas of the Veda, and as related in the Mahābhārata, Rāmāyaṇa or the Purāṇas, the Vedic version of them will mostly be found to be more simple, more primitive, and more intelligible than those of the epic and Paurāṇic poems. This is not meant as a denial, that real epic poetry, that is to say, a mass of popular songs celebrating the power and exploits of gods and heroes, existed at a very early period in India, as well as among the other Āryan nations; but it shows, that, if yet existing, it is not in the Mahābhārata and Rāmāyaṇa we have to look for these old songs, but rather in the Veda itself. In the collection of the Vedic hymns, there are some which may be called epic, and may be compared with the short hymns ascribed to Homer. In the Brāhmaṇas passages occur, in prose and verse, celebrating the actions of old kings.

The following extract from the Sāṅkhāyana-Sūtras (xvi. 1.), throws some light on the literature which the Brāhmaṇas possessed, in addition to what we are accustomed to call the Veda[24]:

"At the Horse-sacrifice (aśvamedha), the Adhvaryu calls upon singers who sing to the lute (*vīṇāgaṇaginas*), and invites them to celebrate the king, who then performs the sacrifice together with other virtuous kings of old. On the first day of the sacrifice, the priest tells the story which begins with Manu Vaivasvata. As the people of Manu were men, and there are men present at the sacrifice, the priest teaches these, the householders, by telling this story. He then says,'The Ṛc-verses are the Veda, this is the Veda,' and recites a hymn.

"On the second day he tells the story which begins with Yama Vaivasvata (from the Śatapatha). As the people of Yama were the fathers, and there are fathers present, he teaches the elders by this story. He then says,'The Yajurveda is the Veda; this is the Veda,' and recites an Anuvāka (āśvamedhika) of the Yajuṣ.

On the third day he tells the story which begins with Varuṇa Āditya. As the people of Varuṇa were the Gandharvas and as they are present, he teaches the young and fair youths by this story. He then says,'The Atharva-veda; is the Veda; this is the Veda,' and recites the Biṣaja,[25] a work on medicine.

"On the fourth day he tells the story which begins with Soma Vaiṣṇava (from the Śatapatha). As the people of Soma were the Apsaras, and as these are present, he teaches the young and fair maids by this story. He then says,'The Āṅgirasa-veda is the Veda; this is the Veda,' and recites the Ghora,[26] another work of the Ātharvaṇikās.

"On the fifth day he tells the story which begins with Arbuda Kādraveya. As the people of Arbuda were the Sarpas (snakes), and as these are present, he teaches the Sarpas, or the snake-charmers, by this story. He then says,'The SarpaVidyā is the Veda; this is the Veda,' and recites the SarpaVidyā[27]

"On the sixth day he tells the story which begins with Kuvera Vaiśravaṇa. As the people of Kuvera were Rakṣas, and as these are present, he teaches *Selagas*, or evil-doers, by this story. He then says,'The Rakṣovidyā is the Veda, this is the Veda,' and recites the Rakṣovidyā.[28]

"On the seventh day he tells the story which begins with Asita Dhānvana.[29] As his men were the Asuras, and as these are present, he teaches the usurers (Kustdin) by this story. He then says,'The AsuraVidyā is the Veda, this is the Veda,' and performs a trick by sleight of hand.[30]

"On the eighth day he tells the story which begins with *Matsya Sāmmada*. As his men were the creatures of the water, and as these are present, he teaches the Matsyas (fishes), or the fishermen by this story. He then says,'The Itihāsa-veda is the Veda, this is the Veda,' and recites an Itihāsa.'[31]

"On the ninth day he tells the story which begins with Tārkshya Vaipaśyata.[32] As his men were the birds, and as these are present, he teaches the birds, or the young students (Brahmāhārin),[33] by this story. He then says,'The Purāṇa-veda is the Veda, this is the Veda,' and recites the Purāṇa.[34]

"On the tenth day he tells the story which begins with Dharma Indra (from the Śatapatha). As his men were the gods, and as these are present, he teaches the young, learned and poor priests by this story.[35] He then says,'The Sāmaveda is the Veda, this is the Veda, and sings the Sāma.[36]"

This extract shows that epic poetry, traditional as well as improvised on the spur of the moment, existed during the Vedic age.

EPIC POEMS

In several parts of the Brāhmaṇas, and Āraṇyakas, when account is given of the literature, known to the ancient Hindus we meet with the names of Gāthā, Nārāśaṅsī. Itihāsa, and Ākhyāna[37] (songs, legends, epic poems, and stories) as parts of the Vedic literature. The occurrence of titles of literary works like these, has been made use of to prove the existence, at that early period, of the writings which afterwards were designated by the same names. But though the Mahābhārata is called an Itihāsa, and the Rāmāyaṇa an Ākhyāna, and though many works have in later times become famous under the name of Purāṇas yet these enumerations of literary works in the Brāhmaṇas do not refer to them.[38] They contain only general names of titles, which have been applied to certain parts of the sacred literature, contanig either stories of gods or men, or cosmogonic traditions.[39] There is no allusion to any of the titles of the Purāṇas or to the Rāmāyaṇa in Vedic works whether Brāhmaṇas or Sūtras. But as in the Sūtras of Āśvalāyana[40] the name of the Bhārata, and according to some manuscripts even the name of the Mahābhārata, is mentioned this may be considered as the earliest trace, not merely of angle epic poems, but of a collection of them. The age of Āśvâlāyana, which will be approximately fixed afterwards would, therefore if we can rely on our manuscripts, furnish a limit below which the first attempt at a collection of a Bhārata or Mahābhārata ought not to be placed. But, there is no hope that we shall ever succeed by critical researches in restoring the Bhārata to that primitive form and shape m which it may have existed before or at the time of Āśvâlāyana. Much has indeed been done by Professor Lassen who, in his Indian Antiquities, has pointed out characteristic marks by which the modern parts of the Mahābhārata can be distinguished from the move ancient; and we may soon expect to see his principles still further carried out in a translation of the whole Mahābharata, which, with the help of all the Sanskrit comamentaries, has been most carefully prepared by one of the most learned and laborious scholars of Germany. If it were possible to sift out from the huge mass of Indian epic poetry as we now possess it in the Mahābhārata and Rāmāyaṇa, those old stories and songs which must have been living for a long time in the mouth of the people before they were collected, enlarged, arranged and dressed up by later hands, a rich mine of information would be opened for the ancient times of India, and very likely also for the Vedic age. But the whole frame of the two epic poems as they now stand, their language and metre, as well as the moral and religious system they contain, show that they were put together at a period when the world of the Veda was living by tradition only, and moreover, partly misunderstood, and partly forgotten. The war between the Kurus and Pāṇḍavas, which forms the principal object of our Mahābhārata, is unknown in the Veda. The names of the Kurus and Bhāratas are common in Vedic literature but the names of the Pāṇḍavas have never been met with. It has been observed,[41] that even in Pāṇini's grammar the name Pāṇḍu or Pāṇḍava does not occur, while the Kurus and Bhāratas are frequently mentioned particulary in rules treating of the formation of patronymics and similar words.[42] If then, Āśvalāyana can be shown to have been a contemporary, or at least an immediate successor, of Pāṇini, the Bhārata which he is speaking of must have been very different from the epic poem which is known to us under the name of the Mahābhārata, celebrating the war of the Kurus and Pāṇḍavas.[43]

EPIC TRADITIONS REMODELLED

In the form in which we now possess the Mahābhārata it shows clear traces that the poets who collected and finished it, breathed an intellectual and religious atmosphere, very different from that in which the heroes of the poem moved. The epic character of the story has throughout been changed and almost obliterated by the didactic tendencies of the latest editors, who were clearly Brāhmanas brought up in the strict school of the

Laws of Manu. But the original traditions of the Pāṇḍavas break through now and then, and we can clearly discern that the races among whom the five principal heroes of the Mahābhārata were born and fostered, were by no means completely under the sway of the Brāhmanical law. How is it, for instance, that the five Pāṇḍava princes, who are at first represented as receiving so strictly Brāhmanic an education, who, if we are to believe the poet, were versed in all the sacred literature, grammar, metre, astronomy, and law of the Brāhmaṇas, could afterwards have been married to one wife ? This is in plain opposition to the Brāhmanic law, where it is said, "they are many wives of one man; not many husbands of one wife".[44] Such a contradiction can only be accounted for by the admission, that, in this case, epic tradition in the mouth of the people was too strong to allow this essential and curious feature in the life of its heroes to be changed. However, the Brāhmanic editors of the Mahābhārata, seeing that they could not alter tradition on this point, have at least endeavoured to excuse and mitigate it. Thus we are told in the poem itself, that at one time the five brothers came home, and informed their mother that they had found something extremely precious. Without listening further, their mother at once told them they ought to divide it as brothers. The command of a parent must always be literally obeyed; and as Draupadi was their newly discovered treasure, they were obliged, according to the views of the Brāhmaṇas, to obey, and to have her as their common wife. Indian lawgivers call this a knotty point[47]; they defend the fact, but refuse to regard it as a precedent.

Neither does the fact that Pāṇḍu is lawfully married to two wives, harmonise with the Brāhmanic law. That law does not prohibit polygamy, but it regards no second marriage as legal, and it reserves the privilege of being burnt together with the husband to the eldest and only lawful wife. Such passages in the ancient epics are of the greatest interest. We see in them the tradition of the people too far developed, to allow itself to be remodelled by Brāhmanic Diaskeuastes. There can be little doubt that polygamy, as we find it among the early races in their transition from the pastoral to the agricultural life, was customary in India. We read in Herodotes (v. 5.), that amongst the Thracians it was usual, after the death of a man, to find out who had been the most beloved of his wives, and to sacrifice her upon his tomb. Mela (ii. 2.) gives the same as the general custom of the Getse. Herodotus (iv. 71.) asserts a similar fact of the Scythians, and Pausanias (iv. 2.) of the Greeks, while our own Teutonic mythology is full of instances of the same feeling.[45] And thus the customs of these cognate nations explain what at first seemed to be anomalous in the epic tradition of the Mahā-Bhārata, that at the death of Pāṇḍu, it is not Kunti, his lawful wife, but Madrī, his most beloved wife, in whose arms the old king dies and who successfully claims the privilege of being burnt with him, andfollowing her husband to another life. [47]

The same remark applies to the Rāmāyaṇa. In this second epic also, we see that the latest editors were shocked by the anomalies of the popular tradition, and endeavoured to impart a more Brāhmanic polish to the materials handed down to them from an earlier age Thus king Daśaratha kills the son of a Brāhmaṇa, which would be a crime so horrible in the eyes of the Brāhmaṇas, that scarcely any penance could expiate it.[48] This is the reason why the young Brāhmaṇa is represented as the son of a Śūdra woman, and tells the king so himself, in order to relieve him from the fear of having killed the son of a Brahmaṇa. The singular relation, too, between Rāma and Paraśu-Rāma, was probably remodelled by the influence of the Brāhmaṇas, who could not bear the idea of their great hero, the destroyer of all the Kṣatriyas, being in turn vanquished by Rāma, who was himself a Kṣatriya.

EARLY CUSTOMS

The Vedic literature, by the very sacredness of its character, has fortunately escaped from the remodeling puritanism of the later Brāhmaṇas. There must, from the first, have been as great a variety in the intellectual, religious and moral character of the Indians, as there is in the geographical and physical character of India. If we look at Greece, and consider the immense diversity of local worship, tradition, and customs, which co-existed within that small tract of country, and then turn our eyes to the map of India, barred as it is by mountain-ranges and livers, it becomes clear that the past ages of such a country cannot be represented in their fulness and reality by the traditions of the later Brāhmaṇas, which as we now possess them in the epic and Paurāṇic poetry of the Hindus, are all tinged with the same monotonous colouring. Such a uniformity is always the result of an artificial system, and not of a natural and unimpeded development. It is indeed acknowledged by the Brāhmaṇas themselves that different customs prevailed in different parts of India. Some were even sanctioned by them notwithstanding their policy of monopolising and (so to speak) brahmanising the whole Indian mind. Although, for instance, in the liturgic works annexed to the Vedas (Śrauta-Sūtras), an attempt was made to establish a certain unity in the sacrifices of the people all over India, yet in the performance of these sacrifices there existed certain discrepancies, based on the traditionary authority of the wise of old, between family and family. This is still mere the case in the so-called domestic ceremonies of baptism, confirmation, marriage, etc., described in the Gṛhya-Sūtras, which, connected as they were with the daily life of the people, give us much more real information on the ancient customs of India than those grand public or private sacrifices which are prescribed in the Śrauta-Sūtras, and could only have been kept up by sacerdotal influence. In these domestic ceremonies everybody is allowed, as a general law, to follow the customs of the family[49] to which he belongs, or of his village and country, provided these customs do not too grossly insult the moral and religious feelings of the Brāhmaṇas.

Although these domestic ceremonies were fully sanctioned by the Brāhmaṇic law, the authority upon which they are founded does not lie directly in the sacred revelation of the Brāhmaṇas, (Śruti), but in tradition (Smṛti), a difference, the historical importance of which will have to be pointed out hereafter. As to the customs of countries and villages, there can be no doubt that in many cases they were not only not founded upon Brāhmaṇic authority, but frequently decidedly against it. The Brāhmaṇic law, however, is obliged to recognise and allow those customs, with the general reser-vation that they must not be in open opposition to the law. Thus Āśvalāyana in his Gṛhya-Sūtras, says—"Now the customs of countries and places are certainly manifold. One must know them as far as marriage is concerned. But we shall explain what is the general custom."[50]

Here the commentator adds—"If there be contradiction between the customs of countries, etc. and those customs which we are going to describe, one must adopt the custom as laid down by us, not those of the country. What we shall say is the general law, this is our meaning. Amongst the Vaidehas, for instance, one sees at once that loose habits prevail. But in the domestic laws continence is prescribed; therefore there is no doubt that the domestic and not the national customs are to be observed."[51]

In the Sūtras of Gautama, too, a similar line of conduct is traced out. After it has been said that the highest authority by which a government ought to be guided consists in the Vedas, Vedāṅgas, Śāstras, and old traditions, it is added (Adhy. 11. Sūtra 20.); that in cases where the customs, of countries, classes and families are not expressly founded upon a passage of the Veda, they are, notwithstanding, to be observed, if they are not clearly against the principles of the sacred writings, such as would be, for instance, marrying the daughter of a maternal uncle.[52]

There is an interesting passage in the Gṛhya-saṅgraha-pariśishṭa, composed by the son of Gobhila, which Dr. Roth quotes in his Essays on the Veda, (p. 120): "The Vaśiṣṭhas wear a braid on the right side, the Ātreyas wear three braids, the Aṅgiras wear five locks, the Bhṛgus have their head quite shaved, others have a lock of hair on the top of the head."[53]

Another peculiarity ascribed to Vaśiṣṭhas is that they exclude meat from the sacrifices. [54]

A similar notice of the customs of neighbouring nations, is found in Raghunandana's quotation from the Harivaṁśa—that the Śakas (Scythians) have half their head shorn, the Yavanas (Greeks ?) and Kambojās the whole, that the Pāradas (inhabitants of Paradene) wear their hair free, and the Pahlavas (Persians) wear beards.[55]

In the same way, then, as different traditions were current in India relative to such observances, it is probable that different families had their own heroes, perhaps their own deities, and that they kept up the memory of them by their own poetic traditions. It is true that such a view is merely conjectural. But when we see that in some parts of the Veda, which are represented as belonging to different illustrious and noble families, certain gods are more exclusively celebrated;[56] that names which in Vedic poetry are known as those of heroes and poets (Pururavas, Kutsa) are afterwards considered as names of infidels and heretics, we have a right to infer that we have here the traces of a widely extended practice.

VEDIC TRADITIONS REMODELLED

In the hymns of the Ṛg-veda we meet with allusions to several legendary stories— afterwards more fully developed by the Brāhmaṇaṣ in their Brāhmaṇas—by which laws that were in later times acknowledged as generally binding, and as based upon the authority of the Veda, are manifestly violated. It is an essential doctrine of the Brāhmaṇas, that the religious education, and the administration of sacrifices, as well as the receiving of rewards for these offices, belong exclusively to their own caste. Kakṣīvat, however, whose hymns are found in the first and ninth Maṇḍala of the Ṛg-veda, and who, whether on account of his name or for some better reason, is said to have been a Kshatriya, or of royal extraction, is represented as receiving from King Svanaya presents, which, according to Manu[57], it would have been unlawful for him to accept. In order to explain this away, a story is told, that although Kakṣīvat was the son of King Kaliṅga, yet his real father was the old Ṛṣi Dīrghatamas, whose hymns have likewise been preserved in the first Maṇḍala of the Ṛg-veda. This poet had been asked by the king to beget offspring for him, according to ancient Indian custom. The queen, however, refused to see the old sage, and sent her servant-maid instead. The son of this servant and the Ṛṣi Dīrghatamas was Kakṣīvat, and as the son of a Ṛṣi he was allowed to perform sacrifices and to receive presents. This story shows its purpose very clearly, and there can be little doubt that it owes its orign to the tender conscience of the Brāhmaṇas, who could not bear to see their laws violated by one of their own sacred Ṛṣis. It is a gratuitous assumption to suppose that the poets of the Veda should have been perfect in the observance of the Brāhmaṇic law. That law did not exist when they lived and composed their songs, for which in later times they were raised to the rank of saints. Whether Kakṣīvat was the son of a Brāhimaṇa or a Kshatriya, of a servant-maid or of a queen, is impossible to determine. But it is certain that in the times in which he lived, he would not have scrupled to act both as a warrior and priest, if circumstances required it. This becomes still more evident, if we accept Professor Lassen's view, who considers Dīrghatamas, the father of Kakṣīvat, as one of the earliest Brāhmanic missionaries in the southern parts of Bengal, among the Aṅgas and Kaliṅgas.[60] Now, under circumstances of this kind, when the Brāhmaṇas were still labouring to establish their supremacy over different parts of India, it can hardly be believed that the different castes and their respective duties and privileges should have been established as strictly as in later times. In later times it is considered a grievous sin to recite the hymns of the Veda in place where a Śūdra might be able to hear them. In the Ṛg-veda we find hymns which the Brāhmaṇas themselves allow to be the compositions of the son of a slave. Kavaṣa Ailūṣa is the author of several hymns in the tenth Book of the Ṛg-veda; yet this same Kavasha was expelled from the sacrifice as an imposter and as the son of a slave (dāṣyāh putraḥ), and he was re-admitted only because the gods had. shown him special favour. This is acknowledged by the Brāhmaṇas of the Aitareyins[59] and Kauṣītakins, and in the Mahābhārata also Kavaṣa is called a Niṣāda.

VEDIC AND PAURĀṆIC WORSHIP

The marked difference between the Vedic and epic poetry of India has been well pointed out by Professor Roth of Tubingen, who for many years has devoted much time and attention to the study of the Veda. According to him, the Mahābhārata, even in its first elements, is later than the time of Buddha.[60] "In the epic poems," he says, "the Veda is but imperfectly known; the ceremonial is no longer developing, it is complete. The Vedic legends have been plucked from their native soil, and the religion of Agni, Indra, Mitra and Varuṇa has been replaced by an altogether different worship. The last fact," he says, "ought to be the most convincing. There is a contradiction running throughout the religious life of India, from the time of the Rāmāyaṇa to the present day. The outer form of the worship is Vedic, and exclusively so;[61] but the eye of religious adoration is turned upon quite different regions.[64] The secondary formation, the religion of Viṣṇu and Brahmā, began with the epic poetry, and remained afterwards as the only-living one but without having the power to break through the walls of the Vedic ceremonial, and take the place of the old ritual."

And if it be unsafe to use the epic poems as authorities, for the Vedic age, it will readily be admitted that the same objection applies with still greater force to the Purāṇas. Although one only of the eighteen Purāṇas has as yet been completely published, enough is known of their character, partly by Professor Burnouf's edition of the Bhāgvata-Purāṇa, partly by extracts given from others Purāṇas by Professor Wilson, to justify our discarding their evidence with reference to the primitive period of Vedic literature. Even the Mānava-dharma-śāstra, the law-book of the Mānavas, a sub-division of the sect of the Taittirīyas, or, as it is commonly called, the laws of Manu, cannot be used as an independent authority. It cannot be said that the compilers of these laws were ignorant of the tradition of the Vedic age. Many of their verses contain a mere paraphrase of passages from the hymns, Brāhmaṇas and Sūtras; but they likewise admitted the rules and customs of a later age, and their authority is therefore valid only where it has been checked by more original and genuine texts.

MANU'S CODE OF LAWS

The Code of Manu is almost the only work in Sanskrit literature which, as yet, has not been assailed by those who doubt the antiquity of everything Indian. No historian has disputed its claim to that early date which had, from the first, been assigned to it by Sir William Jones. It must be confessed, however, that Sir William Jones's proofs of the antiquity of this Code cannot be considered as conclusive, and no sufficient arguments have been brought forward to substantiate any of the different dates ascribed to Manu, as the author of our Law-book, which vary, according to different writers from 880 to 1280 B. C.

If the age of Manu or of the epic poems could be fixed, so as to exclude all possible doubt, our task with regard to the age of the Veda would be an easy one. The Veda is demonstrably earlier than the epic poetry and the legal codes of India. We do not, however, advance one step by saying that the Veda is older than the author of the Mānava-dharma-śāstra, whose date is altogether unknown, or even than the Mahābhārata, if it can be doubted whether that poem in its first elements be anterior to the Buddhistic religion or not; while it is said, at the same time, that the last elements which have been incorporated into this huge work allude to historical events later than the Christian era.[63] Here, then, we must adopt a new course of procedure. We must try to fix the age of the Veda, which forms the natural basis of Indian history; and we must derive our knowledge of the Vedic age from none but Vedic works, discarding altogether such additional evidence as might be obtained from the later literature of India. Let some Vedic dates be once established, and it will probably be possible to draw lines of connection between the Vedic and the rest of the Indian literature. But the world of the Veda is a world by itself; and its relation to all the other Sanskrit literature is such, that the Veda ought not to receive but ought to throw light over the whole historical development of the Indian mind.

The Veda has a twofold interest : it belongs to the history of the world and to the history of India. In the history of the world the Veda fills a gap which no literary work in any other language could fill. It carries us back to times of which we have no records anywhere, and gives us the very words of a generation of men, of whom otherwise we could form but the vaguest estimate by means of conjectures and inferences. As long as man continues to take an interest in the history of his race, and as long as we collect in libraries and museums the relics of former ages, the first place in that long row of books which contains the records of the Āryan branch of mankind, will belong for ever to the Ṛg-veda.

But in the history of India, too, the Veda is of the greatest importance. It has been a standing reproach against our studies that it is impossible to find anything historical in Indian literature.[64] To a certain extent that reproach is well founded; and this accounts no doubt for the indifference with which Sanskrit literature is regarded by the public at large.

We may admire the delicate poetry of Kālidāsa, the philosophical vigour of Kapila, the voluptuous mysticism of Jayadeva, and the epic simplicity of Vyāsa and Vālmīki, but as long as their works float before our eyes like the mirage of a desert, as long as we are unable to tell what real life, what period in the history of a nation they reflect, there is some-thing wanting to engage our sympathies in the same manner as they are engaged by the tragedies of Æschylus, or the philosophical essays of Cicero. We value the most imperfect statues of Lycia and Ægina, because they throw light on the history of Greek art, but we should pass by unnoticed the most perfect mouldings of the human frame, if we could not tell whether they had been prepared in the studio of Phidias, or in the dissecting-room of a London hospital.

In the following sketch of the history of Vedic literature, I cannot promise to give dates such as we are accustomed to find in the literary histories of other nations. But I hope I shall be able to prove that there exist in that large mass of literature which belongs to the Vedic age, clear traces of an original historical articulation; and that it is possible to restore something

like chronological continuity in the four periods of the Vedic literature. If this can be achieved, if we can discover different classes of literary works, and vindicate to them something of a truly historical character, the reproach that there is nothing historical to be found in India will be removed, as far as the peculiar nature of that literature allows.

The modern literature of India, though not yet grouped in chronological order, will find in the literature of the Vedic age something like a past, some testimony to prove that it did not spring up in a day, but clings by its roots to the earliest strata of Indian thought. The laws of the Mānavas, though no longer the composition of a primeval sage, will at least be safe against the charge of being the invention of some unemployed Indian lawgiver. Plays like Śakuntalā and Urvaśī, though no longer regarded as the productions of a Periclean age, will be classed among the productions of what may properly be called the Alexandrain period of Sanskrit literature. But whatever we may have to surrender with regard to the antiquity claimed by these and other Sanskrit works, that portion of the literature of India which alone can claim a place in the history of the world, and which alone can command the attention of those who survey the summits of human intellect, not only in the East but over the whole civilized world, will, we hope, for the future, be safe against the doubts which I myself have shared for many years. It is difficult, no doubt, to believe that the most ancient literary work of the Āryan race, a work more ancient than the Zendavesta and Homer, should, after a lapse of at least three thousand years, have been discovered, and for the first time published in its entirety, not in one of the Parishads on the borders of the Ganges, but in one of the colleges of an English University, It is difficult to believe that sufficient MSS. should have been preserved, in spite of the perishable nature of the material on which they are written, to enable an editor to publish the collection of the Vedic hymns in exactly that form in which they existed at least 800 years before the Christian era; and, still more, that this collection, which was completed at the time of Lycurgus, should contain the poetical relics of a pre-Homeric age; an age in which the names of the Greek gods and heroes had not yet lost their original sense, and in which the simple worship of the Divine powers of nature was not yet supplanted by a worship of personal gods. It is difficult to believe this; and we have a right to be sceptical. But it is likewise our duty to inquire into the value of what has been preserved for us in so extraordinary a manner, and to extract from it those lessons which the study of mankind was intended to teach to man.

HISTORY OF VEDIC LITERATURE.

In taking a survey of the works which belong to the Vedic literature of India, our task would be greatly facilitated if general and characteristic features could be pointed out by which Vedic and non-Vedic works might at once be distinguished. Without entering into a minute analysis of the individual character of a work, a mode of criticism which, with our present knowledge of the earlist Indian literature, must be very uncertain, it will often happen that some external mark presents itself, determining at once the age or class of writing to which it belongs. It is true that there are certain grammatical forms and orthographical peculiarities which Indian grammarians restrict to the Veda, and which, therefore, might be used as distinguishing marks of works belonging to that era. But Manu, or rather the author of the Mānava-dharma-śāstra, has also employed several Vedic forms; because in transforming Vedic verses into epic Ślokas, he is sometimes obliged to retain words and forms which are not in strict accordance with the general character of his language; a fact which accounts in some degree for the strange appearance of many of his verses, which are stiff and artificial, and very inferior in fluency to the older strains which they paraphrase.

There is a strongly marked character in Vedic prose, and no attempt has been made to imitate it in later times. But in order to distinguish Vedic from non-Vedic poetry, we must attend more closely to the metre. Several Vedic metres bave been imitated by later poets, but there are metres which never occur in Vedic works and which may be used as criteria for distinguishing ancient from more modern poetry.

That difference of metre should form a broad line of demarcation between two periods of literature, is not at all without an analogy in the literary history of other nations, particularly in older times. If once a new form of metre begins to grow popular by the influence of a poet who succeeds in collecting a school of other poets around him, this new mode of utterance is very apt to supersede the other more ancient forms altogether. People become accustomed to the new rhythm sometimes to such a degree, that they lose entirely the taste for their old poetry on account of its obsolete measure. No poet, therefore, who writes for the people, would think of employing those old-fashioned meters- and we find that early popular poems have had to be transfused into modern verse in order to make them generally readable once more.

Now it seems that the regular and continuous Anuṣṭubh-Śloka is a metre unknown during the Vedic age, and every work written in it may at once be put down as post-Vedic It is no valid objection that this epic Śloka occurs also in Vedic hymns, that Anuṣṭubh verses are frequently quoted in the Brāhmaṇas, and that in some of the Sūtras the Anuṣṭubh-Śloka occurs intermixed with Trishṭubhs, and is used for the purpose of recapitulating[65] what had been explained before in prose. For it is only the uniform employment of that metre[66] which constitutes the characteristic mark of a new period of literature. Thus rhyme occasionally occurs in English poetry before the Norman period; yet, when we find whole poems written in rhyme and without the old Teutonic system of alliteration, we are sure that they cannot have been composed in an Ante-Norman period. The elegiac measure seems to have been used before Callinus; yet Callinus and Archilochus are always mentioned as the inventors of it : that is, they were the first to sanction the uniform employment of this metre for entire poetical compositions. Hence no elegiac poem can be previous to the close of the 8th century B. C. The same applies to the iambus, the invention of which is commonly ascribed to Archilochus; although iambics occur interspersed in the Margites, a poem ascribed to Homer by no less an authority than Aristotle.[67] In the history of German literature we have several instances where poems of the 12th century[68] had to be recast as early as the 13th, on account of their metre and language; which, during this period of rapid transition had already become obsolete and unreadable.

Excluding, then, from the Vedic period the Mahābhārata, Rāmāyaṇa, Manu, the Purāṇas, all the Śāstras aud Darśanas we have now to see what remains of literary works belonging to the Vedic age.

There are in that age four distinct periods, which can be established with sufficient evidence. They may be called the *Chandas period, Mantra period, Brāhmaṇa period*, and *Sūtra period*, according to the general form of the literary productions which give to each of them its peculiar historical character.

In order to prove that these four periods follow each other in historical order, it is necessary to show that the composition of Sūtra works presupposes the existence of a Brāhmaṇa literature; that the Brāhmaṇa literature again is only possible with the presupposition of a Mantra literature; and lastly, that the form in which we possess the Mantra literaure presupposes a period of Vedic history preceding the collection and final arrangement of the ancient Mantras or hymns.

FOOTE NOTES

1. "Śakuntalā or the Fatal Ring, an Indian drāma, translated from the original Sanskrit and Prakrit. Calcutta, 1789." There have since appeared three editions of the Sanskrit text, and translations in French, German, Italian, Danish, and Swedish.

   A new and very elegant English version has lately been published by Professor Williams. Hertford, 1856.

2. Goethe was one of the greatest admirers of Śakuntalā, as may be seen from the lines written in his Italian Travels at Naples, and from his well-known Epigram : "Willt Du die Bltithe des frühen, die Früchte des späteren Jahres,
   Willt Du, was reizt und entzuckt, willt Du was sättigt und nährt,
   Willt Du den Jlimmel, die Erde mit einem Namen begreifen,

Nenn ich, Sacontala, Dich, und so ist Alles gesagt."
"Will you the blossoms of spring and the fruits that are later in season,
Wilt you have charms and delights, will you have strength and support,
Will you with one short word eneompass the earth and the heaven,
All is said if I name only, Sacontala thee"

3. Professor Gildemeister in his most laborious and accurate work, "Bibliothecse Sanscritee Specimen, Bonnse, 1847," brings the number of books that have been published up to that time in Sanskrit philology to 603, exclusive of all works on Indian antiquities and Comparative Philology. During the last twelve years that number has been considerably raised.
4. Professor Lassen, in his work on Indian Antiquities, now in course of publication, is giving a resumé of the combined labours of Indian philologists during the last seventy years, sifted critically and arranged scientifically by a man of the ' most extensive learning, and of the soundest principles of criticism. His work may indeed be considered as bringing to its conclusion an important period of Sanskrit philology, which had taken its beginning with Sir W. Jones's translation of Śakuntalā- Indische Alterthums-Kunde, von Christian Lassen. Bonn, 1847-1858.
5. Herder's Schriften, vol. ix. p. 226, Zur schönen Literature und Kunst. Tübingen, 1807.
6. Cf. Account of a Discovery of a Modern Imitation of the Vedas, with Remarks on the genuine works, by Fr. Ellis; Asiatic Researches, xiv, p. 1-59 : Calcutta, 1822.
7. Professor H. H. Wilson, in the preface to his translation of the Viṣṇu-Purāṇa, remarks : "It is the boast of inductive philosophy that it draws its conclusions from the careful observation and accumulation of facts; and it is equally the business of all philosophical research to determine its facts before its ventures upon speculation. This procedure has not been observed in the investigation of the mythology and traditions of the Hindus. Impatience to generalise has availed itself greedily of whatever promised to afford materials for generalisation; and the most erroneous views have been confidently advocated, because the guides to which their authors trusted were ignorant or insufficient."

* Ref. Strabo-XV. 1.6. for text Vide Appendix A.

8. "Paraśu-Rāma cleared the earth thrice seven times of the Kṣatriya caste, and filled with their blood the five large lakes of Sāmanta-pañcaka, from which he offered libations to the race of Bhṛgu. Offering a solemn sacrifice to the King of the gods, Paraśu-Rāma presented the earth to the ministering priests. Having given the earth to Kasyapa, the hero of immeasurable prowess retired to the Mahendra mountain, where he still resides; and in this manner was there enmity between him and the race of the Kṣatriyas, and thus was the whole earth conquered by Paraśu-Rāma." (Viṣṇu-Purāṇa, p. 403.) In the Mahābhārata the earth is made to say, "The fathers and grandfathers of these Kṣatriyas have been killed by the remorseless Rāma in warfare on my account."

9. In one of the old hymns of the Ṛg-veda this thought seems to weigh upon the mind of the poet, when he says :
सतो बन्धुमसति निरविन्दन् हृदि प्रतीष्य कवयो मनीषा ṚV. x. 129. 4.
"Poets discovered in their heart, through meditation, the bond of the existing in the non-existing."
10. In the Veda life after death is not frequently alluded to, and it is more for the goods of this world, for strength, long life, a large family, food, and cattle, that the favour of the gods is implored. One of the rewards for a pious life, however, consists in being admitted afer death to the seat of the gods. Thus Kakṣivān (कक्षीवान्) says, "He who gives alms goes and stands on the highest place in heaven, he goes to the gods." (Ṛv. i. 125. 5.) Thus Dīrghatamas (दीर्घतमा:) after having rebuked those who are rich, and do not give alms, nor worship the gods, exclaims, "The kind mortal, O Sage, is greater than the Great in heaven; let us worship thee, O Agni, for ever and ever !" (Ṛv. i. 150, 3,)
11. The technical term pretyabhāva (प्रेत्यभाव), which occurs so frequently in Indian philosophy, and has generally been rendered by "condition of the soul after death" means really the state in which we are while living on earth. Our present life, according to Indian notions, is "bhāva," birth and. growth, "pretya", after a previous death.
12. In the same sense the sun is called *jīvo asuḥ*, "the vital spirit,'cf. Ṛv. i. 113. 16,.
उदोर्ध्व जीवो असुर्न आगादप प्रागात्तम आ ज्योतिरेति:-Rv. ii. 3.14,
"Rise! our life, our spirit, came ; the darkness went off; the light approaches!"
को ददर्श प्रथमं जायमानमस्थन्वन्तं यदनस्था बिभर्ति।
भूभ्या असुरसृगात्मा क्व स्वित्को विद्वांसमुपगात्प्रष्टुमेतत्।।
"Who has seen the first born, when he who has no bones (*i. e.*, form) bore him who had bones ? Where was the life the blood, the sole (self) of the world ? Who went to ask this from any that knew it ?"
13. It is difficult to find a satisfactory etymology for ātmā (nomin), particularly in its older, and possibly more original form, tmā. Bopp (Comp. Grammar, i. 140.) says, "if ātmā, stand for ātma, and derived from a lost root, āh, to think (when it must be remembered that the root nah also changes its final h sometimes into, upanah and upanat), it might be compared with the Gothic ahma, soul." This root, dh, is afterwards traced by Bopp in the Sanskriṭ aha, "he said;" and he observes that to speak and to think are in the Indo-European languages sometimes expressed by one and the same word. The last observation, however, is not quite proved by the ex-ample taken by Bopp from the Zend, *manthra*, speech, For although the Sanskrit mantra is derived from man, to think, it receives its causa! meaning by the termination tra, and has therefore the signification of prayer, hymn, advice, speech (i. e., what makes us think). If *ātmā* come from a root ah, the meaning of this root is more likely that of breathing, which would account for Gothic *ahma*

(πνεvμα), as well as for Sanskrit aha, Greek η and ηXω, Latin ajo and nego, and similar words. If we derive *ātmā*, spirit, soul, self, from this I root, ah, we may also derive from it a-ham, I (cuneiform inscript. adam, ego, εγω, ich). But there always remains a difficulty as regards the elision of 'ā' in the old Vedic form *tmā*, instead of *ātmā*, and the Zend *thmanangh*, which, according to Prof. Burnouf's conjecture, is the Sansk. *tmanas* (Commentaire sur le Yaśna, p. 509.); a difficulty which neither European etymologists (Pott, Etymologische Forschungen, i. 196.; Benfey, Griechisches Wurzellexicon, i. 265.), nor Indian Aupadika scholars (Ugadi Sūtras, 4.152.) have yet explained.

14. Bṛhadāraṇyaka, 2d Adhyāya, 4th Brāhmaṇa, p. 28, edit. Poley; 4th Prapathaka, 4th Brāhmaṇa, p. 444. edit. Röer.
15. Instead of प्रिया बतारे न: सती Dr. Poley reads प्रियावतारे न: सती which he may have meant for" you Avatāra or incarnation of our love." Not to speak however, of the grammatical difficulties of this construction, the Commentary leaves no doubt that we ought to read, (इष्टा) बत (इत्यनुकम्प्याह) अरे (मैत्रेयि)।
16. This last sentence is taken from the fifth Brāhmaṇa of the fourth Adhyāya, where the same story is told again with slight modifications and additions.
17. "Nay, for aught we know of ourselves, of our present life, and death; death may immediately, in the natural course of things, put us into a higher and more en'arged state of life, as our birth does."-Bishop Butler. (Trans, from Strabo-XV, 59; for text Vide Appendix A)
18. The notion of sin is clearly expressed, for instance, in a song of Gṛtsāmadas-

    वि मच्छ्रथाय रशनामिवाग ऋध्यम ते वरुण खामृतस्य।
    मा तन्तुश्छेदि वयतो धियं मे मा मात्रा शार्यपस: पुर ऋतो:।।
    अपो सु म्यक्ष वरुण भियसं मत्सम्राल्ऋतावोऽनु मा गृभाय।
    दामेव वत्साद्विमुमुग्ध्यंहो न हि त्वदारे निमिषश्चनेशे।। (Ṛv. ii. 28. 5.)

    "Deliver me from sin, as from a rope; let us obtain thy path of righteousness. May the thread not be torn while I am weaving my prayer; may the form of my pious work not decay before its season.

    "Varuṇa, take all fear away from me; be kind to me, O just king ! Take away my sin like a rope from a calf; for afar from you 1 am not the master even of a twinkling of the eye."

    And again,

    घृतव्रता आदित्या इषिरा आरे मत्कर्त रहसूरिवाग:। (Ṛv. h. 29. 1.)

    "You quick Ādityas, ye who never fail in your works, carry away from me all sin, as a woman does who has given birth to a child in secret."

    *Ref. Strabo, XV. 59 (for text Vide Appendix).
19. Sāyaṇa in his commentary on the Ṛg-Veda. i. 131. 3., explaining the words वि त्वा ततस्रे मिथुना अवस्यव: "Couples wishing for protection have magnified you, O Indra !" quotes passages from the Brāhmaṇas, the Sūtras, and the Smṛtis, in support of the law laid down in the Pūrva-Mīmānsā that man and

wife should perform sacrifices in common. From the Brāhmaṇas he quotes the beginning of the Agnyādhāna, where it is said that man and wife are to place the sacred fire in common : जायापती अग्निमादधीयीताम्। From the Sūtras he quotes a rule, वेदं पत्न्यै प्रदाय वाचयेत्। This seem to mean, "Let him, after giving the Veda to his wife, make her recite it." The passage is taken from the Āśvalāyana Srauta-Sūtras, i. 11. If the word veda, used by Āśvalāyana, meant the Veda, this passage would be most important, as proving the existence of the Veda, as a written book, at the time of Āśvalāyana. Veda, however, is used here in the sense of "a bundle of grass," and is connected with vedih, an altar made of grass (Root *ve*, Lat. viere). Lastly, Sāyaṇa quotes from the Smṛtis, Manu, V. 155., "Women cannot sacrifice without their husbands.': नास्ति स्त्रीणां पृथग्यज्ञ:।

20. The piety and happiness of a married couple is well described in a hymn ascribed to Manu Vaivasvata, B,v. viii. 31. 5-9.
21. Manu, ix. 18., translated by Sir W. Jones. "Women have i no business with the texts of the Veda, thus is the law fully settled; having; therefore, no evidence of law, and no knowledge of expiatory texts, sinful women must be as foul as falsehood itself"; and this is a fixed rule."
22. M. Troyer, in his valuable edition of the Rājataraṅgiṇī (ii. 399), gives the following data as to the extent of the Buddhistic religion : *'La population de la terre est evaluee par M. Hassel á 921 millions ; par Malte-Brun, a 642 millions; par d'autres, a 737 millions d'habitants. Le Buddhisme est professé dans presque tout l'empire de la Chine, qui, seul d'apres differents computs, contient de 184 a 300 millions d'habitants. f Ajoutons-y les Buddhistes de plusieursT les de l'Est, de la Cochinchine, du Siam, du pays des Birmans, de l'lnde, du Nepal, du Tibet, et de la majeure partie de la Tartarie, etc, et l'on trouveraque je n'exage're pas trop le nombre des Buddhistes actuels."
23 See J. Bird, Historical Researches on the Origin and Principles of the Buddha and Jaina Religion. Bombay, 1847,
24. The same account is given in the Āśvalāyana-sūtras, x. 7, and in the Śatapatha-Brāhmaṇa, xiii 3.1, 1.
25. The commentator insists on this being a distinct book of the Ātharvaṇikās, and not a hymn. या औषधीरित्येतत्सूक्तं केचिदाहु: तदयुक्तम्। समाख्यानाद्द्वेष-जग्रन्थस्याथर्वणिकानाम्।। The Śatapatha says अथर्वणामेकं पर्व।। Āśvalāyana यद्धेषजं निशान्तम्।।
26. घोरमाथर्वणो ग्रन्थ:।। The Śatapatha says अङ्गिरसामेकं पर्व।।
27. गारुडां कङ्कनीयां वा।। The Śatapatha : सर्पविद्याया एकं पर्व।।
28. कुहुकरूपा रक्षोविद्या।। According to the Śatapatha देवजनविद्याया एकं पर्व।। according to Āśvalāyana, पिशाचविद्या।।
29. Asita Dhānva, Śatapatha and Āśvalāyana,
30. असुरविद्येन्द्रजालादिना तन्निर्देशान्मायामपि काश्चित्कुर्यादङ्गलिन्यासरूपाम्।।
31. इतिहासवेदस्य पृथम्भावेन दर्शनात्।।

32. Vaipasśscita, according tp Āśvalāyana.
33. वायोविद्यिका:।। Śatapatha.
34. पुराणं वायुप्रोक्तमत्राख्येयम्। The Vāyu-purāṇa has a more ancient appearance than the other Purāṇas.
35. यूनोऽप्रतिग्राहकाञ्छ्रोत्रियान्।।
36. साम्नां दशतम् Śatapatha.
37. Cf. Taittrīya-Āraṇyaka, ii. 9 : ब्राह्मणानीतिहासान्पुराणानि कल्पान् गाथा नाराशंसी:।। Bṛhadāraṇyaka, ii. 4. 10 इतिहास: पुराणं विद्या उपनिषद:श्लोका: सूत्राण्यनुव्याख्यानानि व्याख्यानानि।। ibid. iv. 1. 2,iv 5 9; Śatap. Brāhm. xi. 7. 1. . Atharv. Saṁhitā, xv. 6. : इतिहासश्च पुराणं च गाथाश्च .नारशंसीश्च।। Cf- Aufrecht, Indische Studien p.133 Sāyaṇa himself is sometimes doubtful and in his Commentary on the Taittirīya-āraṇyaka, for instance, he says that by Purāṇa might be meant the Brahmāṇḍa, etc., and by Itihāsa the Mahābhārata. This, however, is a mistake, and it would'bring Sāyaṇa into contradiction with himself. He has fully proved in his Introduction to the Ṛg-veda that in this passage of the Taittirīya.Āraṇyaka.no works separate from the Veda could be understood. Cf. Ṛg-veda Saṁhitā, p. 23. Dr. Weber - his extracts from Pāṇini (iv. 2 60.), shows that vyākhyāna, ākhyāna, kathā ākhyāyāyikā, itihāsa and *Purāṇa,* were titles of literary works known at the tune of Kātyāyana. But he inclines to the opinion that Kātyāyana did not mean Mahābhārata, Rāmāyaṇa, and the Purāṇas, as we now possess them, by these general names. Cf. Indische Studien, I. p. 147.
38. In the later literature also, names like Itihāsa, Ākhyāna, and Purāṇa are by no means restricted to the Mahābhārata, Rāmāyaṇa, and the Purāṇas. The Mahābhārata is called Purāṇa, Ākhyāna, and Itihāsa. Cf. M. Bh. 1. 17-19. Vyāsa himself calls his poem, the Mahābhārata a Kāvya; and Brahmā sanctions this as its proper title. Cf. M. Bh. I. 72. The passage modifies Professor Lassen's opinion as to Kāvya being the distinctive title of the Rāmāyaṇa. Cf. Indian Antiquities, 1. 485. The Mahābhārata is also called the fifth Veda, or the Kārṣṇa-veda; that is. the Veda composed by Kṛshṇa Dvaipāyana Vyāsa. Cf. M. Bh. I. 2300. Burnouf. Bhāg III. pref. xxi. Lassen, Ind. Antiq I. 789.
39. Cf. Sāyaṇa, Introduction to the Ṛg-veda Saṁhitā, p. 23.
40. Gṛhya-Sūtras, ill. 4. MS. 1978, E. I. H., reads, भरतधर्माचार्या: instead of भारतमहाभारतधर्माचार्या: the reading adopted by Dr. Roth (Zur Literatur, p. 27). Unfortunately the Commentary to this passage is very scanty, which is so much the more to be regretted, as the text itself seems to contain spurious additions. According to the MSS, the passage reads अथ ऋषग: शतर्चिनो माध्यमा गृत्समदो विश्वामित्रो वामदेवोऽत्रिर्भरद्वाजो वसिष्ठ: प्रगाथा: पावमान्य: क्षुद्रसूक्ता महासूक्ता इति। प्राचीनावीती सुमन्तुजैमिनिवैशम्पायनपैलसूत्रभाष्य-भारतधर्माचार्या जानन्तिबाहविगार्ग्यगौतम- शाकल्यवाभ्रव्यमाण्डव्यमाण्डूकेया। गार्गी वाचकन्वी वडवा

प्रातीथेयी सुलभा मैत्रेयी कहोलं कोषीतकं महाकौषीतकं पैङ्ग्य सुयज्ञं शाङ्खायनमैतरेयं शाकलं वाष्कलं सुजातवक्त्रमौदवाहिं सौजामिं शौनकमाश्वलायनं ये चान्ये आचार्यास्ते सर्वे तृप्यन्त्विति।।

According to the commentator we have first, 12 Ṛṣis, who, as Ṛṣis, are to be invoked, when the Brāhmanical thread (यज्ञोपवीत) is suspended round the neck *(nivita)*- These are indeed the Ṛṣis of tbe Ṛg-veda : Best the Satarcbins (शतर्चिन:) the common title of the poets of the first Maṇḍala : then Gṛtsāmada (2d Maṇḍala), Viṣvāmitra (3rd M.), Vāmadeva (4th M), Atṛ (5th M.) Bharadvāja (6th M.), Vasiṣṭha (7th M.); then follow the poets of the Pragātha hymns (8th M.), tbe poets Of the Pavamānis (9th M.), and finally the authors of the 10th and last Maṇḍala, Who are called Kṣudira-sāktas and Mahā-sūktas, authors of short and long hymns, The next class comprises twenty-three invocation;, according to the Commentary, and they arc to be made, when the Brāhmanical cord is suspended over the right shoulder *(prāchīnāviti)*. The text however, contains more than twenty-three names, and it is likely that some of them have been added afterwards, while others are perhaps to be taken collectively. भारतधर्माचार्या: may also be taken as one word, in the sense of the legal authorities of the Bhāratas.

41. Dr. Weber, Indische Studien, p. 148. Kātyana, however, the immediate successor of Pāṇini, knows not only Pāṇḍu, but also his descendants, the Pāṇḍyas.

42. The names of the two wives of Pāṇḍu, Kuntī and Mādrī occur in the commentary on Pāṇini. (Cf. i. 2. 49., iv. 1.65 iv. 1. 176 (text) for Kuntī, iv. 177. for Mādrī). But both these names are geographical appellatives, Kuntī signifying a woman from the country of the Kuntas, Mādrī a Madra-woman. Pṛthā, another name of Kuntī, stands in the Gaṇa Śivādi. As the proper names of the Pāṇḍava princes, we find Yudhisṭhira, Pāṇ. vi. 1. 134, vi. 3. 9., viii. 3. 95. (text); Arjuna, Pāṇ. iii. 1. 119., iv. 3,64 v. 4. 48., vi, 2. 131.; Bhima, Pāṇ. vi. 1. 205.; Nakula, Pāṇ. vi. 3. 75. The name of Sahadeva does not occur; but his descendants, the Sāhadevas, are mentioned as belonging to the race of Kuru, together with the Nākulas, Pap iv. 1. 114. In the same way we find the descendants of Yudhiṣṭira and Arjuna mentioned as members of the eastern Bhāratas, Pāṇ. ii. 4. 66. Draupadī's name does not occur in Pāṇini, but Subhadrā, the sister of Kṛṣṇa and the wife of Arjuna, is distinctly mentioned, Pāṇ. iv. 2. 56, Another passage in tne commentary on Pāṇini (iv. 3. 87) proves even the existence of a poem in praise of Subhadrā, which, if we remember the former mention of a war about Subhadrā (iv. 2. 56.), seems most likely to have celebrated this very conquest of Subhadrā by Arjuna. In the Mahābhārata this story forms a separate chapter, the Subhadrā-haraṇa-parva (Ādiparva, p. 288.), which may be the very work which Pāṇini, according to his commentator, is alluding to. That the chapter in the Mahābhārata belongs to the oldest parts of this

epic, may be seen from its being mentioned in the Anukrāmaṇī of Dhṛtarāṣṭra (i. 149). "When I heard that Subhadrā, of the race of Madhu, had been forcibly seized in the city of Dvārakā, and carried away by Arjuna, and that the two heroes of the race of Vṛshṇi had repaired to Indraprashtha, I then, O Sañjaya, had no hope of success." The Mahābhāṣya, however, does not explain the former Sūtra, (iv. 2. 56.), and for the latter it gives examples for the exceptions only, but not for the rule. The word grantha, used in the Sūtra, (iv. 3. 87.), is always somewhat suspicious. That some of the Sūtras which now form part of Pāṇini's grammar, did not proceed from him, is acknowledged by Kaiyyaṭa. (cf. iv. 3. 131, 132.) अपाणिनीयः सूत्रेषु पाठ इत्याह इति कैय्यटः। कौपिञ्जलहास्तिपादादित्यस्यापाणिनीयत्वात् इति कैय्यटः।। Kṛṣṇa Vāsudeva, who is considered as peculiarly connected with the tradition of the Pāṇḍavas, is quoted as Vāsudeva, of the race of Vṛshṇi (Pāṇ. iv. 1. 114.); as Vāsvdeva, together with Śiva and Āditya (Pāṇ. v. 3. 99.); as Vāsudeva, together with Arjuna (iv. 3. 98. text). In the commentary to Pāṇ. iii. 3. 156., and ii. 3. 72., we have proof of Kṛṣṇa's being worshipped as a god; in i. 4. 92. he is mentioned as a hero. His residence, Dvārakā, however, does not occur in Pāṇini.

43. That Pāṇini knew the war of the Bhāratas, has been rendered highly probable by Prof. Lassen (Ind. Alterthumskunde, i. 691, 837). The words which called forth Pāṇini's special rule, (iv. 2. 56), can scarcely be imagined to have been different from those in the Mahābhāṣya; viz. "Bhārataḥ Saṅgrāmaḥ, Saubhadraḥ Saṅgrāmaḥ." It was impossible to teach or to use Pāṇini's Sūtras without examples, which necessarily formed part of the traditional grammatical literature long before the great Commentary was written, and are, therefore, of a much higher historical value than is commonly supposed. The coincidences between the examples used in the Pratisākhyas and in Pāṇini, show that these examples were by no means selected at random, but that they had long formed part of the traditional teaching. See also Pāṇ. vi. 2. 38., where the word "Mahābhārata" occurs, but not as the title of a poem.

44. वेदेऽप्येवं श्रूयते एकस्य वह्वयो जाया भवन्ति नैकस्या एव बहवः पतयः सन्ति।।

45. धर्मो द्विविधः स्थूलः सूक्ष्मश्च। मन्दमतिभिरपि सुखेन बुध्यमानः स शौचाचमनसन्ध्यावन्दनादिः स्थूलो धर्मः। शास्त्रपारङ्गतैः पण्डितैरेव बोद्धुं योग्य इतरेषामधर्मभ्रान्तिविषयो द्रौपदीविवाहादिः सूक्ष्मो धर्मः। Cf. Sāyaṇa's Com. on Parāśara MS. Bodl. 172, 173. Another explanation is given by Kumārila:

यौवनस्थैव कृष्णा हि वेदिमध्यात्समुत्थिता।
सा च श्रीः, श्रीश्च भूयोभिर्भुज्यमाना न दुष्यति।।

46. Cf. Grimm, History of the German Language, p 139.

47. Other instances of Dharma-vyatikrama are :
कृष्णद्वैपायनस्य गृहीतनैष्ठिकब्रह्मचर्यस्य विचित्रवीर्यदारेष्वपत्योत्पादनप्रसङ्गः।। युधिष्ठिरस्य

कनीयोनिर्जितभ्रातृजायापरिणयनम्।। वासुदेवार्जुनयोर्निषिद्धमातुलदुहितृरुक्मिणी-सुभद्रापरिणयनम्।।-

Kumārila Bhaṭṭ.

48. Cf. Manu, viii, 381 "No greater crime is known on earth than slaying a Brāhmaṇa, and the king, therefore, must not even form in his mind an idea of killing a priest,"

49. Thus it is said, for instance, in the Commentary to Paraśara's Gṛhya-Sūtras, that it is wrong to give up the customs of one's own family and to adopt those of others :

शाखान्तरीयकर्मकरणे दोषमाह वसिष्ठः

न जातु परशाखोक्तं कर्म बुधः समाचरेत्।
आचरन्पर शाखोक्तं शाखारण्डः स उच्यते।
यः स्वशाखोक्तमुत्सृज्य परशाखोक्तमाचरेत्।
अप्रमाणमृषिं कृत्वा सोऽन्धो तमसि मज्जते।
स्मृत्यन्तरेऽपि-स्वकर्म पर्युत्सृज्य तु यदन्यत्कुरुते नरः।
अज्ञानादथवा लोभात्स हतः पतितो भवेत्।।
छन्दोगपरिशिष्टेऽपि-स्वशाखाश्रयमुत्सृज्य परशाखाश्रयं तु यः।
कर्तुमिच्छति दुर्मेधा मोघं तस्य च यत्कृतम्।।

"Vaśiṣṭha declares that it is wrong to follow the rules of another Śākhā. He says 'A wise person will certainly not perform the duties prescribed by another Śākhā; he that does is called a traitor to his Śākhā. Whosoever leaves the law of his Śākhā, and adopts that of another, he sinks into blind darkness, having degraded a sacred Rṣi.' And in another law-book it is said: 'If a man gives up his own customs and performs others, whether out of ignorance or covetousness, he will fall and be destroyed.' And again, in the Pariśiṣṭa of the Chandogas: 'He is a fool who ceases to follow his own Śākhā, wishing to adopt another one, his work will be in vain."

Only in case no special rule is laid down for certain observances in some Gṛhyas, it is lawful to adopt those of other families :

स्वशाखानुक्तमप्यविरुद्धं परशाखोक्तं ग्राह्यम्।। तथा च कात्यायनः-

"यन्नाम्नातं स्वशाखायां परोक्तमविरोधि च।
विद्वद्भिस्तदनुष्ठेयमग्निहोत्रादिकर्मवत्।।"

सूत्रान्तरानुक्तमपि स्मृत्युक्तं ग्राह्यम्।।

50. as'v. S. i. 7.,

"अथ खलूच्चावचा जनपदधर्मा ग्रामधर्माश्च तान्विवाहे प्रतीयाद्यतु समानं तद्वक्ष्यामः।"

51. जनपदादिधर्माणां वक्ष्यमाणानां धर्माणां च विरोधे सति वक्ष्यमाणं धर्ममेव कुर्यान्न जनपदादिधर्ममिति यद्वक्ष्यामस्तत्सर्वत्र समानमित्येवार्थः। वैदेहेषु सद्य एव व्यवायो दृष्टः। गृह्येषु तु ब्रह्मचर्यं विहितम्। तत्र गृह्योक्तमेव कुर्यान्न देशधर्ममिति सिद्धम्।।

52. The commentator Haradatta here mentions the following as customs that prevailed in certain territories, and which had no sanction in the Veda :

"When the sun stands in Aries (Meṣa), the young girls would paint the Sun with his retinue, on the soil, with coloured dust, and worship this in the morning and evening. And in the month Margaśīrṣa (November-December) they roam about the village nicely dressed, and whatever they receive as presents they give to the god. When the sun stands in Cancer (Karkaṭa) in Pūrva Phālguni (February), they worship Uma, and distribute sprouting kidney-beans and salt. When the Sun stands in Aries in Uttarā Phālgunī (?), they worship the goddess Śrī.

As customs of classes he mentions that at the marriage of Śūdras, they fix posts in the ground, put thousands of reflecting lamps upon them, and lead the bride round by the hand.

As customs of families, again, he remarks that some wear the śikhā (lock of hair) in front, some behind, and that passage of the Veda (pravācanas) allow both according to different times.

53. दक्षिणकपर्दा वासिष्ठा आत्रेयास्त्रिकपर्दिनः।
अङ्गिरसः पञ्चचूडा मुण्डा भृगवः शिखिनोऽन्ये।

54. This we learn from the Karma-pradīpa, a supplement to the Sūtras of Gobhila, i. 18.: वसिष्ठोक्तो विधिः कृत्स्नो द्रष्टव्योऽत्र निरामिषः।।

55. अर्द्ध शकानां शिरसो मुण्डयित्वा व्यसर्जयत्।
यवनानां शिरः सर्व कम्बोजानां तथैव च।।
पारदा मुक्तकेशाश्च पह्लवाः श्मश्रुधारिणः।
निःस्वाधयायवषट्काराः कृतास्तेन महात्मना।।।

See also Pāṇ. Gaga Mayūra-vyaṁsakadi.(मयूरव्यंसकादिगणः)।

56. In later times, when the sects of Viṣṇu and Śiva had sprung- up, and the Indian world was divided between them, it seems as if different deities had been ascribed to different castes. Thus it is said in the first Adhyāya of the Vaśishṭha-smṛti:

चतुर्वेदी च यो विप्रो वासुदेवं न विन्दति।
वेदभारभयाक्रान्तः स वै ब्राह्मणगर्दभः।।
तस्मादवैष्णवत्वेन ब्राह्मण्यादि विहीयते।
वैष्णवत्वेन संसिद्धि लभते नात्र संशयः।।
नारायणं परं ब्रह्म ब्राह्मणानां हि दैवतम्।
सोमसूर्यादयो देवाः क्षत्रियाणां विशामपि।।
शूद्रादीनां तु रुद्राद्या अर्चनीया प्रपलतः।
यत्र रुद्रार्चनं प्रोक्तं पुराणेषु स्मृतिष्वपि।।
तदब्रह्मण्यविषयमेवमाह प्रजापतिः।
रुद्रार्चनं त्रिपुण्ड्रश्च पुराणेषु च गीयते।।
क्षत्रविट्शूद्रजातीनां नेतरेषां तदुच्यते।
तस्मात् त्रिपुण्ड्रं विप्राणां न धार्य मुनिसत्तमाः।।

"A Brāhmaṇa versed in the four Vedas, who does not find Vāsudeva, is a donkey of a Brāhmaṇa, trembling for the heavy burden of the Veda. Therefore, unless a man be a Vaiṣṇava, his Brahmahood will be lost; by being a Vaishṇava one obtains perfection, there is no doubt. For Nārāyaṇa (Viṣṇu) the highest Brahma, is the deity of the Brāhmaṇas; Soma, Sūrya, and the rest, are the gods of Kṣatriyas and Vaiśyas; while Rudra and similar gods ought to be sedulously worshipped by the Śūdras.

Where the worship of Rudra is enjoined in the Purāṇas and law-books, it has no reference to Brāhmaṇas, as Prajāpati declared. The worship of Rudra and Tripuṇḍra (the three horizontal marks across the forehead) are celebrated in the Purāṇas, but only for the castes of the Kṣatriya, Vaiśyas, and Śūdras, and not for the others. Therefore, ye excellent Munis, the Tripuṇḍra must not be worn by Brāhmaṇas."

57. Cf. Manu, x. 76.; and Ṛg-veda-bhāṣya, ii., p. 30. Rosen, who has quoted this passage to Ṛv. i 18, 1., reads याजनाध्यापने चैव विशुद्धाच्च प्रतिग्रहात् which he translated by "abstinere jubet a dirigendis sacrificiis, ab institutione sacra et ab impuris donis," referring to Manu. x. 103-110. विशुद्ध however, does not mean impure, but pure. The reading of the commentary ought to be विशुद्धाच्च प्रतिग्रहः, for thus the very words of Manu, x. 76., are restored.

58. In this case, the name of the queen also, Sudeṣṇā, would be significant, for Sudeṣṇā is the name of one of the nations in Bengal. See Viṣṇu-Purāṇa, p. 188. The word "go-dharma," which occurs in the story of Dīrghatamas, in the Mahābhārata, i. 41,95., and which Prof. Lasseo translates by "pastoral law," must have an opprobrious sense, and Indian Paṇḍits explain it by "open and indiscriminate concupiscence."

59. Aitareya-Brāhmaṇa, II. 19. :

''ऋषयो वै सरस्वत्यां सत्रमासत। ते कवषमैलूषं सोमादनयन्दास्या: पुत्र: कितवो ब्राह्मण: कथं नो मध्ये दीक्षिष्टेति। तं बहिर्धन्वोदवहन्नत्रैनं पिपासा हन्तु सरस्वत्या उदकं मा पादिति। स बहिर्धन्वोदूल्हः पिपासयावृत्त एतदपोनटत्रीयमपश्यत्प्र देवत्रा ब्रह्मणे गातुरेत्विति। तेनापां प्रियं धामोपागच्छत्। तमापोऽनूदायँस्तं सरस्वतौ समन्तं पर्यधावत्। तस्माद्धाप्येतर्हि परिसारमित्याचक्षते। यदेनं सरस्वती समन्तं परिससार।। ते वा ऋषयोऽब्रुबन् विदुर्वा इमं देवा उमेपं ह्वयामहा इति तथेति तमुपाह्वयन्त। तमुमहूयैतदपोनपृत्रीयमकुर्वन्त प्र देवत्रा ब्राह्मणे गातुरेत्विति।।''

Kauṣītaki-Brāhmaṇa, XI;

''माध्यमाः सरस्वत्यां सत्रमासत। तद्धापि कवषो मधये निषसाद। तं हेम उपोदुर्दास्या वै त्वं पुत्रोऽसि न वयं त्वया सह भक्षयिष्याम इति। स ह क्रुद्धः प्रद्रवन्सरस्वतीमेतेन सूक्तेन तुष्टाव। तं हेयमन्वेयाय। तत उ हेमे निरागा इव मेरिरे। तं हान्वानृत्योचुर्ऋषे नमस्त अरतु मा मा हिंसीस्त्वं वै नः श्रेष्ठोऽसि यं त्वेयमन्वेतीति। तं ह ज्ञापयाश्चक्रुस्तस्य ह क्रोधं विनिन्युः। स एष कवषस्यैव महिमा सूक्तस्य चानुवेदिता।।

Comment; उपोदुः परुषं वदितवन्तः।। निरागा निकृष्ठो रागो येषाम्।। अन्वानृत्य विनयेन नृतमनुसृता इव।। ज्ञापयाश्चक्रुः सन्तोषयाश्चक्रुः।।

60. Zur Litteratur und Geschichte des Veda. Drei Abband-lungen von R. Roth, Doctor der Philosophie. Stuttgart, 1846.
61. The worship of the Hindus at the present day cannot be called exclusively Vedic, though Vedic remains may be traced in it. In the Introduction to the edition of the Ṛg-veda, by the Tattva-bodhinī-sabhā, it is said, on the contrary, (আদ্যকালিক বৈদিক ধর্মের সহিত ইদানীন্তন প্রচলিত ধর্মের বিভিন্নতা উজ্জ্বলরূপে প্রতীত হইবেক।)

"the difference between the present received law and the early Vedic law, will clearly be perceived by this edition" And again,

(पुराणविहित नर, पशु, पक्षी, सर्प, मत्स्यादि नाना अवयवविशिष्ट देवगणेर, पौराणिक अर्चना एवं लोकविख्यात आधुनिकतम तान्त्रिक क्रियार विस्तारित पद्धतिर सहित वेद विहित यज्ञानुष्ठानेर किपर्यन्त भिन्नता ताहा सम्यक् रूपे इष्ट हइबेक।)

"It will be seen exactly what difference there is between the Paurāṇic worship of the gods, who according to the Purāṇas, are exhibited with the different bodies of men, animals, birds, serpent, and fishes; the widely spread custom of tantric ceremonies, which are the most modern and famous on earth; and the performance of sacrifices as prescribed in the Veda."'
62. Professor Burnouf has treated the same subject in his Review of Prof. Wilson's Translation of the Viṣṇupurāṇa, Journal des Savants, 1840, May, p. 296.
63. That the principal part of the Mahābhārata belongs to a period previous to the political establishment of Buddhism, has been proved by Prof. Lassen, Ind. Ant, i. 489-491. Much has been said since to controvert his views with regard to the age of the Mahābhārata, but nothing that is really valuable has been added to Prof. Lassen's facts or reasonings. "It is not at' all difficult," as Prof. Lassen remarks, "to look at this question from one single point of view, and to start a confident assertion. But in doing this, many persons commit themselves to inconside rate judgments, and show an ignorance of the very points which have to be considered."
64. See Burnouf, Introduction à l'Histoire du Buddhisme, p. iii.
65. Saṇgrah-ślokas. Cf. Weber, Indische Studien, i. p. 47.
66. It is remarkable that in Pāṇini also, the word Śloka is always used in opposition to Vedic literature (Pāṇ. iv. 1. 66., iv. 3. 103., 1., iv. 3. 107.). Ślokas, even if ascribed by Indian tradition to the same author, who is considered as the Ṛṣi of Vedic hymns or Brāhmaṇas, are quoted by a name different from that of his other works. The hymns or Brāhmaṇas ascribed to Kaṭha, for instance, are always to be quoted as "Kaṭhāḥ" (οι περι Κατθον); an expression which could never apply to poetical compositions ascribed to the same Kaṭha, if written in Ślokas. Verses written in this modern style of poetry must be quoted as Kathic Ślokas" (Kaṭhali Ślokah). The Brāhmaṇa promulgated by Tittiri, and kept up in the tradition of the Taittiriyas, is quoted by the name of "the Taittrīyas," but Ślokas composed by Tittiri are never included under this title. (Pāṇ. ii. 4. 21.) Vālmīki-Ślokas are mentioned.

67. See Mure's Critical History, vol. iii. ch. i.
68. For instance, "Reinhard the fox," and old High-German poem of the 13th century, is a new edition of the same Poem written in th 12th century, of which fragments have been found by Grimm. Other poems which are supposed to have been remodelled in the 13th century are "Crescenta", "Duke Ernst," and the "Roland Song." Lachmann supposed the same to have taken place with the "Nibelungen Klage".

THE SŪTRA PERIOD

CHAPTER 1

The *Sūtra period*, with which we have to begin, is of peculiar importance to the history of Indian literature, inasmuch as it forms the connecting link between the Vedic and the later Sanskrit. While on the one hand we must place several works written in Sūtras under the head of the post-Vedic or modern Sanskrit, we shall also find others which, although written in continuous Anushṭubh-Ślokas, or, more frequently, intermixed with Triṣṭubh and other verses (as, for instance, some of the Prātiśākhyas and Anu-kramaṇīs, and the still more modern Pariśiṣṭas) must be considered as the last productions of the Vedic age, trespassing in a certain degree upon the frontier of the later Sanskrit.

It is difficult to explain the peculiarities of the style of the Sūtra literature to any one who has not worked his way through the Sūtras themselves. It is impossible to give anything like a literal translation of these works, written as they are in the most artificial, elaborate, and enigmatical form. Sutra means string; and all the works written in this style, on subjects the most various, are nothing but one uninterrupted string of short sentences, twisted together into the most concise form. Shortness is the great object of this style of composition, and it is a proverbial saying (taken from the Mahābhāṣya) amongst the Paṇdits[1], that "an author rejoiceth in the economising of half a short vowel as much as in the birth of a son." Every doctrine thus propounded, whether grammar, metre, law, or philosophy, is reduced to a mere skeleton. All the important points and joints of a system are laid open with the greatest precision and clearness, but there is nothing in these works like connection or development of ideas." Even apparent simplicity of the design vanishes," as Colebrooke remarks," in the perplexity of the structure. The endless pursuit of exceptions and limitations so disjoins the general precepts, that the reader cannot keep in view their intended connection and mutual relation. He wanders in an intricate maze, and the clue of the labyrinth is continually slipping from his hands." There is no life and no spirit in these Sūtras, except what either a teacher or a running commentary, by which these works are usually accompanied, may impart to them.

Many of these works go even further : they not only express their fundamental doctrines in this concise form of language, but they coin a new kind of language, if language it can be called, by which they succeed in reducing the whole system of their tenets to mere algebraic formulas. To understand these is quite impossible without finding first what each algebraic *x, y,* and *z*, is meant to represent, and without having the key to the whole system. This key is generally given in separate Sūtras, called Paribhāṣā, which a pupil must know by heart, or always have present before his eyes, if he is to advance one step in the reading of such works. But even then it would be impossible to arrive at any real understanding of the subject, without being also in possession of the laws of the so-called Anuvṛtti and Nirvṛtti. To explain the meaning of these technical words, we must remember that the Sūtras generally begin by putting forward one proposition (Adhikāra), which is afterwards never repeated, but always to be understood till a new subject of the same kind is introduced. After the statement of subject, the author goes on by giving a first rule, which may extend its influence over the next following rules, whether these be restrictions or amplifications of it. These restrictive rules exercise again their influence to a certain extent over other rules, so that the whole becomes one continuous chain, each link held and modified by the others, and itself holding to and modifying the rest. The influence of one rule over the others is called Anuvṛtti, its cessation, Nirvṛtti. Without knowing the working of these two laws, which can be only learnt from commentaries, the Sūtras become very much confused. This is particularly the case in those works where the so-called Mīmānsā method of Pūrva-pakṣa (reasons contrā), Uttara-pakṣa (reasons pro), and Siddhānta (conclusion), is adopted. Here the concatenation of pros and cons is often so complicated, and the reasons on both sides defended by the same author with such seriousness, that we sometimes remain doubtful to which side the author himself leans, till we arrive at the end of the whole chapter. It is indeed one of the most curious kinds of literary composition that the human mind ever conceived; and though altogether worthless in an artistic point of view, it is wonderful that the Indians should have invented and mastered this difficult form, so as to have made it the vehicle of expression for every kind of learning. To introduce and to maintain such a species of literature was only possible with the Indian system of education, which consisted in little else except implanting these Sūtras and other works into the tender memory of children, and afterwards explaining them by commentaries and glosses. An Indian pupil learns these Sūtras of grammar, philosophy, or theology by the same mechanical method which fixes in our minds the alphabet and the multiplicationtable; and those who enter into a learned career spend half their life in acquiring and practising them, until their memory is strengthened to such an unnatural degree, that they know by heart not only these Sūtras, but also their commentaries, and commentaries upon commentaries. Instances of this are found among the learned in India up to the present day.

These numerous Sūtra works which we still possess, I contain the quintessence of all the knowledge which the Brāhmaṇas had accumulated during many centuries of study and meditation. Though they are the work of individuals, they owe to their authors little more than their form; and even that form was, most likely, the result of a long-continued system of traditional teaching, and not the invention of a few individuals.

ŚRUTI AND SMṚTI

There is a great difference, according to the notions of the Hindūs themselves, between a work composed previous to the Sūtra period, and a Sūtra composition. The difference of style between a Brāhmaṇa and a Sūtra work (with the exception of some Kalpa-Sūtras, to be mentioned hereafter) would strike every body at first sight, although, as regards the grammatical forms, Vedic irregularities are, according to Sanskrit grammarians, allowed in Sūtras also.[2] But there is another, and more important difference. Literary works, belonging to the preceding periods, the Brāhmaṇas as well as the Mantras, are considered by Indian theologians as forming the Śruti, or divine revelation, in contradistinction to the Sūtras and all the rest of their literature. In the dogmatical language of orthodox Hindūs, the works, which contain the Śruti, have not been composed, but have only been seen or perceived by men, *i. e.*, they have been revealed to men. The Sūtras, on the contrary, although based upon the Śruti, and therefore in some instances also called Śrauta Sūtras, are yet avowedly composed by human authors. Whenever they appear to be in contradiction with the Śruti, their authority is at once overruled, and only in cases where anterior evidence is wanting from the Śruti, can they have any claim to independent authority.

Now, even if we had no other means of proving that the Sūtras could have been composed only after the composition of the Brāhmaṇas, there would be no reason to consider this distinction, drawn by the Indians themselves between their sacred and profane literature, as altogether artificial and devoid of historical meaning, particularly if it can be shown how great an influence that very distinction has exercised on the religious struggles of India.

It is clear that this distinction has ever been the strong-hold of the hierarchical pretensions of the Brāhmaṇas. We can understand how a nation might be led to ascribe a suprehuman origin to their ancient national poetry, particularly if that poetry consisted chiefly of prayers and hymns addressed to their gods. But it is different with the prose compositions of the Brāhmaṇas. The reason why the Brāhmaṇas, which are evidently so much more modern than the Mantras, were allowed to participate in the name of. Śruti, could only have been because it was from these theological compositions, and not from the simple old poetry of the hymns, that a supposed divine authority could be derived for the greater number of the ambitious claims of the Brāhmaṇas. But, although we need not ascribe any weight to the arguments by which the Brāhmaṇas endeavoured to establish the contemporaneous origin of the Mantras and Brāhmaṇas, there seems to be no reason why we should reject as equally worthless the general opinion with regard to the more ancient date of both the Brāhmaṇas and Mantras, if contrasted with the Sūtras and the profane literature of India. It may easily happen, where there is a canon of sacred books, that later compositions become incorporated together with more ancient works, as was the case with the Brāhmaṇas. But we can hardly imagine that old and genuine parts should ever have been excluded from a body of sacred writings, and a more modern date ascribed to them, unless it be in the interest of a party to deny the authority of certain doctrines contained in these rejected documents. There is nothing in the later literature of the Sūtras to warrant a supposition of this kind. We can find no reason why the Sūtras should not have been ranked as Śruti except the lateness of their date, if compared with the Brāhmaṇas, and still more with the Mantras. Whether the Brāhmaṇas themselves were aware that ages must have elapsed between the period during which most of the poems of their Ṛṣis were composed, and the times which gave rise to the Brāhmaṇas, is a question which we need hardly hesitate to answer in the affirmative. But the recklessness with which Indian theologians claim for these Brāhmaṇas the same title and the same age as for the Mantras, shows that the reasons must have been peculiarly strong which deterred them from claiming the same divine authority for the Sūtras.

BRĀHMAṆAS AND SŪTRAS

To ascribe to literary compositions such as the Mantras and Brāhmaṇas a divine origin, and to claim for them a divine and absolute authority, is a step which can hardly pass unnoticed in the intellectual history of a nation, whether for the circumstances which led to it, or for the results which it produced. Now, in India the results of that fatal step are palpable. It may have been intended as a check on religious reforms but it led to a religious revolution. Buddhism would be unintelligible, unless as the overthrow of a system which had tried to maintain its position by an appeal to a divine revelation; and we may be certain that the distinction between Śruti and Smṛti, between revealed and profane literature, was established by the Brāhmaṇas, previous to the schism of Buddha.

If the belief was once established, that not only the simple effusions of the Ṛṣis, but the pointed doctrines of the *Brāhmaṇas* also emanated from a Divine source, and could not therefore be attacked by human reasoning, it is clear that every opposition to the privileges which the Brāhmaṇas claimed for themselves, on the sacred authority of the Veda, became heresy; and where the doctrines of the Brāhmaṇas were the religion of the people, or rather of the king, such opposition was amenable to the hierarchical laws of the State. The Brāhmaṇas themselves cared much more to see the divine authority of the Śruti as such implicitly acknowledged, than to maintain the doctrines of the Ṛṣis in their original simplicity and purity. In philosophical discussions, they allowed the greatest possible freedom; and, although at first three philosophical systems only were admitted as orthodox (the two Mīmānsās and the Nyāya), their number was soon raised to six, so as to include the Vaiśeshika, Sāṅkhya, and Yoga-schools.[3] The most conflicting views on points of vital importance were tolerated as long as their advocates succeeded, no matter by what means, in bringing their doctrines into harmony with passages of the Veda, strained and twisted in every possible sense. If it was only admitted that besides the perception of the senses and the induction of reason, revelation also, as contained in the Veda, furnished a true basis for human knowledge, all other points seemed to be of minor importance. Philosophical minds were allowed to exhaust all possible views on the relation between the real and transcendental world, the Creator and created, the divine and the human nature. It was not from such lucubrations that danger was likely to accrue to the caste of the Brāhmaṇas. Nor was the heresy of Buddha Śākya Muni found so much in his philosophical doctrines, many of which may be traced in the orthodox atheism of Kapila, His real crime lay in his opposition to the exclusive privileges and abuses of the Brāhmaṇas. These abuses were sanctioned by the divine authority of the Veda,[4] and particularly of the Brāhmaṇas. In attacking the abuses, Buddha attacked the divine authority on which they were founded, and the argument was short : he is a heretic; anathema esto.

THE AUTHORITY OF REVELATION ATTACKED

Buddha was a Kshatriya.[5] He was of princely origin, and belonged to the nobility of the land. He was not the first of his caste who opposed the ambition of the Brāhmaṇas. Several centuries before Buddha, Viśvāmitra, who, like Buddha, was a member of the royal caste, had to struggle against the exclusiveness of the priests. At that early time, however, the position of the Brāhmaṇas was not yet impregnable; and Viśvāmitra, although a Kṣatriya, succeeded in gaining for himself and his family the rights for which he struggled, and which the Brāhmaṇas had previously withheld from all but their own caste. King Janaka of Videha again, whose story is given in the Brāhmaṇas, refused to submit to the hierarchical pretensions of the Brāhmaṇas, and asserted his right of performing sacrifices without the intercession of priests. However great the difference may have been between the personal character of these two men and of Buddha, the first principle of their opposition was the same. All three were equally struggling against the over weening pretensions of a selfish priesthood.

But while Viśvāmitra contented himself with maintaining the rights of his tribe or family, and became reconciled as soon as he was allowed to share in the profits of the priestly power, while King Janaka expressed himself satisfied with the homage paid to him by Yājñyavalkya and other Brāhmaṇas, while, in short, successive reformers as they appeared were either defeated or gained over to the cause of the Brāhmaṇas, the seeds of discontent were growing up in the minds of the people. There is a dark chapter in the history of India, the reported destruction of all the Kṣatriyas by Paraśu-Rāmạ. It marks the beginning of the hierarchical supremacy of the Brāhmaṇas. Though the Brāhmaṇas seem never to have aspired to the royal power, their caste, as far as we know the history and traditions of India, has always been in reality the ruling caste. Their ministry was courted as the only means of winning divine favour, their doctrines were admitted as infallible, their gods were worshipped as the only true gods, and their voice was powerful enough to stamp the simple strains of the Ṛṣis and the absurd lucubrations of the authors of the Brāhmaṇas, with a divine authority. After this last step, however the triumph of Brāhmāṇism was preparing its fall, In India, less than in any other country, would people submit to a monopoly of truth; and the same millions who were patiently bearing the yoke of a political despotism threw off the fetters of an intellectual tyranny. In order to overthrow one of the oldest religions of the world, it was sufficient that one man should challenge the authority of the Brāhmaṇas' the gods of the earth (Bhūdeva), and preach among the scorned and degraded creatures of God the simple truth that salvation was possible without the mediation of priests, and without a belief in books to which these very priests had given the title of revelation. This man was Buddha Śākya Muni.

BRĀHMANISM VERSUS BUDDHISM

Now if we inquire how Buddha's doctrines were met by the Brāhamṇas, it is true that here and there in their philosophical works they have endeavoured to overthrow some of his metaphysical axioms by an appeal to reason. An attempt of this kind we have, for instance, in Vācaspati Miśra's commentary on the Vedānta Sūtras. In commenting on the tenet of Buddha, that "ideas like those of being, and not being etc., do not admit of discussion,"[6] Vācaspati observes that the very fact of speaking of these ideas, includes the possibility of their conception; nay, that to affirm they do not admit of reasoning involves an actual reasoning on them, and proves that the mind can conceive the idea of being as different from that of not-being.

Such, however, were not the usual weapons with which

Brāhmāṇism fonght against Buddhism. The principal objection has always been that Buddha's teaching could not be true, because it did not derive its sanction from Śruti or revelation. The Brāhmaṇas, as a caste, would readily have allowed being and not-being, and the whole of Buddha's philosophy, as they did the Sāṅkhya philosophy, which on the most important points is in open opposition to the Vedānta. But while Kapila, the founder of the Sāṅkhya school, conformed to the Brāhmanic test by openly proclaiming the authority of revelation as paramount to reasoning and experience, Buddha would not submit to this, either for his philosophical (abhidharma), or for his much more important moral and religious doctrines (vinaya). No doubt it would have been easy for him to show how some of his doctrines harmonised with passages of the Veda, as in the Veda all possible shades of the human mind have found their natural reflection. If he had done so only for some of his precepts, such, for instance, as, "you shalt not murder,"[7] "you shall not drink,"[8] "you shall eat stand-ing,"[9] the Brāhmaṇas would readily have passed over other doctrines, even such as came into practice after Buddha's death, like "Who longs for heaven, shall worship the holy sepulchre,"[10] "He shall pull out his hair."[11] etc. As he refused to do so, the line of argument taken by the Brāhmaṇas was simply confined to an appeal to revelation, in disproof of the possibility of the truth of Buddha's doctrines.

REVELATION OF THE BUDDHISTS

There must be something very tempting in this 'line of argument, for we see that in later times the Buddhists also endeavoured to claim the same divine character for their sacred writings which the *Brāhmaṇas* had established for the Veda. A curious instance of this is given in the following discussion, from Kumārila's Tantra-vārttika. Here the opponent (*Pūrva-pakṣa*) observes, that the same arguments which prove that the Veda is not the work of human authors, apply with equal force to Śākya's teaching. His authority, he says, cannot be questioned, because his precepts are clear and intelligible; and as Śākya is not the inventor, but only the teacher of these precepts, and no name of an author is given for Śākya's doctrines, the frailties inherent in human authors affect them as little as the Veda.[12] Everything, in fact, he concludes, which has been brought forward by the Mīmāṁsakas to prove the authority of the Veda, proves in the same way the authority of Buddha's doctrine. Upon this, the orthodox Kumārila grows very wroth, and says : "These Śākyas, Vaiśeṣikas, and other heretics, who have been frightened out of their wits by the faithful Mīmānsakas, prattle away with our own words as if trying to lay hold of a shadow. They say that their sacred works are eternal; but they are of empty minds, and only out of hatred they wish to deny that the Veda is the most ancient book. And these would be logicians declare even that some of their precepts (which they have stolen from us), like that of universal benevolence, are not derived from the Veda, because most of Buddha's other sayings are altogether against the Veda. Wishing, therefore, to keep true on this point also, and seeing that not merely human precept could have any authority on moral and supernatural subjects, they try to veil their difficulty by aping our own argument for the eternal existence of the Veda. They know that the Mīmāṁsakas have proved that no sayings of men can have any authority on supernatural subjects; they know also that the authority of the Veda cannot be controverted, because they can bring forward nothing against the proofs adduced for its divine origin, by which all supposition of a human source have been removed. Therefore, their hearts being gnawed by their own words, which are like the smattering of children, and having themselves nothing to answer, because the deception of their illogical arguments have been destroyed, they begin to speak like a foolish suitor who came to ask for a bride, saying, "My family is as good as your family.' In the same manner, they now maintain the eternal existence of their books, aping the speeches of others. And if they are challenged and told that this is our argument, they brawl, and say that we, the Mīmāṁsakas have heard and stolen it from them. For a man who has lost all shame, who can talk away without any sense, and tries to cheat his opponent, will never get tired, and will never be put down!" Towards the end of this harangue, Kumārila adds, what is more to the point, that the Bauddhas, who ascribe to everything a merely temporary existence, have no business, to talk of an eternal revelation.

CHARACTER OF THE SMṚTI

Now, it ought not to be overlooked, that in all these discussions the distinction between Śruti (Mantras and Brāhmaṇas) and Smṛti (Sūtras) is always taken for granted. If, at the time of the first controversies between Bauddhas and Mīmāṁsakas, the authors of the Mantras or Brāhmaṇas and particularly the founders of the so-called ancient Brāhmaṇas, had still been alive, or their names generally known, even a *Brāhmaṇa* could not have ventured to stand up for the divine and eternal origin of this part of the Śruti. On the other hand, nothing could have prevented the Brāhmaṇas from ascribing the same supernatural origin to the Sūtras, if at the time of the rising power of Buddhism their authors also had been lost in oblivion. The distinction, therefore, between Śruti (revelation) and Smṛti (tradition) which is a point of such vital importance for the whole Brāhmanic system will also be found significant in an historical point of view.

It must be observed, however, before we proceed farther, that what is called Smṛti includes not only Sūtras, but also Śloka works, such as the laws of Manu, Yājñavalkya, and Parāśara (the Mānava, Yājñavalkya, and Parāśara dharma-Śāstras), which sometimes are. called the Smṛtis, in the plural. Most of these, if not all, are founded on Sūtras; but the text of the Sūtras have mostly been superseded by these later metrical paraphrases.

How then did the Brāhmaṇas, after they had established the distinction between Śruti and Smṛti, defend the authority of the Smṛti, including Sūtras and the later Śloka works ?

That the Smṛti has no claim to an independant authority but derives its sanction from its intimate connection with the Śruti, is implied by its very name, which means recollection. For, as Kumārila remarks (in the Pūrva-pakṣa), "Recollection is knowledge, the object of which is some previous knowledge;

and if Manu and other authors of Smṛtis had not originally been in possession of an authoritative knowledge, it would be impossible to appeal to their recollection as an authority.[13] It would be as if a man, omitting his son or daughter, was to appeal to the son of a barren daughter. For the original knowledge of Manu might be compared to his son, but his recollection would only be like a grandson. Now as people, if they have reason to doubt the existence of a daughter, would disbelieve every mention of the son of a daughter, thus the recollection (Smṛti) of Manu would be futile, if he himself had not possessed some means of authoritative knowledge."

The following extract from Sāyaṇa's commentary on Parāśara's Code[14] will show the use which the Brāhmaṇas made of this argument, in order to substantiate the authority of their legal text-books.

"Does it not seem after all," he says, "as if this Smṛti (containing as it does the laws of men) hardly deserved a commentary of its own, inasmuch as it is difficult to make out on what grounds it claims any authority ? For, if we appeal to a Sūtra of Jaimini's he founder of the Pūrva-Mīmāṁsā) where he has proved that the Veda possesses an authority irrespective of anything else, these arguments can hardly apply to books which are evidently the work of men, and entirely dependent on the authority of their sources. These sources again if they be considered as the life and strength of that authority, are often very indistinct. First, they could never fall under the cognizance of the senses, because the very nature of duty or law is transcendental. Nor can this ultimate reason or source be found in induction, inasmuch as induction is only possible after observation. Neither can it be looked for in the sayings of other men, because man is exposed to error, and cannot even express things as he has really perceived them. But even if man was free from error, there would always be room for doubt and opposition. And as to finding the authority for these laws in direct precepts of the Śruti (Mantras and Brāhmaṇas) this is out of the question, because such precepts are not to be found there. We have never seen a passage in the Veda where precepts like those of the Smṛti, to keep the body clean, etc., are given.

To admit the right of induction for laws of this kind would be most dangerous, for it would apply with equal force to the precepts of Buddha, to worship the holy sepulchre, etc.

"However, there is an answer to all these doubts. A great difference exists between the Smṛtis of Manu and the Smṛtis of Buddha, because Manu's authority is asserted by the undeniable Veda itself. It is said in the Veda,'Whatever Manu said, was medicine;' but there is no passage there in any way favourable to the Smṛti of Buddha, and therefore the right of applying induction cannot be considered dangerous, because it never could be extended to Buddha's doctrines.

"Quod non,"* says the opponent. "This passage of the Veda,'Whatever Manu said, was medicine,' only an Arthavāda (an explanatory remark), and has no evidence by itself. It only serves to illustrate or recommend another precept, vis., that two verses of Manu's are to be used at a certain sacrifice.[15] Therefore, there is no passage in the Veda to warrant the authority of the Smṛti; and if Śākya's, *i. e.*, Buddha's, Smṛti be exceptionable, the same applies to the Smṛti of Manu. Thus it is said, 'As men speak often untruth and are expossed to error, as no divine precept is given, faith only can be authority.' But further, even admitting that there was a shadow of authority for Manu, what could be said in favour of Parāśara's Smṛti, which is now to be explained ? For, although Veda may praise Manu, it never does the same for Parāśara, and thus Parāśara's authority at least can hardly be defended.

"Against all this our answer is : the Smṛtis are an authority, because that they should have authority is understood by itself; and there is no reason why they should not be considered as having authority. Three reasons are given why Manu and the rest could not claim any authority, viz.,'that men speak untruth, that they are exposed to error, and that no divine precept is given.' These objections, however, are entirely out of order, because nobody would ever think that Manu and Parāśara, who have been perfect from their very birth, could have spoken untruth, and could have erred. So much for the first two objections. And whoever denied that these sages were perfect from their very birth, as Mantras, Arthavādas, Itihāsas, and Purāṇas, prove distinctly not only the existence of Parāśara and others, but also their perfection ? Nay, even if we had not the testimony of the Mantras, how could the perfection; of Parāśara and others be denied, which is involved in their very existence ? A difference of opinion is quite impossible. And has it not been proved in the chapter on the gods[16] in the Uttara Mīmāṁsā, that the Mantras do not require any further proof for what they say ? It is true that in the chapter on the Arthavādas it has been admitted that what the *Arthavādas* contain is not always to be-believed. But this is only on account of some impossible things which are occasionally mentioned therein. Therefore an Arthavāda like this,'Whatever Manu says is medicine,' although it only serves to recommend another rule, must yet be considered as true in itself. With regard to Śākya, nothing similar can be brought forward; and thus it is well said elsewhere,'May a man scorn all the erroneous doctrines of Arhat, Cārvaka, and Buddha.' As regards Parāśara in particular, it is wrong to say that his fame is not equally founded on the Veda, for it is said in the Śruti, 'Thus spoke Vyāsa, the son of Parāśara.' If, therefore, the famous Veda-Vyāsa is praised as the son of Parāśara, how much more famous must not Parāśara, his father, have been ! In the genealogical Brāhmaṇa of the Vājasaneyi-śākhā, the son also and the grandson of Parāśara are mentioned in the succession of pupils and teachers who handed down the Veda,[17]

Ghṛtakauśika received from Pāraśaryāyāṇa, Pāraśaryāyāṇa from Pārāśarya, Pārāśarya from Jātūkarṇya, etc' Therefore Parāśara stands quite on a level with Manu; and the same applies to all the other Ṛṣis, like Vaśiṣṭha and Yājñyavalkya, who are authors of Smṛtis, and are mentioned in the Śruti. Thus we read, 'The Ṛṣis did not see Indra clearly, but Vaśiṣṭha saw him clearly.'[18] 'Atri gave his children to Aurva, who longed for a son.'[19] Yājñavalkya had two wives.'[20] Therefore one must not think of attacking the Smṛtis of Manu and others by any means.

"The third reason also which was brought forward against

the authority of the Smṛti, vis. that the precepts given there are not based upon passages of the Śruti, does not hold good, because passages are met with which are the source of all the laws given in the Smṛti. Thus we read, These five great sacrifices are every day commenced and every day performed : the Deva-yajña (to the gods), the Pitṛ-yajña (to the fathers, the manes), the Bhūta-yajña (to all beings), the Manushya-yajña (to men), the Brāhmā-yajña (to Braḥmān, the divine Self)'[21] And although there is no distinct precept in the Veda for ablutions etc., yet all this is implied. Thus the Bhaṭṭācāryas say, 'It is right to respect the Smṛtis, because they are delivered by Vedic authors, because their origin is well established, and because they derive their authority from the Veda, if but rightly understood.' The Munis see the Śruti, and they deliver the Smṛti; therefore the authority of both is proved on earth by full evidence. A man who despises these two, and adopts fallacious doctrines, is to be avoided by good men as a heretic and Veda-blasphemer.

"But one might object that if these precepts can be learnt from the Śruti, the Smṛti would be unnecessary, because that only which cannot be learnt from other sources forms a fit object for a new work. Here then we say that these precepts, though they can be learnt from the Veda, are nevertheless put together in the Smṛtis for the purpose of making the order of their performance more easy, by leaving out the *Arthavādas*, and by taking from some Śākhās of the Veda particular facts omitted in others. Now it might again be objected that this is done in the *Kalpa-sūtras,* and that therfore there was no necessity for the Smṛtis. But this is wrong, because there are two different kinds of duties to be performed, called Śrauta (based on Śruti) and Smārta (based on Smṛti). The Śrauta ceremonies consist in sacrifices like the Darśa-pūrṇamāsa, etc., which can only be performed after the sacred fire has been placed in the house, and they are clearly based upon the Veda, as we read it. The Smārta Sacraments and traditional customs, on the contrary, consist in ablutions, rinsing the mouth, etc., and they are to be considered as based upon a Śākhā of the Veda which is hidden, but the existence of which must be inferred. Although, therefore, those precepts which regard the placing of the sacred fire, etc., are put together in the Kalpa-sūtras, yet as other duties, such as ablutions, rinsing, etc., are not included in them, the Smṛtis have still their legitimate object."

This discussion has been given here at full length because it is a genuine specimen of Indian orthodox dialectics. Whatever may be thought of this style of argument, we see at all events how great an importance has always been attached by the Brāhmaṇas as to the distinction between Śruti and Smṛti.

SŪTRAS EXCLUDED FROM THE ŚRUTI

It may also have been observed in this extract, that it is not quite in accordance with the language of Sāyaṇa to speak of Sūtra works as Smṛtis in the plural. He applies this term to metrical codes only, like Manu, Yājñavalkya, and Parāśara, but not to Sūtras or Vedāṅgas.[22] This, however, does not affect our present question, because even Sāyaṇa, though he does not call the Sūtras by the name of Smṛtis, places them notwithstanding in the same category with the codes of law, and separates them from the Śruti, upon which they are founded, but with which they are not to be confounded. The Kalpa-sūtras are called by him Śrauta, i. e., based on revelation, but not Śruti (revelation), because although they treat of the same subjects as the Śruti, they are themselves extracts only from the sacred writings. They are arranged by authors whose names are given, while, according to Indian notions, Mantras and Brāhmaṇas were only seen by the Ṛṣis, but neither composed nor arranged by them.[23]

That *Sūtras*, even where they contain Vedāṅga-doctrines, are distinctly excluded from the Śruti, may be seen from the following passage. In the Tantra-vārttika (I. 3,), Kumārila says, "There is a great difference between the Kalpa-sūtras, which teach the performance of sacrifices enjoined by the Vedas, such as we now possess them, and the Smṛtis, which derive their authority from parts of the Veda that have either disappeared or are dispersed, or the existence of which can be proved by induction only. It is easier, therefore, to establish the authority of the Kalpa-sūtras than that of the Smṛtis. The objections which have been raised against the authority of the Smṛtis, and which had to be removed by us before, cannot be thought of with regard to the Kalpa-sūtras, not even if it were only for argument's sake.[24] The question, therefore, is only this, whether the Kalpa-sūtras have the same authority as the Veda, or whether they merely derive their authority from it. As the Veda is called '*ṣaḍaṅga*,' 'having six members,' these six members, and amongst them the Kalpa-sūtras might seem to be implied by the common name of Veda. This, however, would be wrong;[25] for the Kalpa-sūtras, as is well-known, are composed by human authors like Maśaka, etc. They do not take their names, like the Kāṭhaka and other Śākhās of the Veda, from those by whom they were proclaimed, but from their real authors. It is true, no doubt, that the authors of the Kalpa-sūtras have the name of Ṛṣis, and it might be said that as Śiśu Āṅgirasa was not the author of the' Śaiśava hymns in tne Śāmaveda, the Kalpa-sūtras too were not composed, but only proclaimed, by those whose names they bear, particularly as there are even Brāhmaṇas, for instance those of the Aruṇa and Parāśara-śākhā, which have nearly the same form as the Kalpa-sūtras. Nevertheless, nothing can be more mistaken than the opinion of those who would put the Kalpa-sūtras on the same footing as the Veda, because people who teach aid learn the Kalpa-sūtras know that there was a time when these works did not exist, and that they were composed by certain authors like Maśaka, Baudhāyana, Āpastamba, Aśvalāyana, Kātyāyana, and others."[26] They are drawn as he observes in another place, partly from the Veda, but partly also from other sources; and the same applies, according to him, to all the Vedāṅgas and Smṛtis; nay, even to later works, such as the epic and Paurāṇic poems.[27]

ŚRAUTA AND SMĀRTA-SŪTRAS

It might therefore be best to distinguish between Smṛti tradition in general, and the Smṛtis or law-books in particular. We might then speak of Śrauta and Smārta-sūtras, comprehending by the former name all Sūtras, the source of which can be traced in the Śruti; by the latter those of which no such source exists, orsat least, is known, to exist.[28] The title of Smṛtis in the plural (or Smṛti-prahandhās) might be left, for convenience sake, to such works as Sāyaṇa is speaking of, which are composed not in Sūtras but in Ślokas. It ougbt to be remembered, however, that the same subjects which are treated in the metricall Smṛtis of Manu and others, had similarly been treated in Sūtras (Śrauta, Gṛhya, and sāmāyācārika), and that the principal difference between the two lies, not in their matter, but in their age, and their style.

LOST ŚĀKHĀS

An objection against this division and terminology, not unknown to the Brāhmaṇas themselves, is that it is difficult to say whether certain Smārta-sūtras may not be based upon some lost Śākhā of the Veda. The grant a portions of die Kalpa-sūtras, there can be no doubt, are founded on Śruti, if by this name we understand not only the hymns, but also the Brāhmaṇas of the Veda. But there are only few allusions, even in the Brāhmaṇas, the ceremonies described in the Gṛhya-sūtras; and the few passages which are quoted from the Śruti in their support, are chiefly taken from the Āraṇyakas and Upaniṣads, the latest branches of Vedic literature. As to the Ācāras, or the established rules of conduct with regard to particular temporal duties, even Indian writers admit that there are only very vague allusions to them in tbe Śruti, and they try to prove that these laws are based on parts of the Veda which no longer exist. This is a view which is taken for instance by Hara-datta in his commentary on Āpastamba's Sāmayāch-ārika-sūtras and it deserves to be examined more closely. On the first *Sūtra*,[29] "Therefore let us now explain the Sāmayācārika duties," he makes the following observations:

"The word '*therefore*' implies a reason, which is that as the Śrauta (sacrificial) and gārhya (domestic) ceremonies have been explained, and as these ceremonies presuppose other observances, these other observances must now lie explained too. For when it was said before (in the Śrauta and Gṛhya-sūtras), that such and such an act was to be performed by a man after he had rinsed his mouth, by a man who is clean, who holds a pavitra in his hand, who is invested with the sacred thread, etc., an acquaintance with all these things, such as rinsing, etc., is presupposed. The twilight prayers, too, are referred to in the preceding Sūtras, when it is said, that a man who does not perform his twilight prayers is impure, and unworthy of every sacrifice. Several other instances occur; and it is therefore necessary to explain now immediately those other precepts called Sāmāyācārika (temporal). Sāmāyācārika is derived from Sāmaya (agreement) and ācāra (custom). Sāmaya, a human agreement is of three kinds : *vidhi*, injunction; *niyama*, restriction; pratisliedha, prohibition. Rules founded upon Sāmaya are called Sāmāyācāras, from which the adjective Sāmāyācārika, *Dharma* (virtue) is the quality of the individual self, which arises from action, leads to happiness and final beatitude, and is called apūrva, supernatural. But, in our Sūtra, dharma means law, and has for its object dharma as well as adharma : things to be done and things to be avoided.

"It mignt be said, however," continues the Commentator Haradatta, alluding to the same controversy which we saw before treated of by Sāyaṇa, "that if *Samaya* (human agreement) be the authority for the law, it would be difficult to deny the same authority to the Bauddhas and their laws, to worship the holy sepulchre, etc., and therefore Āpastamba has added tbe next Sūtra.[30]

"Those agreements are of authority which were made by men who knew the law."

"We do not say," Haradatta remarks, with regard to these words, "that every agreement becomes of authority, but those only made by men like Manu, etc., who knew the law. But then it might be asked, how it can be found out that Manu knew the law, and Buddha did not ? People answer, that Buddha could not have had a knowledge of the divine law. But the same might be said also of Manu; and if a knowledge of divine things be ascribed to Manu, on account of the excellence which he acquired by his virtue,then, again, it would be the same for Buddha. There is a known verse:[31] 'If Buddha know the law, and Kapila does not, what is truth? If they were both omniscient, how could there be difference of opinion between them ? If this be not so, a distinction must be made; and this has been done by Āpastamba in his next Śutra 'And the Vedas (are of authority).[32]

This Sūtra is explaind by Haradatta in the following manner : "The Vedas are the highest authority for good and bad; and none of the objections made before could apply to the Vedas, which are faultless from all eternity, evident by themselves, and, as they were revealed, unaffected by the faults of human authors. Therefore, while to us those agreements are of authority which were made by men who knew the law, the Vedas, again, were the authority for those men themselves, like Manu, etc. And although we have not before our eyes a Veda, which is the source of these laws, we must still conclude that Manu find the rest had.[33]

It is a matter of considerable interest to know whether this opinion of Haradatta's as to the previous existence of a larger number of Vedic works, deserves credit or not. The opponent of the orthodox Kumārila in the Tantra-vārttika remarks very truly, that to invoke the testimony of lost parts of the Veda is like calling a dead person as a witness.[34] And if we hud no better authority for this opinion than so late a commentator as Haradatta, we should hardly he justified in mentioning it as an argument. Anybody, however, who is acquainted with the character of Indian commentators, will admit that they seldom commit themselves to novel theories, but almost always repeat what existed before in the tradition of their schools; a fact which at once increases and diminishes the usefulness of their works, Thus we find in the case before us that Āpastamba himself, whose sūtras Haradatta explains, entertained a similar opinion on this subject. In the twelfth, section of - his Sūtras, when speaking of some rules on the *Svādhyāya* (praying), he says[35], "that certain rules must be considered as given in Brāhmaṇas of which the tradition or reading has been destroyed. Their former existence," he says, "must be inferred from the simple, fact, that these rules are still followed by men; the only exception being where customs can be proved to depend on selfish motives. In this case, a man who follows such unauthorised customs, shall go to hell."

LOST BRĀHMAṆAS

With regard to the hymns, it is in itself very unlikely that no more should have existed than those which happen to be collected in the Ṛg-veda; and even in the Ṛg-Veda we see that the number of hymns varied in different communities. The ancient poetry of India, however, would hardly have furnished authoritative passages for legal and ceremonial questions; and there is no doubt that the lost tradition which is appealed to by later writers, refers only to Brāhmāṇas. A number of these dogmatic works are still in existence; but others, which are always quoted along with them, are now lost, or known by extracts only. There existed a considerable number of ancient sages who embodied their doctrines, whether on philosophical or ceremonial, on metrical or grammatical questions, in independent works, which were handed down by tradition among their descendants. But, as Kumārila observes, through the carelessness and forgetfulness of men, and also by the extinction of families, these works were necessarily lost; and it is, indeed, less surprising that many of these Brāhamaṇas should have been lost, than that so many should still have been saved, if we remember for how long a time oral tradition was in India the only means of preserving them. Kumārila, however, was too keen-sighted not to perceive the danger of admitting last Śākhās of the Veda as authorities, and he makes several reservations in order to guard against a promiscuous use of this argument. The Buddhists also might appeal to a lost Śākhā, and thus upset all the arguments of the orthodox philosophers. But in spite of the bug-bear of the Buddhists, the general fact that some Śākhās had perished was admitted by Kumārila, as well as by Āpastamba, both endeavouring to prop up the authority of the Smṛti by the broken pillars of the Śruti.[36]

The evidence which has been brought together is sufficient to establish the fact, that the distinction between Śruti and Smṛti, revelation and tradition, had been established by the Brāhmaṇas previous to the rise of Buddhism, or, at all events, previous to the time when the Sūtra style began to be adopted in Indian literature. There existed, previous to the Sūtra period, a body of literary works propagated by oral tradition, which formed the basis of all later writings on sacred subjects, and which by the Brāhmaṇas was believed to be of divine origin. The idea expressed by the verb Śru, to hear, *i.e.* to receive by inspiration, is known in the Brāhmaṇas for the first time in the Taittirīya-Āraṇyaka[37], though it is said to be used there in the sense of Śruti. In the Sūtras, however, the distinction between Śruti and Smṛti is distinctly stated. We find it in the Anupada-sūtras,[38] which we have reason to reckon amongst the earliest specimens of this class of literature. In the Nidāna-sūtras also, ancient tradition is mentioned by the name of Smṛti[39]; and although in Pāṇini the technical distinction between Śruti and Smṛti is not mentioned, it would be wrong to draw any conclusions from this, as there can be little doubt that Pāṇini is later than the Anupada-sūtras.

THE SIX VEDĀṄGAS

We shall now proceed to an examination of those works which belong to the Sūtra-literature of India, as far as they have reference to the Veda.

The Brāhmaṇas say there are six members of the Veda, the six Vedāṅgas. This name does not imply die existence of six distinct books or treatises intimately congested with their sacred writings, but merely the admission of six subjects the study of which was necessary either for the reading, the understanding, or the proper sacrificial employment of the Veda. Manu calls the Vedāṅgas by the name of Pravacanas,[40] which is a, title not unusually applied to the Brāhmaṇas[41] And indeed, instead of looking for the Vedāṅgas to those small and barren tracts which are now known by this name, it is in the Brāhmaṇas and Sūtras that we have to look for the Vedānga doctrines in their original and authentic form. The short Vedāngas which are generally added to the manuscripts of the Veda, and which by several scholars were mistaken for the real Vedangas, represent only the last unsuccessful attempts to faring the complicated and unintelligible doctrines of former sages into an easy and popular form, and to preserve at the same time the names which had been sanctioned by antiquity.

A very clear and rational statement as to the character of the Vedāṅgas in early times, is given in the Bṛhadāraṇyaka and its commentary. According to them the different doctrines of the Vedāṅgas are to be considered as integral parts of the Brāhmaṇas in the same manner as the Purāṇas and Itihāsas. These, as we saw before, were to be taken in the sense of epic or paurāṇic stories, incorporated in the Brāhmaṇas, as illustrations of ceremonial questions. By Itihāsas, as the commentator says, (Bṛhdaraṇy. ii. 4.) we have to understand stories like those of Urvaśī and Purūravas in the Śatapatha-brāhmaṇa; by Purāṇa, passages on creation and the like, for instance, "in the beginning there was nothing,' etc. He then proceeds to quote passages from the Brāhmaṇas which he calls Upaniṣads (mysteries), Ślokas (verses), Sūtras (rules), Anuvyā-khyās (explanations), and Vyākhyās (comments). It is under these heads that the Vedāṅgas had their original place.

It is more difficult to determine where and when the Vedāṅgas were first mentioned as six. In the Muṇḍaka-upaniṣad the number of the Vedāṅgas is given as six, but in a line which is not unlikely to have been interpolated. Yāska (Nir. i. 20.) quotes only the Vedāṅgas, but not the six Vedāṅgas. The number of six occurs in the Caraṇas-vyūha, where we meet with the well-known versus memorialis, containing the titles of the six Vedāṅgas.[42] The same number occurs in Manu (iii. 185). There is a passage in the Chāndogya-Upaniṣad where a mention of the six Vedāṅgas might be expected, at the beginning of the ninth Prapāṭhaka. The number six, however, does not occur there although Vedāṅga doctrines are clearly implied under somewhat unusual names.[43] The earliest mention oi the number six in reference to the Vedāṅgas seems to be contained in one of the Brāhmaṇas of the Śāmaveda. But there again, though the number six is given, the titles of the several Vedāṅgas are not mentioned. It is said there (Ṣaḍvinṁśa, Br. iv. 7.) of Svāhā, that her body consists of the four Vedas, and that her limbs are the six Aṅgas, or members of the Veda.[44] It is possible, however, that more ancient Brāhmaṇas allude to the number of six; at all events we see that it was sanctioned for the Vedāṅgas it before the end of the Brāhmaṇa period.

.The six doctrines commonly comprehended under the title of Vedāṅgas, are Śikṣā (pronunciation), Chandas (metre), Vyākarṇa (grammar), Nirukta (explanation of words), Jyautiṣa (astronomy;, and Kalpa (ceremonial). The first two are considered necessary for reading the Veda, the two next for understanding it, and the last two for employing it at sacrifices.

ŚIKṢĀ, OR PHONETICS

Śāyaṇa, in his Commentary on the Ṛg-veda, defines Śikṣā as the science of the pronunciation of letters, accents, etc.; and he quotes from a work of the Taittrīyas, who have devoted a chapter of their Āraṇyaka to this subject. Now in the seventh book of the Taittrīyas-Āraṇyaka we still find the following headings : "Let us explain the Śikṣā,"[45] "On the Organs of Pronunciation," "On Delivery", "On Euphonic Laws."

Unless we admit that the rules on Śikṣā had formerly their place in this chapter of the Taittirīya-Āraṇyaka, it would be difficult to explain why all the principal subjects of the Śikṣā should be mentioned here, why the whole chapter should be called the Śikṣā chapter (ityuktaḥ śikṣā-dhyāyaḥ), and why it should begin with the words "Let us now explain the Śikṣā." Sāyaṇa, who was certainly acquainted with the Vedic tradition, takes the same view in his Commentary on the Sāṁhiti-upaniṣad.[47] He states that the 'Taittirīya-upaniṣad consists of three parts[48], of the Sāṁhitī, Yājñikī, and Vāruṇī-upaniṣad. Of these the last is the most important, because it teaches the knowledge of the Divine Self. The first serves as an introduction or preparation, in order to bring the mind of the pupil into a proper state for receiving the doctrines on the highest subjects. Now immediately after the first invocation, the Upaniṣad begins with the Śikṣā chapter; and in order to explain this, Say aria remarks that this doctrine 15 necessary here, in order to enable the pupil to read and pronounce the sacred texts correctly, and thus to understand their real meaning.[48] It might be objected,

Sāyaṇa, remarks, that as a correct pronunciation is equally required for the earlier ceremonial portion ef the Veda (Karma-Kāṇḍa), the Śikṣā ought to have been inserted there. But then, he says, this chapter in its present place stands between the ceremonial and the philosophical portion of the Veda, like a lamp on the threshold of a door giving light to both. He adds, that a right pronunciation and understanding is of greater importance for the philosophical part; because mistakes in the sacrifices and the ceremonial can be made good by penance, while there is no penance for a wrong understanding of philosophical principles.

If then there is reason to believe that the doctrine of the Śikṣā was formerly embodied in the Āraṇyakas, perhaps even in the Brāhmaṇas,[49] the question is, why it afterwards lost this place. This can only be accounted for by the appearance of more scientific treatises, which embraced the same subjects, but in a much more systematic style than anything which we could expect to meet with in the Brāhmaṇis and Āraṇyakas.

PRĀTIŚĀKHYAS

These were the Prātiśākhyas, a branch of literature which will claim our particular attention for more than one reason. If we compare the Prātiśākhyas with Brāhmaṇas and Āraṇyakas, they evidently indicate a considerable progress of the Indian mind. They were written for practical purposes; their style is free from cumbrous ornaments, and unnecessary subtleties. It is their object to teach and not to edify; to explain, not to discuss. Where the Brāhmaṇas or Āraṇyakas allude to grammatical, metrical, or etymological questions they give nothing but theological and mystical dreams. So far from receiving elucidation, the points in, question generally become involved in still greater darkness. It is not unlikely that teachers appealed to these passages of the Brāhmaṇas in order to derive from them the highest possible sanction for their doctrines. But these doctrines, if they were intended for use and instruction, must have been delivered in a more homely and more intelligible form. The origin of the Prātiśākhyas may therefore be accounted for in the following manner :

During the Brāhmaṇa period the songs of the Veda were preserved by oral tradition only and as the spoken language of India had advanced and left the idiom of the Veda behind as a kind of antique and sacred utterance, it was difficult to preserve the proper pronunciation of the sacred hymns without laying down a certain number of rules on metre, accent, and pronunciation in general. The necessity, however, of such a provision could hardly have been felt until certain differences had actually arisen in different seats of Brāhmaṇic learning. Thus, when the attempt was made to prevent a further corruption, a certain number of local varieties in accent and pronunciation, and in the recital of the hymns, had actually crept in and become sanctioned by the tradition of different families or schools. These could not be given up, nor was there any means of determining which was the ancient and most correct way of reciting the sacred songs of the Veda. Discussion having arisen on this subject, we find in the Brāhmaṇas occasional mention of verses which, if improperly pronounced, become changed in their meaning. But even where the sense of the Veda was not affected, the respect paid by each teacher, by each family, and by each Brāhmāṇic community to its own established oral tradition, was sufficient to give an imaginary value to the slightest peculiarities of pronunciation, accent, or metre.

A twofold advantage was gained when the rules and exceptions of the old sacred dialect were first reduced to a system. First, ancient dialectical differences, many of which are not so much attributable to corruptions as to the freedom of the old spoken language, were carefully preserved, and even apparent irregularities and exceptions were handed down as such, instead of being eliminated and forgotten. Secondly, a start was made towards a scientific study of language; by the collection of a large number of similar passages, general laws were elicited which afterwards served us the phonetic basis of a grammar like that of Pāṇini; a work which, although ascribed to one author, must have required ages of observation and collection before its plan could be conceived or carried out by one individual. Even the Prātiśākhyas, though they do not refer to grammar properly so called, but principally to the phonetic laws of language, presuppose a longcontinued study of grammatical subjects previous to the lime of their composition. The best proof of this lies in the great number of authors quoted in the Prātiśākhyas, whose opinions are frequently at variance with the precepts contained in the Prātiśākhyas themselves. Though we are not now in possession of the works of these earlier authors, yet we have a right to assume that their doctrines existed formerly in the shape of Prātiśākhyas. In the same way as one only of the different Śākhās or recensions of the Ṛg-veda has been preserved to us in manuscript, the Śākala-śākhā which was followed by Śaunaka, we may understand how one only of the Prātiśākhyas of the Ṛg-veda has come down to us: particularly as its composition is ascribed to the same Śaunnaka who is said to have unitsd the Bāṣkala and the Śākala-śākhās, and who, as far as the Saṁhitā is concerned was a follower of the. Śaiśira-śākhā. Śaunaka's Prātiśākhya of the Śākalas, being one of the latest compositions of this kind, was probably also the most perfect and complete. As Śaunaka states the different opinions of Śākala grammarians on important points, where he himself differs from them, his work was the more likely to supersede previous Prātiśākhyas particularly at the time when the Vedic religion was on its' decline, and Brahmṇic doctrines daily losing influence. Though it is true that as yet only one Prātiśākhya belonging to each Veda has been found in manuscript, yet they all belong not to one of the four Vedas in general, but to one Śākhā of each of them. Prātiśākhya, therefore, does not mean, as has been supposed, a treatise on the phonetic pecu-liarities of each Veda, but a collection of phonetic rules peculiar to one of the different branches of the four Vedas, *i.e.*, to one of those different texts in which each of the Vedas had been handed down for ages in different families and different parts of India. The differences between the Śākhās of the same Veda, as far as the words of the hymns are concerned, seem certainly not to have been very great, if we may judge from the few instances in which different Śākhās of the same Veda have been preserved in manuscripts. Most Śākhās do not differ in the general arrangement or the Saṁhitās, or collections of hymns, but merely in single words or verses. In a few cases only one Śākhā contains some hymns more than another. The Śākhās were not independent collections of the old hymns, but different editions of one and the same original collection, which in the course of a long continued oral tradition had become modified by slight degrees. The texts of the Veda as they existed and lived in the oral tradition of various sets of people became Śākhās differing from other Śākhās somewhat in the same way as the MSS. of ihe New Testament differ from each other. The Prātiśākhyas, besides giving general rules for the proper pronunciation of the Vedic language in general, were intended to record what was peculiar in the pronunciation of certain teachers and their schools. Even in cases where these schools had become extinct, we find the names of their founders, preserved as authorities on matters connected with the pronunciation of certain letters or words.

The real object of the Prātiśākhyas, as shown before, was not to teach the grammar of the old sacred language, to lay down the rules of declension and conjugation or the principles of the formation of words. This is a doctrine which, though it could not have been unknown during the Vedic period, has not been embodied, as far as we know, in any ancient work. The Prātiśākhyas are never called Vyākaraṇas, grammars[50], and it is only incidentally that they allude to strictly grammatical questions. The perfect phonetic system, on which Pāṇini's grammar is built, is no doubt taken from the Prātiśākhyas; but the sources of Pāṇini's strictly grammatical doctrines must be looked for elsewhere.

Although, then, there is no necessity to suppose that every one of the numerous Vedic Śākhās possessed full and complete Prātiśākhyas, like that belonging to the Śākala-śākhā, which was finally collected by Śaunaka, yet the great number of previous authorities quoted in our Prātiśākhyas makes it likely that a large number of similar works did actually exist for the principal Śākhās that are mentioned in earlier writings. In the Pratiñāpariśiṣta[51] it is stated that there were fifteen codes of law for the fifteen Śākhās of the Vājasaneyins; and Kumārila says that the text of these Codes of law and of the Gṛhyas was peculiar in each Caraṇa in the same manner as the formal rules of the Prātiśākhyas.[53] Madhusadana Sarasvatī's definition of Prātiśākhya is perfectly in accordance with this view of the subject. He says: "The Veda[53] consists of two parts : one teaching the sacrifice, the other teaching Brahmān, or the Supreme Being. As there are three different branches of the ceremonial, the Veda is, for the better performance of the sacrifices, divided into three : the Ṛg-veda, Yajur-Veda and Sāma-Veda. The cercmaninal of the Hotṛ priests is performed with the Ṛg-Veda; that of the Adhvaryu priests with the Yajur-Veda; that of the *Udgātṛ priests* wuh ihe Sāma-Veda. The duties of the Brahmā priests, and of him for whom the sacrifice is offered, are also contained in these three Vedas. The Atharva-Veda is not used for solemn sacrifices, and is very different from the others, as it teaches only expiatory, preservative, or imprecatory rites. For each Veda there are several Śākhās, and their differences arise from various readings."[54] Afterwards he goes on to observe that "the rules of pronunciation (*śikṣā*), which apply to all the Vedas in general, have been explained by Pāṇini but that the same rules as they apply to the Śākhās of each Veda, have been taught by other sages under the title of Prātiśākhyas."[55] If we here take the ward Śākhās (branches) in the sense of different traditionary tcxts of the four Vedas, Madhusūdana's words do not require any alteration; they would become obscure if, as has been proposed, we took śākhā either in the sense of "a school" or of "a portion of the Veda."

The word śākhā is used, however, by some writers in so vague a manner that we need not wonder if its meaning has sometimes been misapprehended. "Traditional test (recension) of the Veda" is perhaps the nearest approach to its real meaning.

The word is sometimes applied to the three original Saṁhitās, the Ṛg-veda-saṁhitā, Yajur-Veda-saṁhitā, and Sāma-Veda-saṁhitā[57], in their relation to one another; and without any reference ts subordinate śākhās belonging to each of them. They may be called the original branches or the three stems of the Veda-tree, each of them branching off again in a number of other śākhās. The "branches," as Kumārila says, have all the same root, revelation (Śruti), and they bear all the same fruit, the sacrifice (karma). If otherwise, they would be different trees, not different branches".[57] In the same acceptation the word is used for instance by Āpastamba, where he is giving rules as to the time and place where the Veda ought not to be read. He says there (Sām. Sūtra, 3. 44, 45,) that it aught not to be rehearsed where music or Sāma-hymns are performed, and he adds, that Sāma-hymns ought not to be practised in the neighbourhood of another Śākhā, that is, as the commentator observes, another Veda.[58]

More frequently, however, śākhā is used to signify the various editions, or, more properly, the various traditions, that branched off from each of the three original branches of the Veda. In the latter sense Śākhā seems sometimes synonymous with caraṇa. But there was originally an important difference in the meaning of these two terms.

In order to appreciate the difference between śākhā and caraṇa, it need only be remembered that we find "*śākhām aḍhīte*," "he reads a certain recension of the Veda," but never carṇam adhīte" still less "*pariṣadam adhīte*," "he reads a Carąṇa or a Pariṣad." Hence it is clear that śākhā means originally a literary work, and that Caraṇa does not, If *śākhā* is sometimes used in-tie sense of caraṇa or sect, this because in India the *śākhās* existed in reality not as written books, but only in the tradition of the Caraṇas, each member of a Caraṇa representing what, in our modern times, we should call the copy of a book.

The *Brāhmaṇas* themselves were fully aware of this difference between *śākhā* and *caraṇa*. In a Vārttika to Pāṇini, iv. 1. 63., we find *caraṇa* explained by *śākhādhyetr*, etc., the readers of a śākhā." In a passage of Jugaddhara's Commentary on Mālatīmādhava, Caraṇa is said to mean "a number of men who are pledged to the reading of a certain śākhā of the Veda, and who have in this manner become one body."[59] Pāṇini[60] speaks of Caraṇas as consti-tuting a multitude, that is to say, as comprisiug a number of followers. In Āpastamba's Sāmayacārika-sūtras, where rules are given as to the relative age of persons who ought to be saluted, the Caraṇas or members of the same Caraṇa are mentioned immediately after the Paura-śākhyam, or town acquaintances; and. in the third place stand the Śrotriya-brāhmaṇas.[61] Pāṇini, speaks of the Kāṭhaka and Kalapāka as works belonging to the Caraṇas of the Kaṭhas and Kalāpas.[62] In a Vārttika to iv. 1, 63., women are mentioned as belonging to a Caraṇa; for Kaṇhī is the wife or daughter of a Brāhmaṇa who belongs to the Caraṇa, or reads the Śākhā, of the Kaṭhas. A śākhā, which is always a portion of the Śruti, cannot properly include law books, But followers of certain śākhās might well, in the course of time, adopt a code of laws, which, as it was binding of their Caraṇa only, would naturally go by the name of their Caraṇa. That this actually took place may be seen from a Vārttika to Pāṇ. iv. 3. 120., where it is said that Kāṭhaka may be used not only for the sacred traditions, but also for the laws of the Kaṭhas. Thus the Prātiśākhyas also were called by the name of the Caraṇas, because they were the exclusive property of the readers of certain *śākhās*, and even more, so than the Kuladharmas or family-laws.

As a *śākhā* consisted of a Saṁhitā as well as a Brāhmaṇa, at all events in Infer times, differences in the text of the hymns, us well as discrepancies in the Brāhmaṇas might lead to the establishment of new Caraṇas, founded as they were on sacred texts peculiar to themselves.[64] Śākhās of this kind, which differed through the various readings of the Śruti, were considered by the Brāhmaṇas as eternal śākhās, and the Caraṇas to which they belonged, were not supposed to have founded by human authors.[64] It will be seen hereafter that the Brāhmaṇas admitted another class of *śākhās*, which were founded on Sūtras[65] and derived their names from historical personages, They were confessedly of a later date.

But although, after a careful examination of these passages, we cannot doubt that there was an original difference between *śākhā* and saraṇa, it is not the less certain that these two words were frequently used synonymously;[66] in the same way as we may speak of the Jews when we mean the Old Testament, or of the Koran when we mean the Mohammedans.

After having established the difference between *śākhā* and saraṇa, we have still to inquire how both differ from parishad, in order to determine, the meaning of Pārṣada, another title which is frequently applied to the Prātiśākhyas. Here it is important to observe that although every Prātiśākhya may be called a Pārṣada,[67] *i.e.*, a work belonging to a Pariṣad, not every Pārṣada can be called a Prātiśākhya, but those only which contain the rules of pronunciation for a particular śākhā or text of the Vedic hymns, studied and taught in certain Pariṣads.[68] Amara explains parishad by sabhā or goṣthi, an assembly; but the codes of law lay down more accurately the number, age and qualifications of the Brāhmaṇas necessary to form such an assembly as should be competent to give decisions on all points of which the people, or, if we may say so, the parishioners, might demand advice. That such Pariṣads or Brāhmaṇic settlements existed in old times, we See in the Bṛhadāraṇyaka[69], where it is said that Śvetaketu went to the Pariṣad of the Pañcālas, and many similar passages. The character of a Pariṣad is described in Manu's Code of Laws, xii. 110-113, and by Yājñavalkya, i. 9., where we have the contracted form Pārṣad (पर्षद्) instead of Pariṣad. According to the ideas of these modern .writers a Pariṣad ought to consist of twenty-one Brāhmaṇas well versed in philosophy, theology, and law.[70] This number, however, can be reduced according to circumstances, as will be seen from passages of Parāśara's Dharmaśāstra. It must not be supposed that the rules laid down in these law-books have always, been observed in the formation of a Pariṣad, particularly as regards the early times of India; yet we may be able to form some conception of their original character, by seeing what has become of them in later times. Parāśara says:[71] "Four, or even three able men from amongst the Brāhmaṇas in a village, (grāma-madhye) who know the Veda, and keep the sacrificial fire, form a Pariṣad.

"Or, if they do not keep the sacrificial fire, five or three who have studied the Vedas and Vedāṅgas and know the law, may well form a Pariṣad.

"Of old sages who possess the highest knowledge of the Divine Self, who are twice-born, perform sacrifices, and have purified themselves in the duties of the Veda, one, also, may he considered as a Pariṣad.

Thus, five kinds of Pariṣads have been described by me: but if they all fail, three independent men may form a Pariṣad."

Mādhava, in the Commentary on Parāśara, quotes a similar passage"[72] from Bṛhaspati's Code: "Where seven, five, or three Brāhmaṇas, who know the customs of the world, the Vedāṅgas (or the Vedas and the Aṅgas), and the law, have settled, that assembly is like a sacrifice." The real difference, therefore, between a Caraṇa and a Pariṣad, seems to be that the former signifies an ideal succession of teachers and pupils who learn and teach a certain branch of the Veda; while the latter means a settlement of Brāhmaṇas, a community or college to which members of any Caraṇa might belong. Thus members of the same Caraṇa might be fellows of different Pariṣads, and fellows of the same Pariṣad might be members of different Cāraṇas.[73]

Now as Pārṣada may be used as the title of any work that belonged to a Pariṣad, Or formed,'so to say, the traditional library of the Pārishadyas, it is clear that this title could not be confined to the Prātiśākhyas, though it would necessarily include them. If a follower of the Śākala-saraṇa was a fellow of the Vatsa-parishsd, the Śākala-Prātiśākhya would necessarily be one of the Pārṣada works of the Vatsas, and the Pariṣad of the Vatsas would through this fellow be connected with the Śākala Caraṇa. This is what Durga means when in the Commentary on the Nirukta.[74] he says "that those Pārṣadas only are called Prātiśākhyas which are adopted in a Pariṣad of one's own Caraṇa for teaching certain grammatical doctrines connected with the reading of the Veda according to one or the other Śākhā." The Prātiśākhyas are in fact a sub-division of the Pariṣada books, and in this sense it might well be said that Prātiśākhya is an adjective to Pārṣada.[75]

After the true meaning of Śākhā, Caraṇa, and Pariṣad, of Prātiśākhya and Pārṣada, has thus been determined, we have still to inquire about those other works, which together with the Prātiśākhyas were mentioned as the peculiar property of the Caraṇas. I mean the Kula-dharmas, or law-books. They of course could not be called Prātiśākhyas, but they might claim the title of Cāraṇas, (a name which has not been met with,) or Pārṣadas. Now we saw before that Āpastamba actually refers to the Pariṣads. in his Sāmaya-cārika-sūtras (1. 11), where, after having pointed out the days on which the Veda ought not to be repeated, he remarks, that further particulars on this point are to be found in the Pariṣads.[76] What does this mean ? All that Haradatta has to say in the commentary on this very passage, is that by Pariṣads must here be understood the Mānava, Vāsiṣṭha, and other Dharmaśāstras.[77] These Dharmaśāstras, however, as we now possess them, betray their comparatively modern origin by their form and metre, and occasionally by their matter also. As many of them have been printed at Calcutta, it may be seen that the majority of these small Śloka works are utterly worthless. They were probably made up only in order to fill the gap which had been occasioned by the loss of ancient legal works. This loss was felt the more severely because the names of the old authors retained their celebrity, and were still quoted in common practice and courts of law. I have succeeded, however, in recovering in manuscript large portions of the Kula-Dharmas, which are written in Sūtras, as might be expected in works contemparaneous with the Prātiśākhyas. It has been thought that the sources of Manu and other Dharmaśāstras must be looked for in the Gṛhya-sūtras. This is not quite correct. The Gṛhya-sūtras are concerned chiefly with the Saṁskāras, or domestic sacraments, extending from the birth to tbe marriage of a man, and in so far only as these sacraments form a portion of the subjects treated in the Dharmaśāstras, the Gṛhya-sūtras might be considered as their original sources. But then the same might be said of the Śrauta-sūtras, because the solemn sacrifices prescribed by them are likewise alluded to in the Codes of Law. By far the greatest portion, however, of these codes is taken up with Ācāra, *i.e.*, laws, manners, and customs. The difference between these observances and the ceremonies laid down in the other two branches of Sūtras is this : the domestic sacraments (*gṛhya*), as well as the solemn sacrifices (*śrauta*), are administered by parents or priests for the good of their children and pupils, while the Ācāra comprises all the duties which are to be performed by an individual on his own behalf.[78] These duties refer to the different castes, and to the respective occupations of each. The rules of discipline for the young student, the occupations of the married man, the law of inheritance, the duties of the king, the administration of the law, are accurately detailed in these Sūtras. They are of great importance for forming a correct view of the old state of society in India, and the loss of the larger number of them is greatly to be regretted. Their general title is Sāmayācārika-sūtras or Dharmasūtras, and they form the third part to the Śrauta and Gṛhya-sūtras. Thus we have, beside the Śrauta and Gṛhya-sūtras of Āpastamba, a collection of Sāmayacārika-sūtras belonging to the same Caraṇa of the Āpastambas, the members of which, as Kumārila tells us, followed one of the Śākhās of the Taittirīya Veda. Another collection of Dharmasūtras, which, however, is liable to critical doubts, belongs to the Gautamas, a Caraṇa of the Sāma-veda. It has been printed at Calcutta. A third one bears the name of Vishṇu, and has been printed at Calcutta, enlarged by modern additions written in Ślokas. The Vaśiṣṭha-dharma-śāstra, printed at Calcutta, belongs likewise, at least in part, to this class of Dharmasūtras. Whether we shall succeed in finding still more of thess Sūtraworks is questionable, though prose quotations from other Dharmaśāstras would justify this expectation. There can be no doubt, however, that all the genuine metrical Dharma-śāstras which we possess now, are, without any exception, nothing but more modern texts of earlier Sūtra-works or Kula-dharmas belonging originally to certain Vedic Caraṇas.[80]

To return to those works of the Pārṣada literature which are known by the name of Prātiśākhyas, I may refer for further particulars to Dr. Roth's valuable observations on this branch of literature. To him belongs the merit of having first pointed out in manuscipt four of these works. The first is ascribed to Śaunaka, and belongs to the Śakala-śākhā of "the Ṛg-Veda. I call it the Śākala-Prātiśākhya, not the Śaiśira-Prātiśākhya, though it pretends to follow, like Śaunaka's Anukrnmaṇī the Saṁhitā of the Śaiśirīya-śākhā, which is itself a sobordinate branch of the Sākala-śākhā.[80] Śiśira, however, is never mentioned in this or any other Prātiśākhya, as an authority on grammatical questions.

It is doubtful how far the rules given by Śaunaka in his Prātiśākhya, can be considered as representing the general opinion of the Śākalas. Śaunaka, no doubt, wrote for the Śākalas, to whom he likewise addresses his Anukrnmaṇī. But the author of the Prātiśākhya occasionally quotes the opinions of the Śākalas as different from his own, and speaks of them in the same manner as he alludes to the opinions of other grammarians. He mentions (i. 65.) the Śākalas as observing a certain peculiar pronunciation out of respect for their master, who seems to have sanctioned it in his own rules. Who this muster was is difficult to say. But it is most likely the same who (i. 53) is called the Master, Vedamitra (friend of the Veda), and who (i. 223.) is called Śākalyapitā, the father of Śākalya. His opinions, if we may judge by i. 232., differed from those of the younger Śākalya. In i. 185, we meet with him again under the name of Śākalya Sthavira, Śākalya the elder, and he is there represented as advocating a pronunciation from which Śaunaka, the author of the Prātiśākhya, dissents. In i 199; Śaunaka adopts the opinion of Śākalya, and in i. 208, he likewise mentions him with approbation. But all this would only tend to show that Śaunaka does not consider himself bound to follow either Śākalya, or the father of Śākalya implicitly.[82]

There is not a single MS. at present existing of the Ṛg-veda in which the rules of our Prātiśākhya are uniformly observed, and the same applies to the MSS. of the other Vedas. The rules of the Prātiśākhyas were not intended for written literature, they were only to serve as a guide in the instruction of pupils who had to learn the text of the Veda by heart, and to repeat it, as part of their daily devotions. As Śaunaka was himself a member of the Śākalas, we may quote his Prātiśākhya as the Śākala-Prātiśākhya. But strictly speaking it could only be called one of the Śākala-Prātiśākhyas, preserved by the pupils of

Śaunaka, who, soon after, formed themselves into a new Caraṇa, under the name of Śaunakīyas[83]

The second Prātiśākhya belongs to the ancient text of the Yajurveda. There is only one MS. of it at the Bodleian Library, together with a considerable portion of the Commentary, the Tri-bhāṣya-ratna. Professor Wilson, in his catalogue of the Mackenzie Collection (i. 7. No. xxxiii.) mentions another MS., "The Prātiśākhya of the Yajurveda, with a Bhāṣya or comment, entitled Tri-bhāshya-ratna, from its being said to be the substance of the works of three celebrated sages, Ātreya, Mahiṣa, and Vararuchi." To what parti-cular Śākhā'of the Black Yajur-veda this Prātiśākhya belonged it is difficult to determine. It quotes several of the Caraṇas, belonging to the Black Yajur-veda, such as Taittirīyakas, Āhvarakas, Ukhya, the founder of the Aukhīyas, and Bhāradvāj, the founder of the Bhāradvājins, It also alludes to Mīmāṁsākas, a school of philosophers, mentioned in none of the other Prātiśākhyas, Until we receive some more complete MSS. of this work we can only say that it belongs to some Śākhā of the Taittirīya or Black Yajur-veda. Its grammatical terminoiogy, as might be expected, is less advanced and less artificial than that of the Prātiśākhya of the modern or White Yajur-veda.

The third Prātiśākhya is ascribed to the Śākhā of the Mādhyandinas, one of the subdivisions of the Vājasaneyins;[84] though, perhaps, on the same grounds as those stated above with regard to thc Śākala-Prātiśākhya, it might seem more correct to call it the Prātiśākhya of the Kātyāyanīyas, a sub-division of the Mādhyandinas. It was composed by Kātyāyana, and shows a considerable advance in grammatical technicalities, There is nothing in its style that could be used as a tenable argument why Kātyāyana, the author of the Prātiśākhya should not be the same as Kātyāyana, the contemporary and critic of Pāṇini. It is true that Pānini's rules are intended for a language which was no longer the pure Sanskrit of the Vedas. The Vedic idiom is treated by him as ac exception, whereas Kātyāyana's Prātiśākhya seems to belong to a period when there existed but one recognised literature, that of the Ṛṣis. This, however, is not quite the case. Kātyāyana himself alludes to the fact that there were at least two languages, "There are two words," he says (i. 17.)[85], "om and atha, both used in the beginning of a chapter; but *om* is used in the Vedas, *atha* in the Bhāṣyas." As Kātyāyana himself writes in the Bhāṣya or the common language, there is no reason why he should not have composed rules on the grammar of the profane Sanskrit, as well as on the pronunciation of the Vedic idiom.

Some of Kātyāyana's Sūtras are now found repeated *ipsissimis verbis** in Pāṇini's grammar. This might seem strange; but we know that not all the Sūtras now incorporated in his grammar came from Pāṇini himself, and it is most likely that Kātyāyana, in writing his supplementary notes to Pāṇini, simply repeated some of his Prātiśākhya-sūtras, and that, at a later time, some of these so-called Vārttikas became part of the test of Pāṇini.

The fourth Prātiśākhya belongs to the Atharva-veda. It is called Śaunakīya Cāturādhyayikā, and was, therefore, no doubt the property of the Śaunakīya, a Caraṇa of the Atharva-veda. The name of the author is unknown, and we possess as yet but one MS., and that a very imperfect one, in the Royal Library at Berlin. That it belongs to a Śākhā of the Ātharvaṇa, is indicated by its very beginning,[86] and one of its first rules is quoted by the commentator on the Śākala-Prātiśākhya as belonging to an Ātharvaṇa-Prātiśākhya.[87] Besides, in the fourth chapter of the fourth and last book special reference is made to Ātharvaṇa sacrifices.[87] We can hardly suppose that Śaunaka, the author of the Prātiśākhya of the Ṛg-veda, was at the same time the author of this Śaunakīyā Cāturādhyayikā. Śaunaka, whose name never occurs in the Śākala-prātiśākhya,[88] is quoted in the Cāturādhyayikā, i.1.8.[89] The grammatical terminology of this little tract is far in advance of the technical terms used by Śaunaka. Yet there is a certain connection between the two books, and it is most likely that the author of the Cāturādhyayikā was a member of the Śaunakīyā-saraṇa, founded by the author of the Śākala-Prātiśākhya. Nay it seems as it its author had retained something of the allegiance which Śaunaka owed to

Śākalya and the Śākalas. In one instance, where Pāṇini quotes the opinions of Śākalya, the original is found in the Cāturādhyayikā, and not in the Śākala-prātiśākhya. We are told by Pāṇini, that Śākalya pronounced the 'o' of the vocative to be unchangeable pragṛhya, if followed by the particle iti[90] Exactly the same rule, and in the very same words, is given in the Ātharvaṇa-Prātiśākhya,[91] whereas the Śākala-Prātiśākhya teaches first that the 'o' of the vocative is (pragṛhya), (i. 69)[92]; secondly, that it is liable to certain changes (i. 132, 135); and lastly, that all pragṛhya vowels are unchangeable, if followed by iti (i. 155). In none of these Sūtras do we find the exact words which Pāṇini quotes, and which are found in the Ātharvaṇa-Prātiśākhya. Again, Pāṇini (viii. 3. 19.) ascribes the dropping of *y* and *v* in *Viṣṇv iha* instead of *Viṣṇav iha*, in *hara ehi* instead of *haray ehi*, to Śākalya. Now it is true that this process is not unknown in the Śākala-Prātiśākhya, but it there assumes quite a different aspect (i. 129. 132, 135); whereas, in the Cāturādhyāyikā the explanation is very much the same as in Pāṇini.[93] Pāṇini quotes in the same place (viii. 3. 18.) the spelling adopted in these cases by Śākaṭayana.[94] This is mentioned likewise in immediate connection with the rules which precede it in the Ātharvaṇa-Prātiśākhya; it is not mentioned at all in the Śākala-Prātiśākhya. It has been supposed[95] that a rule, which in Kātyāyana's Prātiśākhya is ascribed to Śaunaka, was taken from the Cāturādhāyikā, and that therefore Kātyāyana's Prātiśākhya was later than that of the Atharva-veda, But the rule ascribed to Śaunaka by Kātyāyana is that a final tenuis, if followed by a sibilant of a *different class*, is changed into the aspirate, whereas according to the Cāturādhyāyikā (II. 1. 6.) a tenuis, followed by a sibilant of its own class, would have to he aspirated.[96] It must be admitted, however, that no such rule as that ascribed by Kātyāyana to Śaunaka is found in the Śākala-Prātiśākhya, and, in other respects, the Prātiśākhya of Kātyāyana shows traces of more modern origin than the Cāturādhyāyikā.

The following list gives the names of the principal authorities quoted in the Śākala-Prātiśākhya, the Taittirīya-Prātiśākhya, the Kātyāyanīya-Prātiśākhya, the Cāturādhyāyikā, the Nirukta and

Pāṇini. I have availed myself of the lists given by Roth, Weber, and Böhtlingk; and though I do not pretend that my own list is complete, it will be sufficient to show the active interest which was taken in grammatical subjects at that early period :

1. Āgniveśya T.
2. Āgniveśyayana. T.
3. Āgrāuaṇa. N.
4. Ātreya. T.
5. Ānyatareya.Ś Ch.
6. Āpiśali. P.
7. Āhvarakas. T.
8. Ukhya. T.
9. Uttamottarīyas. (?) T. (Kramakṛt).
10. Udicyas. P.
11. Audumbarāyaṇa. N.
12. Aupamanyava. N.
13. Aupaśivi. K.
14. Aurṇavābha. N.
15. Kāṇḍāyāna. T.
16. Kāṇva. K.
17. Kātthakya. N.
18. Kāśyapa. K. P.
19. Kauṇḍing T.
20. Kautsa. N.
21. Kauhalīputra. T.
22. Krauṣṭuki. N.
23. Gārgya. S.K.N.P.
24. Gālava. N.P.
25. Gautama. T.
26. Charmaśiras. N.
27. Cākravarmaṇa. P.
28. Jātūkarṇya. K.
29. Taitīki. N,
30. Taittṛīyakas. T.
31. Dalbhya. K.
32. Pañcālas. S.
33. Pauṣkarasādi. T. P. (vart)
34. Prācyas. S. P.
35. Plākṣi. T.
36. Plākṣāyaṇa. T.
37. Bābhravya
38. Bhāradvāja. T. P.
39. Māṇḍūkeya. Ś
40. Māśakīyā. T.
41. Mīmāṁsakas T.
42. Yāska. S.
43. Vāṛabhīkāra. T.
44. Vātsapra.
45. Vātsya Ch.
46. Vārshyāyaṇi.
47. Vālmiki. T.
48. Vedamitra. Ś.
49. Vyāḷi Ś
50. Śatabalāksha Maudgalya. N.
51. Śākaṭāyana. Ś. K. Ch. N. P.
52. Śākapūṇi. N.
53. Śākata (pādakṛt). Ś.
54. Śākalas. S.
55. Śakalya Ś. K. P.

56. Śākalya-pitṛ (sthavira). S.
57. Śaṅkhāyana. T.
58. Śaityāyana. T.
59. Śaunaka. Ś. (?). K. Ch.
60. Sāṅkṛtya. T.
61. Seṅaka. P.
62. Sthaulaṣṭhīvi. N.
63. Sphoṭāyana. P.
64. Hārita. T.

For the Sāma-veda no Prātiśākhya has as yet been discovered. There is a small treatise which I found in the same manuscript of the Bodleian Library which contains the the Taittirīya-Prātiśākhya, and which might be called a Prātiśākhya of the Sāma veda. But it is so badly written, and so unintelligible without a commentary, that little use can be made of it at present. It is called Sāma-tantra,[97] and evidently treats of the same subjects which usually occur in the Prātiśākhyas. Its authenticity is supported by the Caraṇavyūhā, where a Sāma-tantra is mentioned, but without any further particulars.

If it be asked now why all these works, so different in appearance are to be ascribed to one period of literature, the Sūtra-period, the reasons for it are as follows : first, that the style of the majority of these works is the old Sūtra style, for instance, in the Taittirīya-Prātiśākhya, the Kātyāyanīya-Prātiśākhya, and the Cāturādhyāyikā[98] : secondly, that, the manuscripts call these works Sūtras; thirdly, that even works, written in mixed Ślokas, like those of Śaunaka, are quoted as Sūtras,[99] a title which would never be given to works like the Mānava-dharma-śāstra, etc.; and fourthly, that the same men to whom these works are ascribed are known to have composed other works generally written in the style of Sūtras. That the Prātiśākhya of the Śākalas should be written in Ślokas and yet be ascribed to Śunaka, the teacher of Kātyāyana, is no objection. It would have to be excluded from the Sūtra period, if written in regular Anuṣṭubh-ślokas like those of Manu. But the mixture of the Śloka with other ancient metres indicates better than anything else the transition from one period to another, and is quite in accordance with that position which, as will be seen, Śaunaka occupies in the literary history of India.

By comparing Śaunaka's chapters on Śikṣā in his first Prātiśākhya with the small Śloka compilation which is generally quoted as the Vedāṅga, the difference of old and modern Ślokas will at once be perceived. This modern tract which has been printed in India, contains scarcely more than the matter of the Śiva or Śaṅkara-sūtras brought into Ślokas. It mentions the Prākṛt dialects, and represents itself as written after Pāṇini, but not, as Madhusūdana Sarasvatī pretends, by Pāṇini[100]. Yet it is curious to see how great a reputation this small work must have gained, because Sāyaṇa, who knows the Prātiśākhya and quotes both from the Śākala and Taittirīya-Prātiśākhya, regards this small tract as the real Vedāṅga. In a Mīmāṁsā work, which has been mentioned before, Someśvara's Tantravārttika-ṭīkā it seems even as if greater authority had been attributed to this short Śikṣā tract than to the more developed and evidently older works of Śaunaka, Kātyāyana, and others.

Besides these works on Śikṣā which have been enumerated, from the Taittirīyāraṇyaka down to the so called Vedāṅga, we possess another tract on Śikṣā, called the Māṇḍūkī-Śikṣā.[101] But this also is probably a production later than the Sūtra period, and it is important only in so far it bears the name of another Caraṇa of the Ṛg-veda, the Māṇḍūkāyanas,[102] and thus confirms what was pointed out before, that each of the old Śākhās had originally its own Prātiśākhya, although the greater number of them, as well as their Mantra texts, are now lost or preserved only under a more modern form, as may be seen in the case of this Māṇḍūkī-Śikṣā.

II

CHANDAS, OR METRE

The second Vedāṅga doctrine, *Chandas* or *metre*, stands very much in the same position as the Śikṣā. Some names which have been afterwards adopted as the technical designations of metres, occur in some of the Mantras of the Ṛg-veda, and there are frequent allusions to metres in the Brahmāṇas. What is said, however, in tbe Brāhmaṇas with reference to metres, is generally so full of dogmatic and mystical ingredients as to be of scarcely any practical use. In the Āraṇyakas and Upaniṣads whole chapters are devoted to this subject. Yet it is again io the Sūtras only that a real attempt has been made to arrange these archaic metres systematically. We have some chapters on metres at the end of the Śākala-Prātiśākhya, written in Śaunaka's usual style of mixed Ślokas. This treatise is anterior to that of Kātyāyana which we find in the introduction to his Sarvānu-krama, because Kātyāyana is the pupil of Śaunaka, as we shall see hereafter. For the metres of the Śāmaveda we have the Nidāna-sūtra in ten prapāṭhakas, which after plaining the nature and different names of all the Vedic metres, gives a kind of index (*anukramaṇī*) to the metres as they occur in the hymns employed at the Ekāha, Ahīna, and *Saitra* sacrifices. As to Piṅgalanāga's work on Chandas. which is most frequently quoted under the title of Vedāṅga, it does not pretend to be of greater antiquity than the Mahābhāshya, supposing it were admitted that Patañjali, the author of this famous commentary on Pāṇini, was the Same as Piṅgala[103]. There would be nothing extraordinary in the fact that Piṅgala treats of Prākṛt as well as Sanskrit metres. For we have the instance of Kātyāyana-Vararuci, who wrote the Vārttikas on Pāṇini and lived before Patañjali, and is said to be the same who wrote a grammar of the Prākṛt dialects. It must be admitted, however, that Piṅgalanāga's Metric is one of the last works that could possibly be included in the Sūtra period; though there is no sufficient ground for excluding it from this period altogether, merely because those rules which refer to metres not yet employed in the Veda are ascribed to the same Piṅgala. Besides, Piṅgala is quoted as an authority on metres in the Pariśiṣtas[104], a class of literature which does not seem to be separated from the Sūtra period by a long interval.

To the same class of Chandas works to which Piṅgala's treatise belongs, and which are not restricted to certain Śākhās, but are intended for the Veda in general, two other works are added by the commentator on the Śākala-prātiśākhya, the one ascribed to Yāska, the other to Saitava.[105] Both these works, however, seem to be lost at present.

The difference between a Chandas work belonging to one of the Śākhās, and those treatises which are occupied with metre in general, may be seen from the following instance:

According to Piṅgala's Sūtras, a metre of seventy-six syllables is called Atidhṛti, a metre of sixty-eight syllables Atyaṣṭi. Now in Ṛv. i. 127, 6, a verse occurs of sixty-eight syllables which ought therefore to be called an Atyashṭi. According to Piṅgala himself, however, some syllables may be pronounced as two[106], and if we follow his rules on this point, the same verse consists of seventy-six instead of sixty-eight syllables. In order, therefore, to remove the uncertainty attached to the metre of this verse, the Chandas chapter in the Śākala-Prātiśākhya towards the end of the 16th Paṭala) declares that according to the tradition of the bakala or Śaiśira-śākhā, this verse is to be pronounced as an Atidhṛti, *i.e.* with seventy-six syllables. The same direction is given in Kātyāyana's index to the Śākala-saṁhitā.

III

VYĀKARAṆA, OR GRAMMAR

The third Vedāṅga is *Vyākaraṇa or Grammar*. According to the account which Indian authors give of their literature, this branch of Vedic learning would be represented by the Grammar of Pāṇini. Here the contradiction becomes even more glaring. In Piṅgala's Sūtras the Vedic metres were at least treated in the same way as the non-Vedic. But in Pāṇini, the rules which refer to Vedic grammar in particular, form only the exceptions to all the other rules which treat of the regular or classical language. Instead, therefore, of considering the third Vedāṅga doctrine as represented by the grammarians beginning with Pāṇini (Pāṇinyantāḥ), as Indian authors do, it would be more correct to say that it is represented by the grammarians ending with Pāṇini (Pāṇinyantāḥ). It unfortunately happened that Pāṇini's work acquired by its great merits such a celebrity as to supersede almost all that had been written on grammar before him, so that, except the name and some particular rules of former grammarians, we have little left of this branch of literature, except what occurs occnssionally in the Prātiśākhyas. That Pāṇini knew the Prātiśākhyas had been indicated long ago by Professor Böhtlingk; and it can be proved now by a comparison of Pāṇini's Sūtras with those of the Prātiśākhyas, that Pāṇini largely availed himself of the works of his predecessors, frequently adopting their very expressions, though he quotes their names only in cases where they have to serve as authorities for certain rules.

There are two separate treatises on grammatical subject, which belong to a period anterior to Pāṇini: the Sūtras on the *Uṇādi* affixes, and the Sūtras of Śāntanācārya on accents. The *Uṇādi* affixes are those by which nouns are formed from roots, the nouns being used in a conventional sense, find not in strict accordance with their radical meaning, They are called *Uṇādi*, because, in the Sūtras as we now possess them *uṇ* is the first-mentioned affix. That Pāṇini was acquainted with the same arrangements of these formative affixes cannot be doubted, because he uses the same technical name (*uṇādi*) for them. We do not know by whom these Uṇādi affixes were first collected nor by whom the Uṇādi-sūtras, as we now possess them, were first composed. All we can say is that, as Pāṇini mentions them, and gives several general rules with regard to them, they must have existed before his time. But how many of the Sūtras existed before the time of Pāṇini, and how many were added afterwards, is a question that can hardly be solved. In their present form the Sūtras seem to treat the Vedic words as exceptions, at least they give now and then a hint that a certain derivation applies to the Chandas only. Nevertheless it is curious to observe that the greater number of words explained by the genuine Uṇādi-sūtras, are Vedic, some of them exclusively so. If the author of the Sūtras bad intended his rules for the *Bhāṣā* there would have been no reason why be should have paid such prominent regard to words of a purely Vedic character. In fact, I believe, that originally the Uṇādi-sūtras were intended for the Veda only, and that they were afterwards enlarged by adding rules on the formation of non-Vedic words. At last the non-Vedic or *laukika* words assumed such a preponderance that some rules, affecting

Vedic words only, had actually to be inserted as exceptions. If a clear line could be drawn between words purely Vedic, and words never used in the Veda, and if the Sūtras referring to the former were separated from those of the latter class, we might perhaps arrive at the original texts of this interesting work. This, however, is an undertaking which would require a more comprehensive and more critical knowledge of the history of the languages of India, than any scholar at present is likely to command.

As to Śāntana's Phiṭ-sūtras we know with less certainty to what period they belong. A knowledge of them is not presupposed by Pāṇini, and the grammatical terms used by Śāntana are different from those employed by Pāṇini, a fact from which Professor Böhtlingk has ingeniously concluded, that Śāntana must have belonged to the eastern school of grammarians,[107] As, however, these Sūtras treat only of the accent, and the accent is used in the Vedic language only, the subject of Śāntana's work would lead us to suppose that he was anterior to Pāṇini, though it would bo unsafe lo draw any further conclusions from this.

IV

NIRUKTA, OR ETYMOLOGY.

The fourth Vedāṅga is *Nirukta* or *Etymology*. In the same way as, according to Indian authors, Grammar as a Vedāṅga, was represented by Pāṇini's Grammar, we find Nirukta also represented by but one work, generally known by the name of Yāska's Nirukta. Nirukta, however, has had this advantage over Vyākaraṇa, that Yāska's work applies itself exclusively to Vedic etymologies, In the same way as we considered Pāṇini's Grammar as the work where Vyākaraṇa, as a Vedāṅga, took its final shape, so Yāska also would seem to be one of the last authors who embodied the etymological lexicography of Vedic terms in one separate work. Niruktakāras, or authors of Niruktas, are mentioned by Yāska; and some of them must have been as famous as Yāska himself, because we find that their merits in this respect were not forgotten even at the time of the compilation of the Purāṇas.[108] For explanations of old

Vedic words, for etymologies and synonymous expressions, the Brāhmaṇas contain very rich materials, and, with the exception of the Kalpa no other Vedāṅga has a better claim than the Nirukta to be considered as founded upon the Brahmaṇas, Whole verses and hymns are shortly explained there; anil the Āraṇyakas and Upaniṣadas, if included, would furnish richer sources for Vedic etymologies than even ihe Nirukta itself. The beginning of the Aitareya-āraṇyaka is in fact a commentary on the beginning of the Ṛg-veda; and if all the passages of the Brāhmaṇas were collected where one word is explained by another with which it is joined merely by the particle vai, they would even now give a rich harvest for a new Nirukta. It is important, however, not to confouud Yāska's Nirukta with Yāska's Commentary on the Nirukta, although it has become usual, after the fashion of modern manuscripts to call that commentary Nirukta, and to distinguish the text of the Nirukta by the name of Nighaṇṭu. The original Niruktas that formed an integral part of the Vedāṅga literature, known to Yāska himself, can have consisted only of lists of words arranged according to their meaning, like that upon which Yāska's Commentary is based. Whether the same Yāska who wrote the Commentary had some part in the arrangement of the lists of words, is unknown; probably these lists existed in his family long before his time, as Yāska implies himself (Nir i. 20,), But, as he preserved them by his Commentary, it was natural that their authorship too, should have been ascribed to him. Sayaria gives the following account of this matter: "Nirukta is a work where a number of words is given, without any intention to connect them in a sentence. In that book, where a traditional number of words is taught, which begin with "*Gauḥgmā*", and end with "Vasavaḥ, Vājinaḥ, Devapatnyaḥ", there is no intention to state things which are to be understood,[109] because it is only said there that "so many are the names of earth," "so many the names of gold," etc.

This Nirukta consists of three parts, as may be seen from the Commentary on the Anukramaṇikā. Here we read:

"The first part is the Naighaṇṭuka, the second the Naigama, and the third the Daivata, and this must this traditional doctrine be considered as consisting of three parts.

"The *Naighaṇṭuka* begins with *Gauḥ* and goes as far as Apāre.[110] The Naigama begins with *Jahā* and goes as far as *Ulbam* Ṛbīśam[111] The third, or Deity chapter, begins with *Agni* and ends with the *Devapatnīs*[112] Here the gods from Agni to Devī Urjāhutī[113] are gods of the earth; from Vāyu to Bhaga[114] gods of the air; from Sūrya to the Devapatnīs,[115] gods of the sky. People learn the whole traditional number of words, from *Gauḥ* to *Devapatnyaḥ*

"The word Nighaṇṭu applies to works where, for the most pact, synonymous words are taught. Thus, ten Nighaṇṭus are usually mentioned; and this title has been applied to such works as Amarasinha, Vaijayantī, Halāyudha, etc. There-fore[116], the first part of this work also has been called *Naighaṇṭuka*, because synonymous words are taught there. In this part there are three lectures; in the first : we have words connected with things of time and space in this and the other worlds; in the second, we have words connected with men and human affairs : and, in the third, words expressing qualities of the preceding objects, such as thinness, multitude, shortness, etc.

"*Nigama* means Veda. As Yāska has quoted many passages from the Veda, which he usually introduces by the words,'For this there is also a Nigama;' and as, in the second part, consisting of the fourth Adhyāya, words are taught which usually occur in the Veda only, this part is called *Naigama*.

"Why the third part, consisting of the fifth Adhyāya, is called *Daivata* is clear. The whole work, consisting of five Adhyāyas and three parts, is called Nirukta, because the meaning of words is giveu there irrespective of anything else. A commentary on this lias been composed by Yāska in twenty Adhyāyas, This also is called Nirukta, because the real meaning conveyed by each word is fully given therein."[117]

The Nirukta, together with the Prātiśākhyas and Pāṇini's Grammar, supply the most interesting and important information on the growth of grammatical science in India, It would be out of place to enter here into this subject, but I cannot pass it over without at least pointing out the valuable materials preserved in these works, for tracing the origin of one of the most ancient branches of philosophy, *Grammar*.

HISTORY OF GRAMMAR

There are only two tuitions in the whole history of the world which have conceived independently, and without any suggestions from others, the two sciences of logic and Grammar, the Hindūs and the Greeks. Although the Arabs and Jews, among the Semitic nations, have elaborated their own system of grammar, in accordance with the peculiar character of their language they owe to the Greeks the broad outlines of grammatical science, and they received from Aristotle the primary impulse to a study of the categories of thought and speech. Our own grammatical terms came to us from the Greeks; and their history is curious enough, if we trace them back through the clumsy and frequently erroneous translations of the literary statesmen of Rome, to the scholars and critics of Alexandria, and finally to the early philosophers of Greece, the Stoics, Aristotle, Protagoras and Pythagoras. But it is still more instructive to compare this development of the grammatical categories in Greece with the parallel, yet quite independent, history of Grammatical science in India. It is only by means of such a comparison that we can learn to understand what is organic, and what is merely accidental, in the growth of this science, and appreciate the real difficulties which had to be overcome in the classification of words and the arrangement of grammatical forms. The Greeks and Hindūs started from opposite points. The Greeks began with philosophy, and endeavoured to transfer their philosophical terminology to the facts of language. The Hindūs began with collecting the facts of language, and, their generalisations never went beyond the external forms of speech. Thus the Hindūs excel in accuracy, the Greeks in grasp. The grammar of the former has ended in a colossal pedantry; that of the latter still invigorates the mind of every rising generation throughout the civilized world.

Language had become with the Hindūs an object of wonder and meditation at a very early period. In the hymns of the Veda we meet with poetical and philosophical speculations of speech, and Sarasvatī, the goddess of speech, is invoked as one of the most powerful deities. The scientific interest in language, however, dates from a later period. It was called forth, no doubt, by the careful study of a sacred literature, which in India, as elsewhere, called into life many an ancient science. In India the sacred strains of the Ṛṣis were handed down with the greatest care, the knowledge of these songs constituted the only claim and hope of man for a higher life and from a very early time they were looked upon with such a superstitions awe, that a mere error of pronunciation was supposed to mar their miraculous power.[118]

We need not wonder, therefore, that the minutest rules were laid down as to the pronunciation of these hymns, and that the thoughts of the early teachers were led to dwell on the nature of language and its grammatical organisation. Where so much depended on letters, it was natural that words also and their grammatical variations should attract attention. A number of letters, or even a single letter, as Kātyāyana says, may form a syllable (akṣara), a number of syllables or even a single syllable may ierm a word (*pada*).[119] There are many lucubrations on letters, syllables, and words in the Brāhmaṇas, and there are numerous expressions, occuring in the Brāhmaṇas, which mark a certain advance of grammatical knowledge.[120] In the Brāhmaṇa of the Vājasaneyins (xiii. 5.1.18) we meet with the names for Singular, Dual, and Plural. In the Chāndogya-upaniṣad (p. 135, ed. Röer) we find a classification of letters, and technical terms such as *sparśa*, consonants; *svara*, vowels; *uṣman*, sibilants. However, we must not expect in those treatises to find anything sound and scientific. It is in the Sūtra literature that we meet with discussions on language of a purely scientific character; and what we do find in tbe Prātiśākhya, in the Nirukta and Pāṇini, is quite sufficient to show that at their time the science of language was not of recent origin. I can only touch upon one point. It is well known how long it took before the Greeks arrived at a complete nomenclature for the parts of speech. Plato knew only of Noun (ονομα) and Verb (ρημα) as the two component parts of speech, and for philosophical purposes Aristotle too did not go beyond that number. It is only in discussing the rules of rhetoric that he is led to the admission of two more parts of speech, the συνδε σμοι (conjunctions) and αρθρα (articles). The pronoun αυτωνυμια does not come in before Zenodotos, and the preposition (προθε σις) occurs first in Aristarchos. In the Prātiśākhya, on the contrary, we meet at once with the following exhaustive classification of the parts of speech (xii. 5.)

"The noun (nāma), the verb (ākhyāta), the preposition (*upasarga*), and the panicle (*nipāta*), are called by grammarians the four classes of words.[121] The noun is that by which we mark a being, a verb that by which we mark being; the latter is called a root (*dhātu*). There are twenty prepositions, and these have a meaning, if joined with nouns or verbs. The rest of the words are called particles. The verb expresses an action; the preposition defines it; the noun marks a being; particles are but expletives. There are, however, besides the particles which have no meaning, others which have, for we see that some particles are used on account of their sense: but it is impossible to say how many there are of each clhss, whether they, are used in measured or in prose diction,"[122]

The same division is adopted,by most grammarians, and it is more fully explained by the author of the Nirukta, After stating that there are four kinds of words, Yāska says that the verb is chiefly concerned with being, nouns with beings. He then brings in a new definition which reminds us of the first introduction of the προσηλορια as distinct from the ονομα by the Stoics. "The verb," he Says, "when it expresses being, expresses a kind of being which lasts from an earlier to a later time, such as "he walks," "he cooks," the nouns, if they express being (and not a being), express a kind of being that has become embodied in one, from beginning to end, such as "a walking," "a cooking." Here the chief difference between the verb and the noun appellative, is established on a similar ground to that on which Aristotle ascribes to the verb a temporal character, and denies it to the noun.[122]

The distinction of the numbers was first pointed out by Aristotle, the technical terms for singular and plural (αριθμος ∊ντΧος πληθνυτιΧόs) date from a Inter time, In India the terms for the three numbers, Singular, Plural, and Dual were known in the Brāhmaṇa period.

Aristotle had no clear conception of cases, in the grammatical sense of the word. Ptosis, with him, refers to verbs as well as nouns. The introduction of the five cases, in our sense of the word, is due to the Stoics. In the Prātiśāhyas we find not only a name for case, restricted to nouns (vibluikti, i. e. Χλισις) but the number of cases also is fixed at seven.

The distinction of the genders is the only point on which the Greeks may claim a priority to the Hindūs, It was known in Greece to Protagoras; whereas in India the Prātiśākhyas seem to have passed it over, and it appears first in Pāṇini.[123]

There are some discussions in the beginning of the Nirukta which are of the highest interest with regard to etymology; While in Greece the notions of one of her greatest thinkers, as expressed in the Cratylus, represent the very infancy of etymological science, the Brāhmaṇas of India had treated some of the vital problems of etymology with the utmost sobriety. In the Prātiśākhya of Kātyāyana we find, besides tlte philosophical division of speech into nouns, verbs, prepositions and particles, another division of a purely grammatical nature, and expressed in the most strictly technical language. "*Verba* with their conjugational terminations, Nouns, derived from verbs by means of *krt*-suffixes, *Nouns*, derived from nouns by means of taddhita-suffixes, and four kinds of *Compounds*-these constitute language."[124]

In the Nirukta. this division is no longer considered sufficient. A new problem has been started, one of the most important problems in the philosophy of language, whether all nouns, are derived from verbs ? No one would deny that certain nouns, or the majority of norms, weds.' derived from verbs. The early grammarians of India were fully agreed, that *kartṛ*, a doer, was derived from *kṛ*, to do; Pācaka, a cook, from pach, to cook. But did the same apply to all words ? Śākaṭāyana, an ancient grammarian and philosopher, answered the question boldly in the affirmative, and he became the lounder of a large school, called the Nairuktas (or Etymologists,) who made the verbal origin of all words the leading principle of all their researches. They were opposed, and not without violence, by another school, emphatically called the Vaiyākaraṇas or Analysers, who, following the lead of Gārgya, the etymologists,[125] admitted the verbal origin of those words only for which an adequate grammatical analysis could be given. The rest they left unexplained. Let us hear how Yāska states the arguments on both sides. After having explained the characteristics of the four classes of words, he says: "Śākaṭ āyana maintains that nouns are derived from verbs, and there is an universal agreement of all Etymologists (Nairukta) on this point. Gārgya, on the contrary and some of the grammarians say, not all (nouns are derived from verbs). For first, if the accent and formation were regular in all nouns and agreed entirely with the appellative power (of the root), nouns such as go (cow), *aśva* (horse), Puruṣa (man), would be in themselves intelligible.[126] Secondly, if all nouns were derived from verbs, then if any one performed a certain action, he would, as a subject , be called in the same manner. For instance, if aśva, horse were derived from' as", to get through, then any one who got through a certain distance, would have to be called aśva, horse. If *tṛṇa*, grass, were derived from *tṛd*, to pierce, then whatever pierces would have to be called tṛṇa. Thirdly, if all nouns were derived from verbs then everything would take as many names as there are qualities belonging to it. A pillar , for instance, which is now called sthūṇa, might be called dareśaya, hole-rest because it rests in a hole; or sañjanī, joiner, because there am beams joined to it. Fourthly, people would cull things in such a manner that the meaning of nouns might be at least intelligible, whatever the regular formation may be by which the actions of these things are supposed to be expressed. Instead of purusha, man, which is supposed to be formed from Puriśaya, dwelling in the body, they would say Puriśaya, body-dweller; instead of *aśva*, horse, *aṣṭṛ*, pervader; instead of *tṛṇa*, grass, *tardana*, piercer. Fifthly, after a noun tins been formed, these etymologists begin to discuss it, and say, for instance, that the earth is called pṛthivī, broad, from prathana stretching. But, who stretched it, and what was his resting-place while he stretched the earth ? Sixthly, where the meaning cannot be discovered, no modification of the root yielding any proper signification, Śākaṭāyana has actually taken whole verbs, ami put together the halves of two distinct words. For instance, in order to form *'satya'*, true, he puts together the causal of *ī*, to go, which begins with *ya*, as the latter half, and the participle of *as*, to be, which begins with *sa*. Lastly, it is well known, that beings come before being and it is therefore impossible to derive the names of beings which come first, from being, which comes after.

"Now all this arguing, "Yāska continues, "is wrong. For however all this may be, first, with regard to what was said, namely, that, if Śākaṭāyana's opinion were right, all words would be significative, this we consider no objection,[127] because we shall show thai they are all significative. With regard to the second point, our answer is that we see as a matter of fact that it is not so, but that of a number of people who perform the same action, some only take a certain name, and others do not. Not every one that shapes a thing is called *takṣan*, a shaper. but only the carpenter. Not every one that; walks about is called a *parivrājaka*, but only a religions mendicant. Not everything thut enlivens is called *jīvana*, but only the sap of the sugar-cane. Not everything that is born of Bhumi (earth) is called Bhūmija, but only the planet Mars (aṅgāraka)[128] And the same remark serves also as an answer to the third objection. With regard to the fourth objection, we reply, We did not make these words, we only have to explain them; and there are also some nouns of rare occurrence which you, grammarians, derive by means of *kṛt*-suffixes, and which are liable to exactly the same objection. For who could tell, without some help from etymologists, that some of the words mentioned in the Aikapadika-chapter mean what they do mean ? *Vratati* is derived by you from *vṛṇāti*, to elect, but it signifies a garland. The same applies to your grammatical derivations of such words as *damūnas*, *jāṭya*, *āṭṇāra*, jāgarūka, *darvihomin*. In answer to thé fifth objection we say, Of course we can discuss the etymological meaning of such words only as have been formed. And as to the questions, who stretched the earth, and what was his resting-place, all we can say is, that our eyes tell us that the earth is broad, and even though it has not been stretched out by others you all men speak as they see. With respect to the sixth objection, we admit, that he who combines word without thereby arriving at their proper meaning, is to be blamed. But this blame attaches to the individual etymologist, not to the science of etymology. As to the last objection, we must again uppeal to the facts of the case. Some words lire derived from qualities, though qualities may be later than subjects, others not."

I doubt whether even at present, with all the new light which Comparative Philology has shed on the origin of words, questions like these could be discussed more satisfactorily than they were by Yāska. Like Yāska, we maintain that all nouns have their derivation, but, like Yāska, we must confess that this is a matter of belief rather than of proof. We admit with Yāska that every noun was originally an appellative and, in strict logic, we are bound to admit that language knows neither of homonymes nor synonymes. But granting that there are such words in the history of every language, granting that several objects, sharing in the same predicate, may be called by the same name, and that the same object, possessing various predicates, may be called by different names, we shall find it as impossible as Yāska to lay down any rule why one of the many appellatives became fixed in every dialcct as thc propcr namc of the sun, the moon, or any other object; or why generic words (homonyms) were founded on one predicate rather than another. All we can say is what Yāska says, it was so *svabhāvataḥ*, by itself, from accident, through the influence of individuals, of poets or law-givers. It is the very point in the history of language where languages are not amenable to organic laws, where the science of language ceases to be a strict science, arid enters into the domain of history.

We leave this subject not without reluctance, and hope to return to it in some more appropriate place.

V

KALPA, OR THE CEREMONIAL

The most complete Vedāṅga is the fifth, the Kalpa for which we have not only the Brāhmaṇas of the different Vedas, but also their respective Sūtras. The Sūtras contain the miles referring to the sacrifices,[129] with the omission of all things which are not immediately connected, with the performance of the ceremonial. They are more practical than the Brāhmaṇas, which for the most part are taken up with mystical, historical, mythological, etymological, and theological discussions. Thus Sāyaṇa says, in his Commentary on the Baudhāyana-sūtras : "The whole mass of Vedic literature consists of three parts; *Mantras*, *Vidhis* and *Arthavādas*. The *Vidhis* enjoin an act, *Arthavādas* recommend it, the Mantras record, it. In order to make the understanding of the prescribed ceremonies more easy, the Reverend Budhāyana composed the Kalpa. For the Brāhmaṇas are endless, and difficult to understand, and therefore have old masters adopted the Kalpa-sūtras according to different Śākhās. These Kalpa-sūtras have the advantage of being clear, short, complete, and correct.[130]

It is true that some of the Brāhmaṇas also have a more practical tendency, and might almost be taken for productions of the Sūtra period. We saw before that Kumārila in his Tantravārttika spoke at some Brāhmaṇas, for instance, those of the Āruṇā and Parāśara-śākhās[131] as having the form of Kalpa works. Nay, there ore passages in the Brāhmaṇas which, though properly they ought to be called Kalpa or *vidhi*, me quoted by the Commentators, under the name of Sūtra.[132] The same name is used, in the late books of the Śatapatha-brāhmaṇa, as the tiile of literary compositions, which must then have formed part of the Brāhmaṇa literature.[133]

On the other hand., the Sūtras, composed by Śaunaka, were called Brāhmaṇa-sannibha "having the appearance of a Braḥmāmi," an insertion, which to a certain extent, is true as may be seen by comparing the Ṛg-vidhāna, which is ascribed to Śaunaka, with the Sāma-vidhāna-brāhmaṇa. The same might be said of the Sāṅkhāyana-sūtras, particularly of the last books, where we sometimes meet with considerable portions identically the same as in the Aitareya-brāhmaṇa. But no orthodox Brāhmaṇa would for a moment admit that Brāhmaṇa and Sūtras belonged to the same class of literature. They fear the danger of such admission, because, as Kumārila says, If the name of Śruti were once granted to the Sūtras, it would with difficulty be denied to the sacred writings of Buddhists and other heretics. It would be, as he expresses himself in his graphic language, "Like letting in the heretics on the high road, after having driven them out of the village with sticks and fists."

Originally a Brāhmaṇa was a theological tract and it was called brāhmaṇa, not because it treated of the Brahman, the Supreme Spirit, or of sacrificial prayers, sometimes called brāhmaṇi, but because it was composed by and for Brāhmaṇas. These Brāhmaṇas or dicta theologica, were gradually collected in different families or Pariṣads, and gave rise to greater works, which were equally called by the name of Brāhmaṇa. Such a collection became a more or less comprehensive repository of theological lore, and no consideration as to practical usefulness seems to have influenced either the original contributors or the later collectors. In the course of time, however, and particularly during periods of theological controversy, these works began to assume a practical importance, and it was then that the want of proper arrangement was felt as a serious inconvenience. Hence, when new additions were made to the ancient stock of *Brāhmaṇic* learning, or when, as in the case of a controversy or a schism, the founders of a new community were called upon to compose a *Brāhmaṇic* code different from that which belonged to their adversaries, a more systematic and business-like spirit, such as afterwards led to the composition of Sūtras, began to show itself in the arrangement of these Inter Brāhmaṇas.

There was, however, a cartain general system which regulated the composition of the Brāhmaṇas from the very first. Long before ths different Brāhmaṇas were composed, the sacrificial system, which they were chiefly intended to illustrate, had been definitely arranged, and the duties of' the three or four classes of priests engaged at the great sacrifices, had been finally agreed upon. This division of priests and the general order of the sacrifices must have been settled previously even to the composition of the Saṁhitas of the Sāma and Yajur-Vedas; for both follow the established order of the sacrifices, and are neither more nor less than collections, containing the verses which lie second and third classes of priests, the Chandogas and Adhvaryus, had to employ at various sacrifices, They are liturgical song-books, adapted to an already-existing sacrificial canon. The case is different with the Ṛg-veda. The Ṛg-veda-saṁhitā was collected without any reference to sacrificial purposes. The Brāhmaṇas, however, of all the three Vedas, the Ṛgveda as well as the Sāma and Yajur-Vedas, pre-suppose the final division of the three classes or priests. This division, to which we shall have to revert hereafter, may be shortly described as follows: The chief part, or as the Brāhmaṇas say, the body of each sacrifice, had to be performed by the Adhvaryu priests. The preparing of the sacrificial ground, the adjustment of the vessels, the procuring of the animals, and other sacrificial oblations, the lighting of the fire, the killing of the animal, in short, all that required manual labour, was the province of the Adhvaryu priests. They stood lowest in the estimation of the Brāhmaṇas, and as the proper pronunciation of the sacred texts required considerable study, they were allowed simply to matter the verses which they used during the sacrifice. The recitation of Vedic verses was considered as so subordinate a part of their duty that their Saṁhitā, at least the most ancient Saṁhitā[134] of the Adhvaryu Veda priests, is not a collection of hymns, but rather a complete description of the sacrifice, as performed by the Adhvaryus, interspersed with such verses and for mulae as had to be muttered by the officiating priests. It was at a much later time, and probably in imitation of the Sāma-veda-saṁhitā, that a separate collection of the hymns of the Adhvaryu priests was made, and this we possess in the various Śākhā's of the Vājasaneyins, who have embodied the rules and the description of the sacrifice in a separate Brāhmaṇa, known by the name of the Śatapatha. According to the same metaphor, which assigns the Adhvaryu priests the body of the sacrifice, its two most essential limbs fall to the lot of two other classes, the Hotṛ and Udgātṛ priests; or, as Sāyaṇa says, in his introduction to the Taittirīya-saṁhitā: "The Ṛg-veda and Sāma-veda are like fresco paintings whereas the Yajur-veda is the wall on which they stand." The Udgātṛ priests have little to do with the actual performance of the sacrifice. Their chief duty is to chant their hymns in a loud melodious voice, and these hymns, in the order in which they had to be chanted, were collected in a book of songs, called the Sāma-veda-saṁhitā. The third class of priests, who were equally free from purely manual labour had to recite the sacrificial hymns, according to the strict and difficult rules of the ancient pronunciation and accentuation, but without chanting. No collection, however, was made for them, containing the hymns in their sacrificial order; because the Hotṛ priests were supposed to be so throughly versed in the ancient Vedic poetry as contained in the Ṛg-veda-saṁhitā, that they were expected to know the whole of it, and to be able to repeat readily, without the help of a manual, whatever hymn was enjoined at any part of the sacrifice.

This distribution of the ceremonial between the three classes of priests, which, after the collection of the ancient Saṁhitā of the Ṛg-veda, called forth the two Saṁhitās of the Sāma-and Yajur-Vedas, regulated from the first the composition of the Brāhmaṇas. Instead of one code of theology, we find the collections of Brāhmaṇas treating respectively of the performance of those rites, which each of the three classes of priests was more particularly concerned with. The Adhvaryu priests had orginally, as we saw, no Brāhmaṇa in the usual sense of the word, and what is called their Brāhmaṇa is in reality a mere supplement and continuation of their Saṁhitā; originally, therefore, neither of these names was correctly applicable to the Yajur-veda of the Carakas. In later times, however, the duties of the Adhvaryu were incorporated in a separate Brāhmaṇa, the Śatapatha, at the same time that their hymns were collected in a small manual, the later. Saṁhitā of the Yajur-veda. In a similar manner, the sacrificial duties of the Hotṛ priests were discussed in the Bahvṛca-brāhmaṇa, and those of the Udgātṛ priests, in the Chandoga-brāhmaṇa.

Thus we see that the collection, if not the original composition, of the Brāhmaṇas, was not entirely, without system; and that the remarks on certain parts of the. sacrifice, although sometimes extremely diffuse, and mixed up with extraneous matter, were not thrown together at random. As most of the sacrifices were to be performed by two or three classes of priests in common, the same ceremony may be described in different Brāhmaṇas. The *Agniṣṭoma*, for instance, begins with the ceremony of the *Ṛtvig-varaṇa*, the election of priests. This ceremony is performed by the Adhvaryu priests alone, and it was not necessary to explain it in the Brāhmaṇa of the Hotṛ priests. It is wanting therefore in the Bahvṛca-brāhmaṇas. The next following ceremony, the Dīkṣaṇyeṣṭi, is likewise performed by the Adhvaryus together with the Chandoga priests; but as here the Hotṛ priests also have to take a part (the yājyās and anuvākyās), it is described in the beginning of the Aitareya-brāhmaṇa.[135]

The Kalpa-sūtras, with which we are at present concerned, follow the same system as the Brāhmaṇas. They presuppose, however, not only the existence of three distinct collections of Brāhmaṇas but of different Śākhās or recensions, which, in the course of time, had branched off from each of them.

It is a characteristic peculiarity of the Sūtras, that they were intended by their authors for more than one Caraṇa, or adapted to more than one Śākhā. This is remarked upon by Kumārila, when he says : "All authors of Kalpa Sūtras join with the rules of their own Śākhā, the optional commandments of other Śākhās, a proceeding approved of by Jaimini."[136] Or again, "Not one of the Sūtrakāras was satisfied with comprehending his own Śākhā only."[137] The same is maintained still more strongly by the author of the Hiraṇyakeśi-bhāshya. "No single Śākhā," he says, "contains a complete account of the ceremonial, and a reference to other Śākhās is absolutely necessary."[138] That this means a reference to other Śākhās of the same Veda, and not a reference to other Vedas, may be seen from a passage of Kauśika Rāma,[139] where he establishes the general principle, that in a Sūtra a quotation from a different Śākhā makes a rule optional, whereas a quotation from a different Veda confirms it as generally binding. It was not usual that a common Brāhmaṇa knew more than one Śākhā. He might, if he liked study each of the three Vedas, but, as, Kumārila says : "It is not necessary that one man should read different Śākhās, because one Śākhā only is comprehended in that study of the sacred texts which every Brāhmaṇa is bound to pass through. Therefore, if a very clever man should read different Śākhās of one Veda, he may do so, but he might as well, if very rich, sacrifice at the same time with rice and barley,"[140] But, even if a Brāhmaṇa had studied the Saṁhitās and Brāhmaṇas of the three Vedas, according to their various Śākhās, he would still have found it extremely difficult to learn from them the correct performance of every sacrifice. It was, therefore, in order to obviate this difficulty, that the Sūtras were called into existence, as a kind of grammar of the Vedic ceremonial, useful for members of all Caraṇas.

The Kalpa-sūtras for the Hotṛ priests, which were composed by Āśvalāyana, were intended both for the Śākala and Bāṣkala-śākhās,[141] and they contain occasional references to other Caraṇas also. Sāyaṇa, in his introduction to the Ṛg-veda (i. p. 34) says distinctly, that Āśvalāyana teaches the employment of hymns, which do not occur in the Śākala-śākhā. "These" he says, "have been taken from another Śākhā, and their employment, therefore, rests on the authority of a different Brāhmaṇa, although the sacrifice itself (karmi) must be considered as one and the same for all Śākhās, in spite of some differences in its performance (*prayoga*)?[142]"

There is a second, and more ancient, collection of Sūtras for the Hotṛ priests, written by Sāṅkhāyana. They were intended for members of the Kauṣītaki-śākhā, Śākhā of which we still possess the Brāhmaṇa and the Āraṇayaka. The Brāhmaṇa is sometimes quoted under the name of the Śāṅkhāyana-brāhmaṇa, in the same manner as the Aitareya is sometimes quoted as Āśvalāyana-brāhmaṇa. This Sāṅkhāyana text of the Kauṣītaki-brāhmaṇa may be more modern than the Aitareya-brāhmaṇa, but the Sūtras of Sāṅkhāyana are more ancient than the Sūtras of Āśvalāyana. The Sūtras for the Adhvaryu priests were composed by Kātyāyana, adopted by the Kāṇva and Mādhyandina-śākhās.[143]

The ceremonial of the Udgātṛ priests who followed the Sāma-veda was likewise composed by authors who were free from the exclusive influence of one particular Śākhā. The Kātyāyana-sūtras were not originally the Sūtras of a Kātyāna-śākhā, but they were written by Kātyāyana, and afterwards adopted by the numerous branches of the Kauthuma-śākhā. Another collection of Sūtras, almost identical with the former was composed by Drāhyāyaṇa, and was adopted by the different Caraṇas of the Rāṇāyanīyas.[144] Both Sūtras follow the same authority, the Tāṇḍya-brāhmaṇa, its old as well as its more modern portion, and they quote not only the traditional literature of various Caraṇas, such as the Śāṭyāyanins, Śālaṅkāyanins, but the works of individuals also, such as Śāṇḍilya, Śāṇḍilyāyana, Dhānañjayya, Kautsa, Kṣairakalambhin, two Gautamas, Bhāṇḍitāyana, Rāṇāyani-putra, Lāmakāyana, Śaucivṛkṣi, etc.[145]

But although the Sūtras were adopted by different Caraṇas, existing previous to the composition of the Sūtras, and although the author of a new code of Sūtras might himself become the founder of a new Caraṇa or sect, the text of these short rules seems never to have changed. The text of the Āś៲ d'āyana-sūtras was one and the same for a follower of the old Śakala, Bāṣkala or Aitareyi-śākhās. We meet with no authorised *varice letiones* as we do in the Brāhmaṇas. As late as the time of Sāyaṇa the various readings of the Brāhmaṇas were known, and he refers to them frequently in his Commentary on the Aitareyi-brāhmaṇa. Nothing of the kind ever occurs in the commentaries on the Sūtras; still less were the Sūtras liable to those more important changes which the Brāhmaṇas underwent, as they became the property of distinct Caraṇas or sects.

Kumārila's argument, therefore, by which he endeavoured to establish a distinction between the Brāhmaṇas and Sūtras,[146] is fully confirmed by those traces which can still be discovered by philological criticism. We have only to translate what he calls Śruti, or revelation, by "ancient literature handed down by oral tradition," and the distinction between Brāhmaṇas, as Śruti, and Sūtras, as Smṛti, holds perfectly good. There is no doubt a distinction to be made between the manner in which the hymns and the Brāhmaṇas, both included under the name of Śruti, were preserved. But, in spite of Wolf's maxim, that prose literature marks everywhere the introduction of writing, we must claim for the Brāhmaṇas, as well as for the hymns, a certain period during which they were preserved by means of oral tradition only. Without the admission of an oral tradition, carried on for several generations and in several places by different families and Brāhmaṇic colonies, it would seem impossible to account for the numerous recensions of the same Brahmana, and for the various readings of each recension. How the changes, the addition, the re-arrangements of the original collections of the Brāhmaṇas were effected, we have no means of ascertaining; but we can see, that the Kāṇva and Mādhyandina recensions of the Śatapatha-brāhmaṇa presup pose some point from whence they both started in common. The same applies to the Bahvṛca-brāhmaṇa in the widely differing recensions of the Aitareyins, the Saṅkhāynins or the Kauṣītakins. There is a common stock in the Brāhmaṇas of each Veda. The same ceremonial is described, the same doubts are raised, similar solutions are proposed, and many chapters are repeated in the same words. Before each recension took its present shape—and few only of these numerous recensions have been preserved to us they must have rolled from hand to hand, sometimes losing old, some-times gathering new matter; now broken to pieces, now' re-arranged, till at last the name of their author became merged in the name of the Caraṇa that preserved his work. No traces of this kind can be discovered in the Sūtras. We probably read them in our MSS., exactly as they were written down at first by Kātyāyana, Āśvalāyana, and others. They are evidently the works of individual writers, the result of careful and systematic research. They presuppose the Saṁhitās and the Śākhās of the Saṁhitās; they presuppose the Brāhmaṇas and the Śākhās of the Brāhmaṇas. And they also refer to individual writers, whether they had become the founders of Caraṇas, or whether they enjoyed an authority as teachers of law and other subjects connected with the intellectual pursuits of the early Brāhmaṇas.

There is, however, one fact that seems to militate against the distinction between the Brāhmaṇas and Sūtras, in so for as it assigns a very early origin, and a traditionary character, to at least some works which were written in Sūtras. At the time of Kātyāyana, if not at the time of Pāṇini, there existed Sūtras, which were not then considered as the works of modern or at least well-known authors, like Āśvalāyana or Kātyāyana, but indicated by their very name, that they had formed, for a time, part of the traditional literary property of a Caraṇa, or of some learned school. Their titles are formed on the same principle as the titles of ancient Brāhmaṇas. The affix in (*ṇini*) is added to the names of their reputed authors, and this, as we know, is a mark that their authors were considered as Ṛṣis or inspired writers.[147] Their works are not quoted in the singular, like all modern Sūtras (for instance, "this is the ceremonial of Asmaratha" *iti* kalpa āśmarathaḥ but, and this is a characteristic feature of the ancient traditional literature of India-in the masculine plural, the literary works being supposed to have their only substantial existence in the minds or memories of those persons who read or taught them. We find, for instance, "thus say the Parāśarins, the Śailālins, the Karmandins, the Kṛśaśvins." whereas the work even of Pāṇini himself is quoted as "the Pāṇinīyam," as it were "Panineum," not as "the Paṇineyins."[148] But although these quotations refer to Sūtras, it ought to be observed that not one of them refers to Kalpa, or ceremonial Sūtras. Where Pāṇini (iv. 3. 105.), or rather his commentator, quotes works on Kalpa in a similar, though not in exactly the same manner, we must bear in mind that expressions like "Paiṅgī kalpaḥ," "the ceremonial taught by the old sage Kuśika," may refer to portions of the Brāhmaṇas which are called kalpa, ceremonial, in contradistinction to the

Brāhmaṇa or the purely theological discussions;[149] and it is nowhere said that these old Kalpas were written in Sūtras. Unless, therefore, a quotation can be brought forward previous to Kātyāyana, and referring to a collection of Kalpa-sūtras, such quotation calling the Sūtras not by the name of their author, but by the name of a Caraṇa, not in the singular, but in the masculine plural, Kumārila's distinction between Brāhmaṇas and Sūtras remains unshaken, and we are justified in maintaining that the Kalpa-sūtras, in spite of some apparent similarity with the later Braḥmānas, belong to a period of literature different in form and character from that which preceded it, and which gave rise to the traditionary literature of the Brāhmaṇas.

The Kalpa-sūtras are important in the history of Vedic literature for more than one reason. They not only mark a new period of literature, and a new purpose in the literary and religious life of India, but they contributed to the gradual extinction of the numerous Brāhmaṇas, which to us are therefore only known by name. The introduction of a Kalpa-sūtra was the introduction of a new book of liturgy. If it was adopted by different Caraṇas, smaller differences in the ceremonial and its allegorical interpretation, which had been kept up by the Brāhmaṇas, of each Caraṇa, would gradually be merged in one common ceremonial; or, if they were considered of sufficient importance, a short mention, such as we find here and there in the Sūtras, would suffice, and render the tedious discussions of the Brāhmaṇas on the same points, superfluous. If the Sūtras were once acknowledged as authoritative, they became the most important part of the sacred literature which a Brāhmaṇa had to study. Those who had to perform the sacrifices might do so without the Veda, simply by means of the Kalpa-sūtras; but no one could learn the ceremonial from the hymns and Brāhmaṇas alone, without the help of the Sūtras.[150] There remained, indeed, the duty of every Brahmaṇa to learn his Svādhyāya, which comprised the hymns and the Brāhmaṇas. But complaints were made, at least at a later time, that the hymns and the Brāhmaṇas were neglected on account of the Sūtras, and one of the reasons why the Hotṛ priests were never allowed to have a prayer-book, such as the hymn-books of the Yajur-veda and Sāma-veda, was the fear that they would then neglect *svādhyāya*, and learn only those hymns which were enjoined for the sacrifices by the Kalpa-sūtras. We need not wonder, therefore, if, after a short time, the authors of Kalpa-sūtras became themselves the founders of new Caraṇas, in which the Sūtras were considered the most essential portion of the sacred literature; so that the hymns and Brāhmaṇas were either neglected, or kept up under the name of "the hymns and Brāhmaṇas of the new Caraṇa," having ceased to form by themselves the foundation of an independent tradition or school.

In order to make quite clear the influence which the Sūtras exercised on the final constitution of the Vedic Caraṇas we ought to distinguish between three classes of Caraṇas:

(i) Those which originated with the texts of Saṁhitās;

(ii) Those which originated with the texts of Brāhmaṇas;

(iii) Those which originated with the Sūtras.

We need not enter here into the question, whether originally there was but one Veda, and whether this original Veda became afterwards divided into three branches or Śākhās, the Ṛg-vtda, Yajur-veda, and Sāma-veda. This is the view adopted by the Brāhmaṇas, and they consider these three divisions as the three most ancient Śākhās, and their propagators or *pravartakas* as the three most ancient Caraṇas. This is a natural mistake. It is the same mistake which leads to the assumption of common literary language previous to the existence of the spoken dialects, whereas in fact the various dialects existed previous to the establishment of the classical language. The first collection of Vedic hymns is that which we have in the Ṛg-veda, a collection, not made with any reference to the threefold division of the later ceremonial, and therefore not one of three branches, but the original stock, to which the other two, the Yajur-veda and Sāma-veda, were added at a much later period.

The most ancient Śākhās and Caraṇas of which we have any knowledge are those which arose from differences in the text of the Ṛg-veda-saṁhitā, such as the Bāṣkalas and Śākalas. We never hear of either Brāhmaṇas or Sūtras peculiar to these *Śākhās,* and the natural conclusion, confirmed besides by native authority, is that they diverged and became separated on the strength of various readings and other peculiarities, affecting the texts of their Saṁhitās. There is no evidence as to the existence of similar Saṁhitā śākhās for the Yajurveda or Sāmaveda. If we take the two *śākhās* of the Yajur-veda-saṁhitā, that of the Kāṇvas and that of the Mādhyandinas, both presuppose the existence of a Vājasaneyi-saṁhitā, and this Vājasaneyi saṁhitā would have been perfectly useless without a Brāhmaṇa. It was not the saṁhitā, but the Brāhmaṇa of the Vājasaneyins, handed down as it was in various texts, which gave rise to the fifteen Caraṇas of the Vājasaneyins, and among them to the Kāṇva and Mādhyandina-Caraṇas. Their Saṁhitās were of secondary importance, and startling as such an opinion might sound to an orthodox *Brāhmaṇa,* were probably not put together till after the composition of the Vājasneyi-Brāhmaṇa in its original and primitive form. The peculiar differences in the text of *mantras* of the Kāṇvas and Mādhyandinas depend on the differences occurring in their respective Brāhmaṇas, and not *vice versa.* On the same ground, we must doubt the existence of ancient Saṁhitā-śākhās for the Sāma-veda.

The next step which led to the formation of Caraṇas was the adoption of a Brāhmaṇa, and we therefore call this second class the Brāhmaṇa-caraṇas. When the growth of a more complicated ceremonial led to the establishment of three or four classes of priests, each performing peculiar duties, and requiring a special training for their sacerdotal office, there must have been a floating stock of Brāhmāṇas, or dicta theological, peculiar to each class of priest. They treated of the general arrangement of the sacrifice. They handed down the authoritative opinions of famous sages: they gave the objections raised against such opinions by other persons: and gradually they clothed these contradictory statements in the form of a logical argument. Occasionally, an allegorical interpretation was given of the meaning of certain rites, the simple and natural import of which had been forgotten. Rewards were vouchsafed to the pious worshipper, and instances were recorded of such rewards having been obtained by the faithful of former ages. All these sayings and discussions were afterwards collected as three distinct Brāhmaṇas, belonging to the three classes of priests. We still meet with the general names of Bahvṛca-brāhmaṇas for the Ṛg-veda, of Adhvaryu-brāhmaṇas for the Yajur-veda, and of Chandoga-brāhmaṇas for the Sāma-veda, without any further reference to particular Caraṇas by which these Brāhmaṇas were collected or adopted. But those Brāhmaṇas are no longer met with in their original form. They have come down to us, without exception, as the Brāhmaṇas of certain Caraṇas of each Veda. Instead of one Bahvṛcha-brāhmaṇa of the Ṛg-veda, we only find the Bahvṛcha-Brāhmaṇa of the Aitareyins, or the Kauṣītakins, or the Śaṅkhāyanins. Instead of one Chandoga-biahrmma or Chāndogyam, we have the Chandog-brāhmaṇa of the Tāṇḍins or the Tāṇḍya, and we find quotations from other Caraṇas, such as the Śāṛyāyanins[151] or the Kauthumas. Instead of one Adhvaryu-brāhmaṇa, we have the dark code of the old Carakas, or the Taittirīyas and the Kaṭhas, and the new Brāhmaṇa of the Vājasaneyins, and their descendants, the Kāṇvas and Mādhyandinas. We no where find the original collection from which the various recensions might be supposed to have branched off and Deviated in time. In most cases, where we possess the text of a Brāhmaṇa, preserved by different Śākhās, the variations are but small, and they point clearly to one and the same original from which they descended. Sometimes, however, the variations are of a different kind, so much so that we are inclined to admit several independent collections of that floating stock of Brāhmaṇic lore, which went on accumulating in different places and through various generations. If we compare the Brāhmaṇas of the Aitareyins and the Kauṣītakins, we find their wording, even where they treat of the same matters, very different. The order in which the sacrifices are described is not always the same, nor are the ceremonial rules always identical. Illustrations and legends are interspersed in the Brāhmaṇa of the Kauṣītakins of which no trace can be found in the Brāhmaṇa of the Aitareyins. And yet, with all these differences the literal coincidence of whole chapters, the frequent occurrence of the same sentences, the same comparisons and illustrations, render it impossible to ascribe to each of these Brāhmaṇas a perfectly independent origin. The two Brāhmaṇas of the Kāṇvas and Mādhyandinas, in spite of their differences, in spite of additions and omissions that have been pointed out in either, compel us to admit that they had a common starting-point. To judge from frequent quotations, the number of Brāhmaṇas differing from each other more or less considerably, and the number of Caraṇas, founded on these Brāhmaṇas, must have been very large. We can easily imagine how this happened. The name of a famous teacher, who gathered a number of students around himself in a village, or who lived under the protection of some small Raja, was preserved by his pupils for generations. The sacred literature which he was, perhaps, the first to teach in a newly-founded colony, was afterwards handed down under the sanction of his name, though differing but slightly from the traditional texts kept up in the community from which he himself had started. He might, perhaps, add a few chapters of his own composition, a change quite sufficient, in the eyes of the Brāhmaṇas to constitute a new work, or at least to disqualify it for claiming any longer its original title. When these new Caraṇas had once been founded, it was but natural, though they orginated chiefly with a Brāhman a of their own, that the text of their Saṁhitās also should be slightly modified. This was not the case necessarily. The Aitareyins, for instance, and the Kauṣitakins though they differred in their Brāhmaṇas, preserved, as far as we know, the same śākhā of the Saṁhitā, and preserved it each with the same minute accuracy. No Saṁhitā peculiar to the Kauṣītakins and Aitareyins is ever mentioned, and the points on which they differed were from the very first, connected with the subject matter of the Brāhmaṇas. Students following different śākhās as far as their Brāhmaṇas was concerned, might very well follow one and the same Śākhā of the Saṁhitā, though they would no longer call it by its own original name. In most cases, however, and particu-larly in the Caraṇas of the

Yājurveda, a difference in the Brāhmaṇas would necessitate, or, at least, naturally, lead to, corresponding differences in the Saṁhitā, such as we find for instance, in the hymns of the Kāṇvas and Mādhyandinas.[152]

These Brāhmaṇa-caraṇas existed previous to the first composition of the Sūtras, and in the Sūtras belonging to the Sāma-veda, which are the earliest Sūtras we possess, they are quoted. No Sūtra is ever quoted in any of the Brāhmaṇas, but there is no collection of Sūtras in which the various Śākhās of the Brāhmaṇas are not referred to by name. The authorities quoted in the Sūtras on doubtful points of the Vedic ceremonial, are invariably taken from the Brāhmaṇa-saraṇas. In the commentary on Pāṇini, such names as "the Aitareyins, the Śāṭyāyanins, and Bhāllavins" are distinctly explained as supporters of ancient Brāhmaṇas; and the antiquity of the two last is still further confirmed by the fact of their being quoted as Brāhmanic authorities in the Śatapatha-brāhmaṇā.[153]

The third and most modern class of Caraṇas consists of those which derive their origin from the introduction of a new body of Sūtras, such as the Āśvalayanīyas, the Kātyāyanīyas, and many of the sub-divisions of the Taittirīyas. It is not always possible to determine with certainty whether a Caraṇa dates from the Brāhmaṇa period, or from the Sūtra period, because so many of the Brāhmaṇas and Sūtras, have been lost, and some of the Brāhmaṇas have been handed down to us under the names of more modern Sūtra-saraṇas, by which they were adopted. It is easy to determine that the Kauṣītakins date from the Brāhmaṇa period, because there is neither a Kauṣītaki-sūtra nor a Kauṣītaki-saṁhitā, but only a Kauṣītaki-brāhmaṇa; but in other instances our knowledge of the ancient literature of India is too fragmentary to enable us to fix the age of the numerous Caraṇas which are quoted by later authorities. Some of the Sūtras again, as we saw before, are older than others, and seem almost to trespass on the frontiers of the Brāhmaṇa period. How are we to determine, for instance, whether the Sāṅkhāyanas were originally a Brāhmaṇa saraṇa and had their

Sūtras written by one of their own sect, or whether the foundation of their Caraṇa rested on the text of the Sūtras,[154] a new text of the original Brāhmaṇa of the Bahvṛchas being adopted by them in later times, and thenceforth quoted as the Sāṅkhāyana-brāhmaṇa ? In some instances the relative age of certain Sūtras has been preserved by the tradition of the schools. Thus the most ancient Sūtra of the Taittirīyas is said to have been that of Baudhāyana, who was succeeded by Bhāradvāja, Āpastamba, Satyāṣāḍha, Hiraṇyakeśin, Vadhūna and Vaikhānsa; all of whom, with the exception of the two last, have lent their names to different Caraṇas of the dark Yajur-veda.

Although none of the Sūtras seem to have been written with the distinct purpose of founding a new Caraṇa, it can easily be imagined how different communities, after adopting a collection of Sūtras as the highest authority for their ceremonial, become inclined to waive minor points of difference in the Saṁhitās and Brāhmaṇas, and thus coalesced into a new Caraṇa under the name and sanction of their Sūtrakara.

After these new Sautra-saraṇas had once been started, We find that the Saṁhitas and Brāhmaṇas current among their members, were designated by the name of the new Caraṇas. Thus we may explain the title of Āśvalāyana-brāhmaṇa given to the Aitereya-brāhmaṇa in one of the MSS, of the Bodleian library;[155] and we shall not hesitate to ascribe the same meaning to an Āśvalāyana-brāhmaṇa, said to be quoted by Yājñikadeva in his commentary on Kātyāyana,[156] Why such a Brāhmaṇa should not be quoted by early writers, such as the authors of Sūtras, is easily understood. Its title was necessarily of late origin, and it is important as marking the progressive changes in the nomenclature of Indian literature. We have a similar and still better authenticated instance in so-called Āpastamba-brāhmaṇa, which is but a different title of the Taittirīya-brāhmaṇa, as adopted by the followers of the Āpastamba-sūtras. It is in this manner that the Sūtras may be said to have contributed partly to the formation of new Caraṇas, some of which are not mentioned in the ancient lists, as, for instance, the Kātyāyanīyas; partly to the extinc-tion of the more ancient Brāhmaṇa-saraṇas and Saṁhitā saraṇas, many of which are now known to us by name only.

That the introduction of the Sūtras and the foundation of Sūtra saraṇas was felt as an innovation by the Brāhmaṇas themselves, we perceive from the manner in which even modern writers speak of them; half objecting to their authority, yet glad to admit and even to defend what could no longer be prevented. The Sūtras were not indeed, admitted as part of the Śruti, yet they were made part of the Svādhyāya, and had to be learned by heart by the young students. They might, therefore, like the Saṁhitās and Brāhmaṇas, claim a kind of sacred character, and in time become the charter of a new Caraṇa. Thus we read in Mahādeva's Commentary on the Hiraṇyakeśī-sūtras[157] : "The Kalpa-sūtra is sometimes different for different Śākhās, sometimes it is not. The difference of the Śākhās arises partly from the difference of the sacred text (adhyāyana being used in the sense of svādhyāga, perhaps with reference to the peculiar pronunciation taught in the Prātiśākhyas), partly from a difference in the Sūtras. The Sūtras of Āśvalāyana and Kātyāyana, for instance, are the same for two Śākhās whose respective texts are different, while in the Taittirīya-veda we find Śākhās with different Sūtras, but no differences in their sacred texts. Hence it may be said,[158] that sometimes, where there is a difference in the Sūtras, there is also a difference of Śākhā; and, on the other hand, where there is a difference of Śākhā, there may be a difference in the Sūtras." Mahādeva goes even further, and tries to show that, like all the revealed literature of the Brāhmaṇas, the Sūtras also existed previous to the beginning of time and had no historical origin.[159] "As the various Śākhās," he says, "which arise from various readings of the sacred texts are without a a beginning, or eternal, so are also the various Śākhās which arise from different Sūtras. For the titles of certain Sūtras, derived from their authors, are not modern; but being eternal, as inherent in individual Ṛṣis, whose names occur in certain Kalpas or ceremonials, and retaining the same character when applied to the Sūtras, which have been promulgated by the Ṛṣis, they hold good as titles for

Śākhās, which apparently are marked by the names of men.[160]" We may now understand in what sense the same Mahādeva gives to the word Caraṇa the meaning both of Śākhā and Sūtra,. "It is true," he says, "that'śākhā means a part of the sacred tradition, consisting of Mantras and Brāhmaṇas, and that the subordinate Śākhās, of the Veda owe their origin to the differences of either Mantras or Brāhmaṇas. Nevertheless as Veda means the sacred tradition, together with the Aṅgas or subsidiary doctrines, a śākhā may include the Aṅgas and yet remain Veda, and as such become different from other Śākhā, owing to a difference in the Angus. If, therefore, the Sūtra, which is an Anga, differs, there will be difference in the sacred tradition; and thus a difference in the Sūtras may well become the cause of a different name of a Śākhā."[161]

The following list, though far from being complete, contains some of the Kalpa-sūtras which are best known to us either from MSS. or otherwise :

I. YAJUR-VEDA

A. OLD, OR DARK TEXT

1. Āpastamba, text and commentary existing.
2. Baudhāyana, text and commentary existing
3. Satyāṣāḍha Hiraṇyakeśin, text and commentary existing.
4. Mānava-sūtra, large fragments of text existing.
5. Bhāradvāja-sūtra, quoted.
6. Vādhūna-sūtra quoted.
7. Vaikhānasa-sūtra, quoted.
8. Laugākṣi-sūtra, quoted.
9. Maitra-sūtra, quoted.
10. Kaṭha-sūtra, quoted.
11. Vārāha-sūtra, quoted

B. NEW, OR BRIGHT TEXT

1. Kātyāyana, text and commentary existing.

II. SĀMA-VEDA.

1. Maśaka's Ārṣeya-kalpa, text and commentary existing.
2. Lāṭyāyana-sūtra, (Kauthuma), ditto.
3. Drāhyāyaṇa-sūtra (Rāṇāyanīya), ditto.

III. ṚG-VEDA

1. Āśyalāyana-sūtra, text and commentary existing.
2. Sāṅkhyāyana-sūtra, ditto.
3. Śaunaka-sūtra, quoted.

VI. ATHARVA-VEDA

1. Kuśika-sūtra, text existing

SMĀRTA-SŪTRAS

Two other classes of Sūtras have already been mentioned as belonging to the same branch of literature with the Śrauta-sūtras, viz. the Gṛhya, and Sāmayacārika-sūtras.

Both are included under the common title of Smārta-sūtra, in contradistinction to the Śrauta-sūtras; the latter deriving their authority from the Śruti (the Mantras and Brāhmaṇas), the former from Smṛti, or immemorial tradition. The Gṛhya and Sāmayacārika-sūtras have frequently been confounded by European scholars; but the Brāhmaṇas distinguish strictly between the Gṛhya ceremonies, performed by the married house-holder, chiefly for the benefit of his family, and the Sāmayacārika rules, which are to be observed by the rising generation, and which regulate the various relations of every-day life. It is chiefly in the Sāmayacārika, or, as they are sometimes called, Dharma-sūtras, that we have to look for the originals of the later metrical law-books, such as Manu, Yājñavalkya, and the rest; and the statement of Megasthenes, that the Hindūs at his time administered law from memory (απο μνημησ)[162] can only refer to the Smārta-sūtras of the Caraṇas, and to the modern Smṛti-Saṁhitās of Manu, Yājñavalkya, Parāśara, etc.

The Gṛhya-sūtras, belonging to the old Yajur-veda, are

numerous. Quotations have been met with from Baudhāyana Bhāradvāja, Hiraṇyakeśin, the Kāṭhaka,[163] and the Maitrayaṇīyas,[164] all names connected with the Taittirīya-veda, and proving the existence of distinct collections of Gṛhya-sūtras. The number of similar Sūtras for the bright Yajur-veda seems to have been still more considerable. Every one of the fifteen Caraṇas of the Vājasaneyins is said to have been possessed of Kula-dharmas, which may have been either

Gṛhya or Dharma-sūtras.[165] The only collection, however, which has come down to us is that of Pāraskara.[166] Another, ascribed to Vaijvāpin, is quoted, but has not yet been discovered in manuscript. Connected with the Sāma-veda Gṛhya-sūtras of Gobhila, adopted both by the Rāṇāyaṇīyas and the Kauthumas seem to have obtained the greatest celebrity, there being but one other collection, the Khādira gṛhya, which is sometimes quoted as a parallel authority of the Chandogas.[167] The Gṛhya-sūtras of the Ṛg-veda or the Bahvṛcas were written by Śaunaka, and he is quoted as an authority on legal subject by as late a writer as the author of the Mānava-dharma-śāstra (iii. 16). The only two collection, however, which have been preserved in MS. or those of Āśvalāyana and Sāṅkhāyana. Various opinions are expressed by the Brāhmaṇas themselves as to the meaning of *gṛhya*. Gṛha, according to the commentary on Āśvalāyana, signifies not only house, but also wife. In support of the latter meaning he quotes a passage, *sagṛho gṛham āgataḥ* "he is gone to the house with his wife." According to this derivation the *gṛhya* ceremonies would be those which are performed with the sacred fire, first lighted by a husband on the day of his marriage. This fire, or the altar on which it is kept, is called *gṛhya*, and the *gṛhya* sacrifices are all performed on that altar. But it is doubtful whether *gṛha* can ever mean wife. In the passage quoted above, it rather means house or family. Besides, as the Hindūs themselves admit, this domestic fire has sometimes to be lighted by a Brāhmaṇa[168] before his marriage, in case his father should die prematurely.[169] Gṛhya, therefore, probably meant originally the house or the family-hearth, from *gṛha*, house, and it was in opposition to the great sacrifices for which several hearths were required, and which were therefore called *vaitānika*,[170] that the domestic ceremonies were called Gṛhya, as performed by means of the one domestic fire. It should be stated, however, in favour of the former interpretation, that in Gobhila's Sūtra these domestic ceremonies are not called gṛhya, but *gṛhya* karmāṇi and that here also the commentator admits *gṛhya* in the sense of housewife or tradition.[171]

The general name of the sacrifices performed, according to the Gṛhya-sūtras, is Pāka-yajña, where pāka is not to be taken in the sense of cooking, but signifies, according to Indian authorities, either small or good. That pāka is used in the first sense appears from such expressions as *"yo'smat-pākataraḥa,"* "he who is smaller than we." But the more likely meaning is *good* or *excellent* or *perfect*; because, as the commentators remark, these ceremonies impart to every man that peculiar fitness without which he would be excluded from the sacrifices, and from all the benefits of his religion. As it is necessary that the marriage ceremonies should be rightly performed, that the choice of the bride should be made according to sacred rules, prescribed in the Sūtras or established by independent tradition in various families and localities, the first ceremony described in the Gṛhya-sūtras is Marriage, Then follow the; *Sanskāras*, the rites to be performed at the conception of child, at various periods before his birth, at the time of his birth, the ceremony of naming the child, of carrying him out to see the sun, of feeding him, of cutting hair, and lastly of investing him as a student, and handing him to a Guru, under whose care he is to study the sacred writings, that is to say, to learn them by heart, and to perform all the offices of a Brahmacārin, or religious student, It is only after he has served his apprenticeship and grown up to manhood, that he is allowed to marry, to light the sacrificial fire for himself, to choose his priests, and to perform year after year the solemn sacrifices, prescribed by the Śruti and the Smṛti. The latter are described in the later books of the Gṛhya-sūtras, and the last book contains a full account of the funeral ceremonies and of the sacrifices offered to the spirits of the departed.

There is certainly more of human interest in these domestic rites than in the great sacrifices described in the Śrauta-sūtras. The offerings themselves are generally of a simple nature, and the ceremonial is such that it does not require the assistance of a large class of professional priests. A log of wood placed on the fire of the hearth, an oblation poured out to the gods, or alms given to the Brāhmaṇas, this is what constitutes a pāka-yajña. Āśvalāyana quotes several passages from the Veda, in order to show that the gods do not despise those simple offerings, nay, that a mere prayer will secure their favour, and that a hymn of praise is as good as bulls and cows. He quotes from Rv. viii. 19. 5. and 6. : "The mortal who sacrifices to Agni with a log of wood, with an oblatian, with a bundle of grass[172] with a reverence, careful in his performance, his horses will press on quickly, his fame will be the brightest; nowhere will mischief, whether wrought by the gods or wrought by men reach him." Another verse is quoted from Rv. viii. 24. 20., where men are called upon "to speak a mighty speech which is sweeter to Indra than milk (ghṛta, ghee) and honey." And lastly, reference is made to a passage (Ṛv. 16. 47.), where the poet says : "With this hymn of praise, O Agni, we bring you a sacrifice that is fashioned by the heart; may these be your bulls, your oxen, and your cows." All these passages are more applicable to the Gṛhya than to the Śrauta ceremonies, and though the latter may seem of greater importance to the Brāhmaṇas, to us the former will be more deeply interesting as disclosing that deep-rooted tendency in the heart of man to bring the chief events of human life in connection with a higher power, and to give to our joys and sufferings a deeper significance and a religious sanctification.[173]

The third class of the Sūtras, the Sāmayacārika or Dharma-sūtras, are equally interesting on account of the light which they throw on the every day life of the early Brāhmaṇas. According to the commentaries on these works, the existence of the Dharma-sūtras is presupposed by the Śrauta and Gṛhya-sūtras. It is said, for instance, in the former, that a certain act of the sacrifice is to be performed by a man, after he has adjusted his sacrificial cord (*yajñopavītam*); but in what peculiar manner a man ought to adjust that cord is not stated, but is supposed to be known from the Dharma-sūtras. The same remark is made with reference to the exact manner of rinsing the mouth (ācānta), and of performing the morning and evening prayers (*sandhyā-vandana*). These matters are spoken of as generally known from the Sūtras, and, according to Hindū commentators, they could only be known from the Dharma-sūtras. This argument, however, can hardly be considered conclusive as to the historical priority of the Dharma-sūtras. On the contrary, it seems more likely that these matters, such as adjusting the sacrificial cord, etc., were supposed to be so well known at the time when the Śrauta and Gṛhya-sūtras were first composed, that they required no elucidation. Instead, therefore, of considering the Dharma-sūtras as earlier in time, the evidence, as far as it is known at present, would rather point in the opposite direction, and make us look upon these Dharma-sūtras as the latest of the three branches of Sūtras. This impression is confirmed by other reflections. In neither of the other Sūtras is the position of the Śūdra so definitely marked as in the Dharma-sūtras. Āpastamba, in his Sāmayacārika-sūtras, declares distinctly that there are four Varṇas, the Brāhmaṇa, the Kṣatriya, the Vaiśya, the Śūdra, but that the initiatory rites, the *Upanayana* in particular, are only intended for the three first classes. The same is implied, no doubt, in the other Sūtras, which give the rules as to the proper time when a young Brāhmaṇa, a young Kṣatriya, or a young Vaiśya should be apprenticed with their spiritual tutors, but never say at what age this or similar ceremonies should be performed for one not belonging to these three *Varṇas*. Yet they never exclude the Śūdra expressly,[174] nor do they represent him as the born slave or client of the other castes. In the Dharma-sūtras the social degradation of the Śūdra is as great as in the later Law-books, and the same crime, if committed by a

Brāhmaṇa and a Śūdra is visited with very different punishments. Thus, if a member of the three Varṇas commits adultery with the wife of a Śūdra, he is to be banished; if a Śūdra commits adultery with the wife of a member of the three Varṇas he is to be executed.[175] If a Śūdra abuses an honest member of the three Varṇas, his tongue is to be cut.[176] He is to be flogged for not keeping at a respectful distance. For murder, theft, and pillage the Śūdra is executed; the Brāhmaṇa, if caught in the same offences, is only deprived of his eye-sight. This is the same iniquitous law, which we find in the later Law-books. But although the distinction between the Sudras and the other Varṇas is so sharply drawn by Āpastamba, he admits that a Śūdra, if he obeys the law, may be born again as a Vaiśya, the Vaiśya as a Kṣatriya, and the Kṣatriya as a Brāhmaṇa[177] and that a Brāhmaṇa, if he disregards the law, will be born again as a Kṣatriya, the Kṣatriya as a Vaiśya and a Vaiśya as a Śūdra.

It might be supposed that the Dharma-sūtras formed merely an appendix to the Śrauta and Gṛhya-sūtras, and that they should be classed with the Pariśiṣṭa literature. But such a supposition is contradicted by the fact, that the Dharma-sūtras occasionally treat of the same subjects as the Gṛhya-sūtras, and employ almost the same words in explaining some of the initiatory rites, the Saṅskāras. They must, therefore, be considered as independent collections of Sūtras, later perhaps than the Śrauta and Gṛhya-sūtras, but enjoying the same authority on matters belonging to Smṛti or tradition, as the Gṛhya-sūtras.

We have still to mention the Ten Sūtras of the Sāma-veda.[178] Sutras[179] do not all, strictly speaking, treat of the Kalpa, or the ceremonial. Some of them are little more than lists such as we find in the Anukramaṇīs or Indices, appended to the other Vedas. Their style, however, approaches the style of the Sūtras; and, as they are quoted together as the Ten Sūtras, and, as some of them belong decidedly to the earliest productions of the Sūtra literature, it will be more convenient to place them here, than to refer them to the Pariśiṣṭa literature, with which they have little or nothing in common. They are :

I. The Kalpa-Sūtra, or Ārṣeya-kalpa of Maśaka, an index of the hymns used by the Chandoga priests, in the order in which the sacrifices are described in the Tāṇḍya-brāhmaṇa, Eleven Prapāṭhakas: 1–5, on the sacrifices called *Ekāha*; 6–9, on the sacrifices called *Ahīna*; 10–12, on the sacrifices called *Sattra*. Commentary by Varadarāja.

II. The Anupada-sūtra, a gloss to the Tāṇḍya-brāhmaṇa in ten Prapāṭhakas,

III. The Kalpa-Sūtra, already mentioned, either of Lāṭ yāyana or Drāhyāyaṇa, Lāṭyāyana quotes Maśaka, and follows the order of the Tāṇḍya-brāhmaṇa.

IV. The Nidāna-sūtra, on Metres, in ten Prapāṭhakas.

V. The Upagrantha-sūtra, a treatise on the performance of some of the Sāma-veda sacrifices, commonly ascribed to Kātyāyana[181].

VI. The Kṣudra-sūtra or Kṣaudra, in three Prapāṭhakas, equally treating of the ceremonial of the Sāma-veda.[182]

VII. The Taṇḍālakṣaṇa-sūtra.

VIII. The Pañcavidha-sūtra[183], in two Prapāṭhakas.

IX. The Kalpānupada, and

X. The Anustotra-sūtra, in two Prapāṭhakas.

We miss in this list the Pushpa-sūtra, ascribed to Gobhila, and containing rules on the adaptation of the text of the hymns to their musical performance.

JYOTIṢA OR ASTRONOMY

The last of the Vedāṅgas is called *Jyotiṣa*, or Astronomy. Its literatrue is very scanty, and the small treatise, generally quoted as the Jyotiṣa, belongs to the same class of works as the Śikṣā. Colebrooke speaks of different Jyotiṣas for each Veda, and he calls one, which has a commentary, the Jyotiṣa of the Ṛg-veda. Among his MSS, however, which are now deposited at the East India House, there is but one work of this kind. It exists in various MSS., (Nos. 1378, 1743, 1520), and the differences between these MSS. are so small that we could hardly consider them as distinct works. This tract is later than the Sūtra period, and we possess as yet no work on ancient astronomy, composed in the style of the early Sūtras. Notwithstanding its modern form, however, the doctrines which are propounded in this small treatise represent the earliest stage of Hindū astronomy, the theories on which it is founded, and the rules which it lays down, are more simple, less scientific, than anything we find in other astronomical treatises. Nor is it the object of this small tract to teach astronomy. It has a practical object, which is to convey such knowledge of the heavenly bodies as is necessary for fixing the days and hours of the Vedic sacrifices. It was the establishment of a sacred Calendar, which in India, as elsewhere, gave the first impulse to astronomical studies. Thus we meet in the Brāhmaṇas and Āraṇayakas with frequent allusions to astronomical subjects, and even in the hymns we find traces which indicate a certain advance in the observation of the moon, as the measurer of time. The fact that the name of the moon is the same in Sanskrit, Greek and German, and that it is derived from a root which originally means to measure, shows that even before the separation of the Indo-European family, the moon had been looked upon as the chief means of measuring time. And the close connection between the names of moon and month proves that a certain knowledge of lunar chronology existed during the same early pariod. In one passage of the Ṛg-veda[184] the moon is mentioned in connection with the Nakṣatras, and we can hardly doubt that this is an allusion to the Nakṣatras, the well-known name of the Lunar Mansions or the Lunar Zodiac. In the hymns[185] the phases of the moon have not only received proper names but they have been personified, and are invoked as deities to grant progeny to their worshippers. Again, there is a passage in the first book of the Ṛg-veda, where in addition to the twelve months, a thirteenth or intercalary month is mentioned. The poet says there (Ṛv. i. 25.8.), "He (Varuṇa), firm in his work knows the twelve months with their offspring, and knows the month which is produced in addition." It has been objected that the idea of an intercalary month was too scientific for the early poets of the Veda, and a different translation has been proposed : "Varuṇa, who knows the twelve months, and knows those which are to come." But the poet would not have used the singular of the verb, if he meant the plural. He could not have said, "the twelve months and those which are to come," if he meant to say, "the past months and those which are to come." No doubt the acquaintance with an intercalary month presupposes a certain knowledge of lunar and solar astronomy, but not more than what a shepherd or a sailor might gain in the course of his life. The whole idea expressed by the poet is, that Varuṇa maintains the established order of the world, and therefore knows the twelve months aud also the thirteenth. In the hymns of the Yajur-veda the thirteenth month is changed already into a deity. Oblations are offered (Vājasaneya-saṁhitā, vii. 30.,) to each of the twelve months, and at the end one oblation is made to *Anhasaspati*, the deity of the intercalary month. In the Brāhmaṇas[186] likewise the the thirteenth month is mentioned, and in the Jyotiṣa the theory of intercalation is fully explained, Two names for "an astronomer," Nakṣatra-darśa and Gaṇaka, occur as early as the Taittirīyaka and the Saṁhitā of the Yajur-veda[187]; among the sciences of the early *Brāhmaṇas*, *Nakṣatra-Vidyā* or Astronomy is mentioned in the Chāndogyopaniṣad. In the Gaṇapāṭha, appended to Pāṇini's grammar[188] the title of Jyotiṣa occurs together with the titles of other Vedic works; and in the Caraṇa-vyūha we meet not only with the Jyotiṣa, but with an Upa-jyotisha, or a supplementary treatise on astronomy. This supplementary treatise is one of the Pariśiṣṭas, and in the same class of writings we meet with other tracts on astronomical subjects such as the Gobhilīya Navagraha-śānti pariśiṣṭa[189] belonging to the Sāma-veda, and several more belonging to the Atharva-veda.[190]

SŪTRA LITERATURE IN GENERAL

If now we take a comprehensive view of that class of literature which we have just examined we find some characteristic features throughout. All these works were written with a practical object, quite a new phase in the literature of such a nation as the ancient Hindūs. The only authority which the Sūtrakāras, the authors of the Sūtras, claimed for their works was the authority of that ancient, and, as it was then already considered, revealed literature on which their works were founded. These men claimed no inspiration for themselves. They had made a scientific study of the literature handed down to them by former generations, and they wished to make that study easier to their contemporaries and to future generations. The style which they adopted for that purpose was business-like in the extreme. It was the curt and dry style of the Sūtras, a style peculiar to India, which can only be compared with the elaborate tables of contents, or the marginal notes, of some of our own early writers. It has its first beginnings in the Brāhmaṇas, where some subjects, particularly those which had given rise to early controversy, are stated with all the conciseness and neatness of the Sūtra style. But whereas the authors of the Brāhmaṇas screened their poverty behind a constant display of the most insane verbosity, the writers of the Sūtras gloried in every word they could save without endangering the practical usefulness of their manuals. In some instances, they adopted a poetical form, and they succeeded in combining the conciseness of their prose with the rhythm of their early metres, the mixed Ślokas. Thus their position is marked by the very form of their works, as intermediate between the antique style of the Brāhmaṇas, and the modern style of the metrical Śāstras. Their works form a distinct and compact class of literature, and if we succeed in fixing the relative age of any one of these Sūtrakāras or writers of Sūtras, we shall fixed the age of a period of literature which forms a transition between the Vedic and the classical literature of India.

THE ANUKRAMṆĪS

Several of the works mentioned before were ascribed to Śaunaka and his two pupils, Kātyāyana and Āśvalāyana. But we have not yet mentioned a number of treatises, ascribed to the same authors, and belonging to the same sphere of literature as the Sūtras, which, however, on account of their technical character, could not lay claim to the title of Vedāṅga, or "member of the Veda." They are known by the name of the *Anukramaṇīs* from *anu* along, and *Kram* to step. They are systematic indices to various portions of the ancient Vedic literature,

The most perfect Anukramam is that of the Saṁhitā of the Ṛg-veda. It is ascribed to Kātyāyana, an author chiefly known by his works on the Yajur-veda and Sāma-veda. Its name is Sarvānukramaṇī or Sarvānukrarma, *i. e.*, the index of all things.[191] It gives the first words of each hymn, the number of verses, the name and family of the poets, the names of the deities, aud the metres of every verse. Before the time of Kātyāyana, there had been separate indices for each of these subjects, and it was with reference to them that Kātyāyana called his own index the general or comprehensive index. Our authority for this is Ṣaḍguruśiṣya, the author of a commentary on the Index of Kātyāyana; a man who like Devarājayajvan, the author of a commentary on the Nighaṇṭu, was not without a certain appreciation of the historical progress of Indian literature. He tells us in his Vedārthadīpika, that before Kātyāyana, there existed one index of the poets, one of the metres, one of the deities, one Anuvākas, the old chapters of the Ṛgveḍa, and one of the hymns;[192] and that these indices were composed by Śaunaka. Now we know the style of Śaunaka, and as by a happy accident some of these former indices have been preserved, some complete, others in fragments, we are able to test Ṣaḍguruśiṣya's accuracy.

We remarked before, as a distinctive peculiarity of the style of Śaunaka, as contrasted with that of Kātyāyana, that the Prātiśākhya ascribed to the former is composed in mixed Ślokas, whereas the Prātisakhya of Kātyāyana is written in prose or in Sūtras. The same observation applies to the Anukramaṇīs. Those ascribed to Śaunaka are composed in mixed metres, as far as we can judge from quotation; the Anukramaṇī of his pupil Kātyāyana is in prose, and exhibits all the artificial appliances of a Sūtra composition. There is one of Śaunaka's Anukramaṇīs, the Anuvāka-anukramaṇī, which can be restored completely from MSS;[193] and this work bears the most manifest traces of Śaunaka's style, partly in the mixture, partly in a peculiar rudeness, of its metres. The other Anukramaṇīs, ascribed to Śaunaka are lost to us, but they must have existed at the time of Ṣaḍguruśiṣya. He quotes not only from the Anuvāka-anukramaṇī (Bhāṣya, viii. 1.), but also from the Deva-anukrama) (Bhāṣya, viii. 4), and he distinguishes this work from the Bṛhad-devatā, another work attributed to Śaunaka, of which there is one MS, in Europe at the Royal Library of Berlin.[194] Sāyaṇa also, though later than Ṣaḍguruśiṣya, was still in possession of Śaunaka's works, and he quotes particularly the Bṛhad-devatā, in several of his own commentaries. Śaunaka's Ārṣa-anukramaṇī is quoted by Sāyaṇa in his Commentary on the Ṛg-veda, i. 100. 1. If we add to these quotations a reference to Śaunaka's Chando'nukramaṇī, which is found in Ṣaḍguruśiṣya's Vedārthadīpikā (MS. E. I. H. 1823, p. 7. a.), we may consider the authenticity of these works sufficiently established; and it is hardly unreasonable to suppose that the fifth Anukramaṇī also, of which no quotations have as yet been met with, the Sūktānukramaṇī, was in existence as late as Sāyaṇa's time.[195]

This would give us for the Ṛg-veda five Anukramaṇīs by Śaunaka, one by Kātyāyana, and one by an unknown author. The Bṛhad-devatā is a work of too large a compass to be called an Anukramaṇī, and it is even doubtful whether we possess this work in the same form in which Śaunaka left it. To judge from Dr. Kuhn's extracts, the author of the Bṛhad-devatā follows indeed the Śākala-śākhā, but his: text must have differed from that of our MSS. The author may have followed one of the sub-divisions of the Śākalas, the Śaiśira-śākhā, for instance, which we know was followed by Śaunaka. The division of the Saṁhitā which is adopted in the Bṛhad-devatā, is that of Maṇḍalas, Anuvākas, and Sūktas; but the other division into Aṣṭakas is equally known, and even the Khilas are taken into account, whereas both : Śaunaka and Kātyāyana exclude these later hymns distinctly from their indices. Dr. Kuhn concludes from a passage in Ṣaḍguruśiṣya's Commentary, to which we shall revert hereafter, that not Śaunaka, but Āśvalāyana, was the author of our Bṛhad-devatā. This conclusion, however, is not borne out by sufficient evidence, nor is the fact that Śaunaka is quoted by name in the work itself a sufficient argument against

Śaunaka's authorship. According to the line of argument adopted by Dr. Kuhn, it would be equally objectionable to ascribe the Bṛhad-devatā to Āśvalāyana : for in one passage, according to Dr. Kuhn's own emendations, the name of Āśvalāyana also occurs in it. Other authorities which are quoted in this curious work are the Aitareyaka, the Kauṣītakins, the Bhāllavi-brāhmaṇa, the Nidāna (*Nidāna-sañcake granthe*), Śākalas, Bāṣkalas, Madhuka, Śvetaketū, Gālava, Gārgya, Rāthītara, Rāthantarin, Śākaṭāyana, Śaṇḍilya, Romakāyana Sthavira, Kāṭhakya, Bhāgurin, Śākapūni, Bhārmyaśva Mudgala, Aurṇavābha, Krauṣṭukin, Mātrin, and Yāska. The last is most frequently mentioned, and the whole book is dedicated to him. To judge from the style of the Bṛhad-devatā, the work as we now possess it, though originilly written by Śaunaka, seems to have been recast by a later writer.

The following figures, taken from Śaunaka's Anukramaṇīs, will serve to give an idea of the minuteness with which the Veda was studied at his time. According to Śaunaka, the Śākala-śākhā of the Ṛg-veda-saṁhitā consists of 10 Maṇḍalas, or 64 Adhyāyas.

Maṇḍalas.		Anuvākas		Hymns.
The 1st	contains	24	and	191
2nd ś	,,	4	,,	43
3rd	,,	5	,,	62
4th	,,	5	,,	58
5th	,,	6	,,	87
6th	,,	6	,,	75
7th	,,	6	,,	104
8th	,,	10	,,	92 (+ 11 Vālakhilyas)
9th	,,	7	,,	114
10th	,,	12	,,	191
The 10 have		85 and		1017 + 11 = 1028

The Bāṣkala-śākhā had 8 hymns more = 1025 hymns.

The 64 *Adhyāyas* have 2006 *Vargas*. These are arranged

as follows :

	Verses		*Vargas*		Verses
Vargas consisting of	1	=	1	=	1
”	2	=	2	=	4
”	3	=	97	=	291
”	4	=	174	=	696
”	5	=	1,207	=	6,035
”	6	=	346[1]	=	2,076
”	7	=	119	=	833
”	8	=	59	=	472
”	9	=	1	=	9
64 Adhyāyas		=	2,042		10,622

Here we have to observe a difference between the number of verses as deduced from the *Vargas,* and the number stated by Śaunaka. The latter gives the sum total of verses = 10,5801/2, but, immediately afterwards, the sum total of half verses = 21,.2321/2 = 10,616 verses.

How this difference arose it is difficult to say ; but it should be observed that, if we divide the sum total of verses, 21, 232, by 2, we get 10,616 verses, an this number comes very near to 10,622, which the Carana-vyūha gives as the sum total of the verses of the Ṛg-veda. According to the Carana-vyūha (MS. Ch. 785.) the 64 Adhyayas of the Ṛg-veda have:

Verses.

	Verses		*Vargas*		
Vargas consisting of	1	=	1	=	I
”	2	=	2	=	4
”	3 es	=	93	=	279
”	4	=	176	=	704
”	5	=	1,228	=	6,140
”	6	=	357	=	2,142
”	7	=	129	=	903
”	8	=	55	=	440
”	9 *m*	=	1	=	9
			2,042		10,622

The number of padas or words in the Ṛg-veda-saṁhitā is stated as 153,826, which gives an average of between 14 to 15 words to each verse. Another computation brings the number of the charchā-padas (i. e., words which are used in the Krama-pāṭha, omitting the repeated passages or *galitas*) to 110,704, and the number of syllables to 432,000.

In another Anukramaṇī, Śaunaka gives a list of verses, arranged according to the metres in which they are written , and at the end he states the sum total of verses a 10,402; but here again, if we cast up the number of verses in each metre, according to his own statement, we get 10,409 instead of 10,402. These differences are startling if we consider the general accuracy of the exegetical works of the Brāhmaṇas; but they may arise either from faults in the MSS. of the Anukramaṇīs, or from the fact that some of the Khilas were included, though, according to their own professions, both Śaunaka and Kātyāyana would seem to exclude these later hymns from their Anukramaṇīs. The following table will show the distribution of metres according to Śaunaka :

Gāyatrī	...	2,451	Brought forward	...	9793
Uṣṇik	...	341	Aṣṭi	...	6
Anuṣṭubh	...	855	AtyaṣṭI	...	84
Bṛhatī	...	181	Dhṛti	...	2
Paṅkti	...	312	Atidhṛti	...	1
Triṣṭubh	...	4,253	Ekapadā	...	6
Jagatī	...	1,348	Dvipadā	...	17
Atijagatī	...	17	Pragāthā Bārhata	...	194
Śakvarī	...	26	Kākubha	...	55
Atiśakvarī	...	9	Mahā-bārhata	...	251
Carried forward		9,793			10,409

For the Yajur-veda we have three Anukramaṇīs, one for the ātreyīśākhā of the Taittirīyas, the other for the Śākhā of the Carayaṇīyas, the third for the Mādhyandina-śākhā of the

Vājasaneyins. The former[197] differs from other Aunkramaṇīs in so far as it contains an index not of the Saṁhitā only, but also of the Brāhmaṇa and the Āraṇyaka. Its object is not simply to enumerate the Kāṇḍas (Aṣṭakas), Praśnas, Anuvāka and Kāṇḍikas as they follow in the text, but rather to indicate the chief subjects of this Veda, and to bring together the different passages where the same sacrifice with its supplements is treated. Though we do not possess a MS. of the Ātreyī-śākhā, it is possible to identify nearly the whole of the Index with the text of the Saṁhitā[198], the Brāhmaṇa,[199] and the Āraṇyaka[200] which we possess. The Ātreyī-śākhā though not mentioned in the Caraṇa-Vyūha must be considered as a sub-division of the Aukhīya-śākhā; and the Aunkramaṇī says that Vaiśampāyana handed it down to Yāska Paiṅgī, Yāska to Tittiri, Tittiri to' Ukha, and Ukha to Ātreya, who was the author of a Pada-text,[201] while Kuṇḍina composed a Commentary (vṛtti) on the same Śākhā. The Āpastamba-śākhā, of which we possess the complete Brāhmaṇa, is a sub-division of the Khāṇḍikeyas.

There is a curious tradition, preserved in the Kāṇḍānukarma that, although the greater portion of the Ātreyī-śākhā was originally taught by Tittiri, some chapters of it owed their origin to Kaṭha, the founder of the Kāṭhaka śākhā. This assertion is confirmed by Sāyaṇa in his Commentary on the Taittitīyāraṇyaka. The chapters ascribed to Kaṭha and called the Kāṭhakam are found at the end of the Brāhamaṇa and beginning of the Āraṇyaka. They contain

1. The Sāvitrāgnicayana with the Brāhmaṇa, Tait.-br. iii. 10.
2. The Nāciketacayana, Tait.-br. iii. 11.
3. Divahsyenaya iṣṭaya. Tait.-br, iii. 12. 1 & 2.
4. Apadya iṣṭayaḥ. Tait.-br. iii. 12. 3 & 4.
5. Cāturhotra-citi. Tait.-br. iii. 12, 5.
6. Vaisvatrja-citi. Tait.-br. 12.6-9, end of Brāhmaṇa.

7.	Aruṇaketuka-citi.	Tait.-āruyaka, i 1.
8.	Svādhyāya-brāhmaṇa.	Tait.-Āraṇyaka, i. 2.

They are given here as they follow one another in the text of the Āpastamba-śākhā, and this order is confirmed in every particular by Sāyaṇa's Commentary (MS. E. I. H. 1145) which is in fact a commentary intended for the Āpastamba-śākhā of the Taittirīya-brāhmaṇa. According to his introductory remarks prefixed to each Anuvāka, the Savitra-citi occupies the tenth, the Nāciketa-citi the eleventh Prapāṭhaka. In the twelfth Prapāṭ haka, he remarks, the Cāturhotra and Vaiśvasṛja should be explained. But as the *iṣṭis*, called the Divaḥśyenis and Apādyās, form part of the complete Cāturhotra (they stand either in the middle or at the end of it), they are explained first. Thus we find in the beginning of the twelfth Prapāṭhaka (iii. 12.1). the *pratīkas* of the Yajyānuvākyās of the Divaḥśyenis; in iii. 12. 2. the rules for the same iṣṭis; and in the same manner, the Yājānuvākyās of the Apādyās in iii. 12. 3., and the rules in iii. 12, 4. Then follows the Cāturhotra-cayana in iii. 12. 5. and in the last four Anuvākas the Vaiśvasṛija-chayana.

A different order seems to have been observed in the Ātreyī-śākhā of the Taittirīya-brāhmaṇa, for, although the same chapters are here ascribed to Kaṭha, their arrangement must have differed, unless we suppose that the author of the Kāṇḍanukrama introduced an alteration. He writes: "*Tāvat Tittiriḥ provācha*. (Tittiris Taidttīrrya-śākhā-pravartako'nyebhyo munibhyaḥ Śiṣyebhyaḥ provācha.) Athāshṭau Kāṭhakāni (athāmantaram Kāṭhaka-śākhā-pravartakeṇa Kāṭha-ka-muninā proktānyucyante):

1.	Sāvitra, Taitirīya brāhmaṇa,	iii. 10.
2.	Nāciketa ,, ,,	iii. 11.
3.	Cāturhotra ,, ,,	iii. 12. 5.
4.	Vaiśvasṛija	iii. 12. 6-9.
5.	Āruṇa Taitirīya-Āraṇyaka	i. I.
6.	Divaḥśyenīs, Taitirīya brāhmaṇa	iii. 12. 1-2.

7. Apādyās iii. 12. 3-4.

8. Svādhyāya-brāhmaṇa, Taitirīya-Āraṇyaka, i, 2."

The second Anukramaṇīā of the Yajur-veda which we possess, belongs to ihe Cārāyaṇīya-śakha, and is called the Mantrārṣādhyāya.[202] The only copy which we huve of it is found in the same MS. which contains the Carak-śākhā[203] and it is evidently intended as an index to this śākha. Nor is there anything anomalous in this, if we remember that the Cārāyaṇīya-śākhā is a subdivision of the Caraka-śākhā. But what is less intelligible is the title given to the text, which instead, of Yajur-veda, is cniled in the MS. Yajur-veda-kāṭhaka. This title, Kaṭhaka, cannot well refer to the śākhā of the Kaṭhas, for this is itself a sub-division of the Carakas. It must most likely be taken in the same sense in which Kāṭhaka was explained before, *i.e.*, "*Kāṭ hakamuninā proktam*;" though it is strange that the very chapters which in the Āpastambaśākhā of the Taitirīyaka are ascribed to Kaṭha, are wanting in our Śākhā, while all the other sacrifices which are described in the Taittiriyasaṁhitā and Brāhmaṇa, are luid down in very much the same order.

The third Anukramaṇī, that of the Mādhyandina-śākhā of the Vājasaneyaka, is ascribed to Kātyāyana, who is mentioned also as the author of an Anuvākānukramaṇī. It gives the names of the poets, the deifies, and the metres, for all the verses of the Saṁhitā, including the Khila (Adhyāya 26-35.) and the Śukriya portions. (Adhy. 36-40).

For the Sāma-veda we have two classes of Anukramaṇīs, the former more ancient, the latter more modern than those of the other Vedas which we have hitherto examined, One Index to the hymns of the Sāma-veda following the order of the Veya-gāna and Āraṇya-gāna) has been preserved under the name of Ārsheya-brāhmaṇa,[204] a title by which this work is admitted within, the pale of the revealed literature of the Brāhmaṇas, Allusions to the names of poets and deities of different hymns occur in the Brāhmaṇas of other Vedas also; but in none, except the Sāma-veda, have these scattered observations been arranged into regular Anukramaṇīs before the beginning of the Sūtra period, or been incorporated in the body of their revealed literature. What the Brahmāṇas call Śruti or revelation, signifies, as we saw, what is more ancient than the Sūtras; and that the Ārṣeya-brāhmaṇa is earlier at least than Kātyāyana, can fee proved by the fact of Kātyāyana's quoting passages from it,[205] It has been pointed out as a distinguishing mark of the Brāhmṇs of the Sāma-veda that they are never accented, but it is doubtful whether any conclusion could be drawn from this as to their being of later origin than the Brāhamṇas of the other Vedas.[206]

But while the existence of an Ārsheya-brāhmaṇa shows that the Chandogas were the first to compose an index to their sacred literature, we find that their regular Anukramaṇīs' are more modern than those of the Ṛg-veda, and must be referred to a class of works known by the name of Pariśiṣṭas. They are contained in MS. Bodl. Wilson 466, where they form the fifth and sixth of the twenty Pariśiṣṭas attached to the Sāma-veda. There title is, "Naigeyānāmṛkṣu ārṣam," and "Naigeyānām ṛkshu daivatam," and they give respectively the names of the poets find the deities for the verses composing the Ārcika, of the Chandogs according to the Śākhā of the Naigeyas, a subdivision of the Kauthumas. It agrees on the whole, but not in all particulars,[207] with the Śākhā published by Stevenson and Benfey, and it has been supposed that their text is taken from MSS. belonging to the Rāṇāyaṇīya Śākhā. The most characteristic difference between these Pariśishṭas and the Ārṣeya-brāhmaṇa seems to lie in this, that the latter refers to the original prayer-books of the Chandogas, the Veyagāna, and Āraṇya-gāna, while former follow the Saṁhitā, including Ārcika and Staubhika, or as they are also called, Pūrvārcika and Uttarārcika.

For the fourth Veda, the Ātharvarṇa, or Brahma-veda, an Anukramaṇī has been discovered by Professor Whitney in a MS. of the British Muséum, prepared for Col. Polier. A copy of this MS. is found in MS. 2142 of the East India House. It is a complete index to the Saṁhitā in 10 Paṭalas, written in a simple aud intelligible style. Its title is Bṛhat-sarvānukramaṇī.

It is evident, that if it was possible to determine the age of the Anukramaṇīs, we should have a terminus *ad quem* for the Vedic age. The index of tie Ṛg-veda enables us to check almost every syllable of the hymns', and we may safely say that we possess exactly the same number of verses, and words, and syllables in our MSS, of the Ṛg-veda as existed at the time of Kātyāyana. The index of the Ātreyī-śākhā (by Laugākshi ?) authenticates our MSS. not only of the Saṁhitā, but also of the Brāhmaṇa and Āraṇyaka of the Taittirīya-veda, and the index to the Kāṭhaka refers to a work exactly the same as that of which we possess the text in MS. The Ārsheya-brāhmaṇa presupposes the existence of the Gānas of the Sāma-veda, and the Anukramaṇīs of the Naigeyas could only have been written after the text of the more modern Ārcika had branched off into different Śākhās,

The only Anukramaṇīs of which the authors are known are, the Anukramaṇīs of Śaunaka to the Ṛg-veda, and the two Sarvānukramas of Kātyāyana, one to the Ṛg-veda, the other to the white Yajur-veda. We shall see whether it is possible to fix the age of these two writers.

We remarked before, that the Anukraraṇī of Kātyāyana, if compared with the Anuvākānukramaṇī of Śaunaka, shows the same progress in style which we may always observe between these two writers. Śaunaka writes in mixed Ślokas and takes great liberties with the metre; Kātyāyana writes in prose and introduces the artificial contrivances of the later Sūtras. Again, Śaunaka's index follows the original division of the Ṛg-veda into Maṇḍalas, Anuvākas, and Sūktas; Kātyāyana has adopted the more practical and more modern division into Aṣṭakas, Adhyāyas, and Vargas. The number of hymns is the same in Śaunaka and Kātyāyana. They both follow the united Śākhā of the Śākalas and Bāṣkalas, and bring the number of hymns, exclusive of all Khilas, to 1017. Before this union took place, the Bāshkalas counted eight hymns more than the Śākalas, i.e, 1025 instead of 1017 and they read some of the hymns in the first Maṇḍalas in a different order.[209] The khilas, or supplementary hymns, are omitted in the Anukramaṇīs of Śaunaka and Kātyāyana though they were known to both; Śaunaka, however, excludes them more strictly than Kātyāyana.[210] The latter has admitted the eleven Vālkhilya-hymns, and thus brings the total number of hymns to 1028..

From all these indications we should naturally be led to expect that the relation between Śaunaka and Kātyāyana was very intimate, that both belonged to the same Śākhā, and that Śaunaka was anterior to Kātyāyana. We know of only one other writer whose works are equally intended for the united Śākhā of the Śākalas and Bāṣkalas; this is Āśvalāyana, the author of twelve books of Śrauta-sūtras, of four books of Gṛhya-sūtras, and of some chapters in the Aitareyāraṇyaka.[211]

Let us see now, whether these indications can be supported by other evidence.

Ṣaḍguruśiṣya in his Commentary on Kātyāyana's Sarvānukrama, says :

"Śunahotra, the great Muni, was born of Bhāradvāja, and of him was bora Śunahotra, all the world being a witness. Indra himself went to the sacrifice of the Ṛṣi in order to please him. The great *Asuras*, thinking that Indra was alone, and wishing to take him, surrounded the sacri-ficial enclosure. Indra, however, perceived it, and taking the guise of the Ṛṣi, he went away. The *Asuras* seeing the sacrificer again, seized Śunahotra, taking him for Indra. He saw the god that is to be worshipped, and saying 'I am not Indra, there he is, ye fools, not I,' he was released by the *Asuras*, Indra called and spake to him; 'Because you delight in praising, therefore you are called Gṛtsamada, O Ṛṣi; your hymn will be called by the name of *Indrasya indriyam*, the might of Indra. And you, being born in the race of Bhṛgu, shall be Śaunaka, the descendant of Śaunaka, and you shall see again the second Maṇḍala, together with that hymn. He, the Muni Gṛtsāmada, was born again, as commanded by Indra. It was he who saw the great second Maṇḍala of the Ṛg-veda as it was revealed to him together with the hymn Śajanīya; it was he the great Ṛṣi, to whom at the twelve years' sacrifice, Ugraśravas, the son of Romaharṣaṇa, the pupil of Vyāsa recited, in the midst of the sacrifice, the story of the Mahābhārata, together with the tale of the Harivaṁśa, a story to be learnt from Vyāsa alone, full of every kind of excellence, dear to Hari, sweet to hear, endowed with great blessing. It was he who was the lord of the sages, dwelling in the Naimiṣīya forest; he, who to the King Śatānīka, the son of Janamejaya, brought the laws of Viṣṇu, which declare the powers of Hari. That Śaunaka, celebrated among the Ṛṣis as the glorious, having seen the Maṇḍala, and heard the collection of the Mahābhārata, being also the propagator of the laws of Viṣṇu, the great boat on the ocean of existence, was looked upon by the great Ṛṣis as the only vessel in which worshippers might get over the Bahvṛca, with its twenty-one Śākhās, like one who had crossed the Ṛg-veda. There was one Śākhā of Śākala, another of Bāṣkala : taking these two Saṁhitās and the twenty-one Brāhmaṇas, the Aitareyaka, and completing it with others, Śaunaka, revered by numbers of great Ṛṣis, composed the first Kalpa-sūtra."

It need hardly be pointed out that this passage contains a strange and startling mixture of legendary and historical matter, and that it is only the last portion which can be of interest to us. The story of Śaunahotra, the son of Śunahotra, and grandson of Bhāradvāja, being born again as Gṛtsamada-Śaunaka, may have some historical foundation, and the only way in which it can be interpreted, is, that the second Maṇḍala, being originally seen by Gṛtsamada, of the family of Bhṛgu was afterwards preserved by Śaunahotra, a descendant ol Bhāradvāja, of the race of Aṅgiras, who entered the family of Bhṛgu, took the name of Śaunaka, and added one hymn, the twelfth, in praise of Indra, This is partly confirmed by Kātyāyana's Anukramaṇī,[212] and by the Ṛṣyanukramaṇī of Śaunaka.[213] It would by do means follow that Śaunaka was the author of the hymns of the second Maṇḍala. The hymns of that Maṇḍala belong to Gṛtsamada of the Bhṛgu race. But Śaunaka may have adopted that Maṇḍala, and by adding one hymn, may have been said to have made it his own. Again, it does not concern us at present whether Śaunaka, the author of the Kalpa-sūtra, was the same as Śaunaka, the chief of the sages in the Naimiṣīya forest, to whom, during the great twelve-years' sacrifice Ugraśravas related the Mahābhārata, and who became the teacher of Śatānīka, the son of Janamejaya. If this identity could be established, a most important like would be gained, connecting Śaunaka and his literary activity with another period of Indian literature. This point must be reserved for further consideration. At present we are only concerned with Śaunaka, the author of the Kalpa-sūtras and other works composed with a view of facilitating the study of the Ṛgveda.

Ṣaḍguruśiṣya, continues :

"The pupil of Śaunaka was the Reverend Āśvalāyana. He, having learned from Śaunaka all sacred knowledge, made also a Sūtra and taught it, thinking it would improve the understanding and please Śaunaka. Then, in order to please his pupil, Śaunaka destroyed his own Sūtra,[214] which

consisted of a thousand parts find was more like a Brāhmaṇa.'This Sūtra,' like said,'which Āśvalāyana has made and taught, shall be the Sūtra for this Veda.' There are altogether ten books of Śaunaka, written for the preservation of Ṛg-veda;

(i) The index of the Ṛṣis;

(ii) The index of the Metres;

(iii) The index of the Deities;

(iv) The index of the Anuvākas;

(v) The index of the Sūktas;

(vi) The Vidhāna (employment of the Ṛc-verses);

(vii) The employment of the Fādas;[215]

(viii) The Bārhad-daivata;

(ix) The Prātiśākhya[216] of ihe Śaunakas;

(x) His Smārta work an matters of laws[217]

Āśvalāyana having learnt all these ten Sūtras, and knowing also the Gotras, (genealogies[218]), became versed in all the sacrifices by the favour of Śaunaka. The sage Kātyāyana had thirteen books before him; ten of Śaunaka and three of his pupil Āśvalāyana.[219] The latter consisted of the Sūtras in twelve chapters (Śrauta-sūtra), the Gṛhya-sūtras in four chapters, and the fourth Āraṇyaka (of the Aitareyāraṇyaka) by Āśvalāyana.

The sage Kātyāyana, having mastered the thirteen[220] books of Śaunaka and, of his pupil, composed several works himself; the Sūtras of the Vājins,[221] the Upagrantha[222] of the Sāma-veda, the Ślokas[223] of the Smṛti (the Kūrmapradīpa, the Brahma-Kārikās of the Atharvaṇs,[224] and the Mahāvārttika,[225] which was like a boat on the great ocean of Pāṇini's Grammar. The rules promulgated by him were explained by the Reverend Patañjali,[226] the teacher of the Yoga-philosophy, himself the author of the Yoga-śāstra and the Nidāna, a man highly pleased by the great commentary, the work of the descendant of Śāntanu. Now it was Kātyāyana, the great sage, endowed with these numerous excellencies, who composed, by great exertion, this Sarvānukramaṇī. And because it gives the substance of all the works composed by Śaunaka and his pupils, therefore the chief among the Bahvṛcas have called it the General Index."

भरद्वाजसुतो जज्ञे शुनहोत्रो महामुनिः।
शौनहोत्रस्तस्य जज्ञे सर्वलोकस्य पश्यतः।।
इन्द्रो जगाय प्रीत्यर्य पृषेर्यसमपि स्वयम्।
इन्द्रोमेकाकिनं मत्वा जिघृक्षन्तो महासुराः।।
परिवब्रुर्यज्ञवार्ट तदिन्द्रोऽप्यन्वबुध्यत।
इन्द्रोऽपिं यजमानस्य वेषमास्याय निर्गतः।।
यजमानं पुनर्द्दष्टद्वा जगृहुस्ते महासुराः।
शैनहोत्रमिन्द्रबुद्धया यजनीयं ददर्श सः।।
नाहमिन्द्रः स एवाज्ञा नाहमित्यनुवर्णयन्।
मुक्तस्तैरसुरैरिन्द्र आहूयैवमुवाच ह।।
गृणन्मादयसे यस्मात्तस्माद्गृत्समद[२२९] ऋषे।
इन्द्रस्येन्द्रियमित्येत[२३०] न्नम्ना सूक्तं भविष्यति।।
त्वं तु भूत्वा भृगुकुले शुनकाच्छौनको भव।
एतत्सूक्तयुतं पश्य द्वितीयं मण्डलं पुनः।।
स इन्द्रचोदितो जातः पुनर्गृत्समदो मुनिः।
सजनीययुतं[२३१] यो वै द्वितीयं मण्डलं महत्।।
ददर्श यस्मै चाचष्टे[२३२] सत्रे द्वादशवर्षिके।
वेदव्यासप्रसादेन रोमहर्षणनन्दनः।।

उग्रश्रवा व्यासशिष्यः कर्ममध्ये महर्षये।
महाभारतमाख्यानं हरिवंशकथान्वितम्।।
वेदव्यासैकविज्ञेयं[२३३] महागुणगणान्वितम्।
हरिप्रियं श्रुतिसुखं कर्ममध्ये महर्द्धिमत्।।
आसीद्गृहपतिर्यो वै नैमिषारण्यवासिनाम्।
शतानीकाय राज्ञे यो जनमेजयसूनवे।।
उपानयद्विष्णुधर्मान्[२३४] साक्षात्कारकरान्[२३५] हरेः।
स शौनको मुनिगतो श्रूयमाणो महायशाः।।
द्वितीयं मण्डलं दृष्टवा[२३६]। श्रुतभारतसंहितः[२३७]।
संसाराब्धिमहापोतविष्णुधर्मप्रवर्त्तकः।।
एकविंशतिशाखस्य[२३८] बह्वृचस्य महर्षिभिः।
कल्पितः[२३९] कल्पितरोऽभूदृग्वेद इव पारगः।।
शाकलस्य संहितैका वाष्कलस्य तथापरा।
ते संहिते समाश्रित्य ब्राह्मणान्येकविंशतिः।।
एतरेयकमाश्रित्य तदेवान्यैः प्रपूरयन्।
कल्पसूत्रञ्चकाराद्यं[२४०] महर्षगणपूजितः।।
शौनकस्य तु शिष्योऽभूद्भगवानश्वलायनः[२४१]।
स तस्माछ्रुतसर्वज्ञः सूत्रं कृत्वा न्यवेदयत्[२४२]।।
प्रबोधपरिशुद्ध्यर्थं शौनकस्य प्रियं त्विति।
सहस्रखण्डं स्वकृतं सूत्रं ब्राह्मणसन्निभम्।।
शिष्याश्वलायनप्रीत्यै शौनकेन विपाटितम्।
उक्तं तत्तत्कृतं सूत्रमस्य वेदस्य चास्त्विति।।
शौनकीया दश ग्रन्थास्तदा ऋग्वेदगुप्तये।
आर्ष्यनुक्रमणीत्याद्या छान्दसी दैवती तथा।।
अनुवाकानुक्रमणी सूक्तानुक्रमणी तथा।
ऋक्पादयोर्विधाने च[२४३] बार्हद्दैवतमेव च।।
प्रातिशाख्यं शौनकीयं स्मार्त दशममुच्यते।
स सूत्रदशकं ज्ञात्वा तथा[२४४] साकृतगोत्रज्ञः[२४५]।।
शौनकस्य प्रसादेन कर्मज्ञः समपद्यत।
कात्यायनमुनिर्मेने त्रयोदशकमत्र तु।
शौनकीयं च दशकं तच्छिष्यस्य त्रिकं तथा।

द्वादशाध्यायकं सूत्रं चतुष्कगृह्यमेव[२४६] च।।
चतुर्थारण्यकं चेति ह्याश्वलायनसूत्रकम्।
सशिष्यशौनकाचार्यत्रयोदशकविन्मुनिः।।
वाजिनां सूत्रकृत्साम्नामुपग्रन्थस्य कारकः।
स्मृतेश्च कर्ता श्लोकानां भ्राजमानां च[२४७] कारकः।।
अथर्वणां निर्ममे यः सम्यग्वै ब्राह्मकारिकाः।
महावार्त्तिकनौकारः पाणिनीयमहार्णवे।
यत्प्रणीतानि वाक्यानि भगवांस्तु पतञ्जलिः[२४८]।
व्याख्याच्छान्तनवीयेन[२४९] महाभाष्येन[२५०] हर्षितः।।
योगाचार्यः स्वयं कर्ता योगशास्त्रनिदानयोः।
एवङ्गुणगणैर्युक्तः कात्यायनमहामुनिः।।
तपोयोगान्निर्ममे यः सर्वानुक्रमणीमिमाम्।
सशिष्यशौनकाचार्यसर्वग्रन्थार्थवर्तनात्।।
प्राहुर्बह्वृ चसिंहास्तु सर्वानुक्रमणीमिमाम्।

If we accept this statement, of Śaḍgurnśiṣya, and it certainly seems to agree in the main with that we might have guessed from the character of the works, ascribed respectively to Śaunaka, Āśvalāyana and Kātyāyana, we should have to admit at least five generations of teachers and pupils : first Śaunaka; after him Āśvalāyana, in whose favour Śaunka is said to have destroyed one of his works; thirdly, Kātyāyana who studied the works both of Śaunka; and Aśvalāyana ; fourthly, Parañjali, who wrote a commentary on one of Katyayana's works; and lastly Vyāsa, who commented on a work of Patañjali. It does not follow that Kātyāyana was a pupil of Āśvalāyana, or that Patañjali lived immedi-ately after Kātyāyana, but the smallest interval which we can admit between every two of these names is that between teacher and pupil, an interval as large as that between father and son, or rather larger. The question now arises : Can the date of any one of these authors be fixed chronologically ?

Before we attempt to answer this question, it will be necessary to establish the identity of Kātyāyana and Vararuchi.

Kātyāyana was the author of the Sarvānukrāmaṇī, and the same work is quoted us the Sarvānukrāmaṇī of Vararuci,[251] the compiler of the doctrines of Śaunka. In Professor Wilson's Catalogue of the Mackenzie Collection, a Prātisākhya is ascribed to Vararuci, and this can hardly be anything else but the Mādhyandina-Prātiśākhya of Kātyāyana. Hemochandra in his Dictionary gives Vararuci as synonyme of Kātyāyana without any further comment, just as he gives Sālāturīya as a synonyme of Pāṇini.

Let us now consider the information which we receive about Kātyāyana Vararuci from Brahmāhic sources. Somadevabhaṭṭa of Kashmir collected the popular stories current in his time, and published them towards the begin-ning of the twelfth century under the title of Kathā-sarit-sāgara,[252] the Ocean of the rivers of Stories. Here we read that Kātyāyana Vararuci, being cursed by the wife of Śiva, was born at Kauśāmbī, the capital of Vatsa. He was a boy of great talent and extraordinary powers of memory. He was able to repeat to his mother an entire play, after hearing it once in the theatre; and before he was even initiated he was able to repeat the Prātiśākhya which he had heard from Vyāḷi. He was afterwards the pupil of Varṣa, became proficient in all sacred knowledge, actually defeated Pāṇini in grammatical controversy. By the interference of Śiva, however the final victory fell to Pāṇini. Kātyāyana had to appease the anger of Śiva, became himself a student of Pāṇini's Grammar, and completed and corrected it. He afterwards is said to have become minister of King Nanda and his mysterious successor Yogananda at Pāṭaliputra.

We know that Kātyāyana completed and corrected Grammar, such as we now possess it.[253] His Vārttikas are supplementary rules, which show a more extensive and accurate knowledge of Sanskrit than even the work of Pāṇini. The story of the contest between them was most likely intended as a mythical way of explaining this fact. Again we know that Kātyāyana was himself the author of one of the Prātiśākhyas, and Vyāḷi quoted by the authors of the Prātiśākhyas as an earlier authority of the same subject.[254] So far the story of Somadeva agrees with the account of Ṣaḍguruśiṣya and with the facts as we still find them in the works of Kātyāyana. It would be wrong to expect in a work like that of Somadeva historical and chronological facts in the strict sense of the word; yet the mention of King Nanda, who is an historical personage, in connection with our grammarian, many, if properly interpreted help to fix approximately the date of Kātyāyana and his predecessors, Śaunaka and Āśvalāyana. If Somadeva followed the same chronological system as his con temporary and countryman, Kalhaṇa Paṇḍita, the author of the Rājataraṅgiṇi or History of Kashmir, he would, in calling Pāṇini and Kātyāyana, the contemporaries of Nanda and Candragupta, have placed them long before the time which we are wont to call historical.[255] But the name of Candragupta fortunately enables us to check the extravagant system ot Indian chronology. Candragupta, of Pāṭaliputra, the successor Nandas, is Sandrocottus, of Pulibothra, to whom Megasthenes was sent as ambassador from Seleucus Nicator; and, if our classical chronology is right, he must have been king at the turning point of the fourth and third centuries B. C. We shall have to examine hereafter the different accounts which Buddhists and Brāhmaṇas give of Candragupta and his relation to the preceding dynasty of the Nandas. Suffice it for the present that if Candragupta was king in 315, Kātyāyana may be placed, according to our interpretation of Somadeva's story, in the sccond half of the fourth century B. C. We may disregard the story of Somadeva, which actually makes Kātyāyana himself minister of Nanda, and thus would make him on old man at the time of Candragupta's accession to the throne. This is according to its own showing, a mere episode in a ghost story, and had to be inserted in order to connect Kātyāyana's story with other fables of the Kathā-sarit-sāgara. But there still remains this one fact, however slender it may appear, that as late as the twelfth century A.D., the popular tradition of the Brāhmaṇas connected the famous grammarians Kātyāyana and Pāṇini wilh that period of their history which immediately preceded the rise of Candragupta and his Śūdra dynasty; and this, from an

European point of view we must place in the second half of the fourth century B. C.

The question now arises, can this conjectural date, assigned to Kātyāyana, be strengthened by additional evidence ? Professor Böhtlingk thought that this was possible; and he endeavoured to show that the Commentary of Patañjali, which embraces both the Vārttikas of Kātyāyana and the Pāṇini, was known in the middle of the second century B. C. It is said in the history of Kashmir, that Abhimanyu, the king of Kashmir, sent for Brāhmaṇas to teach the Mahābhāṣya in his kingdom. Abhimanyu, it is true, did not reign, as Professor Böhtlingk supposed, in the second century B. C, but, as has been proved from coins by Professor , in the first century A. D, But even thus this argument is important. In the history of Indian literature dates are mostly so precarious that a confirmation even within a century or two is not to be despised, The fact that Patañjali's immense commentary on Pāṇini and Kātyāyana had become so famous as to be imported by royal authority into Kashmir in the first half of the first century A. D., shows at least that we cannot be very far wrong in placing the composition of the original grammar and of the supplementary rules pf Kātyāyana on the threshold of the third century B. C. At what time the Mahābhāshya was first composed it is impossible to say. Patañjali, the author of the Great Commentary, is sometimes identified with Piṅgala; and on this view, as Piṅgala is called the younger brother, or at least the descendant of Pāṇini,[256] it might be supposed that the original composition of like Mahābhāshya belonged to the third century. But the identity of Piṅgala and Patañjali is far from probable, and it would be rash to use it as a foundation for other calculations.

It will readily be seen how entirely hypothetical all these arguments are. If they possess any force it is this, that in spite of the conflicting statements of Brāhmaṇical, Buddhist, and European scholars, nothing has been brought forward as yet that would render the date here assigned to Kātyāynna impossible. Nay more; if we place Kātyāyana in the second half of the fourth century, Āśvalāyana, the predecessor of Kātyāyana, about 350, and Śaunaka, the teacher of Āśvalāyana, about 400; and if then, considering the writers of Sūtras anterior to Śaunaka and posterior to Kātyāyana, we extend the limits of the Sautra period of literature from 600 to 200, we are still able to say, that there is no fact in history or literature that would interfere with such an arrangement. As an experiment, therefore, though as no more than an experiment, we propose to fix the years 600 and 200 B. C. as the limits of that age during which the Brāhmaṇic literature was carried on in the strange style of Sūtras.

In order to try the strength of our supposition we shall ourselves attempt the first attack upon it.

There is a work called the Uṇādi-sūtras, which as it is quoted under this name by Pāṇini, must have existed previous to his time. The author is not known. Among the words formation of which is taught in the Uṇādi-sūtras,[257] we find (iii. 140) dīnāraḥ, a golden ornament; (iii. 2) Jinaḥ synonymous with Arhat, a Buddhist saint; (iv. 184) tirīṭam, a golden diadem; (iii. 25) stupaḥ, a pile of earth.

The first of these words, dīnāra, is derived by the author of the Uṇādi-sūtras from a Sanskrit root, dīn. By other grammarians it is derived from dīna, poor, and ri, to go, what goes or is given to the poor. It is used sometimes in the sense of ornaments and seals of gold. These derivations, however, are clearly fanciful, and the Sanskrit dīnāra is in really the Latin *denarius*[258]. Now, if Pāṇini lived in the middle of the fourth century B. C, and if the Uṇādi-sūtras were anterior to Pāṇini, how could this Roman word have found its way into the Uṇādi-sūtras ? The word denarius, is not of so late a date in India as is generally supposed. Yet the earliest document where it occurs is the Sanchi inscription No. 1.[259] Burnouf remarked that he never found the word *dīnīra* used in what he considered the ancient Buddhist Sūtras. It occurs in the Avadāna-śataka, and in the Divyāvadāna. It would seem to follow, therefore, either that the Uṇādi-sūtras and Pāṇini must be placed later than

Candragupta, or that the Sūtra in which this word is explained is spurious. It would not be right to adopt the latter supposition without showing some cause for it. It is well known that in a literature which is chiefly preserved by oral tradition, corrections and additions are more easily admitted than in works existing in MS. The ancient literature of India was continually learnt by heart; and even at the present day when MSS. have become so common, some of its more sacred portions must still be acquired by the pupil from the mouth of a teacher, and not from MSS. If new words, therefore, had been added to the language of India after the first composition of the Uṇādi-sūtras, there would be nothing surprising in a Sūtra being added to explain such words. Happily, however, we are not left in this instance to mere hypothesis. Ujjvaladatta, the author of commentary on the Uṇādi-sūtras, forms a favourable exception to most Sanskrit commentators, in so far as he gives us in his commentary some critical remarks on the readings of MSS. which he consulted. He states in his introduction that he has consulted old MSS. and commentaries, and he evidently feels conscious of the merit of his work, when he says, "If anybody, after having studied this commentary of mine, suppresses my name in order to put forth his own power, his virtuous deeds will perish."[260] Now in his remarks on our Sūtra, Ujjvaladatta says, "Dinära means a gold ornament, but this Sūtra is not to be found in Sūtīvṛtti and Devavṛtti.'[261] If, therefore, the presence of this word in the Uṇādi-sūtras would have overthrown out calculations as to the age of Pāṇini and his predecessor who wrote the Sūtras, the absence of it except in one Sūtra, which is proved to be of later date, must serve to confirm our opinion, Cosmus Indicopleustes remarked that the Roman denarius was received all over the world; and how the denarius came to mean in India a gold ornament we may learn from a passage in the "Life of Mahāvira."[262] There it is said that a lady had around her neck a string of grains and golden dinars, and Stevenson adds that the custom of stringing coins together, and adorning with them children especially, is still very common in India.

That Ujjvaladatta may be depended upon when he makes such statements with regard to MSS, or commentaries, collated by himself, can be proved by another instance. In the Uṇādi-sūtras IV, 184, we read; "*kṛtṛkṛpibhyaḥ kīṭan*," Out of the three words of which the etymology is given in this Sūtra, *kṛpītam*, water, and *kirīṭam*, a crest, are known as ancient words. The former occurs in the Gaṇa Kṛpaṇīdi (Pān. VIII. 2.18.1); the other in the Gaṇa *arddharcādi*. The third word, however, *kirāṭa*, a tiara, has never been met with in works previous to Pāṇini. Now, with regard to this word, Ujjvaladatta observes that it is left out in the Nyāsa.[263]

The authority of this work, a commentary by Jinendra on the Kāśikāvṛitti, would, by itself, be hardly of sufficient weight; but on referring to the MS. of Mahābhāṣya at the Bodleian Library, I find that there also the Sūtra is quoted exactly as Ujjvaladatta said, *i. e.*, without the root from which *kirīṭa* is derived. Having thus found Ujjvaladatta trustworthy and accurate in his critical remarks, we feel inclined to accept his word, even where we cannot control him, or where the presence of certain words in the Sūtras might be explained without having recourse to later interpolations. Thus *stūpaḥ*, which occurs III. 25, might be explained as simply meaning a heap of earth. Nay, it is a word which, in its more general sense, is found in the Veda. Yet the most common meaning of stūpa is a Buddhist monument, and as we are told by Ujjvala, that this word does not occur in the Satīvṛtti, and that in the Sarvasva it is derived in a different manner, we can have little doubt that it, was not added till after the general spreading of Buddhism and the erection of Topes in India; a negative argument which gives additional strength to the supposition that the original Uṇādi-sūtras were composed before that period.[264]

To add one more instance. In all the editions of the Uṇādi-sūtras, Jina occurs as the name of the founder of a Bauddha sect. As many scholars have assigned to Jina and the Jainas a very modern date, the presence of this name might seem to throw considerable doubt on the antiquity ascribed to the Uṇādi-sūtras. In a passage of Sāyaṇa, however (Ṛv. i. 61. 4.), where he has occasion to quote the Sūtra containing, among other words, the etymology of Jina, all the MSS. omit the root *ji*, from which Jina is said to he derived. It is equally omitted in Nṛsiṃha's Svaramañjarī[265].

The test which has thus been applied to our chrono-logical arrangement of the Sūtra literature in general, in the case of the Uṇādi-sūtras, so far from invalidating, has rather strengthened our argument for placing the whole literature of the Sūtras, at least of those which are connected with the Vedas, between the years 600 and 200 B,C.

PARIŚIṢṬAS

There is one class of works which must be mentioned before we leave the Sūtra period, the so-called Parīśiṣṭas. They are evidently later than the Sūtras, and their very name, Paralipomena, marks their secondary importance. They have, however, a character of their own, and they represent a district period of Hindū literature, which, though it is of less interest to the student, and though it shows clear traces of intellectual and literary degeneracy, is not on that account to be overlooked by the historian. Some of the more substantial Pariśiṣṭas profess to be composed by authors whose names belong to the Sūtra period. Thus Śaunaka is called the author of the Caraṇa-vyūha by the commentator of Pāraskara's Gṛhya-sūtras, Rāma-kṛshṇa[265] (MS. E. I. H. 440. 577. 912); a writer no doubt quite untrustworthy where he gives his own opinions, but yet of some importance where he quotes the opinions of others. Kātyāyana is quoted as the author of the Chhandoga-pariśiṣṭa.[266] The same Kuśika, who is known as the author of the Sūtras for the Ātharvaṇa, is mentioned as the author of the Atharvaṇa-pariśiṣṭas also. Other Pariśishṭas though not ascribed to Kātyāyana, are said to be composed in accordance with his opinions.[267] Again, while the Gṛhya-sūtras of the Chandogas are acknowledged as the work of Gobhila, a Pariśiṣṭa on the same subject is ascribed to the son of Gobhila.[268] The names of Śaunaka and Kātyāyana are frequently invoked at the beginning or end of these works, and though some of them appear to us simply useless mid insipid, it is not to be denied that others contain information which we should look for in vain in the Sūtras. Their style is less concise than that of the Sūtras. The simple Anuṣṭub Śloka preponderates, and the metre is more regular than that of the genuine Anuṣṭubh compositions of Śaunaka. Their style resembles that of the Bārhad-daivata and Ṛg-vidhāna works originally composed by Śaunaka, handed down to us, as it would seem, in a more modern form. But on the other side the Pariśiṣṭas have not yet fallen into that monotonous uniformity which we find in works like the Mānavadharma-śāstra, the *Padhatis*, or the later Purāṇas; and passages from them are literally quoted in the Purāṇas. The Pariśiṣṭas, therefore, may be considered the very last outskirts of Vedic literature, but they are Vedic in their character, and it would be difficult to account for their origin at any time except the expiring moments of the Vedic age.

The following argument may serve to confirm the favourable view which I take of some of the Pariśishṭas, Besides the MSS. of the Caraṇa-vyūha, there is a printed edition of it in Rājā Rādhākanta Deva's Sabda-kalpadruma, This printed test is evidently taken from more modern MSS. It quotes seventeen instead of fifteen Śākhās of the Vājasaneyins; whereas the original-number of fifteen is confirmed by our MSS. of the Caraṇa-vyūha, by the Pratijñā-pariśiṣṭa, and even by so late a work as the Visnu-purāṇa (p. 281), We may therefore suppose that at the time when the Pariśiṣṭa, called the Caraṇa-vyūha, was originally composed, these two additional Śākhā did not yet exist. Now one of them is the Śākhā of the Kātyāyanīyas, a Śākhā, like many of those mentioned in the Purāṇas, founded on Sūtras, not on Brāhmaṇas. The fact, therefore, of this modern Śākhā not being mentioned in the original Caraṇa-vyūha serves as an indication that at the time of the original composition of that Pariśishṭa, sufficient time had not yet elapsed to give to Kātyāyana the celebrity of being the founder of a new Śākhā.

On the other hand it should be stated that Pāṇini does not seem to have known literary works called Parisiahtas.[269]

The number of Pariśiṣṭas is frequently stated at eighteen. This may have been their number at some time, or for one particular Veda, but it is now considerably exceeded, The Caraṇa-vyūha, itself a Pariśishṭa gives the same number; but it seems to speak of the Pariśishṭas of the Yajur-veda only. There is a collection of Pariśiṣṭas for each Veda. Works, such as the Bahvṛca Pariśiṣṭa, Sāṅkhāyana-Pariśiṣṭa, Āśvalāyana-Gṛhya-pariśiṣṭa, must be ascribed to the Ṛg-veda. A MS. (Bodl. 466.) contains a collection of Pariśiṣṭas which belong to the Sāma-veda, At the end of the first treatise'it is and "*iti Sāmagānām chandaḥ Samāptaṁ,*" "here end the metres of the Sāma-singers."[270] Other treatises begin with the invocation, "Namaḥ Sāmavedāya." The second is called Kratu-saṅgraha, on sacrifices; the third, Viniyoga-saṅgraha, on the employment of hymns; the fourth, Somotpattiḥ, on the origin of Soma. The filth and sixth treatises contain the index to the Ārchika of the Sāma-veda after the Naigeya-śākhā. As no pointed allusions to other Vedas occur in these tracts, there can be little doubt that the whole collection of these Pariśiṣṭas may be classed, as Sāma-veda literature. The Chandoga-pariśiṣṭa, however, which is commonly ascribed to Kātyāyana, is not found in this MS. The Pariśiṣṭas of the Yajur-veda are enumerated in the Caraṇa-vyūha, and will have to be examined presently. Those of the Ātharvaṇa are estimated by Professor Weber at seventy-four,[271] and are said to be written in the form of dialogues, in a style similar to that of the Purāṇas, and sometimes, we are told, agreeing literally with chapters of the astrologicial Saṁhitās.

According to the Caraṇa-vyūha[272] the following ate the eighteen Pariśiṣṭas of the Yajur-veda :

(i) The Yūpalakṣaṇam; according to Vyāsa's Caraṇa-vyūha, the Upajyotiṣam.

(ii) The Chāgalakṣaṇam; Māṅgala-lakṣaṇam, (Vyāsa).

(iii) The Pratijñā; Pratijñānuvākyam ? (Vyāsa).

(iv) The Anuvākasāṅkhya; Parisāṅkhya (Vyāsa),

(v) The Caraṇa-vyūhaḥ : Caraṇa-vyūhaḥ (Vyāsa).

(vi) The Śrāddhakalpaḥ; Śrāddhakalpaḥ (Vyāsa).

(vii) The Śulvikāni or Śulvāni.

(viii) The Pārṣadam.

(ix) The Ṛgyajūṁṣi.

(x) The Iṣṭakāpūraṇam.

(xi) The Pravarādhyāyaḥ; Pravarādhyāyaḥ (Vyāsa, No.7)

(xii) The Uktha-śāstram; śāstram (Vyāsa, No. 8),

(xiii) The Kratusāṅkhya; Kratu (Vyāsa, No. 9).

(xiv) The Nigamāḥ; Āgamaḥ (Vyāsa, No. 10).

(xv) The Yajñapārśve or pārśvam; Yajñam (Vyāsa, No. 11); Pārśvān (Vyāsa, No. 12).

(xvi) The Hautrakam; Hautrakam (Vyāsa, No. 13).

(xvii) The Prasavotthānam; Paśavaḥ (Vyāsa, Mo, 14); Ukthāni, (Vyāsa, No. 15).

(xviii) The Kūrma-lakṣaṇam, (Vyāsa, No. 16),

A similar order has evidently been followed, in a collection of the Parisiṣṭas, forming part of Professor Wilson's valuable collection of MSS. now deposited in the Bodleian Library. Thc MS., however, is incomplete, and seems to have been compiled by a person ignorant of Sanskrit from another MS., the leaves of which had been in confusion. Most of the MSS. of these Pariśiṣṭas are carelessly copicd, whcrcas thc MSS. of the Sūtras are generally in excellent condition. The MSS, which Rāja Rādhākāntadeva used seem to have been in an equally bad state, if wc may judge from tbe various readings which he occasionally mentions.[273] But although the Bodleian MS. leaves much to desire, it serves at least to support the authenticity of the titles given in the MS. of the Caraṇa-vyūha against the blunders of the printed test. We find there;

(i) The Yūpalakṣaṇam,[274] a short treatise on the manner of preparing the sacrificial post.

(ii) The Chāga-Lakṣaṇam,[275] on animals fit for sacrifies.

(iii) The Pratijña,[276] begins with giving some definition of sacrificial terms, but breaks off with the fourth leaf, whereas the Pravarādhyāya (No. 11) had already been commenced on the third, and is afterwards carried on the fifth leaf. Thus we lose from tbe fourth to the eleventh Pariśiṣṭa, which formed part of the original MS. if wo may judge from the fact that the Pravarādhyāya is here also called the eleventh Pariśiṣṭa.

(iv) The Anuvāka-saṅkhyā exists in MS. E. I. H. 965,

(v) The Caraṇa-vyūhaḥ is found in numerous copies.

(vi) The Śrāddhakalpaḥ exists in MS. E. I. H, 1201, and MS. Chambers 66. It is there ascribed lo Kātyāyana.

There is also among the Chambers MSS. at Berlin (292-294) a Śrāddha-kalpa-bhāṣya ascribed to Gobhila.

(vii) The Śulvikāni are found in MS. Chambers 66, and a Śulvadīpikā, ES. E. I. H. 1678.

(viii) The Pārṣadam, This must not be mistaken for a Prātiśākhya, nor would it be right to call the Prātiśākhyas Pariśiṣṭas. The Pārṣada is a mnch smaller work, as may be seen from a MS. in the Royal Library at Berlin, Chambers 378.

(ix) The Ṛgyajūṁshi is the only Pariśishṭas, that cannot be verified in MS,; there is no reason for supposing that it was an Anukramaṇī either of ihe Yajur-veda or Ṛg-veda.

(x) The Iṣṭakāpūraṇam has been preserved in MS. Chambers 389 with a commentary by Karka, and in MS. Chambers 392, with a commentary by Yājñikadeva.

(xi) The Pravarādhyāyaḥ is found again in our own MS., and is followed by a small tract, the Gotra-nirṇayaḥ. The seven principal Pravaras are those of the Bhṛgus,

Aṅgiras, Viśvāmitras, Vaśiṣṭhas, Kāśyapas, Atris, and Agastis. The eight founders of Gotras or families are Jamadagni, Bhāradvāja, Viśvāmitra, Atri, Gautama, Vasiṣṭha, Kāśyapa and Agastya,[276] The whole treatise, of which more hereafter, is ascribed to Kātyāyana.[278]

(xii) The Uktha-śāstram is found in our MS. So is

(xiii) The Kratusaṅkhya, which gives an enumeration of the principal sacrifices.

(xiv) The Nigama-pariśiṣṭa, is the last in our MS. It contains a number of Vedic words with their explanations, and forms a useful appendix to Yāska's Nirukta. It alludes not only to the four castes, but ths names of the mixed castes also, according to the Anuloma and Pratiloma order, ate mentioned.

The four Isst Pariśiṣṭas are wanting in our MS.

The fifteenth, however, tlie Yajñapārśvarn is found in MS. E. I. H. 1729, Chambers, 253; the sixtenth, the Hautrakam, exists with a commentary in MS. Chambers 669. The two lost Pariśishṭas have not yet been met with in MS. but we may probably form some idea of the last the Kūrma-lakṣaṇam, from some chapters of Varāhamihira's Bṛhatsaṁhitā, where we find both a Kūrma-vībhāgaḥ and a Kūrma-lakṣaṇam, the last being there followed by a chapter, called by the same name as the second Parisiṣṭa, Chāga-lakṣaṇam.

Although there is little of real importance to be learned from those Pariśiṣṭas, the fact of their existence is important history of the progress and decay of the Hindū mind, As in the first or Chandas period, we see the Āryan settlers of India giving free utterance to their thoughts and feelings, and thus creating unconsciously a whole world of religious, moral, and political ideas; as we find them again during the second or Mantra period, carefully collecting their harvest; and during the third or Brāhmaṇa period busily occupied in systemstising and interpreting the strains of their forefathers, which had already become unintelligible and sacred; as in the fourth or Sūtra period we see their whole energy employed in simplifying the complicated system of the theology and the ceremonial of the Brāhmaṇas; so we shall have to recognise in these Pariśiṣṭas a new phase of the Indian mind, marked by a distinct character, which must admit of historical explanation. The object of the Pariśiṣṭas is to supply information on theological or ceremonial points which had been passed over in the Sūtras, most likely because they were deemed of sufficient importance, or because they were supposed to be well known to those more immediately concerned. But what most distinguishes the Pariśiṣṭas from the Sūtras is this, that they treat everything in a popular and superficial manner; as if the time was gone, when students would spend ten or twenty years of their lives in fathoming the mysteries and mastering the intricacies of the Brāhmaṇa literature. A party driven to such publication as the Pariśiṣṭas, is a party fighting a losing battle. We see no longer that self-complascent spirit which pervades the *Brāhmaṇas*. The authors of the Brāhmaṇas felt that whatever they said must be believed whatever they ordained must be obeyed. They are frightened by no absurdity, and the word "impossible" seems to have been banished from their dictionary. In the Sūtras we see that a change has taken place. Their authors seems to feel that the public which they address will no longer listen to endless theological swaggering. There may have been deep wisdom in the Brāhmaṇas, and their authors may have sincerely believed in all they said; but they evidently calculated on a submissiveness on the part of the pupils or readers, which only exists in countries domineered over by priests or professors. The authors of the Sūtras have learned that people will not listen to wisdom unless it is clothed, in a garb of clear argument I and communicated in intelligible language. Their words contain all that is essential in the Brāhmaṇas, but they give it in a practical, concise and deinite from. These works were written at a time when the Brāhmaṇa were fighting their first battles against the popular doctrines of Buddha. They were not yet afraid. Their language is firm, thought it is no longer inflated, "Buddhism," as Burnouf says,[279] soon grew into a system of etisy devotion and found numerous recruits among those who were frightened by the difficulties of Brāhmaṇical science. At the same time that

Buddhism attracted the ignorant among the Brāhmaṇas, it received with open arms the poor and the miserable of all classes." It was to remove, or at least to simplify, the difficulties of their teaching, that men like Śaunaka and Kātyāyana adopted the novel style of the Sūtras. Such changes in the sacred literature of a people are not made without an object, and the object of the Sūtras, as distinct from that of the Brāhmaṇas, could be no other than to offer practical manuals to those who were discouraged by too elaborate treatises, and who had found a shorter, way to salvation opened to them by the heretical preaching of Buddha. After the Sūtras there is no literature of a purely Vedic character except the Pariśiṣṭas. They still presuppose the law or the Sūtras, and the faith of the Brahmanas. There is as yet no trace of any being accorded to Śiva or Viṣṇu or Brāhmā. New gods, however, are mentioned; vulgar or popular ceremonies are alluded to. The castes have become more marked and multiplied. The whole intellectual atmosphere is still Vedic, and the Vedic ceremonial, the Vedic theology, the Vedic language seem still to absorb the thoughts of the authors of the Pariśiṣṭas. Any small matter that had been over looked by the authors of the Sūtras is noted down as a matter of grave importance. Subjects on which general instructions were formerly considered sufficient, are now treated in special treatises, intended, for men who would no longer take the trouble of reading the whole system of the Brāhmaṇic ceremonial. The technical and severe language of the Sūtras was exchanged for a free and easy style, whether in prose or metre; and however near in time the Brāhmaṇas may place the authors of the Sūtras and some of the Pariśiṣṭas, certain it is that no man who had mastered the Sūtra style would ever have condescended to employ the slovenly diction of the Pariśiṣṭas. The change in the position and the characters of the Brāhmaṇas, such as we find them in the Sūtras, and such as we find them again in the Pariśiṣṭas, has been rapid and decisive. The men who could write such, works were aware of their own weakness, and had probably suffered many defeats. The world around them was moving in a new direction, and the old Vedic age died away in important twaddle.

Consideration like these, in addition to what we found, before in inquiring into the age of Kātyāyana, tend to fix the Sūtra period, as a phase in the literary history of India, as about contemporaneous with the first rise of Buddhism; and they would lead us to recognise in the Pariśiṣṭas the exponents of a later age, that had witnessed the triumphs of Buddhism and the temporary decay of Brāhmaṇic learning and power. The real political triumph of Buddhism dates from Aśoka and his council, about the middle of the third Century B. C. and while most of the Vedic Sūtras belong to this and the preceding centuries, none of the Pariśiṣṭas were probably written before that time.

Before the Council of Pāṭaliputra the Buddhists place, indeed, 300 years of Buddhist history, but that history was clearly supplied from their own heads and not from authentic documents. Buddhism, up to the time of Aśoka, was but one out of many sects established in India. There had been as yet no schism, but only controversy, such as we find in the Brāhmaṇas themselves between different schools and paries. There were as yet no *Brāhmaṇas* opposed to Buddhists, in the later sense of the world. No separation had as yet taken place, and the greatest reformers at the time of Buddha were reforming Brāhmaṇas. This is ackowledged in the Buddhist writings, though they probably were not written down before Aśoka's Council. But even then Buddha is represented as the pupil of the *Brāhmaṇas*, and no slur is cast on the gods and the song of the Veda. Buddha, according to his own canonical biographer, learned the Ṛg-veda and was proficient in all the branches of Brāhmanic lore. His pupils were many of them Brāhmaṇas; and no hostile feeling against the Brāhmaṇas find utterance in the Buddhist Canon. This forms a striking contrast with the sacred literature of the Jains. The Jains, who are supposed to have made their peace with the Brāhmaṇas, yet in their sacred works, written towards the beginning of the fifth century A. D., treat their opponents with marked disrespect. Their great hero Mahāvira, though at first conceived by a Brāhmaṇa woman, is removed from. her womb and transferred to the womb of a Kṣatriya woman, for "surely," as Sakko (Indra) says,[280] "such a thing as this if has never happened in past, happens not in present, nor will happen in future time, that an Arhat, a Cakravarti, a Baladeva, or a Vasudeva should be born in a low caste family, it servile family, a degraded family, a poor family, a mean family, a beggar's family,; but on the contrary, in all time, past, present, and to come, an Aṃat, a Cakravarti, a Vasudeva, receives birth in a noble family, an honourable family, an royal family, Kṣatriya family, as in the family of Ikṣvāku, or the Harivaṁśa or some such family of pure deseent." Now this is mere party insolence, intelligible in the fifth century A. D., when the *Brāhmṇas*, as a, party, were re-establishing their hierarchical sway. Nothing of the kind is to be found in lhe canoṇical books of the Buddhists. Buddha had his opponents, and among them chiefly the Tīrthakas : but so had all eminent sages of whom we read in the Brāhmaṇas. But Buddha had also his friends followers, and they likewise were Brāhmaṇas and Ṛṣis; some of them accepted his doctrines, not excluding the abolition of caste. Buddhism, in its original form, was only a modification of Brāhmaṇism. It grew up slowly and imperceptibly find its very founder could hardly have been aware of the final results of his doctrines. Before the time that Buddhism became a political power, it had no history, no chronology, it hardly had a name. We hear nothing of Buddhas in the Brāhmaṇas, though we meet there with doctrines decidedly Buddhistic, The historical existence of Buddhism begins with Aśoka and the only way to fix the real date of Aśoka is by connecting him with Candragupta, his second predecessor, the Sandrocottus of the Greeks. To try to fix it according to the early Buddhist chronology would be as hopeless us fixing the date of Alexander according to the chronology of the Purāṇas.

It is possible to discover in the decaying literature of Vedic Brahmāṇism the contemporaneous rise of a new religion, of Buddhism. Every attempt to go beyond, and to bring the chronology of the Buddhists and Brāhmaṇas into harmony has proved a failure. The reason, I believe, is obvious. The Brāhmaṇas had a kind of vague chronology in the different capitals of their country. They remembered the names of their kings, find they endeavoured to remember the years of their reigns. But to note the year in which an individual such as Gautama Śākyasiṁha, was born, however famous he may have been in his own neighbourhood or even in more distant Pariṣads, would have entered as little into their thoughts as the Romans, or even the Jews, thought of preserving the date of the birth of Jesus before he had I become the founder of religion, Buddha's immediate followers may have recollected and handed down, by oral communication, the age at which Buddha died; the age of his disciples too may have been recollected, together with the names of some local Rājas who patronised Buddha and his friends; but never, until the adoption of Buddhism as the state religion by Aśoka, could there have been any object in connecting the lives of Buddha and his disciples with the chronology of the Solar or Lunar Dynasties of India. When, at the time of Aśoka, it became necessary to give an account of the previous history of Buddhism, the chronology then adopted for the early centuries of that failh was necessarily of a purely theoretical kind. We possess more than one system of Buddhist chronology, but none of them can be considered authentic witb regard to the times previous to Aśoka, the second successor of Candragupta. There is the system of the Southern Buddhists, framed in Ceylon; there are the various systems of the Northern Bnddhisis, prevalent in Nepal, Tibet, and China; and the system of the Purāṇas, if system it can be called, in which Śākya is made the father of his father, and grandfather of his son. To try to find out which of these chronological systems is the most plausible: seems useless, and it can only make confusion worse confounded if we attempt a combination of the three. It has been usual to prefer the chronology of Ceylon, which places Buddha's death in 543 B. C. But the principal argument in favour of this date is extremely weak. It is said that the fact of the Ceylonese era being used as an era for practical purposes speaks in favour of its correctness. This may be true with regard to the times after the reign of Aśoka. In historical times any era, however fabulous its beginning, will be practically useful; but no conclusion can be drawn from this, its later use, as to the correctness of its beginning. As a conventional era, that of

Ceylon may be retained, but until new evidence can be brought forward to substantiate the authenticity of the early history of Buddhism as told by the Ceylonese priests, it would be rash to use the dates of the Southern Buddhists as a corrective standard for those of the Northern Buddhists or of the Brāhmaṇas. Each of these chronological systems must be left to itself. They start from different premises, and necessarily arrivé at different results, The Northern Buddhists founded their chronology on a reported prophecy of Buddha, that "a thousand years after his death his doctrines would reach the Northern countries."[281] Buddhism was definitely introduced into China, in the year 61 A. D; hence the Chinese fix the date of Buddha's death about one thousand years anterior to the Christian era. The variations of the date, according to different Chinese authorities, are not considerable and may easily be explained by the uncertainty of the time at which Buddhism found its way successively into the various countries north of India, and at last into China. Besides 950 or 949 B. C.,[282] which are the usual dates assigned to Buddha's death by Chinese authorithes, we may mention the years 1130, 1045, 767, for each of which the same claim has been set up. The year 1130 rests on the authority of Tchao-chi, as quoted by Matouanlin in the annals of the Soui.[283] Fahian, also, seems to have known this date; for, according to his editor, he placed the death of Buddha towards the beginning of the dynasty Teheu, and this, according to Chinese chronology, tool; place in 1122.[284] In another place, however, Fahian, speaking of the spreading of Buddhism towards the north, places this event 300 years after Buddha's Nirvāṇa, or in the reign of the Emperor Phing-Wang. As this emperor reigned 770-720, Fahian would seem to have dated the Nirvāṇa somewhere between 1070 and 1020. The date 767 rests on the authority of Matounlin.[285] From Tibetan books no less than fourteen dates have been collected[286] and the Chinese pilgrims who visited India found it impossible to fix on any one date as established on solid evidence. The list of the thirty-three Buddhist patriarchs, first published by Rémurāt (Mélanges Asiatiqnes, i. p. 113), gives the date, of their deaths from Chakia-mouni, who died 950 B. C, to Soui-neng, who died 713 A.D., and bears, like everything Chinese, the character of the most exact chronologicul accuracy. The first link, however, in this long chain of patriarchs is of doublful character, and the lifetime of Buddha, from 1029 to 950, rests on his own prophecy, that a, Millennium would elapse from his death to the conversion of China. If, therefore, Buddha was a, true prophet he must have lived about 1,000 B .C., and this date once established, everything else had to give way before it. Thus Nāgārjuna, called by the Chinese Nāgā Koshuna, or Loung-chou, is placed in their own traditional chronology, which they borrowed from the Buddhists in Northern India, 400 years after the" Nirvāṇa[287] The Tibetans assign the same date to him[288]. In the list of the patriarchs?, however, he occupies the fourteenth place, and dies 738 years after Buddha. The twelfth patriarch, Maning (Deva Bodhistttva), is traditionally placed by the Chinese 300 years alter Buddha. In the list, of the patriarchs he dies 618 years after the Nirvāṇa.

But if in this manner the starting point of the Northern Buddhist choronalogy turns out to he merely hypothetical, based as it is on a prophecy of Buddha, it will be difficult to avoid the same conclusion with regard to the date assigned to Buddha's death by the Buddhists of Ceylon and of Burmah and other countries which received their canonical books from Ceylon. The Ceylonese possess a trustworthy and intelligible chronology beginning with the year 161 B. C.[289] Before that time their chronology is traditional, and full of absurdities. According to Professor Lassen, we ought to suppose that the Ceylonese, by some means or other, were in possession of the right date of Buddha's death; and as there was a prophecy of Buddha that Vijaya should land in Ceylon on the same day on which Buddha entered the Nirvāṇa[290] we are further asked to believe that the Ceylonese historians placed the founder of the Vijayan dynasty of Ceylon in the year 343, in accordance with their sacred chronology. "We are not told, however, through what channel the Ceylonese could have received their information as to the exact date of Buddha's death, and although Professor Lassen's hypothesis would be extremely convenient, and has been acquiesced in my most Sanskrit scholars, it would not be honest were we to conceal from ourselves or from others that the first and most important link in the Ceylonese, as well as in ihe Chinese chronology, is extremely weak, All we know for certain is, that the Ceylonese had an historical chronology after the year 161 B. C., that is to say, long before the Brāhmaṇas or Buddhists of the North can show anything but tradition. If, then, the exact Ceylonese chronology begins with 161 B. C, it is but reasonable to suppose that there existed in Ceylon a traditional native chronology extending beyond that date; and that, at all events, the first conquest of Ceylon, the establishment of the first dynasty, had some date, whether true or false; assigned to it in the annals of the country. Vijay, the founder of the first dynasty, means Conquest, and such a person mast likely never existed. But his name and fame belong to Ceylon; and even the latest tradition have never connected him with the Buddhist dynasties, of India. He is called in the Mahāvaṁśa, the son of Siṃhabāhu, the sovereign of Lain, (supposed to be a subdivision of Magadha, near the Gaṇḍakī river), and he is connected by a miraculous genealogy with the kings of Baṅga (Bengal) and Kaliṅga (Northern Circars), but not with the Buddhist dynasties of Magadha. The only trace of Buddhism that can be discovered in the legends of Vijaya consists in the fact that his head, and the heads of his seven hundred companions, were shaved when they were sent adrift in a ship that was ultimately to bring them to Ceylon. But the author of the Mahāvaṁśa takes care to say that this shaving of their heads was part of the punishment inflicted on Vijaya, by his father, who, when asked by the people to execute his own son for numberless acts of fraud and violence, preferred to send him and his companions adrift on the ocean, after their heads had been shaved. Supposing then that before Duṣṭagamam, *i. e.*, before 161 B. C, the Ceylonese possessed a number of royal names, and that by assigning to each of them a more or less fabulous reign, they had arrived in the year 543 as the probable date of the Conquest, we can Well understand how, under the influence of the later Buddhists, exactly the same thing took place in Ceylon which took place in China. Various temples in Ceylon had their legends, by which their first foundation was ascribed to Buddha himself. Hence the Mahāvaṁśa begins with relating three miraculous visits which Buddha, during his lifetime, paid to Ceylon, At that time, however, it is said that Ceylon was still inhabited by Yakshas. If thus the very earliest history of the island had been brought in connection with Buddha, it is but natural that some sanction of a similar kind should have been thought necessary with regard to the Conquest, A prophecy was therefore, invented, "The ruler of the world, Buddha," so says the Mahāvaṁśa, having conferred blessings on the whole world, and attained the exalted, unchangeable Nirvāṇa, seatd on the throne on which Nirvāṇa is achieved, in the midst of a great assembly of *devatās*, the great divine sage addressed this celebrated injunction to Śakra, who stood near him : 'One Vijaya, the son of Siṁhabāhu, king of the land of Lāla, together with seven hundred officers of state, has landed on Laṅkā. Lord of Devas ! my religion will be established in Laṅkā. On that account thoroughly protect, together with his retinue, him and Laṅkā.' The devoted King of Devas having heard these injunctions of the successor (of former Buddhas), assigned the protection of Laṅkā to the Deva Utpalavarṇa (Viṣṇu). He, in conformity to the command of Śakra, instantly repaired to Laṅkā, and in the character of a *parivrājaka* (devotee) took his station at the foot of a tree.

"With Vijaya at their head the whole party approaching him, inquired, 'Pray, devotee, what land is this ?' he replied, 'The land Laṅkā." Having thus spoken, he blessed them by sprinkling water on them out of his jug, and having tied (charmed) threads on their arms, departed through the air."

At the end of the preceding chapter, the date of the event is still more accurately fixed. "This prince named Vijaya," we read there, "who had then attained the wisdom of experience, landed in the division Tāmraparṇī of this land Laṅkā, on the day that the successor of former Buddhas reclined in the arbour of the two delightful "Śāla-trees, to attain *Nirvāṇa.*" In this manner the conquest of Ceylon was invested with a religious character, and at the same time a connection was established between the traditional chronology of Ceylon and the sacred history of Buddha. If Buddha was a true prophet, the Ceylonese argue quite rightly that he must have died in the year of the Conquest, or 548 B.C.

This synchronism once established, it became necessary to accommodate to it, as well as possible, the rest of the legandary history of the Buddhists. It contained but few historical elements previous to Aśoka's Council, but that, council had again to be connected with the history of Ceylon.

Aśoka was the contemporary of Devānāmpriya Tishya, King of Ceylon. This king adopted Buddhism, and made it, like Aśoka, the state religion of the island. Now, according to the traditional chronology of Ceylon, Devānāmpriya Tishya came to the throne 236 years after the landing of Vijaya,[291] and he reigned forty years (807—267 B.C.). He was intimately connected with Aśoka, as we shall see and it was necessary that the same interval which in the historical traditions of Ceylon separated. Devānāmpriya Tishya from Vijaya should separate Aśoka from Buddha. This was achieved in the following manner : One Aśoka is supposed to have come to the throne ninety years after Buddha, and a council (the second, as it is called) is supposed to have taken place in the tenth year of his reign, or just one hundred years after Buddha. At, that second council a prophecy was uttered that in 118 years a calamity would befall the Buddhist religion. This refers to the reign of the so called second Aśoka, who was at first a great enemy to religion.

Now the first Aśoka is represented to have reigned 18 years after the Council (100 anno Buddhae), and if we cast up these 118 years, the 22 years of Aśoka's sons, the 22 years of the Nine, the 24 years[292] of Candragupta, the 28 years of Bindusāra, and the 4 years which elapsed before Aśoka's inauguration,[293] we find that Aśoka's inauguration would fall just 118 years after the second Council, 218 years after Buddha, or 325 B.C. The

Council of this real Aśoka was held in the 17th year of his reign, or 235 after Buddha. Mahendra, the son of Aśoka, proceeded to Ceylon in the next year, or 236 years after Buddha ; and in this manner the arrival of Mahendra in Ceylon, and the inauguration of Devānāmpriya Tishya as King of Ceylon, are brought together in the same year. It is true that in order to achieve this, it has become necessary to add a first Aśoka,[294] of whom the Northern Buddhists know nothing; it has become necessary to admit another Moggaliputto, and another Council, all equally unknown except in the traditional chronology of Ceylon. The Northern Buddhists know but one Aśoka, the grandson of Chandragupta; they know but one Council, besides the Assembly following immediately on the death of Buddha, viz., the council of Pāṭaliputra under Dharmāśoka, and this they place 110 years after Buddha's Nirvāṇa.[195] Piṇḍola, a contemporary of Buddha, was seen as an old man by Aśoka. But who was to contradict the Ceylonese historians ? They possessed, what the Buddhists of Magadha did not possess, a history of their island and their sovereigns. They valued historical chronology for its own sake forming an exception in this respect to all other nations of India. They were a colony and like most colonies, they valued the traditions of the past. The Buddhists of Magadha, as far as we are able to judge, preserved but a few historical re-collections, frequently in the form of prophecies, which they afterwards forced into the loose frame of the Brāhmaṇic chronology. The Buddhists of Ceylon did not borrow the outlines of their history either from the *Brāhmaṇas* or from the Buddhists of Magadha ; and this is a point which has never been sufficiently considered. Their outlines of history were not constructed originally in order to hold the Buddhist traditions of the North. They may have been slightly modified, so as to avoid glaring inconsistencies between the profane history of Ceylon and the sacred history of Buddhism. But there is evidence to show that, on the other hand, the historical legends of Magadha had to yield much more considerably, the framers of the final chronology finding it impossible to ignore the annals of their island and the reigns of their ancient half-fabulous kings. The chronology of the

Mahāvaṁśa is a compromise between the chronology of Ceylon and that of Magadha, but the latter was the more pliant of the two. There is nothing to prove that the *terminus á quo* of the chronology of Ceylon,—the date of Vijaya's landing—was borrowed from the North. There were Buddhist traditions connecting Vijaya's landing with the death of Buddha, but the date 543 B.C. is never found in the sacred chronology of Buddhism, before it was borrowed from the profane chronology of Ceylon. There were similar, and, as it would seem, better founded traditions, connecting Devānāmpriya Tishya with the great Aśoka ; but the date of Devānāmpriya Tishya was not determined by the date of the great Aśoka, nor was the date of Aśoka's Council, as 110 after Buddha, accepted in Ceylon. On the contrary, the interval between Vijaya and Devānāmpriya Tishya was allowed to remain as it stood in the Ceylonese annals, and the Buddhist traditions were stretched in order to suit that interval. An intermediate Aśoka and an intermediate Council were admitted, which were unknown to the Northern Buddhists. The prophecy that Nāgārjuna should live 400 years after Buddha,[296] had been altered by the Chinese so as to suit their chronology. They placed him 800 years after Buddha. In like manner the Ceylonese Buddhists, having fixed Buddha's death at 543 B. C. changed the traditional date of Nāgārjuna from 400 to 500 after Buddha.[297] All this is constructive chronology, and whether we follow the Chinese or Ceylonese date of Buddha, we must always remember that in both the *terminus á quo* is purely hypo-thetical. This does not interfere with the correctness of minor details, such as the number of years assigned to each king, and in particular the chronological distance between certain events. These may have formed part of popular tradition, long before any system of chronology was established. A very old man, Piṇḍola, was represented in a popular legend to have been a contemporary both of Buddha and of Dharmāśoka. Hence the interval between the founder and the royal patron of Buddhism would naturally be fixed at about 100 years. This is a tradition which may be used for historical purposes. Again, when we see that a date like that of Nāgārjuna fixed in the North of India at 400 after Buddha, is altered to 800 and 500, so as to suit the requirements of two different systems of chronology, we may feel inclined to look up on the unsystematic date as the most plausible. But in order to make use of such indications we must first of all establish a πoυ oτ́ω", and this can only be found in Chandragupta. Everything in Indian chronology depends on the dale of Chandragupta. Chandragupta was the grandfather of Aśoka, and the contemporary of Seleucus Nicator. Now, according to Chinese chronology, Aśoka would have lived, to waive minor difference, 850 or 750 B. C, according to Ceylonese chronology, 3-15 B. C. Either of these dates ia impossible, because it does not agree with the chronology of Greece, and hence both the Chinese and Ceylonese dates of Buddha's death must be given up as equally valueless for historical calculations

There is but one means through which the history of India can be connected with that of Greece, and its chronology be reduced to its proper limits. Although we look in vain in the literature of the *Brāhmaṇas* or Buddhists for any allusion to Alexander's conquest, and although it is impossible to identify any of the historical events, related by Alexander's companions, with the historical traditions of India, one name has fortunately been preserved by classical writers who describe the events immediately following Alexander's conquest, to form a connecting link between the history of the East and the West. This is the name of Sandracottus or Sandrocyptus, the Sanskrit Chandragupta.

We learn from classical writers. Justin, Arrian, Diodorus Siculus, Strabo, Quintus Curtius and Plutarch, that in Alexander's time there was on the Ganges a powerful king of the name of Xandrames, and that soon after Alexander's invasion, a new empire was founded there by Sandracottus or Sandrocyptus. Justin says : "Sandracottus gave liberty to India after Alexander's retreat, but soon converted the name of liberty into servitude after his success, subjecting those whom he had rescued from foreign dominion to his own authority. This prince was of humble origin, but was called to royalty by the power of the gods ; for, having offended Alexander by his impertinent language,[298] he was ordered to be put to death, and escaped only by flight. Fatigued with his journey he lay down to rest, when a lion of large size came and licked off the sweat that poured from him with his tongue, and retired without doing him any harm. The prodigy inspired him with ambitious hopes, and collecting bands of robbers he roused the Indians to rebellion. When he prepared for war against the captains of Alexander, a wild elephant of enormous size approached him, and received him on his back as if he had been tamed. He was a distinguished general and a brave soldier. Having thus acquired power, Sandracottus reigned over India at the time when Seleucus was laying the foundation of his greatness, and Seleucus entered into a treaty with him, and setting affairs on the side of India directed his march against Antigonus.'[299]

Besides this we may gather from classical writers the following statements bearing on Xandrames and Sandrocyptus: "When Alexander made inquiries about the interior of India, he was told that beyond the Indus there was a vast désert of 12 (or 11, according to Curtius,) day's journey, and that at the farthest borders thereof ran the Ganges. Beyond that riwer, he was told, the Prasi *(Prāchyas)* dwelt, and Gangaridse. Their king was named Xandrames, who could bring into the field 20,000 horse, 200,000 foot, 2,000 chariots and 4,000 (or 3,000, Curtius,) elephants. Alexander who did not at first believe this, inquired from king Porus whether this account of the power of Xandrames was true ; and he was told by Porus that it was true, but that the king was but of mean and obscure extraction, accounted to be a barber's son ; that the queen, however, had fallen in love with the barber, had murdered her husband, and that the kingdom had thus devolved upon Xandrames."[300] Quintus Curtius says,[301] "that the father of Xandrames had murdered the king, and under pretence of acting as guardian to his sons, got them into his power and put them to death ; that after their extermination he begot the son who was then king, and who, more worthy of his father's condition than his own, was odious and contemptible to his subjects.' Strabo adds,[302] "that the capital of the Prasii was called Pālibothra, situated at the confluence of the Ganges and another river," which Arrian[303] specifies as the Erannoboas. Their king, besides his birth-name, had to take the name of the city, and was called the Pālibothrian. This was the case with Sandracottus to whom Megasthenes was sent frequently. It was the same king with whom Seleucus Nicator contracted and alliance ceding to him the country beyond the Indus, and receiving in its stead 500 elephants.[304] Megasthenes visited his court several times ;[305] and the same king, as Plutarch says,[306] "traversed India with an army of 600,000 men, and conquered the whole."

These accounts of the classical writers contain a number of distinct statements which could leave very little doubt as to the king to whom they referred. Indian historians, it is true, are generally so vague and so much given to exaggeration, that their kings are all very much alike, either all black or all bright. But nevertheless, if there ever was such a king as the king of the Prasii, and usuṃer, residing at Pāṭaliputra, called Sandrocyptus or Sandracottus, it is hardly possible that he should not be recognized in the historical traditions of India. There is in the lists of the kings of India the name of Chandragupta, and the resemblance of this name with the name of Sandracottus or Sandracyptus was first, I believe, pointed out by Sir William Jones.[307] Wilford, Professor Wilson, and Professor Lassen have afterwards added further evidence in confirmation of Sir W. Jones's conjecture ; and although other scholars, and particularly M. Troyer, in his edition of the Rājātaraṅgiṇi, have raised objections, we shall see that the evidence in favour of the identity of Chandragupta and Sandrocyptus is such as to admit of no reasonable doubt. It is objected that the Greeks called the king of the powerful empire beyond the Indus, *Xandrames,* or *Aggramen.* Now the last name is evidently a mere misspelling for Xandrames, and this Xandrames is not the same as Sandracottus. Xandrames, if we understand the Greek accounts rightly, is the predecessor of Chandragupta or rather the last king of the empire conquered by Sandracottus. If, however, it should be maintained, that these two names were intended for one and the same king, the explanation would still be very easy. For Chandragupta (the protected of the moon), is also called Chandra,[308] the Moon ; and Candrāmas, in Sanskrit, is a synonyme of Chandra. Xandrames, however, was no doubt intended as different from Chandragupta. Xandrames must have been king of the Prasii before Sandracottus, and during the time of Alexander's wars. If this Xandrames is the same as the last Nanda, the agreement between the Greek account of his mean extraction, and the Hindū account of Nanda being a Śūdra, would be very striking. It is not, however, quite clear whether the same person is meant in the Greek and Hindū accounts. At the time of Alexander's invasion Sandracottus was very young, and being obliged to fly before Alexander, whom he had offended, it is said that he collected bands of robbers, and with their help succeeded in establishing the freedom of India. Plutarch says distinctly that Sandracottus reigned soon after, that is soon after Xandrames, and we know from Justin, that it was Sandracottus, and not Xandrames, who waged wars with the captains of Alexander. Another objection against the identification of Chandragupta and Sandracottus was the site of their respective capitals. The capital of Chandragupta, Pāṭaliputra, was no doubt the same as the Pālibothra of Sandracottus, the modern Patna. But exception was taken on the ground that Patna is not situated near the confluence of the Ganges and the Sone or Erannoboas, where the ancient Pālibothra stood. This, however, has been explained by a change in the bed of the river Sone, which is established on the best geographical evidence.

There are several other points on which the histories of Chandragupta and Sandracottus agree. Sandracottus founded a new empire at Pālibothra. Chandragupta was the founder of a new dynasty, the Mauryas[311] at Pāṭaliputra. Sandracottus , gained the throne by collecting bands of robbers. Chandragupta did the same. Sandracottus was called to royalty by the power of the gods and by prodigies. So was Chandragupta, although the prodigy related by Justin is not exactly the same as the prodigies related by Hindū authors. So far, therefore, there is nothing in the Greek accounts that is not confirmed by Hindū tradition. That there should be a great deal more in Hindū tradition than was known to the Greeks is but natural, particularly as many of the Hindū stories were evidently invented at a later time and with a certain object. As the grandson of Chandragupta was the great patron of the Buddhists, attempts were naturally made by Buddhist writers to prove that Chandragupta belonged to the same race as Buddha; while on the other hand the Brāhmaṇic writers would be no less fertile in inventing fables that would throw discredit on the ancestor of the Buddhist sovereigns of India. Some extracts from the writings of these hostile parties will best show how this was achieved. In the Mahāvaṁśo[310] we read : "Kālāśoko had sons: these brothers (conjointly) ruled the empire righteously for twenty-two years. Subsequently there were nine brothers: they also according to their seniority reigned for twenty-two years. Thereafter the Brāhmaṇa Cāṇakko, in gratification of an implacable hatred borne towards the ninth surviving brother, called Dhana-nando, having put him to death, installed in the sovereignty over the whole of Jambudīpo, a descendant of the dynasty of Moriyan sovereigns, endowed with illustrious and beneficent, attributes, and surnamed Chandagutto. He reigned 24 (not 34) yeas."

The commentary on this passage adds the following details:'[311] "Subsequent to Kālāśoko, who patronised those who hold the second convocation, the royal line is stated to have consisted of twelve monarchs to the reign of Dhammā-soko, when they (the priests) held the third convocation. Kālāśoko's own sons were ten brothers. Their names are specified in the Aṭṭhakathā. The appellation of 'the nine Nandos' originates in nine of them bearing that patronymic title.

"The Aṭṭhakathā of the Uttaravihāro priests sets forth that the eldest of these was of an extraction (maternally) not allied (inferior) to the royal family; and that he dwelt in one of the provinces;[312] it gives also the history of the other nine. I also will give their history succinctly, but without prejudice to its perspicuity.

In afor time, during the conjoint administration of the (nine) sons of Kālāśoko, a certain provincial person appeared in the character of a marauder, and raising a considerable force, was laying the country waste by pillage. His people, who committed these depredations on towns, whenever a town might be sacked, seized and compelled its own inhabitants to carry the spoil to a wilderness, and there securing the plunder, drove them away, On a certain day, the banditti who were leading this predatory life having employed a daring, powerful, and enterprising individual to commit a robbery, were retreating to the wilderness, making him carry the plunder. He who was thus associated with them, inquired : 'By what means do you find your livelihood ?' 'your slave' (they replied) 'we are not men who submit to the toils of tillage, or cattle tending. By a proceeding precisely like the present one, pillaging towns and villages, and laying up stores of riches and grain, and providing ourselves with fish and flesh, toddy and other beverage, we pass our lives jovially in feasting and drinking.' On being told this, he thought: 'This mode of life of these thieves in surely excellent; shall I, also, joining them, lead a similar life?' and then said, 'I also will join you, I will become a confederate of yours. Admitting me among you, take me (in your marauding excursions).' They replying *'sādhu,'* received him among them.

"On a subsequent occasion, they attacked a town which was defended by well armed and vigilant inhabitants. As soon as they entered the town the people rose upon and surrounded them, and seizing their leader, and hewing him with a sword, put him to death. The robbers dispersing in all directions repaired to, and reassembled in the wilderness. Discovering that he (their leader) had been slain ; and saying, In his death the extinction of our prosperity is evident; having been deprived of him, under whose control can the sacking of villages be carried on? Even to remain here is imprudent; thus our disunion and destruction are inevitable :' they resigned themselves to desponding grief. The individual above mentioned, approaching them, asked: 'What are ye weeping for ?' On being answered by them, 'We are lamenting the want of a valiant leader, to direct us in the hour of attack and retreat in our village sacks.' 'In that case, my friends,' (said he) 'ye need not make yourselves unhappy; if there be no other person able to undertake that post, I can myself perform it for you; from henceforth give not a thought about the matter.' This and more he said to them. They, relieved from their perplexity by this speech, joyfully replied, '*sādhu*', and conferred on him the post of chief.

"From that period proclaiming himself to be Nando, and adopting the course followed formerly (by his predecessor), he wandered about, pillaging the country. Having induced his brothers also to co-operate with him, by them also he was supported in his marauding excursions, Subsequently assembling his gang, he thus addressed them: 'My men ! this is not a career in which valiant men should be engaged; it is not worthy of such as we are; this course is only befitting base wretches. What advantage is there in persevering in this career, let us aim at supreme sovereignty ?' They assented. On having received their acquiescence, attended by his troops and equipped for war, he attacked a provincial town, calling upon (its inhabitants) either to acknowledge him as sovereign, or to give him battle. They on receiving this demand all assembled, and having duly weighed the message, by sending an appropriate answer, formed a treaty of alliance with them. By this means reducing under his authority the people of Jambudīpo in great numbers, he finally attacked Pāṭaliputta[313] (the capital of the Indian empire), and usurping the sovereignty, died there a short time afterwards, while governing the empire.

"His brothers next succeeded to the empire in the order of their seniority. They altogether reigned twenty-two years. It was on this account that (in the Mahāvaṁśo) it is stated that there were nine Nandos.

"Their ninth youngest brother was called Dhana-nando, from his being addicted to hoarding treasure. As soon as he was inaugurated, actuated by miserly desires the most inveterate, he resolved within himself, 'It is proper that I should devote myself to hoarding treasure;' and collecting riches to the amount of eighty *koṭis,* and superintending the transport thereof, himself, and repairing to the banks of the Ganges, by means of a barrier constructed of branches and leaves interrupting the course of the main stream, and forming a canal, he diverted its waters into a different channel; and in a rock in the bed of the river having caused a great excavation to be made, he buried the treasure there. Over this cave he laid a layer of stones, and to prevent the admission of water, poured molten lead on it. Over that again he laid another layer of stones, and passing a stream of molten lead (over it), which made it like a solid rock, he restored the river to its former course. Levying taxes even on skins, gums, trees, and stones, among other articles, amassed further treasures, which he disposed of similarly. It is stated that he did so repeatedly. On this account we call this ninth brother of theirs, as he personally devoted himself to the hoarding of treasure, 'Dhana-nando,'

"The appellation of 'Moriyan sovereigns' is derived from the auspicious circumstances under which their capital, which obtained the name of Moriya, was called into existence.

"While Buddha yet lived, driven by the misfortunes produced by the war of (prince) Vidhudhabo, certain members of the Sākya line retreating to Himavanto, discovered a delightful and beautiful location, well watered, and situated in the midst of a forest of lofty bo and other trees. Influenced by the desire of settling there, they founded a town at a place where several great roads met, surrounded by durable ramparts, having gates of defence therein, and embellished with delightful edifices and pleasure gardens. Moreover that (city), having a row of buildings covered with tiles, which were arranged in the pattern of the plumage of a peacock's neck, and as it resounded with the notes of flocks of *'konchos'* and *'mayuros'* (pea-fowls), was so called. From this circumstance these Sākya lords of this town, and their children and descendants, were renowned throughout Jambudīpo by the title of 'Moriya.' From this time that dynasty has been called the Moriyan dynasty."

After a few isolated remarks, the Ṭikā thus proceeds in its account of Chāṇakko and Chandagutto :

"It is proper that in this place a sketch of these two characters should be given. Of these, if I am asked in the first place. 'Where did this Chāṇakko dwell ? Whose son was he?' I answer, 'he lived at the city of Takkasilā. He was the son of a certain *Brāhmaṇa* at that place, and a man who had achieved the knowledge of the three Vedas ; could rehearse the *mantos (mantras);* skilful iṇ stratagems; and dexterous in intrigue as well as policy. At the period of his father's death he was already well known as the dutiful maintainer of his mother, and as a highly gifted individual worthy of swaying the *chatta (chatra).*

"On a certain occasion, approaching his mother, who was weeping he inquired, 'My dear mother, why do you weep ?' On being answered by her, 'My child, you are gifted to sway a *chatta.* Do not, my boy, endeavour by raising the *chatta,* to become a sovereign. Princes everywhere are unstable in the attachments. You also, my child, will forget the affection thou owe me. In that case, I should be reduced to the deepest distress. I weep under these apprehensions. He exclaimed: 'My mother, what is that gift that I possess ? On what part of my person is it indicated ?' and on her replying 'My dear, on thy teeth,' smashing his own teeth, and becaming Kaṇḍhadatto' (a tooth broken man) he devoted himself to the protection of his mother. Thus it was that he became celebrated as the filial protector of his mother. He was not only a tooth-broken man, but he was disfigured by a disgusting complexion, and by deformity of legs and other members prejudicial to manly comeliness.

In his quest of disputạtion, repairing to Pupphapura, the capital of the monarch Dhana-nando, (who abandoning his passion for hoarding, becoming imbued with the desire of giving alms, relinquishing also his miserly habits and delighting in hearing the fruits that resulted from benevolence, had built a hall of alms-offering in the midst of his palace, and was making an offering to the chief of the *Brāhmaṇas* worth a hundred *koṭis* and to the most junior *Brāhmaṇa* an offering worth a lac), this *Brāhmaṇa* (Cāṇakko) entered the said apartment, and taking possession of the seat of the chief *Brāhmaṇa,* sat himself down in that alms-hall.

" At that instant Dhana-nando himself decked in regal attire, and attended by many thousands of *'śivakā'* (state palanquins), glittering with their various ornaments, and escorted by a suite of a hundred royal personages, with their martial array of the four hosts, of cavalry, elephants, chariots and infantry, and accompanied by dancing-girls, lovely as the attendants on the *devas,* himself a personification of majesty, and bearing the white parasol of dominion, having a golden staff and golden tassels, with this superb retinue repairing thither, and entering the hall of alms-offering, beheld the *Brāhmaṇa* Cāṇakko seated. On seeing him, this thought occurred to him (Nando): 'Surely it cannot be proper that he should assume the seat of the chief *Brāhmaṇa.* Becoming displeased with him, he thus evinced his displeasure. He inquired : 'Who are you, that you have taken the seat of the chief *Brāhmaṇa* ?' and being answered (simply), 'It is I;' 'Cast from hence this cripple *Brāhmaṇa ;* allow him not to be seated', exclaimed Nando; and although the courtiers again and again implored of him, saying, 'Devo ! let it not be so done by a person prepared to make offerings as you are, extend your forgiveness to this *Brāhmaṇa ,'* he insisted upon his ejection. On the courtiers approaching Cāṇakko, and saying, 'Achariyo ! we come, by the command of the Rājā, to remove your from hence ; but incapable of uttering the words, "Acāriyo, depart hence," we now stand before your abashed." Enraged against him (Nando), rising from his seat to depart, he snapt asunder his Brāhmaṇical cord, and dashed down his jug on the threshold, and thus invoking malediction: 'Kings are impious : may this whole earth, bounded by the four oceans, withhold its gifts from Nando,' he departed. On his sallying out, the officers reported this proceeding to the Rājā. The king, furious with indignation, roared, 'Catch, catch the slave.' The fugitive, stripping himself naked, and assuming the character of an *ajīvako,* and running into the centre of the palace, concealed himself in an unfrequented place, at the Saṅkhārathānan. The pursuers, not having discovered him, returned and reported that he was not to be found.

"In the night he repaired to a more frequented part of (the palace, and meeting some of the suite of the royal prince Pabbato, admitted them into his confidence. By their assistance he had an interview with the prince. Gaining him over by holding out hopes of securing the sovereignty for him, and attaching him by that expedient, he began to search the means of getting out of the palace. Discovering that in a certain place there was a ladder leading to a secret passage he consulted with the prince, and sent a message to his (the prince's) mother for the key of the passage. Opening the door with the utmost secrecy, he escaped with the prince, and they fled to the wilderness of Viñjjhā (Vindhya.)

"While dwelling there, with the view of raising resources, he converted (by recoining) each *kahāpanā*[314] into eight, and amassed eighty *Jeotis* of *Kahāpanas.* Having buried this treasure, he commenced to search for a second individual entitled (by birth) to be raised to sovereign power and met with the aforesaid prince of the Moriyan dynasty called Chandagutto,

"His mother, the queen consort of the monarch of Moriya-nagara, the city before mentioned, was pregnant at the time that a certain powerful provincial Rājā conquered that kingdom, and put the Moriyan king to death. In her anxiety to preserve the child in her womb, she departed for the capital of Pupphapura, under the protection of her elder brothers, and under disguise she dwelt there. At the completion of the ordinary term of pregnancy she gave birth to a son, and relinquishing him to the protection of the *devas,* she placed him in a vase, and deposited him at the door of a cattle pen. A bull named Chando stationed himself by him, to protect him; in the same manner that Prince Ghoso, by the interosition of the *devatā,* was watched over by a bull. In the same manner also, that the herdsman in the instance of that Prince Ghoso repaired to the spot where that bull planted himself, a herdsman, on observing this prince, moved by affection, like that born to his own child, took charge of and tenderly reared him ; and in giving him a name, in reference to his having been watched by the bull

Chando, he called him 'Chandagutto,' and brought him up. When he had attained an age to be able to tend cattle a certain wild huntsman, friend of the herdsman, becoming acquainted with the boy, attached to him, took him from (the herdsman) to his own dwelling, and established him there. He contiérentd to dwell in that village.

"Subsequently, on a certain occasion, while tending cattle with other children in the village, he joined them in a game called, 'the game of royalty.' He himself was named Rājā ; to others he gave the offices of sub-king, etc. Some being appointed judges were placed in a judgment hall; some he made officers of the king's household ; and otheroutlaws or robbers. Having thus constituted a court of justice, he sat in judgment. On culprits being brought up, when they had been regularly impeached and tried, on their guilt being clearly proved to his satisfaction, according the sentence awarded by his judical ministers, he ordered the officers of the court to chop off their hands and feet. On their replying *'Devo* ! we have no axes,' he answered : 'It is the order of Chandagutto that ye should chop off their hands and feet, making axes with the horns of goats for blades, and sticks for handles.' They acted accordingly; and on Striking with the axe, the hands and feet were lopped off. On the same person commanding, 'Let them be reunited' the hands and feet were restored to their former condition.

"Cāṇakko happening to come to that spot, was amazed at thc procccding hc bchcld.' Accompanying (thc boy) to thc village, and presenting the huntsman with a thousand *kahāpaṇās,* he applied for him ; saying ; 'I will teach your son every accomplishment ; consign him to me.' Accordingly, conducting him to his own dwelling, he encircled his neck with a single fold of a woollen cord, twisted with gold thread, worth a lac.

"The discovery of this person is thus stated (in the former works): 'He discovered this prince descended from the Moriyan line.'

"He (Cāṇakko) invested Prince Pabbatto, also with a similar woollen cord. While these youths were living with him, each had a dream, which they separately imparted to him. As soon as he heard each (dream), he knew that of these Prince Pabbato would not attain royalty; and that Chandagutto would, without loss of time, become paramount monarch in Jambudīpo. Although he made this discovery, he disclosed nothing to them.

"On a certain occasion having partaken of some milk-rice prepared in butter which had been received as an offering at a brāhmaṇical disputation, they retired from the main road, and lying down in a shady place, protected by the deep foliage of trees, fell asleep. Among them the Acāriyo awakening first, rose; and for tbe purpose of putting prince Pabbato's qualifications to the test, he gave him a sword, and telling him: 'Brillg me the woollen thread on Chandagutto's neck, without either cutting or untying it, sent him off. He started on the mission, and failing to accomplish it, he returned. On a subsequent day, he sent Chandagutto on a similar mission. He repairing to the spot where Pabbato was sleeping, and cosidering how it was to be effected, decided: 'There is no other way of doing it; it can only be got possession of, by cutting his head off.' Accordingly chopping his head off, and bringing away the woollen thread, he presented himself to the Brāhmaṇa, who received him in profound silence. Pleased with him, however, on account of this (exploit), he rendered him in the course of six or seven years highly accomplished, and profoundly learned.

"Thereafter, on his attaining manhood, he decided: 'From henceforth this individual is capable of forming and controlling an army;' so he repaired to the spot where his treasure was buried, and took possession of it, and employed it, enlisting forces from all quarters, and distributing money among them; and having thus formed a powerful army, he entrusted it to him. From that tittle throwing off all disguise, and invading the inhabited parts of the country, he commenced his campaign by attacking towns and villages. In the course of their (Cāṇakko and Candagutto's) warfare, the population rose to a man, and surrounding them, and hewing their army with their weapons, vanquished them. Dispersing, they reunited in the wilderness; and consulting together, they thus decided: 'As yet no advantage has resulted from war; relinquishing military operations, let us acquire a knowledge of the sentiments of the people.' Thenceforth, in disguise, they travelled about the country. While thus roaming about, after sunset retiring to some town or other, they were in the habit of attending to the conversation of the inhabitants of those places.

"In one of these villages, a woman having baked some *'appalapūva'* (pancakes) was giving them to her child, who leaving the edges would only eat the centre. On his asking for another cake, she remarked ; 'This boy's conduct is like Chandagutto's in his attempt to take possession of the kingdom.' On his inquiring : 'Mother, why, what am I doing; and what has Chandagutto done?' 'You, my boy,' said she, 'throwing away the outside of the cake, eat the middle only. Chandagutto also in his ambition to be a monarch, without subduing the frontiers, before he attacked the towns, invaded the heart of the country, and laid towns waste. On that account, both the inhabitants of the town and others, rising, closed in upon him, from the frontiers to the centre, and destroyed his army. *That* was *his* folly.'

"They, on hearing this story of hers, taking due notice thereof, from that time again raised an army. On resuming their attack on the provinces and towns, commencing from the frontiers, reducing towns, and stationing troops in the intervals, they proceeded in their invasion. After a respite, adopting the same system, and marshalling a great army, and in regular course reducing each kingdom and province, then assailing Pāṭaliputta and putting Dhana-nando to death, they seized that sovereignty.

"Although this had been brought about, Cāṇakko did not at once raise Chandagutto to the throne; but for the purpose of discovering Dhana-nando's hidden treasure, sent for a certain fisherman (of the river); and after deluding him with the promise of raising the *Chatta* for him, and securing the hidden treasure, within a month form that date, put him also to death[315], and inaugurated Chandagutto monarch.

"Hence the expression (in the Mahāvaṁśo) 'a descendant of the dynasty of Moriyan sovereigns ;' as well as the expression 'installed in the sovereignty.' All the particulars connected with Chandagutto, both before his installation and after, are recorded in the Aṭṭhakathā of the Uttaravihāro priests. Let that (work) be referred to, by those who are desirous of more detailed information. We compile this work in an abridged form, without prejudice however to its perspicuity.

"His (Chandagutto's) son was Bindusāro. After his father had assumed the administration, the said father sent for a former acquaintance of his, a Jatilian, named Maniyatappo, and conferred a commission on him. 'My friend, (said he) do you restore order into the country ; suppressing the lawless proceedings that prevail.' He replying *'sādhu,'* and accepting the commission, by his judicious measures, reduced the country to order.

"Cāṇakko, determined that to Chandaguttoṭa monarch, who by the instrumentality of him (the aforesaid Maniyatappo) had conferred the blessings of peace on the country, by extirpating marauders who were like unto thorns (in a cultivated land)—no calamity should befall from poison, decided on inuring his body to the effects of poison. Without imparting the secret to any one, commencing with the smallest particle possible, and gradually increasing the dose, by mixing poison in his food and beverage, he (at last) fed him on poison, at the same time taking steps to prevent any other person participating in his poisoned repasts.

"At a subsequent period his queen consort was pronounced to be pregnant. Who was she ? Whose daughter was she ? 'She was the daughter of the eldest of the maternal uncles who accompanied the Rājā's mother to Fupphapura.'[1] Chandagutto wedding this daughter of his maternal uncle, raised her to the dignity of queen consort.

"About this time, Chāṇakko on a certain day having prepared the monarch's repast sent in to him, himself accidentally remaining behind for a moment. On recollecting himself, in an agony of distress, he exclaimed, 'I must hasten thither, short as the interval is, before he begins his meal;[316] and precipitately rushed into the king's apartment, at the instant that the queen who was within seven days of her confinement, was in the act, in the Rājā's presence, of placing the first handful of the repast in her month. On beholding this, and rinding that there was not even time to ejaculate 'Don't swallow it,' with his sword he struck her head off and them ripping open her womb, extricted the child with its caul, and placed it in the stomach of a goat. In this manner, by placing it for seven days in the stomach of seven different goats, having completed the full term of gestation, he delivered the infant over to the female slaves. He caused him to be reared by them, and when a name was conferred on him-in reference to a spot, (Bindu) which the blood of the goats had left-he was called Bindusāro."

This Bindusāro succeeded his father as king, and, after a reign of 28 years, he was succeeded by the great Aśoka. In this manner, the Buddhists prove that through the Mauryas, Aśoka belonged to the same family as Buddha, the royal family of the Sākyas.

The *Brāhnaṇas,* on the contrary, endeavour to show that Chandragupta belonged to the same contemptible race as the Nandas. Thus we read in the Viṣṇu-purāṇa[317] :—

"The last of the Bṛhadratha dynasty, Ripuñjaya, will have a minister named Śunika (Sunaka, Bh. P.), who having killed his sovereign will place his son Pradyota upon the throne (for 23 years, Vāyu and Matsya P.). His son will be Palaka (24 years, V.; Tilaka or Bālaka, 28 years, M. P.). His son will be Viśākhayupa (50 years V.; 53 M. P.). His son will be Janaka (Ajakd? 21 years V ; Sūryaka, 21 years M.; Rājāka, Bh. P.). And his son will be Nandivardhana (20 years V. and M. P.). These five kings of the house of Pradyota will reign over the earth for 138 years (the same (number in V. and Bh. P.).

"The next prince will be Śiśunāga,[318] his son will be Kākavarna (36 years V, and M.) ; his son will be Kṣemadharman (Kṣemakarman, 20 years V., Kṣemadharman, 36 years M.); his son will be Kṣatraujas (40 years V.; Kshemajit or Kṣemarchis, 36 years M.; Kṣetrajṃa, Bh. P.). his son will be Vidmisāra (Vimbisāra, 28 years V.; Vindusena or Vindhyasena, 28 years M. ; Vidhisāra, Bh.); his son will be Ajatasatru ;[319] his son will be Dharbaka (Harṣaka, 25 years V. ; Vamsaka, 24 years M.); his son will be Udayāśva (33 years V.; Udibhi or Udasin, 33 years M.);[320] his son also will be Nandivardhana ; and his son will be Muhānanda (42 and 43 years V.; 40 and 43 years M.). These ten Śaiśunāgas will be kings of the earth for 362 years.

"The son of Mahānanda will be born of a woman of the Śūdra-class; his name will be Nanda, called Mahāpadma, for he will be exceedingly avaricious. Like another Paraśu-rāma, he will be the annihilator of the Kṣatriya race, for after him the kings of the earth will be Śūdras. He will bring the whole earth under one umbrella, he will have eight sons, Sumālya, and others, who will reign after Mahāpadma; and he and his sons will govern for a hundred years. The *Brahmaṇa* Kauṭilya will root out the nine Nandas.

"Upon the cessation of the race of Nanda, the Mauryas will possess the earth. Kauṭilya will place Chandragupta[321] on the throne; his son will be Vindusāra ;[322] his son will be Aśokavardhana; his son will be Vinduśara; his son will be Daśaratha; his son will be Saṅgata ; his son will be Śāli-śūka ; his son will be Somaśarman; his son will be Śaśi-dharman, and his successor will be Vṛhadratha. These are the ten Mauryas who will reign over the earth for 137 years."

The title of Maurya, which by the Buddhists was used as a proof of Aśoka's royal descent, is explained by the *Brāhmaṇas* as a metronymic, Murā being given as the name of one of Nanda's wives.[323]

If now, we survey the information here brought together from Buddhist, Brāhmaṇic, and Greek sources, we shall feel bound to confess that all we really know is this :[324]

Candragupta is the same person as Sandrocyptus, or Sandracottus. This Sandracottus, according to Justin (xv. 4.), had seized the throne of India after the prefects of Alexander had been murdered (317 B. a). Seleucus found him a sovereign of India when, after the taking of Babylon and the conquest of the Bactrians, he passed on into India. Seleucus however, did not conquer Sandracottus, but after concluding, a league with him, marched on to make war against An gonus.[325] This must have taken place before 312, for in that year, the beginning of the Seleucidan era, Seleucus had returned to Babylon.

We may suppose that Chadragupta became king about 315, and as both the Buddhist and Brāhmaṇic writers allow him a reign of 24 years, the reign of Bindusāra would begin 291 B. C. This Bindusāra again had according to both Brāhmaṇic and Buddhistic authors, a long reign of either twenty-five or twenty-eight years. Taking the latter statement as the better authenticated, we find that the probable beginning of Aśoka's reign took place 263 B. C. ; his inauguration 259 B. C. ; his Council either 240 or 242 B. C. At the time of Aśoka's inauguration, 218 years had elapsed since the conventional date of the death of Buddha. Hence if we translate the language of Buddhist chronology into that of Greek chronology, Buddha was really supposed to have died 477 B. C,, and not 543 B. C. Again, at the time of Chandragupta's accession, 162 years were believed to have elapsed since the conventional date of Buddha's death. Hence Buddha of Bengal, xviii. p. 20 was supposed to have died 315+ 162 = 477 B. C. Or, to adopt a different line of argument, Kaniṣka, according to the evidence of coins, must, have reigned before and after the Christian era. In the Stūpa of Maṅikyāla, which was built by Kaniṣka, Roman coins have been found of as late a date as 35 B. C. How long before that date this Turushka or Indo-scythian king may have assumed the sovereignty of India it is difficult to determine. But under him the Northern Buiddhists place a new Council which was presided over by Ṣisumitra,[326] and the date of which is fixed at *more than* 400 after Buddha's *Nirvāṇa*.[327] If we add 400 and

33, and take to account that the Council took place *more* than 400 years after Buddha, and that Kaniṣka must have reigned some years before he built his Stūpa, we find again that 477 B. C. far more likely than 543, as the conventional date of Buddha's death. All the dates, however, before Chandragupta are to be considered only as hypothetical. The second council under Kālāśoka is extremely problematical, and the date of Buddha's death, as 218 before Aśoka, is worth no more than the date of Vijaya's landing in Ceylon, fixed 218 before Devānāmpriya Tishya. Professor Lassen, in order to give an historical value to the date of 543 assigned to the death of Buddha, adds 66 years to the 22 years of the reign of the Nandas, and he quotes in support of this the authority of the Purāṇas which ascribe 88 years to the first Nanda. The Purāṇas, however, if taken in their true meaning, are entirely at variance with the Buddhist chronology before Chandragupta, and it is not allowable to use them as a corrective. As to the chronology of the Ceylonese Buddhists, so far from becoming more perfect by the addition of those sixty-six years, it would really lose all consistency. The most useful portions of that choronology are the prophecies of Buddha and others, as to the number of years intervening between certain events. All these dates would have to be surrendered if we adopted Professor Lassen's correction. The great Council would not fail 218 years after Buddha's death, Chandragupta would not come to the throne 162 years after the Nirvāṇa : Buddha, in fact, as well as his apostles, would be convicted as false prophets by their very disciples.

Whatever changes may have to be introduced into the earlier chronology of India, nothing will ever shake the date of Chandragupta, the illegitimate successor of the Nandas, the ally of Seleucus, the grandfather of Aśoka. That date is the sheet-anchor of Indian chronology, and it is sufficient for the solution of the problem which occupies us at present. It enables us to place Kātyāyana before Chandragupta, the successor of the Nandas, or, at all events, the founder of a new dynasty, subsequent to the collapse of Alexander's empire. It enables us to fix chronologically an important period in the literature of

India, the Sūtra period, and to extend its limits to at least three generations after Kātyāyana, to about 200 B. C. In doing so, I am far from maintaining that the evidence which connects the names of Kātyāyana and Nanda is unexceptionable. – Nowhere except in Indian history should we feel justified in ascribing any weight to the vague traditions contained in popular stories which were written down more than a thousand years after the event. The most that can be said in favour of these traditions is, first, that there was no object in inventing them ; secondly, that they are not in contradiction with anything we know of the early history of India from other sources ; and thirdly,that the date which from their suggestions we assign to the literary works of Kātyāyana and his predecessors and successors, harmonises with the conclusions derived from the literature of the *Brāhmaṇas,* as to the probable growth and decay of the Hindū mind previous to the beginning of our era.

Although these chronological discussions have occupied so much of our space, it is necessary to add a few words of explanation. It might seem as if, in bringing together all the evidence available for our purpose, certain authorities had been overlooked which might have confirmed our conclusions. Professor Bohtlingk, whose researches with regard to the age of Pāṇini deserve the highest credit, has endeavoured to fortify his conclusions by some additional evidence, derived from the works of Chinese travellers ; and other writers on the same subject have followed his example, though they have given a different interpretation to the statements of those travellers, and have arrivéd at different results as to the probable date of Pāṇini. The evidence of these Buddhist pilgrims, however, yields no real results, either for or against the date assigned to Pāṇini and Kātyāyana, and it is for this reason that it has been entirely discarded in the preceding pages. Professor Bohtlingk relied on the testimony of Hiouen-thsang, a Buddhist pilgrim who travelled through India in the years 629-645 after Christ, and whose travels have lately been translated by M. Stanislas Julien.[328] There we read :

"Apres avoir fait environ cinq cent li, au sud-est de la capitale (de Chīnapati), il arriva au couvent appelè Ta-mo-soufa-na-seng kia Ian *(Tāmaaavana saṅghārāma),* ou le couvent de la Forét Sombre. On y comptait environ trois cent religieux qui suivaient les principes de l'école des Sarvāstivā-das. Us avaient un extérieur grave et imposant, et sedistinguaient par la pureté de leur vertu et I'élévation de . Us approfondissaient surtout 1'e'tude du petit Vehicule. Les mille Buddhas du Kalpa des Sages (Bhadra-kalpa) doivent, dans ce lieu, rassemblér la multitude des Devas et leur expliquer la sublime loi. Dans la trais centime annee Aprés le Nirvāṇa de Sākya Tathagata, il y eut un maitre des Sastras, nommṃ *Kātyāyana,* qui composa, dans ce couvent, le Fa-tchi-lun (Abhidbarma-jñāna-prasthāna)."

At first sight this might seema very definite statement as to the age of Kātyāyana, placing him, if we accept the conventional date of Buddha's death, about 243 B. C. But how can we prove that Hiouen-thsang was speaking of Kātyāyana Vararuchi ? It might be said that the Kātyāyana, so simply mentioned by Hiouen-thsang, must be a person of note. Hiouen-thsang does not mention ancient authors except men of note, and the Kātyāyana whose dates he gives in this place, cannot be a chance person of that name, but must be some well-known author. It could hardly be meant for Mahākātyāyana, because he was the pupil of Buddha, and could not be placed 300 years after this *Nirvāṇa.* Besides Mahākātyāyana, there is certainly no person of the same name of greater literary fame than Kātyāyana Vararuchi. But the Kātyāyana of whom Hiouen-thsang speaks was a Buddhist, and the author of a work on metaphysics, which Hiouen-thsang himself translated from Sanskrit into Chinese. Making all possible allowance for the tendency of later Buddhist writers to refer the authorship of certain works to names famous in ancient Brāhmaṇic history, we can hardly build much on the supposition that the author meant by the Chinese traveller was the old Kātyāyana Vararuchi, the contemporary of Pāṇini. But, even if all these objections could be removed, what use could we make of Hiouen-thsang's chronology, who follows the system of the Northern,' and not of the Ceylonese Buddhists, who makes Aśoka to reign 100 years after Buddha, Kaniṣka 400, the king of Himatala 600, and so on ? We should first have to determine what, according to Hiouen-thsang, was the real date of Buddha's *Nirvāṇa,* and what was the era used at his time in the monasteries of Northern India ; whether he altered the dates, assigned by the Buddhists of India to the various events of their traditional history, according to the standard of the Chinese Buddhist chronology, or whether lie simply repeated the dates, such as they were communicated to him in the different places which he visited. All these questions would have to be answered, and if they could be answered, we should in the end only arrivé at the date of Kātyāyana, but not of the Kātyāyana, with whom we are concerned.

There is another passage in Hiouen-thsang which has been frequently discussed, and according to which it would seem that we should have to place Pāṇini much later, and Kātyāyana, the critic of Pāṇini, could not have lived before the first century after Christ.

M. Reinaud, in his excellent work, ("Mémoire Géographique, Historique et Scientifique sur l'Inde, antérieurement au milieu du XIe. siécle, d'aprés les écrivains arabes, persans et chinois (Paris, 1849)," was the first to call attention to this passage. He says (p. 88.) : "Ainsi qne pour plusieurs autres personnages notables du bouddhis-me, Hiouen-thsang attribue a Pāṇini deux existences, la premiére ā une époque ou la vie de l'homme était plus longuc qu'a present, et la seconde vers l'an 500 aprés la mort de Bouddha, e'est-à dire au temps du second Vikramāditya, un siécle environ apres le regne de Kanika. Dans sa premiére existence, Pāṇini professait le brahminisme; maisdans la seconde il se convertit avec son pére au bouddhisme." M. Reinaud pointed out with great sagacity the various consequences which would follow from such a statement, and he remarked besides that the fact of the Yavanānī *(lipi),* the writing of the Ionians or the Greeks, being mentioned in Pāṇini, would likewise tend to place that grammarian rather later than was commonly supposed.

The same legend, thus partially translated from Hiouen-thsang, was made by Professor Weber the key-stone of a new system of Indian chronology. Admitting the double existence of Pāṇini, he says that his second existence falls 500 years after Buddha, or 100 after Kaniṣka, whom Hiouen-thsang places 400 after Buddha. The date assigned by Hiouen-thsang to Kaniṣka is rejected by Professor Weber. He takes, however, the real date of Kaniṣka, as established on numismatic evidence, about 40 A. D. ; he then adds to it the hund:ed years, which, according to the constructive chronology of the Northern Buddhists, elapsed between Kaniṣka and Pāṇini, and thus deduces 140 A. D. as a new date for Pāṇini.

Without entering into the merits of these calculations, we are enabled by the publication of the complété translation of Hiouen-thsang to show that, in reality, the Chinese pilgrim never placed Pāṇini so late as 500 after Buddha. On the contrary, he represents the reputation of that old grammarian as firmly established at that time, and his grammar as the grammar then taught to all children. I subjoin the extracts from Hiouen-thsang:

"Aprés avoir fait environ vingt li au nord-ouest de la ville de *Ou-to-lcia-han-cha* (Uḍakhāṇda ?), il arriva à la ville de *P'o-lo toulo* ("Śālātura) qui doona le jour an Ṛṣi *Po-ṇi-ṇi* (Pāṇini), auteur du Traité *Ching-ming-lun* (Vyākaraṇam).

Dans la haute antiquité, les mots de la langue étaient extremement nombreux; mais quand le nionde eut été detruit, l'univers se trouva vide et désert. Des dieux d'une Iongévité extraordinaire descendirent sur la terre pour servir de guides aux peoples. Telle fut l'origine des lettres et des livres. A partir de cette époque, leur source s'agrandit et depassa les bornes. Le dieu *Fan* (Brāhmaṇa) et le roi du ciel (Indra) étab-lirent des régies et se conformérent au temps. Des Ṛṣis héré-tiques composérent chacun des. mots. Les hommes les priient pour modéles, continuérent Vent leur ceuvre, et travaillérent a l'envi pour en conserver la tradition ; mais les étudiauts faisaient de yains efforts, et il leur était difficile d'en approfondir le sens.

"A l'époque oú la vie des hommes était réduite á cent ans, on vit paraftre le Ṛṣi *Po-ṇi-ni* (Pāṇini), qui était instruit dés sa naissance et posséadait un vaste savoir. Affligé de 1' ignorance, du siécle il voulut retrancher les notions vagues et fausses. débarrasser la langue des mots superflus et en fixer les lois. Comme il voyngeait pour faire des recherches et s'instruire, il rencoiitra le dien *Tscu-thsa'i* (Īśvara Deva), et lui exposa le plan de l'ouvrage qu'il méditait.

" 'A merveille !' lui dit le dieu *Tseu-Thas'i* (Īśvara Deva); 'vous pouvez compter sur mon secours."

"Aprés avoir recu ses instructions, le Ṛṣi se retira, II se livra alors á des recherches profondes, et déploya toute la vigueur de son esprit. II recueillit une multitude d'express-ions, et composa un *livre de mots*[330] qui renfermait mille *ślolcas*; chaque *śloka* était de trente-deux syllabes. II sonda jusqu'á leurs dernieres litnites, les connaissances anciennes et nouve-lies, et ayant rassemblé', dans cet ouvrage, les letters et les mots, il le mit sous une enveloppe cachetée et le presenta au roi, qui en concut autant d'estime que d'adrairation. II rendit un décretqui ordonnait á tous ses sujets de l'étudier et del'enseigner aux autres. II ajouta que quiconque pourrait le réciter, d'un bout a l'autre, recevrait, pour reéompense, mille piéces d'or. De Iá vient que, grâce aux lecons successives des maîtres, cet ouvrage est encore aujourd'hui en grand honneur. C'est pourquoi les Brāhmaṇes de cette ville out une science solide et des talents élevés, et se distinguent á la fois par l'étendue de leurs connaissances et la richcssc dc lcur Mémoirc.

"Dans la ville de *P'o-lo tou-lo* (lisez *So-lo-tou-lo*—"Śala-tura), il y a un *Stūpa*. Ce fut en cet endroit qu'un *Lo-han* (un Aṁat) convertit un disciple de *Po-ni-ni* (Pāṇini). Cinq cents ans aprés que *Jou-ldÏ* (le Tnthāgata) eut quitté le monde, il y eut un grand *'O-lo-han* (Aṁat) qui, venant du royaume de *Kia-chi-mi-lo* (Cachemire\ voyageait pour convertir les hommes. Quand il fut arrivé dans ce pays, il vit un *Fan-tcJd* (un Brahmachārin) occupé á fouetter un petit gallon qu'il instruisait. 'Pourquoi malTraitézvous cet enfant ?' dit 1' *Aṁat* au *Fan-tcM* (Brahmacārin).

" 'Je lui fais'e'tudier,' repondit-il, 'le *Traité de la Science des Sons* (Ching-ming – Vyākaraṇam), mais il ne fait aucun progrés.'

"L'*arhat* se dérida et laissa échapper un sourire. Le vieux *Fan-tehi* (Brahmacārin) lui dit: 'Les *Cha-men* (Śramaṇas) ont un coeur affectueux et compatissant, et s'apitoient sur les créatures qui souffrent. L'homme plein d'humanité vient de sourire tout á l'heure ; je désirerais en connaitre la cause'. " 'Il n'est pas difficile de vous l'apprendre,' répondit l'Arhat, 'mais je crains de faire naitre en vous un doute

d'incré dulité. Vous avez, sans doute, entendu dire qu'un Ṛṣi, nommé *Po-ni-ni* (Pāṇini) a composé le Traité *Ohiing-ming-lun* (Vyākaraṇam), et qu'il l'a laissé, Aprés lui, pour l'instruction du monde.' Le *Po-lo-men* (le Brāhmaṇe) lui dit: Les enfants de cette ville, qui sont tous ses disciples, révérent sa vertu, et la statue, élevée en son honneur, subsiste encore aujourd'hui.'

" 'Eh bien !' repartit *l'Arhat,* 'cet enfant, á qui vous avez donné le jour, est précisément ce *Ṛṣi* (Dans sa vie anté-rieur), il employait sa forte Mémoire á étudier les livres profanes; il ne parlait que des Traités hérétiques et ne cherchait point la vérité. Son esprit et sa science dépérirent, et il parcourut, sans s'arreter, le cercle de la vie et de la mort. gráce á un reste de vertu, il a obtenu de devenir votre fils bien-aimé. Mais les livres profanes et l'eloquence du siécle ne donnent que des peihes inutiles. Pourraiton les comparer aux saintes instructions de *Jou la'i* (du Tathâgata), qui, par une influence secr&te procurent rintelligence et le bonheur ?

" 'Jadis, sur les bords de la mer du midi, il y avait un arbre desséché dont le tronc creux donnait asile á cinq cents chauves-souris. Des marchands s'arrêtérent un jour au pied de cet arbre. Comme il régnait alors un vent glacial, ces hommes, qui étaient tourmentés par la faim et le froid, amassérent du bois et des broussailles et allumérent du feu au pied de l'arbre. Lo flamme s'accrut par degrés et embrasa bientōt l'arbre desséché.

" 'Dans ce moment, il y eut tin des marchands qui, aprés le milieu de la nuit, se mit á lire, á haute voix, le Receuil de *LO-*

pi-ta-mo (de l'Abhidharma). Les c auves-souries, quoique tourmentées, par l'ardeur du feu, écoutérent avec amour les accents de la loi, supportérent la douleur sans sortir de leur retraite, et y terminérent leur vie. En conséquencesde cette conduite vertueuse, elles obtinrent de renaître dans la classe des hommes. Elles quittérent la famille, se livrlrent á l'étude, et, grâce aux accents de la loi, qu'elles avaient jadis entendus, elles acquirent une rare intelligence, obtinrent toutes ensemble la dignité *d'Aṁat,* et cultive'rent, de siécle en siécle, le champ du bonheur. Dans ces derniers temps, le roi *Kia-ni-se-kia* (Kaniṣka) et l'honorable *Hie* (Ārya Pārśvika) convoquérent cinq cents sages dans le royaume de *Kia-chi-mi-lo* (Kashmir), et composéient le *Pi-po cha-lun* (le Vibhāshāśāstra). Tous ces sages étaient les cinq cents chauves-souris qui habitaient jadis le creux de l'arbre desseche. Quoique j'aie un esprit borné, j'étais moi-meme l'une d'elles. Mais les hommes différent entre eux par la supériorité ou la mediocrité de leur esprit; les uns prennent leur essor, tandis que les autres rampent dans l'obscurité. Maintenant, ô homme plein d'humanité, il faut que vous permattiez *á* votre fils bien-aimé de quitter la famille. En quittant la famille (en embrassant la vie religieuse), on acquiert des merites ineffables.'

"Lorsque *L'Arhat* eut acheve ces paroles, il donna une preuve de sa puissance divine en disparaissant a l'instant

" Le Brāhmane sa sentit pénétré de foi et de respect, et Aprés avoir fait éclater son admiration, il alia raconter cet événement dans tout le voisinage. Il permit aussitôt *á* son fils d'embrasser la vie religieuse et de se livrer *á* l'etude. Lui-même se convertit immêdiatement, et montra la plus grande estime pour les *trois Précieux.* Les hommes de son village suivirent son exemple, et, aujord'hui encore, les habitants s'affermissent de jour en jour dans la foi.

" En partant au nord de la ville de *Ou-to kia-han-t'cha* (Uḍakhāṇda ?), il franchit des montagnes, traversa des vallues, et, Aprés avoir fait environ six cents li, il arriva au royaume de *Ou-tchang-na*[331] (Udyāna[332]).

Whatever the historical value of this legend may be, it is quite clear that it lends no support of any kind to the opinion of those who would place the grammarian Pāṇini 500 years after Buddha, or 100 years after Kaniṣka.

It is possible that the inquiries into the ancient literature of Buddhism, particularly in China, may bring to light some new dates, and help us in unravelling the chronological traditions of the *Brāhmaṇas* of India. The services, already rendered to Sanskrit archeology by the publications of M. Stanislas Julien are of the highest value, and they hold out the promise of a still larger harvest; but for the present we must be satisfied with what we possess, and we must guard most carefully against rash conclusions, derived from evidence that would break' down under the slightest pressure. Even without the support which it was attempted to derive from Hiouen-thsang, Kātyāyana's date is as safe as any date is likely to be in ancient Oriental chronology; and the connection between Kātyāyana and his predecessors and successors, supported as it is not only by tradition but by the character of their works which we still possess, supplies the strongest confirmation of our chronological calculations. As to other works of the Sūtra period, there are no doubt many, the date of which cannot be fixed by any external evidence. Tradition is completely silent as to the age of many of their authors. With regard to them we must trust, at least for the present, to the similarity of their style and character with the writings of those authors whose age has been fixed. It is possible that the works of earlier-authors quoted by Yāska and Pāṇini and others might still come to light, if any systematic search for ancient MSS. was made in different parts of India. Many works are quoted by Séyaṇa, Devarāja, Ujjvaladatta, and other modern writers, which are not to be found in any European Library. Some of them may still be recovered[333]. We must not, however, expect too much. Vast as the ancient literature of India has been, we must bear in mind that part of it existed in oral tradition only, and was never consigned to writing. In India, where before the time of Pāṇini we have no evidence of any written literature, it by no means follows that because an early Ṛṣi is quoted in support of a theory, whether philosophical or grammatical, there ever existed a work written by him with pen and ink. His doctrines were handed down from generation to generation; but, once erased from the tablets of memory, they could never be recovered.

In the Sūtras which we still possess, it is most important to observe the gradual change of style. Śaunaka's style, when compared with that of his successors, is natural, both in prose and verse. His prose more particularly runs sometimes so easily and is so free from the artificial contrivances of the later Sūtras, that it seems a mistake to apply to it the name of Sūtra. It is not unlikely that this title was assigned to his works at a time when its meaning had not yet been restricted either to the long "yarns" of the Buddhists or to the compendious paragraphs of the *Brāhmaṇas,* and we may well believe the statement that Śaunaka's works on the ceremonial resembled more the Brāhmaṇas than the later Sūtras. Aśvalāyana's style is still intelligible, and less cramped by far than style of the Nirukta, a work commonly ascribed to Yāska, the collector of the Nighaṇṭuṣ. Pāṇini is more artificial. He is no longer writing and composing, but he squeezes and distils his thoughts, and puts them before us in a form which hardly deserves the name of style. Kātyāyana is still more algebraic ; but it is in Pirigala that the absurdity of the Sūtras becomes complete. If any writers succeed him they could hardly have excelled, him in enigmatic obscurity, and we may well believe that he was one of the last writers of Sūtras. The authors of the Pariśiṣṭas, unwilling to wear the strait-jacket of the Sūtrakāras, and unable to invent a more appropriate dress, adopted the slovenly metre of epic poetry, well adapted for legendary narration but unfit for scientific discussion.

REFERENCES

1. Benares Magazine, Oct. 1849.
2. Vedic forms occur in the Prātiśākhya-Sūtras, and are pointed out as such by the commentators. For instance, I. Prātiśākhya, iv 33. ता वशंगमानि instead

of तानि वशंगमानि। The Commentator says, तानिशब्दलोपी द्रष्टव्य:। छन्दोवत्सूत्राणि भवन्ति। The same applies also to the Sāmayācārika-Sūtras, for instance, those of Āpastamba i. 53, where we read अधासनशायी। The Commentator explains tis irregular form by अध:शब्दस्य सवर्णदीर्घश्छान्दसोऽपपाठो वा। Again, i. 93, we find अग्लौंस्तु explained by the Commentary as तत्रानुस्वारपाठश्छौंन्दस:। अपपाठो वा। Gautama-Sūtras, p. 40, 1. 20., we read सकारान्तपाठ आर्ष: सुमेध सो दुर्मेधस इत्यादिषु दर्शनात्।।

3. Kumārila quotes Sāṅkhya and Yoga, together with other heretical systems. साङ्ख्ययोगपाञ्चरात्रपाशुपतशाक्यनिर्ग्रन्थपरिगृहीतधर्माधर्मनिबन्धनानि।। As to the Vaiśeṣikas, see page 75.
4. The Buddhists say that the three Vedas were propounded originally by Maha Brahmā, at which time they were perfect truth; but they have since been corrupted by the Brāhmaṇas and now contain many errors. Cf. R. Spence Hardy, Eastern Monachism, p. 185.
5. Kumārila always speaks of Buddha as a Kṣatriya who tried to become a Brāhmaṇa. For instance, स्वधर्मातिरेकेण च क्षत्रियेण सता प्रवक्तृत्वप्रतिग्रहौ प्रतिपन्नौ। And again, बुद्धादे: पुनरयमेवातिक्रमोऽलङ्कारबुद्धौ स्थित:। येनैवमाह कलिकलुषकृतानि यानि लोके मयि निपतन्तु विमुच्यतां तु लोक इति स किल लोकहितार्थ क्षत्रियधार्ममतिकम्य ब्राह्मणवृत्तिं प्रवक्तृत्वं प्रतिपद्य प्रतिषेधातिक्रमसमर्थैर्ब्राह्मणैरननुशिष्टं धर्म बाह्यजनानुशास्तिं धर्मपीडामप्यात्मनोऽङ्गींकृत्य परानुग्रहं कृतवानित्येवं विधैरेव गुणै: स्तूयते।

   "And this very transgression of Buddha and his followers is represented as if it did him honour. For he is praised because he said,'Let all the sins that have been committed in this world fall on me, that the world may be delivered.' It is said that if he thus transgressed the duty of a Kshatriya, and entered the life of a Brāhmaṇa and preached, it was merely for the good of mankind; and that in adopting for the instruction of excluded people a law which had not been taught by the Brāhmaṇas, he took the sin upon himself and was benefitting others,"
6. सदादीनामन्यतमद्विचारं न सहते। (Br.S. 11-ū-)
7. न हन्यात्।
8. न पिबेत्। i.e. "You shall not drink intoxicating liquors."
9. तिष्ठन्भुञ्जीत।
10. चैत्यं वन्देत स्वर्गकाम:।
11. केशान् लुञ्चेत्।
12. अकर्तृकतया नापि कर्तृदोषेण दुष्यति।
    वेदवद्बुद्धवाक्यादि कर्तृस्मरणवर्जणात्।
    बुद्धवाक्यसमाख्यापि प्रवक्तृत्वनिबन्धना।
    तद्दृष्टत्वनिमिता वा काठकाङ्गिरसादिवत्।।
    यावदेवोदितं किञ्चिद्वेदप्रमाण्यसिद्धये।
    तत्सर्व बुद्धवाक्यानामतिदेशेन गम्यते।।

13. पूर्वविज्ञानविषयं विज्ञानं स्मृतिरुच्यते।
पूर्वज्ञानाद्विना तस्याः प्रामाण्यं नावधार्यते।।
and again,
मन्वादीनामपि यदि प्रथमं किञ्चित्प्रमाणं सम्भाव्यते ततः स्मरणं भवेन्नान्यथा कस्मात्पुनः पुत्रं दुहितरं चाधिक्रम्य वन्ध्यादौहित्रोदाहरणम् कृतम्। स्थानतुल्यत्वात्पुत्रस्थानीयं हि मन्वादेः पूर्वविज्ञानम्। दौहित्रस्थानीयं स्मरणम्। अतश्च यथा दुहितुरभावं परामृश्य दौहित्रस्मृतिं भ्रान्ति मन्यन्ते तथा मन्वादिभिः प्रत्यक्षाद्यसम्भवपरामर्शादष्टकादिस्मरणं मिथ्येति मन्तव्यम्।।
14. MS. Bodl. 172, 173.
* What not ?
15. As dhayyās at the Somāraudra Caru, in the middle of the Sāmidhenī, or fire-kindling hymns. The same argument occurs in Kumārila's Tantravārttika, i. 3.,
तथा च मनोर्ऋचः सामिधेन्यो भवन्तीत्यस्य विधोर्वाक्यशेषे श्रूयते मनुर्वै यत्किञ्चिदेव वदेत्तद्भेषजं भेषजताया इति।।
Mahādeva, in his Commentary on the Hiraṇyakeśi-Sūtras, says that the Śruti bears witness to the authority of the Smṛtis by declaring that whatever Manu said was medicine.
श्रुतिरपि स्मृतीनां वेदमूलत्वमाह यद्वै किञ्च मनुरवदत्तद्भेषजमिति, भेषजं यथा हितमेवं मनुवचनमपि प्रमाणत्वेन हितमित्यर्थः।।
16. If this refers to the Saṅkarṣaṇa-kāṇḍa, which is ascribed to Jaimini, and forms an appendix to the Karma-mīmāṁsā-sūtras (cf. Prasthāna-bheda), we ought to read Pūrva-mīmānsā instead of Uttara-mīmāṁsā.
17. Bṛhadāraṇyaka, 5. 6. 3.
18. Taitirīya-Saṁhitā. 3. 5. 2. ऋषयो वा इन्द्रं प्रत्यक्षं नापश्यत् तं वसिष्ठः प्रत्यक्षमश्यत् सोऽब्रवीत् ब्राह्मणं ते वक्ष्यामि यथा त्वत्पुरोहिता. प्रजा. प्रजनिष्यन्तोऽथ मेतरेभ्य ऋषिभ्यो मा प्रवोच इति। तस्मा एतात् स्तोमभागानब्रवीत् ततो वसिष्ठपुरोहिताः प्रजाः प्राजायन्त तस्माद्वासिष्ठो ब्रह्मा कार्यः।
"The Ṛṣis did not see Indra clearly, but Vaśishṭha saw him clearly.
Indra said,'I shall tell you a Brāhmaṇa, so that all men that are born will have you for *Purohita*; but do not tell of me to the other Ṛṣis'. Thus he told him these parts of the hymns; and ever since, men were born having Vaśiṣṭha for their Purohita. Therefore a Vaśiṣṭha is to be chosen as Brahmā."
Cf. Tāṇḍya Brāhmaṇa xv. 5, where it is said of the Bhāratas that they will always have a Vaśiṣṭha as Purohita. The Commentator there observes, that Bhārata may either mean the kings of that name, or men in general.
19. Taittirīya-Saṁhitā, 7. 1. 8.
अत्रिरददादौर्वाय प्रजां पुत्रकामाय स रिरिचानोऽमन्यत निवीर्यः शिथिलो यातयामा स एतं चतूरात्रमश्यत्तमाहरत्तेनायजत ततो वै तस्य चत्वारो वीरा अजायन्त सुह्वाता सूद्गाता स्वध्वर्युः सुसभेयः।।
"Atri gave his children to the son of Urva, who longed for a son. Then he felt lonely, and saw that he was without power, weak, and decrepit. He saw this Caturātra; he took it and sacrificed with it. Four sons were born to him

from it, - a good Sotr, a good Udgatṛ, a good Adhvaryu, and a good Brahmā." ?

20. Śatapatha-brāhmaṇa, XVII, 4.5.
21. Taittirāya-Āraṇyaka, ū, 10.
22. Kumārila remarks that, although the six Vedāṅgas are not called by the name of Smṛti, they are Smṛti in the same sense as the Dharma-sūtras, i. 3. 9.
स्मृतित्वं त्वङ्गानां धर्मसूत्राणाञ्चाविशिष्टम्-
यद्यपि स्मृतिशब्देन नाङ्गानामभिधेयता।
तथाप्येषां न शास्त्रत्वप्रमाणत्वनिराक्रिया।।
Mahādeva, in his Commentary on the Hiraṇyakeśi-sūtras, says distinctly, सूत्रेषु स्मृतित्वं स्मृत्यधिकरणे स्थितम्। तत्सूत्रकारेणैवोक्तं न्यायवित्समय इति मीमांसासिद्धान्तस्वीकारदर्शनेन।।
23. "When we spoke of this (the authorship of Madhuchan das) to a learned Hindū friend, he exhibited very marked dissatisfaction and distress, begging us to write and tell Professor Wilson that the hymn had no author; that it had existed from everlasting; and that Madhuchandas was only the fortunate seer to whom, on the last occasion of its revelation, it had been revealed."- Benares Magazine for June 1851, "On Muller's Edition and Wilson's Version of the Ṛg-Veda."
24. अप्रमाण्यं स्मृतीनाञ्च यदशब्दतयोदितम्।
पूर्वपक्षे न तद्वक्तुं कल्पसूत्रेषु शक्यते।।
प्रत्यक्षवेदशब्दत्वात्तदुक्ता नापशब्दता।
न ह्यत्यन्तानृतं वक्तं शक्यते पूर्वपक्षिणा।।
25. वेदत्वं कल्पसूत्राणां नो वक्तव्यं मनागपि।
26. Kumārila expressly observes that these names signify certain individuals, and not Caraṇas (sects), like those of Kaṭha, by which certain Śākhās of the Veda were promulgated.
"यथा च कठादिचरणैरनादिभिः प्रोच्यमानानामनादिवेदशाखानामनादिसमाख्यासम्भवो नैवं नित्यावस्थितमशकादिगोत्रचरणप्रवचननिमित्तसमाख्योपपत्तिः। मशकबौधायनापस्तम्बादि-शब्दा ह्यादिमदेकद्रव्योपदेशिन इति न तेभ्यः प्रकृतिभूतेभ्योऽनादिग्रन्थविषयसमाख्या-व्युत्पादनसम्भवः।।"
"The branches of the Vedas which were proclaimed by the sects of Kaṭha and others from all eternity, have a fair claim to be called eternal. But this does not apply to works handed down by the sects or families of Maśaka and others, however long they may have been established. For names like Maśaka, Baudhāyana, and Āpastamba, imply an individual being which had a beginning, and therefore it is impossible that a title derived from these names should ever belong to an eternal work."
And again :
"यथैव हि कल्पूसत्रग्रन्थानितराङ्गस्मृतिनिबन्धनानि चाध्येत्रध्यापयितारः स्मरन्ति तथाश्वलायनबौधायनापस्तम्बकात्यायनप्रभृतीन् ग्रन्थकारत्वेन।।"
"For teachers and pupils do not only know by heart the Kalpa-sūtra books,

and the other Vedāṅga and Smṛti composition but they also remember Āśvalāyana, Baudhāyana, Kātyāyana, and others, as the authors of these books."

27. "तत्र यावद्धर्ममोक्षसम्बन्धि तद्वेदप्रभवम्। यत्त्वर्थसुखविषयं तल्लोक व्यवहारपूर्वकमिति विवेक्तव्यम्। एषैवेतिहासपुराणयोरप्युपदेशवाक्यानां गतिः।
"All that has reference to virtue and final beatitude is taken from the Veda, while other matters, the purpose of which consists in pleasure and gain, are according to the customs of men. This distinction applies not only to the Vedāṅgas, but also to authoritative passages in the Purāṇas and Itihāsas."
Uvaṭa, in his commentary on the Śākla Pratiśākya, takes the same view. He says, "that as the Veda was too difficult to be used by itself, learned men have extracted from it different doctrines on the ceremonial, the metre, and grammar, and brought them into a more intelligible form in the Sūtras."
यस्मात्केवलैर्वेदवाक्यैर्न शक्यतेऽनुष्ठानं विक्षिप्तत्वाद्वेदवाक्यानां गूढार्थत्वाच्च अतः कविभिराचार्यैर्वेदार्थकुशलैर्वेदार्थेभ्यो निष्कृष्य कर्मार्थं सुखावबोधनानीमानि विद्यास्थानानि प्रवर्तितानि। शिक्षा कल्पो व्याकरणं निरुक्तं छन्दो ज्यौतिषमितिधार्मशास्त्रं पुराणं न्यायविस्तरो मीमांसादीनि।
And again
अत आचार्यो भगवान् शौनको वेदार्थवित् सुहृद्भूत्वा ब्राह्मणेभ्योऽर्थवादानुत्सृज्य विधिं समाहृत्य पुरुषहितार्थमृग्वेदस्य शिक्षाशास्त्रं कृतवानिति।।

28. Thus smārtam karma is well defined by Ṣadguruśiṣya in the Sarvānukarmanībhāṣya, as 'nishekadi śmaśanāntam smṛti-gṛhya-vihitam-karma.' In the Commentary on Āśvalāyana's Śrauta-Sūtras it is said, that, if observances, like rinsing the mouths, etc., are prescribed in the Śrauta Sūtras (as they are for instance Āśval i. 1. 3,), this is only done in order to show that such observances are acknowledged and presupposed by the Śrauta-Sūtras though they belong to the province of the Gṛhya ceremonies.
स्मातिनां स्नानाचमनयज्ञोपवीतादीनां श्रौतकर्माविरुद्धानामस्मिन् शास्त्रे प्राप्तिप्रदर्शनार्थमिदमाचमनं कर्माङ्ग विंधीयते। शौचार्थस्य गृहप्रवेशात्प्रागेव कृतत्वात्। तदुक्तम्-
"मनःप्रसादात्सत्योक्त्या तमसा स्नानकर्मणा।
आचान्त्या चात्मनः शुद्धिं कृत्वा कर्म समारभेत"-इति।।

29. अर्थातः सामयाचारिकान्धार्मान्व्याख्यास्यामः।।१।।

30. धर्मज्ञसमयः प्रमाणम्।।२।।

31. सुगतो यदि धर्मज्ञः कपिलो नेति का प्रभा।
तावुभौ यदि सर्वज्ञो मतिभेदः कथं तयोः।।
Dr. Weber, in his dissertation on the Upaniṣads, thinks it is not impossible that Kapila, the founder of the Sāṅkhya, and Buddha were in fact one and the same person. (Indische Studien, i. 436.) He afterwards qualifies this conjecture, and calls it not very probable. It is true that the Indians themselves observed a certain similarity between the doctrines of Kapila and Buddha. But this would rather show that the two were different persons. Nor would the legend that Buddha was born at Kapilavastu, the town of Kapila, or

rather of the Kapilas, seem to prove the identity of Kapila and Buddha. By another conjecture, the same ignious scholar makes the founder of the Sāṅkhya (Pañcaśikha Kāpileya) the same person with Kāpya Pātañjala, who occurs in the Śatapatha-Brāhmaṇa; while, in a former article (i. 84), both Kapila aud Patañjali together, the former as the founder of the Saukliya, the latter as the author of the Yoga system, are merged into Kāpya Patañjala. Aferwards, however, this opinion also is retracted, because Dr. Weber thinks that the Yoga system might be a later devolopment of the Sāṅkhya.

32. वेदाश्च ।।३।।

33. Someśvara, who calls himself a son of Mādhava, and of whose work "Tantra-vārttika-ṭīkā" there is a manuscript at the E. I. H, (No. 1030), dated Samvat, 1552, goes even a step farther, and says that, although rules of the Smṛtis may be against the sacred law, the Veda must notwithstanding be considered as their source, because the Smṛtis themselves maintain that the Veda is the highest authority, an admission which the followers of Buddha protest against. Cf. p. 80
ननु याज्ञवक्यादिभिरपि यदुच्यते द्विजातीनां शूद्राद्दारोपसङ्ग्रहः न तन्मम मतं यस्मात्तत्रात्मा जायते स्वयं तेन पुनरित्यादिहेतुदर्शनपूर्वकं धर्माधर्मोपदेशनान्न तन्मात्रेण वेदमूलत्वनिराकरणं युक्तमित्याशंक्य वेद एव द्विजातीनां निःश्रेयसकरः पर इत्यादिना तैः प्राधान्येन वेदमूलत्वाभिधानात् etc. Cf. Yājñavalkya, ed. Stenzler, i. 56., i. 40.; Manu,iii. 12,13., where the Commentator mentions Vaśiṣṭha as having spoken of the marriage of a Brāhmaṇa with a Śudra, the ceremony not being accompanied by sacred hymns, as a kind of morganatic marriage, kāmato vivāḥ, वासिष्ठोऽपि शूद्रामप्येके मन्त्रवर्जभिति मन्त्रवर्जितं शूद्राविवाहमाह।।

34. भृतसाक्षिकव्यवहारवच्च प्रलीनशाखामूलत्वकल्पनायां यस्मै यद्रोचते स तत्प्रमाणीकुर्यात्।
"If a man maintain a lost tradition to have been a source, he may prove what he pleases, for it is like appealing to a dead witnes." And again:

येन यत्नेन मन्वाद्यैरात्मवाक्यं प्रपाठितम्।
कस्मात्तेनैव तन्मूलं चोदना न समर्पिता।।
यस्यैव यदभिप्रेतं स एवतत्प्रलीनशाखामस्तके निक्षिप्य प्रमाणीकुर्यात्।

"Why has divine precept not been established by Manu and the others as the source of their teaching, which would not have cost them more labour than to proclaim their own doctrine ? Anybody may throw whatever he likes into the skull of a lost tradition, and then invoke it as an authority."

35. ब्राह्मणोक्ता विधयस्तेषामुत्सन्नाः पाठाः प्रयोगादनुमीयन्ते। यत्र तु प्रीत्युपलब्धितः प्रवृत्तिर्न तत्र तदनुवर्तमानो नरकाया राध्यति।।

The Commentator says : उत्सन्नाः पाठा अध्येतृदौर्वल्यात्।।

"The original passages were lost by the negligence of the students."
Kumārila obseves :

"शाखानां विप्रकीर्णत्वात्पुरुषाणां प्रमादतः।
नानाप्रकरणस्थत्वात्स्मृतेर्मूलं न दृश्यते"।।

"The original text from which the Smṛti was derived cannot always be found, because the Śākhās are scattered about, students are negligent, and because these rales stand under different heads."

And again : दृश्यते ह्यद्यत्वेऽप्यर्थ (वि) स्मरणं ग्रन्थनाशश्च।।

"As if we did not see in our own time that subjects are forgotten and works lost."

न च प्रलयो न सम्भव्यते। दृश्यते हि प्रमादालस्यादिभि: पुरुषक्षयाच्च।

"And it must not be said that their destruction is impossible, for we see it takes place every day, whether by negligence, idleness, or by the death of men,"

36. यैश्च मन्वादिस्मृतीनाप्युत्सन्नवेदशाखामूलमभ्युपगतं तान्प्रत्प्रति सुतरां शाक्यादिभिरपि शक्यं तन्मूलत्वमेव वक्तुम्। को हि शक्नुयादुत्सन्नानां वाक्यविषयेयत्तानियमं कर्तुम्। ततश्च यावत्किश्चित्कियन्तन्मपि कालं कैश्चिदाद्रियमाणं प्रसिद्धिं गतं तत्प्रत्यक्षशाखाविसंवादेऽप्युत्सन्न-शाखामूलत्वावस्थामनुभवत्तुल्यकक्षतया प्रतिभायात्। 'अत एव विरोधे त्वनपेक्ष्यं स्यादिति'।।

37. Taitt Ār. i. 1, 8. : स्मृति: प्रत्यक्षमैतिह्यमनुमानश्चतुष्टयम्।।

The Commentator explains Smṛti by अनुमेयश्रुतिमूलं मन्वादिशास्त्रम्। "The laws of Manu and others whose source is a revelation the existence of which must be inferred." *Pratyakṣa* sensuous impression) is, according to Sāyaṇa सर्वपुरुषाणां श्रोत्रिये ग्राह्यं वेदवाक्यम्, "the word of the Veda which all men can perceive in their teacher. *Aitihya* (tradition) is explained by इतिहासपुराणमहाभारत ब्राह्मणदिकम्, "Legends, Purāṇas, the Mahābhārata and the Brāhmaṇas." Lastly *Anumāna*, if we believe Sāyaṇa, does not here mean inference, but customs of good men, by which or from which the existence of an authority, that is, of Sruti and Śmṛti, as the source of these customs, is inferred, अनुमान: शिष्टाचार:। तेन हि मूलभूतं श्रुतिस्मृतिलक्षणं प्रमाणमनुमीयते।

38. Anupada-sūtra, ii. 4. श्रुतिस्मृतिदृष्टसम्पन्नै:। Cf Indische Studien i. p. 44.

39. Nidāna-sūtra, ii. 1. आचार्यस्मृतीनाम्। याज्ञिका: स्मृतौ। Cf. Indische Studien, i. p. 45.

40. Manu, iii. 184. अग्र्या: सर्वेषु वेदेषु सर्वप्रवचनेषु च।

"Those priests must be considered as the purifiers of a company who are most learned in all the Vedas and all their Aṅgas" Sir W. Jones.

Kullūka : प्रकर्षेणैवोच्यते वेदार्थ एभिरिति प्रवचनान्यङ्गानि।।

"Because the meaning of the Veda is proclaimed by them, therefore are the Aṅgas called Pravacanas."

41. कालबविनामपि प्रवचनविहित: स्वर: स्वाध्याये।

Com. प्रवचनशब्देन ब्राह्मणमुच्यते। प्रोच्यत इति प्रवचनम्।।

"Among the Kālabavins also the accent exists in the perusal of the Veda enjoined by the Pravacanas. Com. By the word *'Pranachana'* is meant the Brāhmaṇa, and it is called so because it is proclaimed."

There is a passage in the Prasthāna-bheda,

एवं प्रवचनभेदात्प्रतिवेदं भिन्ना भूयस्य: शाखा:।

"For each Veda there are several Śākhās the difference of which arises from different *Pravacanas*."

Here *pravacana* means Brāhmaṇa, because the difference of the Brāhmaṇa-śākhās does arise from Brāhmaṇas peculiar to each. It is. possible, however, that Mādhusūdana used *pravacana* in the sense of pronunciation, the difference of pronunciation being the chief cause of the Saṁhitā-śākhās. *Pravacana* is used in the Kaṭhopaniṣad, ii, 23;, in the sense of "reading."

42. शिक्षा कल्पो व्याकरणं निरुक्तं छन्दो ज्यौतिषम्।। Āpastamba, who occasionally quotes Ślokas in his Sūtras, does oot seem to have known this verse. His words are (ii. 4. 8.) षडङ्गो वद: कल्पो व्याकरणं ज्योतिषं निरुक्तं शिक्षा। What follows, in the only MS. I know, is eaten away by worms; but then comes the word छन्दोविचिति, which was the title of a metrical treatise, and is quoted as much before Piṅgala, in the Śabda-Kalpa-druma, *s. v.* तस्य ग्रन्था: छन्दोविचिति-पिङ्गल-छन्दोमञ्जरी-श्रुतबोघादय: सन्ति।। One of the Pariśiṣtas of the Sāmaveda begins with the words अथातश्छन्दसां विचयं व्याख्यास्याम:। The Pariśiṣtas however, are later than. Āpastamba and Pīṅgala; for the author of the Pariśiṣta declares that he made use of Pīṅgala's work:
ब्राह्मणात्तण्डिनश्चैव पिङ्गलाच्च महात्मन:। निदानादुक्थशास्त्राच्च छन्दसां ज्ञानमृद्धृतम्।
The title छन्दोविचिति refers, therefore, most likely to the Nidāna-sūtra, which also begins with. अथातश्छन्दसां विचयं व्याख्यास्याम:। Cf MS, Berol. 95. In the Commentary on the Śākala-prātiśākhya, at the end of the 14th Book, the Vedāṅgas are enumerated as follows :
कल्पो व्याकरणं निरुक्तं शिक्षा छन्दोविचितिर्ज्योतिषामयनम्।।

43. This passage has been pointed out and translated by Colebrooke (Miscellaneous Essays, i. 12.). "Nārada, having solicited instruction from Sanatkumāra, and being interrogated by him as to the extent of his previous knowledge, says, "I have learnt the Ṛg-veda, the Yajur-veda, the Sāma-veda, the Atharvaṇa (which is) the fourth, the Itihāsa and Purāṇa (which are) a fifth, and grammar, or) the Veda of Vedas, the obsequies of the manes (पित्र्यम्), the art of computation (राशिम्) the knowledge of omens (दैवम्), the revolution of periods (निधिम् com. महाकालादिनिधिशास्त्रम्) the intention of speech (or art of reasoning) (वाकोवाक्यम्) the maxims of ethics (एकायनम्), the divine science (or construction of scriptures) (देवविद्याम्, com. निरुक्तम्) the science appendant on holy writ (or accentuatiou, prosody, and religious rites) (ब्रह्मविद्याम्), the adjuration of spirits (भूतविद्याम् com. भूततन्त्रम्), the art of the soldier (क्षत्रविद्याम् com. धनुर्वेदम्), the science of astronomy (नक्षत्रविद्याम्) the charming of serpents (सर्पविद्याम्), the science of demigods (or music and mechanical arts, गारुडम् see page 39.): all this I have studied; yet do I only know the text, and have no knowledge of the soul."

44. चत्वारांऽस्यै वेदा: शरीरं षडङ्गान्यङ्गानि। ओषधिवनस्पतयो लोमानि।।
"The four Vedas are her body; the six Aṅgas her limbs; herbs and trees her hair." See also the text frequently quoted from the Veda, ब्राह्मणेन षडङ्गो वेदो

निष्कारणोऽध्येयो ज्ञेयश्च ।। "The Veda, with its six members out to be known and understood by a Brāhmaṇa without any further inducement."

45. शीक्षां व्याख्यायाम: The'i'in Śikṣā short (*hrasva*) though it is strong (*guru*). It is only in the Āraṇyaka that Śikṣā occurs instead of Śikṣā. Śikṣā is derived from √*śak*, to be able, and means originally a desire to know. From the same root we have śākta, a teacher (Ṛv. vii. 103. 5.); *śikṣamāṇa*, a pupil (Ṛv. vii. 102. 5.). *Śiṣya*, a pupil, comes from a different root. Sāyaṇa says, शिक्ष्यन्ते वेदनायोपदिश्यन्ते स्वरवर्णादयो यत्रासौ शिक्षा। सैव शीक्षा।। The other headings are, वर्णः। स्वरः। मात्रा। बलम्। साम। सन्तानः।

46. I owe a copy of this Commentary of Sāyaṇa's to the kindness of Dr. Röer, at Calcutta. Seeing, in the catalogue of manuscripts published by the Asiatic Society of Calcutta, a work of Sāyaṇa's called Śikṣā-bhāṣya, and imagining this to be a commentary on this Śikṣā-vedāṅga or one of the Prātiśākhyas, I wrote to Dr. Röer for a copy of it. Though I was ultimately disappointed when I found that it had nothing to do with the Prātiśākhyas, I still consider the Commentary of great interest, particularly Sāyana's introduction to the Vedānta system in it. Dr. Röer has since published the whole Taittirīya-upaniṣed, with the Commentaries of Śaṅkara and Ānanda Giri, in No. 22 of the Bibllotheca Indica.

47. सेयं तैत्तिरीयोपनिषत् त्रिविधा। सांहिती याज्ञिकी वारुणी चेति। तत्र प्रथमे प्रपाठके संहिताध्यानस्योक्तत्वात् जपोपनिषतत्सांहिती। द्वितीयतृतीययोः प्रपाठकयोर्या ब्रह्मविद्या विहिता तस्याम्। etc. तासां तिसृणां मध्ये वारुणी मुख्या।

48. तस्माद्विद्यायामवैकल्याय यथाशास्त्रं बोद्धुमुपनिषत्पाठे प्रयत्नातिशयं विधातुमत्रैव शिक्षाध्यायोऽभिधीयते।। तस्य च ग्रन्थस्यार्थज्ञानप्रधानत्वात्पाठे मा भूदौदासीन्यमित्येतदर्थे द्वितीयानुवाके शिक्षाध्यायोऽभिधीयते।

49. The passage .from the Puṣpa-sūtras (viii. 8.) which was quoted before, कालबविनामपि प्रवचनविहितः स्वरः स्वाध्याये, does not prove that the rules on the acceut were laid down in the Brāhmaṇas of the Kālabavins, because it may also mean that the accented delivery erf sacred text was enjoined in the Brāhmaṇa.

50. According to the first Prātiśākhya, i. 58 पादवच्चैव प्रेषान् their rules would seem to affect passages of the Brāhmaṇas too; like होता यक्षत् etc. and the Commentator adds, ऋक्षु यल्लक्षणं तत्प्रैषेष्वपि। Most of these *Praiṣas*; however, are taken from the hymns; as, for Instance, the word होता यक्षत् (Ṛv.i. 139.10). This is different for the Yajur-veda where the general rules of the Prātiśākhya extend their influence to the sacrificial invocations.

51. Ms. Bodl. W. 510.:
तेषां पञ्चदश यथास्वरं प्रतिष्ठाः प्रतिशाखं च कुलधर्माः।
The meaning of "*Yathāsvaram pratiṣṭhāḥ*" is doubtful. Should it mean "rules with reference to accents?" If so, they would be the rules of Prātiśākhyas. That the Śākhās differed about the accents is seen in the case of the Māṇḍukeyas and Śākalas. Prātiśākhya I. 200. Kātyāyana, as the author of a Prātiśākhya, is called स्वरसंस्कारप्रतिष्ठापयिता।।

52. Tantra V. I. 3. (MS. Bodl. W. .325. p. 15 b.)
धर्मशास्त्राणां गृह्यग्रन्थानाञ्च प्रातिशाख्यलक्षणवत्प्रतिचरणं पाठव्यवस्थोपलभ्यते।

53. Veda is taken here in the general sense of sacred literature, as Uvaṭa says, 'सर्वकालं सर्वदेशेषु प्रतिचरणमविभागेनैकैको मन्त्रराशिर्वेद इत्युच्यते।

"Every single collection of hymns which existed at any time and in any place, without reference to the divisions in each Caraṇa (sect), is called Veda."

54. According to Madhusūdana, the Brāhmaṇa part of the Veda, by which he can only mean the Upaniṣads, is not affected by the peculiarities of the Śākhās. If this were true; it would only prove the late origin of the Upaniṣ ads. Some Upaniṣads, however, show traces of various readings, which must properly be attributed to various Śākhās. This is admitted, for instance, by Sāyaṇa in his Commentary on the Yājñikī or Nārāyaṇīya-upamṣad, "Tadīya-patha-sampradāyo deśaviśeṣu bahuvidho dṛśyate; tatra yadyapi śākhābhedaḥ kātaṇam tathāpi Taittirīyādhyādhyāyakais tat-tad-deśanivāsibhiḥ śiṣṭar ādṛtatvāt, sarvo'pi pāṭha upādeya eva." Ind. Stud. i. 76.

55. See also Someśvara's Tantra-vārttika-ṭikā, MS. E. I. H. 1030, p. 95.)
साधारणी विशेषविषया च द्विविधा शिक्षा। तत्र साधारण्या वेदाङ्गत्वेन धर्मप्रामाण्येऽपि कात्यायनादिप्रणीताया विशेषविषयायाः प्रतिवाक्यं प्रतिपदञ्चोच्चारणं नियच्छन्त्या धर्मप्रमाणाभावाशङ्कानिराकरणार्थं पृथगुपादानेऽपि शिक्षात्वेनैक्यान्नातिरेकापत्तिः।

"There are two kinds of Śikṣā, a general and one which has regard to particulars. It is true that the authority of the general Śikṣā is established, on account of its belonging to the Vedāṅgas; but in order to remove all doubt as to the authority of the particular Śikṣās, published by Kātyāyana and others, which determine the pronunciation of each sentence and each word, it is clear that it is not different from the other, inasmuch as both are one by their common character of Śikṣā, although they are spokeig of separately."

56. It is said of Sāyaṇa that he wrote commentaries on each of the Śākhās of the Ṛk, Yajuṣ and Sāma.
ऋग्यजुःसामशाखानामेकैका व्याकृता त्वया।
तावता तत्समानार्था ज्ञातुं शक्यास्ततः पराः।।

Ekaika could hardly mean "one from among the *Śākhās* of each Veda."

57. यदि प्रतिशाखं कर्मभेदः स्यात् तत एकमूलाभावादादित एवारभ्य भिद्यमानत्वात् समस्तकर्माख्फलान्तरत्वात् वृक्षान्तरवद्वेदान्तराण्येवोच्येरन् न शाखान्तराणि।।

58. गीतिशब्दाश्च सामशब्दाश्च एते श्रूयमाणा अनध्यायहेतवः।। शाखान्तरं च साम्नामनध्यायः।।४५।। वेदान्तरसकाशे साम नाध्येयम्।। The first Sūtra is paraphrased by the Mānavas, iv, 123.–''सामध्वनावृग्यजुषी नाधीयीत कदाचन'।

59. चरणशब्दः शाखाविशेषाध्ययनपरैकतापन्नजनसङ्घवाची। Cf. Zur , Litterature, p.57.

60. Pāṇ. iv. 2. 46. चरणेभ्यो धर्मवत् scil. समूहार्थे।

61. Āp. i. 4. 4. The Commentator says that चारणशब्दः शाखाध्यायिषु रूढः Cāraṇa, therefore, means a member of A Caraṇa. Lassen (Ind. Alterthumsk. i. 640.) takes Cārana in the sense of wandering poets, so named still in Western India.

62. Pāṇ. iv. 3. 126. गोत्रचरणाद्वुञ् scil. इदमर्थे।
63. Mahādeva's Hiraṇyakeśi-bhāṣya :
स्वाध्यायैकदेशो मन्त्रब्राह्मणात्मकः शाखेत्युच्यते। तयोर्मन्त्रब्राह्मणयोरन्यतरः भेदेन वेदेऽवान्तरशाखाभेदः स्यादिति चेत् सत्यम्।।
"Any portion of oral tradition consisting of Mantras and Brāhmaṇas is called a *śākhā*, and it is clear that differences of either the Mantras or Brāhmaṇas will necessarily lead, in the Veda, to a variety of subordinate śākhās,"
64. अध्यपनभेदाच्छाखाभेदोऽनादिः। "The various śākhās which arise from various readings are eternal."
65. "शाखाभेदेध्ययनभेदाद्वा सूत्रभेदाद्वा। आश्वालायनीयं कात्यायनीयञ्च सूत्रं हि भिन्नाध्ययनयोर्द्वयोः शाखायोरेकैकमेव। तैत्तिरीयके समाम्नाये समानाध्ययने नाना सूत्राणि।" Mahādeva's Commentary on the Hiraṇyakeśi-sūtra.
66. Cf. Nirukta, i. 17., where सर्वचरणानां is explained by सर्वशाखान्तराणाम्, and Pāṇ. ii. 4. 3. चरणः शाखा। Pāṇ. vi. 3. 86.
67. Pārṣada, instead of Pāriṣada. Cf. Pāṇ, iv. 3, 123.
68. I doubt the existance of word like माध्यन्दिनपार्षदम् which Dr. Roth mentions (Zur Litteratur, p. 16.). One may speak of पञ्चालानां परिषद् or वत्सानां परिषद् etc., and a Prātiśākhya current in one of these Pariṣads may, perhaps, be called वत्सपार्षदम्। But माध्यन्दिन is not the name of a Pariṣad, but of a Śākhā; and therefore the Commentary on Gobhila speaks of a वत्सशाखीयप्रातिशाख्यम्।।
69. Bṛh Ār. vi. 2.श्वेतकेतुर्ह वा आरुणेयः पञ्यालानां परिषदमाजगाम।।
70. एकविंशतिसंख्याकैर्मीमांसान्यायपारगैः।
वेदाङ्गकुशलैश्चैव परिषत्त्वं प्रकल्पयेत्।।
71. चत्वारो वा त्रयो वापि वेदवन्तोऽग्निहोत्रिणः।
ब्राह्मणानां समर्था ये परिषत्सा विधीयते।।
अनाहिताग्नयो येऽन्ये वेदवेदाङ्गपारगाः।
पञ्च त्रयो वा धर्मज्ञाः परिषत्सा प्रकीर्तिता।।
मुनीनामात्मविद्यानां द्विजानां यज्ञयाजिनाम्।
वेदव्रतेषु स्नातानामकोऽपि परिषद्भवेत्।।
पञ्च पूर्वे मया प्रोक्तास्तेषां वाऽसम्भवे त्रयः।
स्ववृत्तिपरिपुष्टा ये परिषत्सा प्रकीर्तिता।।
72. लोकवेदाङ्गधर्मज्ञाः सप्त पञ्च त्रयोऽपि वा।
यत्रोपविष्टा विप्राः स्युः सा यज्ञसदृशी सभा।।
73. See Gobhila-bhāṣya, MS W. 72. p. 71. a. आचार्य सपरिषत्कं भोजयेत्सब्रह्मचारिणश्च।। com. सह परिषदा शिष्यगणेन वर्तत इति सपरिषत्कः तम्। समानं तुल्यकालं ब्रह्मचारित्वं येषां त इमेऽन्यशाखिनोऽपि सब्रह्मचारिणः सवयसोऽभिधीयन्ते।। The expression इत्येके, "thus say some," which occurs frequently in the Sūtras, is stated to refer to different śākhās, उत्तरामित्येके।। Com. इत्येवमेके शाखिन आहुः। एक इति

स्वमतव्युदासार्थं परशाखाप्रदर्शनार्थञ्च। एवमेके मन्यन्ते न गोभिल इत्यर्थः। Nārāyaṅa's Commentary on Gobhila, MS. W. 72. page 23. b

74. Nir, i. 17. किं पार्षदानि। स्वचरणपर्षद्येव यैः प्रतिशाखं नियतमेव पदावग्रहप्रगृह्यक्रमसंहिता-स्वरलक्षणमुच्यते तानीमानि पार्षदानि प्रातिशाख्यानीत्यर्थः।।
"Those Pārṣada books by which in a Pariṣad (parish or college) ot one's own Caraṇa (sect), the peculiarities of accent, Saṁhitā atsd Krāma-reading, of Pragṛhya-voweis and separation of words, are laid down as enjoined for and restricted to certain Śākhās (branches or recensions of the Veda) are called Pratiśākliyas."
75. Sec Dr. Roth.Zur Litteratur, p. 58.
76. अन्यदतः परिषत्सु।।
77. अत एतस्मादनध्यायप्रकरणादन्यदनध्यायनिमित्तं परिषत्सु मानवादिषु धर्मशास्त्रेषु यथोक्तं तथा द्रष्टव्यम्। तत्र वासिष्ठः। etc.
78. The threefold division of Dharma is pointed out by the Prayoga-vaijayantī. (MS. Bod. W. 68, p. 1 6. a.) तैः प्रत्येकं मितो धर्मस्त्रिविधः परिकीर्तितः ।।४३।। अनेनैवाभिप्रायेणह बोधायनः। उपरिष्ठो धर्मः प्रतिवेदं तस्यानु व्यारत्यास्यामः (sic)। स्मार्तो द्वितीयः। शिष्टाचारस्तृतीय इति।।
"Baudhāyana says, the highest law is that contained in each Veda, which we shall follow to our explanation; the second is the traditional law; the third, the customs of eminent sages."
79. See Prof. Stenzler's introduction to his edition of Yājñavalkya, and his remarks on Indian Law-books iu Indische Studien, i. 232.
80. इदं शास्त्रं पार्षदाख्यमखिलं सम्पूर्णमुत्तरत्र वक्ष्ये वक्ष्याम इत्यर्थः। शैशिरीये पारयणपाठ इति वाक्यशेषः। शैशिरीयायां संहितायामित्यर्थः। शैशिरी संहिता शिशिरदृष्टत्वात्। तथा पुराण उक्तम्।
"मुद्गलो गोकुलो वात्स्यः शैशिरः शिशिररतथा।।
पश्चैतो शाकलाः शिष्याः शाखाभेदप्रवर्तका इति।"
तथा च ऋग्वेदे शैशिरीयायां संहितायामिति। यथा ऋग्वेदे पारायणानाये शाकल्ये शैशिरीयकमिति वा। The verses to which the commentary refers are not in the MS. See also Vishṇu Purāṇa. p. 277 n.
ऋग्वेदे शैशिरीयायां संहितायां यथाक्रमम्।
प्रमाणमनुवाकानां सूक्तैः शृणुत शाकलाः।।
Com. शैशिरीयायां शिशिरनाममहर्षिप्रोक्तयाम्।
81. In xiii. 12. Śākalya is mentioned as one of three Ācāryas, Vyāḷi, Śākalya, Gārgya.
82. This Prātiśākhya has lately been edited by M. A. Regnier, in the "Journal Asiatique."
83. It has been edited by Prof. Weber, Indische Stüdien, vol, iv.
84. Indische Studien, iv. p. 103.
85. नमो ब्रह्मवेदाय। अथाङ्गिरसः।।
86. तथा चाथर्वणप्रातिशख्य इदमेव प्रयोजनमुक्तम्। एवमहेति च विभाषाप्राप्तं सामान्येन।।

87. अथार्वणेषु च कर्मसु यागवर्जितेषु मणिबन्धानादिषु।।
88. In the very same words or *ānupūrvī*.
89. I still doubt the genuineness of the first verse of the Śākala-prātiśākhya where Śaunaka's name has been foisted to at the end. The emendation which I proposed in my edition of the Śākala-prātisākhya, requires the admission of a so-called *iyādi-pūraṇa*
90. The quotation refers to Śākala-pr. i. 114.
91. 1. 1. 16. सम्बुद्धौ शाकल्यस्येतावनार्षे।।
92. 1. 3. 19. आमन्त्रितमितावनार्षे।।
93. 1. 69. ओकार आमन्त्रितजः प्रगृह्यः।
94. ii, 1. 21, स्वराद्यवयोः पदान्तयोः।। ता इमा आपः।। ii. I. 22. नाकाराद्वकारस्य ।। उभाविदम्।। ii. 1. 23. गविष्टौ गवेषण इति।। Forms like *ubhā u*, instead of *ubhāv u*, sanctioned by the Śākala-pr. i-129, would offend rule of the Ātharvaṇa-prātiśakhya.
95. लेशवृत्तिरधिस्पर्श शाकटायनस्य।।
96. Indische Studien, iv. 249.
97. Kātyāyana would write दृषत् साये, विराट् षण्डे; the Cāturādhyāyikā, दृषथ् साये विराठ् षण्डे।।
98. It begins (MS. Bod. W. 505.) श्रीगणेशायनमः।। स्वरोऽनन्त्यः। नीचानाम्। उपान्त्यम्। उपान्त्यम्। त्रिषु। आदिः। उपान्त्यञ्च। द्वितीयम्। अन्तश्च। उपान्त्ये।।१।। आद्ये। अन्त्ये। मध्यम्। विपरीतस्वराणाम्। जारा। माहङ्। शश्व्यु। ऊता। पारिव्वु। दि।।२।। बि। पिबा दधाविदपूवा। जरा परा च। सूष्वा। ईयाङ्। अन्त्ये। शता। तिपौगु।। etc. From my notes taken in the Royal Library of Berlin, I see that the same work exists there with a commentary (?) in 13 Prapāṭhakas. समाप्तमिदं छन्दोग सम्बन्धिकं सामतन्त्राभिधानं व्याकरणम्। The same work I find mentioned in Dr. Weber's interesting article on the Sāma-veda (Indische Studien, i. 48.) It is curious that this Sāmatantra is called Vyākarana, grammar. The same name is also given to the Ṛk-tantra, a small Śiksha treatise, MS. Bodl. W. 375. This MS. contains several small treatises on Śikṣā matters connected with the Sāma-veda, but more in the form of Pariśiṣṭas : one on *Avagraha*, or division of words; another called Sāma-saṅkhyā and a third called Stobhānusaṁhārā, beginning with the words 'अथातो ह्रस्वदीर्घप्लुतमात्राण्यक्षराणि व्याख्यास्यामः'।
99. The title put at the end of the chapters of the Taittirīya-prātiśākhya is "iti prātiśākhya-sutre prathamaḥ praśnaḥ samāptaḥ," etc.
100. Ṣadguru-śiṣya, in his Commentary on the Anukramaṇī, says that Śaunaka first composed a Kalpa-sūtra, consisting of 1000 parts and resembling a Brāhmaṇa, सहस्रखण्डे स्वकृतं सूत्रं ब्राह्मणसन्निभम्। This was aferwards destroyed by himself; but his few remaining works, which are written in verse, are equally called Sūtras, सूत्रदशकम्।
101. अथ शिक्षां प्रवक्ष्यामि, पाणिनीयं मतं यथा।

and again;

शङ्करः शाङ्करीं प्रादाद्दाक्षीपुत्राय धीमते।
वाङ्मयेभ्यः समाहृत्य देवीं वाचमिति स्थितिः।
येनाक्षरसमाम्नायमधिगम्य महेश्वरात्।
कृत्स्नं व्याकरणं प्रोक्तं तस्मै पाणिनये नमः।।

102. Another work on Śikṣā is mentioned by Raja Rādhākānta in the article which he has dedicated to the Vedāṅgas in his Śabda-kalpa-druma, and for which Amara and Bharata are quoted as authorities. तत्र अकारादिवर्णानां स्थानकरणप्रयत्नबोधिका अ कु ए ह विसर्जनीयाः कण्ठ्य इत्यादिका शिक्षा। The Commentary on the Śākala-prātisākhya also seems to speak of two Śikṣās. यथा तावच्छिक्षायां स्युर्मूर्द्धन्या ऋटुरषाः सामान्येन सर्वशाखासु रेफो मूर्द्धन्य इत्युक्तः। तथान्यस्यां शिक्षायां दन्तमूलय इति रेफो दन्तमूलीय उक्तः। एवं सर्वा शिक्षा वर्णेषु स्थानकरणानुप्रदानादि सर्वासु शाखासु विदधाति। न तु नियतः कस्यां शाखायां रेफो मूर्द्धन्यः कस्यां दन्तमूलीय इति। अत एव व्यवस्थापकमारभ्यते। दन्तमूलीयस्तु तकारवर्गः सकाररेफलकाराश्च रेफं वर्त्स्यमेके। शा० प्रा० १-४५ । ४६ । ४७ ।एवमस्यां शाखायां दन्तमूलीयो वा वर्त्स्यो वा रेफ इत्येतदवधारितम्।।

103. Māṇḍukeya is quoted in the Śākala-prātiśākhya, I, 200

104. Colebrooke, Miscellaneous Essays, ii. 63.

105. MS. Bodl. W. 466. सामगानां छन्दः।
ब्राह्मणात्तण्डिनश्चैव पिङ्गलाच्च महात्मनः।
निदानादुक्थशास्त्राच्च छन्दसां ज्ञानमुद्धृतम्।।

106. तथा सर्वैश्छन्दश्चित्यादिभिः पिङ्गलयास्कसैतवप्रभृतिभिर्यत्सामान्येनोक्तं लक्षणम् See Dr. Roth's Preface to the Nirukta, p. 10; and *quaere* whether in the Śākala-prātisi xvii, 25. one might read इति वै यास्कः instead of इति वैयास्कः as the commentator proposes. Saitava is the pupil of Pārāśarya and divided by thirteen teaehets from Yāska. Cf. Bṛh. Āraṇya. Kāṇva. H, 6, 2. 3.; Indische Studien, i. p. 156. n.

107. Piṅgala, 3. 1. पाद इयादिपूरणः।। इयादिः पूरणो यस्य (पादस्य) असावियादिपूरणः। आदिग्रहणे तु उवादयो गृह्यन्ते। तत्रायमर्थः। यत्र गायत्र्यादौ छन्दसि पादस्याक्षरसंख्या न पूर्यते तत्रेयादिभिः पूरयितव्या। यथा तत्सवितुर्वरेणियमिति, दिव्यं गच्छ सुवः पत इत्येवमादयः।।

108. Cf. Böhtlingk, Ein erster Versuch über den Accent mi Sanskrit, p. 64.; and Pāṇini, page xii.

109. Thus Śākapūrṇi is mentioned as a Niruktakṛt in the Viṣṇupurāṇa (p. 277. n, 9.); but this is no reason why Śāka-pūrṇi should be the same as Yāska, as Colebrooke supposed. (Miscell. Essays, i. 15.) In fact Śākapūrṇi is quoted by Yāska himself, for there can be no doubt that Sakapūrṇi is the same name as Śākapūṇi. In later times, also, Yāska and Śakapaṇi are regarded as distinct persons; for instance, in a verse ascribed, to Parāśara (Anukr, Bh. iv. 5, 7.), which occurs in the Bṛhad-devatā शुनासिरमिन्द्रं यास्कस्तु मेने, सूर्येन्द्रौ तु मन्यते शाकपूणिरिति पराशरः।

Another Niruktakṛt mentioned by Sāyaṇa is the son of Sṭhūla-ṣṭhīvī or, as Yāska calls him, Sthaula-ṣṭhīvī,

109. If Sāyaṇa means to give io these lines an etymology instead of a simple definition of Nirukta the attempt would be very unsuccessful. Nirukta comes from *nirvach*, to explain. His definition, however, is right, in so far as the Nirukta does not contain a connected string of ideas, but merely an enumeration of words. There is another definition of Nirukta, which is quoted by Rādhākānta in his Śabda-kalpa-druma and occurs as one of the Kārikās iu the Kāśikā-vṛtti (Pāṇ. vi. 3. 109.) :

वर्णागमो वर्णविपर्ययश्च द्वौ चापरौ वर्णविकारनाशौ।
धातोस्तदर्थातिशयेन योगस्तदुच्यते पञ्चविधं निरुक्तम्।।

"A Nirukta contains the doctrine of five things; of the addition, transposition, change, and dropping of letters and of the use of one particular meaning of a root".

Instances of this are given in another verse :

भवेद्वर्णागमाद्धंसः सिंहो वर्णविपर्ययात्।
गूढोत्मा वर्णविकृतेर्वर्णनाशात्पृषोदरम्।।

"*Hansa* is formed by an aditition, *Sinha* by a transposition, Guḍhotmā by a change, *Pṛṣodara* by a dropping of letters."

110. 1-3 Adhyāya.
111. 4 Adhyāya.
112. 5 Adhyāya.
113. 1-3.
114. 4-6
115. 6.
116. Sāyaṇa inverts here the historical order of things, because Yāska's Nighaṇṭu must have been called by this name before the time of Amara's Dictionary. Several Koṣas arc quoted which have not yet been mat with in manuscript : Sarva Koṣa, Ranti or Rantideva Koṣa, Yādava Koṣa, Bhāguri Koṣa, Bala Koṣa, all of which must have been in existence as late as the Commentary on the Meghadūta.
117. I have translated this passage of Sāyaṇa, because Dr. Roth has adopted a different division of the Nirukta in hia edition, where he calls the first five books, containing the list of words, Naighaṇṭuka; the first six books of Yāska's Commentary, Naigama; and the rest Daivata. It would have been better to preserve the old divisions, which are based not only upon the authority of Yāska himself, but also on his commentators, with this exception; only, that, according to them, the Naigama may also be called the Aikapadika. Thus Durga says,

एतावन्तः समानकर्माणो धातवः एतावन्त्यस्य सत्त्वस्य नामधेयानीति स एकः पदराशिर्नैघण्टुकं नाम प्रकरणम्। यत्र तावर्थौ प्रायेण चिन्त्येते प्रसङ्गतोऽन्यत्किञ्चित्त देतदेवंलक्षणं नैघण्टुकं नाम प्रकरणं गवादि प्राग्जहाशब्दात्।। आ पुनर्यत्रैतावता मर्थानामिदमभिधानमित्यर्थः प्रायेण चिन्त्यते अनवगतसँस्काराश्च निगमा जहादि-प्रागग्निशब्दात्।।

Again, after having defined the third part, the Daitvata, Durga goes on saying :

तान्येतानि त्रीणि प्रकरणानि नैघण्टुकमैकपदिकं दैवतमिति।

अनेन प्रकरणत्रयप्रपञ्चेनेदमवस्थितं नैरुक्तशास्त्रमिति।

And Further on :

यानि पुनर्नैघण्टुकानि गवादीनि नैगमानि जहादीनी......प्रकरणद्वये नैघण्टुके चैकपदिके च व्याख्यास्याम इत्येतदनुवर्तते।।

He afterwards seems to imply that whole may also be called Nighaṇṭu but there is no authority whatever for calling the first part of Yāska's Commentary, as Dr. Roth does, Naigama. Devarāja also takes the same view when he says :

"भगवता यास्केन समाम्नायं नैघण्टुकनैगमदेवताकाण्डरूपेण त्रिविधं गवादिदेवपत्न्यन्तं निर्ब्रुवता नैगमदेवताकाण्डपरिपठितानि पदानि प्रत्येकमुपादाय निरुक्तानि दर्शितानि निगमानि च। नैघण्टुककाण्डपरिपठितानां तु गवाद्यपारेअंतानामेकच-त्वारिंशशतत्रयाधिकं सहस्रं सामान्येन एतावन्त्यस्य सत्त्वस्य नामधेयानीति व्याख्याय तत्र प्रदर्श्य कतिचिदेव निरुक्तानि तथापि कानिचिदेव दर्शितनिगमानि। अन्यानि तु ग्रन्थविस्तरभीत्या सामान्येन निर्वचनलक्षणस्योक्तत्वा-द्बुद्धिमद्भिर्निर्वक्तुं सुशक्यानीत्यभिप्रेत्य प्रायेण चोपेक्षितानि।। etc.

118. An analogous feeling among the Polynesians is mentioned in Sir G. Grey's Polynesian Mythology, p. 32.
119. Kāt.-pr. viii. 98.
120. Ind. Studien, iv. p. 76.
121. नामाख्यातमुपसर्गो निपातश्चत्वार्याहुः पदजातानि शाब्दाः।
तन्नाम येनाभिदधाति सत्त्वं तदाख्यातं येन भावं स धातुः।।
प्राभ्या परा निर्दुरनु व्युपाप सं परि प्रति न्यत्यधि सूदवापि।
उपसर्गा विंशतिरर्थवाचकाः सहेतराभ्यार्मितरे निपाताः।।
क्रियावाचकमाख्यातमुपसर्गो विशेषकृत्।
सत्त्वाभिधायकं नाम निपातः पादपूरणः।।
निपातानामर्थवशान्निपातनादनर्थकानामितरे च सार्थकाः।
नेयन्त इत्यस्ति संख्येह वाङ्मये मिताक्षरे चाप्यमिताक्षरे च ये।।
नेयन्तः is न ईयन्तः; it means तेषामियत्ता नास्ति।।
121. The name for pronoun, *sarvanāman*, occurs in the the Nirukta, vii. 2, and in the Cāturādhyāyikā.
122. Poet C. 20-for text vide Appendix A.
123. Kātyāyanīya Prātiśākhya, iv. 170
124. 1.27. तिङ्कृत्तद्धितचतुष्टयसमासाः शब्दमयम्।।
125. निरुक्ताश्च गार्ग्यवर्जम्। Durga.
126. This construction is against the Commentary, but, if the MS. such as we have it, is correct, it seems to me the only possible construction.
127. The Commentator translates, "even if it were so, even if some remained inexplicable, this would be no objection;" for, boni grammatical est nonnulla etiam nescire.
128. The remarks of the Commentator on this passage are so curious, that they deserve te be copied. "You may well ask, (he says) why this is so. But, my friend, go and ask the world. Quarrel with the world, for it is not I who made this law. For although all nouns are derived from verbs, yet the choice

of one action (which is to be predicated in perference to others) is beyond' any control. Or it may be that there is a certain law with regard to those who perform certain actions more exciusively. A man who performs one particular action more exclusively whatever other actions he may perform will have his name from that particular action. Nor So we say that he who at one time and in one place shapes things is a carpenter but he who at any time or any place is a carpenter, him Site always call carpenter. This, is not a predicate restricted to one, it may freely be given to others. Now and theo there may be other actions, more peculiar to such persons, and they may take other names accordingly, yet their proper name remains carpenter." And with regard to the next problem the Commentator says : "A carpenter may well perform other actions, but he need not therefore take his name from them. If it is said, several thing's might have one and the same name, and one and the same thing might have different names all we can answer is, that this is not proved by the language such as it is. Words are fixed in the world we cannot say how (*svabhāvataḥ* - by nature)." This, together with the text, shows a clearer insight into the nature of Homonyma and Synonyma, or, as the Peripatetics called the latter, Polyonyma, than anything we find in Aristotle,

129. Kumārila Tantravārttika, i. 3. 1.

एवं कल्पसूत्रेष्वर्थवादादिमिश्रशाखान्तरविप्रकीर्णन्यायलभ्यविध्युपसंहारफलमर्थनिरूपणं तत्त्प्रमाणमङ्गीकृत्य कृतम्। लोकव्यवहारपूर्वकाश्च केचिदृत्विगादिव्यवहारा: सुखार्थहेतुत्वेनाश्रिता:।

"Thus the real sense has been ascertained in the Sūtras by means of collecting; the commandments which were to be obtained systematically as they were dispersed in different Śākhās and mixed up with *Arthavādas*, etc. One or the other authority was selected, and, to afford greater facility, some performances of the priests which are connected with worldly matters were also taken in."

130. तत्र तावद्विध्यर्थवादमन्त्रात्मना त्रिधा व्यवस्थितो वेदराशि:। विध विहितमर्थवादप्ररोचितं मन्त्रेण स्मृतमभ्युदयकारि भवतीति। ततश्च चोदितानं कर्मणां सुखावबोधाय भगवान् बौध ायन: कल्पमकल्पयत्। यतो ब्राह्मणानामानन्त्यं दुरवबोधतया........अतो न तै: सुखं कर्मावबोध इति कल्पसूत्राणीमानि प्रतिनियताशाखान्तारानङ्गीचक्रु: पूर्वाचायी:।। कल्पस्य वैशद्यलाघवकात्‍र्न्य प्रकरणशुद्ध्यादिभि: प्रकर्षैर्युक्तस्य etc. MS. E.I. H. 104.

In the beginning of the Commentary on Āpastamba's Sūtras, it is said that the author is going to explain the Yajūrvaidika performance of the whole *vaitānik* sacrifice, which is detached in many *Śākhās* and scattered in different; parts of the Veda.

अत्रभगवानापस्तम्बो वेदभागध्याकीर्ण विभक्तानेकशास्त्रव्यासक्तं च विश्वस्य वैतानिकस्य कर्मणो याजुर्वैदिकं प्रयोगं व्याचिख्यासु:। श्रुतौ संक्षिप्तयोर्दशपूर्णमासयोर्व्याकरणेन शाखान्तरोपसहारादिना च विस्पष्टीकरणं व्याख्यानम्।

"To explain means to separate, for instance, the new moon and the full moon sacrifices, which in the Veda are thrown together and to make them intelligible by comprehending different Śākhās."

131. आरुणपराशरशाखाब्राह्मणस्य कल्परूपत्वम्। See also Sāyaṇa's introduction to

the; Aitareya-brāhmaṇa, where he says कल्पस्त्वारुणकेतुकचयनप्रकरणे समाम्नायते। इति मन्त्राः कल्पोऽत ऊर्द्ध्वं यदि बलिं हरेदिति। Might not the name आरुणपराजी, Pāṇ. iv. 3. 105.be meant for आरुणपराशरी?

132. Indische Studien, i. 149. n.
133. See Śatapatha-brāhmaṇa, xiv. 4. 4. 10. The word is not used in a similar passage, xi. 3. 8. 8. Sea page 40. note 7.
134. According to some commentaries this ancient collection of the *Adhvaryu* priests was called *Kṛṣṇa*, or the dark Yajur-veda, owing to its motley character, whereas the more recent version of the Yajur-veda was called Śukla or bright, on account of the clear separation of hymns and rules, or, according to others, on account of its enabling the reader to distinguish clearly between the offices belonging to the *Hotṛ* and the *Adhvaryu*, a more popular explanation is given by Colebroolce ? from Mahīdhara's Commentary on the Vājasaneyi Saṁhitā. It occurs also in the Purāṇas :"The *Yajush*, in its original form, was at first taught by Vaiśampāyana to twenty seven pupils. At this time, having instructed *Yājñavalkya*, he appointed him to teach the Veda to other disciples. Being afterwards offended by the refusal of *Yājñavalkya* to take on himself a share of the sin incurred by *Vaiśampāyana*, who had unintentionally killed his own sister's son the resentful preceptor bade *Yājñavalkya* relinquish the science which he had learnt. He instantly disgorged it in a tangible form. The rest of *Vaiśampāyana's* disciples receiving his command to pick up the disgorged Veda, assumed the form of partridges, and swallowed the texts which were soiled, and for this reason termed "black;" they are also denominated Taittirīya from *tittiri*, the name of a partridge, *Yājñavalkya*, overwhelmed with sorrow, had recourse to the Sun; and through the fevour of that luminary, obtained a new revelation of the Yajuṣ which is called "white" or pure, in contradistinction to the other, and is likewise named *Vājasaneyin*, from a patronymic, as it should seem, of *Yājñavalkya* himself; for the Veda declares, "these purer texts, revealed by the Sun, are published by Yājñavalkya, the offspring of *Vājasani*." But, according to the Vishṇu-purāṇa, the priests who studied the Yajuṣ are called *Vājins*, because the Sun, who revealed it assumed the form of a horse (*vājin*)." It is elear that these are nothing but late etymological legends *Tittiri* and *Vājin* were, proper names. *Tittiri* was the pupil of *Yāska*; the pupil of *Vaiśam-pāyana* and it is through them that the old or dark Yajurveda was handed down. *Yājñavalkya*, of the family of the *Vāja-saneyin*, was the founder of the more modern or bright Yajur-veda.
135. "The Aitareya-brāhmaṇa consists of forty Adhyāyas; the Āraṇyaka also is reckoned part of the Aitareya and is equally ascribed to Mahūdāsa, the son of Itarā. "In the Brāhmaṇa, the first subject is the Jyotiṣṭoma (Chatuḥsamsthā); then the Gavām-ayana, the Ādityānām-ayana, the Aṅgirasāmayana and the Dvādaśāha. The Jyotishṭoma stands first among the Somayāgas, (such as the Goṣṭoma and Āyuṣṭoma), and it comprises seven sacrifices (saptasaṁsthā). Four of these are the Agniṣṭoma, Ukthya, Ṣoḍaśin and Atirātra; and among these four the Agniṣṭoma is the model, the whole ceremony being here fully

detailed, while for the other sacrifices the peculiar rules only are given, the rest being supplied from the model. The Agaiṣṭoma ought therefore to be explained first. Now it is very true, that at the beginning of the Agniṣṭoma the Ṛtvij priests are to be elected, for Āpastamba says in his Sūtras, he who is going to sacrifice with Soma, let him choose Ārṣeya-brāhmaṇas for Ṛtvij;' but as the Hotṛ priests have nothing to do in the ceremony of this election, and as the Ṛg-veda is only cencerned with rules for the Hotṛ priests, the Dīkṣaṇyeṣṭi is explained first. For although the Iṣṭi, or the sacrifice itself, is performed by *Adhvaryus* yet the *Yājyās* and *Anuvākyās* belong to the Hotṛ priests. In the Ṛg-veda we find the Yājyās, Puronuvākyās, etc.; in the Yajur-veda the Dohanas, Nirvāpas, etc.; in the Sāma-veda the Ājya-stotras, Pṛṣṭhastotras, etc."-*Sāyaṇa*.

136. Kumārila, i. 3. ''स्वशाखाविहितैञ्चापि शाखान्तरगतान्विर्धीन्।
कल्पकारा विबवघ्नन्ति सर्व एव विकल्पितान्।।
सर्वशाखोपसंहारो जैमिनेश्चापि सम्मत:।।''

137. Kumārila, ii. 4. 2 न च सूत्रकाराणामपि कश्चित् स्वशाखोपसंहार-मात्रेणावस्थित:।।

138. अवश्यश्च शाखान्तरोपसंहारोऽपेक्षित:। न ह्येकस्यां ख्शाखायां श्रौतस्मार्तकर्मानुष्ठानं साकल्येन विहितं तन्मन्त्रा वा पठिता: किंतु किश्चित् क्वचित्।।

139. शाखासु विकल्प: वेदेषु समुच्चय इति नयायाद्याजुर्वेदिकानामस्माकं छन्दोग-ब्राह्मणस्य वेदान्तरत्वादवश्यमुपसंहार:। अतो नित्य: प्रश्न:।।

140. Kumārila, T. V. ii.; Jaimini Sūtra, ii. 4. 2. शाखान्तराध्ययनं तावदेकस्य पुंसो नैवेष्यते किं कारणम्। स्वाध्यायग्रहणेनैका शाखा हि परिगृह्यते।। तश्चान्यो नामातिमेघावित्वादेकवेदे गतानि शाखान्तराण्यप्यधीयीत स समृद्ध: सन् व्रीहियवैरपि मिश्रैर्यजेत।।

This does not exclude, however, the obligation of reading different Yedas. न त्वेवं वेदान्तरस्वाध्ययनं न प्रसज्येत न वचनान्तरेण प्रतिप्रस्नवात्। अनया त्रय्या विद्ययेति तथा वेदानधीत्य वेदौ वेति मानवम्।। See also Mitākṣatrā, p. 17. a. b. एकशाखाध्ययनक्षमो वेदपारग:।।

141. निवित्प्रैषुपरोरुक्कुतापवालखिल्यमाहनाम्न्यैतरेयब्राह्मणसहितस्य शाकलस्य वाष्कलस्य चाम्नायद्वयस्यैतदाश्वलायनशास्त्रं नाम प्रयोगशास्त्रम्। Nārāyaṇa Gārgya's Commentary on Āśvalāyana.

142. Hiraṇyakeśi-bhāṣya : सर्वशाखाप्रत्ययमेकं कर्मेति नयायविद:।। नास्ति कर्मभेद:। यथा नानाशाखप्रत्ययमेकं कर्मेति न्यायशास्त्रनिर्णयेऽपि शाखा-पीक्षतानेव विधीन् न्यायांश्चोपसंहृत्य तत्तच्छाखिन: कर्मभेदेऽपि प्रयोगभेदं रचयन्ति। नहि शब्दान्तरादिभि: प्रमाणै: कर्मभेदोऽस्ति।।

143. आश्वलायनीयं कात्यायनीयं च सूत्रं हि भिन्नाध्ययनयोर्द्वयोर्द्वयो: शाखयोरेकमेव।। Mahādeva's Commentary on the Hiraṇyakeśi-sūtra.

144. In a MS. of the Drāhyāyaṇa sūtras, E. I. H. 363, they are called राणायनिशाखीयं द्राह्यायणसूत्रम्।।

145. See Weber, Vorlesungen, P. 74. The Kauthumas seem to be a later Caraṇa than the Rāṇāyanīyas. Lāṭyāyana quotes a Rāṇāyaniputra; Kauthumas are quoted in the Puṣpa-sūtra.

146. अर्थैकत्वेन केषाश्चिदक्षराणाश्च साम्यतः।
साद्रश्याद्ब्राह्मभ्रान्तिर्जातैवमपनीयते।।
Kumārila i. 3. 7.
"The mistake of supposing the Sūtras to be Brāhmaṇas, which arose from their identity of object and occasional literal coincidences, has thus been removed.

147. Cf. Pāṇ. iv. 3. 103-110. The Sūtras from 106 are not explained in the Mahābhāṣya according to the Calcutta edition.

148. Kalpa-sūtras were composed contemporaneously with Pāṇini, and even after his time, as, for instance, the Sūtras of Āśvalāyana and Kātyāyana, which we still posses, and those of Āśmarathya, which are lost. The last are quoted in the commentary to Pāṇini (iv. 3. 105.), as a modern work on Kalpa; yet Āśvalāyana in his Sūtras, v. 13, refers to Āśmarathya as an authority, whom he follows in opposition to other teachers whose opinion he rejects. Cf. Aśv. Sūtras, v. 13.; Indische Studien, i. 45.

149. The wording of the Sūtra. "*Purāṇaprokteṣu brāhmaṇa- kalpeṣu*" seems to confirm this interpretation. The Paiṅgins must be considered as a Brāhmaṇa-saraṇa, for there is a Paiṅgyam, the work of a Paiṅgin, quoted in the Kauṣītaki-brāhmaṇa, and in a doubtful passage of the Aitareya-brāhmaṇa. It is difficult to say anything equally positive about the Kauśikī-kalpaḥ, an expression which may possibly refer to the Kauśika-sūtras of the Atharva-veda,

150. वेदादृतेऽपि कुर्वन्ति कल्पैः कर्माणि याज्ञिकाः।
न तु कल्पैर्विना केचिन्मन्त्रब्राह्मणमात्रकात्।। Kumārila.

151. In one of the most interesting Brāhmaṇas of the Chandogas, the Sāmavidhāna-brāhmaṇa, we see how the two last in a series of teachers became the founders of a Caraṇa, by teaching this Brāhmaṇa, which had been handed down to them through a succession of nine or at least six masters, to a multitude of followers.
अथास्य सामविधानस्य सम्प्रदायप्रवर्तकानाचार्याननुक्रमेण सङ्कीर्तयति। सोऽयं प्राजापत्यो विधिः। तमिमं प्रजापतिर्वृहस्पतये प्रोवाच। वृहस्पतिर्नारदाय। नारदोविष्वक्सेनाय। विष्वक्सेनो व्यासाय पाराशर्याय व्यासः पाराशर्यो जैमिनये। जैमिनिः पौष्पिण्डयाय। पौष्पिडयः ताण्डिशाट्यायनिनौ बहुभ्यः।।
on the Śāṭyāyanins and their relation to the Sāma-veda, see Indische Studien, i. 49.

152. The differences of these schools may be seen in Weber's edition of the Yajur-veda at the end of each Adhyāya.

153. See Weber's Indische Studien, ii. 44.

154. It should be observed, that in some MSS. of the Caraṇa-vyūha the two Caraṇas, which belong most likely to the Sautra period, those of Āśvalāyana and Sāṅkhayāna, are not mentioned.

155. MS. Wilson. 473. The title is आस्वलाएनक ब्राह्मण (sic); it contains the fifth Book of the Aitareya-brāhmaṇa.

156. Kātyāyana, ii, 5. 18.; vi. 6, 5. Indische Studien i. 230.

157. तत्र कल्पसूत्रं प्रतिशाखं भिन्नमभिन्नमपि क्वचित् शाखाभेदेऽध्ययनभेदाद्वासूत्रभेदाद्वा आश्वलायनीयं कात्यायनीयञ्च सूत्रं हि भिन्नाध्ययनयोर्द्वयोः शाखयोरेकैकमेव। तैत्तिरीयके च समाम्नाये समानाध्ययने नाना सूत्राणि। अनेन च सूत्रभेदे शाखाभेदः शाखाभेदे च सूत्रभेद इति परस्पराश्रय इति वाच्यम्।।

158. Afterwards he says again : तथा चेकस्यां तैत्तिरीयशाखायां समान-पाठायां सूत्रभेदादवान्तरशाखाभेदश्चरणव्यूहशास्त्रे दर्शितः। "It has been shown in the Caraṇa-vyūha, that in the Taittirīya śākhā, where there is but one and the same sacred text, subordinate Śākhās arise from different Sūtras."

159. यथाध्ययनभेदाच्छाखाभेदोऽनादिरेवं सूत्रभेदादपि। न हि सूत्राणां कर्तृसम्बन्धिासंज्ञाद्यतनी किन्तु नानाकल्पगतासु तत्तन्नामकर्षिव्यक्तिषु नित्या तत्प्रणीत-सूत्रेषु च नित्यां जातिमवलम्ब्य तिष्ठति यथा पुरुषनामाङ्कितशाखासु संज्ञा।।

"Nānākalpa-gatāsu" cannot refer to the chronological Kalpas, because these are after the beginning of time,

160. Cf. p. 87, n. supra.

161. चरणव्यूहः। चरणाः शाखाः सूत्राणि च। व्यूहो विविच्य भेदः। न चात्राध्ययनभेदोऽस्ति तस्मात्सूत्रभेदादेव शाखाभेदः।। ननु स्वाध्यायैकदेशो मन्त्र-ब्राह्मणात्मकः शाखेत्युच्यते। तयोर्मन्त्रब्राह्मणयोरन्यतरभेदेन वेदेऽवान्तरशाखाभेदः स्यादिति चेत्। सत्यम् यथा साङ्गः स्वाध्यायो वेदशब्दवाच्य एवं शाखापि साङ्गैव वेदैकत्वेन शाखान्तरत्वं लभते। तत्राङ्गस्य सूत्रस्य भेदाद्भिद्यत एव स्वाध्यायाध्ययनमिति भवतु चरणभेद एव शाखाभेदव्यवहारे हेतुः। तथा च यथा शाखध्ययनं नियतं तथा सूत्राध्ययनमपि।।

162. Strabo, xv. 1. 53. seq,, see Appendix A.

163. See Stenzler "On Indian Law Books," Ind. Stud. i. 232, and iii. 159.

164. Weber, Vorlesungen, p, 97.

165. See p. 107, n. 2 supra.

166. In a MS. (Wilson, 451.) Pāraskara's Gṛhya-sūtras are ascribed to the Mādhyandinī śākhā.

167. See Āśāditya in his "Commentary on the Karma-pradipa," Ind. Stud. i. 58. This Karma-pradīpa, a work ascribed to Kātyāyana, is intended as a supplement to Gobhila.

168. "भार्यादिरग्निर्दायादिर्वा तस्मिन्गृह्याणीति गौतमः" This is taken from Gautama, v.1.

169. A Brahmacārin who has not yet finished his religious education, possesses no sacred fires of his own, and if he is obliged to perform ceromonies with burnt offerings, he must do so with common fire and without sacred vessels. Thus the Kātyāyana-sūtra-paddhati says : गवेधुकचरुरवकीर्णिपशुश्च लौकिकेऽग्नौ भवति। तत्रावकीर्णिपशौ पुरोडाशश्रपणं भूमौ भवति न कपालेषु।।

170. वितानोऽग्नीना विस्तारः। तत्र भवातवैतानिकानि बह्वग्निसाध्यानि कर्माणीत्यर्थः।। Nārāyaṇa on Āśv. Gṛhya-sūtra. The three fires are the *Gārhapatya, Āhavaniya, Dakṣiṇa*; the one fire is the Āvasathya or Gṛhya.

171. अथातो गृह्यकर्माण्युपदेक्ष्यामः।।१।। गृह्यशब्देन स्मार्ताग्निरुच्यते। तस्मिन्यानि कर्माणि

तानि गृह्याकर्माणि। दीर्घत्व छान्दसम्। अथवा गृह्या स्मृतिः। तस्यां यानि कर्माणि।। अथवा गृह्या पत्नी। तया सहितस्य यानि कर्माणि।।

172. The Commentator explains veda as the sacred code. Such a code was not known to the authors of the hymns. On the meaning of veda, see page 25, note 1. supra.

173. In addition to a list of literary names quoted in the Gṛhya-sūtras of Āśvalāyana (see p. 38), I subjoin a larger list of a similar character from the Sāṅkhāyana-Gṛhya-sūtras, of which a copy exists at Berlin. (Weber, "Catalogue of Sanskrit MSS." p. 33.) Sumantuh, Jaimini-Vaiśampāyana-Pailasūtrabhāshya-Gārgya-Babhru-Bābhravya-Maṇḍu-Māṇḍavyāḥ, Gārgī Vāchaknavī, Vaḍavā Prātitheyī, Sulabhā Maitreyī; Kaholam, Kauṣītakim, Mahākauṣītakim, Suyajñam, Sāṅkhāyanam, Āśvalāyanam, Aitareyam, Mahaitareyam, Bhāradvājam, Jatūkaraṇyam, Paiṅgyain, Māhāpaiṅgyam, Bāṣkalam, Gārgyam, Śākalyam, Māṇḍūkeyam Māhādamatram, Audavāhim, Mahau-davāhim, Sauyāmim, Śaunakim, Gautamim, Śākapūṇim, ye cānye ācāryas, te sarve tṛpyantviti. See also Karma-pradīpa, MS. W. 465, p. 16 b.

174. Āpast, i. 6. अशूद्राणामदुष्टकर्मणामुपायनं वेदाध्ययनमग्न्याधेयं फलवन्ति च कर्माणि।। शुश्रूषा शूद्रस्येतरेषां वर्णानाम्।। In later works, such as the Sanskāra-gaṇapati, this Sūtra of Āpastamba, which excludes the Śūdras from initation, has been so altered as to admit them. MS. E. I. H. 912, p. 16. अथ शूद्राणामुपनयनम् आपस्तम्बः। शूद्राणामदुष्टकर्मणामुपनयनम्। मद्यपानरहितानामिति कल्पतरुकरः।।

175. ms. p. 163 नाश्य आर्यः शूद्रायां वध्यः शूद्र आर्यायाम्। (नाश्यो निर्वास्यः)

176. MS. p. 164 b जिह्वाछेदनं शूद्रस्यार्य धार्मिकमाक्रोशतो वाचि पथि शय्यायामासन इति समीभवतो दण्डताडनम्।। पुरुषवधे स्तेये भूम्यादान इति स्वान्यादाय वध्यश्चक्षुर्निरोस्त्वेतेषु ब्राह्मणस्य।।

177. MS. p. 125 b. धर्मचर्यया जघन्यो वर्णः पूर्वं पूर्वं वर्णमापद्येत जातिपरिवृत्तौ अध र्मचर्यया पूर्वो वर्णोजघन्यं जघन्यं वर्णमापद्येत जातिपरिवृत्तौ।।

178. The most important among them were first noticed and described by Dr. Weber, on whose authority some of our statements must rest.

179. MS. Chamb. 100.

लाठ्यायनमनुपदं निदानं कल्पमेव च।
उपग्रन्थाञ्च क्षुद्राश्च तण्डालक्षणमेव च।।
सूत्रं पञ्चविधेयञ्च कल्पानुदमेव च।
अनुस्तोत्रञ्च विज्ञेयं दशसूत्रप्रकीर्त्तनम्।।

Varadarāja in his Commentary on Kātyāyana's Pratihāra (MS. Bodl. W. 394). वीक्ष्य ब्राह्मणसूत्रोपग्रन्थनिदानतद्व्याख्या; and again : इह खलु उपग्रन्थकल्पब्राह्मणप्रोक्तानां ज्योतिष्टोमादिविश्वसृजामयनपर्यन्तानामेकाहीन-सत्राणाम्।।

180. Cf. Ind. Studien, i, 43, 54, 56, 58 ; MS. E. I. H. 121. सामवेद उपग्रन्थसूत्रम् copied Samvat, 1586 – 1530 A. D. by Paṇḍita Śrī Lakṣmīdhara, son of Śrī Bhīma. इत्युपग्रन्थसूत्रे चतुर्थः प्रपाठकः।।

181. MS. Bodl. W. 375.

182. MS. Bodl. W. 375. Begins प्रस्तावोग्द्गीथप्रतिहारोपद्रवनिधनानि भक्तय: तत्पाञ्चविध्यं स्मृतं व्याख्यास्याम:।। One of these five *Bhaktis*, the *Pratihāra*, is described in the Pratihāra-sūtra, ascribed to Kātyāyana, and explained by Varadarāja.
183. MS. Bodl. W. 375.
184. Ṛv. viii, 3, 20: átho nákṣatrāṇām eshām upásthe śoma āhitaḥ," "Soma is placed in the lap of these *Nakṣtras*."
185. Ṛv. ii, 32, Rākā, the full moon; Sinīvālī, the last day before the new moon; and Guṅgu, the new moon, are mentioned Ṛv. v. 42, 12, Rākā occurs again; and X. 48. 8. we read Guṅgubhyaḥ. In both these passages, however, the poet is speaking of rivers, and not of the moon.
186. Sāyaṇa, in his Commentary on Ṛv. ii. 40.3, says, that the thirteenth month was called the seventh season, and he quotes from a Brāhmaṇa a passage : "*asti trayodaśo māsa iti śruteḥ*."
187. Taitt.-brāhm. iv; 5; Vāj.-sanh. xxx. 10.; 20.
188. Gaṇa ukthādi. Pāṇ. iii. 1. 143, *graha*, planet, is mentioned as different from *grāha*.
189. MS. Chambers, 404.
190. Nakshtra-kalpa, Graha-yuddha, Ṛāhu-cāra, Ketu-cāra, Ṛtuketu-lakṣaṇa, Nakshātra-grahotpāta-lakshaṅa. Weber, Ind. Stud. i. 87. 100.
191. सर्वज्ञेयार्थवर्णनात्सर्वानुक्रमणीशब्दं निब्रुवन्ति विपश्चित:।।
192. आर्ष्यानुक्रमणीत्याद्या छान्दसी दैवती तथा।
अनुवाकानुक्रमणी सूक्तानुक्रमणी तथा।।
193. Several MSS. contain portions of the Anuvākānukramaṇī; and with the help of Ṣaḍguruśiṣya's Commentary, contained in the introduction to his commentary on Kātyāyana's Sarvānukrama, (MS. Bodl. Wilson, 379), the text might be published in a critical edition.
194. Dr. Kuhn gives the following description of this MS. in Haupt's "Zeitschrifi fur Deutsches Alterthum." The Bṛhad- devatā (Chambers, 192.) composed in epical metre, is ascribed to Śaunaka, and contains an enumeration of the deities invoked in each hymn of the Ṛg-veda. It gives much mythological and other information as to the character of the gods of the Veda. The text of the MS. is so corrupt that we can scarcely think of restoring it without the help of other MSS." Another MS. has since been found in India, and a distinguished Sanskrit scholar is preparing an edition of it.
195. Another Anukramaṇī, containing the last verses of each Maṇḍala, is quoted by Ṣaḍguruśiṣya (Anukr. Bh. viii. 1). मण्डलान्तानामृचामनुक्रमणे प्रतिचक्ष्य विचक्ष्वेत्येष्वपि गृह्यते।। Cf. Ṛv. Maṇḍ, vii. 6. 15; Aṣṭ. v. 7. 9,
196. Triṇi śatāni shaṭkāṇām chatvārimśat shaṭcha Vargāh.
197. MS. E. I. H. 1623, 965.
198. Ibid 1702; name of Śākhā unknown
199. Ibid 293, containing the three books of the Āpastamba-brāhmaṇa.
200. Ibid 1690, etc.
201. See MS. Bodl. Wilson, 361.
202. See Catalogue of the Berlin MSS. No. 142.

203. The title is "*Ekottara-śatādhvaryu-śākhā-prabhedabhinne Yajurvedakāṭhake Carakaśākhā.*"
204. See Beafey, Sāma-veda p. vii.
205. In the first chapter of the Ārṣeya-brāhmaṇa, we read : यो ह वा अवदितार्षेयच्छन्दोदैवतब्राह्मणेन मन्त्रेण याजयतिवाध्यापयति वा स्थाणु' वर्च्छति गर्त वापद्यते (MS. 089 वापद्यते) प्र वा मीयते पापीयान्भवति यातयामान्यस्य छन्दांसि भवन्ति। This passage is referred to by Kātyāyana, when he says: अनेवंविदो यातयामानि छन्दांसि भवन्ति स्थाणुं वर्च्छति गर्ते वा पत्यते प्रमीयते वा पापीयान्भवतीति विज्ञायते।। See also Kātyāyana's Introduction to his Anukramaṇī of the Mādhyandina-śākhā, and Ṛg-veda-bhāṣya, p. 40.
207. Kumārila says :

यत्तु भाष्यकारेण स्वराभावादित्यसन्नियामार्थव्याख्यानं कृतं-

"तन्मन्त्रेष्वप्यवेदत्वं कल्पाधीतेषु साधयेत्।
तथा गृह्योपदिष्टेषु छान्दोग्यब्राह्मणेषु च।।
ब्राह्मणानि हि यान्यष्टौ सरहस्यान्यधीयते।
छन्दोगास्तेषु सर्वेषु न कश्चिन्नियतः स्वरः।
तेन तेष्वप्यवेदत्वं स्वराभावात्प्रसज्यते।।"

208. Cf. Sāma-veda, ed. Beufey, p. xx.
209. In the Śākala-śākhā, the hymns of Getama are followed by those of Kutsa, Kakṣīvat, Parucehepa, and Dīrghatamas; in the Bāṣkala-śākhā their order was, Gotama Kakṣīvat, Parucchepa, Kutsa, Dīrghatamas.
210. खैलिकानामनादेशोऽस्मिन्ग्रन्थेऽनुवाकानाम्; or, according to MS. 502 ऽनुवाकानान्निह स्मृतः।।
211. Thus it is said : एतस्य (समाम्नायस्य इतिशब्दो निवित्प्रैषुपरो रुक्कुतापवालखिल्य. मद्दानाम्न्यैतैरेयब्राह्मणसहितस्य शाकलस्य वाष्कलस्य चाम्नायद्वय-स्यैतदाश्वलायनसूत्रं नाम प्रयोगशास्त्रमित्यध्येतृप्रसिद्धं सम्बधविशेषं द्योतयति।। Śrauta-sūtra-bhāṣya, i. 1.
212. य आङ्गिरसः शौनहोत्रो भूत्वा भार्गवः शौनकोऽभवत्स गृत्समदो द्वितीयं मण्डलमपश्यदिति।।
213. तथा तस्यैव शौनकस्य ऋष्यनुक्रमणे-

"त्वमग्न इति गृत्समदः शौनको भृगुतां गतः।
शौनहोत्रः प्रकृत्या तु य आङ्गिरस उच्चयत इति।।"

214. विपाटितम् means "torn," and corresponds with Sūtra, "a thread." A similar expression is विच्छिन्नम् which is applied, for instance, to the Mahābhāṣya, when it felt into disuse Kashmir. See Rajataraṅgiṇī. Histoire des Rois du Kashmire, traduite at commentée par M. A. Troyer, iv. 487; and Böhtlingk Pāṇini, p. xvi. The true sense seems to be that in which Devarājayajvan uses विच्छन्न in such passages as तच्चाध्यनं कलियुगे प्रायेण विच्छिन्नसम्प्रदायमासीत्।।। A work was lost when the chain of the oral tradition was broken.
215. I read विधाने च, because these must be two different works, the Ṛgvidhāna and Pādavidhāna, in order to complete the number of ten. The Ṛgvidhāna exists in MS. (E. I. H. 1723), and is not only written in Śaunaka's mixed

Ślokas, but distinctly ascribed to him in tlie second verse; कर्मणाभृषिदृष्टानां विधिं प्रोवाच शौनक: The book ends with the words Nevertheless, in the form in which we have it, it is later than Śaunaka. The term Ṛgvidhāna is mentioned in the Taittirī-yāraṇyaka.

216. This must be the Prātiśakhya of the Ṛg-veda and not of the Atharva-veda, which is likewise ascribed to Śaunaka, the Cāturādhyayikām Saunakīyam.

217. See Stenzler. Indische Studien i. p. 243.

218. साकृतगोत्रज: is unintelligible. Should it be व्याकृतगोत्रज्ञ:?

219. All the works of Āśvalāyana still exist, as Ṣaḍguruśiṣya describes them. Instead of चतुष्कगृह्यम्, it would be better to read चतुष्कं गृह्यम्।।

220. If this number is right, Śaunuka's Śrauta-sūtra could not have been destroyed at the time of Kātyāyana.

221. The Kalpa-sūtras of the Yajur-veda. On the Vājins or Vājasaneyins, see Colebrooke, Essays, i, 16.

222. See page 107. Upagrantha is not to be taken in the sense of Pariśiṣṭa.

223. Bhrājamāna, is unintelliyible; it may be Pārṣada.

224. These Vārttikās have not yet been met with.

225. The Vārttikas to Pāṇini.

226. Patañjali, the author of the Mahābhāṣya, according to tradition called by the name of Bhartṛhari also, was the reputed author of the Yoga-sūtras. On these a commentary was written by Vyāsa who might be called a descendant of Śāntanu. The reading may not be quits correct, and Mahābhāṣya is more likely to refer to Patañjali's own work; but the dental *n* of the MSS, speaks rather in favour of the reading *'mahābhāgyena.'*

227. अवबुध्यत Ch. 192. Weber, Catalogue, p. 12,

228. वेवं Ch. 192., W. 379. वेशम्?

229. गृत्समदो Ch., W.

230. त नाम्ना Ch., W.

231. Rv. II. 12; the Sūkta with the refrain, "sa janāsa-indra."

232. वाचस्ते Ch., W,

233. से क Ch., W.

234. द्धि धर्मात् W. द्व धर्मान् Ch.

235. करां Ch., W.

236. दृष्टा W.

237. ता Ch. W.

238. खास्य W. Ch.

239. न: W.

240. द्य Ch. W.

241. गुण Ch., W.

242. यन् Ch., W.

243. ने न W. Ch.

244. तया W. Ch.

245. साकृतगोत्रजः W. साकृतगोत्रज Ch.
246. चातुष्क W.
247. पार्षदस्य?
248. तदञ्जलिः Ch. W.
249. छान्तयनीयेत W. छान्तपनीयेत
250. भाष्येण or भाग्येन?
251. MS. E. I. H. 576. contains a commentator the Ṛg-Veda, where a passage from the Sarvānukramaṇī is quoted as "अत्र शौनकादिमतसङ्गृहीतुर्वररुचेरनुक्रमणिका"।। This commentary of Ātmānand seems anterior to Sāyaṇa. In the introduction different works and commentaries, connected with the Veda are quoted, but Mādhava and Sāyaṇa are never mentioned. We find the Skāndabhāṣya, and commentators such as Udgītha-bhāskara mentioned. (स्कान्दभाष्यादिषु भाष्याकारैरुद्गीथभास्करादिभिः) by Ātmānand, and the same works were known also to Devarājayajvan. Devarājayajvan, however, quotes not only Skandasvāmin and Bhaṭṭa-bhāskara Miśra, but also Mādhava. He therefore was later than Mādhava. Skandasvāmin, and Bhāskara, on the contrary, were anterior to Mādhava, being quoted in his commentary. Ātmānanda, though not quoted by Mādhava, seems anterior to Mādhava, and the authorities which he quotes are such as Śaunaka, Vedamitra (Śākalya), the Bṛhad devatā, Viṣṇu-dharmottara, and Yāska.
252. Kathā sarit-sāgara, edited by Dr. Hermann Brockhaus, Leipzing, 1839.
253. The same question with regard to the probable age of Pāṇini, has been discussed by Prof. Böhtlingk in his edition of Pāṇini Objections to Prof. Böhtlingk's arguments have been raised by Prof. Weber in his Indische Studing. See also Ṛg-veda. Leipzig, 1857, Introduction.
254. Cf. Ṛg-ved, Leipzig, 1857, p. lxvii
255. Lassen-Indische Aiterthumskande, ii, 18.
256. According to the southern Buddhists it was Candra-gupta, and not Nanda, whose corpse was re-animated. As. Res, xx. p. 167.
257. Ṣaḍguruśiṣya : तथा च सूत्र्यते हि भगवता पिङ्गलेन पाणिन्यनुजेन
258. A new and more correct edition of the Uṇādi-sūtras has lately been published by Dr. Aufrecht, Bonn, 1859,
259. J. Prinsep says : "The Roman deuarius, from which Dināra was derived, was itself of silver, while the Persian *Dirhem* (a silver coin) represents the Drachma, or dram weight, of the Greeks. The weight allowed to the dinār of 32 *rattis*, or 64 grains, agrees so closely with the Roman and Greek unit of 60 grains, that its identity cannot be doubted, especially when we have before as the actual gold coins of Chandragupta (?) (didrachmas), weighing from 120 to 130 grains, and indubitably copied from Greek originals, in device as well as weight." Journal A, S. B., vol. vi. p. 455. Notes on the facsimiles of the inscriptions from Sanchi near Bhilsa, by James Prinsep.
260. योऽमुं वृत्तिं समालोच्य स्वपौरुषसमीहया।
मन्त्रामाच्छादनं कुर्यात्सुकृतं तस्य नश्यति।।

261. सूत्रमिदं सूतीवृत्तौ (सतीवृत्तौ?) देववृत्तौ च न दृश्यते।।
262. Kalpa-sūtra, translated by Stevenson, p. 45.
263. कृपो रो लः (पा० ८, २, १८) इत्यत्र न्यासे कृकृपिभ्यां चेति सूत्रं दृश्यते। अतस्तररिन्न नास्तीति लक्ष्यते।। Colebrooke, Miscellaneous Essays, ii. 40, mentions this work in his list of Sanskrit grammars : "Nyāsa or Kaāśkāvṛtti-pañjikā by Jinendra: another exposition of the Kāśikāvritti, which explanatory notes by Rakṣita." He adds, however, with his usual caution : "I state this with some distrust, not having yet seen the book. The Nyāsa is universally cited; and the Bodhinyāsa is frequently so. Vopadeva's Kāvya-kāmadhenu quotes the Nyāsa of Jinendra and that of Jinendra-buddhi."
264. The word stūpa does not occur in Pāṇini or the Gaṇa-pāṭha. Sāyaṇa to Rv. i. 24. 7. does not quote the Uṇādi-sūtra, but derives stūpa from a root *styai*, affix'pa.'
265. तन्निर्णयश्चरणव्यूहे शौनकेन दर्शितः।।
266. छन्दोगपरिशिष्टं कात्यायनमुनिकृतं सामवेदिककर्मबोधाकं गोभिलसूत्राणां परिशेषशास्त्रमिति स्मृतिः।
267. MS. Bodl. W- 510.

अष्टादश परिशिष्टानि तदादौ यूपलक्षणम्।
चातुर्ण्य (चातुर्वर्ण्य) प्रवक्ष्यामि वृक्षाणां पशुभिः सह।।
निन्दाप्रशंसे वक्ष्यामः कात्यायनमतात्तथा।।

268. MS, Bodl. W- 510 14. गृह्यसङ्ग्रहं परिशिष्टं गोभिपुत्रकृतम्।।
269. Pariśiṣta occurs only as a *pratyadāharaṇa* in Pāṇ. iv. 1. 48, but it is used there as a feminine, and in quite a different sense.
270. It is also called *Chandasam vicayaḥ*, and contains quotations from the Tāṇḍya-brāhmaṇa, Piṅgala, the Nidāna, and Uktha-śāstra.
271. According to passages in the Caraṇa-vyūha belonging to the Ātharvaṇa, the number of the Kauśikoktāni Pariśiṣṭāni would amount to 70.
272. Besides the MS, of the E. I. H., and collations of some of the MSS. at Berlin, I have used the printed edition of the 29 Caraṇa-vyūha in Rādhākānta's Sanskrit Encyclopaedia. The MSS. differ so much that it would be hazardous to correct the one by the other. They probably represent different versions of the same text. The name of the author varies likewise. Sometimes he is called Śaunaka, sometimes Kātyāyana, and in Rādhākānta's edition, Vyāsa. The last is, perhaps, meant, for the same whom we found mentioned before as the author of a Commentary on Patañjali's Yoga. The text has since been published by Prof. Weber.
273. For instance पारष्यानुहोत्रकमपि पाठः instead of पार्श्वान्हौत्रकम्।
274. MS, Chambers, 66.
275. MS. Chambers, 136.
276. Called Pratiṣthā-lakṣaṇam in MS, Chambers, 66,
277. जमदग्निर्भरद्वाजो विश्वामित्रोऽत्रिगौतमौ।

वशिष्ठकश्यपागस्त्या मुनयो गोत्रकारिणः।।
एतेषां यान्यपत्यानि तानि गोत्राणि मन्यते।।

278. कात्यायनविरचितो विप्राणां हितकाम्यया।
अध्याय: प्रवराख्योऽयं पुरा ब्रह्मविनिर्मित:।।
279. Burnouf, introduction à 1' Hisloire du Buddhisme, Roth, Abhandlungen, p. 22,
280. Kalpa Sūtra, p. 35.
281. Lassen-Indian Antiquithes, ii., p. 58. Schiefner-Mélanges Asiatiques, i, 436.
282. Lassen, ii. 52. Foucaux, Ṛgya Techer Rol Pa, p. xi.
283. Foucaux, 1. c note communicated by Stan. Julien.
284. Neumann, Zeitschrift für die Kunde des Morgenlandes, ii. 117; Lassen ii.54.
285. Foucaux, 1.c. According to Klaprotk Matouanlin places Buddha 688 to 609.
286. Csoma, Tibetan Grammar, p. 199-201. They are : 2422, 2143, 2139., 2135, 1310,1060, 885, 882, 880, 837, 752, 653, 576, 546.
287. Lassen ii. 58. Burnouf, Introduction, i p. 350. n. 51.
288. As they place Vasumitra more than 400 aner Buddha, the date for Nāgārjuna ought to foe about 450.
289. Turnour, Examination of the Pali Buddhistical Annals, Journal of Asiatic Society of Bengal, vi, p. 721.
290. Mahāvaṁso, p. 46. The Mahāvaṁśa was written in Pāli by Mahānāma. He was a priest and uncle of king Dasenkelleya, or Dhātusena who reigned from a. d. 459 to 477. Mahānāma made use of earlier histories, and mentions among them the Dīpa-vaṁśa. This work, also called Mahāvaṃśa, and written in Pāli, is supposed to be still in existence, and carries the history to the reign of Mahāsena, who died A. D. 302. Mahānāma, though he lived more than a hundred years after Mahāsena's death, does not seem to have carried the history much further. His work ends with the account of Mahāsena's reign, It terminates with the 48th verse of the 37th chapter of what is now known as the Mahāvaṃśa, and it is only from conjecture that Turnour, the editor and translator of the first 38 chapters of the Mahāvaṁśa ascribes the end of the 37th, and the whole of the 38th chapter to the pen of Mahānāma's work was afterwards continued by different writers. It now consists of 100 chapters, and carries the history of Ceylon to the middle of the 11th century. He is likewise the author of a commentary on his own work, which commentary ends at the 48th verse of the 37th chapter.
291. Mahāvaṃso, Pref. p. iii.
292. Not thirty-four years as printed in the Mahāvaṁso. See Lassen, ii, 62. n.
293. As. Res., xx p. 167.
294. This first Aśoka is called Kālāśoka, a name which it would be too bold to explain as the chronological Aśoka.
295. In some instances that date is changed to 200 A. B., by means of a reaction exercised by the literature of Ceylon on the chronology of the Continental Buddhists. Burnouf, Introduction, p. 436, 578
296. As. Res. xx, 513.
297. Turnour, Examination of some points of Buddhist Chronology, Journal of the Ast., S. B. v, 530. Lassen ii 58.

298. Plutarch, Vitā Alex. c. 62, says that Sandracottus saw Alexander when he was a μειρακιον
299. Justini Hist. Philipp, Lib. xv, cap. iv.
300. Diodotus Siculus, xvii. 93. The statement in Photii Biblioth. p. 1579, that Porus was the son of a barber, repeated by Libanius, torn, ii. 632., is evidently a mistake. Plutarch, Vitā Alexandri, c. 62, speaks cf 80,000 horse, 8,000 chariots, and 6,000 elephants.
s301. Quintus Curtius, ix. 2.
302. Strabo, xv. 1. 36
303. Arrian, Indica, x. 5.
304. Strabo, xv. 2. 9.
305. Arrian, Exped. v. 6, Indica, v. 3.
306. Plutarch, Vitā Alexandra, c, 62
307. Asiatic Researches, vol. iv. p. 11.
308. See Wilson's notes on the Mudrā Rākṣasa, p. 132.
309. The name of Maurya seems to have been known to the Greeks, See Cunningham, Journal of the As Soc. of Bengal, xxiii. p. 680.
The wooden house in which the tribe of the Morieis are said to have lived, may refer to the story of the Mauryas living in a forest. See Mahāvaṁśo, p. xxxix.
The statement of Wilford, that Maurya meant in Sanskrit the offspring of a barber and a Śūdra-woman, has never been proved.
310. Mahāvaṃso, p. 21. The Pāli orthography has been preserved in the following extracts.
311. Mahāv., p. 38.
312. It would seem that the eldest son of Aśoka did not participate in the general government of the country, but received a provincial vice-royalty. But in the Burmese histories it is stated distinctly that the eldest son, named Bhadrasena, reigned with nine of his brothers during a period of twenty-two years.
313. Pāṭalipūtra was then governed by the youngest son of Aśoka, called Piñjamakh, and the robber-king who first called himself Nanda, is said to have reigned a short time under the title of Ugrasena. Ast. Res, xx, p. 170.
314. Kahapaṇa-Kārṣāpaṇa.
315. This is probably the Kaivarta-nanda of the Rājaratnākara.
316. See page 259.
317. Vishṇu-purāèa, transtatee by H. H. Wilson, p. 466.
318. Śiśunāka, who according to the Vāyu and Matsya Purāṇa, relinquished Benares to his son, and established himself at Giriraja or Rājagṛha in Bihar, reigned 40 years, V. and M. P.
319. 25 years V.; 27 years M.: the latter inserts a Kaṇvāyana, 9 years, and Bhūmimitra or Bhūmiputra, 14 yars, before him.
320. According to the Vāyu, Udaya or Udayāśva founded Pāṭaliputra, on the sothern angle of the Ganges.
321. The length of this monarch's reign is given uniformly by the Purāṇas and the Buddhist histories, as 24 years. The number is given by the Vāyu-Purāṇa, the Dīpavaṁśa, the Mahāvaṁśa (where 34 is a mistake for 24), and

in Buddhaghosha's Arthakathā. Cf. Mahāv. p. lii.

322. The Vāyu-Purāṇa calls him Bhadrasāra, and assigns 25 years to his reign.

322. Viṣṇu-purāṇa, p. 468. n. 21. This rests only on the authority of the commentator on the Viṣṇu-purāṇa; but Chandragupta's relationship with Nanda is confirmed by the Mudrā-rākṣasa.

323. Lassen, Indische Alterthumskunde, ii. 413.

324. A. Cunningham in the Journal of the Asiatic Society of Bengal, xviii. p. 20

325. Asiatic Researches, xx, 297.

326. Nāgārjuna, who must be somewhat later than Vasumitra, is roughtly placed 400 years after Buddha by the Northern, 500 after Buddha by the Southern Buddhists.

327. Mémoires sur les Contrées occidentales par Hiouenthsang, liv, iv. p. 200

328. Foucaux, Lalitavistara, pp. 3, 415, 417.

329. "Livre de mots" is intended as the title of Pāṇini's grammar, which was "Śabdānuśāsanam." This title is left out in the Calcutta edition, and likewise in Professor Böhtlingk's edition of Pāṇini. See Zeitschrift der Deutschen Morgenländischen Gesellschaft, vii, 162

330. Inde du nord.

331. Mémoires sur les contrées occidentales, traduits du Sanskrit en Chinois, en I'an 648, par Hiouen-thsang, et du Chinois en Francais par M. Stanislas Julien, Membre de Pinstuitut; tome i. p. 125; Voyages des Pélerins Bouddhistes, vol ii. See also the author's editon of the Ṛg-veda and Prātiśākhya, Introduction, p. 12.

332. According to the opinion of M. Fitz-Edward Hall, a scholar of the most extensive acquaintance with Sanskrit literature, the number of distinct Sanskrit works in existence is, probaly, not less than ten thosand. (Journal o the Asiatc Society of Bengal. 1858, p. 305).

THE BRĀHMAṆA PERIOD

2
CHAPTER

Having assigned to the Sūtra literature of India the wide limits of a period extending 600 to 200 B.C. we have now to examine another and confessedly more ancient class of Vedic writings, differing in style both from the Sūtras, which are posterior, and from the *Mantras,* which are anterior to them. These are called by the comprehensive name of Brāhmaṇas. But as between the Sūtras and the later Sanskrit literature we discovered a connecting link in the writings known under the name of Pariśiṣṭas, so we meet on the frontier between the Brāhmaṇas and the Sūtra literature, with a class of works intermediate between the Brāhmaṇas and Sūtras which claim to be considered first. These are the Āraṇyakas, or "The Treatises of the Forest."

THE ĀRAṆYAKAS

The Āraṇyakas are so called, as Sāyaṇa informs us, because they had to be read in the forest[1]. It might almost sccm as if they were intended for the *Vānaprasthas* only, people who, after having performed all the duties of a student and a householder, retire from the world to the forest to end their days in the contemplation of the deity. Thus it is said in the Āruṇikopaniṣad, that the *Sannyāsin,* the man who no longer recites the *Mantras* and no longer performs sacrifices, is bound to read, out of all the Vedas, only the Āraṇyaka or the Upaniṣad. In several instances the Āraṇyakas form part of the Brāhmaṇas, and they are thus made to share the authority of Śruti or revelation. We have seen, however, that part of an

Āraṇyaka Was ascribed to a human author, to Āśvalāyana. Another part is quoted by Sāyaṇa in his Commentary on the Ṛg-veda[2], as being a Sūtra work of Śaunaka's. Colebrooke found, in one transcript of this Āraṇyaka, that it was ascribed to Āśvalāyana; but he remarks, "probably by an error of the transcriber." This is not the case; and it is a good proof of a certain critical conscience even amongst the orthodox dogmatists of the Hindus, that they acknowledged a certain difference between the Brāhmaṇas and Āraṇyakas, although it was of great importance to them, particularly in their orthodox philosophy, to be uble to appeal to passages from the Āraṇyakas as invested with a sacred authority. The most important Upaniṣ ads, which are full of philosophy and theosophy, form part of the Āraṇyakas, and particularly in later times the Āraṇyaka was considered the quintessence of the Vedas.[3] Nevertheles it is acknowledged by Indian authors[4] that a mistake may be made and the work of a human author may be erroneously received as. a part of the sacred book by those who are unacquainted with its true origin. An instance, they say, occurs among those who use the Bahvṛch, a śākha of the Ṛg-veda, by whom a ritual of Āśvalāyana has been admitted under the title of the fifth Āraṇyaka, as a part of the Ṛg-veda.

That the Āraṇyakas presuppose the existence of the Brāhmaṇas may be clearly seen from the Bṛhadāraṇyaka, of which we possess now a complete edition by Dr. Röer, of Calcutta, together with two Sanskrit commentaries. If we take for instance the story of Janaka, who promised a large prize to the wisest *Brāhmaṇa* at his sacrifice, and compare this story, as it is given in the Śatapatha-brāhmaṇa (xi. 4. 6.) with the third Ādhyāya of the Bṛhadāraṇyaka where the same subject occurs, we find in the Āraṇyaka all the details given almost in the same words as in the Brāhmaṇa, but enlarged with so many additions, particularly with respect to the philosophical disputations which take place between Yājñyavalkya and the other *Brāhmaṇas,* that we cannot hesitate for a moment to consider the Āraṇayka as an enlargement upon the Brāhmaṇa.

The chief interest which the Āraṇyakas possess at the present moment consists in their philosophy. The philosophical chapters well known under the name of Upaniṣads are almost the only portion of Vedic literature' which is extensively read to this day. They contain, or are supposed to contain, the highest authority on which the various systems of philosophy in India rest. Not only the Vedānta philosopher, who, by his very name, professes his faith in the ends and objects of the Veda,[5] but the Sāṅkhya, the Vaiśeṣika, the Nyāya, and Yoga philosophers, all pretend to find in the Upaniṣads some Wārranty for their tenets, however antagonistic in their bearing. The same applies to the numerous sects that have existed and still exist in India. Their founders, if they have any pretensions to orthodoxy, invariably appeal to some passage in the Upaniṣads in order to substantiate their own reasonings. Now it is true that in the Upaniṣads themselves there is so much freedom and breadth of thought that it is not difficult to find in them same authority for almost any shade of philosophical opinion. The old Upaniṣads did not pretend to give more than "guesses at truth," and when, in course of time, they became invested with an inspired character, they allowed great latitude to those who professed to believe in them as revelation. Yet this was not sufficient for the rank growth of philosophical doctrines during the latter ages of Indian history; and when none of the ancient Upaniṣads could be found to suit the purpose, the founders of new sects had no scruple and no difficulty in composing new Upaniṣads of their own. This accounts for the large and ever growing number of these treatises. Every new collection of MSS., every new list of Upaniṣads given by native writers, adds to the number of those which were known before; and the most modern compilations seem now to enjoy the same authority as the really genuine treatises.

The original Upaniṣads had their place in the Āraṇyakas and Brāhmaṇas. There is only one instance of a saṁhitā containing Upaniṣads the Vājasaneyi-saṁhitā, which comprises the Īśa-upaniṣadā, forming the 40th book, and the Śivasaṅkalpa, forming part of the 34th book. This, however, so far from proving the grearer antiquity of that Upaniṣad, only serves to confirm the modern date of the whole collection known under the name of Vājasaneyi-saṁhitā.[6] But though the proper place of the genuine Upaniṣads was in the Brāhmaṇas, and here chiefly in those secondary portions commonly called Āraṇyakas, yet in later times, the Upaniṣads obtained a more independent position, and though they still professed to belong more particularly to one or the of the other four Vedas, that relationship became very lax and changeable.

The true etymological meaning of the word Upaniṣad had been forgotten in India. It is generally explained by *rahasya,* or *guhya ādeśaḥ,* mystery; and an artificial etymology is given, according to which Upaniṣad would mean "destruction of passion or ignorance, by means of divine revelation,"[7] The original signification of the word, however, must have been that of sitting down near somebody in order to listen, or in order to meditate and worship. Thus we find *up* + *sad* used in the sense of sitting and worshipping :

Ṛv. ix. 11.6.Namasā it upa sīdata, "Approach him with praise."

Rv. x. 73. 11. Vayaḥ suparṇāḥ upa sedur Indram priyamedhāḥ shayaḥ nādhamānāḥ. "The poets with thoughts have approached Indra begging, like birds with beautiful wings."

The root *ās,* which has the same meaning as *sad,* to if joined with the preposition *upa,* expresses the same idea as *upa-sad, i. e.* to approach respectfully, to worship (Ṛv. x. 153.1.). It is frequently to express the position which the pupil occupies when listening to his teacher,[8] and it clearly expresses a position of inferiority in such passages as, Brāhmaṇa, i. 3. 4. 15 : "tasmād *uparyāsīnam* kṣatriyam, adhastād imāḥ prajā upāsate." "therefore these people below (the *Viś* or *Vaiśyas)* sit under, or pay respect to the Kṣatriya who sits above." Still more decisive is another passage in the same work (ix. 4. 3. 3.). where *upannhādin* is used in the sense of subject : "kshatrāya tad visum adhas upaniṣadāiṇim karoti,[9] "he thus makes the Viś below subject to the Kṣatriya," There can be little doubt therefore that Upaniṣad meant originally the act of sitting down near a teacher,[10] of submissively listening to him; and it is easy to trace the steps by which it came to mean implicit faith,[11] and, at last, truth of divine revelation.

The songs of the Veda contained but little of philosophy or theosophy, and what the Brāhmaṇas call the higher, knowledge is not to be sought for in the hymns of the Ṛṣis "What,"[11] says the author of the Śvetāśvatara-upaniṣadā, "what shall a man do with the hymns. who does not know that eternal word of the hymns in the highest heaven, that in which all the gods are absorbed ? Those who know it, they are blessed." The same sentiment is frequently expressed, but nowhere with greater force than in a passage of the Kaṭha-upaniṣadā[12] a passage most remarkable in many respects. "That divine Self," the poet says, "is not to be grasped by tradition,[13] nor by understanding, nor by all revelation; by him whom He himself chooses, by him alone is He to be grasped; that Self chooses his body as his own." Rammohan Roy when he visited the British Museum and found the late Dr. Rosen engaged in preparing an edition of the hymns of the Veda, expressed his surprise at so useless an undertaking. But the same philosopher looked upon the Upaniṣads as worthy to become the foundation of a new religion, and he published several of them himself with notes and translations. "The adoration of the invisible Supreme Being," he writes, "is exclusively prescribed by the Upaniṣads or the *principal* parts of the Veda, and also by the Vedānta," and if other portions of the Veda, seem to be in contradiction with the pure doctrine of the Upaniṣads, he hints that the whole work must not only be stripped of its authority, but looked upon as altogether unintelligible.[14]

The early Hindus did not find any difficulty in reconciling the most different and sometimes contradictory opinions in their search after truth; and a most extraordinary medley of oracular sayings might be collected from the Upaniṣad even from those which ate genuine and comparatively ancient, all tending to elucIdate the darkest points (philosophy and religion, the creation of the world, the nature of God, the relation of man to God, and similar subject: That one statement should be contradicted by another seem never to have been felt as any serious difficulty. Thus we read in the first verse of the

Śvetāśvatara-upaniṣadā "Is Brahman the cause ? Whence are we born ? By what dl we live ? Where do we go ? At whose command do we Wālk after the Law, in happiness and misery? Is Time the cause, or Nature, or Law, or Chance, or the Elements ? Is Man to be taken as the source of all ? Nor is it their union because there must be an independent Self, and even that independent Self has power over that which causes happiness and pain."[15] The answers returned to such questions are naturally vague and various. Thus Mādhava in his Commentary on Parāśara, quotes first from the Bhavṛcha-upaniṣadā. "In the beginning this world Was Self alone, there Was nothing else winking. He thought, Let me create the worlds, and he created these worlds." From this it would follow that the absolute Self Was supposed to have created everything out of nothing. But immediately afterwards Mādhava quotes from another Upaniṣad, Śvetāśvatara (IV. 10.), where Māyā or delusion is called the principle, and the Great Lord himself, the deluded[16]. This is evidently an allusion to Sāṇkhya doctrines, but Mādhava explains it in a different sense. He maintains that here also the Divine Self is meant by the Great Lord, and that Delusion is only one of his powers, as heat is a power of fire[1]. And he appeals to another passage in the same Upaniṣad (1. 3.), where it is said "that sages endowed with meditation and intuition, saw the power of the Divine' Self, concealed by his own qualities." This same interpretation is adopted in the *Sūtras,* of the Vedānta-philosophy, but it by no means follows that therefore it is the true one. The principal interest of the older Upaniṣads consists in the absence of that systomatic uniformity, which we find in the later systems of philosophy, and it is to be regretted that nearly all scholars who have translated portions of the Upaniṣads have allowed themselves to be guided by the Brāhmaṇic commentators. The commentators wrote all, more or less, under the influence of philosophical systems, and thought themselves justified in explaining the Upaniṣads in such a manner that they should agree, even in the most minute points, with the, *sūtras* of the philosophical schools But the authors of the Upaniṣads were poets rather than philosophers. Truth' itself assumed, in their eyes, an aspect varying according to their own feelings and misgivings. We saw that the Bhavṛcha-upaniṣadā placed *Ātman* or the Self at the beginning of all things. The Taittirīya-upaniṣad speaks of *Brahman*, the true omniscient, and infinite, and derives from it the ether, the air, fire, Water, earth, plantfood, seed, and body.[18] This, in the eyes of the later commentators, may appear substantially the same doctrine as that of the Bhavṛca-upaniṣadā. But to us it is of interest to mark the difference, and to Wātch the various attempts which were made to express the idea of a creator. The Bhavṛcas, by calling him *Āman* in the masculine, showed that they were impressed more strongly with the idea of a personal Being; the Taittirīyas, speaking of *Brahman* as neuter, gave more prominence to the idea of a Power. It was an epoch in the history of the human mind when the identity of the masculine Self and the neutral *Brahman Was* for the first time perceived, and the name of the discoverer has not been forgotten. It was Śāṇḍilya who declared that the Self within our heart is *Brahman* (Chhand-up. Iii. 4. p. 208), and this tenet, somewhat amplified', is quoted as "Śāṇḍilya's wisdom" by the author of the Śatapatha-brāhmaṇa (x. 6. 3.). Other sages among the Chandogas[1] again speak simply of a *Sat,* or a Being, which desired to be many, and created the light, the light flowing into Water? the Water into food, and so on. Ātharvaṇikas speak of the Creator as *Akshara,* and it must remain doubtful whether they connected with this word the idea of the Indestructible or of Element[20], The term used by the Vājasaneyins is *Avyākṛa,* or the undeveloped. Every one of these terms had originally a meaning of its own, and though in later times they may all be used synonymously, they ought to be kept distinct when we are tracing the history of the human mind. Some of the ancient sages, after having arrived at the idea of *Avyākṛta,* Undeveloped, went even beyond, and instead of the *Sat* or το ον, they postulated an *Asat,* το μη ον as the beginning, of all things. Thus we read in the Chāndogya-upaniṣadā :[21] "And some say, in the beginning there was *Asat* (not being), alone, without a second; and from this *Alat* might the *Sat* be born."

But in spite of the Great variety of philosophical thought on this and similar subjects that was to be found in the Upaniṣ ads, the wānt of new Upaniṣads was felt by the sects which sprang up in every part of India,[22] The old Upaniṣads, however, were not rejected, and to the present day the ten which are chiefly studied in Bengal are the BṛhadāĀraṇyaka, the Aitareya, Chāndogya, Taittirīya, Īśa, Kena, Kaṭha, Praśna, Muṇḍaka and Māṇḍūkya-upaniṣadās. Every one of these has been published, and we possess an excellent edition both of the text and commentary by Dr. Röer in the volumes of the Bibliotheca Indica. The whole number of Upaniṣads, however, known to be or to have been in existence, is much larger. It Was commonly stated as 62,[23] but it has lately been brought as high as 108,[24] and even higher. Some of the titles given in various lists belong most likely to smaller portions' of certain Upaniṣads, and these extracts, adopted by some sect or other, were after-wards quoted as independent treatises.[25] May are of very modern origin, and have no right to be mentioned in connection with Vedic literature. In order, however, to have this whole mass of literature together, every work that claims the title of Upaniṣad on any ground whatsoever, has been incorporated in an alphabetical list, which will be printed as an Appendix. There are several works which had to be consulted in drawing up this list. First, Anṇuetil Duperron's Oupnekhat,[26] a work which contains the translation of fifty Upaniṣads from Persian into Latin. [The author of this Persian translation is supposed to be Dārā *Shakoh,* the eldest son of *Shah Jehan,* and pupil of Babu Lal; but in reality the work seems to have been performed by several Paṇḍits, whom that enlightened prince called from Benares to Delhi, ordering them to translate some of their sacred works into Persian. Three years after the accomplishment of their work, their patron was put to death by his brother Aurungzeb.][27] Secondly, there is Colebrooke's Essay on the Vedas, which gives a more complete enumeration of the Upaniṣads. Thirdly,

Weber's Analysis of Duperron's translation of Upaniṣads, in his "Indian Studies." Fourthly, an article by Mr. W. Elliot in the Journal of the Asiatic Society of Bengal, 1851, giving an account of Upaniṣads known in the South of India, among the Telugu *Brāhmaṇas'* Fifthly, Dr. Röer's introductions to the various Upaniṣads, edited and translated by him in the volumes of the Bibliotheca Indica. There are other works, the well-known pamphlets of Rammohun Roy, the Essays of Pauthier, Poley, d'Eckstein, Windiscmann, and the publications of the Tattvabodhinī Society, all of which had to be consulted in drawing up our own alphabetical list.

The names of the authors of the principal Upaniṣads[28] are unknown. This is owing to the very character of these works. They contain authoritative statements on the highest questions, and such statements would lose all authority if they were represented to the people at large as the result of human reasoning and imagination. They, in a higher degree than any other part of the Vedas, must have been considered from the very beginning as revelation, and as directly communicated to the world by the Supreme Spirit. This sentiment is clearly expressed in the beginning of the Muṇdaka-upaniṣadā : "*Brāhman (masc.* =ब्रह्मा), the creator of the universe, the preserver of the world, appeared first among the gods. He taught the knowledge of *Brāhman* (neuter), the foundation of all knowledge, to Atharvan his eldest son. Atharvan long ago imparted the knowledge of *Brāhman,* which Brahmā had explained to him, to Angis; he told it to Sātyāvāha Bhāradvāja, Bharadvaja in succession to Aṅgiras. Śaunaka, the great lord, approached Aṅgiras respectfully, and asked : 'What is it through which if known all this becomes known ?'"[29] It is stated that the text of the Upaniṣads, after it had once been revealed, Was never affected by differences, arising from the oral tradion of various Śākhās; and in one instance where various texts of the same Upaniṣad have been noted by the *Brāhmaṇas,* they, are ascribed to various localities, but not to various *Śākhāa.* Each *Śākhā,* however, Was supposed to be possessed of an

Upaniṣad, and the Muktikā states boldly that, as there are 1180 Śākhās, there ought properly to be as many Upaniṣads.

Another reason why we never bear of the authors of Upaniṣads as we hear of the Ṛṣis of hymns is that in many instances the Upaniṣads are mere compilations from other works. Verses from the hymns are incorporated into various Upaniṣads, and stories originally propounded in the Brāhmaṇas, are enlarged upon by the compilers of these philosphical tracts.

In cases only where the Upaniṣads form part of an Āraṇyaka, the reputed authors of the larger works might likewise be considered as the authors of the Upaniṣads. This authorship, however, is different from the authorship of a Gauḍapāda and Śaṅkara. As the Bṛhadāraṇyaka forms part of the Śatapatha-brāhmaṇa, Yājñavalkya, the reputed author of the Brāhmaṇa, might well be considered as the author of the Upaniṣad known by the name of Bṛhadāraṇyaka. It forms the last five Prapāṭhakas of the 14th book of the Śatapatha-brāhmaṇa in the Mādhyandina-śākhā, whereas in the Kāṇva-śākhā the whole of the. 17th book is comprised under the name of Upaniṣad. Yājñavalkya Vājasaneya is mentioned towards the end of the Bṛhadāraṇyaka as the person who received the whole of the White Yajurveda from Āditya or the Sun. His influential position at the court of Janaka, king of Videha, is alluded to several times, and one portion of the Bṛhadāraṇyaka is called the Yājñavalkīyam Kāṇḍam, as specially celebrating the victories gained by that sage over all his rivals. But even if we accept the traditional opinion that Yājñavalkya was the author of the Brāhmaṇa and the Āraṇyaka, such a supposition would be of very little help to us in determining the probable age of the Upaniṣad portion of the Śatapatha-brāhmaṇa. We need not enter at present into the question whether the supposed authorship of Yājñavalkya implies that he actually composed, or only that he collected the sacred code of the Vājasaneyins. That code is, no doubt, in some peculiar sense, considered as Yājñavalkya's own work. At the time of Pāṇini it was called by a name which, by its very character, indicated that the Śatapatha-brāhmaṇa was a work due to the exertion of *one* individual, and that it was not, like other Brāhmaṇas, simply proclaimed by him (*prokta*), or formed the traditional property of an ancient Vedic Śākhā bearing his name. This, together with a remark in the Vārttika to Pāṇini, iv. 3. 105, may be interpreted as indicating the more modern date of this Brāhmaṇa and its Āraṇyaka, as compared with the Brāhmaṇa and Āraṇyakas of other Vedas. But beyond this, the name of Vājasaneya Yājñavalkya, as the reputed author of these works, will not help us in fixing the age of the Vājasaneyi-brāhmaṇa-upaniṣadā.

Attempts have been made to fix the age of Yājñavalkya, as the author of a Law-book, and to transfer this date to the author of the Vedic works, just mentioned. The versifier, however, of these laws is as distinct from the original Yājñavalkya, as the poetical editor of the Laws of the Mānavas is from the mythic Manu, the founder of the Mānava-śākhā.

Although the poetical editor of this code of laws speaks of the Āraṇyaka[30] as his own work, nobody will be misled by an assertion of this kind.[31] But even the age of the versifier of Yājñavalkīyas code of laws is difficult to determine. Professor Wilson, in his "Ariana Antiqua" (page 364), observes that the word Nānaka, a gold or silver coin having upon it the figure of Śiva, may be derived from Nāna, a term which occurs on the coins of Kanerki, and is supposed to be "the name of a goddess; probably the same as the Anaitis or Anahid of the Persians, or the tutelary goddess of Armenia, Anaia or Nānaca." If so (and I think the explanation extremely doubtful) the age of Yājñavalkya's legal dicta in which the word Nānaka occurs, would be' subsequent to the era of Kanerki, and, as Professor Stenzler remarks in his edition of Yājñavalkya, the second century after Christ would be the earliest date that could be assigned to Yājñavalkya. Now the identification of Nānaka and Nāna (Nanaia, Nana Rao,) is a very ingenious conjecture, but no more. Even if admitted to be true, we should still have to prove that the same goddess did not occur in the same wāy on more ancient oriental coins. As the Hindus derived their knowledge of coined money from foreign nations, Nānaka may have been current in India long before the time of Kanerki, though the Nānakas of Kanerki may be the first known to us as coined in India. The occurrence of a word like Nānaka,[32] therefore, is not sufficient by itself to prove that the second century after Christ is the earliest date of the Yajñavalkiya Code, still less of Yājñavalkya, as Professor Stenzler supposes. But whatever date may be assigned to this Śloka work, the date of Yājñavalkya, the author of the Āraṇyaka and the Śatapatha-brāhmaṇa, would not be affected by it in any. wāy, and the Śatapatha-brāhmaṇa is the only work from which we may expect information on this point.

Another attempt has been made to fix the age of Yājñavalkya, or, at least, to assign certain chronological limits to the first origin of the Śākhā of the Mādhyandinas, a sub-division of the Vājasaneysins. Arrian, when speaking of the course of the Ganges, mentions among the rivers falling into the Ganges, the "Andomatis, flowing from the country of the Mandiadini, an Indian people."[33] Lassen thought he discovered in this the Sanskrit word Mādhyandina, meridional; and, as a mere conjecture, such a remark Was valuable. Professor Weber, however, went beyond this, and, taking for granted the identity of Mandiadini and Mādhyandina, taking for granted also the identity of this Indian people with the Mādhyandina, a subdivision of the Śākhā of the Vājasaneyins, he concluded that the text of this *Śākhā, i. e.,* the Saṃhitā and Brāhmaṇa of the White Yajur-veda, published by himself, must have existed in the third century B. C. Such rapid conclusions are rarely safe. There may have been such a people as the Mādhyandinas at any time before or after Christ, and there may have been such a *Śākhā* as that of the Mādhyandinas at any time before or after Christ, but the people need not have had any connection with that *Śākhā,* as little as the *Prācyas* or Prasii had anything in common with the *Śākhā* of the Prachya-Kaṭhas or the αμχισθολοι, another Indian people, mentioned by Greek writers, with the *Śākhā* of the Kapiṣṭhalas. Granted, however, that the *Śākhā Was* formed in the country of the

Mādhyandinas, and derived its name from it, nothing whatever would follow from this as to the exact date when this was effected.

A second Āraṇyaka is that of the Taittirīyas. As the Taittirīya-veda (or the Black Yajur-veda) is always represented as anterior to the White Yajur-veda, the Taittirīya Āraṇyaka also might be expected to be older then the Bṛhadāraṇyaka. It is more likely, however, that the Taittirīya Āraṇyaka did not yet exist at the time when Yājñavalkya, after seceding from his master, founded a new school, and endowed it with a new Saṁhitā and Brāhmaṇa. The Āraṇyaka of the Taittirīyas may have been added to their Brāhmaṇas subseṇuently to this schism, in the same wāy as the Bṛhadāraṇyaka is certainly later then many portions of the Śatapatha-brāhmaṇa. At all events the Taittirīya-Āraṇyaka represents the latest period in the development of the Vedic religion, and shows a strong admixture of post-Vedic ideas and names. The same applies also to several parts of the Taittrīya-brāhmaṇa, the last part of which does not belong to *Tittiri,* but is ascribed to Kaṭha, the same *Muni* to whom the beginning of the Āraṇyaka is said to have been revealed.[34] There are some traces which would lead to the supposition that the Taittirīya-veda had been studied, particularly in the south of India, and even among people which are still considered as un-Āryan in the Brāhmaṇa of the Ṛg-veda. In the Taittirīya Āraṇyaka different readings are mentioned, which are no longer ascribed to different *Śākhās* but to certain countries in the south of India, like those of the Drāviḍas, Āndhras, and Karnātakas. This fact by itself would throw some doubt on the antiquity and genuineness of this class of Vedic writings,[35] at least in that form in which we now possess them.

The Taittirīya Āraṇyaka consists of ten books, of which the four last are devoted to Upaniṣad doctrines. No author is mentioned, and *Tittiri*, who might seem to hold the same position for the Taittirīya Āraṇyaka which Yājñavalkya holds for the Bṛhadāraṇyaka, is represented by the *Brāhmaṇas* themselves neither as the author nor as the first teacher. He received the tradition from Yāska Paiṅgi, who received it from Vaiśam-pāyana. Tittiri himself handed it on to Ukha, and he to Ātreya.

Tittiri, therefore, was believed to be the founder of a *Śākhā* but not the author of the Āraṇyaka.

A third Āraṇyaka is the Aitareya Āraṇyaka, belonging to the Ṛg-veda. It forms a work by itself, and is not counted as part of the Aitareya-brāhmaṇa. This is an important point. The work consists of five books or Āraṇyakas,[36] the second and third of which form the Bahvṛca upaniṣadā, if by this name we like to distinguish the complete Upaniṣad from a portion of it, *viz* : Adhyāyas 4-6, of the second Āraṇyaka, commonly quoted as the Aitareyopaniṣad. If we ask for the name of the author, we find again the same uncertainty as in the Bṛhadāraṇyaka and the Taittrīya Āraṇyaka. All we know for certain is that there was a *Sākhā* of the Aitareyins, which was in the possession of a Brāhmaṇa and an Āraṇyaka. Both these works were afterwards adopted by the later *Śākhās* of the Ṛg-veda, so that we actually hear of an Āśvalāyana text of the Aitareyakam. We also know from the Chāndogya upaniṣadā (iii. 16) that there was a Mahidāsa Aitareya, who, by means of his sacred knowledge was supposed to have defied death for 1,600 years; and in the Aitareya-Āraṇyaka, not in the Brāhmaṇa, he is several times quoted by the same name as an authority. In the later commentaries, a story is mentioned according to which the Brāhmaṇa and Āraṇyaka of the Ṛg-veda were originally revealed to one Aitareya, the son of Itara. This story, however, sounds very apocryphal, and had a merely etymological origin. Itara, in Sanskrit, means not only the other of two, but also low, rejected. Thus, if the patronymic Aitareya was to be accounted for, it was extremely easy to turn it into a metronymic, and to make Aitareya the son of an Itara, a rejected wife. Thus Sāyaṇa, in his introduction to the Aitareya-brāhmaṇa, tells us that there was once a great Ṛṣi who had many wives. One of them was called Itarā, and she had a son called Mahidāsa. His father preferred the sons of his other wives to Mahidāsa, and once he insulted him in the sacrificial hall, by placing all his other sons on his lap. Mahidāsa's mother, seeing her son with tears in his eyes, prayed to her own tutelary goddess, the Earth *(svīya-kula-*

devatā Bhūmiḥ), and the goddess in her heavenly form appeared in the midst of the assembly, placed Mahidāsa on a throne, and gave him on account of his learning the gift of knowing the Brāhmaṇa, consisting of forty Adhyāyas, and, as Sāyaṇa calls it, another Brāhmaṇa, treating "of the Āraṇyaka duties."

This, and similar stories mentioned by Colebrooke,[37] are not calculated to inspire much confidence. On the contrary we feel inclined to attach more value to the accidental admissions of the *Brāhmaṇas* who ascribe the later portions of the AitareyāĀraṇyaka to such well known authors as Śaunaka and Āśvalāyana. There may have been an Aitareya, the founder of the *Śākhā* of the Aitareyins, and himself the expounder of those ceremonial, philological, and philosophical tracts which are incorporated in the Brāhmaṇa and the Āraṇyaka of the Aitareyins. He is quoted himself as an authority in those works, but nothing is said in them of his degraded descent, nor of the erudition granted to him by the goddess of the earth.

Another Āraṇyaka, belonging to another *Śākhā* of the Ṛg-veda, is the Kauṣītaki-Āraṇyaka. Colebrooke stated in his Essay on the Veda that "the original of the Kauśitakam was among the portions of the Veda which Sir Robert Chambers collected at Benares, according to a list which he sent to me some time before his departure from India." According to the catalogue of Sir Robert's MSS. which are now at the Royal Library at Berlin, there is in that collection not only the text and commentary of the Kauṣītaki-brāhmaṇa, but likewise the Āraṇyaka in three *Adhyāyas,* of which the third constitutes the Kauṣītaki-upaniṣadā. "Here again we know nothing as to the name of an author, Kauṣītakin being simply the name of that sect in which the text of these works was handed down from teacher to pupil.

There are no Āraṇyakas for the Sāma-veda, nor for the so called fourth Veda, the Ātharvaṇa.

Traces of modern ideas are not wanting in the Āraṇyakas, and the very fact that they are destined for a class of men who had retired from the world in order to give themselves up to the contemplation of the highest problems, show an advanced, and already declining and decaying society, not unlike the monastic age of the Christian world. They problems, indeed, which are discussed in the Āraṇyakas and the old Upaniṣads are not in themselves modern. They had formed the conversation of the old and the young, of Wārriors and poets, for ages. But in a healthy state of society these questions were discussed in courts and camps : priests were contradicted by kings, sages confounded by children, women were listened to when they were moved by an unknown spirit.[38] This time, which is represented to us by the early legends of the Āraṇyakas, was very different from that which gave rise to professional anchorites, and to a literature composed exclusively for their benefit. As sacrifices were performed long before a word of any Brāhmaṇa or Sūtra had been uttered, so metaphysical speculations were carried on in the forests of India long before the names of Āraṇyaka or Upaniṣad were thought of. We must carefully distinguish between a period of growth, and a period which tried to reduce that growth to rules and formulas. In one sense the Āraṇyakas are old, for they reflect the very dawn of thought; in another, they are modern, for they speak of that dawn with all the experience of a past day. There are passages in these works, unequalled in any language for grandeur, boldness, and simplicity. These passages are relics of a better age. But the generation which became the chronicler of those Titanic Wārs of thought was a small race: they were dwarfs, measuring the footprints of departed giants.

Chronologically we can see with great clearness that the Āraṇyakas are anterior to the Sūtras. It is only in their latest portion that they show traces of the style of Sūtra compositions. We can likewise see that they are later than the Brāhmaṇas, to which they themselves, in several instances, form a kind of appendix. Beyond this we cannot go and an impartial consideration of the arguments adduced in favour of a much earlier or a much later date of this class of Vedic literature, will show a complete absence of facts and arguments, such as are required for inductions. Whether Pāṇini knew the Āraṇyakas as a branch of sacred literature is uncertain. Although he men-tions the word "Āraṇyaka," he only uses it in the sense of "living in the forest;" and it is the author of the Vārttikas[39] who first remarks that the same word is also used in the sense of "read in the forest." The word *Upaniṣad,* besides, being used in the Upaniṣads themselves[40], occurs in the Sūtras of Pāṇini (i. 4. 79.), but there is nothing to prove that Pāṇini knew Upaniṣad as the name of a class of sacred writings.

It is hardly necessary to remark that at the time when the Āraṇyakas were written, the hymns of the Saṁhitās were not only known, but known in the same form in which we now possess them.[41] The Ṛg-veda is quoted as a whole, and consisting of ten Maṇḍalas. Though the name of Maṇḍala is not used, the names assigned to each of the ten books are the same as those used in the Anukrāmaṇīs, and they follow each other in the same succession. Nay, these names had evidently been current for some time before, for the author of the Āraṇyaka assigns the most extra-ordinary etymologies to them, and uses them in support of the wildest speculations. He first mentions the Śatarcins (शतर्चिन:) or the poets of the first Maṇḍala. He then comprehends the poets of Maṇḍala ii. to IX. under the common name of the Mādhyamas, assigning to the poets of the tenth and last Maṇḍala the name of Kṣudra-sūktas and Mahāsūktas. The middle books are enumerated more in detail under their usual names, Gṛtsamada, (ii), Viśvāmitra (iii), Vāmadeva (iv), the' Atris (v), Bhāradvāja (vi), the Vasiṣtha (vii), the Pragāthas (viii), the Pāvamānīs (ix). The names also of Ṛg-veda, Yajur-veda, and Sāma-veda occur as literary titles in this Āraṇyaka.[42]

The etymologies assigned to these names are not perhaps more absurd than those which we find in the Brāhmaṇas. But there are other etymological explanations in the Āraṇyakas such as we scarcely find in any genuine Brāhmaṇa. Part of the first Āraṇyaka (i. 4) reads almost like a commentary on the first hymns of the Ṛg-veda, and the short glosses scattered about in these books of the forest might well be considered as the first elements of a Nirukta.

The grammatical study of the hymns of the Veda was evidently far advanced, and scholastic pedantry had long taken the place of sound erudition, when the early portions of the Āraṇyaka were composed. Not only the ten books of the Ṛg-veda are mentioned, but likewise their sub-divisions, the hymns *(sūkta),* verses *(ṛc),* half verses *(arddharca),* feet *(pada),* and syllables *(akṣara).* Sometimes the syllables of certain hymns and classes of hymns are counted, and their number is supposed to possess a mys terous significance. In one passage (ii. 12.) speculations are propounded on the division of letters into consonants (व्यञ्जने), vowels (घार्ष), and sibilants (उष्माणः).

Admitting, therefore, that the Āraṇyakas represent the latest productions of the Brāhmaṇa period, and that in some cases their authors belong to the age of Śaunaka, in others even to a more modern age, we have now to consider the character of the genuine Brāhmaṇas, in order to point out the differences which distinguish the Brāhmaṇas from the Sūtras by which they are followed, and from the *Mantras* by which they are preceded,

THE BRĀHMAṆAS

The difficulty of giving an exhaustive definition of what a Brāhmaṇa is has been felt by the *Brāhmaṇas* themselves. The name given to this class of literature does not teach us more than that these works belonged to the *Brāhmaṇas.* They were *Brāhmaṇic i.e.,* theological tracts, comprising the knowledge most valued by the *Brāhmaṇas,* bearing partly on their sacred hymns, partly on the traditions and customs of the people. They profess to teach the performance of the sacrifice; but for the greater part they are occupied with additional matter; with explanations and illustrations of things more or less distantly connected with their original faith and their ancient ceremonial.

Sāyaṇa, in his introduction to the Ṛg-veda,[1] has given such extracts from the Pūrva-Mīmāṁsā philosophy as may furnish a pretty correct idea of the Brāhmaṇas, and he has treated the same subject again in his Introduction to the Aitareya-brāhmaṇa.

"A Brāhmaṇa," he says," is twofold, containing either commandments (fafe), or additional explanations (विधि). This is confirmed by Āpastamba, saying : 'The Brāhmaṇas are commandments for the sacrifices; all the rest consists of additional explanations.' The commandments, too, are of two kinds, either causing something to be done which was not done before, or making something known which was not known before. Of the former kind are all those commandments occurring in the practical part, such as, 'At the Dīkṣaṇīya ceremony he presents a *Puroḍāśa* (पुरोडाश) oblation to Agni and Viṣṇu.' Of the latter kind are all philosophical passages, such as, 'Self was all this alone in the beginning.'

"But how can it be said,"Sāyaṇa goes on, "that the Veda consists of Mantras and Brāhmaṇas, as the essential qualities neither of the one nor of the other part can be satisfactorily defined ? For if it be said that a *Mantra* alludes to those things which are commanded, this definition would not comprehend all *Mantras* because there are some which are themselves commandments, as, for instance, 'He takes Kapiñjals for the Spring.' Again, if it be said that a *Mantra* is what makes one think (मन् to think), this definition would comprehend the Brāhmaṇas also. Other definitions have been given, that a *Mantra* ends with the word 'you are, or that it ends with the first person plural; but none of these definitions can be considered as exhaustive. The only means, then, by which *Mantras* can be distinguished from Brāhmaṇas lies in their general sacrificial appellation, which comprehends the most different things under the one common name of *Mantras*. There are some recording the performance of sacrifices; some contain praises, some end with the word you (त्वा), some are invocations, some are directions, some contain deliberations, some contain complaints, some are questions, some are answers, etc. All these attributes are so heterogeneous, that none of them can be used for a definition. Knowing, however, that the Veda consists only of two parts, we may say that whatever does not come under the name of *Mantra* is Brāhmaṇa, whether it contains reasons, explanations, censures, recommendations, doubts, commandments, relations, old stories or particular determinations. Not one of these subjects belongs to the Brāhmaṇas exclusively, but they occur more or less frequently in the *Mantras* also, and could therefore not be used as definitions of the Brāhmaṇas. The same objection applies to all other definitions which have been attempted. Some have said that the frequent occurrence of the particle *iti* (इति = thus) constitutes a Brāhmaṇa; others, that a Brāhmaṇa closes with the words *ityāha* (इत्याह = thus be said) others that a Brāhmaṇa contains stories, etc.; but all this would apply with equal force to some of the *Mantras*. The only division therefore of the Veda that holds good consists in comprehending one part under the old traditional appellation of Mantra, and consider-ing all the rest as Brāhmaṇas.

"But it might be objected," Sāyaṇa continues, " that for instance in the chapter on the Brāhmayajña (ब्रह्मयज्ञ), other part of the Veda are mentioned besides the Brāhmaṇas and Mantras, under the title of Itihāsas (epic stories), Purāṇas (cosmogonic stories), Kalpas (ceremonial rules), Gathas (songs), Narāsaṅsis, (heroic poems). This however would be the same mistake, as if we should place a *Brāhmaṇa* co-ordinate with a *Brāhmaṇa* who is a mendicant. For all these titles, like Itihāsa, etc., apply only to sub-divisions of the Brāhmaṇas. Thus, passages from the Brāhmaṇas, like 'The gods and the Āsurās were fighting,' etc., would be called Itihāsas; other passages like 'In the beginning there was nothing', would be called Purāṇas; therefore, we may safely say, that the Vedas consist of two parts only, of *Mantras* and *Brāhnaṇas*. "[44]

If after these not very satisfactory definitions of what a Brāhmaṇa is and how it differs from a *Mantra,* we turn to the Brāhmaṇas themselves, such as we possess them in MS, we find that their number is much smaller than we should have expected.

If every *Śākhā* consisted of a Saṁhitā and a Brāhmaṇa, the number of the old Brāhmaṇas must have been very considerable. It must not be supposed, however, that the Brāhmaṇas which belonged to different Śākhās, were works composed independently by different authors. On the contrary, as the Saṁhitās of different Sākhās were nothing but different recensions of one and the same original collection of hymns, and could be distinguished from each other only by a number of authorised *varies lectiones* or by the addition and omission of certain hymns, the Brāhmaṇas also, which were adopted by different Caraṇas of the same Veda, must be considered not as so many independent works, but in most instances as different recensions of one and the same original. There was originally but one body of Brāhmaṇas for each of the three Vedas; for the Ṛg-veda, the Brāhmaṇas of the Bahvṛcas, for the Sāma-veda the Brāhmaṇas of of the Chhandogas, and for the Yajur-veda in its two forms the Brāhmaṇas of the Taittirīyas, and the Śatapatha-brāhmaṇa. These works were not written in metre, like the Saṁhitās, and were therefore more exposed to alteration in the course of a long continued oral tradition.

We possess the Brāhmaṇa of the Bahvṛcas, in the *Śākhās* of the Aitareyins and the Kauṣītakins. The various readings of other *Śākhas* quoted by the commentator on the Aitareya-brāhmaṇa, show evidently that there were other *Śākhās* of the Bahvṛcas, which differed but little in the wording of their Brāhmaṇas. But even the Brāhmaṇa of the Kauṣītakins which has been preserved to us as a distinct work, different from the Brāhmaṇa of the Aitareyins, can only be considered as a branch of the original stock of Brāhmaṇa literature, current among the Bahvṛcas. Its arrangement differs considerably from that of the Aitareya-brāhmaṇa. The sacrifice described in the beginning of the Aitareya-brāhmaṇa forms the seventh Adhyāya of the Kauṣītaki-brāhmaṇa,[45] and most of the other sacrifices are equally displaced. Others which are discussed in the Aitareya-brahmaṇa are altogether wānting in the Kauṣītaki-brāhmaṇa, and must be supplied from the Sūtras of the Śāṅkhāyana-śākhā, a sub-division of the Kauṣītakins. But whenever parallel passages occur, it becomes clear that the coincidences in the description of sacrifices and the wording of legends cannot be accidental.

Most of the Brāhmaṇas which are left to us are collective works. A tradition has been preserved in confirmation of this fact. The Brāhmaṇa of the Taittirīyas in the Śākhās both of the Apastambiyas and the Ātreyas, contains some portions which bear the name of Kaṭha, and were formerly the property of his followers. The component parts are frequently called Brāhmaṇas, instead of chapters or sections. The same applies to the Āraṇyakas and Upaniṣads. In some cases, these smaller Brāhmaṇas are quoted by their special titles[46]; and in their collected form they are handed down, not always by the name of the Caraṇa by which they were adopted, but more frequently by that of the Caraṇa in which their original collection took place. Thus the Aitareya-brāhmaṇa, though adopted by the Āśvalayanlyas, is more frequently quoted by its original name than by that of Āśvalāyana-brāhmaṇa.[47] The Brāhmaṇa of Kauṣītakin or the Kauṣītakins is more usually referred to by this name than by that of the later Caraṇa of the Śāṅkhāyanas.

In the Brāhmaṇa of the Chandogas it is evident that after the principal collection was finished (called the Prauḍha or Pañcaviṁśa-brāhmaṇa *i.e.,* consisting of twenty-five sections), a twenty-sixth Brāhmaṇa Was added which is known by the name of Shadvirhsa-brāhmaṇa. This Brāhmaṇa together with the Adbhuta-brāhmaṇa must be of very modern date. It mentions not only temples *(Devāyatanāni),* but images of gods *(daivata-pratimā)* which are said to laugh, to cry, to sing, to dance, to burst, to sweat, and to twinkle. These two have long been supposed to be the only Brāhmaṇas of the Chandogas, and they constitute, no doubt, the most important part of that class of literature. It is curious, however that whenever the Brāhmaṇas of the Chhandogas are quoted, their number is invariably fixed at eight. Kumārila Bhaṭṭa, i. 3,[48] says, "in the eight Brāhmaṇas, together with the Upaniṣads, which the Chandogas read, no single accent is fixed." Still more explicit is a statement by Sāyaṇa which I quoted in the introduction to the first volume of my edition of the Ṛg-veda.[49] Here Sāyaṇa says: "There are eight Brāhmaṇas; the Prauḍha is the first, (this means the large Brāhmaṇa, or the Pañcaviṁśa); the one called Ṣaḍvirśa or Ṣaḍvirśad-brāhmaṇa, is the second; then follows the Sāmavidhi; then the Ārṣeya-brāhmaṇa, the Devatādhyaya-brāhmaṇa, and the Upaniṣad. These with the Saṁhitopaniṣad and the Varim are called the eight books." Of these the Sāmavidhana-brāhmaṇa was well known, the very ṇuotation of Sāyaṇa has been taken from his commentary on this very curious work. It might have been difficult, however, to identify the other five works if there had not been among the MSS, of Professor Wilson's collection at the Bodleian Library, one (No. 45 containing four of these small tracts, the Sanhitopanishadam-brāhmaṇam, the Devatādhyāyaḥ, the Vaṁśa-brāhmaṇam, and the Ārsheya-brāhmaṇam.[50] The only Brāhmaṇa, therefore, on which any doubt could remain, was the Upaniṣad, and here we shall probably not be wrong if we adopt one of Professor Weber's less bold conjectures, that Sāyaṇa intended this for the Chāndogya-upaniṣadā.[51] With the exception of this and the Sāmavidhana, which contains most important information on questions connected with *Aoliara* or customs, all the other tracts are of comparatively small importance.

It is in the Śatapatha-brāhamaṇa, however, that we can best observe the gradual accumulation of various theological and ceremonial tracts which were to form the sacred code of a new Çaraṇa. The text of this work has been edited by Professor Weber, and we can likewise avail ourselves of several essays on this branch of Vedic literature, published from time to time by that, industrious scholar. According to Indian traditions, Yājñavalkya Vājasaneya. the founder of the new Caraṇa of the Vajasaneyins is himself, if not the author, ot least the first who proclaimed the saṁhitā and Brāhmaṇa of the Vājasaneyins. We can see clearly that the composition of both the saṁhitā and Brāhmaṇa was guided by the same spirit, and it is not at all unlikely that in this the most modern of all Vedas, the final arrangement of the saṁhitā may have been contemporaneous with, or even later than, the composition of the Brāhmaṇa.

First of all, it ought to be remarked that the story which has been preserved by tradition of the schism introduced by Yājñavalkya among the followers of the *Adhvaryu* or Yajur-veda is confirmed by internal evidence. The general name of the ancient *Śākhās* of the Yajur-veda is Caraka, and the Taittirīyas, therefore together with the Kaṭhas and others are called by a general name, Caraka-śākhās. This name Carakas is used in one of the Khilas of the Vājasaneyi-saṁhitā as a term of reproach. In the 30th. Adhyāya a list of people is given who are to be sacrificed at the *Purusha-medha,* and among them we find the Carakacārya, the teacher of the Caraka, as the propel victim to be offered to *Duṣkṛtā* or sin. This passage,-together with the similar hostile expressions in the Śatapatha-brāhamaṇa were evidently dictated by a feeling of animosity against the ancient schools af the *Adhvaryus,* whose sacred texts we possess in the Taittirīya Veda, and from whom Yājñvalkaya seceded in order to become himself the founder of the new Caraṇas of the Vājasaneyins.

If we compare the saṁhitā and Brāhmaṇa of the Vājasaneyins with those of the Carakas, we see that the order of the sacrifices is on the whole the same, and that the chief difference between the two consists in the division of *Mantras* and Brāhmaṇas, which is carried out more strictly by Yājñavalkya than in the ancient text of the Taittirīyas. This Was most likely the reason why the text of Yājñavalkya was called Sukla Yajur-veda which is generally translated by the White Yajur-veda. But some commentators explain Śukla more, correctly by *śuddha,*[52] and translate it by "cleared," because in this new text the Mantras had been cleared and separated from the Brāhmaṇas and thus the whole had been rendered more lucid and intelligible. In opposition to this they suppose that the old text was called *Kṛṣṇa* or dark, because in it the verses and rules are mixed together, and less intelligible; or because as Vidyāraṇya says, it contains the rules of the *Hotṛ* as well as of the *Adhvaryu* priests, and thus bewildered the mind of the student.[1]

It was in the nature of the duties which the *Adhvaryuis* had to perform at the sacrifices, that their hymns and invocations could hardly be separated from the rules *(vidhi)* contained in the Brāhmaṇas. It was not a more accident therefore that in the Vedas of the ancient *Adhvaryus* the hymns and rules were mixed up, and it must be considered as a mere innovation if what is now called the saṁhitā of the Black Yajurveda is distinguished by this name from the Brāhmaṇa, which in reality is a continuation of the same work. It is not unlikely that it was the very wish to have, like the Bavhṛcas and Chandogas, a saṁhitā, *i. e.* a collection of hymns distinct from the ceremonial rules which led to the secession of the Vājasaneyins, and, by a kind of reaction, to the absurd adoption of the titles of saṁhitā and Brāhmaṇa among the Taittirīyas. In the new code of the Vājasaneyins, the most important part Was nevertheless the Brāhmaṇa, the saṁhitā being a mere collection of verses extracted and collected for the convenience of the officiating priest. The difference in the text of these verses and formulas would be marked in Brāhmaṇa, and transferred from the Brāhmaṇa into the saṁhitā. This is, therefore the very opposite of what happened with the text of the saṁhitā and Brāhmaṇa of the Bahvṛcas. Here the saṁhitā existed long before the Brāhmaṇa of the Aitareyins was composed. The Vājasaneyi-saṁhitā may possibly represent various readings which existed in the *Śākhās* of the Taittirīyas; but these verses were collected and formed into a saṁhitā only as an appendix to the Śatapatha-brāhmaṇa, the real code of the Vājasaneyins. Where the sacrificial invocations of the Vājasaneyins differ from those of the Taittirīyas we ought to recognize in those differences the last traces of *Śākhās* which existed previous to the establishment of the Vājasaneyins. In the beginning, for instance, of the Darśa-pūrṇamāsa sacrifice, the *Adhvaryu* priest, having called the cows and calves together, has to touch the calves with a branch. This act of the sacrifice was originally accompanied by the words "vāyava stha, upāyava stha, "you are like the winds," and the whole ceremony, together with these invocations, is contained in the Taittirīya-saṁhitā. In the Mādhyandina śākhā, on the contrary, not only are the words "upāyava stha" omitted in the saṁhitā, but a distinct wārning is given in the Brāhmaṇa not to use these words, belonging to a different *Śākha*.[54]

A comparison of the text of the Taittirīyas and Vājasaneyins shows that it would be a mistake to call Yājñavalkya the author, in our sense of the word, of the Vājasaneyi-saṁhitā and the Śatapatha-brāhmaṇa, the ancient Mantras and Brāhmaṇas into their present form, and considering the differences between the old and new text, we must admit that he had a greater right to be called an author than the founders of the Caraṇas of other Vedas whose texts we possess. In this sense, Kātyāyana says, in his Anukrāmam, that Yājñavalkya received the Yajur-veda from the Sun.[1] In the same sense the Śatapatha-brāhmaṇa ends with the assertain that the White Yajur-veda was proclaimed by Yājñavalkya Vājasaneya;[5] and in the same sense Pāṇini, or rather his editor, says in the first Vārttika to iv. 3. 105. that there were modern Brāhmaṇas proclaimed by Yajñayalkya, and that their title differed by its formation from the title given to more ancient Brāhmaṇas. At the time when these titles were framed Yājñavalkya Was still alive; and his work, therefore, was not yet considered as one handed down by tradition through several generations. There might seem to be some difficulty in making Yājñavalkya the author or editor of the whole Yajur-veda, because there are several portions of the Brāhmaṇa where Yājñavalkya himself is introduced as one of the chief interlocutors, so much so that part of the Bṛhadāraṇyaka, the last book of the Śatapatha-brāhmaṇa, is designated by the name of Yājñavalkiyam Kāṇḍam. But similar instances occur in several of the traditional works of the Brāhmaṇas, and in this case the decided traces of ar later origin which are to be found in the Bṛhadāraṇyaka would justify us in supposing that these portions were added after Yājñavalkya's decease, particularly as it is called Yājñavalklya not Yājñavalkya-kāṇḍa.[8] ;

That Yājñavalkya, though deserting the Carakas, derived great advantage from their Veda, is seen at once by the whole arrangement of his work. I give a list of the various subjects treated in the Vājasaneyi-saṁhitā, according to Mahīdhara. saṁhitā of the Vājasaneyins begins with The Darśa-purṇamāsa-mantrās (दर्शपूर्णभासमन्त्राः), Adhyāya, i.ii. 28,

Then follow:

Pitṛyajṃa-mantrāḥ, (पितृयज्ञमन्त्राः), ii. 29-34.

Agnyādheya-mantrāḥ (अग्न्याध्येयमन्त्राः) ii. 1-8.

Agnihotram (अग्निहोत्रम्), ii. 9-10.:

Agnyupasthānam (अग्न्युपस्थानम्), ii- 11-43.

Cāturmāsyāni (चातुर्मास्यानि), ii- 44-63.

Soma :

Agniṣṭomaḥ (अग्निष्टोमः), iv. 1-viii. 23.

Śālāpraveśaḥ (शालाप्रवेशः), iv. 1-37.

Atithyeṣhau havir-grahaṇādi-mantrāḥ, (yūpa-nirmāṇam) आतिथ्येष्टौ हविर्ग्रहणमन्त्राः (यूपनिर्माणम्), v. 1-fin. .

Yūpasaṅskāraḥ : (āgnishomāya-paśu)-somābhishava-mantrāḥ यूपसंस्कारः (अग्निषोमीयपशु-सोमाभिषवमन्त्राः) vi. 1-fū.

Graha-grahana-mantrāḥ (upāṁśvādi-pradānānta) (ग्रहग्रहणमन्त्राः उपांश्वादिप्रदानान्त),vi. 1-fū.

Tṛtīya-savānagatā āditya-grahādi-mantrāḥ (तृतीयसवनगता आदित्य ग्रहादिमन्त्राः), viii. 1-23.

Prāsaṅgikāḥ (प्रासङ्गिकाः), viii. 24-63.

Vājapeyaḥ (वाजपेयः), ix. 134.

Rājāsuyah (राजसूयाः), ix. 35-10.

Rājāsuya-abhiṣekārtha-jalādānādi-rājasūyaśeṣaś Caraka-sautrāmaṇiḥ Ca. (राजसूयाभिषेकार्थजलादानादिराजसूयशेषः चरकसौत्रामणिः), x. 1-fin.

Agnichayanam (अग्निचयनम्), ix-xviii.

Ukhādhāraṇā-mantrāḥ (उखासम्भरणादिमन्त्राः), xi.

Ukhādhāraṇā, gārhapatya-chayaua, kshetra-karshaṇam, ausha-dhavapanādiḥ (उखाधारणम् गार्हपत्यचयनम्, क्षत्रकर्षणम्, औषधवपनादि) xii.

Puṣkara-parṇādyūpadhāna-mantrāḥ (prathamā chitiḥ) पुष्करपर्णाद्युपणनमन्त्राः (प्रथमा चिति), xiii.

Dvitīyadi-citi-trayam (द्वितीयादिचितित्रयम्), xiv.

Pañcama-chitiḥ (पञ्चमचितिः), xv.

Śatarudriyākhya-homa-mantrāḥ (शतरूद्रियाख्यहोममन्त्राः), xvi. Citya-pariṣekādi-mantrāḥ (चित्यपरिषेकादिमन्त्रा), xvii. Vasordhārādimantrāḥ (वसोर्धारादिमन्त्राः), xviii.

Sautrāmaṇiḥ (सौत्रामणिः), xix.ṭxxi.

Surādīndrābhishekāntam (सुरादीन्द्राभिषेकान्तम्), xix.

Sekāsandyādi-hautrāntarn (सेकासन्द्यादिहौत्रान्तम्), xx.

Yājyādi-preshaṇāntam (याज्यादिप्रेषणान्तम्) xxi.

Aśvamedhas (अश्वमेघः), xxii.ṭxxv.

Home-mantrāḥ (होममन्त्राः), xxii

Śiṣṭam āsvamedhikam (शिष्टमाश्वमेविकम्),, xxiii.[1]

Śruti-rūpa-mantrā āśvamedhikānām paśūnām (श्रुतिरूपमन्त्रा आश्वमेघिकानां पशूनाम्) xxiv

Khilāni (खिलानि), xxvi-xxxv.

Anukta-mantra-Kaṭhanam (अनुक्तमन्त्रकथनम्) xxvi. . . .

Paṃcha-chitika-mantrāḥ (पञ्चचितिकमन्त्राः), xxvū.

Sautrāmaṇi - sambandhi - prayājānuyaja - praiṣa - nirūpaṇam (सौत्रमणिसम्बन्धिप्रयाजानुयाजप्रैषनिरूपणम्), xxviii.

Śiṣṭāśvamedha-mantrāḥ (शिष्टाश्वमेघमन्त्राः)j xxix.

Purusha-medhaḥ (पुरूषमेघः), xxx-xxvi.

Sarva-medhaḥ (सर्वमेघः), xxxii-xxxiii.

Brahma-yajñaḥ (ब्रह्मयज्ञाः), xxxiii. 55-xxxiv. fin.

Pitṛ-medhaḥ (पितृमेघः), xxxv.

Śukriyam (Pañcādhyāyī [शुक्रियम्-(पञ्चाध्यायी)], xxxi.ṭxl.[1]
Pravargya-Śāntipāṭhaḥ (प्रवर्ग्यशान्तिपाठः), xxxvi.

Abhryādi-rauhiṇāntam (अभ्रयादिरोहिणान्तम्), xxxvii.

Mahāvīra-nirūpaṇam (महावीरनिरूपणम्), xxxviii.

Gharmādi-nishkṛtih, lix. (धार्मादिनिष्कृतिः),

Jṃāna-Kāṇḍam, (ज्ञानकाण्डम्), xl.

According to this list the Vājasaneyi-saṁhitā may be divided into different sections. The first section comprises the Darśapūrṇamāsa, etc. I–iii.; the second the Soma sacrifices, iv–x.; the third the Agnicayanas, xi.-xviii.

These eighteen Adhyāyas, which correspond to the

Taittirīya-saṁhitā are explained in the first nine books of the Śatapatha-brāhmaṇa and the first eighteen chapters of Kātyāyana's Sūtras. They form, no, doubt, the most important part of the Adhvaryu-veda, but there is no evidence to show that they ever existed in a separate form. It has been well remarked, however, by the editor of the Śatapatha-brāhmaṇa, that the first nine books consist altogether of sixty Adhyāyas, "and that the name of Ṣaṣṭipatha (षष्टिपथ), the Sixty Paths, which is mentioned in the Vārttika to Pāṇ. iv. 2. 60., may refer to this portion, whereas the whole Brāhmaṇa, consisting of one hundred Adhyāyas, received the title of Śatapatha, the Hundred Paths.

The Sautrāmaṇī ceremony, which begins with the 19th Adhyāya, has nothing corresponding to it in the Taittirīya-saṁhitā, but, like the following sacrifices, it has been incorporated in the Taittirīya-brāhmaṇa. There is a difference also in the treatment which this sacrifice receives in the Śatapatha-brāhmaṇa. Adhayaya xix. and xx. are indeed explained there, in the 12th book, but they do not receive the same careful explanation which was given to the preceding sacrifices. The last Adhyāya, containing verses of the Hotṛ is not explained at all. Kātyāyana treats these three Adhyāyas in the 19th book of the Sūtras.

The Aśvamedha, which fills Books xxii-xxv. of the the Vājasaneyi-saṁhitā, is but partially contained in the Taittirīya-saṁhitā, and the Śatapatha also, though it devotes to this ceremony a considerable part of the 13th book, treats it in a much more superficial manner than the former sacrifice. Kātyāyana explains it in his 20th book.

The Adhyāyas, which follow the Aśvamedha, are distinctly called Khilas or supplements by Kātyāyana. They are relegated to the Brāhmaṇa by the Taittirīyas, and explained with less detail in the Śatapatha-brāhmaṇa. Adhyāyas xxvi.-xxix contain some hymns belonging to sacrifices previously explained, and they are passed over entirely by the Śatapatha-brāhmaṇa and by Kātyāyana. Adhyāyas xxx. and xxxi. contain the Puruṣa-medha, which the Taittirīyas treat in their Brāhmaṇa. The

Śatapatha-brāhmaṇa devotes but a short space to it in its 13th book, and Kātyāyana explains Adhyāya xxxi. in his 21st book,

The ceremonies comprised in the three following Adhyāyas, xxxii. to xxxiv. Sarva-medha and Brāhma-yajña, are passed over by the Śatapatha-brāhmaṇa and Kātyāyana. The Taittirīyas allow them no place in their Brāhmaṇa, but include them in their Āraṇyaka.

The Pitṛ-medha which follows in the 35th Adhyāya, finds its place in the Brāhmaṇa of the Taittirīyas. The Śatapatha and Kātyāyana explain it, the former in the 13th, the latter in the 21st book.

The Śukriya portion of the Vājasaneyi-saṁhitā, xxxvi.-xl., is excluded from the Brāhmaṇa of the Taittirīyas, and treated in their Āraṇyaka. The Śatapatha-brāhmaṇa explains three of these Adhyāyas, xxxvii.ṭxxxix., in full detail in its 17th Kāṇḍa, and Kātyāyana devotes to them the Sūtras of his last book.

Those who only take into account the general object of the Śatapatha-brāhmaṇa have called it a running commentary on the Vājasaneyi saṁhitā. But this applies strictly to the first nine books only, and with the tenth book the Brāhmaṇa assumes a new and more independent character. The tenth book is called *Agni-rahasyam,* the mystery of the fire, and it refers to no particular portion of the saṁhitā, but enlarges on the ceremonies which have been described in the four preceding books. Towards the end (x. 4. 6.), it contains two chapters, which in the Kāṇva-śākhā, form the beginning of the Bṛhadāraṇyaka-upaniṣadā, and are there followed by the Madhu-kāṇḍa, the Yājñavalkīya-kāṇḍa, and Khila-kāṇḍa of the 14th book of the Madhyandina-śākhā. The tenth book or *Agni-rahasyam* closes with its own genealogy or Vaṁśa.

With the 11th book begins, according to Sāyaṇa, the second part of the Śatapatha-brāhmaṇa. It is called Aṣṭādhyāyī, and gives additional information on all the sacrifices mentioned before, beginning with the *Agnyādhāna.*

The 12th book, which is called Sautrāmaṇi, treats of *prāyaścitta,* or penance in general, and it is only in its last portion that it refers to the text of the saṁhitā, and to that ceremony in particular from which it has derived its names. Besides this name of Sautrāmaṇi, the 12th book is also known by the name of Madhyama or the middle book, and this title can only be explained if we begin the second part of the Śatapatha, not, as Sāyaṇa suggests, with the 11th, but with the 10th book.

The 13th book is chiefly concerned with the *Aśvamedha,* and its first three Adhyāyas may again be considered as a kind of commentary on the saṁhitā. Towards the end some sacrifices, beginning with the *Puruṣa-medha,* which the saṁhitā treats in its Khila portion, are explained, but other ceremonies also are mentioned, for which there is no precedent in the saṁhitā. The Bṛhadāraṇyaka, the last book of the Śatapatha, contains in its first three Adhyāyas, a close commentary on the *Pravargya* of the saṁhitā, but becomes quite independent afterwards. Its object is no longer the sacrifice, but the knowledge of *Brāhman,* without any particular reference, however, lo the last Adhyāya of the saṁhitā, which, as we saw, was equally devoted to the doctrine of the Upaniṣads.

It is clear, therefore, that the Śatapatha-brāhmaṇa was not simply a running commentary on the saṁhitā; nay there is nothing to prove that the hymn-book of the Vājasaneyins existed previous to their Brāhmaṇa. The Śatapatha-brāhmaṇa may have been edited by Yājñavalkya, but its component parts, like the component parts of the other Brāhmaṇas, must have been growing up during a long period of time in different localities before they were collected. The collecticn of ancient Brāhmaṇas must always have been the work of individual teachers, and their Brāhmaṇas, in their new and complete form, were at first the exclusive property of that one Caraṇa to which the collectors belonged, or of which they became the founders. Afterwards these collective Brāhmaṇas were adopted by the members of other Caraṇas, who either added some chapters of their own, or introduced certain modifications, by which we now find that different texts of one and the same Brāhmaṇa differ from one another. We must distinguish, therefore, between old and new

Brāhmaṇas, the former being those which from time immemorial had been living in the oral tradition of various Caraṇas, the latter comprising the great collective works. Some of the latter vary slightly in the editions adopted in various Caraṇas; others, and these the most modern, show the distinct influence of individual editors. Pāṇini, whose views are not shackled by the inspiration-doctrine which blinded and misled all the followers of the orthodox Mimāṁsā school, broadly states the fact, that there are old and new Brāhmaṇas; whereas, according to the doctrine of later divines, the Brāhmaṇas are neither old nor new, but eternal; and of divine origin. Pāṇini, who is a grammarian, rests his opinion as to the different dates of the Brāhmaṇas on the evidence of language. "A book," he says, "composed by a certain author, may be called by an adjective derived from the author's name."[61] For instance, a book composed by Vararuchi, may be called *"Vararucho granthaḥ."*[62] A work, on the contrary, which has only been taught and promulgated by a person, is not to be called his book *(grantha),* but bears its own title, such as " grammar," or, whatever else it may be, together with an adjective, derived from the author's name. Pāṇini's grammar, for instance, is not to be called *"Pāṇinīyo granthaḥ"* but *" Pāṇinīyam Vyākaraṇam:"* because it is a canonical work, revealed to Paṇini but not invented by him. It may also be called *"Pāṇinīyam,"* in the singular neuter; *i.e.,* Pāṇineum.[63] In the same wāy it is perfectly correct to speak of an "Āpiśalam", a work composed by Āpiśala, of a "Paiṅgī Kalpaḥ," an old ceremonial of Piṅga's, of a "Mādhurī Vṛttiḥ," a commentary of Madhura,[64] and of "Cārakāḥ Ślokāḥ," verses composed by Caraka. "But," says Pāṇini, "if the work referred to consists either of Vedic hymns *(Chandas),* or of old Brāhmaṇas *(purāṇa prokteṣu Brāhmaṇeṣu),* then it is not correct to use these derivative adjectives in the singular (unless we employ secondary derivatives, such as Taittirīyakaṁ, Kaṭhakam), but it is necessary to use the masculine plural." It is wrong to use the word Kaṭham as an adjective from Kaṭha; in the sense of hymns promulgated by Kaṭha; or to use Taittirīyam (from Tittiri, like Pāṇinīyam from Pāṇini), or Taittirīyam Brāhmaṇam, in the sense of a Brāhmaṇa promulgated by Tittiri, Even Kalpas and Sūtras like the Kalpas of Kāśyapa, and Kauśika, or the Sūtras of Pārāśrya, Śilāla, Kaimanda, and Kṛśāśva, are better quoted as "the Kāśyapins," etc. if they are old works.[65] According to Pāṇini, we must speak of "the Kaṭhas," *i.e.,* those who study and know the hymns promulgated by Kaṭha;[66] of "the Taittirīyas," those who study and know the Brāhmaṇa promulgated by Tittiri. This peculiarity of the Sanskrit language, which reminds us of the Greek expression of οι περι admits of a very natural explanation, if we remember that in these old times literary works did not exist in writing, but were handed down by oral tradition in different communities, which represented, so to say, different works, or even different recensions of one and the same work, like so many manuscripts in later times. It Was much more natural, therefore, to say, "the Taittirīyas relate," than to speak of a Taittirīyam, a work proclaimed by Tittiri, who was perhaps a merely nominal ancestor of the Taittirīyas, or to refer to a Taittirīya *grantha i. e.,* Tittirī's book, which in reality never existed. That this is the real ground for this Sanskrit idiom becomes more evident by the exceptions, mentioned by Pāṇini himself. There are no exceptions with regard to the names of hymns, or rather of the supporters of their texts; but there are Brāhmaṇas, Kalpas, and Sūtras, spoken of in the same Wāy as Pāṇini's own work. It is wrong, for instance, to speak of the Yājñavalkyas in the same sense as we speak of the Taittirīyas, and the works promulgated by Yājñavalkya, although they are Brāhmaṇas, arc callcd Yājñavalkyani Brāhmaṇani.[67] "And why ?" says Kātyāyana; "because they are of too recent an origin; that is to say, they are almost contemporaneous with ourselves."Here, then, we see that as early as Pāṇini and Kātyāyana a distinction was made, not only by learned men, but in common language, between old and modern Brāhmaṇas. We see that the Brāhmaṇas of Yājñavalkya, whose works, as those of a seceder, we had reason to consider as modern, are by their very name classed as moden . What other Brāhmaṇas belong to the same class, it is not so easy to say, because the only other instance quoted, besides the Brāhmaṇas of Yājñavalkya, are the Saulabhāni

Brāhmaṇani; and they have not yet been met with. It is not unlikely, however, that the so-called Anubrāhmaṇani,[69] or supplimentary Brāhmaṇas, which we have, for instance, in the Sāma-veda,[70] may come under this category.[71]

That different Brāhmaṇas existed at the time when the great collective Brāhmaṇas were composed, might be proved, even without the testimony of Pāṇini, by quotations occurring in the Brāhmaṇas themselves. The original Caraṇas were not all rival sects, and it Was natural that one Caraṇa should be ready to accept Brāhmaṇas of another, if they contained any additional traditions or precepts which seemed to be valuable. Thus we find the Brāhmaṇas of the Kaṭhas added to the Brāhmaṇas of the Taittirīyas. In other cases we find that one Brāhmaṇa quotes the opinion of another Śākhā, not in support of its own doctrines, but in order to refute it. Thus the Kauṣītakins are frequently attacked in the Tāṇḍya-brāhmaṇa. Now, if these quotations of different authorities, which we meet with in Brāhman as, alluded only to the opinions of certain individuals we might still be doubtful whether these opinions had formerly been laid down in separate Brāhmaṇa works. But when we see quotations like *"iti Kauṣītakcam," "iti Paiṅgyam,"* "so says the work of the Kauṣītakins or Paiṅgīns," there can be little doubt that separate Brāhmaṇas, propagated by separate Caraṇas, are here intended, whatever commentators may say to the contrary.[72]

What became of these numerous Brāhmaṇa-Caraṇas which are quoted both in the Brāhmaṇas and in the Sūtras, is not quite clear. Most likely they were absorbed or replaced by a more modern class of Caraṇas, the Sūtra-Caraṇas. When the Sūtras once came to be regarded as part of the sacred canon, they gave rise to a large number of new Caraṇas.[73] Their members would preserve the text of the saṁhitā and Brāhmaṇa of an earlier Caraṇa from which they originally branched off.[74] The ground of division being in the Sūtras, the minor differences between the texts of the Saṁhitās and Brāhmaṇas might be waived in these modern Caraṇas and this would gradually lead to the loss of many of the old Śākhās. We saw before, in the case of the Śākalas and Bāṣkalas, that at the time when Sūtras began to be composed there was a tendency to reunite different

Śākhās into one. That the introduction of Sūtras encroached on the study of the Brāhmaṇas and Saṁhitās in the school of the *Brāhmaṇas,* becomes evident from passages in which the custom of performing sacrifices after the prescriptions of Sūtras only declared to be without merit and without effect. Kumārila in one passage simply states the fact that priests perform sacrifices by means of the Kalpa Sūtras only, and without the Veda, that they could not do the same by means of the Mantras and the Brāhmaṇas, and without the Kalpas.[75] In another place[76] he declares that the reason why the Smṛtis or law-books, which he considers to be founded on the Veda, had not been made up of literal extracts, Was because this would have endangered the sacred study of the whole Veda. The Veda would thus have been read in a different order, or small extracts only would have been studied instead of the whole Veda. Now this is what seems to have happened to a certain extent by the introduction of the Sūtras, and it would account for the loss of many of the old Śākhās, Saṁhitās as well as Brāhmaṇas.

In order to show more clearly to how great an extent the Vedic literature was fostered by means of the Caraṇas I shall give a list from the Caraṇa-vyūha. This *Pariśiṣṭa* is a document of a comparatively late period, though it may'be one of the oldest works belonging to this class of literature.[77] It is, therefore, no good authority as to the number of the old saṁhitā-Caraṇas and Brāhmaṇa-Caraṇas, many of which were lost or merged into others during the Sūtra period; but it is of interest as the first attempt at a complete enumeration of Sūtra-Caraṇas, and may be trusted particularly with regard to the Sūtra-charanis, which, at the time of its composition, were still of recent origin. The number of the old Caraṇas would, no doubt, have to be increased considerably, if the quotations of different Śākhās were taken into account, which occur in the Brāhmaṇas as well as in the Sūtras. But at the same time we may conclude from the lists given in the Caraṇavyūha that most of these old Caraṇas were extinct shortly after the Sūtra-period, and that their works as well as their names, began to be forgotten.

Of the Ṛg-veda five Caraṇas are mentioned :

1. The Śākalas[78] (शाकला:)
2. Bāshkalas[79] (वापकला:)
3. Āśvalāyanas[80] (भाश्वलायना:)
4. Śāṅkhāyanas[81] (शाङ्खायना:)
5. Māṇḍukāyanas[82] (माण्डूकायना:)

We miss the names of several old Śākhās such as the Aitareyins, Śaiśiras,[83] Kauṣītakins, Paiṅgins, while the Āśvalāyanas, who are mentioned, must be considered as the founders of one of the latest Śākhās of the Ṛg-veda.

The number of Śākhās of the Yajur-veda is stated at eighty-six. We have first the twelve Caraṇas comprehended under the common name of Carakas. They are, according to the MS. of the Caraṇa-vyūha;

1. Charakas.[84] (चरका:)
2. Āhvarakas.[85] (आह्वरका:)
3. Kaṭhas.[86] (कठा:)
4. Prācya-Kaṭhas.[87] (प्राच्यकण्ठा:)
5. Kapiṣṭhala-Kaṭhas.[88] (कपिष्ठलकठा:)
6. Cārāyanīyas.[89] (चारयणीया:)
7. Vāratantavīyas.[90] (वारतन्तवीया:)
8. Śvetāśvataras.[91] (श्वेताश्वतरा:)
9. Aupamanyavas. (औपमन्यवा:)
10. Pātas.[92] (पाता:)
11. Aiṇḍineyas.[93] (ऐण्डिनेया:)
12. Maitrāyaṇīyas.[94] (मैत्रायणीया:)

The Maitrāyaṇīyas are subdivided into seven Caraṇas

13. Mānavas.[95] (मानवा:)
14. Vārāhas.[96] (वाराहा:)

15. Dundubhas. (दुन्दुभाः)

16. Chāgaleyas.[97] (छागलेयाः)

17. Hāridravīyas.[98] (हारिद्रवीयाः)

18. Śyāmas.[99] (श्यामाः)

19. Śyāmāyanīyas.[100] (श्यामायनीयाः)

Then follow

20. Taittirīyas (तैत्तिरीयाः), subdivided into

21. Aukhīyas[101] (औखीयाः)

22. Kbāṇḍikīyas[102] (खाण्डिकीयाः)

The Khāṇḍikīyas are again subdivided into :—

23. Kāleyas[103] (कालेयाः)

24. Śāṭyāyanins. (शाट्यायनिनः)

25. Hiraṇyakeśins. (हिरण्यकेशिनः)

26. Bhāradvājins.(भारद्वाजिनः)

27. Āpastambins. (आपस्तम्बिनः)

This gives altogether twenty-seven Śākhās, the same number which is mentioned in the Viṣṇu-purāṇa,[104] although the maner of computing them is different.

Then follow the fifteen Śākhās of the Vājasaneyins, a number which is confirmed by the Pratijmā-pariśiṣṭa, and has also been preserved in the Viṣṇu-purāṇa, while the Caraṇa-vyūha of the Śabdakalpi-druma brings their number to seventeen.

They are :

28. Jābālas.[105] (जाबालाः)

29. Baudheyas[106]. (बौधेयाः)

30. Kāṇvas.[107] (काण्वाः)

31. Mādhyandinas.[108] (माध्यन्दिनाः)

32. Śāpheyas.[109] (सोफयाः)

33. Tāpanīyas.[110] (तापनीयाः)

34. Kapolas.[111] (कपोलाः)

35. Pauṇḍravatsas.[112] (पौण्ड्रवत्साः)

36. Āvaṭikas.[113] (आवटिकाः)

37. Paramāvaṭikas.[114] (परमावटिकाः)

38. Pārāśaryas.[115] (पाराशर्याः)

39. Vaineyas.[116] (वैनेयाः)

40. Vaidheyas.[117] (वैधेयाः)

41. Auḍheyas.[118] (औढेयाः)

42. Mauneyas.[119] (मोनेयाः)

Though the number of the Śākhās of the Yajur-veda is stated as eighty-six by the Caraṇa-vyūha, the names given, including the Vājasaneyins, amount only to forty-three, exactly half the number expected.[120] It is difficult to account for this, for although some other names are mentioned, for instance the Prācya, Udīcya and Nairṛtya Kaṭhas, yet this would not increase the number of Śākhās sufficiently.

The largest number of Śākhās is ascribed to the Sāma-veda. It is said to have been a thousand. The author of the Caraṇa-vyūha, however, confesses that the greater part of them no longer exists. Those remaining at the time when the Caraṇa-vyūha was composed were the seven Śākhās of the

1. Rāṇāyaṇīyas.[121] (राणयणीयाः)
2. Sāṭyamugryās.[122] (साट्यमुग्ध्याः)
3. Kālāpas.[123] (कालापाः)
4. Mahākalopas.[124] (महाकलोपाः)
5. Lāṅgalāyanas.[125] (लाङ्गलायनाः)
6. Śārdūlas.[126] (शार्दुलाः)
7. Kauthumas.[127] (कौथुमः)

The Kauthumas are again subdivided into the

8. Āśurāyaṇas.[128] (आशुरायणाः)

9. Vātāyanas.[129] (वातायनाः)

10. Prāñjalidvaitabhṛts.[130] (प्राञ्जलिद्वैतभृतः)

11. Prācīnayogyas.[131] (प्राचीनयोग्याः)

12. Naigeya-Kauthumas.[132] (नैगेयकौथुमाः)

The account given by the Ś. K. D. is very different and in many places corrupt. Here we have,

1. the Asurāyaṅīyas or Śurāyaṇīyas,
2. Vārtāntaveyas,
3. Prāñjalas,
4. Ṛgvarṇa-bhedas,
5. Prācīnayogyas,
6. Jñānayogyas,
7. Rāṇāyaṇīyas.

The Rāṇāyaṇīyas are subdivided into nine; Rāṇāyaṇīyas,

8. `Śāṭhyāyanīyas (or Śārāyaṇīyas, Śāṭhyamugryās)
9. `Śātvalas (or Sātyamudbhavas),
10. Maudgalas (not mentioned in the Bhāṣya),
11. Khallalas,
12. Mahākhallavas,
13. Lāṅgalas,
14. Kauthumas,
15. Gautamas,
16. Jaiminīyas.

Of the Atharva-veda nine divisions are mentioned, but the names given are incomplete and corrupt. They are given here, with some conjectural emendations from the MSS.[133]

1. Paippalādas.[135] (पैप्पलावाः)

2. Śaunakas.[3] (शौनकाः)

3. Dāmodas. (दामोदाः)

4. Tottāyanas. (तोत्तयनाः)
5. Jayālas. (जयालाः)
6. Brāhmapalāsas. (ब्राह्मपलाशाः)
7. Kaunakhins. (कौनखिनः)
8. DevaDarśanins.[136] (देवदर्शनिनः)
9,. Cāraṇavidyās. (चारणविद्याः)

This list makes no distinction between old and new Caraṇas. If we had the whole Vedic literature before us, as it was living during ancient times in the traditions of numerous Brāhmaṇic families, it would be possible to determine which of these Caraṇas owe their origin to Sūtras, which to Brāhmaṇas or saṁhitās. As it is, we can only infer that some Caraṇas, like those of the Āśvalāyanas, Hiraṇyakeśins, Bhāradvājins, Āpastambins, Baudhāyanas, Pārāśaryas, etc. are in all probability of modern origin, because the only works ascribed to their founders are Sūtra compilations. Their saṁhitās and Brāhmaṇas, whenever they are mentioned, seem to be the same as those of older Caraṇas, with but small modifications. Other Caraṇas, like those of the Paiṅgīns, Kauṣītakins, Aitareyins, Sātyāyanins etc. are not mentioned in connection with any Sūtras composed by authors bearing these names; and it is most likely, therefore, that they derive their origin from authors whose names have been perpetuated in the titles of certain Brāhmaṇas. Whether these Caraṇas were in possession of Sūtras is doubtful, nor have we any means of determining whether, for instance, a member of the Aitareyi-Caraṇa, after adopting the Kalpascitras of Śaunaka, would retain his allegiance to the Aitareyins or not. The ancient saṁhitās used in these Brāhmaṇa-Caraṇas, and originally adopted from older Caraṇas, were not likely to be affected by considerable differences after their adoption. The fact that we never find a Kauṣītaki-saṁhitā or Paiṅgi-saṁhitā quoted tends to show that the Caraṇas, which owe their independent constitution to the introduction of a Brāhmaṇa, retained in most instances the original text of their

Saṁhitās. Caraṇas, lastly, like those of the Śākalas, Bāṣkalas, Śaiśiras, etc. whose names are connected neither with Sūtras nor Brāhmaṇas, but with saṁhitās only, mast be referred to the earliest period of the formation of Vedic communities, and must have existed, as the bearers of their own traditional collection of hymns, before the composition of either Brāhmaṇas or Sūtras. With regard to many Caraṇas, however, it will remain doubtful to which of these three classes they belong, until a larger number of Vedic works peculiar to each Caraṇa becomes available. Caraṇas like those of the Mādhyandinas and Kāṇvas must be referred to the Brāhmaṇa period, because their Saṁhitās and Brāhmaṇas are ascribed to one and the same teacher. This teacher, Yājñavalkya, is represented as the author of modern Brāhimaṇas and we saw that, in all probability, his saṁhitā was even more modern than his Brāhmaṇas. The fact however, that the Sūtras adopted by the Mādhyandina and Kāṇva-Caraṇas are ascribed to Kātyāyana, shows that these Caraṇas existed certainly previous to the Sūtra period. With regard to the saṁhitā Caraṇas it will always be difficult to determine how far their differences were fixed, if not originally called forth by the introduction of the Brāhmaṇas. Most likely the saṁhitā-Caraṇas are restricted to the Ṛg-veda. It is certain, at least, that no Brāhmaṇa belonging to any Veda was composed before the division of priest into *Hotṛs, Udgātṛs,* and *Adhvaryus,* had taken place. Before that division there was but one collection of hymns, that of the Bahvṛcas, and it is among the Bahvṛchas only that we have any distinct traces of saṁhitā-Caraṇas.

It will always be very difficult to assign a distinct meaning to such terms as Carana and Śākhā, because we have nothing that exactly corresponds to them in our own experience. Literary works, such as the Śākhās were, have assumed with us a much more tangible shape. They exist as books and not merely as a body of thought handed down in schools, or in families. To read a *Śākhā* meant not only tc go over it, but to take possession of it, to guard it in the memory, and to enable others to read it by repeating it to them. A man who had read a book was himself the book : the song of a poet had no outward existence except through those who heard and remembered it. A work once composed, might either wither for wānt of an audience, or grow, like a tree, of which every new listener would become a new branch. The idea of representing what we should call an edition of a hundred copies, by the simile of a branch, was a very natural one, and if we once adopt it and enter into the spirit of this Sanskrit idiom, we see that it is difficult to distinguish between the branch, as the book, and the branch, as the reader; between the trust, and the trustee. It would be well, however, to speak of the former only as *Śākhā,* and of the latter as the reader of a *Śākhā,* while we should reserve the name of Caraṇa for those ideal successions or fellowships to which all those belonged who read the same *Śākhā.*

If it is difficult to describe what a Śākhā and a Caraṇa were, it is all the more necessary to state what they were not. Now a Caraṇa was not the same as a *Gotra* or *Kula. Gotra* or *Kula* means a family, and the number of families that had a right to figure in the Brāhmaṇic Peerage of India was very considerable. The *Brāhmaṇas* were proud of their ancestors, and preserved their memory with the most scrupulous care, as may be seen by the numerous treatises on the subject which are preserved to the present day. Mādhava, for instance, after stating who his father, mother, and brothers were, what Śākhā he followed, what Sūtra he had adopted, adds at the end that his family descended from Bhāradvāja.[137] *Gotras,* or families existed among *Kṣatriyas* and *Vaiśyas* as well as among *Brāhmaṇas}* Caraṇas were confirmed to the priestly caste. *Gotras* depended on a real or imaginary community of blood, and thus correspond to what we call families. Caraṇas depended on the community of sacred texts. They were ideal fellowships, held together by ties, more sacred in the eyes of a *Brāhmaṇa* than the mere ties of blood. They were the living depositories of the most sacred texts, and with the extinction of a Caraṇa, the words which were believed to be the breath of God would have been lost without the hope of recovery. Members of different *Gotras* might belong to the same Caraṇa. When the member of a *Gotra* became the founder of a new Caraṇa, the new Caraṇa might bear the name of its founder, and thus become synonymous but not identical, with a *Gotra.*

The names of the Caraṇas were naturally preserved as long as the tests which they embodied continued to be studied. The names of the *Gotras* were liable to confusion, particularly in later times, when their number had become very considerable. But the respect which the *Brāhmaṇas,* from the very earliest time, paid to their ancestors, and the strictness with which they prohibited marriages between members of the same family, lead us to suppose that the genealogical lists, such as we find in the Brāhmaṇas, in the Sūtras; in the Mahābhārata, in the Purāṇas and even at the present day, present in their general outlines a correct account of the priestly familes of India. All Brāhmaṇic families who keep the sacred fires are supposed to descend from the Seven Ṛṣis. These are:*Bhṛgu, Aṅgiras, Visvāmitra, Vaśiṣṭha, Kaśyapa, Atri, Agasti.* The real ancestors, however, are eight in number :*Jamadagni, Gautama and Bharadvāja, Visvāmitra, Vasiṣṭha, Kāśyapa, Atri, Agastya.* The eight *Gosas,* which descend from these Ṛṣis, are again subdivided into forty-ṇine *Gotras,* and these forty-ṇine branch off into a still larger number of families. The names *gotra, vaṁśa, varga, pakṣa,* and *Gaṇa* are all used in the same sense, to express the larger as well as the smaller families descended from thc cight Ṛṣis.

A *Brāhmaṇa,* who keeps the sacrificial fire, is obliged by law to know to which of the forty-nine *Gotras* his own family belongs, and in consecrating his own fire he must invoke the ancestors who founded the *Gotra* to which he belongs. Each of the forty-ṇine *Gotras* claims one, or two, or three, or five ancestors, and the names of these ancestors constitute the distinctive character of each *Gotra.*[139] A list of these forms part of most of the Kalpa-sūtras, and I here give one of them from the 12th Book of Āśvalāyana's Śrauta-sūtras.[140]

List of the Forty-nine *Gotras,*, according to Āśvalāyana, xii, 10. seq.

1. THE BHṚGUS.

Nome of Gotra.	No. of Ancestors.	Invocation o[1] Ancestors.
1. Jāmadagnāḥ	Vntsāḥ 5	Bhārgava, Chyāvāna, Āpnavām, Aurvn, Jāmadagneti.
2. Jāmadagnyāḥ or Jāmadagnāh.	5	Bhārgava, Chyāvāna, Āpnavāna, Ārshṭisheṇa, Anupeti.
3. Bidāḥ	5	Bhārgava, Chyāvana, Āpna-vāni, Aurva, Baideti.
4. Yaska Bādhaula Mauna Mauka Sarkarākṣi (शर्करादिन) Śārṣtī Sévarṇi Śālaṅkāyana Jaimini Devantyāyanāḥ	3	Bhārgava, Vaitahavya, Sāvetaseti.
5. Śyaitāḥ	3	Bhārgava, Vainya, Pāreheti.
6. Mitrayuvaḥ	1	Bādhryasveti. I or 3 Bhārgava, Daivodāsa, Bédhryaśvet.
7. Śunakāḥ	1 3	Gārtsamadeti or Bhārgava, SaunaHotṛa, Gartsama-deti.

THE ĀṄGIRASAS.

II a. THE GOTAMAS.

Name of Gotra.	No. of Ancestors.	Invocation of Ancestors.
8. Gotamāh (गौतमाः) गीतमाः	3	Āṅgirasa, Āyāsya, Gautameti. अङ्गिरसायास्यगौतमेति।
9. Ucathyāh	3	Auchathya,Gautameti.

उच्थ्याः		अङ्गिरसौचथ्यगौतमेति।
10. Rahūgaṇāh	3	Rāhūgaṇya, Gautameti.
रहूगणाः		अङ्गिरसराहूगण्यगौतमेति
11. Somarājakayah	3	Somarājya, Gautameti.
सोमराजकयः		अङ्गिरससोमराण्ज्गौतमेति।
12. Vāmadevāh		Vāmadevya, Gautameti.
वामदेवाः		अङ्गिरसवामदेवगौतमेति।
13. Bṛhadukthāḥ		Bārhadukthya, Gautameti
बृहदुक्थाः		अङ्गिरसबार्हदुक्थयगौतमेति।
	3	Āngirasa, Pārasadaśva,
14. Pṛṣadaśvaḥ		or Vairūpeti.
पृषदश्वाः		3 Ashṭādanshṭra, rshadaśva, Vairūpeti.
15. Rikṣāḥ	5	Āṅgirasa, Bārhaspatya. Bhāradvāja, Vāndana, Mātavachaseti.
रिक्षा		
16. Kakṣīvantaḥ	5	Auchathya, Gautama,
कक्षीवन्तः		Auśija, Kākṣīvateti.
17. Dirghatamāsaḥ	3	Aucathya, Dīrgha-tamaseti.
दीर्घतमसः		

II b. THE BHĀRADVĀJAS.

18. Bharadvājāgni-1 veśyāḥ	3	Āṅgirasa, Bārhaspatya, Bhāradvājeti.
भरद्वाजाग्निवेश्याः		
19. Mudgalāḥ Bhārmyaśiva,		Maudgalyeti.
		or Tarkshya, Bhārmyaśva,
मुद्गलाः		Mudgalyeti.
20. Viṣṇuvṛddhāḥ …	3	Āṅgirasa, Paurukutsya,
विष्णुघृद्धाः		Trāsadasyaveti.
21. Gargāh icargya,	5	Bārhaspatya, Bhāradvāja,
गर्गाः		Śainyeti.
	3	or śnainya, Gargyeti.
22. Hārita		
हारितः		
Kutsa	3	Āmbarīṣa, Yauvanāśveti.
कुत्सः		

Piṅga
पिङ्गः
or
Śaṅkha 3 Māndhātr, Āmbarīṣa, Yauvānaśveti.
शङ्खः
Durbhya
दर्भ्यः
Bhaimagavāḥ
भैमगवाः

23. Saṅkṛtiḥ
संकृतिः 3 Āṅgirasa, Gaurivīta Sankṛtyeti.
Pūtimāshaḥ
पूतिमाषः
Taṇḍiḥ
तण्डिः
Śambhuḥ
Śaivagaṇāḥ
शम्भुः

or
3 Śāktya, Gaurivita, Sānkṛtyeti

24. Kaṇvāḥ Āṅgirasa, Ajāmīḍha, Kāṇveti. or
कण्वाः 3 ,, Ghaura,

25. Kapayaḥ 3 ,, Māhīyava, Urukṣayaseti
कपयः

26. Śauṅga-Śaiśiryāḥ or 3 Bārhaspatya, Bhāradvāja, Kātya, Atkileti.
शौङ्गशैशीर्याः Kātya, Atkileti.

III. THE ATRIS.

27. Atrayaḥ 3 Ātrya, Arcanānasa, Śyavāśveti.
अत्रयः

28. Gaviṣṭhirāḥ 3 Gaviṣṭhira, Paurvātitheti.
गविष्ठिराः

IV. THE VIŚVĀMITRAS

29. Chikita- 3 Vaiśvamitra, Ḍevarāta, Audaleti.

Gālava-
Kālabava-
Manutantu-
Kuśikaḥ

30. Śraumata-kāmakā- 3 yanāḥ.
31. Dhanañjayāḥ 3 Mādhuchhandasa,
Dhānañjayyeti.
32. Ajāḥ 3 Mādhuchhandasa, Ajyeti.
33. Rohiḥāḥ 3 Mādhuchhandasa, Rauhiṇeti
34. Aṣṭakāḥ 3 Mādhuchhandasa, Aṣṭaketi.
35. Purāṇa-Vāridhāpa yantāḥ. 3 Devarāta, Pauraṇeti.
36. Kaṭāḥ 3 Kātyā, Atkileti.
37. Aghamarṣaṇāh 3 Aghamarṣaṇa, Rauśketi.
38. Reṅavaḥ 3 Gāthina, Raiṇaveti.
39. Veṇavaḥ 3 Gāthina, Vaiṇaveti.
40. Śālaṅkāyana-
Śālākṣa-
Lohitākṣa-
Lohitajānavaḥ 3 Śāloṅkāyana, Kauśiketi.
41. Kāśyapah
42. Nidhruvāḥ
43. Rebhāḥ
44. Śaṇḍilāḥ
V. The Kāśyapa 3 Kāśyapa, Āvatsāra, Āsiteti.
3 Naidhruveti.
3 Raibhyeti.

Śāṇḍila, Āśita, Daivaleti,
or
3 Kāśyapa,

VI. THE VASIṢṬHAS

45. Vaśishṭhāḥ 1 Vasistheti.
46. Upamanyavaḥ 3 Vasiṣṭha, Ābharadvasu,
Indraprāmadeti.
47. Parāśarah 3 Vasiṣṭha, Śāktya, Pārāśaryeti.

48. Kundinah 3 Maitrāvaruṇa,
Kauṇḍinyeti.

VII. THE AGASTIS

3 Āgastya, Dārḍhacyuta,
49. Agastayah or Idhamavāheti.
3Āgastya, Dārdhacutya,
Somavāheti.

There are other lists of much greater extent, which may become useful in time for chronological calculations. In them the first branch of the Bhṛgus, the Vatsas, count 75 names; among them such names as Śaunakavānah (8), Pailah(13), Paingalayanah (14), Pāṇiniḥ (29), Vālmīkayaḥ (30). The Vidās comprise 13, the Ārṣṭiṣeṇas 8, the Yāskas 20, the Mitrayus 11, the Vainyas 3, and the Śunakas 9 names. It would occupy too much space to print these lists here.

In order to prove that these lists were not merely arbitrary compositions, their practical bearing on two very important acts of the ancient Brāhmaṇic society, the consecrating of the sacrificial fires, and marriage, should be borne in mind.

When the fire is to be consecrated, *Agni Havyavāhana,* the god who carries the libations to heaven, must be invoked. This invocation or invitation of *Agni,* is called *pravara*[141]. Agni himself or the fire is called *Ārṣeya,* the offspring of the Ṛṣis, because the Ṛṣis first lighted him at their sacrifices. He is the Hotṛ as well as the *Adhvaryu* among the gods. Like the *Hotṛ* and *Adhvaryu* priests, he is supposed to invite the gods to the sacrifice, and to carry himself the oblation to the seat of the immortals. When therefore a *Brāhmaṇa* has his own fire consecrated, he wishes to declare that he is as worthy as his ancestors to offer sacrifices, and he invites *Agni* to carry his oblations to the gods as he did for his ancestors. The names of these ancestors must then be added to his invitation, and thus the invitation or invocation of the ancestors came to be called *pravara.* For instance, if a *Brāhmaṇa* belongs to the family of the Māṇḍūkeyas, he must know that the Māṇḍūkeyas belong to the Vatsas, and that the Vatsas are descended from Bhṛgu, and invoke five ancestors. He must, therefore, like all members of the Vatsa-gotra, invoke Agni by the names of Bhārgava, Cyāvāna, Āpnavāna, Aurva, and Jāmadagna. If he belong to the family of Yājñavalkya, a branch of the Kuśakas, descendants of Viśvāmitra, he must invoke Agni by the name of Viśvāmitra, Devarāta and Udala. This, at least, is the rule laid down in the Baudhāyana-Sūtra, with which the Āśvalāyana-Sūtra, coincides, expect that it does not mention Yājñavalkyas as a subdivision of the Kuśakas. This custom was known at the time of the composition of the Brāhmaṇas. and we have no reason to doubt that ever since the first establishment of Vedic sacrifices, the forty-nine families preserved the tradition of their sacred pedigree, and that their genealogies possess a certain historical value[142].

This is confirmed still further if we consider the ancient Brāhmaṇic marriage laws. To marry a woman belonging to the same Gotra, or having the same Pravara, was considered incest, and visited with severe penance,. Āśvalāyana (xū. 15) says : *"Asamāna pravarair vivāhaḥ"* "Marriage takes place with persons who have not the same *Pravara,* i.e., who do not invoke the same Ṛṣis as their ancestors." Āpastamba says : *"Sagotrāya duhitaram na prayacheta,')* "You shall not give thy daughter to a man belonging to the same *Gotra* or family." Yājñavalkya says : *"Arogiṇīm bhrātṛmatim asamānarshagotrājam udvahet."* "Let a man marry a woman who is free from disease, who has brothers, and who is not the daughter of a man having the same ancestors and belonging to the same *Gotra* as himself." In each case severe punishments are threatened if a man transgress these rules knowingly, or even unknowingly. There are some special rules with regard to marriage, which differ again according to different Sūtras; of which the following, taken from Āśvalāyana, may serve as a specimen :

1. Persons who have the same *Pravara* must not inter marry. Hence a Parāśara must not marry the daughter of a Parāśara.
2. Persons belonging to the same *Gotra* must not intermarry. Hence a Viśvāmitra must not marry the daughter of a Viśvāmitra.
3. There are exceptions to this rule among the Bhṛgus and

> Āṅgirasas. As a general rule, persons are called *sagotra,* if but one of the Ṛṣis whom they invoke is the same.

Hence an Upamanyu must not marry the daughter of a Parāśara, because the name of Vasiṣṭha occurs in the *tryārsheya pravara* of both. But the three Gotras of the Bhṛgus, from the Śyaitas to the Śunakas, may intermarry. The first four Gotras of the Bhṛgus must not, neither tbe six first Gotras of the Gotamas. The Pṛṣadaśvas, Mudgalas, Viṣṇuvṣddhas, Kāṇvas, Āgastyas, Hāritas, Saṅkṛtis, Kapis, and Yāskas may intermarry among themselves, and with the Jāmadagnyas, etc. Dhīrghatamāsas', on the contrary, Auchathyas and Kakṣlvats are to be considered as members of one *Gotra,* nor are marriages allowed between the Bhara-dvājāgniveśis, Ṛikṣas, Śuṅga-Śaiśiris, (or Śuṅgas, Śaiśiris), Katas, and, according to some, the Gargas.

It is clear from this that the science of genealogy, being so intimately connected with the social and ecclesiastical system of the *Brāhmaṇas,* must have been studied with great care in India, and that the genealogical lists which have been preserved to us in ancient works represent something real and historical.

LITERARY MERITS OF THE BRĀHMAṆAS

After we have thus gained an insight into the system by which the Brāhmaṇas were handed down from generation to generation, we now return to a consideration of the literary merits of these works. The Brāhmaṇas represent no doubt a most interesting phase in the history of the Indian mind, but judged by themselves, as literary productions, they are most disappointing. No one would have supposed that at so early a period, and in so primitive a state of society, there could have risen up a literature which for pedantry and downright absurdity can hardly be matched anywhere. There is no lack of striking thoughts, of bold expressions, of sound reasoning, and curious traditions in these collections. But these are only like the fragments of a *torso,* like precious gems set in brass and lead. The general character of these works is marked by shallow and insipid grandiloquence, by priestly conceit, and

Antiquarian pedantry. It is most important to the historian that he should know how soon the fresh and healthy growth of a nation can be blighted by priestcraft and superstition. It is most important that we should know that nations are liable to these epidemics in their youth as well as in their dotage. These works deserve to be studied as the physician studies the twaddle of idiots, and the raving of mad men. They will disclose to a thoughtful eye the ruins of faded grandeur, the memories of noble aspirations. But let us only try to translate these works into our own language, and we shall feel astonished that human language and human thought should ever have been used for such purposes. The following is a small specimen, and it has not been chosen to give an unfavourable idea of the Brāhmaṇas. It is the beginning of the Aitareya-brāhmaṇa, and explains a sacrificial act in itself full of meaning. Originally the Dīkṣaṇīyā, as this ceremony is called, was meant to represent, by simple and natural emblems the new birth through which a man, on his first admission to the sacrifice, was believed to enter a new life. Let us see what became of this act in the hands of the Brāhmaṇas.

AITAREYA BRĀHMAṆA-DĪKSHAṆĪYA

Agni is the first among the Gods, Viṣṇu the last[1]. Between them stand all the other deities.

They offer a Puroḍāśa to Agni and Viṣṇu which has been prepared for the Dīkṣāṇīyā in eleven jars.[144]

They offer it indeed to all the deities of this ceremony, without any difference.[145]

For Agni is all the deities, Viṣṇu is all the deities;[146]

They are the two extremities of the sacrifies, Agni and Viṣṇu. Thus when men offer the Puroḍāśa to Agni and Viṣṇu, they worship the deities at both ends.[147]

Here they say, if there be a Puroḍāśa prepared in eleven jars, and there be two gods, Agni and Viṣṇu, what rule is there for the two, or what division ?[148]

The Puroḍāśa of eight jars belongs to Agni, for the Gayattrī verse consists of eight syllables, and the Gāyatrī is Agni's metre. That of three jars belongs to Viṣṇu, for Viṣṇu strode thrice through this universe. This is their rule here, and this the division.[149]

He who thinks himself without wealth, may offer *Caru* in *ghee* (clarified butter).[150]

On this earth no one succeeds who has no wealth?[151]

The *ghee* in the *Caru,* is the milk of the woman, the grains belong to the man; both together are a pair. Thus the *Caru* increases him by this very pair with progeny and cattle, so that he may prosper.[152]

He who knows this is increased with progeny.[153] He who performs the New-moon and Full-moon sacrifices, has commenced with the sacrifice and with the gods.[154] After having sacrificed with the New-moon or Full-moon oblation, he may perform the *Dīkṣā* on the same oblation and the same sacrificial seat.[1]

This is one *Dīkshā.*[156]

The *Hotṛ* must recite seventeen *Sāmidhenī* verses.[157]

The Prajāpati, the Lord of the World, is seventeen-fold, the months are twelve, and the seasons five, by putting the *Hemanta* and *Śiśira* seasons as one. So much is the year, and the year is Prājāpati.[158]

He who knows this prospers by these verses which reside in Prājāpati.[159]

The sacrifice went away, from the gods. They wished to find it by means of the *Iṣṭis*. The *Iṣṭitis* are called *Iṣṭis* because with them they wished (✓*ish,* to wish) to find it.[160] They found it.[161]

He who knows this prospers after having found the sacrifice.[162]

What are called oblations *(ābhūti)* are invocations *(ābhūti);* with them the sacrificer calls the gods, this is why they are called *(ābhūtis).*[163]

They are called *Utis,* for by their means the gods come to the calling of the sacrificer *(ayanti,* they come). Or because they are the paths and the ways they are called *ūtis* (ऊतय:) ; for they are the way to heaven for the sacrificer.[164]

There they say, as another priest makes the oblation *(gcil.* the *'Adhvaryu),* then why do they call him the *Hotṛ* (the offerer), who recites tke prayers and formulas [165] Because he causes the deities to be brought near according to their station, saying, "Bring him, bring him." this is the reason why he is called *Hotṛ*; he is a *Hotṛ* (from *avah,* to bring near.)[166]

He who knows this, is called a *Hotṛ.*[167]

He whom the priests initiate (by means of the *Dīṣkā* ceremony), he is made again to be an embryo (he is born again.)[168]

They sprinkle him with Water.[169]

Water is seed; having thus given this to him, they initiate him.[170]

They anoint him with fresh butter *(navanīta).* Clarified butter for the gods is (called) *Ājya;* for men *Surabhi-gh'ta;* for the mancs *Ayuta,* for the embryos *Navanīta.* Therefore by anointing him with *navānita,* they increase him with his own portion.[171]

They anoint his eyes with a collyrium.[172]

Anointing is light for the eyes. Having thus imparted light to him, they initiate him.[173]

They rub him clean with twenty-one handful of Kuśa grass.[174]

Him who is pure and has thus been cleaned, they initiate,[175]

They take him to the hall.[176]

The hall is the womb for the pupil *(dīkshīta).* By taking him to the hall they take him (who Was before represented as an embryo) into his womb.[177]

In this true womb he sits, and hence he departs.[178]

Therefore the fruit is borne in the true womb and brought forth from it.[179]

Therefore let not the sun shine upon him in its rising or setting away from the hall nor let the priests speak to him.[180]

They cover him with a cloth.[181]

This cloth is the caul in which the pupil is to be born; thus they cover him with the caul.[182]

The skin of a black antelope is his next cloak.[183]

Next to the caul is the *Jarāyu;* thus they cover him with the *Jarāyu?*[184]

He closes his hands.[185]

With closed hands the embryo lies, with closed hands the child is born. As he closes his hands, he holds the sacrifice, and all its gods between his hands.[186]

They say. there is no confusion for him who has first finished his *Dīkshā,* for his sacrifice is held fast (between his hands), and the gods are so likewise. Therefore there can be no loss for him, like that which falls on him whose *Dīkshā was* finished later.[187]

After having put off his cloak, he descends to the bath. Therefore an embryo is born after he is separated from the *Jarāyu.*[188]

He descends together with his cloth—therefore a child is born together with the caul.[189]

For him who has not offered a sacrifice before, let (the *Hotṛ* recite two *puronuvākyās* (पुरोनुवाक्य), *"tvam agne sapratha asi,"* (v. 18. 4.) for the first, *"soma yās te mayohiuvaḥ"* (i. 91. 9.) for the second portion of the *ghee*[190]

(The third line of the first verse is) "through you they carry out the sacrifice"; and by reciting this line the *Hotṛ* carries out the sacrifice for the pupil..[191]

For him who has offered a sacrifice before, let the Hotṛ recite instead *"Agniḥ pratnena manmanā,"* (viii. 44. 12.) and *soma gīrbhiṣṭvā* vayam"(i. ū. 91. ii.).[192]

By saying *"pratnam"* (former) a word which occurs in the first verse, he alludes to the former sacrifice.[193]

Both these rules (of using certain verses for a man who has not and for a man who has, sacrificed before) are not to be observed.[194]

Let him rather use the two verses on the destruction of Vṛtra *"Agnir vṛitrāṇī jaṅghanat,"* (vi. 15. 24.) and *"tvam Somaśi satpatiḥ"* (i. 91. 5.).[195]

For he whom the sacrifice approaches destroys Vṛtra; therefore verses on the destruclion of Vṛtra are to be used.[196]

Having enjoined these two verses for the introductory ceremony of the offering of *ghee,* the *Brāhmaṇa* now proceeds to detail the *yājyānuvākyās* for the principal offering.

"Agnir mukham prathamo devatānām," etc., is the Puronuvākyā, *"Agniś ca Viṣṇo tapa uttamam mahaḥ,"* etc., the Yājyā verse. These two verses on Agni and Viṣṇu are correct in form. The correctness of a sacrifice consists in its correctness of form; it consists in this that the verse recited alludes to the act performed.[197]

Agni and Viṣṇu are the guardians of the *Dīkṣā* among the gods. They are the lords of the *Dīkṣā.* Therefore as the oblation is to Agni and Viṣṇu, they who are the lords of the *Dīkṣā* are pleased and grant the *Dīkṣā* saying, "Let those who perform this rite be initiated."[198]

They are *Trīṣṭubhs* (by their metre), in order that they may give bodily strength.[199]

Having explained the verses used by the *Hotṛ* at the principal part of the sacrifice, the Brāhmaṇa adds some rules on the *Svishṭakṛt* verses.

He who wishes for beauty and for wisdom, let him use the two Gāyatrī verses[200] of the *Svishṭakṛt.*[201]

The *Gāyatrī* is beauty, full of wisdom.[202]

He who knowing this uses the two *Gāyatrī* becomes possessed of beauty and wisdom.[203]

He who desires long life, let him use two *Uṣṇih* verses.[206] *Uṣṇih* is life.[205]

Dvandva compound. The verses are not in the *śākala-śākhā* of the Ṛg-veda.

He who knowing this uses the two *Ushṇihs,* arrivés at any age.[206]

He who desires heaven, let him use two *Anuṣṭubhs*[207]

There are sixty-four syllables in the two *Anuṣṭubhs,* and three are those worlds, (earth, sky and heaven) each of twenty-one parts. With each twenty-one syllables he ascends to these worlds, and with the sixty-fourth he stands firm in heaven.[208]

He who knowing this uses the two *Anuṣṭubhs,* stands firm.[209]

He who desires wealth and glory, let him use two *Bṛhatīs*[210]

The *Bṛhatī* is wealth and glory.[211]

He who knowing this uses two *Bṛhatīs* gives himself wealth and glory.[212]

He who loves the sacrifice, let him use two *Paṅktis.*[213]

The sacrifice is like a *Paṅkti.*[214]

The sacrifice comes to him who, knowing this, uses two *Paṅktis.*[215]

Let him, who desires strength use two *Triṣṭubhs.*[216] *Triṣṭubh* is strength, which is vigour and power.[217]

He who knowing this uses two *Triṣṭubhs,* becomes strong, vigorous and powerful.[218]

Let him, who desires cattle, use two *Jagatīs*[219] Cattle is *Jagatī-like.*[220]

He who knowing this uses two *Jagatīs,* becomes rich in cattle.[8]

Let him, who desires food, use two *Virāj* verses.[222]

Virāj is food.[223] (*Virāj,* to shine.) Therefore he who has the largest food here shines most on earth; this is the reason why it is called *Virāj* (shining).[224]

He who knows this shines forth among his own people; he is the best of his friends.[225]

All these are voluntary verses. We now come to those which are always to be used.

Now the metre *Virāj* possesses five powers.

Because it has three lines, therefore it is *Gāyatrī* and *Ushṇih* (which also have three lines). Because its lines have each eleven syllables, therefore it is *Triṣṭubh.* Because it has thirty three syllables, therefore it is *Anuṣiṭubh.* (If it be said that that the two Virāj verses in question, *i. e., "preddho agne,"* etc. and *"imo agne,"* etc. have only thirty-one and thirty-two syllables, it must be remembered thaṇ metres do not change by one syllable or by two. The fifth power is that it is *Virāj* (shining).[226]

He who knowing this uses the two *Virāj* verses, obtains the power of all metres, retains the power of all metres, obtains union, uniformity and unison with all metres, eats and has to eat, has food together with his family.[227]

Therefore the two *Virāj* verses are certainly to be used, those which begin with *"Preddho agno"* and *"Imo agne.'*[228]

Dīkṣā is right, *Dīkhsā* is truth, therefore a man who performs the *Dīkṣā* must speak the truth.[229]

Now they say, what man can speak all truth ? Gods are full of truth, men are full of falsehood,[230]

Let him make each speech with the word *"Vicakṣaṇa."* (which means, let him put *vicakṣaṇa"* at the end of the name of a person whom he addresses,)[231]

The eye is *vicakṣaṇa,* for with it he sees clearly *(J vi-calcskṣa* to perceive.)[4]

The eye is established as truth among men.[233]

Therefore people say to a man who tells something, "Have you seen it ? And if he says "I saw it,"then they believe him. And if one sees a thing oneself, one does not believe others, even many.[234]

Therefore let a man make each speech with the word *"Vichakshaṇa"*; then his uttered speech bcomes full of truth.[235]

AN EPISODE FROM KAUṢĪTAKĪ-BR.

The next extract is from the Kauṣītaki-Brāhmaṇa (xxvi, 5.). It will show how completely the true character of the sacrifice had been forgotten, and how much importance was attached to mere trifles. It is intelligible, wherever there is an established ceremonial, and priests appointed to wātch over it, that certain rules should be laid down for remedying any mistakes that may have occurred in the performance of a sacrifice. The chapter of accidents is a large one, and the *Brāhmaṇas* have spared no pains in laying down the most complicated rules, to counteract the consequences of a real mistake. The rules of penance or *prāyaścitta* occupy, in' several instances, one-third of the whole collections of ceremonial rules. But this was not enough. Discussions were raised, not only how to remedy mistake?, that had been observed at the time; but how to counteract the effects of mistakes, unobserved during the performance of the sacrifice. To settle this question, the Kauṣītakins ṇuote the following story :

"And then Pratardana, the son of Divodāsa, (a famous king) having gone to the Sacrifke of the Ṛṣis of Nimiṣa, sat down in their presence and asked the question : 'If the *Sadasya* (the superintending priest, according to the ceremonial of the Kauṣītakins) should make known a past blunder, or any one of the priests should observe it, how would you be free from sin ?' The priests were silent. Their *Brāhmaṇa was* Allkayu, the descendant of Vachaspati. He said, 'I do not know this, alas ! Let us ask the teacher of our fathers, the elder Jātukarṇya. He asked him: 'If the performer himself should observe a past blunder, or some one else should make it known, how could that blunder become not a blunder ? by saying the passage again, or by an offering ?' Jātukarṇya said, 'The passage must be said again.' Alikayu asked him again : Should he say again the *Śastra,* the *Anuvacana,* the *Nigada,* the *Yājyā,* or whatever else it may be, from beginning to end ? Jātukarṇya said : As far as the blunder extends, so far let him say it again whether a verse, a half verse, a foot, a word, or a letter. Then said Kauṣītaki : Let him not say the passage again, nor let him perform a penance offering (Kauṣ.-br. vi. 11.) It is not a blunder,'so said Kauṣītaki; 'for what-ever blunder the *Hotṛs* commit at the sacrifice without being aware of it, all that, Agni, the divine *Hotṛ,* makes whole; and this is confirmed by a verse from the Ṛg-veda.' "[236]

There are, however, other passages in the Brāhmaṇas, full of genuine thought and feeling, and most valuable as pictures of life, and as records of early struggles, which have left no trace in the literature of other nations. The story of Sunaḥaśepha, for instance, which we find in the Aitareya-brāhmaṇa, and in the Śāṅkhāyana-Sūtras is in-teresting in many respects. It shows that at that early time, the *Brāhmaṇas* were familiar with the idea of human sacrifices, and that men who were supposed, to belong to the caste of the *Brāhmaṇas* were ready to sell their sons for that purpose. The text of this story, together with the various readings, as gathered from the Śāṅkhāyanasūtras will be printed in the appendix.[237]

"Hariścandra,[238] the son of Vedhas, of the family of the Ikṣvākus, was a king without a son. He had a hundred wives, but had no son by them. In his house lived Parvata and Nārada. He asked Nārada : 'Tell me, O Nārada, what do people gain by a son, whom they all wish for, as well those who reason as those who do not reason ?'

Being asked by one verse, Nārada[239] replied in ten verses : 'If a father sees the face of a son, born alive, he pays a debt in him, and goes to immortality.

'The pleasure which a father has in his son is greater than all the pleasures that are from the earth, from the fire, and from the waters.

Always have the fathers overcome the great darkness by a son; for a Self is bom from his Self; it (the new-born Self, the son) is like a ship, full of food, to carry him over.

'What is the flesh ? What is the skin ? What are the hairs ? What the heat ?' Try to get a son, you *Brāhmaṇas* he is undoubtedly the world.

'Food is life for men, clothing his protection, gold his beauty, cattle his strength. His wife is a friend, his daughter is a pity[240]; but the son is his light in the highest world-

'As husband he embraces a wife, who becomes his mother, when he becomes her child, having been renewed in her, he is born in the tenth month.

'A wife is a wife *(jāyā)* because man is born *(jāyāte)* again in her. She is a mother *(ābhūti);* because she brings forth *(ābhūti);* a germ is hidden in her.

'The gods and the old ages brought great- light unto her.. The gods said to men : "In her you will be born again."

'There is no life for him who has no son, this the animals also know.

'The path which those follow who have sons and no sorrows, is widely praised and happy. Beasts and birds know it, and they have young ones everywhere.'

Having thus spoken, he said to him : 'Go to Varuṇa the king, and say : May a son be born to me, and I shall sacrifice him to you.' The king assented, he went to Varuṇa the king, and said : 'May a son be born to me and I shall sacrifice him to you.' Varuṇa said, 'Yes.' A son was born to him, called Rohita. Then Varuṇa said to Hariścandra : 'A son is born to thee, sacrifice him to me.' Hariścandra said : 'When an animal is more than ten days old, it can be sacrificed. May he be older than ten days and I shall sacrifice him to you.'

Varuṇa assented. The boy was more than ten days old, and Varuṇa said : 'He is older now than ten days, sacrifice him to me.' Hariścandra said : 'when an animal's teeth come, then it can be sacrificed. May his teeth now come, and I shall sacrifice him to you.'

Varuṇa assented. His teeth came, and Varuṇa said : 'His

teeth have come, sacrifice him to me.' Hariścandra said : 'When an animal's teeth fall out, then it can be sacrificed. May his teeth fall out, and I shall sacrifice him to you.'

Varuṇa assented; his teeth fell out and Varuṇa said : 'His teeth have fallen out, sacrifice him to me. Hariścandra replied : 'When an animal's teeth come again, then it can be sacrificed. May his teeth come again, and I shall sacrifice him to you.'

Varuṇa assented. His teeth came again, and Varuṇa said : 'His teeth have come again, sacrifice him to me.' Hariścandra said : 'When a wārrior *(kṣatriya)* is girt with his armour, then he can be sacrificed. May he be girt, and I shall sacrifice him to you.'

Varuṇa assented. He was girt, and Varuṇa said : 'He has been girt, let him be sacrificed to me.'

Hariścandra assented. He addressed his son and said : 'Child, he gave you to me; Death ! that I sacrifice you to him.' The son said, 'No !', took his bow, and went to the forest and lived there for a year.

And Varuṇa seized Hariścandra, and his belly swelled. This Rohita heard and went from the forest to the village *(grāma)*. Indra, in the form of a man, went round him, and said : 'For a man who does not travel about there is no happiness, thus we have heard, O Rohita ! A good man who stays at home is a bad man. Indra is the friend of him who travels. Travel.

Rohita thought, a *Brāhmaṇa* has told me to travel, and thus he travelled a second year in the forest. When he went from the forest to the village, Indra, in the form of a man, went round him, and said :

'A traveller's legs are like blossoming branches, he himself grows and gathers the fruit. All his wrongs vanish, destroyed by his exertion on the road. Travel !'

Rohita thought, a *Brāhmaṇa* has told me to travel, and thus he travelled a third year in the forest. When he went from the forest to the town, Indra, in the form of a man, went round him, and said :

'The fortune of a man who sits, sits also; it rises, when he rises; it sleeps, when he sleeps; it moves well when he moves, Travel !'

Rohita thought, a *Brāhmaṇa* has told me to travel, and thus he travelled a fourth year in the forest. When he went from the forest to the town. Indra, in the form of a man, went round him, and said :

'A man who sleeps is like the *Kali* age;[241] a man who awakes is like *Dvapara* age; a man who rises is like the *Treta* age; a man who travels is like the *Kṛta* age. Travel!'

Rohita thought, a *Brāhmaṇa* has told me to travel, and thus he travelled a fifth year in the forest. When he went from the forest to the town, Indra, in the form of a man, went round him, and said :

'A traveller finds honey, a traveller finds sweet figs. Look at the happiness of the Sun, who travelling never tries. Travel !'

Rohita thought, a *Brāhmaṇa* has told me to travel, and thus he travelled a sixth year. He met in the forest a starving Ṛṣi, *Ajigarta,* the son of *Śuyavasa.* He had three sons. *Śunaḥpucha, Śunaḥśepha* , and *Śunolāṅgūla.* Rohita said to him : 'Ṛṣi, I give you a hundred cows, I ransom myself with one of these thy sons.' The father'embraced the eldest son, and said: 'Not him.' 'Nor him,' said the mother, embracing the youngest. And the parents bargained to give Śunaḥśepha , the middle son. Rohita gave a hundred, took him, and went from the forest to the village. And he came to his father, and said : 'Father, Death ! I ransom myself by him.' The father went to Varuṇa said :

'I shall sacrifice this man to you.' Varuṇa, said, 'Yes, for a *Brāhmaṇa* is better than a Kṣatriya.' And he told him to perform a Rājasūya sacrifice. Hariścandra took him to be the victim for the day, when the Sotna is spent to the gods.

Viśvāmitra was his *Hotṛ* priest, *Jamadagni* his *Adhvaryu* priest, Vasiṣṭha, the *Brahmā, Ayāsya,* the *Udgātṛ* priest. When Śunaḥśepha had been prepared, they found nobody to bind him to the sacrificial post. And Ajīgarta, the son of Śūyavasa said : 'Give me another hundred, and I shall bind him.'[242] They gave him another hundred and he bound him. When he had been prepared and bound, when the *Āprī* hymns had been sung, and he had been led round the fire, they found nobody to kill him. And Ajīgarta, the son of Śūyavasa said : 'Give me another hundred, and I shall kill him.' They gave him another hundred, and he came whetting his sword, Then Śunaḥśepha thought, 'They will really kill me as if I Was not a man.[243] Death ! I shall pray to the gods.' He went with a hymn to *Prajāpati* (Lord of the World), the first of gods. Prajāpati said to him : 'Agni (fire) is the nearest of gods, go to him.' He went with a hymn to Agni, and Agni said to him: '*Savitṛ* (the progenitor) rules all creatures, go to him.' He went with a hymn to Savitṛ, and Savitṛ, said to him.' You are bound for *Varuṇa* the king, go to him.' He went with a hymn to Varuṇa the king, and Varuṇa said to him : '*Agni* is the mouth of the gods the kindest god, praise him, and we shall set you free.' Thus he praised Agni, and Agni said to him : 'Praise the Viśve Devāḥ, and we shall set you free.' Thus he praised the Viśve Devāḥ, and they said to him : 'Indra is the greatest, strongest, mightiest, and friendliest, of the gods, praise him, and we shall set you free.' Thus he praised Indra, and Indra was pleased, and gave him in his mind a golden car, which Śunaḥśepha acknowledged by another verse. Indra said to him; 'Praise the *Aśvinau,* and we shall set you free.' Thus he praised the Asvinau, and they said to him 'Praise *Uṣas* (dawn) and we shall set you free.' Thus he praised Ushas with three verses. While each verse Was delivered, his fetters were loosed, and Hariścandra's belly grew smaller, and when the last verse was said, his fetters were loosed, and Hariścandra well again."

This story is chiefly interesting as revealing to us three distinct elements in the early social life of India. These are represented by the royal or reigning family of the Ikṣvākus, by their priests or ministers belonging to several famous *Brāhmaṇical* races, and by a third class of men, living in the forests, such as Ajīgarta and his three sons. It is true that Ajīgarta is called a Ṛṣi, and one of his sons a *Brāhmaṇa*. But even if we accept the Āryan origin of Ajigarta, the seller and butcher of his own son, it is important to remark how great a difference there must have been between the various Āryan settlers in India. Whether we ascribe this difference to a difference in the time of immigration, or whatever other reason we may assign to it, yet there remains the fact, that, with all the vaunted civilization of the higher Āryan classes, there were Āryan people in India to whom not only a young prince could make the offer of buying their children, but where the father offered himself to bind and kill the son, whom he had sold for a hundred cows. This was a case so startling to the later Brāhmaṇas, that the author of the Laws of *Manu Was* obliged to allude to it, in order to defend the dignity of his caste.[244] Manu says, that hunger is an excuse for many things, and that Ajīgarta, although he went to kill his own son, was not guilty of a crime, because he did so to appease his hunger. Now the author of the Aitareya-brāhmāṇa certainly does not adopt this view, for Ajīgarta is there, as we shall see, severely abused for his cruelty, so much so, that his son, whom he has sold, considers himself at liberty to leave the family of his parents, and to accept the offer made by Viśvāmitra of being adopted into his family. So revolting, indeed, is the description given of Ajīgarta's behaviour in the Brāhmaṇa, that we should rather recognise in him a specimen of the un-āryan population of India. Such a supposition, however, would be in contradiction with several of the most essential points of the legend, particularly in what regards the adoption of Śunaḥśepha by Viśvāmitra. Viśvāmitra, though arrivéd at the dignity of a *Brāhmaṇa,* clearly considers the adoption of Śunaḥśepha Devarāta, of the famous *Brahmānio* family of the Aṅgir, as an advantage for himself and for his descendants; and the Devarātas are indeed mentioned as a famous branch of the Viśvāmitras. (V.P. p. 405, 23.). Śunaḥśepha is made his eldest son, and the leader of his brothers, evidently as the defender and voucher of their

Brahmahood, which must have been then of very recent date, because Viśvāmitra himself is still addressed by Saunaḥśepha as *Baja-putra,* and *Bharatnṛṣabha,*

The Aitareya-brāhmaṇa goes on to state that the priest asked Śunaḥśepha to perform the sacrifice of the day. Śunaḥśepha then invented the ceremony called *Aḥjaḥsava* and prepared the Soma, accompanied by four verses.[245] He poured the Soma into the *Droṇa-kalaśa* vessel with one verse and made the libations with the four first verses of the same hymn accompanied by *Svāhā* exclamations, as the sacrifice had been begun by Hariścandra. Afterwards he carried out all the things belonging to the *Avabhṛtha* ceremony, employing two verses, and made Hariścandra go to the *Āhavanīya* fire with another hymn.

"When the sacrifice had thus been performed Śunaḥśepha sat down on the lap of Viśvāmitra. Ajīgarta, the son of Śuyavasa, said: "Ṛṣi, give me back my son." Viśvāmitra said, "No, for the gods have given him to me." He became Devarāta (Theodotus) the son of Viśvāmitra, and the members of the families of Kapila and Babhru became his relations. Ajīgarta, the son of Śuyavasa said : "Come you, O son, we, both I and your mother, call you away." Ajīgarta, the son of Śuyavasa said : "You art by birth an Āṅgirasa, the son of Ajīgarta, celebrated as a poet. O Ṛṣi, go not away from the line of thy grandfather, come back to me." Śunaḥśepha replied; "They have seen you with a knife in your hand, a thing that men have never found even amongst Śūdras; you have taken three hundred cows for me, O Aṅgiras." Ajīgarta, the son of Śūyavasa said : "My old son, it grieves me for the wrong that I have done; I throw it away, may these hundred cows belong to you.' Śunaḥśepha replied; "Who once commits a sin will commit also another sin; you will not abstain from the Wāys of Śūdras; what you hast committed cannot be redressed." "Cannot be redressed," Viśvāmitra repeated. "Dreadful stood the son of Śūyavasa when he went to kill with his knife. Be not his son, come and be my son." Śunaḥśepha said : "Tell us thyself, O son of a king, thus as thou art known to us, how I, who am an Āṅgirasa, shall become thy son." Viśvāmitra replied : "You shall be the eldest of my sons, thy offspring shall be the first, you shalt receive the heritage which the gods have given me, thus I address thee." Śunaḥśepha replied : "May the leader of the Bharatas say so, in the presence of his agreeing sons, for friendship's and happiness' sake, that I shall beeome your son." Then Viśvāmitra addressed his sons : "Hear me, Madhuchandas, Ṛshabha, Renu, Aṣṭaka, and all ye brothers that you are, believe in his seniority."

This Viśvāmitra had a hundred sons, fifty older than Madhuchandas and fifty younger. The elders did not like this, and Viśvāmitra pronounced a curse upon them, that they should become outcasts. They became Āndhras, Puṇḍras, Śabaras, Pulindas, Mūṭibas, and many other outcast tribes, so that the descendants of Viśvāmitra became the worst of the Dasyus. But Madhuchandas, together with the other fifty sons, said : "What our father tells us, in that we abide; we place thee before us and follow you." When Viśvāmitra heard this, he praised his sons and said : "You sons will have good children and cattle, because you have accepted my will, and have made me rich in brave sons. You, descendants of Gādhin![246] are to be honoured by all, you brave sons ! led by Devarāta; he will be to you good counsel. You, descendants of Kuśika, follow Devarāta. He is your hero, he will give you my riches, and whatever knowledge I possess. You are wise, all you sons of Viśvāmitra together; you are rich, you stood to uphold Devarāta, and to make him your eldest, descendants of Gādhin, Devarāta[247] (Śunaḥśepha) is mentioned as a Ṛṣi of both families, in the chiefdom of the Jahnus, and in the divine Veda of the Gādhins.".

The same chapter of the Aitareya-brāhmaṇa, where this story of Śunaḥśepha is told, contains many curious details on the mutual relation of the Brāhmaṇas and the Kṣatriyas. The story of Sunaḥśepha is said to form a part of the inauguration of a king, to whom it is related by the *Hotṛ* priests, the *Adhvaryu* priest acting the second part; perhaps an early attempt at dramatic representation.

It does not necessarily follow from this legend that the Ṛṣis, the authors of the Vedic hymns, offered human sacrifices. No one would conclude from the willingness of Abraham to sacrifice his own son in obedience to a supposed command from Jehovah, that the Jews had been in the habit of offering their sons as victims. It is not, however, because human sacrifices seem to belong only to the most savage races of men that we doubt the prevalence of this custom among the ancient Hindus. Human sacrifices are not incompatible with a higher stage of civilization, particularly among people who never doubted the immortality of the soul, and at the same time felt a craving to offer whatever seemed most valuable on earth to the gods in whom they believed. There are few nations in the history of the world whose early traditions do not exhibit some traces of human sacrifices. And though I doubt the continuance of that custom during the *Chandas* period, I see no reason to doubt its previous existence. A passage from the Aitareya-brāhmaṇa offers a striking confirmation of this opinion. It is said there (Ait.-br. 6. 8.) that the gods took man for their victim. "As he was taken, *medha,* (the sacrifice or the spiriṇ went out of him. It entered the horse. Therefore the horse became the sacrificial animal. Then the gods took the horse, but as it Was taken, the *medha* went out of him. It entered the ox. Therefore the ox became the sacrificial animal. The same happened with the ox. Afterwards the sheep, then the goat, and at last the earth became the victim. From the earth rice was produced, and rice was offered in the form of *Puroḍāśa* in lieu of the sacrificial animal. The other beings which had formerly been offered and then been dismissed, are supposed to have become changed into animals unfit for sacrifice; man into a savage, the horse into a Bos Gaurus, the ox into a Gayal ox, the sheep into a camel *(uṣṭra),* the goat into a śarabha. All these animals are *amedhya* or unclean, and should not be eaten."

The drift of this story is most likely that in former times all these victims had been offered. We know it for certain in the case of horses and oxen, though afterwards these sacrifices were discontinued. As to sheep and goats they were considered proper victims to a still later time. When vegetable offerings took the place of bloody victims, it was clearly the wish of the author of our passage to show that, for certain sacrifices, these rice-cakes were as efficient as the flesh of animals. He carries over his argument still further, and tries to show that in the rice the beard corresponds to the hair of animal; the husk to the skin; the *phalīkaraṇas* to blood; the meal to the flesh and the straw to the bones.

AN EPISODE FROM ŚATAPATHA-BRĀHMAṆA

The next story, from the Śatapatha-brāhmaṇa[248] serves to illustrate the relations between the priestly and royal families in the early history of India, and allows us an insight into the policy of the Brāhmaṇas in their struggle for political influence.

"Janaka of Videha once met with some Brāhmaṇas who had just arrivéd. They were Svetaketu Āruṇeya, Soma-śuṣma Sātyāyajñi, and Yājñavalkya. He said to them 'How do you perform the *Agnihotra* ?' Śvetaketu replied: 'O king, I sacrifice to two heats in one another which are ever shining and pervading, the world with their splendour.' 'How is that ?' said the king. Svetaketu replied : '*Āditya* (the sun) is heat; to him do I sacrifice, in the evening in the fire *(Agni), Agni* is heat; to him do I sacrifice in the morning in the sun *(Āditya).*' 'What becomes of him who sacrifices thus ?' said the king. The Brāhmaṇa replied : 'He becomes evershining with happiness and splendour, and has his dwelling with these two gods and is one with them,'

Then Somnśuṣma began : 'O king, I sacrifice to light in light.' 'How is that ?' said the king. Somaśuṣma replied : '*Āditya* is light, to him do I sacrifice, in the evening in *Agni*. Agni is light, to him do I sacrifice, in the morning in *Āditya*.' What becomes of him who sacrifices thus ?'

Said the king. The Brāhmaṇa replied : He becomes full of

light and splendour in this life, and has his dwelling with these two gods and is one with them.'

Then said Yājñavalkya : 'I offer the Agnihotra in taking out the fire (from the house-altar) : for when Āditya sets, all the gods follow him, and if they see that I take out the fire, they come back, and, after having cleaned the sacrificial vessels, having filled them again, and after having milked also the sacred cow, I shall delight them, when I see them again, and they see me.'

Janaka said : 'You, O Yājñavalkya, hast come very near to the *Agnihotra;* I shall give you a hundred cows. But you do not know what becomes afterwards of these twin libations (in the morning and evening). So he said, then mounted his car and went away.

The priests said : 'This fellow of a *Rājānya* has insulted us; let us call him out for a Brāhmaṇa-dispute.' Yājñavalkya observed, We are Brāhmaṇas, he a fellow of *Rājanya.* If we vanquished him whom should we say we had vanquished ? But if he vanquished us, people would say of us that a *Rājanya* had vanquished Brāhmaṇas. Do not think of this.' They allowed what he said, and Yājñavalkya mounted his car, and followed the king. He reached the king, and the king said to him, Yājñavalkya, do you come to know the *Agnihotra* ? 'The *Agnihotra* O king,' replied Yājñavalkya.",

Here the king begins to explain to Yājñavalkya his own view of the two morning and evening libations, called *Agnihotra.* He says, that these two sacrifices rise into the air, and are there again performed; the wind being the fuel and the rays the bright libation. Then he goes on explaining how these two sacrifices, after having delighted the air, enter the sky, where they are performed by sun and moon; how they come back to the earth, and are performed by fire (warmth) and plants; how they enter the man, and are performed by his tongue and food; how they enter the woman, and a son is born. ' This is the true *Agnihotra,* O Yājñavalkya.' said the king; 'there is nothing higher than this.' Yājñavalkya granted him a boon; and the king said, 'May I be allowed, Yājñavalkya, to ask you what I wish.' Since then Janaka became a *Brāhmaṇa.* "

The two following stories are of a more mythological character, and contain curious traditions about Manu, the supposed ancestor of mankind. The first is from the Aitareya-brāhmaṇa, v. 14.

Nābhānediṣṭha, the son of Manu, had been deprived of the paternal share by his brothers, while he was pursuing his studies (in the house of his Guru). When he came home, he said, 'What is my share ?' They replied (pointing to Manu). 'The father, who is our governor and arbitrator.' (Therefore sons call now their father, governor *(niṣṭhāva*[249] and arbitrator *(avavaditṛ)*. He went to his father and said, 'Father, they have made you to be my share.' The father replied, 'Do not believe it, my son, by any means. The Aṅgiras' there perform a sacrifice in order to go to heaven, but every time they come to the sixth day, they get confused. Let them recite these two hymns (of thine[250]) on the sixth day, and when they go to heaven they will give you all the great riches which they have brought together for the sacrifice.' The son said, 'Yes'; went to them, and spoke: 'Ye sages, receive me, the son of Manu.'[1] They replied, 'What is your wish that thou speak thus ? He answered, 'I shall teach you this sixth day, and you shall give me, when you go to heaven, all these great riches which you have brought together for the sacrifice,' They agreed, and he recited for them these two hymns on the sixth day. Thus the Aṅgiras' understood the sacrifice and the life in heaven. Therefore, when the *Hotṛ* priest recites these two hymns on the sixth day, it leads to an understanding of the sacrifice and of the life in heaven.

When the Aṅgiras' were going to heaven they said, "All these great riches are your, O *Brāhmaṇa*. "[252] While he was putting them together, a man in dark dress came up from the north, and said, 'This is mine, mine is what is left on the sacred spot.[253] Nābhānediṣṭha replied, 'They gave it to me.' The man said, 'Then let us ask your father about it.' He went to his father, and the father said, 'Have they given you nothing my son ? Nābhānedishṭha replied, 'They gave me a portion, but then a man in dark dress came up from the north and said, "This is mine; mine is what is left on the sacred spot," and took it.' The father said, 'It belongs to him, indeed, my son, but he will give it to your.' Thereupon Nābhānedishṭha went back and said, 'This is your indeed, O reverend sir; thus spoke my father. 'This I give to you,' replied the man, 'who have spoken the truth. Therefore the truth must be spoken by a man who knows it. These verses of Nābhānediṣṭha give great riches. They give great riches; and he understands on the sixth day the life in heaven who knows this."

"The next extract is taken from the Śatapatha-brāhmaṇa, i. 8. I. 1. (Prap. vi. 3. 1.) :

"To Manu they brought in the morning Water to wash. As they bring it with their hands for the washing, a fish comes into the hands of Manu as soon as he has washed himself.

He spoke to Manu the word : Keep me, I shall preserve you.' Manu said, 'From what will you preserve me ?' The fish said, 'The flood will carry away all these creatures. I shall preserve you from it.' "How canst you be kept ?' said, Manu.

The fish replied, 'As long as we are small there is much destruction for us; fish swallows fish. First, then, you must keep me in a jar. If I outgrow it dig a hole, and keep me in it. If I outgrow this, take me to the sea, and I shall be saved from destruction.

He became soon a large fish. He said to Manu, 'When I am full-grown, in the same year the flood will come. Build a ship then, and worship me, and when the flood rises go into the ship, and I shall preserve you from it.'

Manu brought the fish to the sea, after he had kept him thus. And in the year which the fish had pointed out Manu had built a ship, and worshipped the fish. Then when the flood had risen, he went into the ship. The fish came swimming to him, and Manu fastened the rope of the ship to a horn of the fish. The fish carried him by it over the northern moutain.

The fish said, 'I have preserved you. Bind the ship to a tree. May the water not cut you asunder while your art on the mountain. As the water will sink, you wilt slide down.' Manu slid down with the water; and this is called the Slope of Manu on the northern mountain. The flood had carried away all these creatures, and thus Manu was left there alone.

He went along meditating a hymn, and wishing for offspring. And he sacrificed there also (a *pāka-yahñā*).Taking clarified butter, coagulated milk, whey and curds, he made an offering to the waters. In a year a woman was brought forth from it. She rose nuctuous and trickling; and where she stood there was clarified butter. Mitra and Varuṇa came to meet her.

They said to her, 'Who are you?' She said, 'The daughter of Manu.' 'Say you are ours,' they said. 'No' she replied; 'He who has begotten me to him I belong.' Then they asked her to be their sister, and she half agreed and half did not agree. She went off and came to Manu.

Manu said to her, 'Who are you?' She said, 'I am your daughter.' 'How are you my daughter?' he asked. She replied. 'The oblations which thou hast thrown into the waters, clarified butter, coagulated milk, whey and curds, by them thou hast begotten me. I am a blessing. Praise me at the sacrifice. If you praise me at the sacrifice you will be rich in offspring and cattle. Whatever blessing you will ask by me, will all be given to you,' thus he praised her in the middle of this sacrifice; for the middle of the sacrifice is that which comes between the introductory and the final prayers *(prayājās* and *anuyājās)*.

Manu went along with her, meditating a hymn, and wishing for offspring; and by her he begat this offspring, which is called the offspring of Manu, and whatever blessing he asked was all given to him.

She is indeed *Iḍā*. Whoever knows this, and goes with *Iḍā*, he begets the offering which Manu begat; and whatever blessing he asks by her, is all given to him."

These extracts from the Brāhmaṇas will be sufficient to show that here is much curious information to be gathered from these compilations. In spite of their general dreariness, the Brāhmaṇas, well deserve to be preserved from destruction, which can only be done by the help of European editors. It is true that the ceremonial, the *vidhis,* can be better studied in the *Sūtras,* but if we want to know what meaning was assigned to every act of the sacrifice, such as it had been handed down and become fixed in the *Brāhmaṇic* society of India, long before the composition of any Brāhmaṇa, we must consult these works. Though their professed object is to teach the sacrifice, they allow a much larger space to dogmatical, exegetical, mystical and philosophical speculations, than to the ceremonial itself. They appeal continually to earlier authorities, and in some of them, particularly in the Kauṣītaki-brāhmaṇa, the conflcting opinions of ancient sages are so well confronted, and their respective merits so closely discussed, that we sometimes imagine ourselves reading the dogmatic philosophy of Jaimini. According to the views of native commentators, the characteristic feature of the Brāhmaṇas consists in doubt, deliberation, and discussion, and the word Mimāṁsā which afterwards became the title of Jaimini's philosophy, is frequently used in the Brāhmaṇas to introduce the very problems which occupy the attention of Jaimini and his followers. Of course the discussion is not a *bona fide* discussion. The two sides of every question are stated, but they only serve to lead us on to the conclusion which the author of the Brāhmaṇa considers in the light of a divine revelation. We are reminded of the disputations of two Doctors of Theology who defend for a time the most heretical propositions with the sharpest weapons of logic and rhetoric, though they would extremely regret the final victory of that cause which, for argument's sake, they are called upon to maintain. Never was dogmatism more successfully veiled under the mask of free discussion than in the Mimānsā or discussion of the Brāhmaṇas.

ORIGIN OF THE BRĀHMAṆAS

The fact of so many authorities being quoted by name in these works show that the Brāhmaṇas exhibit the accumulated thoughts of a long succession of early theologians and philosophers. But the very earliest of these sages follow a train of thought which gives clear evidence of a decaying religion. The Brāhmaṇas presuppose, not only a complete collection of the ten Maṇḍalas of the Ṛg-veda, not only the establishment of a most complicated ceremonial, not only the distribution of the ceremonial offices among three or four classes of priests but a complete break in the primitive tradition of the Āryan settlers of India, At the time when the law laid down about the employment of certain hymns at certain parts of the sacrifice, the original meaning of these hymns, and the true conception of the gods to whom they were addressed, had been lost. The meaning also of the old and sacred customs by which their forefathers had hallowed the most critical epochs of life and the principal divisions of the year, had faded away from the memory of those whose lucubrations on the purport of the sacrifices have been emblamed in the so-called *Arthavādas* of the Brāhmaṇas. It is difficult to determine whether, before the beginning of the Ḅrāhmaṇa period, there existed various *Śākhās* among the Bahvṛchas. The collection of the Ṛg-veda-saṁhitā must no doubt have been completed long before the age which led to the composition of Brāhmaṇas. Various readings also may have found their way into that collection before the ·Brāhmaṇa period. But the scrupulous preservation of such variations, which were the natural result of oral tradition, seems more akin to the spirit of the Brāhmaṇas than to that of an earlier age. There is less room for doubt as to the date of the Śākhās of the *Adhvaryus* and *Chandogas*. They belong to the Brāhmaṇa period. What is called the Taittirīaya-saṁhitā is no saṁhitā, in the usual sense of the word, but was originally the Brāhmaṇa of the ancient *Adhivaryus*. It contains the description of the sacrifice, such as it would be reṇuired by the Adhvaryus. The composition of a separate saṁhitā in their behalf, the so-called saṁhitā of the White Yajur-veda, is contemporaneous with, if not later than, the collection of the Śatapatha-brāhmaṇa. We therefore consider all the Śākhās of the *Adhvaryus,* with the exception of their Sūtra-śākhās, as Brāhmaṇa-śākhās which had grown up during the Brāhmaṇa period. And if we feel more hesitation with regard to the saṁhitā of the Chandogas, it is not with reference to what is usually called the Sāma-veda-saṁhitā but with regard to the *Gānas,* These collections of hymns, though they have a purely ceremonial object, have an air of antiquity, and we could hardly understand how the Tāṇḍya-brāhmaṇa, even in its original component parts, could have arisen, unless we suppose that there existed previously collections and groups of hymns, comprised under special names, such as we find in the *Gānas*. Without, therefore, pronouncing a definite opinion on the existence of any Śākhās of the two minor Vedas, previous to the first appearance of Brāhmaṇa literature, we confine ourselves to the assertion, that not one line of any of the Brāhmaṇas which we possess could have been composed, until after the complete collection of the Ṛg-veda, and after the threefold division of the ceremonial. Not one of the Brāhmaṇas Was composed by a Brāhmaṇa who was not either a Bahvṛcha, an Adhvaryu, or Chhandoga. There was a fourth class of superintending priests, who were supposed to be cognisant of the duties of all the three other classes : but there was, as we shall see, neither Brāhmaṇa, nor saṁhitā for their special benefit. According to the opinion of some, the superintendent or Brāhmaṇa might indeed be an *Adhvaryu,* or even a *Chandoga,* but the general rule is that he should be a Bahvṛcha,[254] because the Bahvṛca had the widest knowledge of Vedic hymns. There must have been a time when every Brāhmaṇa who had to act as a priest, what-ever offices he had to perform at the sacrifice, was acquainted with the complete body of the sacred hymns, collected in the Ṛg-veda. But of that time no traces are left in our Brāhmaṇas. Our Brāhmaṇas know of no hymns which are not the property of *Hotṛ, Adhvaryu,* or *Udgātr,* they know of no priests, except the four classes which have divided between themselves all the sacrifices, and have distinct duties assigned to them, whether they officiate singly or jointly. Such a system could only have been carried out by a powerful and united priesthood; its origin and continuance can hardly be conceived without the admission of early councils and canons. Originally every sacrifice was a spontaneous act, and as such had a meaning. When the sacrifices fell into the hands of priests, the priest Was at first the minister, afterwards the representative, of those who offered the sacrifice. But it is only in the last stage of priestcraft that the spoils are divided, and certain acts made the monopoly of certain priests. All this had taken place before the rising of what we call the Brāhmaṇa literature, and we may well conceive that but few traces are left in these works of the thoughts and feelings which had suggested the first spontaneous acts of the early worshippers of India.

The transition from a natural worship to an artificial ceremonial may take place gradually. It had taken place long before the beginning of the Brāhmaṇa period, and the process of corruption continued during this and the succeeding periods, till at last the very corruption became a principle of new life. But there is throughout the Brāhmaṇas such a complete misunderstanding of the original intention of the Vedic hymns, that we can hardly understand how such an estrangement could have taken place, unless there had been at some time or other a sudden and violent break in the chain of tradition. The author of the Brāhmaṇas evidently imagined that those ancient hymns were written simply for the sake of their sacrifices, and whatever interpretation they thought fit to assign to these acts, the same, they supposed, had to be borne out by the hymns. This idea has vitiated the whole system of Indian exegesis. It might be justified, perhaps, if it had only been applied to the purely sacrificial hymns, particularly to those which are found in the Saṁhitās of the Sāma-veda and Yajur-veda. Ṛg-veda too has experienced the same treatment at the hands of Indian commentators, and the stream of tradition, flowing from the fountain-head of the original poets, has, like the waters of the Sarasvatī, disappeared in the sands of a désert. Not only was the true nature of the god, as conceived by the early poets, completely lost sight of, but new gods were actually created out of words which were never intended as names of divine beings. There are several hymns in the Ṛg-veda containing questions as to who is true or the most powerful god. One in particular is well known, in which each verse ends with the innuiring exclamation of the poet; *"Kasmai devāya haviṣa vidkerm ?"* "To which god shall we sacrifice with our offering?" This, and similar hymns in which the interrogative pronoun occured, were employed at various sacrifices. A rule had been laid down, that in every sacrificial hymn, there must be a deity addressed by the poet. In order to discover a deity where no deity existed, the most extra-ordinary objects, such as a present, a drum, stones, plants, were raised to the artificial rank of deities. In accordance with the same system, we find that the authors of the Brāhmaṇas had so completely broken with the past, that, forgetful of the poetical character of the hymns and the yearning of the poets after the unknown god, they exalted the interrogative pronoun itself into a deity, and acknowledged a god *Ka* or Who ? In the Taittirīyaṁnhitā[255] (i. 7. 6. 6.), in the Kauṣītaki-brāhmaṇa (xxiv. 4.), in the Tāṇḍya-brāhmaṇa (xv. 10.), and in the Kauṣītaki-brāhmaṇa, wherever interrogative verses occur, the author states, that *Ka* is Prajāpati, or the Lord of Creatures *(Prajāpatir vai Kaḥ)*. Nor did they stop here. Some of the hymns in which the interrogative pronoun occured were called *kadvat, i. e.* having *Kad* or *quid*. But soon a new adjective Was formed, and not only the hymns, but the sacrifice also, offered to the god, were called *Kaya,* or who-ish. This word, which is not to be identified with the Latin cujus, cuja, cujum, but is merely the artificial product of an effective mind, is found in the Taittirīya-saṁhitā (i. 8. 3, 1.), and in 'the Vājasaneyi-saṁhitā (xxiv. 15.). At the time of Pāṇini this word had acquired such legitimacy as to call for a separate rule explaining its formation (Pāṇ. iv. 2. 25.). The Commentator here explains *Ka* by *Brahmā*. After this, we can hardly wonder that in the later Sanskrit literature of the Purāṇas, *Ka* appears, as a recognised god, as the supreme god, with a genealogy of his own, perhaps even with a wife; and that in the laws of Manu, one of the recognised forms of marriage, generally known by the name of the Prajāpati-marriage, occurs under the monstrous title of Kāya.

What is more natural that the sun should be called in the hymns, golden-handed ? The Brāhmaṇa, however, affected with a kind of voluntary blindness, must needs explain this simple epithet by a story of the sun having lost his hand and having received instead a hand made of gold.

DATE OF THE BRĀHMAṆAS

It would be useless to multiply these instances, as every page of the Brāhmaṇas contains the clearest proof of that spirit of the ancient Vedic poetry, and the purport of the original Vedic sacrifices, were both beyond the comprehension of the authors of the Brāhmaṇas. But although we thus perceive the wide chasm between the Brāhmaṇa period and that period by which it is preceded, we have still to answer the question whether any probable limits can be assigned to the duration of this literary period. The Brāhmaṇas are not the work of a few individuals. By whomsoever they were brought into that form in which we now possess them, no one can claim the sole authorship of the dogmas which are incorporated in each Brāhmaṇa. The Brāhmaṇas represent a complete period during which the whole stream of thought flowed in one channel, and took, at least in that class which alone sustained intellectual activity, the form of prose, never before applied to literary productions, There are old and new Brāhmaṇas, but the most modern hardly differ in style and language from the most ancient. The old Brāhmaṇas passed through several changes, represented by the Brāhmaṇa-śākhās, and even the most modern were not exempt from these modifications. Considering, therefore, that the Brāhmaṇa period must comprehend the first establishment of the threefold ceremonial, the composition of separate Brāhmaṇas, the formation of Brāhmaṇa-Caraṇas and the schism between old and new Caraṇas, and their various collections, it would seem impossible to bring the whole within a shortcr space thon 200 years. Of course this is merely conjectural; but it would reṇuire a greater stretch of imagination to account for the production in a smaller number of years of that mass of Brahmāṇic literature which still exists, or is, known to have existed. Were we to follow the traditions of the Brāhmaṇas themselves, we should have much less difficulty in accounting for the great variety of authors quoted, and of opinions stated in the Brāhmaṇas. They contain lists of teachers through whom the Brāhmaṇas were handed down, which would extend the limits of this age to a very considerable degree. The Chandogas have assigned a separate Brāhmaṇa to the list of their teachers, viz., the Vaṁśa-brāhmaṇa, a work the existence of which ought not to have been called into question, as a copy of it existed in the Bodleian Library.[256] In the Śatapatha-brāhmaṇa these lists are repeated at the end of various sections. There seems to be no imaginable object in inventing these long lists, as in the eyes of the Brāhmaṇas they would have been much too short for the extravagant antiquity assigned to their sacred books. With the exception of the highest links in each chain of teachers, the lists have an appearance of authenticity rarely to be met with in Indian compositions. The number of teachers in the Vaṁśa-brāhmaṇa amount to 53, the last of them, Kāśyapa, the father having received the tradition from Agni, or the god of fire. From Agni the tradition is further traced to Indra, Vāyu (wind), Mṛtyu (death) Prājāpati (the Lord of Creation) and lastly to Brahmā, the Self existing. From Kāśyapa, down to Rādha Gautama, his 26th successor the line of teachers seems to have been undivided. Rādha Gautama had two pupils, who apparently became the founders of different schools. One is called Ansu Dhānañjayya, who received instruction from Rādha Gautama and Amāvāsya Śāṇḍilyāyana; the other, Gobhila, had no teacher besides Rādha. The successors of Gobhila are eleven in number, while those of Ansu Dhānañjayya are twenty-five.

BRAHMĀṆIC TEACHERS

In the Śatapatha-brāhmaṇa we find four *Vaṁśas*. The most important of them stands at the end of the whole work, and consists of fifty-five names; the last of the human teachers being again Kāśyapa, who here is supposed to have received his revelation from *Vāc,* the goddess of speech. She received it through *Ambhiṇī* from *Āditya,* the sun. Among the successors of Kāśyapa we mark the 10th, Yājñavalkya, the pupil of Uddālaka and the teacher of Āsuri; and the 15th, Sāṁjīvīputra; Sañjiviputra seems to have united two lines of teachers; he was the pupil of Kārśakeyīputra, and, according, to the Vamsa of the 10th book, he was likewise the pupil of Māṇḍūkayani, the 9th successor of Tur Kāvaṣeya, who is fabled to have received his revelation, not through the agency of Vach, Ambhiṇī, and Āditya, but direct from Prājāpati and the self-existing Brahmā. There are two other Vaṁśas, one at the end of the Madhukāṇḍa, the other at the end of the Yājñyavalkīyakāṇḍa. Both are, in reality, varieties of one and the same Vaṁśa, their differences arising from the confusion caused by the recurrence of similar names. That of the Madhukāṇḍa consists of sixty names, only forty-five or forty-six of which have an historical appearance. The principal divine teachers after Brahmā, the Self-existing, are Parameṣṭhin, (Prajāpati ?), Mṛtyu (death), Dadhyach Ātharvaṇa, and the two Aśvins.

At the end of the Khila-kaṇḍa a fifth list is found, not a Vaṁśa, but a list of teachers who handed down the Vaṁśa. This seems to be ascribed to Uddalaka Aruneya, the teacher of Yājñavalkya, as its original author.

List of Teachers from the Śatapatha-brāhmaṇa

Madhukāṇḍa.	*YājṃyavalMya-kaṇḍa*
1. Śaurpaṇāyya सौर्पणाय्य:	The same as in the Madhu-kāṇḍa,
2. Gautama गौतम:	
3. Vātsya वात्स्य:	
4. Vātsya and Pārāśarya[257] वात्स्यपाराशरौ	
5. Sāṅkṛtya and Bhāra-dvāja सांकृत्यभारद्वाजौ	
6. Audavāhi and Śāṇḍilya औदवाहिशाण्डिल्यौ	
7. Vaijavāpa and Gautama वेजवापगौतमौ	
8. Vaijavāpāyana and Vaiṣṭapureya वैजवापायन-वैष्टपुरेयौ	
9. Śāṇḍilya and Rauhiṇā-yana शाण्डिल्य-रौहिणयनौ	
10. Śaunaka and Ātreya and Raibhya शौनकात्रेय-रैभ्या:	Jaivantayana instead of Ātreya शौनक:, जैवन्तायन:, रैभ्य:
11. Pautimāṣyāyana and Kauṇḍinyāyana पौतिमाष्यायण-कौण्डिन्यायनौ	The same as in the Madhu kāṇḍa. Kauṇḍinyau कौण्डिन्यौ Aurṇāvābhāh और्णवाभ:
12. Kauṇḍinya कौण्डिन्य:	Kauṇḍinya कौण्डिन्य:
13. Kauṇḍinya कौण्डिन्य:	Kauṇḍinya कौण्डिन्य:
14. Kauṇḍinya and Agni-veśya कौण्डिन्याग्निवेश्यौ:	Kauṇḍinya and Agniveśya कौण्डिन्याग्निवेश्यौ:

15. Saitava (सैतवः)	Saitava vesya (सैतवः)
16. Pārāśarya (पाराशर्यः)	The same as in the Madhu-kāṇḍa.
17. Jātukarṇya (जातूकर्ण्यः)	
18. Bhāradvāja (भारद्वाजः)	
19. Bhāradvāja and Āsurāyaṇa and Gautama Āsurāyaṇa (भारद्वाजासुरायणगौतमाः)	Saukarāyaṇa.
20. Bhāradvāja (भारद्वाजः)	
21. Vaijavāpāyana (वैजवापायनः)	
22. Kauśikayani (कौशिकायनिः)	Valākākauśika (वलाकाकौशिकः)
23. Ghṛtakauśika. (घृतकौशिकः)	
24. Pārāśaryāyaṇa. (पाराशर्यः)	
25. Pārāśarya. (पाराशर्यायणः)	desunt.
26. Jātūkarṇya. (जातूकर्ण्यः)	
27. Bhāradvāja. (भारद्वाजः)	
28. Bhāradvāja and Āsurāyaṇa and Yāska. (भारद्वाजासुरायणौ यास्कश्च)	
29. Traivaṇi. (त्रैवणिः)	Traivaṇi.
30 Aupajandhani. (औपजन्घनिः)	Aupajandhani.[288]
31. Āsuri. (आसुरिः)	Āsuri.
32. Bhāradvāja. (भारद्वाजः)	
33. Ātreya. (आत्रेयः)	
34. Māṇṭi. (माण्टिः)	
35. Gautama. (गौतमः)	
36. Gautama. (गौतमः)	
37. Vātsya. (वात्स्यः)	
38. Śāṇḍilya. (शाण्डिल्यः)	
39. Kaiśorya Kāpya. (कैशौर्यकाप्यः)	

40. Kumārahārita. (कुमारहारीतः)
41. Gālava (गालवः)
42. Vidarbhīkauṇḍinya. (वेदर्भीकौण्डिन्यः)
43. Vatsanapāt Bābhrava. (वत्सनपाद्बाभ्रवः)
44. Pathas Saubhara. (पथः सौभरः)
45. Ayāsya Āṅgirasa.(अयास्याङ्गिरसः)
46. Ābhūti Tvāṣṭra.(आभूतित्वाष्ट्रः)
47. Visvarūpa Tvāṣṭra. (विश्वरूपत्वाष्ट्रः)
48. The two Aśvins. (अश्विनौ)
49. Dadhyac Ātharvaṇa.(दध्यङथर्वणः)
50. Atharvan Daiva.(अथर्वणदैवः)
51. Mṛtyu Prādhvaṅsana.(मृत्युप्राध्वंसनः)
52. Prādhvaṅsana. (प्राध्वंसनः)
53. Ekarṣi.(एकर्षि)
54. Viprajitti. (विप्रजित्तिः)
55. Vyaṣṭi. (व्यष्टिः)
56. Sanāru. (सनारुः)
57. Sanātana. (सनातन)
58. Sanaga. (सनगः)
59. Parameṣṭhin.(परमेष्ठी)
60. Brahmā Svayambhu. (ब्रह्मा स्वयम्भूः)

LAST BOOK

1. Bhāradvājī-putra. (भारद्वाजीपुत्रः)
2. Vatsīmāṇḍavl-putra. (वात्सीमाण्डवीपुत्रः)
3. Parāśarī-putra (पाराशरीपुत्रः)
4. Gārgī-putra. (गार्गीपुत्रः)
5. Pārāśarī-kauṇḍinī-putra (पाराशरीकौण्डिनीपुत्रः)
6. Gārgī-putra.(गार्गीपुत्रः)
7. Gārgī-putra. "
8. Bāḍeyī-putra. (वाडेयीपुत्रः)
9. Mauṣikī-putra. (मौषिकीपुत्रः)

10. Hārikarṇī-putra. (हारिकर्णीपुत्रः)
11. Bhāradvājī-putra (भारद्वाजीपुत्रः)
12. Paiṅgī-putra. (पैङ्गीपुत्रः)
13. Śaunakī-putra (शौनकीपुत्रः)
14. Kāśyapī-vālākyā-māṭharī-putra (काश्यपीवालाक्यामाठरीपुत्रः)
15. Kautsī-putra (कौत्सीपुत्रः)
16. Baudhl-putra (बौधीपुत्रः)
17. Śālaṅkayanī-putra (शालाङ्कायनीपुत्रः)
18. Vārshagaṅī-putra. (वार्षगणीपुत्रः)
19. Gautamī-putra. (गौतमीपुत्रः)
20. Ātreyī-putra. (आत्रेशीपुत्रः)
21. Gautamī-putra. (गौतमीपुत्रः)
22. Vatsī-putra. (वात्सीपुत्रः)
23. Bhāradvājī-putra (भारद्वाजीपुत्रः)
24. Pārāśarī-putra. (पाराशरीपुत्रः)
25. Vérkāruṇī-putra (वार्करुणीपुत्रः)
26. Ārtabhāgī-putra (आर्त्तभागीपुत्रः)
27. Śauṅgī-putra. (शौङ्गीपुत्रः)
28. Sāṅkṛtī-putra. (साङ्कृतीपुत्रः)
29. Ālambī-putra. (आलम्बीपुत्रः)
30. Ālambāyanī-putra (आलम्बायनीपुत्रः)
31. Jayantī-putra (जयन्तीपुत्रः)
32. Māṇḍūkayanī-putra (माण्डूकायनीपुत्रः)
33. Māṇḍūkī-putra. (माण्डमकीपुत्रः)
34. *Sāṇḍilī-Putra.* (शाण्डिलीपुत्रः)
35. Rāthītarī-putra (राथीतरीपुत्रःपुत्रः)
36. Krauñcikī-putrau (कौञ्चिकीपुत्रः)
37. Vaidabhṛtī-putra. (वेदभृतीपुत्रः)
38. Bhālukī-purta (भालुकीपुत्रः)

Yāñvalkīya-kāṇḍa

X BOOK

39. Prācinayogī-putra. (प्राचीनयोगीपुत्र:)	
40. Sāñjīvī-putra (साञ्जीवीपुत्र:)	*Sāñjīvī-putra* (साञ्जीवीपुत्र:)
41. Kārśakeyī-putra. कार्षकेयीपुत्र:)	
42. Prāśnī-putra Āsurivāsin. (प्राश्नीपुत्र: आसुरिवासी)	Māṇḍavya. (माण्डव्य:)
43. Āsurāyaṇa. (आसुरायण:)	Kautsa. (कौत्स:)
44. Āsuri. (आसुरि:)	Mahitthi. (महित्थि:)
45. Yājñavalkya, (Vājasaneya Yajnovalkya, Kh).	Vamakakṣayana.
46. Uddāka. (Uddālaka Aruneya Kh.). (उद्यालक आरुणेय:)	Vātsya. (वात्स्य:)
47. Āruṇa. (आरुण:)	*Sāṇḍlya.* (शाण्डिल्य:)
48. Upaveśi. (उपवेशि:)	Kuśri. (कुश्रि:)
49. Kusri. (कुश्रि:)	Yajñavacas[250] Rājāstambayana (यज्ञवचो राजस्तम्बायन:)
50. Vājasravas. (वाजश्रवा:)	*Tura Kāvasheya.*[1] (तुरकावषेय:)
51. Jihvavat Badbyoga. (जिह्वावद्वाध्योग:)	Prājāpati. (प्रजापति:)
52. Āśita VarshaGaṇa. (असितवार्षगण:)	Brahmā Svaymbhu. (ब्रह्मा स्वयम्भू:)
53. Harita Kāśyapa. (हरितकश्यप:)	
54. Silpa Kāśyapa. (शिल्पकश्यप:)	
55. Kāśyapa Naidhruvi. (कश्यपनैध्रुवि:)	
56. Vāc. (वाक्:)	
57. Ambhiṇī. (अम्भिणी:)	
58. Āditya. (आदित्य:)	

KHILA-KĀṆḌA

Sātyākama Jābāla (सत्यकाम: जाबाल:)

Jānaki Āyasthūṇa (जानकिः आयस्थूणः)
Cūḍā Bhagavitti. (चूडभागवितिः)
Madhuka aingya (मधुकपैङ्ग्यः)
Vājasaneya Yājñavalkya, (वाजसनेययाज्ञवल्क्यः)
Uddālaka Aruneya. (उद्यालकारुणेयः)

VAṀŚA OF THE SĀMA-VEDA

1. Śarvadatta Gārgya. (सर्वदत्तगार्ग्यः)
2. Rudrabhūti Drāhyāyaṇi. (रुद्रभूतिः द्राह्यायणिः)
3. Trāta Aiṣumat. (त्रातः ऐषुमतः)
4. Nigada Pārṇavalki. (निगदपार्णवल्किः)
5. Giriśarman Kāṇṭheviddhi. (गिरिशर्मा काण्ठेविद्धिः)
6. Brahmavṛddhi Chandogamāhāki. (ब्रह्मवृद्धिःछन्दोगमाहकिः)
7. Mitrāvarcas Sthairakāyana. (मित्रावर्चाः स्थैरकायन)
8. Supratīta Auluṇḍya. (सुप्रतीत बालुण्डयः)
9. Bṛhaspatīgupta Śāyasthi. (ब्रहस्पतिगुप्तः शायस्थिः)
10. Bhavatrāta Śāyasthi. (भवत्रातः शायस्थिः)
11. Kustuka Sārkarākṣa. (कुस्तुकः सार्कराक्षः)
12. Śravaṇadatta Kauhala. (श्रवणदत्तः कौहलः)
13. Suśārada Śālaṅkāyana. (सुशारदः शालङ्कायनः)
14. Ûrjayat Aupamanyava. (ऊर्जयदौपमन्यवः)
15. Bhānumat Aupamanyava. (भानुमान् औपपमन्यवः) Aryamabhūti Kālabava. (अर्यमभूतिः कालबवः)
16. Ānandaja Chāndhanāyana. (आनन्दजः चान्धन्यायनः) Bhadraśarman Kauśika. (भद्रशर्मा कौशिकः)
17. Śāmba Śārkarākṣa, and Kāmboja Aupamanyava. (शाम्बशार्कराक्षः काम्बाज बौपमन्यवश्च) Pushyayaśas Audavraji. (पुष्ययशाः औदव्रजी)
18. Madragāra Śaungāyani. (मद्रगारः शौङ्गायनिः) Saṅkara Gautama. (शङ्करगौतमः)
19 Sāti Austrākshi. grief: Aryamarādha Gobhila & Pūṣamitra Gobhila

	(अर्यमराधगोभिलपूषमित्रगोभिलौ:)
20. Suśravas Vārṣagaṇya. (सुश्रवा: वार्षगण्य:)	Aśvamitra Gobhila. (अश्वमित्रगोभिल:)
21. Prātarāhṇa Kauhala. (प्रातराह्णकौहल:)	Varuṇamitra Gobhila. (वरुणमित्रगोभिल:)
22. Ketu Vājya (केतुविजय:)	Mūlamitra Gobhila. (मलमित्रगोभिल:)
23. Mitravinda Kauhala (मित्राविन्द: कोहल:)	Vatsamitra Gobhila. (वत्समित्रगोभिल:)
24. Sunītha Kāpaṭava (सुनीथकापटव:)	Gaulgulavīputra Gobhila. (गौलगुलवीपुत्रो: गोभिल:)
25. Sutemanas Śāṇḍilyāyana. (सुतेमना: शाण्डिल्यायन:)	Bṛhadvasu Gobhila (pita) (घृहद्वसुगोभिल: पिता)
26. Anśu Dhānañjayya (अंशुधानञ्जय्य:)	Gobhila (गोभिल:)

27. Amāvāsya Śāṇḍilyayana and Rādha Gautama.
(अमावास्यशाण्डिल्यायनो राधगौतमश्च:)
28. Gātṛ Gautama. (गातृगौतम:)
29. Samvargajit Lāmakāyana. (समवर्गजिल्लामकायन:)
30. Śākadāsa Bhāḍitāyana. (शाकदासो भाड़ितायन:)
31. Vicakṣaṇa Tāṇḍy. (विचक्षणताण्डय:)
32. Gardabhīmukha Śāṇḍilyāyana. (गर्दभीमुख: शाण्ल्यायन:)
33. Udaraśaṇḍilya (the father). (उदरशण्डिल्य: पिता)
34. Atidhanvan Śaunaka and Maśaka Gārgya. अतिधन्वा शौनक: मशकगार्ग्यश्च
35. Sthiraka Gārgya (the father). स्थिरकगार्ग्य: (पिता)
36. Vāśiṣṭha Caikitāneya. वासिष्ठचैकितानेय:
37. Vāśiṣṭha Araihaṇya (a prince) वासिष्ठ: अरैहण्य: (क्षत्रिय:)
38. Sumantra Bābhrava Gautama. सुमनत्रबाभ्रवगौतम:
39. Śūṣa Vāhneya Bhāradvāja. शूषवाहनेयभारद्वाज:
40. Arāla Dārteya Śaunaka. अरालदार्तेयशौनक:

41. Dṛti Aindrota Śaunaka (the father). दृतिः ऐन्द्रोतशौनकः (पिता)

42. Indrota Śaunaka (the father).[1] इन्द्रोतशौनकः (पिता)

43. Vṛṣaśuṣṇa Vātāvata. वृषशुष्णः वातावतः

44. Nikothaka Bhāyajātya. निकोथकभायजात्यः

45. Pratithi Devataratha. प्रतिथिः देवतरथः

46. Devataras Śāvasāyana (the father). देवतराः शावसायनः (पिता)

47. Śavas (the father). शवाः (पिता)

48. Agnibhū Kāśyapa. अग्निभूः काश्यपः

49. Indrabhū Kāśyapa. इन्द्रभूः काश्यपः

50. Mitrabhū Kāśyapa. मित्रभूः काश्यपः

51. Vibhaṇḍaka Kāśyapa (the father). विभण्डककाश्यपः (पिता)

52. Ṛiṣyaśṛṅga Kāśyapa (the father). ऋष्यशृङ्गः काश्यपः

53, Kāśyapa (the father). काश्यपः (पिता)

54, Agni (fire), अग्निः

55. Indra. इन्द्रः

56. Vāyu (wind). वायुः

57. Mṛtyu (dcath), मृत्युः

58. Prajāpati (Lord of Creation). प्रजापतिः

59. Brahmā Svayambhu. ब्रह्मा स्वयम्भूः

It would be difficult to tell how these long strings of names are to be accounted for, whatever system of chronology we adopt. If we were in possession of the *Vaṁśa* of the *Bahvṛcas* and the ancient *Adhvaryus,* we might perhaps see more clearly. But it is important to observe that these two, which are decidedly the two most ancient Vedas, seem to have had no *Vaṁśas* at all. However this may be explained hereafter, certain it is, and these long lists of names teach at least this one thing, that the Brāhmaṇas themselves looked upon the Brāhmaṇa period as a long continued succession of teachers, reaching from the time when these lists were made and received to the most distant antiquity, back to the very dynasties of their gods. If, therefore, we limit the age of the Brāhmaṇas to the two centuries from

600 to 800 B. C, it is more likely that here-after these limits will have to be extended than that they will prove too wide.

THE GOPATHA-BRĀHMAṆA

There is one work which ought to be mentioned before we leave the Brāhmaṇa period, the Gopatha Brāhmaṇa. It is the Brāhmaṇa of the Brahmā-Veda, the Veda of the Atharvāṅgiras' or Bhṛgu-Aṅgiras'. This Veda does not properly belong to the sacred literature of the Brāhmaṇas, and though in later times it obtained the title of the fourth Veda, there was originally a broad distinction between the magic formulas of the Atharvāṅgiras' and the hymns of the *Bahvrohas,* the *Chandogas,* and the *Adhvaryus.* Madhu-sūdana states the case simply and clearly. "The Veda," he says, "is divided into Ṛc, Yajuṣ and Sāman for the purpose of carrying out the sacrifice under its three different forms. The duties of the *Hot?* priests are performed with the Ṛg-veda, those of the *Adhvaryu* priests with the Yajur-veda, those of the *Udgātṛ* priests with the Sāma-veda. The duties of the Brahmā and the sacrificer are contained in all the three. Atharva-veda, on the contrary, is totally different. It is not used for the sacrifice, but only teaches how to appease, to bless, to curse, etc." But although the hymns of the *Atharvans* were not from the first looked upon as a part of the sacred literature of the Brāhmaṇas, the Brāhmaṇa of the Atharvans belong clearly to the same literary period which saw the rise of the other Brāhmaṇas; and though it does not share the same authority as the Brāhmaṇas of the three great Vedas, it is written in the same language, and breathes the same spirit. The MSS. of this work are extremely scarce, and the copy which I use (E. I. H. 2142) is hardly legible. The remarks, therefore, which I have to offer on this work will necessarily be scanty and incomplete.

The original division of the Veda, and of the Vedic ceremonial, was, as we have seen, a threefold division. The Brāhmaṇas speak either of one Veda or of three; of one officiating priest, or of three. *"Trayī vidyā,"* the threefold knowledge, is constantly used in the Brāhmaṇas[261] with reference to their sacred literature. This, however, proves by no means that at the time when the Brāhmaṇas were composed the songs of the Atharvāṅgiras' did not yet exist. It only shows that originally they formed no part of the sacred literature of the Brāhmaṇas. In some of the Brāhmaṇas, the Atharvāṅgiras' are mentioned. The passage translated before (p. 34) shows that at the time when the Śatapatha-brāhmaṇa was composed the songs of the Atharvāṅgiras' were not only known, but had been collected, and had actually obtained the title of Veda. Their original title was the Atharvāṅgiras', or the Bhṛgvāṅgiras', or the *Atharvans,* and these very titles show that songs which could be quoted in such a manner,[262] must have been of ancient date, and must have had a long life in the oral tradition of India. Their proper position with reference to the other Vedas is well marked in a passage of the Taittirīyrāṇyaka (viii. 3.), where the *Yajuṣ* is called the head, the *Reh* the right, the Sāman the other side, the *Adeśa* (the Upaniṣad) the vital breath, and the Atharvāṅgiras' the tail.

The songs known under the name of the Atharvāṅgiras' formed probably an additional part of the sacrifice from a very early time. They were chiefly intended to counteract the influence of any untoward event that might happen during the sacrifice. They also contained imprecations and blessings, and various formulas, such as popular superstition would be sure to sanction at all times and in all countries. If once sanctioned, however, these magic verses would soon grow in importance, nay, the knowledge of all the other Vedas would necessarily become useless without the power of remedying accidents, such as could hardly be avoided in so complicated a ceremonial as that of the Brāhmaṇas. As that power Was believed to reside in the songs of the Athar-vaṅgiras', a knowledge of these songs became necessarily an essential part of the theological learning of ancient India.

According to the original distribution of the sacrificial offices among the four classes of priests, the supervision of the whole sacrifice, and the remedying of any mistake that might have happened belonged to the *Brahmā.* He had to know the three Vedas, to follow in his mind the whole sacrifice, and to advise the other priests on all doubtful points.[263] If it Was the office of the Brahmā to remedy mistakes in the performance of the sacrifice, and if, for that purpose, the formulas of the Atharvāṅgiras' were considered of special efficacy, it follows that it was chiefly the Brahmā who had to acquire a knowledge of these formulas. Now the office of the Brahmā was contested by the other classes of priests. The Bahvṛcas maintain that the office of Brahmā should be held by a Bahvṛcha *(Hotṛ),* the *Adhvaryus* maintain that it belongs to one of their own body, and the *Chandogas* also preferred similar claims. It was evidently the most important office, and in many instances, though not always, it Was held by the *Purohita,* the hereditary family priest. Certain families also claimed a peculiar fitness for the office of *Brahmā,* such as the Vasiṣṭhas and Viśvāmitras. (See p. 82).

Because a knowledge of the songs of the Atharvāṅgiras' was most important to the Brahmā or *Purohita*[164] these songs themselves, when once admitted to the rank of a Veda, were called the Veda of the Brahmā, or the Brahmā-veda. In the Gopatha-brāhmaṇa the title of the Brahmā-veda does not occur.[265] But the songs of the Atharvāṅgiras[1] are mentioned there. They are called both Ātharvaṇa-veda (i. 5.), and Āṅgirasa-veda (i. 8.), and they are repeatedly represented as the proper Veda for the *Brahmā.* Thus we read (iii.1.): "Let a man elect a *Hotṛ* who knows the Ṛc, an *Adhvaryu* who knows the *Yajus,* an *Udgātṛ* who knows the Sāman, a Brahmā who knows the Atharvāṅgiras'." It seems in fact the principal object of the Gopatha to show the necessity of four Vedas. A carriage, we are told, does not proceed with less than four wheels, an animal does not Wālk with less than four feet, nor will the sacrifice be perfect with less than four Vedas.[266] But although a knowledge of the fourth Veda is thus represented as essential to the *Brahmā,* it is never maintained that such a knowledge would be sufficient by itself to enable a person to perform the offices of a *Brahmā.* Like the Chandogas (R.v. Bh. vol. i. page 3.), the Atharvānikas also declare that the whole sacrifice is performed twice, once in words, and once in thought. It is performed in words by the *Hotṛ, Udgātṛ* and *Adhvaryu* separately; it is performed in thought by the Brahmā alone (Gop. Br. vol. üi. 2.). The *Brahmā,* therefore, had to know all the three Vedas and in addition the formulas of the

Atharvāṅgiras'. It is a common mistake in later writers to place the Atharva-veda co-ordinate with the other Vedas, and to represent it as the Veda of the *Brahmā*. The Gopatha-brāhmaṇa raises no such claims; when it describes the type of the sacrifice, it says :

Agni (fire) was the Hotṛ,

Vāyu (wind) the Adhvaryu,

Sūrya (sun) the Udgātṛ,

Chandrāmas (moon) the Brahmā,

Parjanya (rain) the Sadasya,

Oshadhi and Vānaspati (shrubs and trees) the Chamasadhvaryus (चमसाध्वर्यू)

The Viśve Deva were the Hotṛakas,

The Atharvāṅgiras', the Goptrs or protectors,

In another place (v. 24.) the persons engaged in the sacrifice are enumerated as follows :

Hotṛ, Maitrāvaruṇa, Achāvāka, Gravastut (Ṛg-veda), 1-4.

Adhvaryu, Pratiprasthātṛ, Neshṭṛ, Unnetṛ (Yajur-veda), 5–8.

Udgātṛ, Prastotṛ, Subrahmānya, Pratihartṛ (Sāma-veda), 9–12.

Brahmā, Brāhmaṇachhansin, Potr, Agnīdhra (Atharvaṅgiras'), 13–16.

Sadasya, 17.

Patnī dīkṣitā (the wife), 18.

Śamitṛ (the immolator), 19.

Gṛhapati (the lord), 20.

Aṅgiras, 21.

Here we see that besides the four Brāhmaṇa-priests to whom a knowledge of the Atharvāṅgiras' is recommended, there were other priests who are called *Gopt's, i. e.* protectors or Aṅgiras', and whose special office it was to protect the sacrifice by means of the magical formulas of the Atharvāṅgiras', against the effects of any accidents that might have happened. Such was the original office of the Atharvans at the Vedic sacrifices, and a large portion of the Gopatha-brāhmaṇa (i. 13; i. 22.) is taken up with what is called the Virişta (विरिष्ट), the Una, (ऊन) the Yatayama (यातयाम) or whatever else the defects in a sacrifice are called which must be made good (सन्धान) by certain hymns, verses, formulas, or exclamations. There are long discussions on the proper way of pronouncing these salutary formulas, on their hidden meaning, and their miraculous power. The syllable Om, the so-called Vyahrtis (व्याहृतय:) and other strange sounds are recommended for various purposes, and works such as the Sarpa-veda, Piśāca-veda, Āsurā-veda, Itihāsa-veda, Purāṇa-veda, are referred to as authorities (i. 10.).

Although, however, the Gopatha-brāhmaṇa is more explicit on the chapter of accidents than the Brāhmaṇas of the other Vedas, the subject itself is by no means peculiar to it. The question of expiation or penance *(prāyaścitta)* is fully discussed in the other Vedas and remedies are suggested for all kinds of mishaps. The ceremonial in general is discussed in the Gopatha in the same manner as in the other Brāhmaṇas. There is, in fact, very little, if any, difference between the Gopatha and the other Brāhmaṇas, and it is not easy to discover any traces of its more recent origin. It begins with a theory of the creation of the world, such as we find in many places of the other Brāhmaṇas. There is nothing remarkable in it except one idea, which I do not remember to have seen elsewhere. *Brāhmn* (neuter), the self-existing, burns with a desire to create, and by means of his heat, sweat is produced from his forehead, and from all the pores of his body. These streams of sweat are changed into Water. In the Water *Brahmān* perceives his own shadow, and falls in love with it. This, however, is only one phase in the progress of creation, which is ultimately to lead to the birth of Bhṛgu and Atharvan. Atharvan is represented as the real Prājāpati, or Lord of Creation. From him twenty classes of poets, the same as those mentioned in the Anukra-manl, are produced, and their poems are said to have formed the Ātharvaṇa-veda.

Then follows a new series of creation. *Brahman* creates the earth from his feet, the sky from his belly, heaven from his skull. He then creates three gods : Agni (fire) for the earth, Vāyu (wind) for the sky, and Āditya (sun) for the heaven. Lastly, he creates the three Vedas : the Ṛg-veda proceeds from Agni, the Yajur-veda from Vāyu, the Sāma-veda from Āditya. The three *Vyāhṛtis* also, or sacred syllables *(bhūḥ bhuvaḥ svaḥ),* are called into existence. It is important to remark, that nothing is here said of the fourth Veda; its origin is described separately, and its second name, Āṅgirasa, is explained in detail. We look in vain for any traces of more modern ideas in the Gopatha-brāhmaṇa, till we come to the end of the fifth Prapathaka. This is the last Prapathaka of the Gopatha-brāhmaṇa, properly so called. The text is very corrupt, but it seems to contain an admission that, besides the twenty-one sacrifices which are acknow-ledged in all the Vedic writings, the Aṅgiras' had some new sacrifices of their own.[267] That the Gopatha-brāhmaṇa was composed after the schism of the Carakas and Vājasaneyins, after the completion of the Vājasaneyi-saṁhitā, may be gathered from the fact that where the first lines of the other Vedas are quoted in the Gopatha, the first line of the Yajur-veda, is taken from the Vājasaneyins, and not from the Taittirīyas.

The five Prapāṭhakas which we have hitherto discussed, form only the first part of the Gopatha-brāhmaṇa. There is a second part, called the Uttara-brāhmaṇa which consists of more than five Prapāṭhakas. It is impossible to fix their exact numbers as the MS. breaks off in the middle of the sixth book. It is likewise reckoned as belonging to the Atharva-veda, and quoted by the name of Gopatha. In this second part we meet repeatedly with long passages which are taken from other Brāhmaṇas. Sometimes they coincide literally, sometimes the differences are no greater than what we find in different *Śākhās* of the same Brāhmaṇa. Thus the legend of the sacrifice running away from the gods, which is told in the Aitareya-brāhmaṇa, i. 18, is repeated in the Uttara-brāhmaṇa, ii. 6. The story of Vasiṣṭha receiving a special revelation from Indra which is told in the Taittirīyaka[268] (ūi. 5. 2.) is repeated in the Uttara-brāhmaṇa, (ū. 13.). And here a difference occurs which is characteristic. The Taittirīyas relate that owing to this special revelation which Vasiṣṭha had received from Indra, the Vasiṣṭhas had always acted as *Purohitas*. So far both the Taittirīyas and the Atharvans agree. But when the Taittirīyas contiérent that therefore a Vasiṣṭha is to be chosen a *Brahmā,* the Atharvans demur. The sentence is left out, and it is inculcated on the contrary that the office of Brahmā belongs by right to a Bhṛgu, or to one cognisant of the songs of the Atharvāṅgiras."[269]

If, as we have .little reason to doubt, these passages in the second part of the Gopatha-brāhmaṇa were simply copied from other Brāhman as, we should have to assign to the Uttara-brāhmaṇa a later date than to the Brāhmaṇas of the other Vedas. But this would in no way affect the age of the original Gopatha-brāhmaṇa. In it there is nothing to show that it was a more modern composition than, for instance, the Śatapatha-brāhmaṇa. In the saṁhitā of the Atharva-veda we find something very similar.[270] Here also the last, if not the last two books, betray a more modern origin, and are full of passages taken fiom the Ṛg-veda. The Anukrāmanl calls the nineteenth book the Brahmākāṇḍa and the hymns of the last book *'yajñīyaśaṁsana-mantras* (यज्ञियशंसनमन्त्राः) *i.e.* hymns for sacrificial recitations. The collection of the saṁhitā Was probably undertaken simaltaneously with the composition of the Gopatha-brāhmaṇa, at a time when through the influence of some of the families of the Bhṛgus and Aṅgiras' the magic formulas of the Atharvans had been acknowledged as an essential part of the solemn ceremonial. With the means at present at our disposal it is impossible to trace the history of these verses back to the earlier period of Vedic literature, and I shall not return to them again. What is known of their origin and character has been stated by Professor Whitney in several very careful articles in the Journal of the American Oriental Society.[271] "The Ātharvaṇa," he says, "is like the *Ṛc,* historical and not a liturgical collection. Its first eighteen books, of which alone'it was originally composed, are arranged upon a like system throughout; the length of the hymns, and not either their subject or their alleged authorship, being the guiding principle: those of about the same number of verses are combined together into books, and the books made up of the shorter hymns stand first in order. A sixth of the mass, however, is not metrical, but consists of longer or shorter prose pieces, nearly akin in point of language and style to passages of the Brāhmaṇas. Of the remainder, or metrical portion, about one-sixth is also found among the hymns of the *Ṛch,* and mostly in the tenth book of the latter: the rest is peculiar to the Ātharvaṇa". And again,[272] "The most prominent characteristic feature of the Ātharvaṇa is the multitude of incantations which it contains; these are pronounced either by the person who is himself to be benefitted, or more often, by the sorcerer for him, and are directed to the procuring of the greatest variety of desirable ends; most frequently, perhaps, long life, or recovery from grievous sickness, is the object sought: then a talisman, such as a necklace, is sometimes given, or in very numerous cases some plant endowed with marvellous virtues is to be the immediate external means of the cure; further, the attainment of wealth or power is aimed at, the downfall of enemies, success in love or in play, the removal of petty pests, and so on, even down to the growth of hair on a bald pate."

FOOT NOTE

1 Sāyaṇa on the TaittiriyāĀraṇyaka.
अरण्याध्ययनादेतदारण्यकमितीर्यते।
अरण्ये तदधीयीतेत्येवं वाक्यं प्रचक्ष्यते।।
And again, एतदारण्यकं सर्व नाव्रती श्रोतुमर्हति।। Part of the Taittiriyāraṇyaka are exempted from the restriction that they should be read in the forest only : नारण्याधीतिनियम: सावित्रादिचतुष्टये। and hence they are ranged with the Brāhmaṇas अतस्तद्ब्राह्मणग्रन्थे श्रुतं वयाख्यातमप्यद:।।

2. P. 112. पञ्चमारण्यक औष्णिहतृचाशीतिरिति खण्डे शौनकेन सूत्रितं सुरूपकृत्नुमूतय इति त्रीण्यन्द्रं त्रीण्यन्द्रं सानसिं रयिमिति द्वे इति। These words occur in the AitareyāĀraṇyaka, v. 2. 11. सुरूपकृत्नुमूतय इति त्रीण्येन्द्रं सानसिं रयिमिति सूक्ते। Other passages quoted by Sāyaṇa from this Āraṇyaka can always be identified in the AitareyāĀraṇyaka. Cf. Colebrooke,Misc. Essays, i. 46.

3. Mahābhārata i. 258. : "This body of the Mahābhārata (the index) is truth and immortality ; it is like new butter from curds, like the Brāhmaṇa among men, like the Āraṇyaka the Vedas, like nectar from medicinal plants, like the sea, best among lakes, like the cow, the highest among animals." Thus the Upaniṣad is called the essence of the Veda; Śatap.-brāhm. x. 3. 5. 12. तस्य वा एतस्य यजुषो रस एवोपनिषत्।

4. This is taken from Colebrooke's extracts from the Pūrva-mīmāṁsā ; a system of philosophy of which it would be most desirable to have a complete edition. (Miscellaneous Essays, i. 307.) Dr. Goldstücker of Königsberg, has collected large materials for such a work, and I trust he will shortly find

an opportunity of publishing the important results of his studies.

5. Vedānta is used, but not yet in its technical sense, Taittirīya-āraṇyaka, x. 12.; a verse frequently repeated elsewhere.
   वेदान्तविज्ञानसुनिश्चितार्थाः संन्यासयोगाद्यतयः शुद्धसत्त्वाः।
   ते ब्रह्मलोकेषु परान्तकाले परामृताः परिमुच्यन्ति सर्वे॥
6. Mahīdhara maintains that some parts of the Upaniṣad were aimed at the Buddhists, who denied the existence of an intelligent Self, called life a water busble, and knowledge intoxication.
7. Colebrooke, Essays, i. 92.
8. Pāṇ. iii. 4. 72. comment : Upāsi to gurum bhavān; and upāsito gurur bhavatā.
9. In this sense Upaniṣad is frequently used in the plural, and signifies sessions.
10. Chāndogya-upaniṣadā, i.*1.9. यदेव विद्यया करोति श्रद्धयोपनिषदा तदेव वीर्यवत्तरम्। "What a man peforms with knowledge, trust, and faith, that is effectual."
11. Śvetāvatara-upaniṣadā, ed. Röer, Bibliotheca Indica vii. 339.
12. II. 23. It is also found in the Muṇḍaka.
13. *Pravacana* tradition, the Brāhmaṇas; see p.97 ; Fn. Commentary; "*eka*-veda-svīkaraṇena," "by learning one Veda."
14. Translation of the Kena-upaniṣadā by Rammohan Roy, Calcutta, 1816, p. 6.
15. किं कारणं ब्रह्म कुतः स्म जाता जीवाम केन क सम्प्रतिष्ठिताः।
    अधिष्ठिताः केन सुखेतरेषु वर्तामहे ब्रह्मविदो व्यवस्थाम्॥
    कालः स्वभावो नियतिर्यदृच्छा भूतानि योनिः पुरुष इति चिन्तयाः।
    संयोग एषां न त्वात्मभावादात्माप्यनीशः सुखदुःखहेतोः॥
16. मायां तु प्रकृतिं विद्यान्मायिनं तु महेश्वरम्।
    तस्यावयवभूतैस्तु व्याप्तं सर्वमिदं जगत्॥
17. नुन श्वेताश्वतरोपनिषदि मायायाः प्रकृतित्वं परात्मनस्तन्नियन्तृत्वं श्रूयते यान्तु० इति। नायं दोषः। मायायाः परात्मशक्तित्वेन शक्तिमतोऽप्यात्मनः कृतित्वावश्यम्भवात्। दहनशक्तियुक्तेऽग्नौ दाहकत्वे व्यवहारदर्शनात्। आत्मक्तित्वं च मायायास्तस्यामेवोपनिषदि श्रुतं, 'ते ध्यानयोगानुगता अपश्यन्देवाशक्तिं स्वगुणैर्निगूढामिति'॥
    Bibl. Ind. vii. 56.
18. *Puruṣa* is body rather than man, Mādhava तत्र पुरुषशब्देन शिरःपाण्याद्याकृतियुक्तो देहोऽभिधीयते। स च देहो ब्रह्मादि बहुप्रकारः॥
19. Chānd.-up. vi. 2.; Bibl. Ind. iii. 394. सत्त्वेव सोम्येदमग्र एकमद्वितीयम्। तदैक्षत बहु स्यां प्रजायेयेति। तत्तेजऽसृजत। तत्तेज ऐक्षस्यां प्रजायेयेति तदपोऽसृजत॥
20. See Goldstücker's Dictionary, s. v. Mādhava says : अश्नुत इति वा, न क्षरतीति वा परमात्मानमाचष्टे॥
21. Chhānd.-up. vi. 1. तद्धैक आहुरसदेवेदम्र आसौदेकमेवाद्वितीयं अस्मादसतः सज्जायेत।
22. Ward, A view of the History, Literature, and Mythology of the Hindus, ii. 61.

23. Ward, loco cit. p. 61.

24. W. Elliot, Journal of the As. Soc. of Bengal, 1851, p. 607.

25. The Maitreyī-upaniṣadā (29. 89.) is probably meant for the Dialogue between Yājñāvalkya and Maitreyī in the BṛhadāĀraṇyaka. The Śāṇḍilya-upaniṣ adā (57. 105.) seems to be a portion of the Chāndogya-upaniṣadā.

26. Oupnekhat, Id est, Secretum tegendum : opus ipsa in India raūssimum continens antiṇuam et arcanam, seu theologicam et philosophicam doctrinam, e quatuor sacris Indorum libris, Rak beid, Djedjer baid, Sam baid, Atharban baid, excerptam; ad verbam, e Persico idiomate, Samskreticis vocabulis intermixto, in Latinum conversum : Dissertationibus et Annotationibus difficiliora explanantibus, illustratum ; studio et opera Anṇuetil Duperron, Indicopleustas. Argentorati, typis et impensis fratrum Levrault, vol. i. 1801 : vol. ii. 1802.

    Duperron received a MS. of the Persian translation of the Upanibhads from M. Gentil, the French resident at the court of Saudjaēēdaulah. It was brought from Bengal to France by M. Bernier, in the year 1775. Duperron, after receiving another MS., collated the two, and translated the Persian into French (not published) and into literal Latin.

    The Persian translation, of which several other MSS. exist, bears the following title in Duperron's translation : "Hanc interpretationem TSD Oupneknathai ṇuorumvis ṇuatuor librorum Beid, ṇuod, designatum cum secreto magno (per secretum magnum) est, et integram cognitionem luminis luminum, his Fakir sine tristitia (Sultan) Muhammad Dara Schakoh ipse, cum significatione recta, cum sinceritate, in tempore sex mensium, (postremo die, secundo rov Schonbeh, vigesimo,) sexto mensis TOV Rāmazzan, anno 1067 rov Hedjri (Christi, 1657) in urbe Delhi, in mansione nakhe noudeh, cum absolutione ad finem fecit perventre."

    The MS. was copied by Ātmā Ram in the year 1767 A. D. Duperron adds: Absolutum est hoc Apographum versionis Latinæ των quinquaginta Oupnekhatha, ad verbum, e Persico idiomate, Samscreticis vocabulis intermixto, factas, die 9 Octobris, 1795, 18 Brumaireanni 4. Reipubl. Gall, Parisiis.

27. Elphinstone, History of India, ū. 446. An earlier instance of a translation of the Upaniṣads is mentioned in Elliot's Historians of India, i. 260. "Abdul Kadir, author of the Tari-khbadaum, who died at the close of the 16th century, says that he was called upon to translate the Atharvana-veda from the Hindi, which he excused himself from doing on account of the exceeding difficulty of the style and abstruseness of meaning ; upon which the task devolved on Hajt Ibrahim Sirhindi, who accomplished it satisfactorily."

29. Some of the most modern Upaniṣads are confessedly the works of Gauḍapāda, Śaṅkara, and other more recent philosophers.

29. See Muṇḍaka-up-ed. Röer.

30. This can only mean the Bṛhadāraṇyaka, as the commentator also observes.

31. Yājñ. Dh. iii. 110.

    ज्ञेयं चारण्यकमहं यदादित्यादवाप्तवान्।
    योगशास्त्रं च मत्प्रोक्तं ज्ञेयं योगमभीप्सता।।

    "He who wishes to attain Yoga (union with the Divine Spirit) must know the Āraṇyaka, which I have received from ditya, and,the Yoga-śāstra, which I have taught." I thought, at first, that there might have been old Dharma-Sūtras of Yājñavalkya, and that the versifier of these Sūtras took this sentence simply from the Sūtras. I have not yet found, however, Yājñavalkya-suttas on Ācāra. The so called Vaiṣṇava-dharma-śāstra or Srī-bhagavad-Viṣṇu-saṁhitā, which has been printed at Calcutta, contains large portions of Sūtras which have been worked up in a very crude manner into a law treatise. The whole chapter on the anatomy of the human body, which in the Yajūavalklya Code precedes the verse in question (iii-110), a chapter which does not stand in the Mānava code, exists, still in prose, in the Viṣṇu-saṁhitā (fol. 28. a. line 11. The simile of the lamp, also, representing the mind in the middle of the body, is borrowed by the editor of the Yajñavalkiya Code from the Viṣṇu-saṁhitā (fol. 29. a. line 11. Yet, although the Viṣṇu-saṁhitā, like the Code of Yājñavalkya, goes on describing the Yoga, no mention is made here of the Āraṇyaka, nor does the author speak of himself in the first person, as the author of the metrical Code does.

32. In the same way it might be said that the Ṛg-veda-saṁhitā could not have been collected before the second century after Christ, because the word Niṣka occurs in the hymns. *Niṣka* is a weight of gold or gold in general, and it certainly has not satisfactory etymology in Sanskrit. Nothing seems to be more likely than that it should be derived from Kaniṣka, the Sanskrit name of Kanerki, as we speak of a "Sovereign" the French of a "Louis". The first syllable Ka may be taken as the usual royal prefix, particularly as Fahian calls the same king Kanika and Nika. (Cf. Reinaud Mamoirs surl'Inde, p. 76.) Yet nobody would draw from this the conclusion that the Veda was written after the time of Kaniṣka. If Niṣka be really derived from the name Kaṇiṣka, Kaṇiṣka must have been the name or title of more ancient kings, whose money became known in India. But Niṣka may have a very different etymology, and at all events it does not furnish any solid basis for chronological conclusions. Nishka does once occur in Pāṇini's Sūtras, v. 2. 119 ; and it is frequently quoted as an example. Pan. iv. 3. 156.

    निष्केण क्रीतं नैष्किकम्। निष्कस्य विकार: नैष्किक:। द्विनिष्का।

    Pāṇini. i 4. 87. उप निष्के कार्षापणम्। v. 2. 119. नैष्कशतिक:। vi. 2. 55. निष्कमाला। iv. 3. 153. हाटको निष्क:। Cf. v. 1. 37.

33. Indische Alterthumskunde, i. 130.; Schwanbeck, Me-gasthenis Indica, p. 106.

34. See page 99 ff.

35. I find that Harisvamin also, in his commentary on the Śatapatha-Brāhmaṇa, quotes the Dakṣinatyas and Saurāṣṭras together with the Kāṇvas, as authorities on Vedic subjects. See Dr. Weber's Ind. Studien; i. 77. In the same place Dr. Weber attempts to prove the late origin of this work by the contraction of "sa indraḥ into sendrah" This contraction, however, occurs already in the Ṛg-veda-saṁhitā. See also Pāṇ, vi. i. 134.

36. The first Āraṇyaka consists of five Adhyāyas and twenty-two Khaṇḍas. The second Āraṇyaka consists of seven Adhyāyas and twenty-six Khaṇḍas. The Upaniṣad begins with the fourth Adhyāya and the twenty-first Khanda. The third Āraṇyaka consists of two Adhyāyas and twelve Khaṇḍas. The fourth Āraṇyaka consists of one Adhyāya and one Khanda (ascribed to Āśvalāyana in Ṣadguruśiṣya's commentary on the Sarvānukrama.) The fifth Āraṇyaka consists of three Adhyāyas and fourteen Khaṇḍas (ascribed to Śaunaka).

37. Miscllaneous Essays, i. 46. p.

38. A Kumārī gandharva-gṛhītā is quoted as an authority in the Kauṣītaki-brāhmaṇa, and it is explained by "viśeṣābhijñā" Kauṣ.Br. ii. 9.; Ait. Br. v. 29, Ind. Studien, i. 84. 217.

39. IV. 2. 129.

40. Ait-ār, iii. i.; ibid, i. 11. Upaniṣasāda,

41. Ait.-ar. ii. 9.

42. "भूर्भुवः स्वरित्येता वाव व्याहृतय इमे त्रयो वेदाः, भूरित्येव ऋग्वेदः, भुव इति यजुर्वेदः स्वरिति सामवेदः।" [Ait.-ar. ii. 10]

43. Ṛg-Veda-bhāṣya-Bhūmikā, p. 11.

44. According- to Madhusūdana's view, the Brāhmaṇas consist of three parts ; of commandments, additional explanations, and Vedānta doctrines, the latter being more particularly represented by the Upanisbads. The same author speaks of four classes of commandments, "A commandment may consist,' he says, "either in a simple definition '(the oblation to Agni is given in eight cups,') ; or it may include the aim ('he who wishes for life in heaven may perform the sacrifice of the new and full moon)' ; or it may detail the means by which the sacrifice is performed ('let him sacrifice with rice') ; or it may contain all this together."

45. Aitareya-Br. i. 1. अग्निर्वै देवानामवमो विष्णुः परमः etc. Kauṣ.-br. vii. 1. अग्निर्वै देवानामवरार्द्ध्यः etc. Ait.-brāh. ii. 2.=Kauṣ.-br. x. 2.; ii. 6 = x. 4 (Śāṅkh-sūtra, v. 17.); ii 3 = xii. 1.

46. Maitreyī-brāhmaṇa is the title given to that portion of the Bṛhadāraṇyaka which contains the dialogue between Yājñavalkya and Maitreyī. The Saulabhant Brāhmaṇani, quoted by "Āśvalāyana and Pāṇini as modern com-

positions, may refer to sections containing a dialogue similar to that between Janaka and Sulabha, which exists in the Mahābhārata. ūI. v. 11,854 Cf. Lassen, Irid. Alterth. xv.note. According to Pāṇini, however, they ought to be taken as Brāhmaṇas composed by Sulabha.

47. Quoted as such by Yājñikadeva on Kāty. 2.5. 18,; 6, 6, 25. Weber, Ind. Stud. i. 230.

48. ब्राह्मणानि हि यानि अष्टौ सरहस्यानि अधीयते छन्दोगास्तेषु सर्वेषु न कश्चिन्नियत स्वरः।

49. P. xxvii. Note.

50. See also "A Catalogue Raisonée, (sic) of Oriental Manuscripts in the Library of the late College Fort St. George," by the Rev. W. Taylor, Madras, 1857, p. 69.

51. The Vaṁśa-brāhmaṇa has lately been printed, with some valuable remarks, by Prof. A. Weber, Ind. Stud. iv. 371.

52. Dvivedagaṅga explains शुक्लानि यजूंषि by शुद्धानि, यद्वा ब्राह्मणेनामिश्रितमन्त्रात्मकानि।

53. विद्यारण्यश्रीपादैर्व्याख्यातत्वेनाध्वर्यवं क्वचिद्धौत्रं क्वचिदित्यव्यवस्थया बुद्धिमालिन्य-हेतुत्वात्तद्यजुः कृष्णमीर्यते।। Rāmakṛṣṇa's Saṅskāra-gaṇapati. Weber, Ind. Stud. i. 27. 84.

* "वायव स्थ, उपायव स्थ"

54. Cf. Sāyaṇa, Ṛg-veda-bhāshya, p. 12.; Śātapatha-brāhmaṇa, i. 7. 3. तस्मादाह वायव स्थेत्युपायव स्थेत्यु हैक आहुरूप हि द्वितीयोऽयतौति तदु तथा न ब्रूयात्।। In the commentary on Baudhāyana's Sūtras, a passage from a Brāhmaṇa is quoted, which may have belonged to the Baudhāyanīya-śākhā. इषे त्वोर्जे त्वेति शाखामाच्छिनत्ति वायव स्थोपायव स्थेति वत्सानपाकरोति।।

The Baudhāyana-sūtras enjoin the first sentence for male calves, the second for female ones, वाचस स्थेति पुंस, उपायव स्थेति स्त्रियः।

55. शुक्लानि यजूंषि भगवान्याज्ञवल्क्यो यतः प्राप तं विवस्वन्तम्।

56. आदित्यानीमानि शुक्लानि यजूंषि वाजसनेयेन याज्ञवल्क्येनाख्यायन्ते।।

57. See Pāṇ. v. 4. 105, on the purport of this difference.

58. According to the forty-eighth Atharva-pariśishṭa, the thirty-second verse of the twenty-third Adhyāya would be the last verse of the Saṁhitā. See Weber. Ind. Stud, iv, p. 432.

59. According to the Mitākṣarā commentary on Yājñavalkya's Dharma-śāstra, xxxvi-1. forms the beginning of an Āraṇyaka. Weber, Vorlesungen, p. 103.

60. A similar ingenious remark has been made by the same savant with regard to the Aitareya and Kauṣītaki, or, as he calls it, Śāṅkhāyana-brāhmaṇa. The former consists of forty, the latter of thirty Adhyāyas, and it is not unlikely

that the rule in Pāṇini, v. 1. 62, how to form the names of Brāhmaṇas, consisting of thirty and forty Adhyāyas, had special reference to these works, The names are "traiṁśāni and chātvāriṁśāni brāhmaṇāni*; the explanation, "triṁśad adhyāyāḥparimāṇam eṣām brāhmāṇanām."

त्रैंशानि च चात्वारिंशानि ब्राह्मणानि।
त्रिंशदध्याया: परिमाणमेषां ब्राह्मणानाम्।'

61. Pāṇ. iv. 3, 116. कृते ग्रन्थे।। Kaiyyaṭa says that this Sūtra does not belong to Pāṇini. See page 94.

62. Pāṇ. iv. 3. 115 उपज्ञाते Bhāṣya : विनोपदेशेन ज्ञातम्। iv. 3. 101, तेन प्रोक्तम्। Bhāṣya : यत्तेन प्रोक्तं न च तेन कृतम्।

63. Cf, iv. 3. 101 ; iv. 2.64.

64. Cf. Pāṇ. iv. 3. 108.

65. Cf. Pāṇ. iv. 2. 66. छन्दांसि ब्राह्मणानि च प्रोक्त प्रत्यययानान्यच्येतृवेदितु-प्रत्ययं विना न प्रयोक्तव्यानि।।

66. That the Kaṭhas were an old Caraṇa possessing their own tradition and laws, is seen from the 11th Vārttīka to Pāṇ. iv. 3. 120. and from Pāṇ. iv. 3. 126.

67. Pāṇ. iv. 3.105. याज्ञवल्क्यादिभ्य: प्रतिषेधस्तुल्यकालत्वात्।

68. There is no Gaṇa, Yājñavalkyādiḥ.

69. Cf. Pāṇ. iv. 2. 62.

70. The Anubrāhmaṇinaḥ (अनुब्राह्मणिन:) are mentioned in the Nidāna-Sūtra belonging to the Sāmaveda. Cf Ind. Stud. i. 45.

71. Ancient Chandas (Saṁhttā-śākhās) are those of the Kaṭhas, Carakas, Maudas, and Paippalādas, Śaunakins, Vajasaneyins, etc., iv 2- 65. Ancient Brāhmaṇas are those of the Bhāllavins, Taittirīyas, Vāratantavīyas, Khāṇḍikīyas, Aukhīyas; the lambins, Pālaṅgins, Kāmalins, Ārcābhins, ruṇins, Tāṇdins, Śyāmāyanins, Kahas, and Kālāpas (these descended from the nine pupils of Vaiśampāyana); the Hāridrāviṅs, Taumburaviṇs, Aulapins, and Chāgileyins (these derived their origin from the four pupils of Kalāpin); the Śāyāyanins. Old Kalpas are those of the Kāśyapins, Kauśikins, the Paiṅgī and Āruṇaparāji Kalpaḥ. Old Sūtras are those of the Pārāśarins, Śailālins Karmandins, and Kṛśāśvins.

72. Indische Studien, i. 393.

73. Colebrooke has taken a different view with respect to the Sūtras. He says, "But those numerous Śākhās did not differ so widely from each other as might be inferred from the mention of an equal number of Saṁhitās, or distinct collections of texts. In general, the various schools of the same Veda seem to have used the same assemblage of prayers; they differed more in their copies of the precepts or Brāhmaṇas; and some received into their canon of scripture portions which do not appear to have been acknowledged

by others. Yet the chief difference seems always to have been the use of particular rituals taught in aphorism (*sūtras*) adopted by each school; and these do not constitute a portion of the Veda, but, like grammar and astronomy, are placed among its appendages.-Misc. Essays, i. 18.

74. तैत्तिरीयके समाम्नाये समानाध्ययने नाना सूत्राणि। तस्मादपि शाखामेद:।। तथा चैकस्यां तैत्तिरीयशाखायां समानपाठायां सूत्रभेदादवान्तरशाखाभेद:।।

75. Kumārīla, i. 3.

    वेदादृतेऽपि कुर्वन्ति कल्पै: कर्माणि याज्ञिका:।
    न तु कल्पैर्विना केचिन्मन्त्रब्राह्मणमात्रकात्।।

76. Kumārīla, i. 3. यत्त किमर्थं वेदवाक्यान्येव नोपसङ्गृहीतानीति। सम्प्रदायविनाशभीते:। विशिष्टानुपूर्व्यव्यवस्थितो हि स्वाध्यायोऽध्येतव्य: श्रूयते स्मार्ताश्चाचारा: केचित्क्वचित्कस्याञ्चिच्छाखायाम्। तत्रापि तु के चित्पुरुषमेवाधिकृत्या-म्नायन्तेऽपरे क्रतुप्रकरणाम्नाता: केनचिन्निमित्तेनोत्कृष्यमाणा: पुरुषधर्मतां भजते। तावत्तान्येव वाक्यान्युद्धृत्याध्यापयेयुस्तत: क्रमान्यत्वात्स्वाध्यविधिविरोध: स्यात्। अनेन च निदर्शनेनान्येऽप्यर्थवादोद्धारेण विधिमात्रमधीयीरन् कमौपायिकमात्रं वा तत्र वेदप्रलय: प्रसज्येत।।

77. It has been printed by Prof. Weber in his Indische Studien. I possess the collation of some of the Berlin MSS., but not of all. In addition to the MSS., collated by Prof. Weber, I have used the text and various readings given in Rādhākānta-deva's Śabdakalpadruma.

78. Pāṇ. iv. 3. 128 ;iv. 2. 117.

79. Bāṣkala. Not mentioned in Pāṇini. As to its etymology, cf. Pāṇ. ii. 1. 65.

80. Pāṇ. iv. 1. 99. Gaṇa naḍādi (नडादिगण).

81. This Śākhā is spelt Sāṅkhyāyana, Śāṅkhyāna, and Śāṅkhāyana. The last, however, is the most correct spelling. See Pāṇini, Gaṇapatha, aśvādi (अश्वादि), and kuñjādi (कुञ्जादि). This Śākhā is omitted by accident in MS. E. I. H.

82. Pāṇ. iv. 1. 19 (tex), Māṇḍūka ; derivative, Māṇḍūkayana, See also Pāṇ, iv. 1. 119.

83. The Śaiśira Śākhā, however, may perhaps be considered as a subdivision of the Śākala-śākhā. Śaiśira, or Śaiśira is mentioned in the Purāṇas as one of the five Śākala pupils, who propagated different Śākhās of the Ṛg-veda, all of them derived from the original recension of Śākalya Vedamitra. In the Viṣṇu-purāṇa these five pupils or descendants of Śākalya Vedamitra are called Mudgala, Gosvalu, Vātsya, Śālīya, and Śiśra (Viṣṇu-pur. 277). In the Vāyu-purāṇa their names are Mudgala, Golaka, Khālīya, Mātsya, Śaiśireya. In the commentary on the Śākala-prātiśakhya they are called Mudgala, Gokula, Vātsya, Śārīra, and Śaiśira, according to the Paris MS.; or Mudgala, Gokhula, Vātsya, Śārīra and Śaiśira, according to the MS. at the E. I. H.

इदं शास्त्रं पार्षदाख्यमखिलं सम्पूर्णमुत्तरत्र वक्ष्ये वक्ष्याम इत्यर्थ:। शैशिरीये पारायणपाठ इति वाक्यशेष:। शैशिरीयायां संहितायामित्यर्थ:। शैशिरी संहिता शिशिरदृष्ठत्वात्। तथा पुराणे उक्तम्-

मुद्गलो गोकुलो वात्स्य: शैशिर: शिशिरस्तथा।
पश्चैते शाकला: शिष्या: शाखाभेदप्रवर्तका:। इति
तथा च ऋग्वेदे शैशिरीयायां संहितायामिति।
यथा ऋग्वेदे पारायणाम्नाये शाकल्ये शैशिरीयकमिति वा।

The verses to which this commentary refers are not in the MS.

84. Pāṇ. iv. 3. 107. text; v. 1. 11. text Gaṇa Kshipakādi (क्षिपकादिगण).

85. *Ahvarakas*, Ś. K. D. Āhūrakas, Sansk. G. P. Hvarakas, MS. Berol. 785. Cf. Pāṇ, ii. 4. 30 ; vi. 2. 124. ; iii. 2. 1-35. comment. Several of these names are very problematical.

86. Pāṇ. iv. 3. 107. text ; ii. 1. 65. com. ; vii. 4. 38. text vi. 3. 42. com.; ū. 4. 3. com. ; i. 3. 49. com.; ū. 1. 163 com.

87. Cf. Pāṇ. vi, 2.10.

88. Pāṇ. viii, 91, Kapiṣthalah and Kapishthalam. Gaṇa krauḍyādi (क्रौड्यादिगण) and upakādi (उपकादि). As to Καμξισ'θολοι, see Megasthenes, edit. Schwaubeck p. 33. note, and p. 108.

89. Pāṇ. iv. 1, 89, com.; iv. 1, 63. com.; iv. 1. 99 com. iv. 3. 80. com. Gaṇa nadādi (नडादिगण).

90. Vārtantavīya, MSS. See, however, Pāṇ. iv. 3. 102.

91. A different reading is mentioned in the S. K. D, namely, Śvetāśvetatarāh. MS. Chamb. 785, has Śvetāḥ Śvetantarāḥ ; 376. Śvetā Aśvataraḥ-Sansk. G. P. Śvetāḥ Svetatarāḥ.

92. See Gaṇa Viḍādi (विडादिगण)

93. Āṣṭhalakāṭhas, Ś. K. D. Pātāṇḍinīyas, Chamb. 785. Vārāyaṇīyas, Ś. K. D.

94. See Gaṇapāṭha, *arihaṇādi* (अरिहणादि).

95. Pāṇ. iv. 1. 105, Gaṇa Gargādi (गर्गादिगण), unless the reading be manutantu.

96. Pāṇ. iv. 2. 80. Gaṇa Varāhādi. Pāṇ. iv. 1. 78.

97. Chaikeyas Ś. K. D. MSS. Chamb. 376. 785, have Chāgeyas. MS. 785, places the Hāridravīyas at the end, adding five new divisions. तत्र हारिद्रवीया नाम पञ्च भेदा भवन्ति। हारिद्रवमासुरं गार्ग्यं शार्कराक्षसमाग्रावसवीयं पञ्चमश्चेते हारिद्रवसंग्रहा:। Pāṇ. *iv.* 1.117, Chāgala, atreyaś chet, chāgalir anyah, ; iv. 8, 109, Chāgaleyinah; vii. 1. 2, Gaṇa takshaśilādi. Chāga leyāḥ Pāṇ. iv, 2. 30, Gaṇa Saṅkhyadi, [संख्यादि: गण:]

98. Pāṇ. iv. 3. 104, Haridru and hāridraviṇaḥ; iv, 4. 53, Gaṇa kisarādi [किसरादिगण]

99. Gaṇa āśvāpi. [अश्वादिगण:]

100. Pāṇ. iv. 3. 104.

101. Aukṣyas and Aukhyas, Ś. K D.; Aukhīyas, Ch. 785 ; Auṣeyas, Ch. 376. Cf. Pāṇ. iv. 3, 102.

102. Khāṇḍikīyas, Ch. 785.; Shāṇḍikeyas, Ch. 376.; Pāṇ. iv. 3. 102.

103. The Caraṇavyūha of the Ś. K. D. has, 23. Āpastambins; 24. Baudhāyanins; 25. Satyāshāḍhnis ; 26. Hiraṇyakeśins ; 27. Aukheyas or Auḍheyins. MS. Ch, 785. has,-23. Kāleyas (Kāleyāh, Pāṇ. iv. 2. 8.); 24. Śāṭyāyanas (Pāṇ. iv. 3. 105.) ; 25. Hiraṇyakeśas ; 26 Bhāradvājas ; 27. Āpastambīyas. MS. 376, Kaletas, Śāṭyāyinins, Hiraṇyakesins, Bharadvajins, Apastambins.

104. p. 279. "Of the tree of the Yajur-veda there are twenty-seven branches, which Vaiśampāyana, the pupil of Vyāsa, Compiled and taught to as many disciples,"

105. Pāṇ. vi. 2, 38. text ; ii. 4. 58. I.

106. Baudheyas, P.-p. Ch. 755.; Augheyas, Ś. K. D.; Gaudheyas, S. G. P.; Baudhayānas, Ch. 376. E. I. H. ; Baudhiḥ. Pāṇ. ii. 4. 58. 1.

107. Pāṇ. iv. 2. 111. text.

108. Mādhyandineyas, Ch. 376. See Gaṇa *utsādi*. [उत्सादिगण:]

109. Sāpeyas, P.-p.; Śāplyas, Ś.K.D.; Sāpeya, Gaṇa śaunakādi. (शौनकादिगण:)

110. Tāpāyanāyas, Ś. K. D.; Ch. 376 Tāpāyanāyas. Ch. 785.

111. Kālāpas, P.-p.; Kapālas, Ś. K. D. ; Ch. 785. ; Kapolas, Ch. 376.

112. Pauṇḍravachas (पौण्ड्रवच्छा:), P.-p.; Ch. 376. Cf. Pāṇ. vii. 3. 24.

113. Cf. Gaṇa Gargādi [गर्गादिगण:], Pāṇ. iv.1.17.; iv. 1. 75, text.

114. Pāmāvaṭikas or Paramāvaṭikas, Ś. K. D.

115. Parāśaras, P.p.; Ch. 785. 376.; Pārāśarīyas, Ś. K. D,; kṛśāvādi; gargādi.

116. Vaidheyas, Ch, 785.; Vaiṇeyas, Ch. 376.

117. Vaidheyas, Ch. 376.; Vaineyas, Ch. 785.

118. Aukhyas, P. p. ; Addhas. Ch. 376.; Ugheyas, Ś. K. D.; See Pāṇ. ii. 4. 7.; Aukhīyas, Ch. 785.

119. Baudhyaśvas, P.-p. ; Mauneyas, Ch. 785. ; Bodheyas, Ch. 376. The Ś. K. D. adds here.-42. Gālavas ; 43. Vaijaras ; 44 Kātyāyanīyas.

120. In a MS. of the Caraka-śākhā of the Kaṭhaka, 101 śākhās of the Yajur-veda are mentioned. Catalogue of the Berlin MSS., p. 38. "*Ekottara-śatādhvaryu śākhā-prabheda-bhi-nne yajurveda-Kaṭhake.*" (एकोत्तरशताध्वर्य शाखाप्रभेदभिन्ने यजुर्वेदकाठके)

121. Gaṇa pailādi.[पैलादिगण:]

122. Sātyamurgyas and Śāṭyamugrryas, Ch. 785. ; Śāṭyamur-gryas, Ch. 376.; Pāṇ. iv. 1. 81.

123. Kālopas, Ch, 785. 376, Pāṇ iv. 3. 108.

124. Mahākālopas, Ch. 785. 376; probably Mahākālāpas.

125. Lāṅgalas, Ch. 785.

126. Śārdūlas, Ch. 376.; wanting in Ch. 785.

127. Gaṇa-Kārtakaujapādi (कार्त्तकौजपादि:)

128. Kauthumas, Ch. 785.; Gaṇa taulvalyādi (तौलव्यादि:)

129. Śāṛdulas, Ch. 785.

130. Surāṇāyaṇīyas. Ch. 785.

131. Prājvalanādvaitabhṛts (प्रज्जवलनाद्वैतभृत:) Ch. 785.; Prāñjali-dvenabhṛts (प्राञ्जलिद्वेनभृत:), Ch. 376. Gaṇa Gargādi. (गर्गादिगण:)

132. Prācīnayogyas and Naigeyas.

133. The text in the Ś.K.D. has पैंप्पला:। दान्ता: प्रदान्ता:। स्नाता:। स्नैता इति च पाठ:। स्नैला:। ब्रह्मदावला:। शौनकी। देविदर्शती। चरणविद्याश्चेति। दाता प्रदाता औता ब्रह्मदीपशो वेदशौ इति भाष्ये नामान्तरम्।। M.S. Ch. 785. reads शौनका दामोदा तोत्तायना जायला ब्रह्मपला शकुनखी देवदर्शी चारणविद्याश्चेति।। MS. Ch. 378. reads शौनका दामोदा तोत्तायना जावला ब्रह्मपलाशा शौनकी देवर्षिचारणविद्याश्चेति।।

134. Pāṇ. iv. 2. 66.

135. Pāṇ. iv. 3. 106.

136. Gaṇa Śaunakādi.(शौनकादिगण:)

137. श्रीमती जननी यस्य सुकीर्तिर्मायिण: पिता।
सागणो भोगनाथश्च मनोबुद्धी सहोदरौ।।
यस्य बोधायनं सूत्रं शाखा यस्य च याजुषी।
भारद्वाजं कुलं यस्य सर्वज्ञ: स हि माधव:।।

138. Baudhāyana-sūtra-bhāṣya, MS. E. I. H. 104, p, 91.

139. सर्वगोत्राणि प्रवरगणायत्तानि।
गोत्राणां तु सहस्राणि प्रयुतान्यर्बुदानि च।
ऊनपश्चाशदेतेषां प्रवरा ऋषिदर्शनात्।।

140. These lists vary considerably in the different Sūtras. Puruṣottama, in his Pravarāmanjari, has made an attempt at collecting and explaining them. He uses the Kalpa sūtras of Baudhayana, Āpastamba, Sātyāṣāḍha, Kuṇḍina, Bhāradvāja, Laugākshi, Kātyāyana, and Āśvalāyana, the Mātsya-purāṇa, the

Bhārata, Manu's Law-book and their commentaries. For Baudhāyana he quotes a commentary by Amala ; for Āpastamba, Dhūrta-svāmin, Kapardi-svāmin, Gurudeva-svāmin ; for Āśvalāyana, Deva-svāmin.

141. तस्य (अग्नेराहवनीयस्य) प्रकर्षेण प्रार्थनानि तैस्तैमन्त्रदृग्भिरेकद्वित्रि-पञ्चसङ्ख्याकैर्विशिष्टानि एकार्षेयास्त्र्यार्षेया: पञ्चार्षेया: प्रवरा इत्युच्यन्ते।।

142. Thus we read in the Śrauta-sūtras, of the Manavas, that the Dikṣita must say his name, of the Gotra, of his father, grandfather and great grandfather; a custom which, if observed as a sacred law, must have preserved a genealogical knowledge for many generations. दीक्षितोऽयमसाविति नाम गृह्णाति। आमुष्यायणमिति गोत्रम्। अमुष्य पुत्र इति पितुर्नाम्ना। अमुष्य पौत्रेति पितामहस्य। अमुष्य नप्त्रेति प्रपितामहस्य।।

143. अग्निर्वै देवानामवमो विष्णु: परमस्तदन्तरेण सर्वा अन्या देवता:।।
The commentator says that the gods among whom Agni and Viṣṇu are the first and last, are the gods to whom prayers are offered at the ceremonies belonging to the Agniṣṭoma. There are 12 prayers (*śastra*), and the first is addressed to Agni (*bhūr Agnir jyotiḥ*); the last, which is an āgnimāruta, contains a verse in praise of Viṣṇu (*Vishṇor nu kam*), See Kauṣītkaki-brāhmaṇa, viii. 1. This passage proves nothing as to the relative dignity of Agni and Viṣṇu. In Kaush.-br. Agni is called *avarārddhya* (अवराद्र्ध्य), Viṣṇu. In parārddhya (परादृर्ध्य), and the Com. explains these terms as signifying the first in the former, and the first in the latter half.

144. आग्नावैष्णवं पुरोळाशं निर्वपति दीक्षणीयमेकादशकपालम्।।

A *Puroḍāśa* is a baked flour cake (*pakvaḥ piṣṭapiṇḍaḥ*) and ✓ *nirvap* to strew, means originally to take four handfuls of rice from the cart and throw them into a winnowing basket. Here, however, it means the offering of the oblation which has been prepared in that manner. The original meaning of Dīkṣa is said to be "shaving or cleansing."

145. सर्वाभ्य एवैनं तद्देधताभ्योऽनन्तरायं निर्वपति।।

146. अग्निर्वै सर्वा देवता विष्णु: सर्वा देवता:।।

147. एते वै यज्ञस्यान्त्ये तन्वौ यदग्निश्च विष्णुश्च तद्यदाग्नावैष्णवं पुरोळाशं निर्वपन्त्यन्तत एव तद्देवानृध्नुवन्ति।।

148. तदाहुर्यदेकादशकपाल: पुरोळाशो द्वावग्रविष्णू कैनयोस्तत्र क्लृप्ति: का विभक्तिरिति।।

149. अष्ठाकपाल आग्नेयोऽष्ठाक्षरा वै गायत्री गायत्रमग्नेश्छन्दस्त्रिकपालो वैष्णवस्त्रिर्हीदं विषुणर्विचक्रमत सैनयोस्त्रत्र क्लृप्ति: सा विभक्ति:।।

150. घृते चरुं निर्वपेत योऽप्रतिष्ठितो मन्येत।।

151. अस्यां वाव स न प्रतितिष्ठति।।

152. तद्यदृघृतं तत्स्त्रियै पयो ये तण्डुलास्ते पुंसस्तन्मिथुनं, मिथुनेनैवैनं तत्प्रजया पशुभि: प्रजनयति प्रजात्यै।।

153. प्रजायते प्रजया पशुभिर्य एवं वेद।।

154. आरब्धयज्ञो वा एष आरब्धदेवतो यो दर्शपूर्णमासाभ्यां यजत आमावास्येन वा हविषेष्टा पौर्णमासेन वा तस्मिन्नेव हविषि तस्मिन्वर्हिषि दीक्षेतैषा एका दीक्षा।।

The commentator tries to show that the Darśa-pūrṇa-māsa sacrifices are connected with all other rites. Although the Soma sacrifice is not a modification of the Darśa-pūrṇa-māsa, still the Iṣṭis, as, for instance, the Dīkṣāṇīya (दीक्षणीया) and Prāyaṇīyā (प्रायणीया), are, and they form part of the Soma sacrifice. The Agnihotra also, with all its parts, does not follow the rules of the D. P. (दर्शपूर्णमास), but it has reference to the Āhavaniya and the other sacred fires, and these fires must be placed by means of the Pavamāna-iṣṭi. Now, as all the Iṣṭis are modifications of the D.P. (दर्शपूर्णमास), the relation is established ; and therefore the D.P. (दर्शपूर्णमास), may be called the beginning of all sacrifices.

155. The commentator says; haviḥ means the sacrifice and barhiḥ means the same, and he takes the two locatives in the sense of "after this new-moon and full-moon sacrifice has been performed."

हवि:शब्दवद्बर्हि:शब्दोऽपि यज्ञोपलक्षक:। तस्मिन्नामावास्याख्ये तस्मिन्पौर्णमासाख्ये वर्हिषि यज्ञाऽनुष्ठिते सति पश्चादेव दीक्षेत।।

156. The last words, "this is one Dīkṣa," indicate that there is another; that is to say, some allow the Soma sacrifice, which begins with the Dīkṣā, before the Darśa-pūrṇa-māsa.

157. सप्तदश सामिधेनीरनुब्रूयात्।।

The number is stated, because generally the Sāmidhenis are only fifteen in number. These fifteen were originally but eleven verses, of which the first and last are repeated three times.

158. सप्तदशो वै प्रजापतिर्द्वादश मासा: पञ्चर्तवो हेमन्तशिशिरयो: समासेन तावत्संवत्सर: संवत्सर: प्रजापति:।।

159. प्रजापत्यायतनाभिरेवाभी राध्नोति या एवं वेद।।१।।

160. The Brāhmaṇa gives here three fanciful etymologies of *ishṭi*, the technical name of the sacrifice ; of *ahuti*, the oblations enjoined at the sacrifice; and of *ūti*, another name for the same. The real etymology of *ishṭi* is not *ish*, to wish, but ✓*yaj*, to sacrifice ; of *āhuti*, not *hvayati*, to call, but *juhoti*, to offer ; of *ūti*, not ayati, to come, but *avati*, to protect.

161. यज्ञो वै देवभ्य उदक्रामत्तमिष्ठिभि: प्रैषमैच्छन्यदिश्रिभि: प्रैषमैच्छँ-स्तदिष्ठीनामिष्ठित्तं तमन्वविन्दन्।।

162. अनुधित्तयज्ञो राध्नोति य एवं वेद।।

163. आहूतयो वै नामैता यदाहुतय एताभिर्वै देवान्यजमानो ह्वयति तदाहुतीना-माहुतित्वम्।।

164. ऊतयो खलु वै ता नाम याभिर्देवा यजमानस्य हवमायन्ति ये वै पन्थानो याः स्रुतयस्ता वा ऊतयस्त उ एवैतत्स्वर्गयाणा यजमानस्य भवन्ति॥

165. तदाहुर्यदन्यो जुहोत्यथ योऽनु चाह यकति च कस्मात्तं होतेत्याचछत इति॥

The commentator says, that the proper name for the Hotṛ would seem to be Anuvaktṛ or Yaṣṭṛ, because पुरोनुवाक्यां चानुब्रूते याज्यां च पठति॥

166. यद्वाव स तत्र यथाभाजनं देवता अमुमावहामुमावहेत्यावाह्यति तदेव होतुर्होतृत्वं होता भवति॥

167. होतेत्येनमाचक्षते य एवं वेद॥२॥

168. पुवर्वा एनमृत्विजो गर्भं कुर्वन्ति यं दीक्षयन्ति॥

169. अद्भिरभिषिञ्चन्ति॥

170. रेतो वा आपः सरेतसमेवैनं तत्कृत्वा दीक्षयन्ति॥

171. नवनीतेनाभ्यञ्जन्ति॥

आज्यं वै देवानां, सुरभिघृतं मनुष्याणामायुतं पितृणां, नबवीतं गर्भाणां तद्यन्नवनीतेनाभ्यञ्जन्ति स्वेनैवैनं तद्भागधेयेन समर्धयन्ति।

The commentator quotes a verse to the effect that molten *ghee* is called *ājya*; hardened, it is called *ghṛta*; slightly molten, it is called ayuta; and well seasoned it is called *surabhi*. But the Taittirīyas say, "*ghṛta* is for the gods, *astu* for the manes) *nishpakva* for men."*Astu* is here the same as *ayuta*, slightly molten, and *nishpakva*, quite liquid.

172. आञ्जत्येनम्॥

173. तेजो वा एतदक्ष्योर्यदाञ्जनं सतेजसमेवैतं तत्कृत्वा दीक्षयन्ति।

174. एकविंशत्या दर्भपिञ्जूलैः पावयन्ति॥

175. शुद्धमेवैनं तत्पूतं दीक्षयन्ति॥

176. दीक्षितविमितं प्रपादयन्ति॥

The hall is called *Dīkṣit-vimita*, because it was made (*vimita*) for the initiated (*dīkshita*). It is commonly called Prācīna-vaṁśa.

177. योनिर्वा एषा दीक्षितस्य यद्दीक्षितविमितं योनिमेवैनं तत्स्वां प्रपादयन्ति॥

178. तस्माद्ध्रुवाद्योनेरास्ते च चरति च॥

179. तस्माद्ध्रुवाद्योनेर्गर्भा धीयन्ते च प्र च जायन्ते॥

180. तस्माद्दीक्षितं नान्यत्र दीजिक्षविमितादादित्योऽभ्युदियाद्वाभ्यस्तमियाद्वापि वाभ्याश्रावयेयुः॥

181. वाससा प्रोर्णुवन्ति॥

182. उल्वं वा एतद्दीक्षितस्य ताद्वास उल्बेनेवैनं तत्प्रोर्णुवन्ति॥

183. कृष्णाजिनमुत्तरं भवति॥

184. उत्तरं वा उल्वाज्जरायु जरायुणैवैनं तत्प्रेर्शुवन्ति।

185. मुष्टी कुरुते॥

186. मुष्टी वै कृत्वा गर्भोऽन्तः शेते मुष्टी कृत्वा कुमारो जायते तद्यन्मुष्टी कुरुते यज्ञ चैव तत्सर्वांश्च देवता मुष्ट्यो कुरुते।

187. तदाहुर्न पूर्वदीक्षिण: संसवोऽस्ति परिगृहीतो वा एतस्य यज्ञ: परिगृहीता देवता नैतस्यार्त्तिरस्त्यपरदीक्षिण एव यथा तथेति।।

It is said by the commentator that if two or more Brāhmanns perform the Soma sacrifice on the same spot and at the same time, they commit a sin, which is called *sansava*, confusion of libations. They ought to be separated by a river or a mountain. He, however, who has finished his Dīkshā first and holds the gods between his closed hands, is not exposed to the consequences of the sansava, because the gods will be with him and not with the other man whose was finished later.

188. उन्मुच्य कृष्णाजिनमवभृथमभ्यवेति तस्कान्मुक्ता गर्भ जरायोर्जायन्ते।।

189. सहैव वाससाभ्यवैति तस्मात्सहैवोल्बेन कुमारी जायते।।३।।

190. 'त्वमग्ने सप्रथा असि सोम यास्ते मयोमुव' इत्याज्यभागयो: पुरोनुवाक्ये अनुब्रूयाद्य: पूर्वमनीजान: स्यात्तस्मै।।

After the general remarks on tha Dīkṣaṇīyeṣṭi (दीक्षणीयेष्टि:) which were given in the first three sections, without any particular regard to the offices of the *Hotṛ*, the fourth section begins with the ceremonial rules for the *Hotṛ*. The *Hotṛ* has to recite certain verses on being ordered to do so by the *Adhvaryu*.

191. त्वया यज्ञं वितन्वत इति यज्ञमेवास्मा एतद्वितनोति।।

192. अग्नि: प्रत्नेन मन्मना सोम गीर्भिष्ट्वा वयमिति य: पूर्वमीजान: स्यात्तस्मै।।

193. प्रत्नमिति पूर्व कर्माभिवदति।।

194. तत्तन्नदृत्यम्।।

195. अग्निर्वृत्राणि जङ्घनत्त्वं सोमासि सत्पतिरिति वार्त्रघ्नावेव कुर्यात्।।

196. घृत्रं वा एष हन्ति यं यज्ञ उपनमति तस्माद्वार्त्रघ्नावेव कर्तव्याविति।।

The reason which the commentator gives for his extraordinary proceeding is, that in each of the two couples of verses which were first recommended, the first verse only contained an allusion to the peculiarities of the sacrifices, while the two verses now enjoined both treat of the destruction of Vṛtra.

197. अग्निर्मुखं प्रथमो देवतानामग्निश्च विष्णो तप उत्तमं मह इन्याग्नावैष्णवस्य हविषो याज्यानुवाक्ये भवत:। आग्नावैष्णव्यौ रूपसमृद्धे एतद्वै यज्ञस्य समृद्धं तद्रूपसमृद्धं यत्कर्म क्रियमाणमृगभिवदति।।

Instead of saying "*anuvākyāyājye*," because the anuvāhya comes before the *yājyā*, the compound *yājyānuvākys* is formed, the shorter word, according to grammar, standing first in a *Dvandva* compound. The verse are not in the *śākala-śākhā* of the Ṛg-veda.

198. अग्निश्च ह वै विष्णुश्च देवानां दीक्षापालौ तौ दीक्षाया ईशाते तद्यदाग्नावैष्णवं हविर्भवति यौ दीक्षाया ईशाते तौ प्रीतौ दीक्षां प्रयच्छतां यौ दीक्षयितारौ तौ दीक्षयेतामिति।।

199. त्रिष्टुभौ भवत: सेन्द्रियत्वाय।।४।।

200. They are "Sa havyavāḷ amartyaḥ," (iii. 11. 2.) and "Agnir Hotā purohitaḥ" (iii. 11. 1.)

201. गायत्र्यौ स्विष्टकृतः संयाज्ये कुर्वीत तेजस्कामो ब्रह्मवर्चसकामः।।
202. तेजो वै ब्रह्मवर्चसं गायत्री।।
203. तेजस्वी ब्रह्मवर्चसी भवति य एवं विद्वान् गायत्र्यौ कुरुते।।
204. उष्णिहा वायुःकामः कुर्वीत।।
They are "*Agne* vājasya gomataḥ," (i. 79. 4.) and "Sa idhāno vasusḥ kaviḥ," (i. 79. 5)
205. आयुर्वा उष्णिक्।।
206. सर्वमायुरेति य एवविद्वानुष्णिहौ कुरुते।।
207. अनुष्टुभौ स्वर्गकामः कुर्वीत।।
They are "Tvam Agne vasūn." (i. 45. 1.)
208. द्वयोर्वा अनुष्टुभोश्चतुःषष्टिरक्षराणि त्रय इम ऊद्ध्र्वा एकविंश लोका एकविंशत्यैकविंशत्यैवेमाल्लोकान्रोहति स्वर्ग एव लोके चतुःषष्टितमेन प्रतिष्ठित।।
209. प्रतितिष्ठिति य एवं विद्वाननुष्टुभौ कुरुते।।
210. बृहत्यौ श्रीकामो यशस्कामः कुर्वीत।।
They are "Enā vo agnim (v. 16. 1.), and Udasya śochiḥ"!
211. श्रीर्वै यशश्छन्दसां बृहती।।
212. श्रियमेव यश आत्मन्धत्ते य एवं विद्वान्बृहत्यौ कुरुते।।
213. पङ्क्ती यज्ञकामः कुर्वीत।।
They are "Agnim tam manye." (v. 6. 1.)
214. पाङ्क्तो वै यज्ञः।।
215. उपैनं यज्ञो नमति य एवं विद्वान् पङ्क्ती कुरुते।।
216. त्रिष्टुभौ वीर्यकामः कुर्वीत।
They are "Dve virūpe charataḥ (i. 95 1.)
217. ओजो वा इन्द्रियं वीर्यं त्रिष्टुप्।।
218. आजस्वीन्द्रियवान् वीर्यवान्भवति य एवं विद्वाँस्त्रिष्टुभै कुरुते।।
219. जगत्यौ पशुकामः कुर्वीत।।
They are '*Janasya gopa*." (v. 11. 1.)
220. जागता वै पशवः।।
221. पशुमान्भवति य एवंविद्वान् जगत्यौ कुरुते।।
222. विराजवन्नाद्यकामः कुर्वीत।।
The are "*Preddho agne*" (vii. 1. 3.) "*Imo agne*"," (vii. 1.18.)
223. अन्नं वै विराट्।।
224. तस्माद्यस्यैवेह भूयिष्ठमन्नं भवति स एव भूयिष्ठं लोके विराजति तद्विराजो विराट्त्वम्।
225. वि स्वेषु राजति श्रेष्ठः स्वानां भवर्ा य एवं वेद।।५।।
226. अथो पञ्चवीर्य वा एतच्छन्दो यद्विराट्।।
यत् त्रिपदा तेजोष्णिहागायत्र्यौ यदस्या एकादशाक्षराणि पदानि तेन त्रिष्टुप् यत् त्रयस्त्रिंशदक्षरा तेनानुष्टुम्न वा एकेनाक्षरेण छन्दांसि वियन्ति न द्वाभ्यां, यद्विराट् तत्पञ्चमम्।।

227. सर्वेषां छन्दसां वीर्यमवरुन्द्धे सर्वेषां छन्दसां वीर्यमश्नुते सर्वेषं छन्दसां सायुज्यं सरूपतां सलोकतामश्नुतेऽन्नादोऽन्नपतिर्भवत्यश्नुते प्रजयान्नाद्यं य एर्वविद्वान् विराजौ कुरुते।।

228. तस्माद्विराजावेव कर्तव्ये। पत्रेद्धो अग्र इमो अग्र इत्येते।।

229. ऋृतं वाव दीक्षा सत्यं दीक्षा तस्माद्दीक्षितेन सत्यमेव वदितव्यम्।।
Right (*rta*) and truth (*sātyā*) are said to differ, inasmuch fta means a true conception, satya, a true speech.

230. अथो खल्वाहु: कोऽर्हति मनुष्य: सर्व सत्यं वदितुं सत्यसंहिता वै देवा अनृतसंहिता मनुष्या इति।।

231. विचक्षणवतीं वाचं वदेत्।।
For instance, instead of saying, "Devadatta, bring the cow," let him say, "Devadatta. *vichaṣaṇa* bring the cow." According to Āpastamba, *vichakṣana* ought to be used after the names of a Kṣatriya and Vaiśya, but "*chanśita*" after the name of a *Brāhmaṇa*.

232. चक्षुर्वै विचक्षणं वि ह्येनेन पश्यतीति।। Kausha-br. चक्षुर्वै विचक्षणं चक्षुषा हि विपश्यति।।

233. एतद्ध वै मनुष्येषु सत्यं निहितं यच्चक्षु:।।

234. तस्मादाचक्षाणमाहुरद्रागति स यद्यदर्शमित्याहाथास्य श्रद्दधति यद्यु वै स्वयंपश्यति न बहूनां च नान्येषां श्रद्दधाति।।

235. तस्माद्विचक्षणवतीमेव वाचं वदेत्सत्योत्तरा है वास्य वागुदिता भवति भवति।।६।।

236. अथ ह स्माह दैवोदासि: प्रतर्दनो नैमिषीयाणां सत्रमुपगम्योपासद्य विचिकित्सां पप्रच्छ यद्यतिक्रान्तमुल्वणं सदस्यो बोधयेतर्त्विजां वान्यतमो बुध्येत कथं वोऽनुल्बणं स्यादिति त उ ह तूष्णीमासुस्तेषामलीकयुर्वाचस्पतो ब्रह्मास, स होवाच नाहमेतद्वेद हन्त पूर्वेषामाचार्य स्थविरं जातुकर्ण्य पृच्छानीति। तं ह पप्रच्छ यद्यतिक्रान्तमुल्बणं कर्ता वा स्वयं बुध्येतान्यो वा बोधयेत कथं तदुल्बणमनुल्बणं भवेत्पुनर्वचनेन वा मन्त्रस्य हामेन वेति पुनर्वाच्यो मन्त्र इति ह स्माह जातुकर्ण्यस्तमलीकयु: पुन: पप्रच्छ शस्त्रं वानुवचनं वा निगदं वा याज्यां वा यद्वान्यत्सर्वं तत्पुनर्ब्रूयादिति यावन्मात्रमुल्बणं ताबद्ब्रू यादृचं वार्द्धर्चं वा पादं वा पदं वा वर्ण वेति ह स्माह जातुकर्ण्योऽथ ह स्माह कौषीतकिर्न मन्त्रं पुनर्ब्रूयान्नाहुतिं जुहुयादनुल्बणमेतदिति ह स्माह कौषीतकिर्यद्धि होतारो यज्ञस्य किञ्चिदुल्बणमबुद्ध्यमाना: कुर्वन्ति सर्व तदग्निर्देवो होतानुल्बणं करोति तदेतदृचाभ्युदितम्।।

237. See Professor Wilson's Eassay on Human sacrifices in the Veda, and Professor Roth, in Weber's Ind. Studien, i. p. 457.

238. Hariśchandra was, according to the Purāṇas, the son of Triśaṅku, king of Ayodhyā whom Vaśiṣtha had cursed, and who made Viśvāmitra his Purohiṭa. Viśvāmitra in the Brāhmaṇa is represented as one of Hariścandra's priests, but the office, of Brahmā is held by Vaśishṭha. In the Rāmāyāṇa, the sacrifice of Śunaḥśepha takes place under King Ambarīṣa.

239. *Nārada* is known as a frequent interlocutor in the epic and purāṇic poetry, particularly in dialogues where moral and legal precepts are given. Cf. Burnouf Bhārgavata-purāṇa, vol. iii. preface.

240. The commentator gives a very different version of this line, He takes mala, which usually means matter, or mud to signify the state of life of a Gṛhastha, or householder,. *Ajina*, the skin, particularly of the antelope (*aja*), he takes as a symbol of the Brahmacārin state, because the pupil wears a skin. Śmaśrūṇi, used in the singular for beard; he takes as a symbol for the Vānaprastha, because he does not shave any more ; and tapas he explains to mean the penance practised by the Parivrājaka .
Why the birth of a daughter was considered a pity we learn from the following verse (metre Rathoddhatā) :

सम्भवे स्वजनदुःखकारिका
सम्प्रदानसमयेऽर्थहारिका।
यौवनेऽपि बहुदोषकारिका
दारिका हृदयदारिका पितुः।।

241. This is one of the earliest allusions to the four ages of the world.
242. Langlois, in his translation of the Harivaṁśa (i. 124.), takes a different view of this circumstance. According- to his translation Śunaḥśepha ' avait etc dans une autre existence un des coursiers atteles au char du soleil." Langlois reads in the text Haridaśva, which he takes as a name of the sun with green horses.
243. The commentator observes here, that although at a sacrifice men and wild beasts were bound to the post, yet both beasts and men were set free immediately after the *paryagni-karaṇam* (purification by fire, carried round), and only animals like sheep, etc., were killed.
244. Manu, x. 105,
245. These verses are to be found in the sixth Anuvāka of the first Maṇḍala of the Ṛg-veda.
246.

```
                 Purūravas
                 Jahnu
. . . . X        Gādhin Kauśika (Bhṛgus)
   |                |                 |
Viśvāmitra.     Satyavati   ×   Ṛcīka (Ikṣvākus)
                            |
                 Jamadagni  ×          Reṇukā
                            |
                       Paraśu-rāma
```

247. This last verse, which is also attributed to Viśvāmitra, ought to be taken rather as a recapitulation of the whole story. Jahnu is one of the ancestors of Viśvāmitra, belonging to the Lunar Dynasty ; Gādhiṅ is considered as Viśvāmitra's father. The commentator gives Jahnu as a Ṛṣi of the family of Ajīgarta, which seems better to agree with the Vedic story.
248. Śatapatha-Brāhmaṇa, Mādhyandina-Śākhā, xi. 4. 5. The same story is alluded to in the Bṛhadāraṇyaka, iv. 3. 1.
249. The commentary explains, निष्ठाव: by धनविभागादेर्धर्मरहस्यं निःशेषेण स्थितिनिर्णयो

निष्ठा। सा यस्मिन्नस्ति स निष्ठावः। तादृशं धर्मरहस्यनिर्णेतारमित्यर्थः।। अववदितारम् ज्येष्ठपुत्रस्यैतावत् द्वितीयस्यैतावत् अन्यस्यैतावदित्यवच्छिद्य वेदितुं समर्थोऽववदिता। तादृशम्।। अयमर्थः। अयं मनुर्धर्मशास्त्रकर्तृत्वाद्धर्मरहस्यनिर्णयवान् पितृत्वेन तवैतावदित्यवच्छिद्य वक्तुं समर्थश्च।।

250. Two hymns ascribed to Nābhānedhiṣṭha occur in Ṛg-veda. x, 5. 1. & 2.
251. These words are taken from the second hymn of Nābhānediṣṭha.
252. The text is एतत्ते ब्राह्मण-सहस्रमिति। but the commentary says, it is to be understood of a thousand cows or animals, left on the spot of the sacrifice, and that in a different Śākhā of this Brāhmaṇa the text is ते सुवर्णं लोकं यन्तो य एषां पशव आसन् तानस्मा अददुरिति।।
253. The commentator says, that this is Rudra, the lord of animals, and that this is clearly indicated in a different Śākhā, where the text is तं पशुभिश्चरन्तं यज्ञवास्तौ रुद्र आगच्छदिति।।
254. Kauṣ.-br, vi. तदाहुः किंविदं किंछन्दसं ब्रह्माणं वृणीत इत्यध्वर्युमित्येके स परिक्रमाणां क्षेत्रज्ञो भवतीति छन्दोगमित्येके तथा हास्य त्रिभिर्वेदैर्हविर्यज्ञाः संस्क्रियन्त इति बह्वृचमिति त्वेव स्थितम्। Some allowance must be made for the fact that the Kauṣītakins are Bahvṛchas,
255. See Böhtlingk and Roth's Dictionary, s. v,
256. Prof. Weber's recent edition of this tract, is the best *amende* he could have made for his former scepticism with regard to the existence of this and other Brāhmaṇas of the Sāma-veda.
257. When there are two teachers, it is always the second through whom the tradition was carried on, except in No. 28, where there has evidently been a great confusion.
258. The Yājñavalkiya-kāṇḍa inserts here :

Sāyakāyana.	सायकायनः
Kauśkāyani (22).	कौशिकायनिः
Ghṛtakauśika (23).	घृतकौशिकः
Pārāśaryāyana (24),	पाराशर्यायणः
Pārāśarya (25).	पाराशर्यः
Jātukarṇya (26).	जातूकर्ण्यः
Bhāradvāja (27).	भारद्वाजः
Bhāradvāja and Āsurāyaṇa and Yāska	भाक्षजासुरायणौ यास्कश्च
Traivaṇi (29)	त्रैवणिः
Aupajandhani (30).	औपजन्धनिः

259. The priest of Janamejaya Pārīkṣit, at his *Abhisheka* sacrifice, is called Tura Kāvasheya in the Aīt. br. viii. 21.
260. The priest of Janamejaya Pārīkṣit, at his Horse sacrifice, is called Indrota

(Daivāpa) Śaunaka in the Śatapatha, xiii, 5. 4.1., and in the Mahābh. xii. 5595, seq. Cf. Weber, Ind. Stud, i, pp. 203, 483.

261. Nirukta-pariśiṣṭa, I, 10.

262. See page 326,

263. Sāyaṇa's Introduction to the Ṛg-veda, p. 3.1.3.

264. Yajñavalkya's Lawbook ; i. 312.

265. See, however, i. 22.

266. At the end of the fifth Prapāṭhaka we read :

ऋग्भि: पृथिवी यजुषान्तरिक्षं
साम्ना दिवं लोकजित्सोमजम्भा:।
अथर्वभिरङ्गिरोभिश्च गुप्तो
यज्ञश्चतुष्पाद्दिव...............।।

267. सप्त: सुत्या: सप्त च पाकयज्ञा हविर्यज्ञा: सप्त तथैकविंशति:। सर्वे ते यज्ञा अङ्गिरसोऽपि यन्ति नूतना यानृषयो (?) सृजन्ति ये च सृष्टा: पुराणै:। And again याँश्च ग्रामे याँश्चारण्ये जपन्ति मन्त्रान्नानार्थान्वहुधा जनास:। सर्वे ते यज्ञा अङ्गिरसोऽपि यन्ति नूतना सा हि गतिर्ब्रह्मणो यावराद्धर्या।। त्रिविष्टपं त्रिदिवं नाकमुत्तमं तमेतया त्रय्या विद्ययैति। अत उत्तरे ब्रह्मलोका महान्तोऽथर्वणामङ्गिरसा च सा गति:।।

268. See page 82, note.

269. See also Uttara-brāhmaṇa ii. 1. = Ait. br. iii, 5.; Utt.-br. v. 14 = Ait.-br. vi. 17.; Utt.-br. vi. 1. = Ait.-br. vi. 18.; Utt.br. vi. 3- Ait.-br, vi. 21.

270. Atharva-veda-saṁhitā, herausgegeben von Roth und Whitney. Berlin, 1855, and 1856.

271. Journal of the American Oriental Society, iv. p. 254.

272. Loc, cit. iii, p. 308

3 CHAPTER

THE MANTRA PERIOD

Having ascribed to one period the first establishment of the threefold ceremonial *(trayī vidyā),* the composition, and collection of the Brāhmaṇas, and the ramification of the Brāhmaṇa-Caraṇas, we have now to see whether we can extend our view beyond the limits of this period and truce the stream of Vedic literature still further back to its source and its earliest diffusion. According to its general character, the Brāhmaṇa period must be called a secondary period. It exhibits a stratum of thought, perfectly unintelligible without the admission of a preceding age, during which all that is misunderstood, perverted, and absurd in the Brāhmaṇas, had its natural growth, its meaning, and purpose. But can it be supposed that those who established the threefold ceremonial, and those who composed the threefold Brāhmaṇas, followed immediately upon an age which had known poets, but no priests; prayers, but no dogmas; worship, but no ceremonies ? Or are there traces to show that, even previous to the composition of the Brāhmaṇas, a spirit was at work in the literature of India, no longer creative, free, and original, but living only on the heritage of a former age, collecting, classifying, and imitating ? I believe we must decidedly adopt the latter view. The only document we have, in which, we can study the character of the times, previous to the Brāhmaṇa period, is the Ṛg-veda-saṁhitā. The other two *Saṁhitās* were more likely the production of the Brāhmaṇa period. These two Vedas, the Yajur-veda and Sāma-veda, were, in truth, what they are called in the Kauṣītaki-brāhmaṇa, the attendants of the Ṛg-veda,[1] The Brāhmaṇas presuppose the

Trayz vidyā, the threefold knowledge, or the threefold Veda, but that *Trayū vidyā* again presupposes one Veda, and that the Ṛg-veda. We cannot suppośe that the hymns which are found in the Ṛg-veda. and in the *Saṁhitās* of the two supplementary Vedas, the Sāma and Yajur-veda, were collected three times by three independent collectors. If so, their differences would be much greater than they are. The differences which do exist between the same hymns and verses as given in the three *Saṁhitās,* are such as we should expect to find in different *Śākhās,* not such as would naturally arise in independent collection or *Saṁhitās.*

The principle on which the *Saṁhitā* of the Ṛg-veda was made is different from that which guided the compilers of the *Saṁhitās* of the *Adhvaryus* and Udgātṛs. These two *Saṁhitās* follow the order of an established ceremonial. They presuppose a fixed order of sacrifices. This is not the case in the *Saṁhitā* of the *Bahvṛcas.* There is, as we shall see, a system in that *Saṁhitā* also, but it has no reference to the ceremonial.

The different character of the Ṛg-veda-Saṁhitā, as compared with the *Saṁhitās* of the other two Vedas, has attracted the attention of the Brāhmaṇas, and we may quote on this subject the remarks of Sāyaṇa, in his Introduction to the Rg-veda.[2]

"Has Āśvalāyana," he says, "when composing the ceremonial Sūtras, followed the order of the *Saṁhitā* of the Ṛg-veda, or of the Brāhmaṇa ? He could not have followed the order of the hymns, because he says at the beginning of his Sūtras, that first of all he is going to explain the new and full-moon sacrifices *(Darśa pūrṇamāsa),* while the first hymns of the Ṛg-veda are never used at that sacrifice. Nor does he seem to have followed the Brāhmaṇa. For the Brāhmaṇa begins with the Dīkṣaṇīyā ceremony. Here then it must be observed that the collection of hymns follows the order which is observed at the *Brāhmayajña* and on other occasions where prayers are to be recited. It does not follow the order in which hymns are employed at the different sacrifices. *Brāhmayajña* is the name given to the act of repeating by heart one's own sacred text or even a single verse of it, whether a Ṛc, Yajuṣ or Sāman. This repeating of all the Ṛc, Yajuṣ or Sāman verses is enjoined by many passages of the Brāhmaṇas, and whenever hymns are thus enjoined to be repeated, that order is to be observed in which they have been handed down by an uninterrupted tradition. But as Āśvalāyana teaches the particular employment of particular hymns, basing it upon the authority of what are termed indicative passages of the revelation, it is but natural that he can not follow the order of the hymns of the Ṛg-veda. The texts of the Yajurveda, however, are given, from the first beginning, according to their order at the performance of sacrifices, and thus bave Āpastamba and others proceeded in the same order in the composition of their Sūtras. As this order has once been received, it is likewise adopted in the *Brahmayajña*. That Āśvalāyana should explain in the first place the Darśa-pūrṇamāsa sacrifice, while the Brāhmaṇa. begins with the Dīkṣaṇīyā sacrifice, is no objection, because the Dīkṣāṇīya is only a modification of the Darśa-pūrṇamāsa, and many of its rules must be supplied from the typical sacrifice. Thus the Kalpa-Sūtra of Āśvalāyana assists in teaching the performance of the sacrifice by showing the employment of the hymns. That Āśvalāyana should teach the employment of passages which do not occur in the *SanMta* of the Ṛg-veda,[3] is no fault, because these hymns occur in different *Śākhās,* and their employment is prescribed by a different Brāhmaṇa, so that their being mentioned can only increase the value of his Sūtras. Those who know the logic of this subject say, that there is but one sacrifice and that it is to be learnt from all the different Śākhās."

Here then we see that even so late a writer as Sāyaṇa is fully aware of the peculiar character of the Ṛg-veda, as compared with the other Vedas. In his eyes the collection of hymns, preserved in the Ṛg-veda, has evidently something anomalous. He, brought up in the system of a stiff liturgical religion, looks upon the Saṁhitās simply as prayer-books to be used at the sacrifices. The sacrifices as taught in the Brāhmaṇas and Sūtras, are. to him a subject of far greater importance than the religious poetry of the Ṛṣis. It is but natural, therefore, that he should ask, what is the use of this collection of hymns, in which there is no order or system, as in the hymn books of the Yajur-veda and Sāma-veda ? His answer, however, is most unsatisfactory. For if the other two collections of hymns can be used for private devotion although they follow the order of the sacrifices, why should not the same apply to the hymns of the Ṛg-veda ?

Whenever we find in the ancient literature and theology of the Brāhmaṇas anything that is contrary to their general rules, anything that seems anomalous to them and is yet allowed to exist, we may be sure that it contains some really historical elements, and that it was of too solid a nature to receive the smooth polish of the Brāhmaṇic system. It is so with the Ṛg-veda-saṁhitā. It belongs to a period previous to the complete ascendancy of the Brāhmaṇas; it was finished before the threefold ceremonial had been worked out in all its details.

And yet there is some system, there is some priestly influence, clearly distinguishable in that collection also. It is true that the ten books of the Ṛg-veda stand before us as separate collections, each belonging to one of the ancient families; but were these collections undertaken independently in each of these families, at different times, and with different objects ? I believe not. There are traces, however faint, of one superintending spirit.

Eight out of the ten Maṇḍalas begin with hymns addressed to Agni, and these hymns, with the exception of the tenth Maṇḍala, are invariably followed by hymns addressed to Indra.[4] After the hymns addressed to these two deities we generally meet with hymns addressed to the Viśve Devāḥ. This cannot be the result of mere accident, nor is there anything in the character of the two gods Agni and Indra, which would necessitate such an arrangement. Agni is indeed called the lowest of the gods, but this neither implies his inferiority nor his superiority.[5] It simply means that Agni, as the god of fire on the hearth, is the nearest god, who descends from his high station to befriend men, and who, in the form of the sacrificial fire, becomes the messenger and mediator between god and men.[6] This would not be sufficient to account for the place assigned to him at the beginning of eight out of the ten Maṇḍalas of the Ṛg-veda. Indra, again, is certainly the most powerful of the Vedic gods,[7] but he never enjoys that supremacy which in Greece and Rome was allowed to Zeus and Jupiter. We can hardly doubt, therefore, that the place allowed to hymns addressed to Agni and Indra, at the beginning of the Maṇḍalas, was the result of a previous agreement, and that the Maṇḍalas themselves do not represent collections made independently by different families, but collections carried out simultaneously in different localities under the supervision of one central authority.

Another indication of the systematic arrangement of the Maṇḍalas is contained in the Āprī hymns.

There are ten Āprī-sūktas in the Ṛg-veda :

1. I. 13, by Medhātithi, of the family of the Kāṇvas (ii. b.); 12 verses.

2. I. 142, by Dīrghatamas son of Uchathya, of the family of the Āṅgirasas (ū. a.); 13 versse. (Indra.)

3. I. 188, by Āgastya, of the family of the Agastis (vii); 11 verses, (Tanūnapāt.)

4. II. 3, by Gṛtsamada, son of Sunahotṛa, *(Āṅgirsa)* adopted by *Śunaka* (Bhārgava) (i. 7.); 11 verses. *(Narāśaṅsa)*

5. III. 4, by Viśvāmitra, son of Gāthin, of the family of the Viśvāmitra (iv.), 11 verses, *(Tanūnapāt,)*

6. V. 5, by Vasuśruta, son of Atri, of the family of the Ātreyas (iii); 11 verses. *(Narāśaṅsa)*

7. Vū. 2, by Vasiṣṭha, son of Mitrāvaruṇau, of the family of the Vasiṣṭhas (vi.); 11 verses. *(Narāśaṅsa)*

8. IX. 5i by Āśita or Devala, of the family of the Kāśyapas (v.); 11 verses. *(Tanūnapāt)*

9. X. 70, by Sumitra, of the family of the Bādhryaśvas (i. 6.); 11 verses *(Narāśaṅsa)*

10. X. 110, by Rāma, the son of Jamadagni, or by Jamadagni, of the family of the Jāmadagnyas (i. *2.);* verses. *(Tanūnapāt)*

These hymns consist properly of 11 verses, each of which is addressed to a separate deity. Their order is as follows :

First verse, to *Agni Idhma* (अग्नि इध्म) or Susamiddha (सुसमिद्ध) the lighted fire,

Second verse, to *Tanūnapāt,* the sun hidden in the waters or the clouds, or to *Narāśaṅsa* (नराशंस) the rising sun, praised by men.

Third verse, to the *Iḷas,* the heavenly gifts, or *Īḷita, Agni,* implored to bring them.

Fourth verse, to *Barhiṣ,* the sacrificial pile of grass. Fifth verse, to *Devīr dvāraḥ,* the gates of heaven.

Sixth verse, to *Uṣāsā-nahtau,* dawn and night.

Seventh verse, to *Daivyau hotārau praehetasau, (i. e., Agni* and *Āditya,* or *Agni* and *Varuṇa,* or *Varuṇa* and *Āditya;* Śaḍguruśiṣya).

Eighth verse, to the three goddesses Sarasvatī, Iḷā, Bhāratī.

Ninth verse, to *Tvaṣṭr,* the creator.

Tenth verse, to *Vānaspati,* the tree of the sacrifice.

Eleventh verse, to the *Svāhākṛtis.* (Viśve Devāḥ, Śaḍguruśiṣya.).

The only differences in the ten *Āprī* hymns of the Ṛg-veda arise from the name by which the second deity is invoked. It is *Tanūnapāt* in hymns 3, 5, 8, 10; *Narāśaṅsa* in hymns 4, 6, 7, 9; whereas in hymns 1 and 2,'the second deity is invoked under either name in two separate verses. This raises the number in these two hymns to twelve, and this number is again raised to thirteen in hymn 2, by the end of a separate invocation of Indra.

The whole construction of these hymns is clearly artificial.

They share the character of the hymns which we find in the Sāma and Yajur-veda, being evidently composed for sacrificial purposes. Nevertheless, we find these artificial hymns in seven out of the ten Maṇḍalas, in I , ū., Ill , V., Vū., IX., X. This proves a previous agreement among the collectors. For some reason or other, each family wished to have its own *Āprī* hymn, a hymn which had to be recited by the *Hotṛ* priest, previous to the immolation of certain victims,[8] and such a hymn was inserted, not once for all in the Saṁhitā, but ten times over. Some of the verses in the *Āprī* hymns are mere repetition, and even families so hostile to each other as the Vasiṣṭhas and Viśvāmitras have some verses in common in these *Āprī* hymns. But, if on one side the presence of the *Āprī* hymns in different Maṇḍalas proves a certain advance of the ceremonial system in the Mantra period, and the influence of a priestly society even in the first collection of the hymns; it proves likewise, that the traditional distribution of the Maṇḍalas among various Vedic families is not a merely arbitrary arrangement. These families insisted on having each their own *Āprī* hymn recorded, and whereas for the general ceremonial, as fixed in the Brāhmaṇas and Sūtras, the family of the poet of certain hymns employed at the sacrifices, is never taken into account, we find an exception made in favour of the *Āprī* hymns. If a verse of Viśvāmitra is once fixed by the Brāhmaṇas and Sūtras as part of any of the solemn sacrifices, no sacrificer, even if he were of the family of the Vasiṣṭhas, would have a right to replace that verse by another. But with regard to the *Āprī* hymns that liberty is conceded. The Aitareya-brāhmaṇa records this fact in the most general form.[9] "Let the priest use the *Āprīs* according to the Ṛṣi. If he uses the *Āprīs* according to the Ṛṣi, he does not allow the sacrificer to escape from the relationship of tha Ṛṣi." Āśvalāyana enters more into details.[10] He says that those who belong to the Śunakas, should use the hymn of Gṛtsamada; those who belong to tho Vasiṣṭhas, that of Vasiṣṭha. The *Āprī* hymn of Rāma or Jamadagni he allows to be used by all families, (excepting the Śunakas and Vasiṣṭhas) but, he adds, that each family may choose the *Āprī* hymn of its own Ṛṣi. How this is to be done is explained in a *Sloka,* ascribed to Śaunaka.[11] He ascribes the first *Āprī* hymn to the Kāṇvas; the second to the Aṅgiras,' with the exception of the Kāṇvas; the third to the Agastis; the fourth to the Śunakas; the fifth to the Viśvāmitras; the sixth to the Atris; the seventh to the Vasiṣṭhas; the eighth to the Kāśyapas; the ninth to the Badhryaṣvas; the tenth to the Bhṛgus, with the exception of the Śunakas and Badhryasvas.[12]

The original purpose of the *Āprī* hymns, and the motive for allowing the priest to choose among them according to the family to which his client belonged, are difficult to discover. An ancient author of the name of Gāṅagari,[13] endeavoured to prove from the fact that one and the same *Āprī* hymn *may* be used by all, that all people belong really and truly to one family. It is possible, indeed, that the *Āprī* hymns may have been songs of reconcilation, and that they were called *Āprī, i. e.* appeasing hymns, not from their appeasing the anger of the gods, but the enmities of members of the same or different families. However that may be, they certainly do prove that there had been an active intercourse between the ancient families of India long before the final collection of the ten books, and that these ten books were collected and arranged by men who took more than a merely poetical interest in the ancient sacred poetry of their country.

Although we see from these indications that the collection of the hymns which we possess in the Ṛg-veda took place during a period when the influence of the Brāhmaṇas, as a priestly caste, had made itself felt in India, we must claim, nevertheless, for this collection a character not yet exclusively ceremonial. Not only is the order of the hymns completely independent of the order of the sacrifices, but there are numerous hymns in our collection which could never have been used at any sacrifice. This is not the case with the other Vedas. Every hymn, every verse, every invocation in the *Saṁhitās* of the Sāma and Yajur-vedas are employed by the Udgātṛs and *Adhvaryus,* whereas the hymns of the Ṛg-veda are by no means intended to be all employed by the *Hotṛ* priests. If we speak of the sacred poetry of the Brahman as, that of the Sāma and Yajur-vedas is sacred only because it is used for sacrificial purposes, that of the Ṛg-veda is sacred, because it had been handed down as a sacred heir-loom from the earliest times within the memory of man. The sacredness of the former is matter of system and design, that of the latter is a part of its origin.

There is an objection that might be raised against this view, and which deserves to be considerd. No one acquainted with the ceremonial of the *Brāhmaṇas* could well maintain that, after the final division of that ceremonial among the three classes of priests, a collection like that of the Ṛg-veda could have been conceived. The Ṛg-veda is not a Veda for the *Hotṛ* priest, in the same sense in which the Sāma and Yajur-vedas are for the *Udgātṛ* and *Adhvaryu* priests. But it might be said that there is a fourth class of priests, the Brahmā class, and that the Ṛg-veda might have been collected for their special benefit. In order to answer this objection, we shall have to examine more closely the real character of the four classes of priests.

Āśvalāyana (iv. 1.), says that there are four priests, each having three men under him. These are :

I. Hotṛ, with Maitrāvaruṇa, Achhavaka, Gravastut.[14]

II. Adhvaryu, with Pratiprasthātṛ, Neshṭṛ, Unnetṛ.

III. Udgātṛ, with Prastotṛ, Agnīdhra or Agnīdh, Potṛ

IV. Brahmā, with Brāhmaṇachhansin, Pratihartṛ, Subrahmānya.

These sixteen priests are commonly called by the name of *Ṛtvij*, and are chosen by the man in whose favour the sacrifice is offered, the *Yajamāna* or Svāmin. There are other priests, such as the *Samitṛ*, (the slayer,) the *Vaikartat*, (the butchers) the *Chamāsadhvaryus*, (the assistaats of the Adhvaryus,) but they do not rank as Ṛtvij. The Kauṣītakins admit a seventeenth Ṛtvij, the so-called Sadasya, who is to superintend the whole sacrifice.[15] This large array of priests was only wanted for certain grand sacrifices. In the Gautama-Sūtra-Bhāṣya (p. 30.) we are told that for the *Agnihotra* and *Aupāsana* one priest, the Adhvaryu, was sufficient; for the *Darśapūrṇamāsa,* four; for the *Cāturmāsyas* five; for the *Pasūbandha* six; for the *Jyotiṣṭoma* sixteen. Āśvalāyana prescribes the sixteen priests for the sacrifices called *Ahīna* (sacrifices lasting from two to eleven days), and *Ekāha* sacrifices of one day), and restricts the seventeen priests to the *Sattras* (sacrifices lasting from thirteen to one hundred days.) Each of the four classes of these priests had peculiar duties to perform. These duties were prescribed in the Brāhmaṇas. The duties of the *Hotṛ* are laid down in the Brāhmaṇas of the·Bahvṛchas, such as the Kauṣītaki and Aitareya-brāhmaṇas; those of the *Adhvaryu* in the Brāhmaṇas of the Carakas (the Taittirīyaka) and in the Brāhmaṇas·of the Vājasaneyins (the Śatapatha); those of the *Udgātṛ* in the Brāhmaṇas of the Chhandogas (the Tāṇḍya). Āpastamba, who describes the sacrifice in his Paribhāsha-Sūtras,[1] says that it is prescribed by the three Vedas, the Ṛg-veda, Yajur-veda, and Sāma-veda.* "The *Hotṛ*" he says, "performs his duties with the BṚg-veda, the *Udgātṛ* with the Sāma-veda, the *Adhvaryu* with the Yajur-veda; the Brahmā with all the three Vedas."

The Adhvaryus were the priests who were entrusted with the material performance of the sacrifice. They had to measure the ground, to build the alter *(vedi),* to prepare the sacrificial vessels, to fetch wood and water, to light the fire, to bring the animal and immolate it. They formed, as it would seem, the lowest class of priests, and their acquirements were more of a practical than an intellectual character. Some of the offices which would naturally fall to the lot of the *Adhvaryu,* were considered so degrading, that other persons besides the priests were frequently employed in them. The *Śamitṛ,* for instance, who had to slay the animal, was not a priest, he need not even be a *Brāhmaṇa*[18], and the same applies to the *Vaikartas,* the butchers, and the so-called *Camāsadhvaryus.* The number of hymns and invocations which they had to use at the sacrifices was smaller than that of the other priests. These, however, they had to learn by heart. But as the chief difficulty consisted in the exact recitation of hymns, and in the close observance of all the euphonic rules, as taught in the Prātiśākhyas, the *Adhvaryus* were allowed to mutter their hymns,[19] so that no one at a distance could either hear or understand them. Only in cases where the *Adhvaryu* had to speak to other officiating priests, commanding them to perform certain duties,[20] he was of course obliged to speak with a loud and distinct voice. All these verses and all the invocations which the *Adhvaryus* had to use, were collected in the ancient liturgy of the *Adhvaryus* together with the rules of the sacrifice. In this mixed form they exist in the Taittirīyaka. Afterwards the hymns were collected by themselves, separated from the ceremonial rules, and this collection is what we call the *Yajur-veda-Saṁhitā* or the prayer-book of the *Adhvaryu* priests.

There were some parts of the sacrifice, which according to ancient custom, had to be accompanied by songs, and hence another class of priests arose whose particular office it was to act as the chorus. This naturally took place at the most solemn sacrifices only. Though as yet we have no key as to the character of the music which the *Udgātṛs* performed, we can see from the numerous and elaborate rules, however unintelligible, that their music was more than mere chanting. The words of their songs were collected in the order of the sacrifice, and this *libretto* is what we possess under the name of Sāma-*veda-Saṁhitā*, or the prayer-book of the *Udgātṛ* priests.[21]

Distinct from these two classes, we have a third class of priests, the *Hotṛs,* whose duty it was to recite certain hymns during the sacrifice in praise of the deities to whom any particular act of the sacrificer was addressed. Their recitation was loud and distinct, and required the most accurate knowledge of the rules of euphony or *Śikṣā*. The *Hotṛs,* as a class, were the most highly educated order of priests. They were supposed to know both the proper pronunciation and the meaning of their hymns, the order and employment of which was taught in the Brāhmaṇas of the Bahvṛcas. But while both the *Adhvaryus* and *Udgātṛs* were confessedly unable to perform their duties without the help of their prayer-books, the *Hotṛs* were supposed to be so well versed in the ancient sacred poetry, as contained in the ten Maṇḍalas of the Ṛg-veda, that no separate prayer-book or Saṁhitā was ever arranged for their special benefit.

There is no *Saṁhitā* for the *Hotṛs* corresponding to the *Saṁhitās* of ths *Adhvaryus* and Udgātṛs. The *Hotṛ* learnt from the Brāhmaṇa, or in later times, from the Sūtra, what special duties he had to perform. He knew from those sources the beginnings or the names of the hymns which he had to recite at every part of the service. But in order to be able to use these indications, he had previously to know the whole body of Vedic poetry, so as to be ready to produce from the vast store of his memory whatever hymn or verse was called for at the sacrifice. There exists among the MSS. of walker's Collection a work entitled, Āśvalāyana-śākhokta-mantrā-saṁhitā, a collection of hymns of the Āśvalāyana-śākhā, which contains the hymns as required according to the Gṛhya-Sūtras of Aśvalāyana. It would have been easy to construct a similar collection for the Śrauta-Sūtras, but such a collection was never made, and it is never alluded to in the ancient literature of the Brāhmaṇas[22].

If then the Ṛg-veda-saṁhitā was not composed for the special benefit of the *Hotṛs,* much less of the other two classes of priests, it might he supposed that it had nevertheless a sacrificial character, and was intended to assist the fourth class of priests, or the *Brahmā,* properly so called. The *Brahmā,* as we saw, had to watch the three classes of priests and to correct any mistake they might commit. He was therefore, supposed to know the whole ceremonial and all the hymns employed by the *Hotṛ, Adhvaryu* and *Udgātṛ*. Now the Ṛg-veda does contain most of the hymns of the other two Vedas,[23] and in several places it is maintained that the *Brahmā* ought properly to be a *Hotṛ*. All this would render it not improbable that the Ṛg-veda-Saṁhitā belonged to the same age as the other two *Saṁhitās*: that its collection was suggested by the same idea which led to the collection of the hymns of the other two classes of priests, and that, for the special benefit of the *Brahmā,* it comprehended in one body all the hymns which the *Hotṛ,* the *Adhvaryu,* and *Udgātṛ* were expected to know singly. In this case the Ṛg-veda-Saṁhitā, instead of being more ancient, would in fact represent the latest collection of a sacred poetry.

It would be of no avail to appeal to the testimony of later authorities, such as the Purāṇas, in order to refute this theory. The Viṣṇu-purāṇa (p. 276), for instance, has the following remarks on this subject; "Vyāsa," it is said, "divided the one sacrificial Veda into four parts, and instituted the sacrificial rite administered by the four kinds of priests, in which it was the duty of the *Adhvaryu* to recite the *Yājuṣ* verses or direct the ceremony, of the *Hotṛ* to repeat the, *Ṛc;* of the *Udgātṛ* to chant the Sāman; and of the Brahmā to pronounce the formula called *'Atharvan.'* Then the Muni, having collected together the hymns called Ṛc, composed the Ṛg-veda. etc , and, with the Atharvans, he composed the rules of all the ceremonies suited to kings, and the function of the Brahmā agreeably to practice." This passage only serves to show that the authors of the Purāṇas were entirely ignorant of the tone and character of the Vedic literature, For although the Brahmā priest was the only Ṛtvij who had occasionally to use passages from the Atharva-veda, blessings, imprecations, etc.; yet the so called Atharva-veda had nothing in common with the three ancient Vedas, and contained no information on the general features of the great sacrifice, such as would have been indispensable to the superintendent of the other priests.[24]

The real answer to a supposition which would assign the Ṛg-veda-Saṁhitā to the Brahmā is, that to him also that collection of hymns would have been of no practical utility. He would have learnt from it many a hymn never called for, never used at any sacrifice; and he would have had to unlearn the order both of hymns and verses whenever he wished to utilise his knowledge for the practical objects of his station.

We may, therefore, safely ascribe the collection of the Ṛg-veda, or, as Professor Roth calls it, the historical Veda, to a less practical age than that of the Brāhmaṇa period; to an age, not entirely free from the trammels of a ceremonial, yet not completely enslaved by a system of mere formalities; to an age no longer creative and impulsive, yet not without some power of upholding the traditions of a past that spoke to a later generation of men through the very poems which they were collecting with so much zeal and accuracy.

The work of the Mantra period is not entirely represented by the collection of the ancient hymns. Such a work would be sufficient in itself to give a character to an age, and we might appeal, in the history of ancient Greek literature, to the age of the Diaskeuasts. A generation which begins to collect has entered into a new phase of life. Nations, like individuals, become conservatives when they cease to trust implicitly in themselves, and have learnt from experience that they are not better than their fathers. But though the distinctive feature of the Mantra period consisted in gathering the fruits of a bye-gone spring, this was not the only work which occupied the Brāhmaṇas of that age. Where poems have to be collected from the mouth of the people, they have likewise to be arranged. Corrections are supposed to be necessary; whole verses may have to be supplied. After collecting and correcting a large number of poems, many a man would feel disposed to try his own poetical powers; and if new songs were wanted, it did not reṇuire great talent to imitate the simple strains of the ancient Ṛṣis. Thus we find in the Ṛg-veda, that after the collection of the ten Maṇḍalas was finished, some few hymns were added, generally at the end of a chapter, which are known by the name of Khilas. We can hardly call them successful imitations of the genuine songs : but in India they seem to have soon acṇuired a certain reputation. They found their way into the Saṁhitās of the other Vedas; they are referred to in the Brāhmaṇas; and though they are not counted in the Anukramaṇīs, together with the original hymns, they are there also mentioned as recognised additions.

Besides these hymns, which were added after the collection of the ten books had been completed, there is another class of hymns, actually incorporated in the sacred Decads, but which nevertheless must be ascribed to poets who were imitators of earlier poets, and whose activity, whether some-what anterior to, or contemporaneous with the final edition of the Ṛg-veda-Saṁhitā, must be referred to the same Mantra period. We need not appeal to the tradition of the *Brāhmaṇas,* who, in matters of this kind, are extremely untrustworthy. They place a very small interval between the latest poets of the hymns and the final collection of the ten books. The latter they ascribe to Kṛṣṇa Dvaipāyana Vyāsa, the embodiment of the Indian *διασκευη,* whereas one of the poets whose hymns form part of the Saṁhitā, is Parāśara, the reputed father of Vyāsa.

But we have better evidence in the hymns themselves, that some of their authors belonged to a later generation than that of the most famous Ṛṣis. The most celebrated poets of the Veda are those who are now called the Mādhyamas,[25] from the fact of their hymns standing between the first and the last books of our collection. They ere Gṛtsamada, (2d Maṇḍala), Viśvāmitra (3d Maṇḍala), Vama-deva (4th Maṇḍala), Atri (5th Maṇḍala), Bharadvāja (6th Maṇḍala), and Vasiṣṭha (7th Maṇḍala). Added to these are, in the beginning, the hymns of various poets, collected in the first Maṇḍala, called the book of the *Śatarcins,* from the fact that each poet contributed about a hundred verses; and at the end, the book of the Pragātha hymns (8th Maṇḍala), the book of the Soma hymns (9th Maṇḍala), and the book of long and short hymns, ascribed to the Kshudra-sūkta and Mahāsākta poets, which, in accordance with its very name, is a miscellaneous collection.

It by no means follows that all the hymns of the seven middle Ṛṣis are more ancient than those of the first and the last books; or that these books contain nothing but modern hymns. But the very name of *Mādhyama,* given to the poets of the books from the second to the seventh, shows that they were considered, even by the Brāhmaṇas, as distinct from the first and the three last books. They are not the middle books numerically, but they are called so because they stand by themselves, in the midst of other books of a more miscellaneous character.

Traces, however, of earlier aud later poems are to be found through the whole collection of the Ṛg-veda; and many hymns have been singled out by different scholars as betrayaing a later origin than the rest. All such hymns I refer to the Mantra period, to an age which though chiefly occupied in collecting and arranging, possessed likewise the power of imitating, and carrying on the traditions of a former age.

It is extremely difficult to prove the modern origin of certain hymns, and I feel by no means convinced by the arguments which have been used for this purpose. At present, however, I need not enter into the minutiae of this critical separation of ancient and modern poetry. It is not my object to prove that this or that hymn is more modern than the rest; but I only wish to establish the general fact that, taken as a whole, the hymns do contain evidence of having been composed at various periods.

In order to guard against misconceptions it should be understood that if we call a hymn modern, all that can be meant is that it was composed during the period which succeeded the first spring of Vedic poetry, *i.e.,* during the Mantra period. There is not a single hymn in the Ṛg-veda that could be ascribed to the Brāhmaṇa period. Even a few of the *Khilas,* modern as they appear to us, presupposed by the Brāhmaṇas and quoted, together with other more ancient hymns. The most modern hymns in the Ṛg-veda-Saṁhitā, if our calculations are right, must have been composed previous to 800 B. C, previous to the first introduction of prose composition,

In order to prove that the hymns which are now thrown together into one body of sacred poetry, were not the harvest of one single generation of poets, we have only to appeal to the testimony of the poets themselves, who distinguish between ancient and modern hymns. Not only has the tradition of the Brāhmaṇas, which is embodied in the Anukramaṇīs, assigned certain hymns to *Ṛṣis,* who stand to each other in the relation of father and son, and grandson, but the hymns themselves allude to earlier poets, and events which in some are represented as present, are mentioned in others as belonging to the past. The argument which Dr. Roth[26] has used in order to prove the comparatively' modern date of the Atharvaṇa, applies with equal force to some of the hymns of the Ṛg-veda. Here, also, the names of Purumīḷha, Vasiṣṭha, Jamadagni, and others, who are known as the authors of certain hymns, are mentioned in other hymns as sages who in former times enjoyed the favour of the gods.

" As our ancestors have praised thee, we will praise thee," is a very frequent sentiment of the Vedic poets. A new song was considered a special honour to the gods. The first hymn of the Ṛg-veda gives utterance to this sentiment. "Agni," says Madhuchandas, " you who are worthy of the praises of ancient, and also of living poets, l bring hither you the gods."

Viśvāmitra the father of Madhuchandas, and himself one of the ancient Ṛṣi*s*. concludes his first hymn[27] with the words, "I have proclaimed, O Agni, these thy ancient songs,[28] and new songs for thee who art old. These great. libations have been made to him who showers benefits upon us : the sacred fire has been kept from generation to generation."

In another hymn,[29] Viśvāmitra distinguishes between three classes of hymns, and speaks of Indra as having been magnified by ancient, middle, and modern songs.

The sacrifice itself is sometimes represented as a thread which unites the living with the departed, and through them, with the first ancestors of man, the gods.[30] The son carries on the weaving which was interrupted by the death of his father,[31] and the poet, at the beginning of a sacred rite,[32] exclaims. I believe I see, with the eye of the mind those who in bye-gone days performed this sacrifice." With a similar feeling, Viśvāmitra, in his morning prayer, looks back to his fathers, who have gazed on the rising sun before him, and have exalted the power of the gods :[33]

" To Iadra goes my thought, spoken out from the heart, to him, the Lord, it goes, fashioned by the bard. It awakes you when it is recited at the sacrifice; Indra ! take heed of that which is made for you.

" Rising even before the day, awakening you when recited at the sacrifice, clothed in sacred white raiments,[34] this is our prayer, *the old, the prayer of our fathers.*

" The Dawn, the mother of the twins, has given birth to the twins *(i. e.* Day and Night the top of my tongue fell, for he (the Sun) came. The twins, who have come near the root of the Sun, assume their bodies as they are born together, the destoyers of darkness.

" Amongst men there is no one to scoff at them who were our fathers, who fought among the cattle. Indra the mighty and powerful, has stretched out their firm folds."[35]

Vasiṣṭha, another of the ancient Ṛṣis, speaks likewise of ancient and modern hymns by which others, besides his own family, secured the favour of the gods.[36] "Whatever poets, ancient or modern, wise men, made prayers to thee, O Indra ! ours may be thy propitious friendship : protect us, O god ! always with your blessings !"

One of ihe greatest in the life of Vasiṣṭha was the victory which King Sudās achieved under his guidance. But in the Maṇḍala of the Vasiṣṭhas, the same event is sometimes alluded to as belonging to the past, and in one of the hymns ascribed to the same Vasiṣṭha we read : "Committing our sons and offspring to the same good protection which Aditi, Mitra, and Varuṇa, like guardians, give to Sudās, let us not make our gods angry."

These passages, which might be greatly increased, will be sufficient to show that there were various generations of Vedic poets. The traces of actual imitations are less considerable than we might expect under such circumstances; and where we do meet with stereotyped phrases, it is often difficult to say which poet used them for the first time. When we find Dīrghatamas Aucathya, beginning a hymn to Viṣṇu with the words, "Let me now proclaim the manly deeds of Viṣṇu;" and another hymn of Hiraṇyastūpa Āṅgirasa to Indra, beginning with, "Let me now proclaim the manly deeds of Indra," we may suppose that the one hymn was composed with a pointed reference to the other; but we cannot tell which of the two was the original, and which the copy.

The fact, however, of ancient and modern hymns being once admitted, we may hope to arrivé gradually at some criteria by which to fix the relative age of single hymns. Some of the hymns betray their comparatively modern origin by frequent allusion to ceremonial subjects. I do not mean to say that the sacrifice as such, was not as old and primitive an institution as sacred poetry itself. Most of the hymns own their origin to sacrifices, to public or domestic holydays. But those sacrifices were of a much more simple nature than the later Vedie ceremonial. When the father of a family was priest, poet, and king, in one person, there was no thought as yet of distributing the ceremonial duties among sixteen priests, each performing his own peculiar office, or of measuring the length of every log that should be put on the fire, and determining the shape of every vessel in which the libations should be offered. It was only after a long succession of sacrifices that the spontaneous acts and observances of former generations would be treasured up, and established as generally binding. It was only after the true meaning of the sacrifice was lost, that unmeaning ceremonies could gain that importance which they have in the eyes of priests. If a hymn addressed to the gods had been heard, if a famine had ceased after a prayer, an illness been cured with a charm, an enemy been vanquished with war songs; not only would these songs, however poor, be kept and handed down in a family as the most precious heirloom, but the position in which the poet recited them, the time of the day, the most minute circumstances of every act, would be superstitiously preserved, in order to insure the future efficiency of the prayer. This was the origin of a ceremonial so complicated as that of the Brāhmaṇas. Now, we find in some of the hymns allusions which refer, not to a naturally growing, but to an artificial and a decaying ceremonial.

The most ancient name for a priest by profession was *Purohita,* which only means *prcepositus* or *prmses.* The *Purohita,* however, was more than a priest. He was the friend and counsellor of a chief, the minister of a king, and his companion in peace and war. Vasiṣṭha and Viśvāmitra, who with their families have both been the *Purohitas* of King Sudās, did more for the king than chanting hymns to implore the aid of their gods. Vasiṣṭha was with the army of Sudās when that king conņuered the ten kings who had crossed the Paruṣṇi (Hydraotis, Ravi); Viśvāmitra, when Sudās himself crossed the Vipaś (Hyphasis, Beyah) and the Śatadru (Hesudras, Sutlej).[37] The importance of their office is best shown by the violent contest which these two families of the Vasiṣṭhas and Viśvāmitras carried on, in order to secure for themselves the hereditary dignity of Purohita. There was a similar contest between the priest at the Court of Asamāti, a descendant of Ikṣvāku. He, not satisfied with his four Purohitas, Bandhu, Subandhu, Śrutabandhu, and Viprabandhu, who were brothers and belonged to the family of the Gaupāyanas, dismissed them, and appointed two new priests *(Māyāvinau).* Those new Purohitas, seeing that the Gaupāyanas used incantations against the life of King Asamāti, retaliated, and caused, by their charms, the death of one of them, Subandhu. Thereupon the other three brothers composed a song to appease the wrath of the two priests, and to save their own lives. This song and some others connected with the same contest, form part of the 8th Ashtaka of the Ṛg-veda.

The very fact of the office of Purohita being hereditary shows that it partook of a political character. It seems to have been so at an early time. In a hymn of the Ṛg-veda, i. 94. 6, where *Agni* is invoked under several priestly names, he is called, *Januṣā* Purohita or Purohita by birth. Cf. i. 102. 8. And we find several instances where priests, if once employed by a royal family, claim to be employed always. When Janamejaya Pārikṣita ventured to perform a sacrifice without the Kāśyapas, he was forced by the Asitamṛgas, a family of the Kaśyapas to employ them again. When Viśvāntara Sauṣadmana drove away the Syāparṇas from his sacrifice, he was prevailed upon by Rāma Mārga-veya to call them back.[38] All this shows that the priestly office was of great importance in the ancient times of India.

The original occupation of the *Purohita* may simply have to perform the usual sacrifices; but with the ambitious policy of the *Brāhmaṇas,* it soon became a stepping-stone to political power. Thus we read in the Aitareya-brāhmaṇa : "Breath does not leave him before time; he lives to an old age; he goes to his full time, and does not die again who has a *Brāhmaṇa* as guardian of his land, as *Purohita.* He conquers power by power; obtains strength by strength; the.people obey him, peaceful and of one mind."

Vāmadeva, in one of his hymns,[39] expresses the same sentiment; and though he does not use the word *Purohita,* there can be little doubt that the Aitareya-brāhmaṇa is right in explaining the words Bṛhaspati and Brahmā by *Purohita.*

"That king withstands his enemies with strong power who supports a Bṛhaspati[40] in comfort, praised him, and honours him as the first.

"The king before whom there walks a priest, lives well established in his own house; to him the earth yields for ever, and before him the people bow of their own accord.

"Unopposed he conquers treasures, those of his enemies and his friends, himself a king, who makes presents to a *Brāhmaṇa* : the gods protect him."

This shows that the position of the *Brāhmaṇas* at the courts of the Kṣatriya kings was more influential than that of mere chaplains. They walked before the king, and considered themselves superior to him. In later times, when the performance of the ceremonies no longer devolved on the *Purohita,* the chief priest took the place of the so called Brahmā priest, who was the *episcopos* of the whole, though he himself took little active part in it. Thus at the sacrifice of Hariścandra, described in the Aitareya-brāhmaṇa (vū. 16-), Āyāsya acts as Udgātṛ, Jamadagni as Adhvaryu, Viśvāmitra as Hotṛ, and Vasiṣṭha, who is known as the Purohita of the Ikṣvāku dynasty, as Brahmā. In the Taittirīya-saṁhitā (ūi. 5. 2.), we read : "Men were born, having a Vasiṣṭha for Purohita, and therefore Vasiṣ ṭha is to be chosen as Brahmā." In the Aitareya-brāhmaṇa again the Brāhmaṇa is identified with Bṛhaspati, who was the *Purohita,* or *pura-etr* of the gods.

The original institution of a *Purohita,* as the spiritual adviser of a king or a chief, need not be regarded as the sign of a far advanced hierarchical system. The position of the Brāhmaṇas must have been a peculiar one in India from the very beginning. They appear from the very first as a class of men of higher intellectual power than the rest of the Āryan colonists; and their general position, if at all re-cognized, could hardly have been different from that of Vasiṣṭha in the camp of Sudās. The hymns, therefore, which only allude to a *Purohita,* or priests in general, need not be ascribed to a late age. But when we meet in certain hymns not only with these, but with various grades of priests, we may be sure that such hymns belong to the Mantra period, and not to the age of primitive Vedic poetry.

This is a question of degree. If we find such verses as "the singers sing you, the chaunters chaunt you,"[41] where the singers are called not by their technical name of Udgātṛ, but Gāyatrins, and the chaunters not by their technical name of Hotṛ, but Arkins, all we can say is that the later division of the sacrifice between Hotṛ and Udgātṛ priests is here found in its first elements. It does not follow that there existed at that time two recognised classes of priests, still less that the Udgātṛs were then in possession of their own Saṁhita. But in Rg. v. 44. we read :

"The Ṛc verses long for the god who watches; the Sāman verses go to him who watches; this Soma libation calls for him that watches : I, O Agni ! am at home in thy friendship."[1]

"[J] Here it is clear that the distinction between Ṛc verses, that were recited, and Sāman verses that were sung, must have been established, though again we need not go so far as to maintain the actual existence of a prayer-book for the Udgātṛ priests.

The third class of priests, the Adhvaryus, who performed the principal acts of the sacrifice, are likewise alluded to in the hymns. We read, Rv. iii. 36. 10: "Accept, O Indra! what is offered you from the hand of the Adhvaryu, or the sacrifice of the libation of the Hotṛ."

There are several hymns which contain allusions to the Darśapūrṇamāsa, the famous New and Full Moon sacrifices. These sacrifices in themselves may have been of the greatest antiquity, as old as any attempt at a regulated worship of the gods. Passages therefore, where we only meet with allusions to the phases of the moon, and their recurrent appeal to the human heart to render thanks to the unknown Powers that rule the chances of nature, and the chances of human life, prove by no means, as the Indian commentators suppose, that at the time of the ancient Vedic poets the lunar ceremonies were of the same solemn and complicated nature as in Inter times. We read, Rv. 1. 194. 4 : " Let us bring fuel, let us prepare oblation remembering you at each conjunction of the moon.[43] Do you perfect our sacred acts that we may live long. Let us not fail in thy friendship, O Agni."[44] Passages like this do not necessitate the admission of a full-grown ceremonial, the only point to its natural beginnings. The same remark applies to the three daily prayers, at sun-rise, noon, and sunset. Nature herself suggests these three periods as the most appropriate for rendering thanks to the heavenly givers of light and life. Thus Manu Vaivasvata[45] alludes several times to the three periods of the day which the gods themselves have fixed for their sacrifice, sunrise *(Sūrya udayati,* or *sūra udite),* mid-day *(madhyandine divaḥ or madhyandine),* and sun-set *(nimruci,* or *ātuci),* and he calls this established order of the sacrifice *ṛta,* the law or the truth.

But when these sacrifices are mentioned with their technical names, when the morning, and noon, and evening prayers are spoken of as first, second, and third libation, we feel that we move in a different atmosphere, and that listening to priests rather than to poets. Thus Rv. iii. 28. 1 :

" Agni, accept our offering, the cake, O Jātavedas, at the *morning libation,* you rich in prayer.

" The baked cake, O Agni, is prepared for you alone indeed; accept it, O youngest of all the gods.

" Agni, eat the cake offered to you *when the day is over,* you art the son of strength, stationed at the sacrifice.

" At the *mid-day libation,* O Jātavedas, accept here the cake, O sage ! Agni, the wise do not diminish at the sacrifices the share of you, who art great.

" Agni, as you love at *the third libation* the cake, O son of strength, that is offered to you, therefore, moved by our praise, take this precious oblation to the immortal gods to rouse them.

" Agni, you who art growing, accept, O Jātavedas, the offering cake, at the *close of day.* "

This hymn contains in reality nothing but a set of invocations for the three daily libations; it uses the very words used in the ceremonial, and it would hardly have been written except by some pious priest brought up under the system of the Brāhmaṇic ceremonial.

The technical names of the priests are of frequent occurrence. The name of Ṛtvij would not prove a great development of the ceremonial. It would only mean the priest who officiates at the various seasons. It was then that sacred fire was kindled by friction. It was lighted in the morning day after day *(dive dive),* it was lighted at the full and new moon, and it was lighted likewise to each of the great natural divisions of the year. Thus it is said, Rv. iii. 29. 10 : " This wood is thy mother every season, born from which you shinest. Do you sit there, as you know it, and make our prayers prosper."

There is nothing artificial in this. But when we meet with the names of the Ṛtvij priests, such as *Potṛ,* Āgnīdhra, Praśāstṛ, Neshṭṛ, *Hotṛ, Adhvaryu, Brahmā,*[46] we can no longer doubt that here we have to deal with late and artificial poetry. These names of priests afterwards still further generalised, and transferred to Agni, who, as the gods of fire, if supposed to carry the offerings of men to the seats of the gods. He is called the *purohita,* or high-priest *Sapta-Hotṛ* also and *Sapta-mānuṣa,* acting as seven priests,[47] are names applied to the god of the sacrificial flame.

There is a whole class of hymns commonly called *dāna-stutis,* or praises of gifts. They are the thanksgivings of certain priests for presents received from their royal patrons. All of these, like the Latin panegyrics, betray a modern character, and must be referred to the Mantra period. In the Brāhmaṇa period, however, not only are these panegyrics known but the liberality of these royal pntrons is held up to the admiration and imitation of later generations by stories which had to be repeated at the sacrifices. In the Śāṅkhāyana-Sūtras (xvi. 11.), the following stories called Nārāśaṅsa (neuter), are mentioned as fit for such occasions. The story of Śunaḥśepha; of Kakṣīvat Auśija who received gifts from Svānaya Bhāvyaya; of Śyāvāsava Ārcanānasa who received gifts from Vaiḍadaśvi; of Bharadvāja who received gift from Bṛbu the carpenter, and Prastoka Sārñjaya; for Vasiṣṭha who was Purohita of King Sudās Paijavana; of Medhāthi, and bow Āsaṅga Plāyogi having been a woman became a man; of Vatsa Kāṇva who received gifts from Tirindira Pāraśvavyaya; of Vaśa Aśvya who received gifts from Pṛthuśravas Kānīna; of Praskaṇva who received gifts from Pṛṣadhra Medhya Métariśva (sic); of Nābhānediṣṭha Mānava, who received gifts from the Aṅgirasa. All these acts of royal liberality are recorded in the hymns of thc Ṛg-vcda, but thc hymns themselves may safely be referred to the second age of Vedic poetry.

Another and most convincing proof that some of our hymns belong to a secondary period of Vedic poetry, is contained in a song, ascribed to Vasiṣṭha, in which the elaborate ceremonial of the *Brāhmaṇas* is actually turned into ridicule. The 103rd hymn in the 7th Maṇḍala, which is called a panegyric of the frogs, is clearly a satire on the priests; and it is curious to observe that the same animal should have been chosen by the Vedic satirist to represent the priests, which by the earliest satirist of Greece was selected as the representative of the Homeric heroes.

" After lying prostrate for a year, like *Brāhmaṇas* performing a vow, the frogs have emitted their voice, roused by the showers of heaven. When the heavenly waters fell upon them as upon a dry fish lying in a pond, the music of the frogs comes together, like the lowing of cows with their calves.

" When, at the approach of the rainy season, the rain has wetted them, as they were longing and thirsting, one goes to the other while he talks, like a son to his father, saying, *akkhala βρεχεχέξ χοάεχοάξ*

" One of them embraces the other, when they revel in the shower of water, and the brown frog jumping after he has been ducked, joins his speech with the green one.

" As one of them repeats the speech of the other, like a pupil and his teacher, every limb of them is as it were in growth, when they converse eloquently on the surface of the water.

" One of them is Cow-noise, the other Goat-noise, one is brown, the other green; they are different though they bear the same name, modulate their voices in many ways as they speak.

" Like *Brāhmaṇas* at the Soma sacrifice of Atirātra, sitting round a full pond and talking, you, O frogs, celebrate this day of the year when the rainy season begins.

" These *Brāhmaṇas* with their Soma have had their say, performing the annual rite. These *Adhvaryus,* sweating whilst they carry the hot pots, pop out like hermit.

" They have always observed the order of the gods as they are to be worshipped in the twelvemonth; these men do not neglect their season; the frogs who had been like hot pots themselves are now released when the rainy season of the year sets in.

" Cow-noise gave, Goat-noise gave, the Brown gave, and the Green gave us treasures. The frogs who give us hundreds of cows, lengthen our life in the rich autumn."

There seems thus to be little room for doubt, if we consider the character of this and similar hymns, that we must make a distinction between two periods in the history of Vedic poetry, the one primitive, the other secondary. Poems, like those which we have just examined, are not the result of an original, free, and unconscious inspiration.

They belong to an imitative, reflecting, and criticising age. An exact division between the ancient and the modern portions of the Ṛg-veda will probably be impossible even after these ancient relics have been studied with a much more searching accuracy than hitherto. The language which might be expected to contain the safest indications of the more ancient or more modern date of certain hymns, has, owing to the influence of oral tradition, assumed an uniformity which baffles the most careful analysis. Nor would it be safe to trust to our preconceived notions as to the peculiar character of genuine and of artificial poetry. Some of the very latest poets may have been endowed with a truly poetical genius, when the originality and freshness of their thoughts would seem to place them in a better age. Nor is the fact that the ancient poets enunciate thoughts entirely their own, and with the full consciousness that what they say has never been said before, sufficient to give to all their productions so deep a stamp of truth and faith that our weakened eyes should always discern it. But although we may hesitate about single hymns, whether they are the productions of ancient or modern Ṛṣis, we cannot hesitate as to the general fact that the ten books of the Ṛg-veda at the time they were finally collected, comprised the poetry of two different periods. This is the only important point for our purpose. We ascribe the later poets of the Veda to the Mantra period, so that we com-prise within that period two apparently distinct, yet, in reality, very cognate tendencies. We suppose that the Mantra period was an age of Epigonoi, occupied at first in imitating the works of their father, and towards the end engaged in the more useful employment of collecting all that was within reach, modern as well as ancient, and handing it down to the careful guardianship of later generations. Two hundred yeárs will not be too long a time for the gradual progress of this work. There are several generations of modern poets, and probably two classes of collectors to be accommodated, and the work of the last collectors, the collectors of the Maṇḍalas, could not have commenced before the last line of every poem which now forms part of the ten Maṇḍalas was written. I there for fix the probable chronological limits of the Mantra period between 800 and 1000 B.C.

Before we leave the Mantra period there is one question which if it cannot be fully answered, requires at least to be carefully discussed. was the collection of the ten books of Vedic hymns the work of' persons cognisant of the art of writing or not ? Were the 1017 hymns of the Ṛg-veda, after they had been gathered into one body, preserved by memory or on paper ?

We can hardly expect to find answer to this question in the hymns themselves. Most persons acquainted with the history of popular poetry among the principal nations of antiquity would be ready to admit that the original composition and preservation of truly national poetry were everywhere due to the unaided efforts of memory. Where writing is known, it is almost impossible to compose a thousand hymns without bringing in some such words as, writing, reading, paper, or pea. Yet there is not one single allusion in these hymns to anything connected with writing.

Let us consider the Old Testament.

The Ten Commandments were not only proclaimed by the voice of God but Moses "went down from the mount, and the two tables of the testimony were in the hand : the tables were written on both their sides; on the one side and on the other were they written, And the tables were the work of God, and the writing was the writing of God, graven upon the tables." (Exodus xxxii. 15. 16.) Here we can have no doubt that the author of the book of Exodus, and the people to whom it was addressed, were acquainted with the art of writing. Again we read (Exodus xxiv. 7), that "Moses took the book of the covenant, and read in the audience of the people;" and (Exodus xxv. 16.), the Lord commanded Moses, saying, "You shall put into the ark the testimony which I shall give you. The covenant here spoken of must have existed as a book, or, at least, in some tangible form.

A nation so early acquainted with letters and books as the Jews would naturally enjoy some of the terms connected with writing in a metaphorical sense. Thus we read in the Psalms (lvi. 9.), "Put you my tears into your bottle : are they not in your book ?"

lxix. 28. "Let them be blotted out of the Book of the living, and not be written with the righteous."

xl. 7. "Then said I, Lo I, come; in the volume of the book it is written of me."

xlv. 1. "My tongue is the pen of a ready writer."

In the Book of Job (xix. 23.), we actually read, "Oh that my words were now written ! oh that they were printed in a book ! That they were graven with an iron pen and lead in the rock for ever !" "Printed" here can only mean "written."

Proverbs iii. 3. "Write them upon the table of your heart."

In the Homeric poems, on the contrary, where the whole Grecian life lies before us in marvellous completeness and distinctness there is not a single mention of writing. The carried by Bellerophon instead of a letter, are the best proof that, even for such purposes, not to speak of literary composition, the use of letters was unknown to the Homeric age. The art of writing, when it is not only applied to short inscriptions but to literature, forms such a complete revolution in the history of a nation, and in all the relations of society, both civil and political, that, in any' class of ancient literature, the total absence of any allusion to writing, may safely be supposed to prove the absence of the art at the time when that literature arose. We know the complete regeneration of modern Europe which was wrought by the invention of printing. Every page of the literature of the sixteenth century, every pamphlet or fly-sheet of the Reformation, tells us that printing had been invented. The discovery of writing, and more specially the application of writing to literary purposes, was a discovery infinitely more important than that of printing. And yet we are asked to believe that Homer has hidden his light under a bushel, and erased every expression connected with writing from his poetical dictionary !

But though it is certain that the Homeric poets did not write, or, if we are to adopt the legendary language of certain critics, though it is certain that blind Homer did not keep a private secretary, there is no doubt that, at the time of Peisistratos, when the final collection of the Homeric poems took place., this collection was a collection of written poems. Peisistratos possessed a large library, and, though books were not so common in his time as they were in the time of Alcibiades, when every schoolmaster had his Iliad,[45] yet, ever since the importation of paper into Greece, writing was a common acquirement of the educated classes of Greeks. The whole civilisation af Greece, and the rapid growth of Greek literature, has been ascribed to the free trade between Egypt and Greece, beginning with the Saidic dynasty.[49] Greece imported all its paper from Egypt; and without paper no Greek literature would have been possible. The skins of animals were too rare, and their preparation too expensive, to permit the growth of a popular literature. Herodotus mentions it as a peculiarity of the barbarians, that at his time some of them still wrote on skins only. Paper (papyrus or byblus) was evidently to Greece what linen paper was to Europe in the middle ages.[50]

Now, if we look for any similar traces in the history of Indian literature, our search is completely disappointed. There is no mention of writing-materials, whether paper, bark, or skins, at the time when the Indian Diaskeuasts collected ths songs of their Ṛṣis; nor is there any allusion to writing during the whole of the Brāhmaṇa period. This upsets the common theories about the origin of prose literature. According to Wolf,[51] prose composition is a safe sign of a written literature. It is not so in India. The whole of the Brāhmaṇa literature, however incredible it may seem, shows not a single vestige of the art of writing. Nay, more than this, even during the Sūtra period all the evidence we' can get would lead us to suppose that even then, though the art of writing began to be known, the whole literature of India was preserved by oral tradition only.

It is of little avail in researches of this kind to say that such a thing is impossible. We can form no opinion of the powers of memory in a state of society so different from ours as the Indian *Pariṣads* are from our universities. Feats of memory, such as we hear of now and then, show that our notions of the limits of that faculty are quite arbitrary. Our own memory has been systematically undermined for many generations. To speak of nothing else, one sheet of "The Times" newspaper every morning is quite sufficient to distract and unsettle the healthiest memory. The remnants of our own debilitated memory cannot furnish us with the right measure of the primitive powers of that faculty. The Guaranies, who are represented by Missionaries as the lowest specimens of humanity, evinced such powers of memory when they were once taught to listen and to reason, that it became a custom to make the chief Indian of of the town, or one of the magistrates, repeat the sermon just delivered from the pulpit before the people in the street, or in the court-yard of a house, and they almost all did it with the utmost fidelity, without missing a sentence.[52] Even at the present day, when MSS. arc neither scarce nor expensive, the young *Brāhmaṇas* who learn the songs of the Veda and the Brāhmaṇas, and the Sūtras, invariably learn them from oral tradition, and know them by heart. They spend year after year under the guidance of their teacher learning a little, day after day, repeating what they have learnt as part of their daily devotion, until at last they have mastered their subject, and are able to become teachers in turn. The ambition to master more than one subject is hardly known in India. This system of educatian has been going on ever since the Brāhmaṇa period, and as early as the Prātiśākhyas we find the most minute rules on the mnemonic system to be followed by every teacher. The only difference in modern times, after the invention of writing, is that a *Brāhmaṇa* is not only commanded to pass his apprenticeship at the house of his Guru, and to learn from his mouth all that a *Brāhmaṇa* is bound to know, but the fiercest imprecations are uttered against all who would presume to acquire their knowledge from written sources. In the Mahābhārata we read, 'Those who sell the Vedas, and even those who write them, those also who defile them, they shall go to hell."[53] Kumārila says, "That knowledge of the truth is worthless which has been acnuired from the Veda, if the Veda has not been rightly comprehended, if it has been learnt from writing, or been received from a Śūdra.[54]

How then was the Veda learnt ? It was learnt by every *Brāhmaṇa* during twelve years of his studentship or *Brahmacharyā*. This according to Gautama, was the shortest period, sanctioned only for men who wanted to marry, and to become *Gṛhasthas*. *Brāhmaṇas* who did not wish to marry were allowed to spend forty-eight years as students. The Prātiśākhya gives us a glimpse into the lecture-rooms of the Brāhmaṇic colleges. "The Guru," it is said,[55] "who has himself formerly been a student, should make his pupils read. He himself takes his seat either to the east, or the north, or the north-east. If he has no more than one or two pupils, they sit at his right hand. If he has more, they place themselves according as there is room. They then embrace their master, and say, 'Sir, read !' The master gravely says 'Om,' *i. e.* 'Yes.' He then begins to say a *Praśna* (a question), which consists of three verses.[56] In order that no word may escape the attention of his pupils, he pronounces all with the high accent,[57] and repeats certain words twice, or he says 'so' *(iti)* after these words.

The chief difficulties in the pronounciation of the Veda are the changes of the final and initial letters.[58] The pupils are' instructed in these euphonic rules independently (the Śiksha), but whenever a difficult case of *sandhi* occurs, the Guru examines his audience and explains the difficulties. And here the method followed is this. After the Guru has pronounced a group of words, consisting of three or sometimes (in long compounds) of more words, the first pupil repeats the first word, and when anything is to be explained, the teacher stops him; and says, "Sir."[59] After it has been explained by the pupil who is at the head of the class, the permission to contiérent is given with the words, "Well, Sir." After the words of the teacher have thus been repeated by one, the next pupil has to apply to him with the word, "Sir."[60] When there is no difficulty, the rule seems to be that the Guru says two words at a time, which are then repeated by the pupil. If it is a compound, one word only is to be pronounced by the Guru, and to be repeated by the pupil. After a section of three verses has thus been gone through, all the pupils have to rehearse it again and again. When they have mastered it, they have to recite the whole without any break, with an even voice, observing all the rules of *sandhi,* marking slightly the division in the middle of compounds, and pronouncing every syllable with the high accent.[61] It does not seem as if several pupils were allowed to recite together, for it is stated distinctly that the Guru first tells the verses to his pupil on the right, and that every pupil, after his task is finished, turns to the right, and walks round the tutor. This must occupy a long time every day, considering that a lecture consists of sixty and more *Praśnas*, or of about 180 verses. The pupils are not dismissed till the lecture is finished. At the end of the lecture, the tutor, after the last half-verse is finished, says, "Sir," the pupil replies, "Yes, Sir." He then repeats the proper verses and formulas, which have to be repeated at the end of every reading, embraces his tutor, and is allowed to withdraw.

These rules speak for themselves. They show that at the

time when young *Brāhmaṇas* had to spend from twelve to forty-eight years of their life in doing nothing but learning and rehearsing the Veda,[62] such a system must have had an object worthy of such efforts. Such an object existed, if, in the absence of writing, the sacred songs, which were believed to be the only means to salvation were to be preserved and guarded against loss and corruption. If, at the time of the Prātiśākhyas, writing had been known, some mention of a book as a sacred object would surely have occurred somewhere. We know from the Gṛhya-Sūtras every event in the life of a *Brāhmaṇa,* from his birth to his death. Not a word is ever said about his learning to write.

The earliest allusion to this system of oral teaching occurs in a hymn of the Ṛg-veda which must be ascribed to the Mantra period. In the primitive poetry of the Chandas period there is no mention either of writing or teaching. But in a satirical hymn of the Vasiṣṭhas (vū. 103, 5) in which the frogs are compared with Brāhmaṇas, teaching their pupils, it is said: "One frog repeats the words of another, like a pupil who repeats the words of his teacher." (See p. 453.) No similar allusion to writing is to be found even in the latest hymns, the so-called Khilas. If writing had been known during the Brāhmaṇa period, is it likely that these works, which are full of all kinds of mystic lucubrations on the origin of all things, should never with a single word have alluded to the art of writing, an art so wonderful that the Greeks would fain ascribe its discovery to one of the wisest gods of the wisest nation on earth ? If letters had been known during the period when men in India were still able to create gods, the god of letters would have found his place in the Vedic pantheon side by side with Sarasvatī, the goddess of speech, and Pūṣan, the god of agriculture. No such god is to be found in India, or in any of the genuine mythologies of the Āryan world.

But there are stronger arguments than these to prove that, before the time of Pāṇini, and before the first spreading of

Buddhism in India, writing for literary purposes was absolutely unknown.

If writing had been known to Pāṇini, some of his grammatical terms would surely point to the graphical appearance of words. I maintain that there is not a single word in Pāṇini's terminology which presupposes the existence of writing. The general name for letters is *varṇa.* This does not mean colour in the sense of a painted letter, but the colouring or modulation of the voice.[63] *Akṣara,* which is used for letter and syllable, means what is indestructible, radical, or an element. We speak of stops as signs of interpunction; Pāṇini only speaks of *virāmas,* stoppages of the voice. The names of the letters are not derived from their shape, as in the Semitic names of Alpha, Beta, Gamna. With the exception of the *r,* their names are their sounds. The name for *r, Repha,* does not occur in Pāṇini. Kātyāyna, however (iii. 3, 108. 4), explains the derivation of *Repha,* and in iv. 4, 128, 2, he uses it for *ra.* In the Prātiśakhyas likewise, the word is well-known, and as- the participle *riphita* is used in the same works, there can be little doubt that *Repha* is derived from a root *riph,* to snarl or hiss.

The terms for the three accents show no traces of writing, such as the Latin word "circumflexus."

What would have been more natural, if writing had been known in Pūṇini's time, than that he should have called the dot of the Anusvāra, *vindu i.e.,* dot, and the Visarga, *dvi-vindu,* the double dot ? Let us take a later grammarian, Vopadeva, and we find such words at once. In Vopadeva, the Anusvāra is called *vindu,* the Visarga, *dvi-vindu.* What the Prātiśākhyas and Pāṇini called the *Jihvāmulīya* (X). the sibilant formed near the base of the tongue, and *Upadhmānīya (X),* the labial flatus, Vopadeva calls *Vajrākrti,* having the shape of the thunderbolt (x), and *Gajakumbhākrti,* having the shape of an elephant's two frontal bones (ω).

The term *arddhacandra* (̐), or half-moon, belongs to the

same class of grammatical terms. Why should these words occur in later grammarians, and not one of them be found in the Prātiśākhyas or Pāṇini ?

Another class of words which would be sure to betray the existence of writing where writing was known, are the words expressive of reading, composing, book, chapter, paragraph, etc. The most usual word for reading in Sanskrit is *adhyeti* or *adhīte,* and at first sight the very existence of such a word might seem to prove the existence of books that could be read. But we have seen in the Prātiśākhyas what was meant when the pupils asked their tutor to make them read. *Adhyeti* and adhīte, from *adhi,* over, and √ i, to go, mean "he goes over a thing, he conquers it, acquires it;" and the very expression "to read a work from the mouth of the tutor," would be sufficient to show that the work existed, not as a book, but in men's memory. Another expression of the same kind is found in Manu (x. ṇ: "All the three castes may read the Veda, but the *Brāhmaṇa* alone is allowed to proclaim, *i. e;* to teach it *(prabrūyāt).* To teach is expressed by causative of the verb *adhyeti, adhyāpayati,* he makes read *i. e.,* he teaches.[64] The ancient Hindus distinguish between two kinds of reading, the *grahaṇādhyayana,* the acquisitive reading, and the *dhāraṇādhyayana,* the conservative reading; the former being the first acquisition of a work, the latter its rehearsing in order not to lose a volume that once belonged to one's mental library. This rehearsing, or *svādhyāya,* self-reading, was as sacred a duty as the first acquisition. It was by means of this *svādhyāya* alone that works could be said to live. We meet with similar ex-pressions in other literatures of the ancient world. Ahura masdā, when he wishes-his law to live among men, requires jimo to be not only the "rememberer" *(mereta)* but the bearer and preserver *(bhereta)* of the Zarathustrian revelation. And many centuries later, Mahāvīra,[65] the founder of the Jaina religion, is called *sāraê, vāraê,* and *dhāraê* of sacred knowledge, *smāraka,* a rememberer, *vāraka,* a guardian who keeps it from profane eyes, and *dhāraka,* a holder who does not forget the knowledge which he once acquired.

Even so late a writer as Kumārila, when he speaks of the material existence of the Veda, can only conceive of it as existing in the minds of men. "The Veda," he says, "is distinctly to be perceived by means of the senses. It exists, like a pot or any other object, in man. Perceiving it in another man, people learn it and remember it. Then others, again perceiving it, as it is remembered by these, learn it and remember it, and thus hand it on to others. Therefore, the theologian concludes, the Veda is without a beginning."[66] These theological arguments may be passed over : but immediately afterwards, in order to show that the Veda has a material existence, Kumārila uses another curious expression, which shows again that to him the Veda existed only in the memory of men. "Before we hear the word Veda," he says, " we perceive, as different from all other objects, and as different from other Vedas, something in the form of the Ṛg-veda that exists within the readers, and things in the form of Mantras and Brāhmaṇas, different from others." Such arguments would not occur to people who were accustomed from time immemorial to appeal to a book as the sacred authority of their faith. When contemporaneously with our Reformation, Nānaka founded the religion of the Sikhs, we find in India, as well as elsewhere, that a book, a real book, was considered as the firmest foundation of a new faith. "At their assemblies, when the chiefs and principal leaders are seated, the Ādi-Grantha (the first book) and Daśama Pādshāka Grantha are placed before them; they all bend their heads before these scriptures, and exclaim, Wā ! Gurujikā Khālsā ! Wā ! Gurujikī Fateh!" A greater ṇuantity of cakes, made of wheat, butter, and sugar, are then placed before the volumes of their sacred writings, and covered with a cloth. These holy cakes, which are in commemoration of the injunction of Nānaka to eat and to give to others to eat, next receive the salutation of the assembly, who then rise, and the Akālis, pray aloud while the musicians play. The Akālis, when the prayers are finished, desire the council to be seated. They sit down, and the cakes being uncovered are eaten of by all classes of Sikhs; those distinctions of original tribes, which are on other occasions kept up, being on this occasion laid aside, in token of their general and complete union in one cause, The Akālis then exclaim, "Sirdars (chiefs) ! this is a Gurumatā" (a great assembly); on which prayers are again said aloud. The chiefs, after this, sit closer, and say to each other : "The. sacred Grantha (book) is betwixt us, let us swear by our scriptures to forget all external disputes, and to be united."[67]

Such a scene would be impossible among pure Brāhmaṇas. They never speak of their *granthas* or books. They speak of their *Veda,* which means "knowledge." They speak of their *Śruti,* which means what they have heard with their ears. They speak of *Smṛti,* which means what their fathers have declared unto them. We meet with the Brāhmaṇas, i.e. the sayings of Brāhmaṇas; with *Sūtras, i. e.,* the strings of rules; with *Vedāṅgas, i. a.,* the members of the Veda : with *Pravācanas, i. e.,* preachings; with *Śāstras, i.e.,teach*ings; with *Dar'śanas, i. e.,* demonstrations; but we never meet with a book, or a volume, or a page.

If we take the ordinary modern words for book, ink, writing, etc , not one of them has as yet been discovered in any Sanskrit work of genuine antiquity. Book, in modern Sanskrit, is *pustam* or *pustakam,* a word most likely of foreign origin.[68] It occurs in such works as the Hitopadeśa, where we read of a person, "neither read in books nor taught by a tutor." The Hitopadeśa itself is said to be written *(likhyate)* as an extract from the Pañcatantra and another book.'[69]

To write is *likh* and *lip,* the former originally used in the sense of scratching, whether on stone or leaves, the latter, in the sense of covering a surface with ink. Thus in the Śākuntala, the chief heroine, when advised to write a love-letter *(madana-lekha),* complains that she has no writing-materials *(lekhana-sādhanāni),* and.her friend tells her to take a lotus-leaf as smooth as the breast of a parrot, and with her nails to scratch the letters on it. This is clearly writing. In the Vikarmorvaśr, again Urvaśi, not daring to face her lover writes a letter *(lekha)* on a birch-leaf *(bhūrja-patra)*. The king, who sees it, calls it *bhūrjagato akṣara-vinyāsah,* "letters put down on a birch leaf;" and when he reads it, he is said to make the leaf speak *(vācayati)*. The leaf *(patra)* is used here not in the sense in which we found it in the Śākuntala, as the leaf of a tree, but as a leaf or sheet of paper. This paper was made of the bark of the birch-tree; and hence, when the queen picks up the love-letter, she thinks "it is a strip of fresh bark which the south wind has blown thither." [70]

Passages like these, to which we might add the well-known introduction to the Mahābhārata leave little doubt that at the time when these modern plays were composed, writing was generally practised by women as well as men. Why should there be no such passage in any of the genuine early Sanskrit works, if writing had then been equally known ?

In Manu's Code of Laws we read (viii. 168.) : "What is given by force, what is by force enjoyed, by force caused *to be written (lekhita),* and all other things done by force, Manu has pronounced void." Here again we have clearly writing. But this is only another proof that this metrical, parapharase of the laws of the Mānavas is later than the Vedic age.

In the Laws of Yājñāvalkya also written documents are mentioned; and the Commentator (ū. 22.) quotes Nārada and other authorities, all in Ślokas, on several minor points connected with the signing *(cihnita)* of papers, and the treatment of witnesses who cannot write *(alipijṃa)*. But I have found no such traces of written document in any of the ancient Dharma-Sūtras.

The words for ink *mati*[71] *kālī, mela, golā,* and pen[72] *(kalama)* have all a modern appearance; and, as to *Kāyastha,* the name of the writer-caste, proceeding from a Kṣatriya father and a Śūdra mother, it does not even occur in Manu.

Another class of words which would be likely to contain allusions to writing are those used for the various sub-divisions of literary compositions : but these too point to a literature kept up by oral tradition only. We observed before that a lecture *(Adhyāya)* consisted of sixty questions or *praśnas*. We find these very words used instead of chapters and paragraphs in the Saṁhitās, Brāhmaṇas, and Sūtras. In the Ṛg veda we have the ancient division into *sūktas,* hymns; *Anuvākas,* chapters *(i.e.,* repetition); and *Maṇḍalas,* books *(i.e,* cycles) : and the later division into *vargas,* classes; *Adhyāyas,* lectures : and *Asht akas,* Ogdoads. In the Taittirīyaka, the division is into *Kaṇḍikas* (sections), *Anuvākas, Praśnas* and *aṣṭakas*. In the Kāṭhuka we have *granthas,* compositions, and *sthānakas,* places. The name of the *Śatapatlia-brāhmaṇa* is derived from its 100 *pathas* or Wālks; and *Śaṣṭipatha* is used for a work consisting of sixty walks or chapters. Other words of the same kin are *prapāṭ haka,* a reading, a lecture; *āhnika,* a day's work; *parvan,* a joint, etc. We look in vain for such words as *volumen,* a volume, *liber, i.e.,* the inner bark of a tree; or βίλβos i.e., βùβλos, the inner bark of the papyrus; or *book, i.e.,* beech-wood.

,*It* is clear, from the evidence which we have examined, that it is far easier to prove the absence of writing during the early period of Sanskrit literature, than to discover any traces of writing even at the time when we are inclined to suppose that it was known in India. Writing was practised in India before the time of Alexander's conquest; and though it may not have been used for literary purposes, we can hardly doubt that a written alphabet was known during the greater part of the Sūtrā period. The Greek writers tell us exactly what we should expect under these circumstances. Megasthenes declared that the Indians did not know letters, that their laws were not written, and that they administered justice from memory.[73] This is perfectly true, if, as has been pointed put,[74] we restrict their ignorance of letters to the fact that they did not employ them for literary purposes. Strabo himself, when quoting the statement of Nearchus that the Indians wrote letters on cotton that had been well beaten together, points out the contradiction between this author and others *(i.e.,* Megasthenes), who declared that the Indians used no letters at all.[75] There is, however, no real contradiction between these two statements, if we only distinguish between the knowledge of letters and their use as a vehicle of literature. Nearchus fully agrees with Megasthenes; for he also states that the laws of the Indians were not reduced to writing.[76] And Megasthenes agrees with Nearchus; for the also shows himself perfectly acquainted with the fact that the Indians used letters for inscriptions on milestones, iudicating the resting-places and distances.[77] Nothing could offer a stronger confirmation of our opinion that the Indians had become acquainted with the art of writing during the Sūtra period and before the conquest of Alexander, but that they abstained from using it for literary purposes, than this apparent contradiction in the accounts of Nearchus and Megasthenes. Curtius, differing from Nearchus, maintains that they wrote on the soft rind of trees,[78] a custom which we saw preserved in the play of Urvaśī. We can hardly believe that the Indians could have used skins for writing. And, though Nicolaus Damascenes declares that he saw the ambassadors of Porus presented to Cæsar Augustus in Antiochia, and that they brought a letter written *ευ διφθρα,* we must remember that this letter was written in Greek,[79] and that the word *ευ διφθερα* may have been used for paper in general.[80]

We shall not be able to trace the Indian alphabet back much beyond Alexander's invasion. It existed, however, before Alexander. This we know from Nearchus himself, who ascribes to the Indians the art of making paper from cotton. Now, in looking for traces of writing before Alexander's time, we find in the Lalita-vistara, which contains the life of Buddha, that the young Śākya is represented as learning to write. Though the Lalita-vistara cannot be regarded as a contemporaneous witness, it is nevertheless a canonical book of the Buddhists, and, as such must be ascribed to the third council. It was translated into Chinese 76 A.D. As we have seen, before, the system of instruction practised in the lecture-rooms of the Brāhmaṇas it will perhaps be of interest to glance at the schools in which Buddha was educated, or supposed to have been educated.

"When the young prince had grown, he was led to the writing-school *(lipi śālā).*[81] We may leave out all the wonderful things that happened on this occasion, how he received a hundred thousand blessings, how he was surrounded by ten thousand children, preceded by ten thousand chariots full of sweetmeats, of silver and gold; how the town of Kapilavastu was cleansed, how music sounded everywhere, and showers of flowers were poured from the roofs, windows, and balconies; how, not satisfied with this, celestial ladies walked before him to clear the road, and the daughters of the wind scattered celestial flowers, besides other fabulous beings who all came to honour the Bodhisattva as he went to school. These marginal illustrations may be dropped in ail Buddhist books, though they leave but little room for the text. When Buddha entered the school, Viśvāmitra, the school-master *(dārakācārya),* unable to bear the majesty of the Bodhisattva's presence, fell to the ground, and had to be lifted up by an angel, named Śubhāṅga. After the king Śuddhodana and his suite had left, the nurses and attendants sat down, and the Bodhisattva took a leaf to write on *(lipi-phalaka)* made of sandal-wood *(uraga-sāra-candana-Mayam).* He then asked Viśvāmitra what writing he was going to teach him. Here follow sixty four names, apparently names of alphabets,[82] all of which the Bodhisattva is acquainted with, whereas Viśvāmitra is obliged to confess his ignorance.. Nevertheless the Bodhisattva stays at school, and learns to write, together with ten thousand boys.[83]

The alphabet which he learns is the common Sanskrit alphabet, with the omission of the letter 1, ṛ and ṛ. It consists of 45 letters, and, as in our own primers, every letter is followed by a word containing that letter at the beginning or in the middle. These words in the Lalita-vistara are so chosen as to illustrate some of the chief points of Buddha!s own doctrines. The alphabet is:ṭa, ā, i, ī, u, ū, e, ai, o, au, am, aḥ; k, kh, g, gh, ṃ; ch, chh, j, jh, *n; ṭ,* ṭh, ḍ, ḍh, ṇ; t, til, d, dh, n; p, ,ph, b, bh, m; y, r, v; ś, ṣ, s, h, kṣ.

Though the further education of Buddha is not fully

described, we see him soon afterwards, in a general competition, the most distinguished scholar, arithmetician, musician, and everything else.[84] This comprehensive system of education, through which Buddha is here represented to have passed, is the very opposite of that followed by the Brāhmaṇas. We nowhere meet in the Buddhist literature with those strong imprecations against book-learning which we found among the Brāhmaṇas, and which may be heard, I believe, even at the present day.

If, thus, the first, though rather legendary, trace of writing, as a part of the elementary education in India, is[85] discovered in the life of Buddha, it is curious to observe that the first actual writing, the first well authenticated inscription in India, is likewise of Buddhist origin. There are no Brāhmaṇic inscriptions earlier than the Buddhist inscriptions of Aśoka on the rocks of Kapurdigiri, Dhauli, and Girnar. They belong to the third century before Christ. They call themselves *lipi,* a writing,[86] or *dharma-lipi,*[87] a sacred writing; and they mention the writer or engraver by the name of *lipi-kara*[88]. This last word *lipi-kara* is an important word, for it is the only word in the Sūtras of Pāṇini which can be legitimately adduced to prove that Pāṇini was acquainted with the art of writing. He teaches the formation of this word, iii. 2,21. There is indeed another passage, which has frequently been quoted, where Pāṇini teaches the formation of the adjective *yavanārī.* This is simply the feminine of *yavana,* as *Indrāṇī.* is of *Indra.* Kātyāyana, however, and the Commentator, both maintain that *yavanānī* is used as a name of *lipi,* and that it meant the writing of the Yavānas. I see no reason to doubt that most of the examples which we find in the Commentaries go back to the very time of Pāṇini, and I am quite willing to admit that Pāṇini, gave his rule on yavanārī simply in order to explain this word as the name of a cartain alphabet. But I must demur to any further conclusions. Yavana is by no means the exclusive name of the Greeks or Ionians. Professor Lassen has proved that it had a much wider meaning, and that it was even used of Semitic nations. There is nothing to prove that Pāṇini was later than Alexander, or that he was acquainted with Greek literature. In the Lalita-vistara, where all possible alphabets are mentioned, nothing is said of a Yāvanānī or a Greek alphabet. The Sanskrit alphabet, though it has always ben suspected to be derived from a Semitic source, has not certainly been traced back to a Greece source. It shows more similarity with the Arāmaean than with any other variety of the Phoenician alphabet.[89] *Yavanānī lipi* most likely means that variety of the Semitic alphabet which, previous to Alexander, and previous to Pāṇini, became the type of the Indian alphabet. But all this is merely conjectural. It is impossible to arrivé at any certain interpretation of *Yavanānī*, as used by Pāṇini, and it is much better to confess this, than to force the word into an argument for any preconceived notions as to the origin of the Indian alphabet.

There is another word in Pāṇini which might seem to prove that, not only the art of writing, but written books were known at his time. This is *grantha*. *Grantha* occurs four times in our texts of Pāṇini.[90] In I. 3, 75., it is so used as to apply to the Veda. In IV. 3, 87. it may refer to any work. In IV. 3, 116, it is applied to the work of any individual author. In VI. 3, 79, it may refer to any work that is studied. I do not attribute much importance to the fact that I. 3, 75, and IV. 3, 116 are marked as not explained in the commentaries; for I confess that in none of these four passages can I discover anything to prove that *grantha* must mean a written or a bound book. *Grantha* is derived fiom a root *grath,* which means *nectere, serere. Grantha,* therefore, like the later *sandxrbha,* would simply mean a composition.[91] It corresponds etymologically with the Latin *textus*. Thus it is used by the Commentator to Nir. 1, 20, where he says that former teachers handed down the hymns *grantliato'rthataśca,* according to their text and according to their meaning." In the later literature of India *grantha* was used for a volume, and in *grantha-kuṭī,* a library, we see clear.. that it has that meaning. But in the early literature *grantha* does not mean *pustaka,* or book; in means simply a composition, as opposed to a traditional work.

This distinction between traditional works and works composed by individual authors is of frequent occurence in Pāṇini, and we attempted, in a former part of this work, to draw some historical conclusions from this distinction. From IV. 3, 101. to 111. the grammarian gives rules how to derive the titles of works from the names of those by whom they were proclaimed *(tena proktam).* But in most cases these derivations are used by Pāṇini as intermediate links only, in order to form the names of Caraṇas who read and preserve these works. Never, he says (IV. 2, 66.), use the derivative, which would be the title of a work in the case of hymns *(chandas)* or Brāhmaṇas. Do not call a work proclaimed by Kaṭha, Kaṭham, but only speak of Kaṭhas, *i. e.,* those who hand down the works proclaimed by Kaṭha. Another still more significant restriction is made by Pāṇini. With reference lo modern works, he says, you may use the neuter in the singular or plural, instead of thes plural of the masculine. The Brāhmaṇas taught by Yājñavalkya may be spoken of as such. But the ancient Brāhmaṇas first proclaimed by Bhallava etc, can only be spoken of as "the Bhāllavins" (Bhallavidse), because it is only in the tradition of his descendants that the works of Bhallava and other ancient ages may be said to live.

However we examine the ancient Sanskrit phraseology with regard to books and their authors, we invariably arrivé at the same results. In the most ancient literature, the idea even of authorship is excluded. Works are spoken of as revealed to and communicated by certain sages, but not as composed by them. In the later literature of the Brāhmaṇa and Sūtra period the idea of authorship is admitted, but no trace is to be found anywhere of any books being committed to writing. It is possible I may [illegible] overlooked some words in the Brāhmaṇas and Sūtras, [illegible] would prove the existence of written books previous to Pāṇini. If so, it is not from any wish to suppress them. I believe, indeed that the Brāhmaṇas were preserved by oral tradition only, but I should feel inclined to claim an aquaintance with the art of writing for the authors of the Sūtras. And there is one word which seems to strengthen such a supposition,

We find that several of the Sūtras are divided into chapters called *paṭalas*. This is a word never used for the subdivisions of the Brāhmaṇas. Its meaning is a covering, the surrounning skin or membrane; it is also used for a tree. If so, it would seem to be almost synonymous with *liber* and *βίβλος*, and it would mean *book* after meaning originally a sheet of paper made of the surrounding bark of trees. If writing came in towards the latter half of the *Sūtra* period, it would no doubt be applied at the same time to reducing the hymns and Brāhmaṇas to a written form. Previously to that time, however, we are bound to maintain that the collection of the hymns, and the immense mass of the *Brāhmaṇa* literature, were preserved by means of oral tradition only.

REFERENCES

1. तत्परिचरणावितरौ वेदौ।। vi, 11.
2. Ṛg. bh. bhū. page 34.
3. Our MSS. represent, according to tradition, the text of the Śākala-śākhā and the same text is followed by Āśvalāyana in his Sūtras. Now, whenever Āvalāyana quotes any verses which form part of the Śākala-śākhā, he only quotes the first words. Every member of his Caraṇa was supposed to know the hymn of the Śākala-śākhā by heart, it was sufficient, therefore, to quote them in this manner. But when he has occasion to refer to the verses which are found in the Brāhmaṇa of the Aitareyins, without being part of the Śākala-saṁhitā, Āśvalāyana quotes them in full. As these verses are not quoted in full in the text of the Aitareya-brāhmaṇa, we may fairly suppose that the text of the Ṛg-veda-saṁhitā, current among the Aitareyins, was different from that of the Śākala-śākhā, and contained the full text of these hymns. Sāyaṇa, in his Commentary, does not state that these additional verses belonged to the Śākhā of the Aitareyins, but there can be little doubt that at his time the text of their Saṁhita was lost and forgotten. He says, however, that these verses belonged to a different Śākhā, and that they must be supplied from Āśvalāyana's Sūtras, where, for this very reason, they were given in full. At the time of Āśvalāyana, therefore, the text of the Saṁhitā of the Aitareyins was still in existence, and he likewise notices in his Sūtras peculiarities in the ceremonial of the Aitareyins. Dr. Roth has pointed out one of these verses (Nirukta, xlv.). The passage in the Aitareya-

brāhmaṇa from which the verse is taken, is, i. 4. 2. ; and Sāyaṇa says there ता एताश्चतस्त्र ऋचः शाखान्तरगता आश्वलायनेन पठिता द्रष्टव्याः।। In a similar manner the modern Sūtras of the Fratres Attidii (Tab. vi. vii.) contain the Mantras in

4. [1]First Maṇḍala, Anuvāka 1, = Agni,
Anuvāka 2. 3 =2 Indra.
Second Maṇḍala, Anuvāka 1. = (Agni-1ṇ
Anuvāka 2. = Indra.
Third Maṇḍala, Anuvāka 1.2 = Agni.
Anuvāka 3. 4 = Indra.
Fourth Maṇḍala, Anuvāka 1.-2, 5. = Agni.
Anuvāka 2. 3. ss Indra.
Fifth Maṇḍala, Anuvāka 1.-2, 14. = Agni.
Anuvāka 2, 15.ṭ3, 8 .= Indra.
Sixth Maṇḍala, Anuvāka 1.2, 1. - Agni.
Anuvāka 2, 1.ṭ4, 4. = Indra.
Seventh Maṇḍala, Anuvāka 1 - Agni.
Anuvāka 2. = Indra.
Eighth Maṇḍala, Pragātha hymns.
Ninth Maṇḍala, Soma hymns. ṇ
Tenth Maṇḍala, Anuvāka 1. - Agni

full which in the ancient statutes (Tab. i.) are only indicated as generally known. See Aufrecht und Kirchhoff, Die Umbrischen Sprachdenkmäler.

5. Schol. ad Pind Nem. x. 59. See Appendix A.

6. Ṛv. iv. 1. 5. सत्वं नो अग्नेऽवमो भवोती नेदिष्ठो अस्या उषसो व्युष्टौ। "Come down to us, O Agni, with thy help ; be you most near to us to-day as the dawn flashes forth."

7. इन्द्रो वै देवानामोजिष्ठो बलिष्ठः Kausītaki-brāhmaṇa, vi. 14.

8. Burnouf, Journal Asiatique, 1850, p. 249. Roth, Nirukta, p. xxxvi.

9. यथऋष्याप्रीणीयात् यद्यथऋष्याप्रीणाति यजमानमेव तद्बन्धुताया नोत्सृजति Ait.-br. ii. 4.

10. Āśv.-sūtra, iii. 2.

11. तत्र भगवता शैनकेन यथर्षिपक्ष आप्रीविवेकार्थमेव श्लोक उक्तः।
कण्वोऽङ्गिरोऽगस्त्यः शुनको विश्वामित्रोऽत्रिरेव च।
वसिष्ठः कश्यपो वध्र्यश्वो जमदग्निरथोत्तमः।।

12. सगोत्राणामपि भिन्नार्षेयत्वसम्भवात् Nārāyaṇa on Āśv.Śrauta-sū.iv.1.

13. सर्वे समानगोत्राः स्युरिति गाणगरिः कथं ह्याप्रीसूक्तानि भवेयुः। Āśv. sūtras, xii 10. See also Anuvākānukramaṇi-bhāṣya, śloka 7. हे शाकलाः! के ते। सर्वेषां शाकलात्वमाप्रीद्वारेण।।

14. This is not the order as given in Āśvalāyana; he places the *Brahmā* and his three men before the *Udgātṛ* and his attendants. Some would seem to place the Brahmā first of all, but Āśvalāyana (Gṛhya, i. 22.) remarks that the Brahmā is first chosen when there is an election of four priests only. If all the sixteen are chosen, then the *Hotṛ* comes first, afterwards the *Brahmā*, thirdly the *Adhvaru* and lastly the *Udgātṛ*.

15. Āsv. Gṛhya i. 22. सदस्यं सप्तदशं कौषीतकिनः समामनन्ति स कर्मणामुपद्रष्टा भवतीति। सप्तदशग्रहणमृत्विक्सधर्मो भवतीति ज्ञापनार्थात्। This is confirmed by the Kauṣītaki-brāhmaṇa. Other authorities admit several *Sadasyas*, (शास्त्रान्तरेऽके दृष्टाः) For the *Sattra* sacrifices a seventeenth priest, called the *Gṛhapati*, lord of the house, is admitted. He is not considered as the *Yajamāna*, but seems to be the actual sacrifices (गृहपतिसंज्ञकेन केवलयजमानपदार्थ- कारिणा सप्तदशेन पुरुषेन सहिताः Nārāyaṇa on Āśv. Śrauta-Sūtra, iv. 1.) In the Aitareya-brāhmaṇa (vii 1.), where the division of the animal among the various priests is described we have the sixteen Ṛtvij, and besides one *Sadasya*, three *Gṛhapatis* (probably the sacrificer himself, one who acts for him and who acts for his wife), one *Śamitṛ* (a slayer, who need not be a *Brāhmaṇa*, two *Vaikartas* (butchers), several *Upagātṛs* (choristers), and an *Ātreya*. Other wives *(patnīs)* besides the *Bhāryā* are mentioned as present. In the Tāṇdya-brāhmaṇa (25. 15.) the *Prati-prasthālṛ* is left out, but two *Adhvaryus*, two Unnetṛs and two Abhigarā-*pagarau* are mentioned.

16. Translated by me in the ninth volume of the German Oriental Society.

17. स त्रिभिर्वेदैर्विधीयते ।।३।।

    ऋग्वेदयजुर्वेदसामवेदैः ।।४।।

    ऋग्वेदन होता करोति ।।१६।।

    सामवेदेनोद्गाता ।।१७।।

    यजुर्वेदेनाध्वर्युः ।।१८।।

    सर्वैर्ब्रह्म ।।१९।।

18. Ait.-brāhmaṇa, vii. 1.

19. उपांशु यजुर्वेदेन।।९।। करणवदशब्दममनः प्रयोगमुपांशु। अन्यत्राश्रुत-प्रत्याश्रुतप्रवरसंवाद-सम्प्रेषैश्च ।।१०।। एतेषामुच्चारणस्य परार्थत्वादुच्चैष्टमेव।।

19. An instance of this occurs in a passage of the Altareya-brāhmaṇa translated by Prof. Roth. The first words (ii 2.) अंज्मो यूपमनुब्रूहि are spoken by the *Adhvaryu*, and not, as Professor Roth supposes, by the *Hotṛ*. It is the *Adhvaryu* only who can say, "We anoint the sacrificial stake, do you accompany us with the hymns." A passage like this, as it is addressed to another priest, the *Adhvaryu* would have to pronounce with a loud voice. The Brāhmaṇa itself says, इत्याहाध्वर्युः "so says the Adhvaryu". The *preṣa*, or command, "*anubrūhi*," can only be addressed to the *Hotṛ*, and there was no ground

for placing the following verses in the mouth of the *Adhvaryu*. Roth, Nirukta, xxxiv.

21. The Saṁhitā consists of two parts ; the Ārciha and Staubhika. The Ārcika, as adopted to the special use of the priests, exists in two forms, called Gānas, or Song-books, the Veya-gāna and Āraṇya-gāna. The Staubhika exists in the same manner as Uha-gāna and Uhya-gāna, Cf. Beufey, Preface to his edition of the Sāma-veda-ārcika, Leipzig, 1848, and Weber, Ind. Studien, i. 30. The supposition that the modern origin of some of the Ṛgveda, could be proved by their not occurring in the Sāma-veda, has been well refuted by Dr. Pertsch.

22. Sāyaṇa (Ṛv. Bh. i. p. 23.) remarks that some verses of the Yajurveda are called Ṛc in the Brāhmaṇas of the *Adhvaryus*. Thus the verses देवः सवितोतोपुनातु is called a Ṛc addressed to Savitṛ. Sāmans also are mentioned, as when it is said, "Singing- the Sāman he sits down." In the Sāma-veda there are not only Ṛch verses, but also Yājuṣ invocations, such as अक्षितमसि, अच्युतमसि, प्राणशंसितमसि। The Hotṛ priests have likewise to use invocations which would more properly be called Yajush, such as अवैरपोऽध्वर्या३उ "*Adhvaryu*, have you got the water ?" to which the *Adhvaryu* replies : उतेमनंनमुः "Yes, it has come." Here the Commentator says, होतुर्यजुरात्मकं कञ्चिन्मन्त्रं विधत्ते।।

23. The invocations, properly called Yajuṣ, are of course not to be found in the Ṛg-veda. Some of the hymns of the Sāma and Yajur-veda, which have a more modern appearance, are to be found in the tenth Maṇḍala of the Ṛg.veda, or among the latest additions, such as the Vālakhilyas. There are, however, some, which, though they occur in the Sāma and Yajur-veda, are not to be found in the Ṛg-veda. This may possibly be accounted for by the fact that we do not possess all the Śākhās, of the Ṛg-veda. The differences also in the text of hymns, as read in the three Vedas, must be ascribed to the influence of early Śākhās, and cannot be used as an argument for determining the more or less ancient date of the three Vedas.

24. Prasthāna-bheda, p. 16., 1. 10, अथर्ववेदस्तु यज्ञानुपयुक्तः शान्ति-पौष्टिकाभिचारादि-कर्मप्रतिपादकत्वेनात्वन्तविलक्षण एव। Against this statement that of Kumārila should be taken into account : (1. 3,) शान्तिपुष्ट्यभिचारार्था ह्येकब्रह्मर्त्विगाश्रिताः क्रियास्तत्र प्रमीयन्तेऽत्राप्येवात्मीय-गोचराः।।

25. 1. See page 38, note 3, and page 53.

26. Abhandlungen, p. 43.

27. Ṛv. in 1. 20.

28. Janima, originally creations, ποιηματα; it is likewise explained as works. Cf. iii. 39. 1.

29. Ṛv. iii. 32. 13.

30. See my Essay on the Funeral Ceremonies, p. xxii. note.

31. Ṛv. x. 130. 1.
32. Ibid. 7.
33. Ṛv. iii. 39.
34. The Viśvāmitras wore white raiments. Their colour, called arjuna, can hardly be distinguished, however, from the colour of the dress of the Vaśiṣṭhas, which is called *śveta*.
35. *Gotra*, originally a hurdle, then those who live within the same hurdles or walls ; a family, a race,
36. Ṛv. vi, 23, 9,
37. See Prof. Roth's excellent essay on Vasiṣṭha and Viśvāmitra, in his work, "Zur Literatur und Geschichte des Veda," published as early as 1846.
38. Aitareya Br. vii. 27. Roth, Abhandluingen, p. 118 Weber, Ind. Studien, 1.39. Margaveya is a difficult name. It may be simply, as Sāyaṇa says, the son of his mother Mrgu; but Mṛgū may be a variety of Bhṛgu, and thus confirm Lassen's conjecture that this Rāma is Rāma, the son of Jamadagni, of the race of Bhṛgu, commonly called Paraśu-rāma. Cf. Weber, Ind. Stud. i'. 216. Marghu is the name of Margiana in the Cuneiform Inscriptions.
39. Sv. iv. 5077.
40. "Bṛhaspati," says the Aitareya-brāhmaṇa, "was the *Purohita of* the gods, and the *Purohitas* of human kings are his successors."
41. Ṛv. i. 10. गायन्ति त्वा गायत्रिणोऽर्चन्त्यर्कमर्किण:।
42. यो जगार तमृच: कामयन्ते वो जगार तमु सामानि यन्ति।

    यो जगार तमर्थ सोम आह तवाहमस्मि सख्ये न्योका:।।

    Rv. viii. 3 22. ऋक्सामाभ्याम्।।
43. I translate *parva* by conjunction, because *parvaṇi*, the dual, is used for the full and new moon ; Āśvalāyana-sūtras, i. 3. 12. Mr. Weigle, in his interesting articleon Kanarese literature (Zeitschritit der Deutschen Morgenländischen Gesellschaft), states that *habba* or *pabba* means a festival in Kanarese, whereas in Sanskrit its usual signification is a chapter of a book. Mr. Weigle therefore refers *pabba* to a class of words, which in being transferred from the Sanskrit into the Dravidian languages, have changed their meaning. We see, however, that the old meaning of *parva* new and full moon, would account very well for the meaning attached to *pabba* in Kanarese, a festival.
44. भरामेध्मं कृणवाम हीवषि ते चितयन्त: पर्वणा पर्वणा वयम्।

    जीवातवे प्रतरं साधया धियोऽग्ने सख्ये मा रिषामा वयं तव।।
45. Ṛv. viii. 27. 19 :

    यदद्य सूर्य उद्यति प्रियक्षत्रा ऋतं दध।

    यन्निम्रुचि प्रबुधि विश्वेदसो यद्वा मध्यन्दिने दिव:।।१९।।

    यद्वाभिपित्वे असुरा ऋतं यते छर्दिर्येम वि दाशुषे।

वयं तद्वो वसवो विश्ववेदस उप स्थेयाम मध्य आ॥२०॥

यदद्य सूर उदिते यन्मध्यन्दिन आतुचि।

वार्म धत्थ मनवे विश्ववेदसो जुह्वानाया प्रचेतसे॥२१॥

वयं तद्वः सम्राज आ वृणीमहे पुत्रो न बहुपाय्यम्।

अश्याम तदादित्या जुह्वतो हविर्येन वस्योऽनशामहै।२२॥

46. Ṛv. ii. 36. ; ii. 37.

47. These seven priests seem to be Hotṛ, Potṛ, Neṣṭṛ, Agnīdha, Praśāstṛ, Adhvaryu and Brahmā.

48. Plutarch, Alcibiades, c. vii.

49. See Grote, History of Greece, ii. p. 201.

50. Plin. Hist Nat. xiii. 13. 27. : "Cum chartae usu maxime humanitas vitas constet et memoria."

51. Wolf, Prolegomena. lxx-lxxiii. : "Scripturam tentare et communi usui aptare plane idem videtur fuisse atque porsam tentare et in ea excolenda se ponere".

52. Dobrizhoffer's Account of the Abipones, vol. ii. p. 63.

53. वेदविक्रयिणश्चैव वेदानाञ्चैव लेखकाः।

वेदानां दूषकाश्चैव ते वै निरयगामिनः॥

54. Kumārīla, Tantra-Vārttika, i. 3. p. 86.

यथैवान्यायविज्ञाताद्वेदाल्लेख्यादिपूर्वकात्।

शूद्रेणाधिगताद्वापि धर्मज्ञानं न सम्मतम्॥

55. Prātiśākhya du Ṛg-veda, par A. Regnier, Journal Asiatique, 1856, Chapitre XV.

56. If the metre is *paṅkti* the *praśna* may consist of two or three verses ; if the metre is longer than *Paṅkti*, two verses only constitute a Praśna ; if a hymn consists of one verse, that by itself forms a praśna. *Samayas*, i. e. passages which have occurred before (and are sometimes left out in the MSS.), are counted, if they consists of a complete verse. Two *Dvipadās* are counted as one verse, and as the Commentator adds (v. 12.), the two half-verses of each *Dvipadā*-line are to be joined in recitation, and only if there is one odd *Dvipada*-line remaining, a pause is to be made at the end of the first half-verse. If there are some verses remaining at the end of a hymn, they may be joined to the last *praśna* ; if there are more than two verses, this is optional.

57. The only words which, in the Saṁhita-pātha, would be likely to escape the pupil's attention are monosyllables consisting of one vowel only, and that a vowel not changed into a semi vowel in which form it would be more audible, This would restrict the rule regarding repetition of the two words a and M. Thus for *prā*, which is *pra* + ā, the Guru would have to say *prā* ā or *prā ā iti*, instead of *ud u shya diva*, *ud u u shya deva*. This repetition would not take place in *udv eti* because *u* is changed into *v*. If sarvodātta

could mean a word being wholly *udātta*, then u would be excluded, and the rule would refer to only. But sarvoddtta means recitation when the accent is disregarded, and all syllables are pronounced with a high tone. The Commentary construes the rule differently. I construe इह प्रवचने सर्वोदात्तत्वम्। तस्मिन् सर्वोदात्तप्रयुक्ते प्रवचनेऽपृं तच्चाक्षैप्रयुक्तं द्विः प्रोक्तव्यमथवेतिकरणान्तम्।।

58. These are chiefly the change of a final m into *Anusvāra* before *r* and the *ūṣmans* ; the common *sandhi* of the *ūṣmans* ; the suppression of a final *n* ; its transition into *r* ; its transition into a sibilant ; the absence of sandhi where *r* follows ; the sandhi of *r*, and the hiatus.

59. The text is निर्वाच्ये तु etc.

60. Here again I differ from the commentator, who takes parasya as an adjective referring to *etad, i.e.*, guroḥ. At the end of a half-verse, this address, *bho* ! is to be dropped ; at the end of an *Adhyāya* it is optional,

61. According to some Śākhās, not the Śākalas, certain words (prepositions) are, in this final recitation also, to be followed by the particle *iti* ; *abhi* is even, in some cases, to be pronounced *abhītyabhi*. Some other rules are given, all of which are optional. The text of the Veda, as repeated in the lecture-room, is neither Saṁhitā, Pada, nor Krāma text. Some few Śākhās only maintain that the Saṁhitā-text should be used *pure et simple.*

62. Csesar (de Bello Gallico, vi. 14), speaking of the Druids, says : "Magnum ibi numerum versuum ediscere dicuntur, itaque nonnulli annos vicenos in disciplina permanent, neṇue fas esse existimant ea literis mandare,"

63. Aristotle, Probl. x. 39.; τα δε γραμμαα παθη εστι τῆς φωνῆς

64. Āpastatmba, Dharrna-sūtra; iii. 86.

65. Kalpa-sūtra, ed. Stevenson, s. 29.

66. वेद: पुन: सविशेषप्रत्यक्षगम्य:। तत्र घटादिवदेव पुरुषान्तरस्थमुपलभ्यस्मरन्ति। तैरपि स्मृतमुपलभ्यान्येऽपि स्मरन्तोऽन्येभ्यस्तथैव समर्थयन्तीत्यनादिता।। सर्वस्य चात्मीयस्मरणात्पूर्वमुपलब्धि: सम्भवतीति निर्मूलता।। शब्दसम्बन्धाव्युत्पत्तिमात्रमेव चेह वृद्धव्यवहाराधीनम्।। प्रागपि हि वेदशब्दादन्यवस्तुविलक्षणं वेदान्तरविलक्षणं चाध्येतृस्थमृग्वेदादिरूपं मन्त्रबाह्मणादिरूपाणि चान्यविलक्षणा-न्युपलभ्यन्ते सर्वेषां चानादय: संज्ञा:।।

67. Asiatic Researches, xi, 255.

68. Could it be *apestak*, originally the Sanskrit *avasthāna* ? See Spiegel, Grammar of the Parsi Language, p. 204.

69. पश्चतन्त्रात्तथान्यस्माद्ग्रन्थादाकृष्य लिख्यते।

70. There are, I believe, but two Sanskrit MSS. in Europe which are written on birch bark ; one in the Royal Library of Berlin, the other in the Library of All Souls College, Oxford.

71. Lalita Vistara, Adhyāya, ix. p. 139. 1. 17.

72. Uṇādi-sūtras iv, 84. calamus, reed.

73. Strabo, xv. 53.:................ For text see Appendix A.
74. Schwanbeck, Megasthenis Fragmenta, p. 50.
75. Strabo, xv. 67. : For text see Appendix A.
76. Strabo.xv. 66. : For text see Appendix A,
77. Οι αγορανομοι.................For text see Appendix A.
78. Curtius. 8, 9. "Libri arborum teneri, haud secus quam chaitse literarum notas capiunt."
79. Strabo, XV. 73 τγϖ δε επιστολην ελληνιξειν εν διφθερα γεγραμμενην.
80. Herodotus, v. 58.
81. Lalita-Vistara, Adhyāya, x.- This work has lately been edited and partially translated by Babu Rajendralal Mitra, one pf the most distinguished Sanskrit scholars in India,
82. The most interesting names are Aṅga (Bhagalpur), Baṅga (Bengal), Magadha, Drāviḍā, Dakshiṇa (Dekhan), Darada, Khāsya (Cassia hills), Chīna (Chinese), Hūṇa, Deva (Devanāgatī), Bhaumadeva (Brāhmaṇa), Uttarakurus, *anudruta* (cursive).
83. The following passage from the Evangelium Infantiæ (ed. Sike, p. 143.) offers a curious paralled : "Erat porro Hiero-solymis quidam Zachæus nomine, qui juventutem erudiebat. Dicebat hie Josepho : quare non mittis ad me Jesum, utliteras discat ? Annuebat illi Josephus, et ad Divam Mariam hoc referebat. Ad magistrum itaque ilium ducebant ; qui simulatque eum corispexerat Alphabetum ipsi-conscripsit, utque Aleph diceret piaecepit. Et cum dixisset Aleph, magister ipsum pronunciare jubebat. Cui Dominus Jesus : Die mihi pritis significationem literse Aleph, et turn Beth pronunciabo. Cumque magister vetbera ipsi intentaret, exponebat illi Dominus Jesus significationes literarum Aleph et Beth ; item, quaenam litecarum figure essent rectse, quaenam obliṇuae, quasnum. duplicates, ṇuae punctis insignitas, quae ūsdem carentes ; quare una litera aliam precedetet ; aliaque plurima enarrare coepit et elucIḍāre, qua? magister ipse nee audiverat unṇuam nee in libro ullo legerat. Dixit porro magistro Dominus Jesus: Attende, ut dicam tibi, coepitṇue clare et distincte recitare, Aleph, Beth, Gimel, Daleth, usque ad fiaem Alphabeti. quod miratus magtster, Hunc, inquit, puerum ante Noachum natum esse existimo; conversusque ad Josephum, Adduxisti, ait, ad me erudiendum puerum, magistris omnibus doctiorem. Divas quoque Marias inquit: Filio tuo nulla doctrina opus est." The Gospel of Thomas the Israelite, or the Book of Thomas the Israelite, the philosopher, concerning the acts which the Lord did, when a child, was most popular in the east.
84. Among the subjects in which he shows his learning, figure Nighaṇṭu, Nigama, Purāṇa, Itihāsa, Veda, Vyakarana, Nirukta, Śikshā, Chandas, Kalpa, Jyotiṣa, Sāṅkhya, Yoga, Vaiśeṣika.
85. In an ancient inscription of Khandagiri (Journal of the Asiat. Soc. of Bengal, vi. 318), a king is mentioned who in his youth learned to write, and was

taught, besides, arithmetic, navigation, commerce, and law ("*tato likha-rūpa-gāṇa-nāva-vyapāra-vidhi-visaradena*").

86. *Etāya athāya iyam lipi likhitā* ; for this purpose was the writing written.
87. *Iyam dhammalipi Devānām piyena piyadasinā rānā likhāpitā asti eva.* (p. 752).
88. Burnouf, Lotus, p. 752.
89. Lepsius, Zwli sprochvergleichende Abhandlungen, p. 78., Schulze's conjecture about Mesnud. Weber, Indische Skizzen.
90. समुद्राङ्भ्यो यनोऽग्रन्थे॥१. ३. ७५॥

    अधिकृत्य कृते ग्रन्थे॥ ४. ३. ८७॥

    कृते ग्रन्थे ॥ ४. ३. ११६॥

    ग्रन्थान्ताधिके च ॥६. ३. ७१॥
91. Thus the Commentator to the Ṛg-veda, 1, 67, 4, explains *chṛtanti by agnim udiśya stutir grathnanti, kurvantityarthaḥ.*

THE CHHANDAS PERIOD

4
CHAPTER

The three periods of Vedic literature which we have examined, the Sūtra, Brāhmaṇa, and Mantra periods, all point to some earlier age which gave birth to the poetry of the early Ṛṣis. Here was a time, doubtless, when the songs which were collected with such careful zeal in the Mantra period, commented upon with such elaborate pedantry during the Brāhmaṇa period, and examined and analysed with such minute exactness during the Sūtra period, lived and were understood wiyout any effort by a simple and pious race. There was a time when the sacrifices, which afterwards became so bewildering a system of ceremonies, were dictated by the free impulse of the human heart, a yearning to render thanks to some Unknown Being, and to repay, in words or deeds, a debt of gratitude, accumulated from the first breath of life. There was a time when the poet was the leader, the king, and priest of his family or tribe, when his songs and sayings were listened to in anxious silence and with implicit faith, when his prayers were repeated by crowds who looked up to their kings and priests, their leaders and judges, as men better, nobler, wiser than the rest, as beings nearer to the gods in proportion as they were raised above the common level of mankind. These men themselves living a life of perfect freedom, speaking a language not yet broken by literary usage, and thinking youghts unfettered as yet by traditional chains, were at once teachers, lawgivers, poets, and priests. There is no very deep wisdom in their teaching, their laws are simple, their poetry shows no very high flights of fancy, and their religion might be told in a few words. But what there is of their language, poetry, and religion has a charm which no other period of Indian literature possesses : it is spontaneous, original, and truthful.

We cannot say this of all the hymns : nay, the greater portion of what we now possess of Vedic poetry must, no doubt, be ascribed to a secondary period, the so-called Mantra period. But after we have discarded what bears the stamp of a later age, there remains enough to give us an idea of an earlier race of Vedic poets. It is true, no doubt, in one sense, that even those earliest specimens of Vedic poetry belong, as has been said by Bunsen, to the modern history of the human race. Ages must have passed before the grammatical texture of the Vedic Sanskrit could have assumed the consistancy and regularity which it shows throughout. Every tense, every mood, every number and person of the verb is fixed, and all the terminations of the cases are firmly established. Every one of these terminations was originally an independent word with an independent meaning. Their first selection was more or less the result of individual choice, their techqical character the result of long usage. There was more than one word for I, and more than one expression for the verb *to be.* The selection of *mi,* as the termination of the first person singular, the selection of as in the sense of *to be,* and the joining of the two so as to produce the auxiliary veib, *asmi* = I am, all this was a conventional act, the act of one or two individuals, fixed by circumstances which were more or less accidental. If then, we find the same combination in the ancient Greek *eopl* and the modern Lithuanian *esmi,* it is clear that the origin of that form goes back to times long anterior to the separate existence of Sanskrit, Greek, and Lithuanian. As *soy, suis,* and *sono* are modern modifications that point back to an earlier type, the Latin *sum,* the Sanskrit *asmi,* Greek *iapl,* Lithuanian *esmi,* are likewise but the modern representatives of some earlier typical form, which existed in the undivided language of the Āryan race.

The same applies to the religion of the Veda. Words like *deva* for 'god' mark a more than secondary stage in the Āryan religion. To use the root √ *div* 'to shine,' with reference to the heavenly bodies, was the result of a free choice. There were other roots which might have been used instead. Nor was it by any means a necessity that the presence of a Divine Power should be felt exclusively in the bright manifestations of nature. All this was the result of a historical growth; and the early periods of that growth had passed away long before the Ṛṣis of India could have worshipped their *Devas* or their bright beings, with sacred hymns and invocations.

From this point of view the Vedic language and poetry may be ascribed to a modern or secondary period in the history of the world, if only it be understood that what preceded that period in India, or in any other part of the Āryan world, is lost to us beyond the hope of recovery, and that, therefore, to us the Veda represents the most ancient chapter in the history of the human intellect. We find no traces in the Veda, or in any Āryan work, of a growing language, growing in the sense in which some of the Turanian languages may be said to be still growing at the present day.[1] The whole grammatical mechanism is finished, the most complicated forms are sanctioned, and the only changes of which the Āryan speech, arrivéd at the point where we find it in the Veda, admits, are those of gradual decay and recomposition. Nor do we find any traces, in the Veda, of a growing religion. We look in vain for the effect produced on the human mind by the first rising of idea of God. To the poets of the Veda that idea is an old and familiar idea : it is understood, never questioned, never denied. We shall never hear what was felt by man when the image of God arose in all its majesty before his eyes, assuming a reality before which all other realities faded into a mere shadow. No whisper will ever reach us of that sacred colloquy when God for the first time spoke to man, and man to God; when man within his own heart heard that still voice through which the Father of mankind revealed himself to all his children, to the Jew first, and also to the Gentile; and when God received the first response from human lips : "Who are you, Lord ?"

That first recognition of God, that first perception of the real presence of God-a perception wiyout which no religion, whether natural or revealed, can exist or grow, belonged to the past when the songs of the Veda were written. The idea of God, though never entirely lost, had been clouded over by errors. The names given to God had been changed to gods, and their real meaning had faded away from the memory of man. Even the earlist hymns of the Veda are not free from mythological phraseology. How far the poets retained a vague consciousness of the original purport of the names of the gods is difficult to say. To our eyes the science of language has disclosed the smallest fibres in the tissue of these names, and allowed us an insight into the darkest secrets of their growth. We can see *nomina,* where even the most keen-sighted native could discover nothing but *numina.* Sometimes, however, we feel surprised at the precision with which even such modern writers as Kumārila are able to read the true meaning of their mythology. When Kumārila is hard pressed by his opponents about the immoralities of his gods, he answers with all the freedom of a comparative mythologist :[2] "It is fabled that Prajāpati, the Lord of Creation, did violence to his daughter. But what does it mean ? Prajāpati, the Lord of Creation, is a name of the Sun; and he is called so, because he protects all creatures. His daughter Uṣas is the dawn. And when it is said that he was in love with her, this only means that, at sunrise, the sun runs after the dawn, the dawn being at the same time called the daughter of the Sun, because she rises when he approaches. In the same manner, if it is said that Indra was the seducer of Ahalyā, this does not imply that the god Indra committed such a crime; but Indra means the sun, and Ahalyā (from *alan* and *li)* the night; and, as the night is seduced and ruined by the sun of the morning, therefore is Indra called the paramour of Ahalyā."

But in spite of the mythological character which the religion of India has assumed in the Veda, in spite of other traces which show that even its most primitive hymns rest on numerous underlying strata of more primitive youghts and feelings, we should look in vain, in any other literature of the Āryan nations, to Greece or Rome, for documents from which to study that important chapter in the history of mankind which we can study in the Veda, the transition from a natural into an artificial religion.

In a history of Sanskrit literature the Chandas period, yough the most interesting from a philosophical point of view, can occupy but a small place. It is represented by a very limited literature, by those few hymns which show none of the signs of a more modern origin which we discussed when treating on the Mantra period. Their number will necessarily vary according to the rules which critics follow in testing the age and character of earlier and later hymns. This critical separation can be carried out successfully only after a comprehensive examination of the leading ideas of the whole Vedic poetry, and it could not be attempted within the small compass of this work. All I can do in this place is to give a few hymns which in yought and language represent the general character of genuine Vedic poetry, and to contrast them with some other hymns which decidedly belong to a later period.

The following hymn is ascribed to Manu Vaivasvata : viii. 30.

1. Among you, O gods, there is none that is small, none that is young : you all are great indeed.

2. Be thus praised, ye destroyers of foes, you who are thirty and three, you the sacred gods of Manu.

3. Defend us, help us, bless us ! do not lead us far away from the path of our fathers, from the path of Manu !

4. You who are here, O gods, all of you, and worshipped by all men, give us your broad protection, give it to cow and horse.

There is nothing striking, nothing that displays any warmth of feeling or power of expression in this hymn. The number of thirty-three assigned to the gods of Manu; would rather tend to refer its composition to a time when the gods of old had been gathered up and had been subjected to a strict census. Nevertheless, the hymn is simple and primitive in yought and language; and the fact of its being ascribed to Manu Vaivasvata shows that the Brāhmaṇas themselves looked upon it as a relic of one of their earliest sages. That Manu himself should be mentioned in the hymn seems to have caused no scruple to the Brāhmaṇas; nor is it any real difficulty from our own point of view. No man of the name of Manu ever existed. Manu was never more than a name one of the oldest mimes for man; and it was given in India, as elsewhere, to the supposed ancestor or ancestors of the human race. The Brāhmaṇas, however, like most Āryan nations, changed the appellative into a proper name. They believed in a real Manu, or in several real Manus, to whom they assigned various cognomina, such as Vaivasvata, Āpsava (Ṛv. ix. 7, 3), Sāmvaraṇa (Ṛv. ix. 6. 5). All of these they naturally counted as among the earliest of human Ṛṣis; and the hymns which they ascribed to them must have belonged in their eyes to the earliest and most important class.

In one sense it is true, no doubt, that invocations of all the gods, the Viśve Devas[3] as they are called, represent a later phase of yought then invocations of single deities. Nevertheless, there is nothing to show that this comprehensive view of all the deities belongs to an age later than that which gave rise to the most ancient hymns which we possess, and which celebrate the power and majesty of individual deities, such as Varuṇa, Indra, Agni (fire), the Maruts (the winds), Uṣas (dawn), etc. When these individual gods are invoked, they are not conceived as limited by the power of others, as superior or inferior in rank. Each god is to the mind of the supplicant as good as all the gods. He is felt, at the time, as a real divinity'—as supreme and absolute, in spite of the necessary limitations which, to our mind, a plurality of gods must entail on every single god. All the rest disappear for a moment from the vision of the poet, and he only who is to fulfil their desires stands in full light before the eyes of the worshippers. "Among you, O gods, there is none that is small, none that is young; you are all great indeed," is a sentiment which, yough, perhaps, not so distinctly expressed as by Manu Vaivasvata, nevertheless, underlies all the poetry of the Veda. Alyough the gods are sometimes distinctly invoked as the great and the small, the young and the old (Ftv. i. 27. 13), this is only an attempt to find the most compre-hensive expression for the divine powers, and nowhere is any of the gods represented as the slave of others. It would be easy to find, in the numerous hymns of the Veda, passages in which almost every single god is represented as supreme and absolute. In the first hymn of the second Maṇḍala, Agni is called the ruler of the universe,[4] the lord of men, the wise king, the father, the brother, the son, and friend of men;[5] nay, all the powers and names of the others are distinctly ascribed to Agni. The hymn belongs, no doubt, to the modern compositions; yet, yough Agni is thus highly exalted in it, nothing is said to disparage the divine character of the other gods. Indra is celebrated as the strongest god in the hymns as well as in the Brāhmaṇas, and the burden of one of the songs of the tenth book[6] is: *Viśvasmād Indra uttaraḥ,* "Indra is greater than all." Of Soma it is said that he was born great, and that he conquers every one.[7] He is called the king of the world,[8] he has the power to prolong the life of men,[6] and in one sense he is called the maker of heaven and earth, of Agni, of Sūrya, of Indra, and of Viṣṇu.[9]

If we read the next hymn, which is addressed to Varuṇa *(ουρόυς)* we perceive that the god here invoked is, to the mind of the poet, supreme and all-mighty. Nevertheless, he is one of the gods who is almost always represented in fellowship with another, Mitra; and even in our hymn there is one verse, the sixth, in which Varuṇa and Mitra are invoked in the dual. Yet what more could human language achieve, in trying to express the idea of a divine and supreme power, than what our poet says of Varuṇa; "You art lord of all, of heaven and earth." Or, as is said in another hymn (ū. 27. 10.), "You are the king of all; of those who are gods, and of those who are men." Nor is Varuṇa represented as the Lord of nature only. He knows the order of nature, and upholds it; for this is what is meant by *dhṛtavrata.*[11] Varuṇa, therefore, knows the twelve months, and even the thirteenth; he knows the course of the wind,; the birds in the air, and the ships of the sea. He knows all. the wondrous works of nature, and he looks not only into the past but into the future also. But, more than all this, Varuṇa Watches over the order of the moral world. The poet begins with a confession that he has neglected the works of Varuṇa, that he has offended against his laws. He craves his pardon; he appeals in self-defence to the weakness of human nature; he deprecates death as the reward of sin. His devotion is all he has where-with to appease the anger of his god; and how natural the feeling, when he hopes to soothe the god by his prayers as a horse is soothed by kind words. The poet has evidently felt the anger of Varuṇa. His friends, wishing for booty elsewhere, have left him, and he knows not how to bring back Varuṇa, who is the only giver of victory. He describes the power of his god, and he praises him chiefly as the guardian of law and order. Like a true child of nature, he offers honey, sweet things, which the god is sure to like, and then appeals to him as to a friend : "Now be good, and let us speak together again." This may seem childish, but there is a real and childish faith in it; and, like all childish faith, it is rewarded by some kind of response. For, at that very moment, the poet takes a higher tone, He fancies he sees the god and his chariot passing by; he feels that his prayer has been heard. True, there is much that is human, earthly, coarse, and false in the language applied to the deity as here invoked under the name of Varuṇa. Yet there is something also in these ancient strains of yought and faith which moves and cheers our hearts even at this great distance of time; and a wise man will pause before he ascribes to purely evil sources what may be, for all we know, the working of a love and wisdom beyond our own.

The hymn is ascribed to Śunaḥśepha, according to the legend of the later Brāhmaṇas, the victim offered to Varuṇa by his own father Ajīgarta Sauyavasi. (See page 375.)

1. However we break your laws from day to day, men as we are, O god, Varuṇa.

2. Do not deliver us unto death, nor to the blow of the furious; not to the anger, of the spiteful !

3. To propitiate you, O Varuṇa we bind your mind with songs, as the charioteer a weary steed.

4. Away from me they flee dispirited, intent only on gaining wealth; as birds to their nests.

5. When shall we bring hither the man who is victory to the warriors, when shall we bring Varuṇa, the wide-seeing, to be propitiated ?

6. This they take in common with delight, Mitra and Varuṇa; they never fail the faithful giver.

7. He who knows the place of the birds, that fly through the sky, who, on the waters knows the ships,

8. He, the upholder of order, who knows the twelve months with the offspring of each, and knows the month[12] that is engendered afterwards,

9. He who knows the track of the wind,[13] of the wide, bright, and mighty; and knows those who reside on high,[14]

10. He, the upholder of order, Varuṇa sits down among his people; he, the wise, sits there to govern.

11. From thence perceiving all wondrous things, he sees what has been and what will be done.

12. May he, the wise son of time (āditya), make our paths straight all our days; may he prolong our lives !

13. Varuṇa, wearing golden mail, has put on his shining cloak; the spies[15] sat down around him.

14. The god, whom the scoffers do not provoke, nor the tormentors of men, nor the plotters of mischicf,

15. He, who gives to men glory, and not half glory, who gives it even to our own bodies,

16. Yearning for him, the far-seeing, my youghts move onwards, as kine move to their pastures.

1 7. Let us speak together again, because my honey has been brought : you eat what you like, like a friend.[16]

18. Now I saw the god who is to be seen by all, I saw the chariot above the earth : he must have accepted my prayers.

19. O hear this my calling, Varuṇa, be gracious now; longing for help, I have called upon you.

20. You, O wise god, are lord of all heaven and earth :

listen on your way.

21. That I may live, take from me the upper rope, loose the middle, and remove the lowest !

The one hymn to Varuṇa would be sufficient to show the mistake of those who deny the presence of moral truths in the ancient religions of the world and more particularly, in the so-called nature-worship of the Āryans. On the contrary, whatever we find of moral sentiments in those ancient hymns is generally as true to-day as it was yousands of years ago; while what is false and perishable in them has reference to the external aspect of the deity, and to his supposed working in nature. The key-note of all religion, natural as well as revealed, is present in the hymns of the Veda, and never completely drowned by the strange music which generally deafens our ears when we first listen to the wild echoes of the heathen worship. There is the belief in God, the preception of the difference between good and evil, the conviction that God hates sin, and loves the righteous. We can hardly speak with sufficient reverence of the discovery of these truths, however trite they may appear to ourselves; and, if the name of revelation seems too sacred a name to be applied to them, that of discovery is too profane, for it would throw the vital truths of all religion, both ancient and modern, into the same category as the discoveries of a Galileo or a Newton. Theologians may agree in denying that any man in possession of his reason can, wiyout a crime, remain ignorant of God for any length of time. Missionaries, however, who held and defended this opinion, have been led to very different convictions after some intercourse with savage tribes. Dobrizhoffer,[17] who was for eighteen years a Missionary in Paraguay, states that the language of the Abipones does not contain a single word which expresses God or a divinity. Penafiel, a Jesuit theologian declared, that there were many Indians who, on being asked whether, during the whole course of their lives they ever yought of God, replied, *no, never.* Dobriz-hoffer says, "Travelling with fourteen Abipones, I sat down by the lire ia the open air, as usual on the high shore of the river Plata. The sky, which was perfectly serene, delighted our eyes with its twinkling stars. I began a conversation with the Cacique Ychoalay, the most intelligent of all the Abipones I have been acquainted with, as well as the most famous in Wār, 'Do you behold', said I, 'the splendour of Heaven, with its magnificent arrangement of stars ? Who can suppose that all this is produced by chance ? Whom do you suppose to be their creator and governor ? What were the opinions of your ancestors on the subject ?, 'My father', replied Ychoalay, readily and frankly, 'our grandfathers and great-grandfathers, were wont to contemplate the earth alone, solicitious only to see whether the plain afforded grass and water for their horses. They never troubled themselves about what went on in the Heavens, and who was the creator and governor of the stars." The Guaranies, who had an expression for the supreme Deity whom they call *tupa,* a word composed of two particlestu, a word of admiration, and *pa,* of inter-rogation, nevertheless worshipped only an evil spirit. Let us turn our eyes from the Indians of America to the Indians of India, and we shall perceive the immense distance by which these noble races are separated from the savage tribes to whom our Missionaries are still trying, and trying in vain, to impart the first principles of religion. The language of their simple prayers is more intelligible to us, their whole world of yought and feeling is nearer to us, than anything we find in the literature of Greece and Rome, and there are here and there, short expressions of faith and devotion in which even a Christian can join wiyout irreverence. If the following were not addressed to Varuṇa one of the many names of the deity, it would seem to contain nothing strange or offensive to our ears :

1. Let me not yet, O Varuṇa, enter into the house of clay; have mercy, almighty, have mercy

2. If I go along trembling, like a cloud driven by the wind; have mercy, almighty, have mercy

3. Through wānt of strength, you strong and bright god, have I gone to the wrong shore; have mercy, almighty, have mercy

4. Thirst came upon the worshipper, yough he stood in the midst of the Waters; have mercy, almighty, have mercy !

5. Whenever we men, O Varuṇa, commit an offence before the heavenly host: whenever we break your law through youghtlessness; have mercy, almighty, have mercy !

Here we have the two ideas, so contradictory to the human understanding, and yet so easily reconciled in every human heart : God has established the eternal laws of the moral world, yet he is willing to forgive those who offend against them; just yet merciful; a judge, and yet a father. "He is merciful even to him who has committed sin."[1]

The next hymn allows us a still deeper insight into strange ideas which the Ṛṣis had formed to themselves as to the nature of sin. (Ṛv. vii. 86).

1. Wise and mighty are the works of him who stemmed asunder the wide firmaments. He lifted on high the bright and glorious heaven; he stretched out apart the starry sky and the earth.

2. Do I say this to my own soul ? How can I get unto Varuṇa ? Will he accept my offering wiyout displeasure ? When shall I, with a quiet mind, see him propitiated ?

3. I ask, O Varuṇa, wishing to know this my sin. I go to ask, the wise. The sages all tell me the same : Varuṇa it is who is angry with you.

4. was it an old sin, O Varuṇa, that you wishs to destroy your friend, who always praises you ? Tell me, you unconquerable lord, and I will quickly turn to you with praise, freed from sin.

5. Absolve us from the sins of our fathers, and from those which we committed with out own bodies. Release Vasiṣtha.,[19] O king, like a thief who has feasted on stolen cattle; release him like a calf from the rope.

6. It was not our own doing, O Varuṇa, it was necessity, an intoxicating draught, passion, dice, youghtlessness. The old is near to mislead the young; even sleep brings unrighteousness.

7. Let me wiyout sin give satisfaction, like a slave to the bounteous lord, the god, our support. The lord god enlightened the foolish; he, the wisest, leads his worshipper to wealth.

8. O lord, Varuṇa, may this song go well to your heart ! May we prosper in keeping and acquiring ! Protect us, O gods, always with your blessings !

These ideas preponderate in hymns addressed to Varuṇa but they likewise occur in the prayers to the other gods. Varuṇa is one of the Ādityas, the sons of time, the Kroniones, the heavenly gods, The hymns addressed to these Ādityas in general are full of moral sentiments, because these gods are believed to protect men, not only against the assaults of nature, against disease and suffering, but al=o against the temptations of sin.

Rv. viii. 13. 14. "May evil betide him, the cursing mortal, the enemy who, double'tongued, would deal us a felon's blow.

15. You gods are with the righteous; you know men in their hearts. Come to the true man, and to the false, ye Vasus.

16. We implore the protection of the mountains, and the protection of the Waters.[20] Heaven and earth, remove from us all evil.

17. Carry us, O Vasus, by your blessed protection, as it were in your ship, across all dangers,

18. To our offspring, to our race, and thus to ourselves, make life longer to live, ye valiant Ādityas !

21. O Mitra, Aryaman, Varuṇa, and ye Winds, grant us an abode free from sin, full of men, glorious, with three bars.

22. We, who are but men, the bondsmen of death, prolong our time well, O Ādityas, that we may live !

Indra, one of the principal gods of the Veda, is likewise invoked, together with the Ādityas, as a god who may pardon sin. " Whatever sin we have committed against you,"[21] the poet says," let us obtain, O Indra, the broad safe light of day; let not the long darkness come upon us !" Indra is clearly conceived as a moral being in the following verse (Ṛv. viii. 21. 14.,)

" You never find a rich man to be your friend; wine-swillers despise you. But when you thunder, when you gather (the clouds), then you are called like a father."

Out of a large number of hymns addressed to the same god, we select one that is ascribed to Vasiṣṭha. (Ṛv. vii. 32).

1. Let no one, not even those who worship you, delay you far from us ! Even from afar come to our feast ! Or, if you are here, listen to us !

2. For these here who make prayers for you, sit together near the libation, like flies round the honey. The worshippers, anxious for wealth, have placed their desire upon Indra, as we put our foot upon a chariot.

3. Desirous of riches, I call him who holds the thunderbolt with his arm, and who is a good giver, like as a son calls his father.

4. These libations of Soma, mixed with milk, have been prepared for Indra : you armed with the thunderbolt, come with the steeds to drink of them for your delight; come to the house!

5. May he hear us, for he has ears to hear. He is asked for riches; will he despise our prayers ? He could soon give hundreds and yousands;—no one could check him if he wishes to give.

6. He who prepares for you, O Vṛtra-killer, deep libations, and pours them out[22] before you, that hero thrives with Indra, never scorned of men.

7. Be you, O mighty, the shield of the mighty (Vasiṣṭ has) when you dūvest together the fighting men. Let us share the wealth of him whom you have slain; bring us the household of him who is hard to vanquish.

8. Offer Soma to the drinker of Soma, to Indra, the lord of the thunderbolt; roast roasts; make him to protect us: Indra, the giver, is a blessing to him who gives oblations.

9. Do not grudge, ye givers of Soma; give strength[23] to the great god, make him to give wealth ! He alone .who perseveres, conquers, abides, and flourishes: the gods are not to be trifled with.

10. No one surrounds the chariot of the liberal worshipper, no one stops it. He whom Indra protects and the Maruts, he will come into stables full of cattle.

11. He will, when fighting, obtain spoil,[24] O Indra, the mortal, whose protection you should be. O hero, be you the protection of our chariots, and of our men !

12. His share is exceeding great, like the wealth of winner. He who is Indra with his steeds, him no enemies can subdue; may he give strength to the sacrificer !

13. Make for the sacred gods a hymn that is not small, that is well set and beautiful ! Many snares pass by him who abides with Indra through his sacrifice.

14. What mortal dares to attack him who is rich in you ? Through faith in you, O mighty, the strong acquires spoil in the day of battle.

15. Stir us mighty Vasiṣṭhas in the slaughter of the enemies, stir us who give their dearest treasures. Under your guidance, O Haryaśva, we shall with our wise counsellors overcome all hardships.

16. To you belongs the lowest treasure; you rear the middle treasure; you are king always of all the highest treasure; no one withstands you in the flock.

17. You are well known as the benefactor of every one, whatever battles there be. Every one of these kings of the earth implores your name, when wishing for help.

18. If I were lord of as much as you, I should support

the sacred bard, you scatterer of wealth, I should not abandon him to misery.

19. I should award wealth day by day to him who magnifies, I should award it to whosoever it be.[25] We have no other friend but you, no other happiness, no other father, O mighty !

20. He who perseveres acquires spoil with his wife as his mate; I bend India, who is invoked by many, for you, as a wheelwright bends a wheel made of strong wood.

21. A mortal does not get riches by scant praise : no wealth comes to the grudger. The strong man it is, O mighty, who in the day of battle is a precious gift to you live as to me.

22. We call for you, O hero, like cows that have not been milked; we praise you as ruler of all that moves, O Indra, as ruler of all that is immoveable.

23. There is no one like you in heaven or earth; he is not born, and will not be born. O mighty Indra, we call upon you as we go righting for cows and horses.

24. Bring all this to those who are good, O Indra, be they old or young;' for you, O mighty, art the rich of old, and to be called in every battle.

25. Push away the unfriendly, O mighty, make us treasures easy to get ! Be the protector of ourselves in the fight, be the cherisher of our friend !

26. Indra, give wisdom to us, as a father to his sons. Teach us in this path, let us living see the son !

27. Let not unknown wretches, evil-disposed and unhallowed, tread us down. Through your help, O hero, let us step over the rushing eternal waters !

In this hymn Indra is clearly conceived as the supreme god, and we can hardly understand how a people who had formed so exalted a notion of the deity and embodied it in the person of Indra, could, at the same sacrifice, invoke other gods with equal praise. When Agni, the lord of fire, is addressed by the poet, he is spoken of as the first god, not inferior even to Indra. While Agni is invoked, Indra is forgotten; there is no competition between the two, nor any rivalry between them or other gods. This is most important feature in the religion of the Veda, and has never been taken into consideration by those who have written on the history of ancient polytheism.

There are other hymns, again, in which the notion of a deity is much less prominent. Indra is there represented like a hero fighting against enemies. He is liable to defeat, his heart fails him in the combat, and yough at last he invariably conquers, he does so rather by an effort than by the mere assertion of his power. Agni, again, in many hymns, is simply described as a power of nature, as the fire, such as it is seen in heaven and on earth. Many things that have become to us familiar, struck the poets of the Veda as wonderful and mysterious. They describe the power of the fire with an awe which, to the natural philosopher of the present day, must appear childish. The production of fire by the friction of wood, or its sudden descent from the sky in the form of lightning, is to them as marvellous as the birth of a child. They feel their dependence on fire; they have experienced what it is to be wiyout it. They were not yet acquainted with lucifer-matches, and hence, when describing the simple phenomena of fire, they do it naturally with a kind of religious reverence. The following verses taken from a hymn of Vasiṣṭha (vii. 3.) may serve as a specimen :

" Neighing like a horse that is greedy for food, when it steps from the strong prison; then the wind blows after his blast; your path O Agni, is dark at once.[27]

O Agni, you from whom, as a new-born male, undying flames proceed, the brilliant smoke goes towards the sky, for as messenger you art sent to the gods.

You whose power spreads over the earth in a moment when you hast grasped food with your jaws,ṭlike a dashing army your blast goes forth; with your lambent flame you seemest to tear up the grass.

Him alone, the ever-youthful Agni, men groom like a horse in the evening and at dawn; they bed him as a str.nger in his couch; the light of Agni, the worshipped[2] male, is lighted.

Thy appearance is fair to behold, you bright-faced Agni, when like gold you shin at hand; your brightness comes like the lightning of heaven; you show splendour like the bright sun."

The human, and afterwards divine qualities ascribed to Agni arise chiefly from his character as messenger between gods and men, or, as high-priest, when he is supposed to carry the oblation to the gods. It is one of the most favourite themes of the Vedic poets, yough perhaps of the modern rather than of the ancient, to celebrate Agni as a priest, as endowed with all priestly powers, and enjoying all the honorific titles given to the various persons who minister at the great sacrifices. The following hymns, one of Vatsa (Ṛv. viii. 11, the other of Gotama (R.v. i. 74), are rather simple as compared with others of the same class, yough there are expressions in which both indicate their more modern character.

1. You Agni art the guardian of sacred rites : you art a god among mortals;[1] you art to be praised at the sacrifices.

2. You, strong Agni, art to be praised at the festivals, you who like a charioteer carriest the offerings to the gods.

3. Fight and drive you away from us the fiends, O Jātavedas, the ungodly enemies, O Agni !

4. You, Jātavedas, desirest not the offering of a hostile man, be it ever so nigh to you.

5. We mortals and sages worship the great name of you, the immortal Jatavedas.

6. We sages call the sage to help, we mortals call on the god for protection, we call on Agni with songs.

7. May the poet draw your mind even from the most distant abode with the song that longs for you, O Agni.

8. You art the same in many places, a lord among all people: we call upon you in battles.

9. In battles we call upon you, Agni, for help when we want strength; we call in struggles upon the giver of precious gifts.

10. You art ancient, to be praised at the sacrifices; you sit as priest from of old and to-day. Replenish your own body, O Agni, and grant happiness to us !

1. As we go to the sacrifice let us say a song to Agni, to him who hears us even from afar.

2. He who, existing from of old, defended the house for the sacrificer when hostile tribes were gathering together.

3. Let even the nations confess, " Agni was born, the slayer of the enemy, the winner of booty in every battle."

4. He whose messenger you art in the house, whose offerings you art pleased to accept, and whose sacrifice you render efficient.

5. Of him indeed, O Aṅgiras, son of strength, people say that his offerings are good, his gods are good and his altar is good.

6. Bring hither, O serene Agni, these gods, bring them that they may be praised, that they may accept the offerings.

7. When you, O Agni, go on a mission, the sound of the horses of your moving chariot is never heard.

8. If protected by you, the warrior is unwashed. Onward he goes, one after another, forward he steps, O Agni, who offers oblations.

9. You, O bright god, bestow with increase a briliant array of heroes upon him who offers oblations to the bright gods.[30]

It is curious to watch the almost imperceptible transition by which the phenomena of nature, if reflected in the mind of the poet, assume the character of divine beings. The dawn is frequently described in the Veda as it might be described by a modern poet. She is the friend of men, she smiles like a young wife, she is the daughter of the sky. She goes to every house, (i. 123. 4.) ; she thinks of the dwellings of men (i. 123. 1; she does not despise the small or the great (i. 124. 6.); she brings wealth (i, 48. 1.); she is always the same, immortal, divine, (i. 124. 4.; i. 123. 8.); age cannot touch her, (i. 113. 15.); she is the young goddess, but she makes men grow old, (i. 92. 11.). All this may be simply allegorical language. But the transitions from *devī,* the bright, to devī, the goddess, is so easy; the daughter of the sky assumes so readily the same personality which is given to the sky, Dyaus, her father, that we can only guess whether in every passage the poet is speaking of a bright apparition, or of a bright goddess; of a natural vision, or of a visible deity. The following hymn of a Vasiṣṭha, (vū. 77.), will serve as an instance :

"Shc shines upon us, like a young wife, rousing every living being to go to his work. The fire had to be kindled by men[31]; she brought light striking down darkness.

She rose up spreading far and wide, and moving towards every one. She grew in brightness, wearing her brilliant garment. The mother of the cows (of the morning clouds), the leader of the days, she shone gold-coloured, lovely to behold.

She, the fortunate, who brings the eye of the god, who leads the white and lovely steed (of the sun), the Dawn was seen, revealed by her rays, with brilliant treasures she follows every one.

You, who art a blessing where you art near, drive far away the unfriendly; make the pastures wide, give us sefety ! Remove the haters, bring treasures ! Raise up wealth to the worshipper, you mighty Dawn.

Shine for us with your best rays, you bright Dawn, you who lengthen our life, you the love of all, who give us food, who givest us wealth in cows, horses, and chariots.

You, daughter of the sky, you, high born Dawn, whom the Vasiṣṭhas magnify with songs, give us riches high and wide : all ye gods, protect us always with your blessings !"

This hymn addressed to the Dawn is a fair specimen of the original simple poetry of the Veda. It has no reference to any special sacrifice, it contains no techqical expressions, it can hardly be called a hymn, in our sense of the word. It is simply a poem expressing, wiyout any effort, wiyout any display of far-fetched yought or brilliant imagery, the feelings of a man who has watched the approach of the dawn with mingled delight and awe, and who was moved to give utterance to what he felt, in measured language. We have heard the same youghts and feelings expressed by so many poets, that we can hardly enter into the pleasure with which those early singers spoke their hearts out for the first time. We have become so accustomed to the rules of the most complicated metres that we hardly consider how mysterious is that instinct which suggested to the first poets the extraordinary variety of rhythm which we find in the Veda. But there is a charm in these primitive strains discoverable in no other class of poetry. Every word retains something of its radical meaning, every epithet tells, every yought, in spite of the most intricate and abrupt expressions, is, if we once disentangle it, true, correct, and complete. But this is not the case with all the poems of the Veda. It would be tedious to translate many specimens of what I consider the poetry of the secondary age, the Mantra period. These songs are generaliy intended for sacrificial purposes, they are loaded with techqicalities, their imagery is some-times more brilliant, but always less perspicuous, and many youghts and expressions are clearly borrowed from earlier hymns. One specimen may suffice, a hymn describing the sacrifice of the horse with the full detail of a supersititious ceremonial. (Ṛv. i. 162.).

" May Mitra, Varuṇa, Aryaman, Āyu, Indra, the Lord of the Ṛbhus, and the Maruts not rebuke us because we shall proclaim at the sacrifice the virtues of the swift horse sprung from the gods.

When they lead before the horse, which is decked with pure gold ornaments, the offering, firmly grasped, the spotted goat[32] bleats while walking onward; it goes the path beloved by Indra and Puṣan.

This goat, destined for all the gods, is led first with the quick horse, as Pūṣan's share; for Tvaṣṭṛ himself raises to glory this pleasent offering which is brought with the horse.

When thrice at the proper seasons men lead around the sacrificial horse which goes to the gods, Pūṣan's share comes first, the goat, which announces the sacrifice to the gods.

Hotṛ, Adhvaryu, Āvayaj (Pratiprasthātṛ), Agnimindha (Agnīdhra), Grāvagrābha (Grāvastu), and the wise Śaṅstṛ (Praśastṛ)[33], may you fill the streams (round the altar) with a sacrifice which is well prepared and well accomplished.

They who cut the sacrificial post, and they who carry it, they who make the ring for the post of the horse, and even they who bring together what is cooked for the horse, may their work be with us. .

He came on—(my prayer has been well performed), the bright-backed horse goes* to the regions of the gods. Wise poets celebrate him, and we have won a good friend for the love of the gods.

The halter of the swift one, the heel-ropes of the horse, the head-ropes, the girths, the bridle, and even the grass that has been put into his mouth, may all these which belong to you be with the gods !

What the fly eats of the flesh, what adheres to the stick, or to the axe, or to the hands of the immolator and his nails, may all these which belong to you be with the. gods!

The ordure that runs from the belly, and the smallest particle of raw flesh, may the immolators well prepare all this, and dress the sacrifice till it is well cooked.

The juice that flows from your roasted limb on the spit after you have been killed, may it not run on the earth or the grass; may.it be given to the gods who desire it.

They who examine the horse when it is roasted, they who say "it smells well, take it away," they who serve the distribution of the meat, may their work also be with us.

The ladle of the pot where the meat is cooked, and the vessels for sprinkling the juice, the vessels to keep off the heat, the covers of the vessels, the skewers, and the knives, they adorn the horse.

Where he walks, where he sits, where he stirs, the foot-fastening of the horse, what he drinks, and what food he eats, may all these which belong to you be with the gods !

May not the fire with smoky smell make you his, may not the glowing cauldron smell and burst. The gods accept the horse if it is offered to them in due form.

The cover which they stretch over the horse, and the golden ornaments, the head-ropes of the horse, and the foot-ropes, all these which are dear to the gods, they offer to them.

If some one strike you with the heel or the whip that you mayest lie down, and you art snorting with all your might, then I purify all this with my prayer, as with a spoon of clarified butter at the sacrifices.

The axe approaches the thirty-four ribs of the quick horse, beloved of the gods. Do you widely keep the limbs whole, find out each joint and strike.

One strikes the brilliant horse, two hold it, thus is the custom. Those of your limbs which I have seasonably prepared, I sacrifice in the fire as balls offered to the gods.

May not your dear soul burn you while you art coming near, may the axe not stick to your body. May no greedy and unskilful immolator, missing with the sword, throw your mangled limbs together.

Indeed you diest not thus, you suffer not; you go to the gods on easy paths. The two horses of Indra, the two deer of the Maruts have been yoked, and the horse come to the shaft of the ass (of the Aśvins.)

May this horse give us cattle and horses, men, progeny, and all sustaining wealth. May Aditi keep us free from sin; may the horse of this sacrifice give us strength!

A comparison of the general tone of this hymn with that of the hymns to Varuṇa, Indra, and Uṣas, translated before, can leave little doubt in the mind of critical historians as to its more modern character. We must be careful, how-ever, not to judge the poetry of the ancient bards of India according to our own standard of what is simple and natural and what is not. The great importance attached to what to us seem mere trifles in the performance of a sacrifice would not be sufficient to stamp this hymn as modern. The superstitious feeling about ceremonial minutiae is natural in a primitive state of civilization, and there are numerous hymns in the Veda which must be adjudged to the earliest period, and where, nevertheless, we meet with sentiments woryour of the most advanced ceremonials.

The same caution is still more necessary with regard to another criterion which has been used to prove the modern date of certain hymns, the presence of philosophical ideas. It has been the custom to regard any hymn in which the nature of the deity, the problems of existence, the hope of immortality are expressed, as decidedly modern. The whole tenth Maṇḍala has been assigned to a later period, chiefly because it contains many hymns the language of which approaches the philosophical diction of the Upaniṣads and of the still later systems of philosophy. This is a mistake.

There is very little to guide us in forming a judgment of what is genuine and primitive in the ancient poetry of so peculiar a race as the Āryans of India. We have nothing to compare with the poetical relics of the Vedic age. Because we find in some hymns ideas or expressions which, in the literatures of other nations, such as the Jews, or Greeks and Romans, we have accustomed ourselves to regard as of comparatively modern growth, we have no right to conclude that they are equally modern in the history of the Indian mind. The Veda opens to us a chamber in the labyrinth of the human mind through which the other Āryan nations had passed long before they become visible to us by the light of history. Whatever the age of the Veda may be, in one sense it is the oldest book in existence. If this collection had been written but fifty years ago, in some distant part of the world untouched by the general stream of civilization, we should still call it more ancient than the Homeric poems, because it represents an earlier place of human yought and feeling. Names ' which in Homer have become petrified and mythological, are to be found in the Veda as it were in a still fluid state. They next appear as appellatives, not yet as proper names; they are organic, not yet broken and smoothed down. Nor can we compare that earlier, lower, and more savage phase of yought which we find in the Veda, with what we know of really barbarous tribes, such as the Negroes of Africa or the Indians of America. For, however inferior to the Greeks of Homer and the Jews of Moses, the Āryas of the Seven Rivers are far above those races, and had long crossed the bounds of an unconscious barbarism, when they worshipped *Dyaus* and the other bright gods of nature.

Let us consider but a single point. We have accustomed ourselves to regard a belief in the unity of God as one of the last stages to which the Greek mind ascended from the depths of a polytheistic faith. The one unknown God was the final result which the pupils of Plato and Aristotle had arrivéd at when they came to listen to the strange teaching of St. Paul at Athens. But how can we tell that the course of yought was the same in India ? By what right do we mark all hymns as modern in which the idea of one God breaks through the clouds of a polytheistic phraseology ? The belief in a Supreme God, in a God above all gods, may in the abstract seem later than the belief in many gods. Yet let one poet but once perceive how he is drawn towards the Divine by the same feelings that draw him towards his father, let such a poet in his simple prayer but once utter, yough it be youghtlessly, the words, "My father," and the dreary désert through which philosophy inarches step by step, is crossed at a single bound. We must not compare the Āryan and the Semitic races. Whereas the Semitic nations relapsed from time to time into polytheism, the Āryans of India seem to have relapsed into Monotheism. In both cases these changes were not the result of a gradual and regular progress, but of individual impulses and peculiar influences. I do not think, therefore, that the mere occurrence of monotheistic ideas, and of other large philosophical conceptions, is sufficient to stamp any class of hymns as of modern date. A decided preponderance of such ideas, coupled with other indications in the character of the language, might make us hesitate before we used such as witnesses for the Chandas period. But there is a monotheism that precedes the polytheism of the Veda, and even in the invocations of their innumerable gods the remembrance of a God, one and infinite, breaks through the mist of an idolatrous phraseology, like the blue sky that is hidden by passing clouds.

There is a hymn of peculiar interest in the tenth Maṇḍala, full of ideas which to many would seem to necessitate the admission of a long antecedent period of philosophical yought. There we find the conception of a beginning of all things, and of a state previous even to all existence. " Nothing that is, was then," the poet says; and he adds, with a boldness matched only by the Eleatic thinkers of Greece, or by Hegel's philosophy, "even what is not (το μη ου) , did not exist then." He then proceeds to deny the existence of the sky and of the firmament, and yet, unable to bear the idea of an unlimited nothing, he exclaims, "What was it that hid or covered the existing" Thus driven on, and asking two questions at once, with a rapidity of yought which the Greek and the Sanskrit languages only can follow, he says, "What was the refuge of what" After this metaphysical flight the poet returns to the more substantive realities of yought, and, throwing out a doubt, he continues, "was Water the deep abyss, the chaos, which swallowed everything ?" Then his mind, turning away from Nature, dwells upon man and the problem of human life. "There was no death," he says, and, with a logic which perhaps has never been equalled, he subjoins, " therefore was there nothing immortal." Death, to his mind, becomes the proof of immortality. One more negation, and he has done. " There was no space, no life, and lastly, there was no time, no difference between day and night, no solar torch by which morning might have been told from evening." All these ideas lie imbedded in the simple words, *"Na rātryā ahna āsīt praketaḥ."* Now follows his first assertion : "That One," he says, and he uses no other epithet or nualificationt " That One breathed breathless by itself : other than it, nothing since has been." This expression, "it breathed breathless" seems to me one of the happiest attempts at making language reflect the colourless abstractions of the mind. "That One," the poet says, " breathed, and lived; it enjoyed more than mere existence; yet its life was not dependent on anything else, as our life depends on the air which we breathe. It breathed breathless." Language blushes at such expressions, but her blush is a blush of truimph.

After this the poet plunges into imagery, "Darkness there was , and all first was veiled in gloom profound, as ocean wiyout light." No one has ever found a truer expression of the Infinite, breathing and heaving within itself, than the ocean in a dark night, wiyout a star, wiyout a torch. It would have been easy to fill out the picture, and a modern writer would have filled it out. The true poet, however, says but a single word, and, at his spell, pictures arise within our own mind, full of a reality beyond the reach of any art.

But now this One had to be represented as growing—as entering into reality—and here again Nature must supply a similitude to the poet. As yet, the real world existed only as a germ, hidden in a husky shell; now, the poet represents the one substance as borne into life by its own innate heat. The beginning of the world was conceived like the spring of nature; one miracle was explained by another. But, even then, this Being, or this nature, as conceived by the poet, was only an unconscious substance, wiyout will and wiyout change. The question how there was generation in nature, was still unanswered. Another miracle had to be appealed to, in order to explain the conscious act of creation : this miracle was Love, as perceived in the heart of men. " Then first came love upon it," the poet continues, and he defines love, not only as a natural, but as a mental impulse. Though he cannot say what love is yet he knows that all will recognise what he means by love, a power which arises from the unsearchable depths of our nature, making us feel our own incompleteness, and drawing us, half-conscious, half-unconscious, towards that far off and desired something, through which alone our life seems to become a reality. This is the analogy which was wanted to explain the life of nature, which he knew was more than mere existence. The One Being which the poet had postulated was neither self-sufficient nor dead : a desire fell upon it,—a spring of life, manifested in growth of every kind. After the manifestation of this desire or will, all previous existence seemed to be unreal, a mere nothing as compared with the fullness of genuine life, A substance with out this life, wiyout that infinite desire of production and reproduction, could hardly be said to exist. It was a bare abstract conception. Here, then, the poet imagines he has discovered the secret of creation, the transition of the nothing into the something,—the change of the abstract into the concrete. Love was to him the beginning of real reality, and he appeals to the wise of old, who discovered in love, "the bond between created things and uncreated." What follows is more difficult to understand. We hardly know into what new sphere of yought the poet enters. The growth of nature has commenced, but where was it ? Did the piercing ray of light come from below, or from above ? This is the question which the poet asks, but to which he returns no answer, for he proceeds at once to describe the presence of male and female powers, nor is it likely that what follows, *"svadhā avastāt, prayatiḥ parastāt,"* is meant as an answer to the preceding inquiry. The figure which represents the creation as a ray entering the realm of darkness from the realm of light, occurs again at a much later time in the system of Manichaeism,[37] but like all attempts at clothing transcendental ideas in the imagery of human yought, it fails to convey any tangible or intelligible impression. This our poet also seems to have felt, for he exclaims "Who indeed knows? Who proclaimed it here, whence, whence this creation was produced? The gods were later than its production, therefore who knows whence it came ? " And now a new yought dawns in tho mind of the Ṛṣi, a yought for which we were not prepared, and which apparently contradicts the whole train of argument or meditation that preceded. Whereas hitherto the problem of existence was conceived as a mere evolution of one substance, postulated by human reasoning, the poet now speaks of an *Adhyakṣa,* an overseer, a contemplator, who resides in the highest heavens. He, he says, knows it. And why ? Because this creation came from him, whether he made it or not. The poet asserts the fact that this overseer is the source of creation, yough he shrinks from determining the exact process, whether he created from himself, or from nothing, or from matter existing by itself. Here the poet might have stopped; but there are yet four more words of extreme perplexity which close the poem. They may be interpreted in two ways. They either mean " Or does he not know ?" and this would be a question of defiance addressed to all who might doubt his former assertion; or they mean " Or he knows not," and this would be a confession of doubt on the part of the poet, startling perhaps after the firm assertion of his belief in this one overseer and creator, yet not irreconcilable with that spirit of timidity displayed in the words, " whether he made it himself or not," which shrinks from asserting anything on a point where human reason, left to herself, can only guess and hope, and, if it venture on words, say in last resort, " Behold, we know not anything."

I subjoin a metrical translation of this hymn, which I owe to the kindness of a friend :

"Nor aught nor naught existed; yon bright sky
Was not, nor heaven's broad woof outstretched above.
What covered all ? what sheltered ? what concealed ?
Was it the water's fathomless abyss ?
There was not deaththence was there naught immortal,
There was no confine betwixt day and night;
The only One breathed breathless in itself,
Other than it there nothing since has been.
Darkness there was , and all at first was veiled
In gloom profound,—an ocean wiyout light.
The germ that still lay covered in the husk

Burst forth, one nature, from the fervent heat.
Then first came Love upon it, the new spring
Of mind-yea, poets in their hearts discerned,
Pondering, this bond between created things
And uncreated. Comes this spark from earth,
Piercing and all-pervading, or from heaven ?
Then seeds were sown, and mighty power arose
Nature below, and Power and Will above.
Who knows the secret ? who proclaimed it here,
Whence, whence this manifold creation sprang ?
The gods themselves came later into being.
Who knows from whence this great creation sprang ?
He from whom all this great creation came.
Whether his will created or was mute,
The Most High seer that is in highest heaven,
He knows it, or perchance e'en He knows not."

Many of the youghts expressed in this hymn will, to most readers, appear to proceed rather from a school of mystic philosophers than from a simple and primitive clan of shepherds and colonists. Meditations on the mysteries of creation are generally considered a luxury which no society can indulge in before ample provision has been made for the lower cravings of human nature ; such is no doubt the case in modern times. Philosophers arise after the security of a state has been established, after wealth has been acquired and accumulated in certain families, after schools and universities have been founded, and a taste created for those literary pursuits which, even in the most advanced state of civilization, must necessarily be confined to but a small portion of our ever-toiling community. Metaphysics, whether in the form of poetry or prose, are, and always have been, the privilege of the limited number of independent thinkers, and youghts like those which we find in this ancient hymn, yough clothed in a form of argument more in accordance with the requirements of our age, would fail to excite any interest except among the few who have learnt to delight in the speculations of a Plato, a Tauler, or a Coleridge. But it would be false to transfer our ideas to the early periods of oriental life. First of all, the merely physical wants of a people living in the rich plains of India were satisfied wiyout great exertions. Secondly, such was the simplicity of their life, that nothing existed which could absorb the energies of the most highly gifted among them. Neither war, nor politics, nor arts, opened a field for the exercise of genius, and for the satisfaction of a legitimate ambition. Nor should it be forgotten that, in the natural course of human life, there is after all nothing that appeals with greater force to our deepest interests than the problem of our existence, of our beginning and our end, of our dependence on a Higher Power, and of our yearnings for a better life. With us these keynotes of human yought are drowned in the din of our busy society. Artificial interests have supplanted the natural desires of the human heart. Nor less should we forget how in these later ages most of us have learnt from the history of the past that our reason, in spite of her un-extinguishable aspirations, consumes this life in a prison the the walls of which she cannot pierce, and where we only see light by lifting our eyes on high. All this was different in ancient times, and particularly among a people so remarkably gifted for philosophical abstraction as the Hindus. Long before they began to care for the laws of nature, the return of the seasons, the course of the stars, or any other scientific or practical subject, their youghts were fixed on the one great and ever recurring question, What am I ? What does all this world around me mean ? Is there a cause, is there a-creatorṭa God ? or is it all illusion, chance, and fate ? Again and again the Ṛṣis express their doubts, and the one knowledge which they value as wonderful and excellent is the knowledge of το ταμεγιστα. It cannot be right to class every poem and every verse in which mystic or metaphysical speculations occur as modern, simply because they resemble the language of the Upaniṣads. These Upaniṣads did not spring into existence on a sudden : like a stream which has received many a mountain torrent, and is fed by many a rivulet, the literature of the Upaniṣads proves, better than anything else, that the elements of their philosophical poetry came from a more distant fountain. The evidence of language is the most decisive for setting the relative age of Vedic hymns ; and the occurrence of such a word as *tadanlm,* then, is more calculated to rouse doubts as to the early date of this hymn than the most abstruse metaphysical ideas which may be discovered in it. Hymns like that ascribed to *Dīrghatamas* (i. 164.) contain, no doubt, many verses full of the most artifical conceptions, the lucubrations rather of conceited dreamers than of simple and original thinkers. But even in those large collective poems there are lines which look like relics of a better age, and bear the stamp of true and genuine feeling. Thus we read in the 37th verse : "I know not what this is that I am like ; turned inward I walk, chained in my mind. When the first-born of time comes near me, then I obtain the por-tion of this speech."

In the 30th verse of the same hymn we read : "Breathing lies the quick-moving life, heaving, yet firm, in the midst of its abodes. The living one walks through the powers of the dead : the immortal is the brother of the mortal." Sometimes when these oracular sayings have been pronounced, the poet claims his due, " One who had eyes," he says, "saw it ; the blind will not understand it. A poet, who is a boy, he has perceived it ; he who understands it will be the father of his father."

In the same hymn one verse occurs which boldly declares the existence of but one Divine Being, yough invoked under different names. (Ṛv. i. 164. 46.) "They call (him) Indra, Mitra, Varuṇa, Agni ; then he is the well-winged heavenly Garutmat ; that which is One the wise call it many ways ; they call it Agni, Yama, Mātariśvan". Many of these verses have been incorporated in the Upaniṣads, and are there explained by later sophists who wish to represent them as a guarantee for the scholastic doctrines of the Vedānta philosophy. It was in the Upaniṣads and in the Sūtras of Vyasa that most Sanskrit scholars became first acquainted with these quotations from the Veda, and hence, even after they had been discovered in their original place in the hymns of the Ṛg-veda-Saṁhitā, a prejudice remained against their antiquity. The ideas which they expressed were supposed to be of too abstract a nature for the uneducated poets of the Vedic age. I am far from defending the opinion of those who maintained the existence of a school of priests and philosophers in the remotest ages of the world, and who discovered the deepest wisdom in the religious mysteries and mythological traditions of the East. But the reaction which these extravagant theories has produced goes too far, if every yought which touches on the problems of philosophy is to be marked indiscriminately as a modern forgery, if every conception which reminds us of Moses, Plato, or the Apostles, is to be put down as necessarily borrowed from Jewish, Greek or Christians ources, and foisted thence into the collections of the ancient poetry of the Hindus.

There is what Leibnitz called *perennis qucedam philosophia,* a search after truth which was not confined to the schools of priests or philosophers. Its language, no doubt, is less exact than that of an Aristotle, its tenets are vague, and the light which it sheds on the dark depths of human yought resembles more the sheet-lightning of a sombre evening, than the bright rays of a cloudless sunrise. Yet there is much to be learnt by the historian and the philosopher from these ' ancient guesses at truth ; and we should not deprive ourselves of the new sources which have so unexpectedly been opened for studying the history of man, fearful and wonderful as his structure, by casting wanton doubts on all that conflicts with our own previous conclusions. I add only one more hymn, in which the idea of one God is expressed with such power and decision, that it will make us hesitate before we deny to the Āryan nations an instinctive Monotheism. (Ṛv. x. 121.)

"In the beginning there arose the Source of golden light—He was the only born Lord of all that is. He established. the earth, and this sky ; Who is the God to whom we shall offer our sacrifice ?

He who gives life, He who gives strength ; whose blessing all the bright gods desire ; whose shadow is immortality ; whose shadow is death ; Who is the God to whom we shall offer our sacrifice ?

He who through His power is the only King of the breathing and awakening world;—He who governs all, man and beast; Who is the God to whom we shall offer our sacrifice ?

He whose power these snowy mountains, whose power the sea proclaims, with the distant river He whose these regions are as it were His two arms ; Who is the God to whom we shall offer our sacrifice ?

He through whom the sky is bright and the earth firm—He through whom the heaven was stablished, nay, the highest heaventHe who measured out the light in the air; Who is the God to whom "we shall offer our sacrifice ?

He to whom heaven and earth, standing firm by His will, look up, trembling inwardly He over whom the rising sun shines forth ; Who is the God to whom we shall offer our sacrifice ?

Wherever the mighty water-clouds went, where they placed the seed and lit the fire, thence arose He who is the only life of the bright gods ; Who is the God to whom we shall offer our sacrifice ?

He who by His might looked even over the Water-clouds, the clouds which gave strength and lit the sacrifice, He *who is God above all gods ;* Who is the God to whom we shall offer our sacrifice ?

May He not destroy us—he the creator of the earth ; or He, the righteous, who created the heaven ; He who also created the bright and mighty Waters ;—Who is the God to whom we shall offer our sacrifice ?"

There is nothing to prove that this hymn is of a particularly ancient date. On the contrary, there are expressions in it, especially the name of Hiranyagarbha, which seem to belong to a later age. But even if we assign the lowest possible date to this and similar hymns, certain it is that they existed during the

Mantra period, and before the composition of the Brāhmaṇas ; certain it is that every verse and every syllable was counted in the Anukrāmaṇīs of the Sūtra period. With our received notions on the history of the human mind it may be difficult to account for facts like these ; but facts must not be made to evapo-rate in order to maintain a theory. The difficulty, such as it is, will be felt by all who think seriously and honestly on these problems. But it is better to state this difficulty than to conceal it. Even if we assign all philosophical hymns to the last years of the Mantra period, we have to account, in the 9th century B. C, for youghts which, like the stems of forest trees, disclose circles within circles, almost impossible to count. There are hymns which are decidedly modern if compared with others ; but if the most modern be ascribed to the Mantra period, what must be the date of the earliest relics of the Chandas age ? There can be little doubt, for instance, that the 90th hymn[1] of the 10th book, a hymn which is likewise found in the 31st book of the Vājasaneyi-Saṁhitā, and in the 19th book of the Atharva-veda, is modern both in its character and in its diction. It is full of allusions to the sacrificial ceremonials, it uses techqical philosophical terms, it mentions the three seasons in the order of *Vasanta,* spring, *Grīṣma,* summer, and *Śarad,* autumn ; it contains the only passage in the Ṛg-veda where the four castes are enumerated. The evidence of language for the modern date of this composition is equally strong. *Grīṣma,* for instance, the name for the hot season, does not occur in any other hymn of the Ṛg veda ; and *Vasanta* also, the name of spring, does not belong to the earliest vocabulary of the Vedic poets. It occurs but once more in the Ṛg-veda x. 161.4., in a passage where the three seasons are mentioned in the order of *Śarad,* autumn, *Hemanta,* winter, and *Vasanta,* spring. But io spite of all the indications of a modern date, this hymn, if our argument holds good, must have existed before the beginning of the Brāhmaṇa period. I see no possibility how we could account for the allusions to it which occur in the Brāhmaṇas, or for its presence in the Saṁhitās of the Vājesaneyins, and Atharvans, unless we admit that this peom formed part of the final collection of the

Ṛg-Veda-Saṁhitā, the work of the Mantra period. There are no traces anywhere of hymns having been added after that collection was closed, exeept in the case of the Khilas, and no secret is ever made as to their spurious character. Oriental scholars are frequently suspected of a desire to make the literature of the eastern nations appear more ancient than it is, As to myself, I can truly say that nothing would be to me a more welcome discovery, nothing would remove so many doubts and difficulties, as some suggestion as to the manner in which certain of the Vedic hymns could have been added to the original collection during the Brāhmaṇa or Sūtra periods, or, if possible, by the writers of our MSS., of which most are not older than the 15th century. But these MSS., yough so modern, are checked by the Anukrāmaṇīs. Every hymn which stands in our MSS. is counted in the Index of Śaunaka, who is anterior to the invasion of Alexander. The Sūtras, belonging to the same period as Śaunaka, prove the previous existence of every chapter of the Brāhmaṇas : and I doubt whether there is a single hymn in the Saṁhitā of the Ṛg-veda which could not be checked by some passage of the Brāhmaṇas and Sūtras. The chronological limits assigned to the Sūtra and Brāhmaṇa periods will seem to most Sanskrit scholars too narrow rather than too wide, and if we assign but 200 years to the Mantra period, from 800 to 1000 B. C, and an equal number to the Chandas period, from 1000 to 1200 B. C, we can do so only under the supposition that during the early periods of history the growth of the human mind was more luxuriant than in later times, and that the layers of yought were formed less slowly in the primary than in the tertiary ages of the world.

REFERENCES

1. See my Letter on the Classification of the Turanian languages, p. 30.
2. प्रजापतिस्तावत्प्रजापालनाधिकारादादित्य एवोच्यते। स चारुणोदय-वेलायामुषसमुद्यन्नभ्येति, सा तदागमनादेवोपजायत इति तद्दुहितृत्वेन व्यपदिश्यते। तस्यां चारुणकिरणाख्यबीजनिक्षेपात् स्त्रीपुरुषसंयोगवदुपचारः। एवं समस्ततेजाः परमेश्वरत्वनिमित्तेन्द्रशब्दवाच्यः सवितैवाहनि लीयमानतया रात्रेरहल्याशब्दवाच्यायाः क्षयात्मक-जरणहेतुत्वाज्जीर्यत्यस्मादनेन वोदितेन वेत्यहल्याजार इत्युच्यते, न परस्त्रीव्यभिचारात्।

3. Viśve Devāḥ, yough treated as a plural, has sometimes the meaning of a *pluralis majestaticus*. See Ewald, Ausführliches Lehrbuch,.178,b
4. त्वं विश्वानि स्वनीक पत्यसे। ii. 1.8. See Nirukta-pariśiṣṭa, i
5. ii. 1. 9.
6. x. 86.
7. ix. 59.
8. ix. 96. 10., *bhuvanasya rājā*.
9. ix. 96. 14.
10. ix. 96. 5.
11. *Vrata* means what must be done, and these *Vratas* or laws are not (aprachyuta) because" they rest on Varuṇa as on a rock."(Ṛv. ii. 28. 8.)
12. The thirteenth or intercalary month ; see page 189.
13. Ṛv. vii. 87. 2., the wind is called the breath of Varuṇa.
14. The gods.
15. These spies or watchers are most likely the other Ādityas, of whom it is said (ii. 27. 3.) that "they see into what is evil and what is good, and that everything, even at the greatest distance, is near to them." "With them the right is not distinguished from the left nor the east, nor the west." (Ṛv. ii. 27. 11.) See Roth, Zeitschrift der Deutschen Moigen-ländischen Gesellschaft, vi. 72.
16. *Hotṛ* does not mean friend, but the priest who is chosen to invite the gods. Perhaps it means poet and priest in a more general sense than in the later hymns.
17. Dobrizhoffer, Account of the Abipones, vol. ii. p. 58.
18. Ṛv. vii. 87. *yaḥ mṛlayāti chakruśc chit āgaḥ*. (य: मृलयातिचक्रुशे चित् आग:।)
19. Name of the poet.
20. Ṛv. viii, 31.10.
21. Ṛv. ii. 27. 14.
22. *Dhāvati* is explained as a neuter verb by the commentary, "he who runs towards you."*Dhāvati*, however, is a techqical term, applied to the libations of the Soma-juice, as may be seen, Rv. viii. 1. 17. "Sota hi somam adrbhih a im enam apsu *dhāvata*," " Press the Soma with stones, make it run into the water.
23. *Dakṣata* is construed with the dative, and the caesura forbids to join make with raye, A similar construction occurs vii. 97. 8., *Dakṣuyyāya dahṣata*. where the commentator explains it rightly.
24. This verse shows signs of a later origin; the ideas are taken from the preceding verse.
25. According to the Commentator *Kuhachidvid* means "wherever he be." It may perhaps mean the ignorant.
26. *Jyāyaḥ* stands for *Jyāyasaḥ*.
27. The construction of this verse is very abrupt, parti cularly the transition from the simile of the horse, which is put in the third person to the address to Agni in the second person. The idea, however, is clear. Agni, the fire,

when first lighted, is compared with a neighing horse, on account of the crackling noise. He is greedy for food as soon as he steps out of his prison, *viz.*, from the wood from which fire is produced by friction, like a horse stepping out of his stable. Then the wind is supposed to kindle the blaze of the fire, and as the path of the horse is darkened by dust, the path of Agni is darkened by smoke.

28. *Ahuta* is used in the general sense of worshipped, well-attended, with special reference to a guest. Cf. Ṛv. i, 44, 4.
29. Might be "deveṣv a nuirtyeṣv" "among gods and among men ?"
30. Every word of this verse baffles translation. Vivāśasi is not simply "you bestow," but', you spread out as the sun spreads out his rays." Suvītrya is not "an array of heroes," but an abstract, signifying the possession of good strength, only that this good strength means "the chief of all their strength," and has special reference to the sons and all the males born in the house. Dyumad, brilliant, corresponds with the verb *vivāsi*. Bṛhat should be taken as an adverb, signifying the ever increasing nature of the gift bestowed by Agni.
31. The fire of the altar for the morning prayers.
32. The goat is the victim or the offering which is led before the horse, and sacrificed to Indra and Pūṣan.
33. All names of priests.
34. In these hymns it is sometimes difficult to say whether the horse be meant, or the sun, of which it is the emblem.
35. The verb in the singular *(astu)* with the substantive in the plural *(sarvā)* finds an analogy in Greek.
36. See Essai de Mythologie Comparée, traduit de 1' Anglais de Max Müller, Paris, 1859, p. 47.
37. Lassen, Indische Alterthumskunde, iii. p. 409.
38. A very careful discussion on this hymn, together with its text, translation, various readings and notes, is to be found in Dr. John Muir's "Original Sanskrit Texts," pp. 6-11.

❑❑

APPENDIX

THE STORY OF ŚUNAḤŚEPHA, ACCORDING TO THE ŚĀKHĀ OF THE AITAREYINS, COLLATED WITH THE TEXT IN THE ŚĀṄKHĀYANA-ŚĀKHĀ.

The upper line shows the various readings of the Śāṅkhāyana-sūtras

हरिश्चन्द्रो

हरिश्चन्द्रो ह वैधस ऐक्ष्वाको राजापुत्र आस तस्य ह शतं

ह

जाया बभूवुस्तासु पुत्रं न लेभे तस्य ह पर्वतनारदौ गृह

ऊषतुः स ह नारं-पप्रच्छ।।

च

यन्निवमं पुत्रमिच्छन्ति ये विजानन्ति ये च न।

तन्नः प्रब्रुहि

किंस्वित्पुत्रेण विन्दते तन्म आचक्ष्व नारदेति[१]।।१।।

स एकया पृष्टो दशभिः प्रत्युवाच।।

विन्दते

ऋणमस्मिन्तसन्नयत्यमृतत्वं च गच्छति।

पिता पुत्रस्य जातस्य पश्येच्चेज्जीवतो मुखम्।।२।।

यावन्तः पृथिव्यां भोगा यावन्तो जातवेदसि।

यावन्तो अप्सु प्राणिनां भूयान्पुत्रे पितुस्ततः।।३।।

शश्वत्पुत्रेण पितरोऽत्यायन्बहुलं तमः।

यज्ञ[२]

आत्मा हि जज्ञ आत्मनः स इरावत्यतितारिणी।।४।।

किं नु मलं किमजिनं किमु श्मश्रूणि किं तपः।
पुत्रं ब्रह्माण इच्छध्वं स वै लोको वदावदः।।५।।
अन्नं ह प्राणः शरणं ह वासो रूपं हिरण्यं पशवो विवाहाः।
सखा ह जाया कृपणं ह दुहिता ज्योतिर्ह पुत्रः परमे व्योमन्।।६।।

त्वाथ

पतिर्जायां प्रविशति गर्भो भूत्वा स मारतम्।
तस्यां पुनर्नवो भूत्वा दशमे मासि जायते।।७।।
जज्जाया जाया भवति यदस्यां जायते पुनः।
आभूतिरेषाभूतिर्वीजमेतन्निधीयते।।८।।
देवाश्चैतामृषयश्च तेजः समभरन्महत्।
देवा मनुष्यानब्रुवन्नेषा वो जननी पुनः।।९।।
नापुत्रस्य लोकोऽस्तीति तत्सर्वे पशवो विदुः।

तीति।।१७।।

तस्मात्तु पुत्रो मारतं स्वसारं चाधिरोहति[३]।।१०।।
वितता देवयानो येनाक्रमन्ते पुत्रिणो ये विशोकाः।
एष पन्था उरुगायः सुशेवो यं पुत्रिण आक्रमन्ते विशोकाः।
तर्यपि मिथुनं चरन्ति।।
तं पश्यंति पशवो वयांसि च तस्मात्ते मात्रापि मिथुनीभवन्ति।।११।।
इति ह स्मा आख्याय।।१३।।
स होवाच स वै मे ब्रूहि यथा मे पुत्रो जायेतेति तं
....अथैन
होवाच वरुणं
मुवाच वरुणं राजानमुपधाव पुत्रो मे जायतां तेन त्वा यजा इति तथेति स वरुणं राजानमुपससार पुत्रो मे जायतां तेन त्वा यजा इति तथेति तस्य ह पुत्रो जज्ञे
वरुण उवाचाज-
रोहितो नाम तं होवाचाजनि वै ते पुत्रो यजस्व मानेनेति स होवाच यदा वै

पशुर्निर्दशो भवत्यथ स मेध्यो भवति निर्दशो न्वस्त्वथ त्वा यजा इति तथेति स ह नि निर्दशो आस

वा अभू

तं होवाच निर्दशो न्वभूद्यजस्व मानेनेति स होवाच यदा वै पशोर्दन्ता जायन्तेऽथ स मेध्यो भवति दन्ता न्वस्य जायन्तामथ त्वा यजा इति तथेति तस्य ह दन्ता जज्ञिरे तं होवाचाज्ञत वा अस्य दन्ता यजस्व मानेनेति स होवाच यदा वै पशोर्दन्ताः पद्यन्तेऽथ स मेध्यो भवति दन्ता न्वस्य पद्यन्तामथ त्वा यजा इति तथेति तस्य ह दन्ताः पेदिरे तं होवाचापत्सत वा अस्य दन्ता यजस्व मानेनेति स होवाच यदा वै पशोर्दन्ताः पुनर्जायन्तेऽथ स मेध्यो भवति दन्ता न्वस्य पुनर्जायन्तामथ त्वा यजा इति तथेति तस्य ह दन्ताः पुनर्जज्ञिरे तं होवाचाज्ञत वा अस्य पुनर्दन्ता यजस्व मानेनेति सन्नाहं प्राप्नोत्य

स होवाच यदा वै क्षत्रियः सान्नाहको भवत्यथ स मेध्यो भवति सन्नाहं नु प्राप्नोत्वथ त्वा यजा इति तथेति स ह प्रापद्वै सन्नाहं

सन्नाहं प्रापत्तं होवाच सन्नाहं नु प्राप्नोद्यजस्व मानेनेति यां चक्रे

स तथेत्युक्ता पुत्रमामन्त्रयामास ततायं वै मह्यं त्वामदस ने

दाद्धन्त त्वयाहमिमं यजा इति स ह नेत्युक्त्वा धनुरादामु राथ

यारण्यमपातस्थौ स संवत्सरमरण्ये चचार।।१४।।

कं राजानं व

अथ हैक्ष्वाकं वरुणो जग्राह तस्य होदरं जज्ञे तदु ह रोहितः शुश्राव सोऽरण्याद्गममेयाय तमिन्द्रः पुरुषरूपेण पर्येत्योवाच।।१८।।

श्रू

नानाश्रान्ताय श्रीरस्तीति रोहित शुश्रुम।

निषड्वरो चरैव रोहितेति

पापो नृषद्वरो जन इन्द्र इच्चरतः सखा चरैवेति[४]।।१।।

चरै स

वरैवेति वैमा ब्राह्मणोऽवोचदिह द्वितीयं संवत्सरमरण्ये चचार।

सोऽरण्याद्ग्राममेयाय तमिन्द्रः पुरूषरूपेण पर्येत्योवाच॥

ले

पुष्पिण्यौ चरतो जङ्घे भूष्णुरात्मा फलग्रहिः।

शेरते श्चरैव रो० स तृती०

शेरेऽस्य सर्वे पाप्मानः श्रमेण प्रपथे हताश्चरैवेति॥२॥

स

चरैवेति वै मा ब्राह्मणोऽवोचदिति ह तृतीयं संवत्सरमरण्ये चचार

सोऽरण्याद्ग्राममेयाय तमिन्द्रः पुरुषरूपेण पर्येत्योवाच॥

आस्ते भग आसीनस्योद्ध्र्वस्तिष्ठति तिष्ठतः।

व रो०

शते निपद्यमानस्य चराति चरतो भगश्चरैवेति॥३॥

स

चरैवेति वै मा ब्राह्मणेऽवोचदिति ह चतुर्थं संवत्सरमरण्ये

चचार सोऽरण्याद्ग्राममेयाय तमिन्द्रः पुरुषरूपेण पर्येत्योवाच॥

नः पुरुषः

कलिः शयानो भवति सञ्जिहानस्तु द्वापरः।

उत्थित

उत्तिष्ठँस्त्रेता भवति कृतं सम्पद्यते चरँश्चरैवेति॥४॥

स

चरैवेति वै मा ब्राह्मणोऽवोचदिति ह पञ्चमं संवत्सरमरण्ये

चचार सोऽरण्याद्ग्राममेयाय तमिन्द्रः पुरुषरूपेण पर्येत्योवाच॥

र पक्कमुटुं

चरन्वै मधु विन्दति चरन्त्स्वादुमुदुम्बरम्।

श्रयमाणं चरैव०

सूर्यस्य पश्य श्रेमानं यो न तन्द्रयते चरँश्चरैवेति॥५॥

स र० च०

चरैवेति वै मा ब्राह्मणोऽवोचदिति ह षष्ठं संवत्सरमरण्ये

चरन्वै मधु विन्दत्यपजिन्वन्परूषकम्। उत्तिष्ठन्विन्दत श्रियं न
निषत्किच नावति। चरैव० स सप्तमं संव. चचार सोऽजीगर्त
.... चचार सोऽजीगर्तं
नाया परीतं पुत्रं भक्ष्यमाणमरण्य ।।१९।।
सौयवसिमृषिमशनया परीतमरण्य................उपेयाय......................
तस्य ह त्रयः पुत्रा आसुः शुनःपुच्छः शुनःशेपः शुऋषे हंताहमेषामेकेना
नोलांगूल इति तं होवाच ऋषेऽहं ते शतं ददाणा अहं ते गवां शतं ददानीति
म्यहमेषमेकेनात्मानं निष्क्रीणा..इति स ज्येष्ठं
स ज्येष्ठं पुत्रं निगृह्णान उवाच न न्विममिति नो एवेममिति
कनिष्ठं माता तौ ह मध्यमे सम्पादयाञ्चक्रतुः शुनःशेपे
तस्य ह शतं दत्वा स तमादय सोऽरण्याद्ग्राममेयाय स पितरमेत्योवाच तत
हन्ताहमनेनात्मानं निष्क्रीणा इति स तथेत्युक्ता वरु० मामन्त्रयाञ्चक्रेऽनेन
स वरुणं राजानमुपससारानेन त्वा यजा इति तथेति श्रेया
भूयान्वै ब्राह्मणः क्षत्रियादिति वरुण उवाच तस्मा एतं स एतं राजसूये
पुरुषपशुमाराजसूयं यज्ञक्रतुं प्रोवाच तमेतमभिषेचनीये पुरुषं पशुलेभे।।२०।।
मालेभे।।१९।।

तासायास्य उद्गाता जम०

तस्य ह विश्वामित्रो होतासीज्जमदग्निरध्वर्युर्वसिष्ठो ब्रह्मायास्य उद्गाता। तस्मा
उपाकृताया नियोक्तारं न विविदुः।

त्वा

स होवाचाजीगर्तः सौयवसिर्मह्यमपरं शतं दत्ताहमेनं नियुयोज
नियोक्ष्यामीति तस्मा अपरं शतं ददुस्तं स निनियोज।
य पर्यग्नि..........शास्तारं
तस्मा उपाकृताय नियुक्तायाप्रीताय पर्यग्निकृताया विशसितारं न विविदुः।
स होवाचाजीगर्तः सौयवसिर्मह्यमपरं शतं त्वा
दत्ताहमेनं विशसिष्यामीति तस्मा अपरं शतं ददुः सोऽसिं
निश्यान इक्षामासा मा

नि:शान एयायाथ ह शुन:शेप ईक्षां चक्रे मानुषमिव वै हन्त दे नीति।।२१।।
मा विशसिष्यन्ति हन्ताहं देवता उपधावामीति स प्रजापतिमेव
प्रथमं देवतानामुपससार कस्य नूनं कतमस्यामृतानामित्येतग्नेर्वै
नेदिष्ठोऽसि तमे

यर्चा तं प्रजापतिरुवाचाग्निर्वै देवानां नेदिष्ठस्तमेवोपधावेति सोऽग्नि-मुपससाराग्नेर्वयं प्रथमस्यामृतानामित्येतयर्चा। तमग्निरुवाच सविता वै प्रसवानामीशे तमेवोपधावेति स सवितारमुपससाराभि त्वा देव सवितरित्येतेन तृचेन तंसवितोवाच वरुणाय वै राज्ञे नियुक्तोऽसि तमेवोपधावेति। स वरुणं राजानमुपससारात उत्तराभिरेकत्रिंशता तं वरुण यं स्त न्नु
उवाचाग्निर्वै देवानां मुखं सुहृदयतमस्तं नु स्तुह्यथ त्वोत्सृक्ष्यामीति भिरेव द्वात्स्त्रक्ष्याम इति सोऽग्निं तुष्टावात उत्तराभिर्द्वाविंशत्या।

वां स्तु त्सृक्ष्यामीति

तमग्निरुवाच विश्वान्नु देवान्स्तुह्यथ त्वोत्स्त्रक्ष्याम इति स श्वान्नु देवाँस्तु
विश्वान्देवाँस्तुष्टाव नमो महद्भ्यो नमो अर्भकेभ्य इत्येतयर्चा।

रिन्द्रं नु स्तुह्य.............................

तं विश्वे देवा ऊचुरिन्द्रो वै देवानामोजिष्ठो बलिष्ठ: सहिष्ठ:

....त्सृ

सत्तम: पारयिष्णुतमस्तं नु स्तुह्यथ त्वोत्स्त्रक्ष्याम इति स

इत्येतेन.............................

इन्द्रं तुष्टाव यच्चिद्धि सत्य सोमपा इति चैतेन सूक्तेनोत्त नो मनसा...........
रस्य च पञ्चदशभिस्तस्मा इन्द्र स्तूयमान: प्रीतो मनसा यर्चा
हिरण्यरर्थ ददौ तमेतया प्रतीयाय शश्वदिन्द्र इति तमिन्द्र त्सृक्ष्यामीति
उवाचाश्विनौ नु स्तुह्यथस्त्रत्वोत्स्त्रक्ष्याम इति सोऽश्विनौ तुष्टावात उत्तरेण तृचेन तमश्विना ऊचतुरुषसं नु स्तुह्यथ त्सृक्ष्याव इति णैव त्वोत्स्त्रक्ष्याम इति स उषसं तुष्टावात उत्तरेण तृचेन नितरां पाशो
तस्य ह स्मर्च्युक्तायां विपाशो मुमुचे कनीये ऐक्ष्वाकस्योदरं बभूवोत्तमायां ह स्मर्च्यु

भवत्युत्तमस्यामेवर्च्युक्तायां विपाशो मुमुचेऽगद ऐक्ष्वाक बभूवाथा हैनमृ मेवैतस्याह्नः

आसा॥१६॥ तमृत्विज ऊचुस्त्वमेव नोऊस्याह्नः संस्थामधिगच्छे:॥२२॥

अथ हैनमंज:सवं शुन:शेपो ददर्श यच्चि...................

गच्छेत्यथ हैतं शुन:शेपोंऽज:सवं ददर्श। तमेताभिश्चतसृ...................

.... इति तमेताभिश्चतसृभिरभिसुषाव यच्चिद्धि त्वं गृहे गृह इत्यथैनं द्रोणकलशखभिरभिषुत्योच्छिष्टं रेति द्रोणकलशे समवनिनायामभ्यवनिनायोच्छिष्टं चम्वोर्भरेत्यतयर्चाथ हा................

थास्मिन्नन्वारब्धाा एतस्यैव सूक्तस्य पू भिर्जू ....स्मिन्नन्वारब्धो.. ....पूर्वाभिश्चतसृभि: सस्वा................थ है सत्वं हाकाराभिर्जुहवां चकाराथैनमवभृथमभ्यवनिनाय त्वं नो अग्ने वरुणस्य विद्वानित्येताभ्यामथैनमत ऊर्ध्वमग्निमाहवनी..................यामास स शु त्येतयमुपस्थापयां चकार शुनश्चिच्छेपं निदितं सहस्त्रदित्यथ ह यर्चा॥२३॥ अथ ह स्योपस्थमाससाद रतं .... शुन:शेपो विश्वामित्रस्यांकमाससाद। स हो सि: पुन होवाचाजीगर्त: सौयवसिर्ऋषे पुनर्मे पुत्रं देहीति नेति होवाच विश्वामित्रो देवा वा इमं मह्यमरासतेति स ह देवरातो

आस तं होवाचाजीवगर्त:........................

वैश्वामित्र आस तस्यैते कापिलेयबाभ्रवा: स होवाचाजीगर्त:

वै वि महा इति तथेत्यांगि......................

सौयवरिरत्वं वेहि विह्वयावहा इति स होवाचाजीगर्त: सौर्त:

यवसिरांगिरसो जन्मनास्याजीगर्ति: श्रुत: कवि:। ऋषे पैतामहात्तंतोर्मापगा: पुनरेहि मामिति॥ स होवाच शुन:शेपोऽदाक्षु लि दर्शुस्त्वा शासहस्तं न यच्छूद्रेष्वलप्सत। गवां त्रीणि शतानि तं

त्वमवृणीथा मदंगिर इति स होवाचाजीगर्त: सौयवसिस्तद्वैह्लुमा तात तपति पापं कर्म मया कृतं। तदहं निह्नवे तुभ्यं ती

प्रतियंतु शता गवामिति। स होवाच शुन:शेपो य: स तकं स्त मापगा छौद्राण्यायाद कृत्पापकं कुर्यात्कुर्यादेनत्ततोऽपरं। नापागा: शौद्रान्नयायादवा अवोचदिति ह वि

सन्धेयं त्वया कृतमित्यसन्धेयमिति ह विश्वामित्र उपपाद ।।२४।। भीम... ...

स होवाच विश्वामित्रो भीम एव सौयवसिः शासेन विशिसिषत्। शसिषुः। अस्थान्मैतस्य पुत्रो भूर्भमैवोपेहि पुत्रतामिति स य त्रं

होवाच शुनःशेपः स वै यथा नो ज्ञपया राजपुत्र तथा तं

वद। यथैवांगिरसः सन्नुपेयां तव पुत्रतामिति। स होवाच विश्वामित्रो ज्येष्ठो मे त्वं पुत्राणां स्यास्तव श्रेष्ठा प्रजा दुने स्यात्। उपेयादैव मे दायं तेन वै त्वोपमन्त्रय इति स र्दा

होवाच शुनःशेपः संज्ञानानेषु वै ब्रूयात्सौहार्द्याय मे श्रियै। यथाहं भरतऋृषभोपेयां तब पुत्रतामित्यथ ह वियां चक्रे।।२५।।

श्वामित्रः पुत्रानामन्त्रयामास मधुच्छन्दाः शृणोतन ऋषभो रेज्येष्ठाय तिष्ठध्वमितिणुरष्टकः। ये के च भ्रातरः स्थ नास्मै ज्यैष्ठयाय कल्पध्वमिति।।१७।। हैक................

तस्य ह विश्वामित्रस्यैकशतं पुत्रा आसुः पञ्चाशदेव ज्यायांसो मधुच्छन्दसः पञ्चाशत्कनीयांसस्तद्ये ज्यायांसो न ते कुशलं रांतं वः ते

मेनिरेताननुव्याजहारांतान्वः प्रजा भक्षीष्टेति त एते अंध्राः पुंढ्राः रा मूचिपा दञ्चो बहुदऽन्ध्राः पुण्ड्राः शबराः पुलिन्दा मूतिवा इत्युदन्त्या बहवो स्यवो यिष्ठा इत्युदाहरन्त्यथ ये मधुच्छभवन्ति वैश्वामित्रा दस्यूनां भूयिष्ठाः। स होवाच मधुच्छन्दाःन्दःप्रभृतयः कनीयांसस्ते कुशलं मेनिरे स ह जगौ मधुपञ्चाशता सार्धं यन्नः पिता...............................च्छन्दा यन्नः पिता सञ्जानीते स्तात्... ....सञ्जानीते स्मिँस्तिष्ठामहे वयम्। पुरस्तवा सर्वे कुर्महे त्वामन्वञ्चो वयं स्मसीत्यथ ह विश्वामित्रः प्रतीतः व ।।२६।। ते वै प्रजा

पुत्राँस्तुष्टाव ते वै पुत्राः पशुमन्तो वीरवन्तो भविष्यथ। ये मानं मेऽनुगृह्णन्तो वीरवन्तमकर्त मा।। पुरएत्रा वीरवन्तो वस्तद्धि वादेवरातेन गाथिनाः। सर्वे राध्या स्थ पुत्रा एष वः सद्विवाचकः।

चनं।। एष वः कुशिका वीरो देवरातस्तमन्वित। युष्माँश्च वोपेतां चामुत

दायं म उषेता विद्यां यामु च विद्यसि।। ते सभ्यश्चो ज्यैष्ठे वैश्वामित्राः सर्वे साकं सरातयः। देवरातय तस्थिरे घृत्यै श्रैष्ठे च

श्रेष्ठ्याय गाथिना:।। अधीयत देवरातो रिक्थयोरुभयोर्ऋषि:।

तस्थिरे ना:।। च्छौन:शेजह्नूनां चाधिपत्ये दैवे वेदे च गाथिनाम्।।

तदेतत्परऋृक्शपमाख्यानं परशतर्गाथमपरिमितं तद्धोताभि

तगाथं शौन:शेपमाख्यानं....................तद्धोता राज्ञेऽभिषिक्तायाचष्टे

हिरण्यकशिपावासीन आचष्टे हिरण्यकशिपावासीन: णात्योमि................

प्रतिगृणाति यशो वै हिरण्यं यशसै वैनं तत्समर्धयत्योमित्यृच:

प्रतिगर एवं तथेति गाथाया ओमिति वै दैवं तथेति मानुषं

सर्वस्मादेनस: सम्प्रमुच्येते

दैवेन चैवेनं तन्मानुषेण च पापादेनस: प्रमुञ्चति तस्माद्यो जी

राजा विजिती स्यादप्ययजमान आख्यापयेतैवैतच्छौन:शेपमाख्यानं न ह्यस्मिन्नल्पं

चनैन: परिशिष्यते सहस्रमाख्यात्रे शतं..................... पुत्रकामा

हाप्याख्या-दद्याच्छतं पतिगरित्र एते चैवासने श्वेतश्वतरो रथो पयन्ते लभन्ते

ह............

होतु: पुत्रकामा हाप्याख्यापयेरँल्लभन्ते ह पुत्राँल्लभन्ते ह पुत्रान्।।१८।।

❑❑

INDEX

S

Y

Z

***